authoritative books on antiques & collectibles

PRICE • GUIDE
TO
ANTIQUES

SPECIAL ANNIVERSARY
10TH
EDITION

INCLUDING
THE TOP-RATED SECTION ON
PATTERN GLASS

EDITED BY ROBERT W. MILLER

Other books by Robert W. Miller

American Primitives
The Art Glass Basket
Clock Guide Identification with Prices
Clock Guide Identification with Prices, Book II
Fabulous Houston Museum
Mary Gregory and Her Glass
Oriental Primer
Pictorial Guide to Early American Tools and Implements
Wallace-Homestead Flea Market Price Guide
Wallace-Homestead Price Guide to Dolls
Wallace-Homestead Price Guide to Toys

Cover Design: Heather Miller
Cover Photography: Perry Struse

Other photography: Tom Needham, Panama City Beach, Florida
Marshall Thurman, Knoxville, Tennessee, and
John Shuman III, Pottstown, Pennsylvania

ISBN 0-87069-386-7
Library of Congress Catalog No. 78-84521

Published by

Wallace-Homestead Book Company
1912 Grand Avenue
Des Moines, Iowa 50305

Contents

Introduction

As we go to press with this Special Anniversary Tenth Edition of the WALLACE-HOMESTEAD PRICE GUIDE TO ANTIQUES AND PATTERN GLASS, it is amazing to see how we've grown since the first Price Guide was compiled in 1972. We were pleased with that bright red, 372-page first edition, but we are very proud of the improvements and additions that have been added since then. This Tenth Edition is almost twice as big as the first, and we think its more than twice as helpful!

Are you tired of hearing us say, "This is just a *guide?*" You, the collector, you, the seller, establish the prices of antiques and collectibles. It's called "fair market value" when a willing buyer and a willing seller, neither under any pressure to buy or sell, arrive at a mutually satisfactory trading price. We report these fair market values.

We *do* use price ranges, simply because prices vary so much from one part of the country to the other. Attend a show in San Francisco; then go to one in New England.

You will find there's no such thing as just adding or subtracting 10 percent to find the regional difference in prices. It's not that simple.

As always, we get our prices by going to and participating in the major shows, countrywide. We study the auction catalogs, talk to museum personnel, private collectors, knowledgeable dealers, and professional writers. Then we use common sense. We don't have a board of directors *or* a crystal ball. We do have a lot of friends in the industry we've been associated with for more than forty years.

So far most of the reports and indications we've received point to an exciting market this year. As early as June 24, Austin Kiplinger in his *Washington Newsletter* was saying the "Antique business is picking up again. The auctions are crowded. Serious collectors are coming back in droves." If the general economy continues to improve, trading in antiques will be much more brisk in the next twelve months. And, as competition increases for the more desirable and scarce items, prices will rise accordingly. Use your own good judgment, but right now may be an excellent time to get that special piece you've been thinking about.

Thanks for buying the best and most helpful price guide on the market. While every effort has been made to avoid them, the editor and publisher cannot be held responsible for errors in typography or in judgment as applied to prices.

How to Buy by Mail

One of the most popular methods of buying and selling antiques is through the U.S. mails. Most antiques publications, whether weekly or monthly, will not knowingly accept advertisements from dishonest people. Unfortunately, some questionable ads slip by the editors, and for that reason we list here some basic rules to follow when you decide to buy or sell by mail.

1. The licensed antiques dealer should guarantee the condition and the authenticity of the merchandise in his ad. This same rule applies to an individual advertising a particular item for sale.

2. When you decide to purchase something that is advertised in one of the many antiques publications, mail your check at once and *always* include a SASE (self-addressed, stamped envelope) in the event the item you order has already been sold. Don't expect the dealer to pay the postage when returning your check. If you especially desire the item, telephone the seller, person-to-person; also, for faster service, send a certified check or a money order. Your personal check may be good locally, but a dealer who doesn't know you has every right to wait until your check clears his bank

before mailing you your merchandise.

3. Ask for five-day approval. You won't always get it, but if you do you have the right to return the merchandise if you aren't satisfied.

4. *Unpack Carefully.* Careless unwrapping of merchandise can cost you money, and don't be foolish enough to think you can blame your mistake on the post office. If the post office is responsible, that's one thing—trying to cheat them is a sad mistake.

5. *Pack Carefully.* If you're filling an order, that extra paper and extra time taken can save you lots of grief when the buyer notifies you that your merchandise arrived in a damaged and/or broken condition. If you do receive damaged and/or broken merchandise, save all the wrappings and take the package immediately to your local post office and file a claim. Save the nasty notes and give those responsible time to make good on your purchase.

6. Remember also that buying by mail does *not* include United Parcel Service. Check with the bus lines with respect to saving the wrapping or filing a claim, if you are mailing and/or shipping by bus. Call them and ask what requirements they have for handling your package.

7. Misrepresented merchandise is just that, and you should take every action to get your money back. First, write to the person or persons from whom you made your purchase, sending your letter by Registered Mail, Return Receipt Requested. It will cost you a little more, but you'll know your letter of complaint was received. If your letter fails to get action, check with your local post office to see what, if any, action can be taken. Also, write to the publisher of the publication from whose ad you ordered your merchandise. Most publications are sincere and will honestly try to get your money back. They won't be in business long if they don't.

8. Don't be afraid to order by mail. It's big business and those using the mails to defraud usually end up in court. Reading the advertisement carefully *before* you order can save you a lot of trouble. Buy with confidence and be fair if a disagreement arises between you and the buyer and/or seller. If you're still not satisfied, then follow suggestions in No. 7 above.

How to Buy at Auctions

Whether you're buying at Sotheby Park Bernet, Adam Wecheler & Sons, or Richard A. Bourne Co., to mention just a few of the top auction houses in this country, it doesn't mean a thing unless you understand the chant of the auctioneer.

Few auctioneers' chants are the same. To the uninitiated, it's all a bunch of unintelligible gibberish. Also, the rules of buying vary from state to state, so here are a few basic rules to help you when you attend your first auction:

1. Learn how to bid *before* you bid by listening to the auctioneer's chant for a time, keeping in mind that innocent scratching of your ear or nose or a casual wave to a friend across the aisle may purchase you a genuine toilet seat!

2. You can bid by voice or by the wave of a hand; those known to the auctioneer may bid by a slight nod of the head or some other signal prearranged with the auctioneer. It depends upon the particular auction.

3. Most auction houses will not be responsible for the correctness of description, authenticity, genuineness or condition of the property being sold, so go early and look over the items being offered. When an auctioneer says, "It looks like walnut," he's not saying it *is* walnut. You may be buying a piece of furniture made of poplar. Know what you're buying.

4. The highest bid accepted by the auctioneer is usually the buyer's. If there's a dispute between two bidders, the auctioneer will usually reopen the bidding, but only between disputing bidders. Then, when the hammer falls, the person with the highest bid is the buyer and thereafter the property is the purchaser's sole risk and responsibility. At most auctions, someone will usually assist you in loading your purchases. Some auction houses will put what you've purchased in a warehouse, at your expense, if you don't claim it within a specified period of time.

5. At an unrestricted sale, or a sale without reserve, the consignors of the items being sold are not supposed to bid. If the consignors bid back their own items, they still pay the full sales commission.

6. Most auctioneers reserve the right to refuse a bid if it is not commensurate with the value of the article or if the next bid is merely a nominal advance over the previous bid. It's the auctioneer's job to get as much as he can for an item, and he's not going to injure the sale by accepting too-low bids.

7. Be knowledgeable from the beginning. Go to the auction in time to get a bidder's number and a good seat. Popular auctioneers with a following will usually fill the house long before the auction begins.

8. Most auction houses will accept your personal check locally, but if you're attending an auction out-of-town, arrange beforehand for credit or take travelers' checks.

There is a National Association of Auctioneers and most states have their own organizations. It's fun to buy by auction and they're becoming more and more popular because of the lure of instant cash to the seller. Most auction houses charge 15 percent of the gross. If you're interested in selling your merchandise by auction, find a reliable firm with which to do business. And, as in any other business transaction, read the contract *before* you sign it and understand what it says *before* you sign it.

How to Buy from Mail Auction Houses

More and more mail auction houses are popping up in the field of antiques and collectibles, and as the rules seem rather confusing to us, we thought we'd list a few and let you judge for yourself.

One firm states that the highest bidder wins at the highest bid sent in. This firm doesn't allow phone calls and there are no reductions given over lower underbidders.

Another mail auction house reduces winning high bids to 10 percent above the second highest bid, except that no bid will be reduced by more than 20 percent, and bids under $5 are not lowered. Phone calls are allowed by this house, and the caller is given the current high bid which, if the caller chooses to overbid, must be topped by a minimum of 10 percent.

Still another firm sells to the highest bidder, except that if more than 15 percent separates the high bid from the next highest, the high bid is reduced by a maximum of 15 percent. During the last two days callers are given the current high bid and are allowed to raise it in 15 percent increments if they have previously bid on the item. Otherwise they must raise by 20 percent.

Sounds like a high stakes crap game at Las Vegas, and as we said, a bit confusing. But mail auction houses are here to stay, so if you're interested in buying antiques and collectibles by this method, learn the rules *before* you bid.

Auction Galleries

Auction galleries that advertise nationally and will, on request, send a catalog are indicated by (C) following the business name. As always, *before* you sign a contract with *any* gallery, make sure you understand what you are signing. We are pleased to see that many of our competitors are now offering gallery listings similar to the list we have been offering for the past five years.

Arizona
Jack Sellner
P. O. Box 1113
Scottsdale, AZ 85251

Arkansas
James E. Wilson & Son
1019 Airport Rd.
Hot Springs, AR 71901

California
Backer's Auction
14100 Paramount Blvd.
Paramount, CA 90723

Bowers & Ruddy Galleries, Inc. (C)
  (coins)
6922 Hollywood Blvd., Suite 600
Los Angeles, CA 90028

Butterfield & Butterfield (C)
1244 Sutter St.
San Francisco, CA 94109

Colorado
Broughton Auction Co.
1645 S. Tejou
Colorado Springs, CO 80906

Wagon Wheel Auctions
Niwot, CO 80544

District of Columbia
C. G. Sloan & Co., Inc. (C)
715 13th St. NW
Washington, DC 20005

Adam A. Weschler & Sons (C)
905 E St. NW
Washington, DC 20004

Florida

Col. Marty Higgenbotham
1702 Edgewood Dr.
Lakeland, FL 33803

Schrader Galleries
211 3rd St. S.
St. Petersburg, FL 30901

Urich's Auction Gallery
3628 Washington Ave.
Fort Myers, FL 30901

Georgia
ABCD Auction Gallery (C)
1 N. Clarendon Rd.
Avondale Estates, GA 30002

Atlanta Galleries
1405 Spring St. NW
Atlanta, GA 30300

Trosby Auction Gallery (C)
81 Peachtree Dr. NE
Atlanta, GA 30309

Illinois
Dunning's Auction Service
755 Church Rd.
Elgin, IL 60120

Hanzel Galleries (C)
1120 S. Michigan Ave.
Chicago, IL 60605

Tom Sapp Auction Co.
Springfield, IL 62700

Stumpf Auction Co.
Mascoutah, IL 62258

Indiana
Kruse Classic Auction Co. (C)
  (old cars)
300 S. Union
Auburn, IN 46706

Lewis & Lambright
112 Detroit St.
La Grange, IN 46761

Iowa
Brannian-Niemann Auction Service
Brooklyn, IA 52211

Hamilton's Complete Auction Service
Leon, IA 50144

Gene Harris
P. O. Box 294
Marshalltown, IA 50158

Richard's Auction Gallery
527 Locust St.
Des Moines, IA 50309

Kansas
Woody Auction Co. (C)
P. O. Box 618
Douglas, KS 67039

Kentucky
Kenneth S. Hays & Associates (C)
4740 Bardstown Rd.
Louisville, KY 40218

Louisiana
Morton's Auction Exchange (C)
701 Magazine St.
New Orleans, LA 70190

Maine
Barridoff Galleries
242 Middle St.
Portland, ME 04101

James D. Julia (C)
Skohegan Rd.
Fairfield, ME 04937

Maritime Auctions
Rt. 2, Box 45A
York, ME 03909

Massachusetts
Richard A. Bourne Co. (C)
Corporation St.
Hyannis, MA 02647

Douglas Galleries (C)
S. Deerfield, MA 01373

Robert C. Eldred Co. (C)
P. O. Box 796
E. Dennis, MA 02641

Robert W. Skinner Gallery (C)
Rt. 117
Bolton, MA 01740

Michigan
C. B. Charles Galleries (C)
825 Woodward
Pontiac, MI 48053

Du Mouchelle Art Galleries (C)
409 E. Jefferson Ave.
Detroit, MI 48226

Stalker & Boos (C)
280 N. Woodward Ave.
Birmingham, MI 48011

Minnesota
The Summer Auction Galleries
Owatonna, MN 55060

New Hampshire
Philip E. Fitanides
Hooksett, NH 03106

Young Fine Arts Gallery
56 Market St.
Portsmouth, NH 03801

New Jersey
Matthew's Galleries
186 Veterans Dr.
Northvale, NJ 07647

New York
Christie's USA (C)
502 Park Ave.
New York, NY 10022

William Doyle Galleries (C)
175 E. 87th St.
New York, NY 10028

Kenneth R. French & Co. (C)
166 Bedford Rd.
Armonk, NY 10504

O. Rundle Gilbert (C)
Rt. 9D
Garrison, NY 10524

Sotheby's New York (C)
1334 York Ave.
New York, NY 10021

Ohio
Paul Aronoff
1117 Vine St.
Cincinnati, OH 45210

Early's Antiques & Auction Co. (C)
123 Main St.
Milford, OH 45150

Garth's Auctions, Inc. (C)
2690 Stratford Rd.
Delaware, OH 43015

Pennsylvania
Black Brothers, Ltd.
Carlisle, PA 17013

Samuel T. Freeman & Co. (C)
1808 Chestnut St.
Philadelphia, PA 19103

Pennypacker Auction Centre (C)
1540 New Holland Rd.
Kenhorst, Reading, PA 19603

Bob, Chuck & Rich Roan, Inc. (C)
R. D. 2
Cogan Station, PA 17728

Frank Roan III, Auctioneer (C)
P. O. Box 112
McEwensville, PA 17749

Tennessee
Clement's Antiques
Hixson, TN 37343

Texas
E & M Alexander
1285 N. Post Rd.
Houston, TX 77055

Clement's Antiques
Forney, TX 75126

Garrett Galleries
1800 Irving Blvd.
Dallas, TX 75207

Virginia
Wilson Galleries (C)
P. O. Box 102
Fort Defiance, VA 24437

Wisconsin
Milwaukee Auction Galleries
5466 N. Port Washington Rd.
Milwaukee, WI 53217

Repairs and Services

Overwhelming! In one word, that's been the positive reaction to this exclusive-to-our-price-guide feature. Now, in this Tenth Edition of our WALLACE-HOMESTEAD PRICE GUIDE TO ANTIQUES AND PATTERN GLASS, there are more than 400 places to help you get your favorite antique repaired or find a part for same.

Always inquire first and *always* enclose a SASE (self-addressed, stamped envelope) if you expect a reply. Please tell us if you received prompt and quality service. This service is for *you* because we feel a Price Guide should do something more than just list a bunch of prices.

Note: If your firm isn't listed here it doesn't mean that you don't do quality work or sell a quality product. It does mean that we don't know about you. So, write!

Suppliers of Repairs and Services

1 B & L Antiquerie
25011 Little Mack
St. Clair Shores, MI 48080
2 Henry F. Witzenberger
15 Po Lane
Hicksville, NY 11801
3 T-K Michael Stained Glass
28200 Florence
St. Clair Shores, MI 48081
4 LEMiniatures
2615 Gravenstein Hwy.
Sebastopol, CA 95472

5 Studio Hannah
Star Route A, Box 93
Flemington, NJ 08822
6 Thompsons
Back Meadows Rd.
Damariscotta, ME 04543
7 Wilson Bergerud
30 Herring St.
Harrington Park, NJ 07640
8 Hector Olszewski
140 W. Houston
New York, NY 10003

9 Globes by Chick
  328 Danville Pike
  Hillsboro, OH 45133
10 Colonial "out-of-print" Book Service
  23 E. 4th St.
  New York, NY 10003
11 Horton Brasses
  P. O. Box 95
  Cromwell, CT 06416
12 Nowell's Inc.
  P. O. Box 164
  Sausalito, CA 94965
13 Noel Wise Antiques
  6503 St. Claudia Ave.
  Arabi, LA 70032
14 T & B Sales Co.
  P. O. Box 30
  Old Hickory, TN 37138
15 Al Meekins
  P. O. Box 161
  Collingswood, NJ 08108
16 "My Grandfather's Shop" LTD
  940 Sligo Ave.
  Silver Springs, MD 20910
17 Ronald's Woodcarving
  434 W. 4th St.
  W. Islip, NY 11795
18 Morgan, Dept. A03K11
  915 E. Ky.
  Louisville, KY 40204
19 Antique Trunk Supply Co.
  3706 W. 169th St.
  Cleveland, OH 44111
20 J & S Co.
  P. O. Box 4840
  Chattanooga, TN 37405
21 Sierra Studios
  P. O. Box 1005
  Oak Park, IL 60304
22 Paul W. Bowser
  1618 W. Main St.
  New Lebanon, OH 45345
23 Les Gould
  391 Tremont Pl.
  Orange, NJ 07050
24 The Genealogical Helper
  526 N. Main St.
  Logan, UT 84321
25 Mike Wells
  30½ W. Wheelock St.
  Hanover, NH 03755

26 The Bedpost
  Rt. 1, Box 155
  Pen Argyl, PA 18072
27 Schoepfer Eyes
  138 W. 31st St.
  New York, NY 10001
28 Wood & Leather Craft
  Star Route
  Callicoon, NY 12723
29 The Clarks
  P. O. Box 434
  Oceanside, CA 92054
30 Constantine
  2050 Eastchester Rd.
  Bronx, NY 10461
31 Whittemore-Durgin
  P. O. Box H2065
  Hanover, NH 02339
32 PECO
  P. O. Box 777
  Smithville, TX 78957
33 Replica Products
  610 57th St.
  Vienna, WV 26105
34 Trans World Trading Co.
  509 S. Cross
  Robinson, IL 62454
35 Appraisers Association of America, Inc.
  60 East 42nd St.
  New York, NY 10017
  (Note: A Membership Directory is available at a cost of $3 to persons seeking the services of a professional appraiser.)
36 Mildred E. Webster
  P. O. Box 37114
  Los Angeles, CA 90037
37 Adams Antiques
  426 Main Ave.
  Northport, AL 35476
38 Doll & Craft World
  125 8th St.
  Brooklyn, NY 11215
39 Waymar, Inc.
  6015 S. Lindbergh
  St. Louis, MO 63123
40 Gaston Wood Finishes, Inc.
  3630 E. 10th St.
  Bloomington, IN 47401
41 Seeley's Ceramic Service, Inc.
  9 River St.
  Oneonta, NY 13820

42 Dolls By Rene
8228 Allport
Santa Fe Springs, CA 90670

43 Costume Quarterly
38 Middlesex Dr.
Brentwood, MO 63144

44 Jeannette Strauss
3705 Chapel Forge Dr.
Bowie, MD 20715

45 John J. Mesterhazy
12917 Westwood Lane
Omaha, NB 68144

46 Hess Repairs
200 Park Ave. S.
New York, NY 10003

47 Williams' Antiques
Albion, IL 62806

48 BMS Materials
P. O. Box 222
Windsor, NY 13865

49 Hardwood Grove Mfg.
Rt. 2, Box 200
West Fork, AR 72774

50 Pat & Hanks Antiques
410 Don Tyler
Dewey, OK 74029

51 DiPonziano & Associates
P. O. Box 23356
San Jose, CA 95153

52 Bill E. Berger
29 E. 12th St.
New York, NY 10003

53 Museum Services
P. O. Box 119
Hingham, MA 02043

54 American Assn. of Conservators
1250 E. Ridgewood Ave.
Ridgewood, NJ 07450

55 Graphics International
P. O. Box 13292, Station E
Oakland, CA 94661

56 Ms. Micheline Masse
Stock Market Information Services,
Inc.
Montreal, Canada

57 Accelerated Indexing Systems, Inc.
3346 S. Orchard Dr.
Bountiful, UT 84010

58 Michael Sissman
Buttonshop Rd.
Williamsburg, MA 01096

59 Lorraine Boyce
15 Bruce Dr.
Newton, NJ 07860

60 Genealogical Bookshelf
P. O. Box 468
New York, NY 10028

61 John Crary
Rt. 1
Canton, NY 13617

62 W.H.M.
2686 McAllister
San Francisco, CA 94118

63 Donna Vernal
217 E. First
Waconia, MN 55387

64 Sandy Ritchie
Rt. 1, Box 17
Scottsville, VA 24590

65 Clark Mfg. Co.
Rt. 2
Raymore, MO 64083

66 Wallin Forge
Rt. 1, Box 65
Sparta, KY 41086

67 The Sobys
P. O. Box 180
W. Springs, IL 60558

68 Irvin Hoover
Rt. 1
Mt. Pleasant Mills, PA 17853

69 The Canery
250 Brookstown Ave.
Winston-Salem, NC 27101

70 Haviland Corner Matching Service
P. O. Box 82
Belmont, CA 94002

71 Berkley, Inc.
2011 Hermitage Ave.
Wheaton, MD 20902

72 Helt's Antiques
Durhamville, NY 13054

73 Strawflower, Inc.
801 W. Eldorado
Decatur, IL 62522

74 House of Antiques
202 N. 5th St.
Springfield, IL 62701

75 Helen Lawler
Rt. 1, Box 334
Blytheville, AR 72315

76 Antique Hardware Co.
P. O. Box 877
Redondo Beach, CA 90277

77 Porter Music Box Co.
5 Mound St.
Randolph, VT 05060

78 American International Galleries
17792 Fitch St.
Irvine, CA 92714

79 The Shade Tree
1318 S. Peoria Ave.
Tulsa, OK 74120

80 Peter Michaels
1922 South Rd.
Baltimore, MD 21209

81 Nicholas Fiscina
20-17 Jackson Ave.
W. Islip, NY 11795

82 Neumann Miller
5482 Lakeview
Yorba Linda, CA 92686

83 Karl Frick
940 Canon Rd.
Santa Barbara, CA 93110

84 Doe's Treasures
P. O. Box 6505
Providence, RI 02940

85 Marleda's
P. O. Box 2308
San Bernadino, CA 92406

86 Bob McCumber
201 Carriage Dr.
Glastonbury, CT 06033

87 Warden's Clock Supply
103 N. Boling
Claremont, OK 70017

88 Musical Americana
354 E. Campbell
Campbell, CA 95008

89 William D. Gilstrap
Rt. 2
Bevier, MO 63532

90 Vintage Patterns II
5304 Thrasher Dr.
Cincinnati, OH 45239

91 McKenzie Art Restoration Studio
2907 E. Monte Vista Dr.
Tucson, AZ

92 Calligraphic Ink
Crystal City Underground
Arlington, VA 22202

93 Emerson Hardwood Co.
2279 NW Front Ave.
Portland, OR 90710

94 Glass Masters Guild
621 6th Ave.
New York, NY 10009

95 Paul Baron Co.
2825 E. College Ave.
Decatur, GA 30030

96 Grady Stewart
2019 Sansom St.
Philadelphia, PA 19103

97 All-Art Restorers
140 W. 57th St.
New York, NY 10019

98 Rikki's Studio
2256 Coral Way
Miami, FL 33145

99 Mr. William and Co.
14 Garfield Pl.
Cincinnati, OH 45202

100 Bostonia Furniture Co.
183 Friend St.
Boston, MA 02114

101 Marcey Medgepeth
Rt. 179
Ringoes, NJ 08551

102 W. B. Lewis
231 Chatham Ave.
Pooler, GA 31322

103 Dorothy Briggs
410 Ethan Allen Ave.
Takoma Park, MD 20012

104 Helen Von Rosenstiel
88 Prospect Park West
Brooklyn, NY 11215

105 Rosemary Evans
9303 McKinney
Loveland, OH 45140

106 Billard's Old Telephones
21710 Regnart Rd.
Cupertino, CA 95014

107 Ritter & Son
P. O. Box 907
Campbell, CA 95008

108 Heritage Clocks of Mass.
P. O. Box 336
Sturbridge, MA 01566

109 Antique Music Box
1015 S. Teljon
Colorado Springs, CO 80906

110 The Broderick Gallery
119 Allandale St.
Jamaica Plain, MA 02130

111 Howard's Stained Glass
2602 S. 11th St.
Gadsden, AL 35901

112 American Lamp
100 Elm Hill Pk.
Nashville, TN 37210

113 Eleanor Sopp
15144 Chamisal
Ballwin, MO 63011

114 The Yankee Drummer
23 Burnham Rd.
Hudson, NH 03051

115 TEC Specialties
P. O. Box 909
Smyrna, GA 30081

116 Modern Technical Tools
Box 681
Hicksville, NY 11801

117 Wedgwood Studio
2522 N. 52nd St.
Phoenix, AZ 85008

118 Elaine L. Mooza
286 Wilson Ave.
Rumford, RI 02916

119 White's
P. O. Box 680
Newberg, OR 97132

120 Jacquelynn's China
4770 N. Oakland Ave.
Milwaukee, WI 53211

121 Oscar Black
1940 Old Taneytown Rd.
Westminster, MD 21157

122 Mrs. Emily Troutman
325 N. 6th St.
Reading, PA 19601

123 Bob Depenbrok
6638 Van Noord Ave.
North Hollywood, CA 91606

124 Pie Galinat
41 Perry St.
New York, NY 10014

125 Stephen W. Weston
Winthrop, ME 04364

126 Play It Again Sam's
5343 W. Devin
Chicago, IL 60646

127 James Broaddus
1635 S. 4th
Terre Haute, IN 47802

128 Silver Plated Flatware Matching
Service
142 Hampshire Rd.
Waterloo, IA 50701

129 Zephyr Glassworks
P. O. Box 42
Santa Cruz, CA 95060

130 Ross Jasper
2213 W. 2nd St.
Davenport, IA 52802

131 Best Books
2034 Empire Blvd.
Webster, NY 14560

132 Oak Knoll Books
680 S. Chapel St.
Newark, DE 19713

133 Yankee Peddler Bookshop
94 Mill St.
Pultneyville, NY 14538

134 Bailes
P. O. Box 150
Eureka Springs, AR 72632

135 Ron-Dot Bookfinders
P. O. Box 44
Greensburg, OH 44232

136 Carriage Association of America
P. O. Box 3788
Portland, ME 04103

137 The Fan Man
4606 Travis
Dallas, TX 75205

138 Carolina Caning Supply
P. O. Box 2179
Smithfield, NC 27577

139 Pat's Etcetera Co.
P. O. Box 777
Smithville, TX 78957

140 The Finishing Touch
5636 College Ave.
Oakland, CA 94618

141 Nostalgia
McHenry, IL 60050

142 Berkley, Inc.
2011 Hermitage Ave.
Wheaton, MD 20902

143 Irene Foukes
5170 Kitson
Orchard Lake, MI 48033

144 Mariana Redwine
756 Bluebird Cyn. Dr.
Laguna Beach, CA 92651

145 Char-Mar's
909 N. 7th
Garden City, KS 67846

146 E. Black
6130 SW 12th St.
Miami, FL 33144

147 Busy "B" Antiques
Rt. 1, Box 99
Zumbro Falls, MN 55991

148 Blue Plate Antiques
P. O. Box 124
Sherborn, MA 01770

149 Leslie
1359 Williamsburg
Flint, MI 48507

150 Stained Glass School
1705 S. Pearl
Denver, CO 80210

151 J & L's Jewelry
1915 Central St.
Evanston, IL 60201

152 R & K Weenike Antiques
Rt. 7
Ottumwa, IA 52501

153 Chicago Old Telephone Co.
P. O. Box 189
Lemon Springs, NC 28355

154 Thomas Malone Studio
12 Ashwood Rd.
Port Washington, NY 11050

155 Family Tree Antiques
P. O. Box 93
Merrick, NY 11566

156 Timesavers
P. O. Box 171
Wheeling, IL 60090

157 Al Bar Wilmette Platers
127 Green Bay Rd.
Wilmette, IL 60091

158 Connecticut Cane & Reed Co.
P. O. Box 1276
Manchester, CT 06040

159 Helt's Antiques
Durhamville, NY 13054

160 Vera L. Phillips
6427 S. Prince
Littleton, CO 80120

161 Lynne-Art's Glass House
P. O. Box 54-6014
Miami Beach, FL 33154

162 Cordier's Fine Arts
1619 S. La Cienga Blvd.
Los Angeles, CA

163 Daniel Zalles
580 Sutter St.
San Francisco, CA

164 Simms & Associates
18311 SW 95th Ct.
Miami, FL 33157

165 Diamonds by Terry
Burnsville, MI 55337

166 19th Century Co.
P. O. Box 1455
Upland, CA 91786

167 Fagan's
P. O. Box 329
Piedmont, AL 36272

168 DB Musical Restorations
230 Lakeview Ave. NE
Atlanta, GA 30305

169 Peggy's Matching Service
P. O. Box 476
Ocala, FL 32670

170 Reed Arts & Crafts
233 W. 5th Ave.
Columbus, OH 43201

171 Inez Pianos, Inc.
2473 Canton Rd.
Marietta, GA 30066

172 Art Reblitz Pianos
3916 N. Azalea
Colorado Springs CO, 80907

173 American Billiards
Suffern, NY 10901

174 Den of Antiquity
810 Rangeline
Columbus, MO 65201

175 Rand & Openshaw
3222 Larga Ave.
Los Angeles, CA 90039

176 The Sterling Fox
P. O. Box 398
Richmond, KY 40475

177 The Silver Queen
778 N. Indian Rocks Rd.
Belleair Bluffs, FL 33540

178 Senti-Metal Co.
1919 Memory Lane
Columbus, OH 43209

179 Ron Steidinger
Forrest, IL 61741

180 Woodsmith Classics
4021 California Ave.
Carmichael, CA 95608

181 Phoneco
Rt. 2
Galesville, WI 54630

182 Pierre et Jacqueline
1223 Green Bay Rd.
Wilmette, IL 60091

183 Paul Jones
429 S. Fredonia
Longview, TX 75601

184 Gary Bradley
Rt 3, Box 606
Corvallis, OR 97330

185 Sarah Bustle
   1701 Central St.
   Evanston, IL 60201
186 Triple X Chemical Co.
   841 Skokie Highway
   Lake Bluff, IL 60044
187 Herbert K. Goodkind
   25 Helena Ave.
   Larchmont, NY 10538
188 Park Place Antiques
   Long Grove, IL 60047
189 Kings Mill Services
   Highway 64
   Wasco, IL 60183
190 Specialized Repair Service
   2406 Bryn Mawr
   Chicago, IL 60659
191 Squaw Alley
   Main and Water Sts.
   Naperville, IL 60540
192 Lead 'n' Glass
   357 Stone Place
   Wheeling, IL 60090
193 Midwest Burnishing
   208 E. Main
   Round Lake Park, IL 60073
194 The Little Corner
   3939 W. Main
   McHenry, IL 60050
195 Wiebold, Inc.
   413 Terrace Pl.
   Terrace Park, OH 45174
196 Mountain Lumber
   1327 Carlton Ave.
   Charlottesville, VA 22901
197 Leslie Brooks
   166-25 Powells Ave.
   Beechhurst, NY 11357
198 Lafayette
   111 Jericho Turnpike
   Syosset, NY 11791
199 Robert W. Miller
   c/o Wallace-Homestead Book Co.
   1912 Grand Ave.
   Des Moines, IA 50309
200 Radio Shack
   2617 W. 7th St.
   Fort Worth, TX 76107
201 Sam Faust
   Changewater, NJ 07831
202 Musical Museum
   Deansboro, NY 13328

203 Ross's Antiques
   Rt. 6
   Milford, PA 18337
204 Porter Music Box Co.
   Randolph, VT 05060
205 Jukebox Junction
   P. O. Box 1081
   Des Moines, IA 50311
206 Gloria Kluever
   P. O. Box 124
   Sherborn, MA 01770
207 John Martin Antiques
   Rt. 3
   Clarksville, GA 30523
208 Paul N. Smith
   408 E. Leeland Heights Blvd.
   Lehigh Acres, FL 33936
209 K. Parry
   17557 Horace
   Granada Hills, CA 91344
210 Slot Machine Repair Service
   2404 W. 111th St.
   Chicago, IL 60655
211 Mort Jacobs Restorations
   231 S. Green St.
   Chicago, IL 60607
212 Mechanical Music Center
   25 Kings Highway North
   Darien, CT 06820
213 Harris Woodcarving
   120 E. Main St.
   Falconer, NY 14733
214 Art Scan, Inc.
   310 State St.
   Albany, NY 12210
215 Estes-Simmons Silverplating, Ltd.
   1168 Howell Mill Rd. N.W.
   Atlanta, GA 30318
216 Nu-Cane Seat Co.
   P. O. Box 995
   Lawrence, MA 01842
217 Landers Co.
   429 Memorial Ave.
   W. Springfield, MA 01089
218 Fan Motors
   3901 Sapling
   Mesquite, TX 75180
219 Art Essentials, Ltd.
   P. O. Box 260
   Monsey, NY 10952
220 19th Century Co.
   P. O. Box 599
   Rough and Ready, CA 95975

221 Ritter & Son Hardware
Dept. 923
Gualala, CA 95445

222 Antique Apparatus Co.
13355 Ventura Blvd.
Sherman Oaks, CA 91432

223 Burdoch Silk Lampshade Co.
3283 Loma Riviera Dr.
San Diego, CA 92110

224 MLB Novelty Works
P. O. Box 416
Exton, PA 19341

225 Chicago Antique Slot Machine Co.
1778 W. Algonquin Rd.
Arlington Heights, IL 60005

226 Tom Krahl
238 Hecker Dr.
Dundee, IL 60118

227 Charlotte Ford Trunks
P. O. Box 536
Spearman, TX 79081

228 Hamlin's Haviland
3510 W. 47th Terrace
Shawnee Mission, KS 66205

229 The Renovator's Supply, Inc.
Miller's Falls, MA 01349

230 Weber Furniture Service
5704 N. Western Ave.
Chicago, IL

231 International Silver Plating Co.
364 Park Ave.
Glencoe, IL 60022

232 Searjeant's Historical
Print & Restoration
P. O. Box 23942
Rochester, NY 14692

233 The Renovation Source
3512 N. Southport
Chicago, IL 60657

234 Wood 'N' Wonders
110 W. 2nd St.
Elmhurst, IL 60126

235 The Lamp Shader
222 Waukegan Rd.
Glenview, IL 60025

236 Adourian Bros.
2114½ W. Lawrence Ave.
Chicago, IL 60625

237 Seven Acres Antique Village &
Museum
Rt. 20 & S. Union Rd.
Union, IL 60181

238 Antique Bazaar
924 Ogden Ave.
Lisle, IL 60532

239 House of Martin, Inc.
4719 Woodward
Downers Grove, IL 60515

240 Midwest Stripping
102 E. Main St.
Round Lake Park, IL

241 Village Strip Shop
211 S. Main St.
Wauconda, IL 60084

242 Yankee Stripper
1283 E. Oakwood
Des Plaines, IL 60016

243 F.P. Turnip & Co.
2566 Prairie Ave.
Evanston, IL 60201

244 The Oak Peddlers
Spring Rd. and Montrose
Elmhurst, IL 60126

245 Victorian House Antiques
320 N. York St.
Elmhurst, IL 60126

246 Klavier Music Roll
10520 Burbank Blvd.
N. Hollywood, CA 91601

247 QRS Music Rolls
1026 Niagara St.
Buffalo, NY 14213

248 Paul C. Burgess
P. O. Box 12
Friendship, MA 04547

249 Carl A. Tessen
1620 Columbia Ave.
Oshkosh, WI 54901

250 Dennis Devine
722 E. Pierce St.
Council Bluffs, IA 51501

251 Arthur Sanders
Musical Museum
Deansboro, NY 13328

252 Paul Crist Studios
14903 Marquardt Ave.
Santa Fe Springs, CA 90670

253 Richard Simonton
4209 Burbank Blvd.
Burbank, CA 91602

254 Sheffield Knifemakers Supplies
P. O. Box 141
DeLand, FL 32720

255 Knife & Gun Finishing Supplies
P. O. Box 13522
Arlington, TX 76013

256 Ben Kelley, Jr.
4726 Chamblee-Tucker Rd.
Tucker, GA 30084

257 Cecil E. Clark
10903 Sharondale Rd.
Cincinnati, OH 45241

258 Bob Cargill
14401 136 St.
Lockport, IL 60441

259 Adrian A. Harris
Rt. 1, Zion Lane
Columbia, TN 38401

260 American Assn. of Conservators &
Restorers
1250 E. Ridgewood Ave.
Ridgewood, NJ 07450

261 Miss Louise G. Bluhm
Fogg Art Museum
Harvard University
Cambridge, MA 02138

262 Archival Restoration Associates, Inc.
510 School Rd.
Blue Bell, PA 19422

263 Miss Linda Shaffer
827 Ocean Front Walk
Venice, CA 90291

264 Ms. Wynne H. Phelan
3721 Ella Lee Lane
Houston, TX 77027

265 Insurance Information Institute
110 William St.
New York, NY 10038

266 Jordan Specialty Co., Inc.
95 University Place
New York, NY 10003

267 Ultra-Violet Products, Inc.
Walnut Grove Ave. at Grand
San Gabriel, CA 91776

268 Peters Antiques
110 Irving St.
Woodstock, IL 60098

269 The Hollinger Corp.
3810 S. Four Mile Run Dr.
Arlington, VA 22206

270 Musical Americana
Talking Machine Co.
561 Washington St.
Santa Clara, CA 95050

271 Mechanical Music Center
P. O. Box 88
Darien, CT 06820

272 A. P. S. Strippery
3421 W. Pearl St.
McHenry, IL 60050

273 Doyle H. Lane
Daniel Boone Village
Hillsborough, NC 27278

274 Forbes
1024 E. Willow Grove Ave.
Philadelphia, PA 19118

275 Antiques Etc. Ltd.
My Grandmother's Dolls
Rt. 47 and North St.
Huntley, IL 60142

276 The Carol Co.
612 S. Hawley Rd.
Milwaukee, WI 53214

277 Saf-Pak Sales Co.
P. O. Box 126
Oak Park, IL 60303

278 Mountain Lumber Co.
P. O. Box 285
Charlottesville, VA 22902

279 Victorian Reproductions, Inc.
1601 Park
Minneapolis, MN 55404

280 Mylan Enterprises, Inc.
P. O. Box 194
Morris Plains, NJ 07950

281 Wraptiques
P. O. Box 353
Larchmont, NY 10538

282 Dave Pierson
806 W. Market St.
Akron, OH 44303

283 Antique Slot Machine Co.
238 Hecker Dr.
Dundee, IL 60118

284 Pro-Pak
527 Dundee Rd.
Northbrook, IL 60062

285 Reisch College of Auctioneering
P. O. Box 949
Mason City, IA 50401

286 Mason City College of Auctioneering
P. O. Box 1463
Mason City, IA 50401

287 Missouri Auction School
1600 – 36 Genessee St.
Kansas City, MO 64102

288 Jim Graham School of Auctioneering
204 U.S. 1
N. Palm Beach, FL 33408

289 Free Play
35 E. St. Joseph St.
Arcadia, CA 91006

290 Sandler Products, Inc.
2229 S. Halsted
Chicago, IL 60608

291 Silver & China Exchange
P. O. Box 4601
Springdale, CT 06907

292 Les McGinnis
P. O. Box 3411
Amarillo, TX 79106

293 The China Match
9 Elmford Rd.
Rochester, NY 14606

294 Wedgwood China Cupboard
740 N. Honey Creek Pkwy.
Milwaukee, WI 53213

295 Marvetia Jack
148 12th St.
Silvis, IL 61282

296 Dialcraft
305 N. High St.
Columbus Grove, OH 45830

297 Fred Catterall
54 Short St.
New Bedford, MA 02740

298 D. E. Myers
430 Virginia Ave.
Sanford, FL 32771

299 L. Hulphers
3153 W. 110th
Inglewood, CA 90303

300 Beverly Sims
421 Plymouth St.
E. Bridgewater, MA 02333

301 Victory Glass Co.
P. O. Box 119
Des Moines, IA 50301

302 Burns Forge
11 N. John St.
Pearl River, NY 10965

303 Thomas M. Edmondson
79 Main St.
Torrington, CT 06790

304 Old Fashioned Milk Paint Co.
Groton, MA 01450

305 Antiques Mechanical Ltd.
605 Ethan Allen Hwy.
Ridgefield, CT 06877

306 Rawburn Hall
Rt. 341 at Brick School Rd.
Warren, CT 06754

307 Ruby Harrison Photographic
Inventory
1916 Lee St.
Evanston, IL 60202

308 Home in Focus
1919 Colfax St.
Evanston, IL 60201

309 Greg Spiess
246 E. Washington
Joliet, IL 60433

310 Tom & Judy's Chair Caning
1201 Florence
Evanston, IL 60202

311 Jeffrey R. Husar
6159 N. Nassau
Chicago, IL 60631

312 Pro-Strip & Long Ago Antiques
132 S. Lincoln Ave.
Carpentersville, IL 60110

313 Colonial Strip Shop
22 N. 29 Pepper Rd.
Lake Barrington, IL 60010

314 The Renovation Source, Inc.
3512 – 14 N. Southport
Chicago IL 60657

315 Galerie de Porcelain
520 Hillside Ave.
Glen Ellyn, IL 60137

316 H. J. M. Arts
1230 Elm St.
St. Charles, IL 60174

317 Guzzo's Crossland Studio
812 E. Main St.
St. Charles, IL 60174

318 Don Daley, Goldsmith
1210 E. State St.
Sycamore, IL 60178

319 Compleat Caning Workshop
4719 Woodward
Downers Grove, IL 60515

320 Nissan Oriental Rugs
7217 W. Lake St.
River Forest, IL 60305

321 Klug & Schumacher
3604 Waterfield P'Way
Lakeland, FL 33801

322 Weber Furniture Service
5704 N. Western Ave.
Chicago, IL. 60645

323 The Crystal Cave
1141 Central Ave.
Wilmette, IL 60091

324 Antique Watch Co. of Atlanta
P. O. Box 450066
Atlanta, GA 30345

325 Vintage Cash Register & Scale Co.
13448 Ventura Blvd.
Sherman Oaks, CA 91423

326 Stock Search Services
6320 74th Ave.
Summit, IL 60501

327 Custom House
6 Kirby Rd.
Cromwell, CT 06416

328 The Metal Mender
7 Silver Spring Park Rd.
Ridgefield, CT 06877

329 Byran Keysor
Main St.
Wolcott, NY 14590

330 Johnson Watch Repair
Box 121 F
Keenesburg, CO 80643

331 Freemont Glass Works
401 Bidwell Ave.
Freemont, OH 43420

332 Bob Patton
6400 Wurzbach #505
San Antonio, TX 78240

333 Joseph A. Flannery
219 W. Church St.
Galion, OH 44833

334 Master's Pieces Antique Cash
Registers
418 N. El Camino
San Clemente, CA 92672

335 Chili Doll Hospital
4332 Buffalo Rd.
North Chili, NY 14514

336 Charles D. Pheiffer
514 Philadelphia Ave.
Takoma Park, MD 20012

337 Eldred Schutt
Clarion, IA 50525

338 M. Lynn Reid
110 Highland Dr.
Union, SC 29379

339 Bennett Antiques
417 Marine Blvd.
Suisun City, CA 94585

340 Ragola Piano Co.
1111 Las Vegas Blvd.
Las Vegas, NV 89101

341 Elbinger Laboratories Inc.
220 Albert St.
E. Lansing, MI 48823

342 Craig Willardson
P. O. Box 8296
Spokane, WA 99203

343 Puett Electronics
P. O. Box 28572
Dallas, TX 75228

344 "Good Ole Stuff" Antique Lamp
Supply
610 N. Meridian St.
Lebanon, IN 46052

345 B & L Antiquerie
6217 S. Lakeshore Dr.
Lexington, MI 48450

346 Muffs Antiques
135 S. Glassell
Orange, CA 92666

347 E.R. Clair
Box 171, R.D. 2
Howard, PA 16841

348 Back Number Wilkins
Box 247
Danvers, MA 01923

349 Grandpa's Attic
112-A E. Washington
Goshen, IN 46526

350 PAB
2915A Atlantic
Atlantic City, NJ 08401

351 Eugene Brown
Box 477
Dodge City, KS 67801

352 Reggio Register Co.
Box 511
Ayer, MA 01432

353 Helen Von Rosenstiel
382 11th St.
Brooklyn, NY 11215

354 M. McDowell
Box 138
Granger, WY 82934

355 Handcrafted Walls
P. O. Box 844
New Canaan, CT 06840

356 Geisers
Rt. 1, Box 426
Rolla, MO 65401

357 Judy Giangivli
R. D. 6, Box 152
New Castle, PA 16101

358 Gen. Finley
6331 Shields Dr.
Huntington Beach, CA 92647

359 S-E Repair Services
Rt. 7, Box 147
Marshall, TX 75670

360 Dolls, Inc.
Rt. 3, Box 64-C
Sandpoint, ID 83864

361 Barb Barker
18 Farmstead Dr.
S. Windsor, CT 06074

362 This 'N That Shoppe
721 Jackson Ave.
Dixon, IL 61021

363 McKenzie Art Restoration Studio
2907 E. Monte Vista Dr.
Tucson, AZ 85716

364 Old Hotel Antiques
68 Main St.
Sutter Creek, CA 95685

365 The Silver Lady
P. O. Box 792
Friday Harbor, WA 98250

366 Sterling Locators
3300 W. Mockingbird, Suite B-101
Dallas, TX 75235

367 Smith's Book Service
Sunsmith House
Brewster, MA 02631

368 Atticana
P. O. Box 437
Sidney, OH 45365

369 Vintage Silver
33 LeMay Ct.
Williamsville, NY 14221

370 Betty Maki
1155 Willow St. #2
Faribault, MN 55021

371 Maurer TV
29 S. 4th
Lebanon, PA 17042

372 The Treasure Hunter
3783 Vivian Rd.
Monroe, MI 48161

373 Old Mill Books
Box 12353
Charleston, SC 29412

374 Marcy's Antiques
6777 Dumeny Rd.
Greencastle, PA 17225

375 Yesterday's Yankee
Lakeville, CT 06039

376 L. Pergl
Colesville Rd., R.D. 6
Binghamton, NY 13904

377 Vince's Glass Refurbishing
73 Rivermount Terrace
Burlington, VT 05401

378 Dori Miles
P. O. Box 159
Remsen, NY 13438

379 Grey Owl Indian Craft Co.
113-15 Springfield Blvd.
Queens Village, NY 11429

380 Havran's Navajo Rug Cleaners
48 West Main
Cortex, CO 81321

381 John N. Lewis
156 Scarboro Drive
York, PA 17403

382 Den of Antiquity
138 Charles St.
Boston, MA 02114

383 Santa Fe Glass & Mirror Co.
P. O. Box 2002
Santa Fe, NM 87501

384 Archival Conservation Co., Inc.
8225 Daly Rd.
Cincinnati, OH 45231

385 The Book Doctor
984 High St.
Harrisburg, OH 43126

386 Abercrombie & Co.
8227 Fenton St.
Silver Spring, MD 20910

387 Carrousel Midwest
Highway 83, Box 97
North Lake, WI 53064

388 Gray Sales, Inc.
P. O. Box 4732
Surfside Beach, SC 29577

389 Just Enterprises
2790 Sherwin Ave., Unit 10
Ventura, CA 93003

390 Rosene Green Associates, Inc.
1622A Beacon St.
Brookline, MA 02146

391 Chimney Farm Carriages
R.F.D. 2
North Canaan, NH 03741

392 Kromer's Carriage Shop
Box 115, R.R. 4
Hodgenville, KY 42748

393 Furniture Revival and Co.
P. O. Box 994
Corvallis, OR 97330

394 A. Beshar & Co.
49 E. 53rd St.
New York, NY 10022

395 George N. Kulles
115 Little Creek Drive
Lockport, IL 60441

396 Marc King
Rt. 5, Box 48
Bluntstown, TN 37617

397 L Eagle Feathers
758 E. Yale St.
Ontario, CA 91764

398 J & J Chrome Plating & Metal
Finishing Corp.
101 Orange Ave.
West Haven, CT 06516

399 The Wicker Shop
2011 Cleveland Rd.
Sandusky, OH 44870

400 Paxton Hardware Co.
Upper Falls, MD 21156

401 Custom Book Binding
1618 W. Main St.
New Lebanon, OH 45345

402 Clock Wheel Cutting
1039 Route 163
Oakdale, CT 06370

403 The Jukebox Junkyard
P. O. Box 181
Lizella, GA 31052

404 Wicker King
8241 Highway 70 South
Nashville, TN 37221

405 Trunks by Paul
411 Marion Dr.
Longview, TX 75602

406 George Studios
45-04 97th Place
Corona, NY 11368

407 R. Bruce Hamilton
551 Main St.
W. Newbury, MA 01985

408 Gary's Restorations
P. O. Box 3843
San Bernardino, CA 92413

409 Noel Bennett
P. O. Box 1175
Corrales, NM 87048

410 Century Glass & Mirror, Inc.
1417 N. Washington
Dallas, TX 75204

411 Crystal Mountain Prisms
P. O. Box 31
Westfield, NY 14787

412 Glassmasters Guild
621 Avenue of the Americas
New York, NY 10011

413 John Morgan
443 Metropolitan Ave.
Brooklyn, NY 11211

414 All-Tek Finishing Co.
355 Bernard St.
Trenton, NJ 08618

415 Baron-Rolen Jewelry
2825 E. College Ave.
Decatur, GA 30030

416 Sandra Brauer/Stained Glass
235 Dean St.
Brooklyn, NY 11217

417 The Condon Studios
33 Richdale Ave.
Cambridge, MA 02140

418 Fred & Nancy Dikeman
42-66 Phlox Place
Flushing, NY 11355

419 Harry A. Eberhardt & Son, Inc.
2010 Walnut St.
Philadelphia, PA 19103

420 Ita H. Aber Co.
1 Fanshaw Ave.
Yonkers, NY 10705

421 International Antique Repair Service,
Inc.
8350 Hickman, Suite 14
Des Moines, IA 50322

422 Keystone
P. O. Box 3292
San Diego, CA 92103

423 Anglo-American Brass Co.
Box 9792
San Jose, CA 95157

424 Aiku Amber Center
760 Market St., No. 617
San Francisco, CA 94102

425 The Clock Shop
806 Main St.
Lake Geneva, WI 53147

426 The Consortium
5 S. Wabash, Suite 1210
Chicago, IL 60603

427 Burdoch Silk Lampshade Co.
3283 Loma Riviera Dr.
San Diego, CA 92110

428 Paul Crist Studios
14903 Marquardt Ave.
Santa Fe Springs, CA 90670

429 Schutte's Lamp Supply
503 W. Spring St.
Lima, OH 45801

430 Van Parys Studio
6338 Germantown Ave.
Philadelphia, PA 19144

431 Timothy J. Somers Leathers
1340 W. School St.
Chicago, IL 60657

432 Jack T. Irwin, Inc.
601 E. Gude Dr.
Rockville, MD 20852

433 New York Marble Works, Inc.
1399 Park Ave.
New York, NY 10029

434 New York Nautical Instrument &
Service Corp.
140 W. Broadway
New York, NY 10012

435 Dorothy Badeu Elliot
3655 Egerton Circle
Sarasota, FL 33583

436 Joseph DeVoren, Silversmiths
6350 Germantown Ave.
Philadelphia, PA 19144

437 Michael J. Dotzel & Son
402 E. 63rd St.
New York, NY 10021

438 Elizabeth Crumley
2208 Derby St.
Berkeley, CA 94705

439 Karekin Beshir Ltd.
1125 Madison Ave.
New York, NY 10028

440 McMaster Fine & Antique Oriental
Carpets
997 Roxwood
Boulder, CO 80303

441 Art Ltd.
Stonecroft 2210
Grafton, WI 53024

442 Larry G. Harmon
1731 Pine Knoll
Caro, MI 48723

443 Andrew Hurst
2423 Amber St.
Knoxville, TN 37917

444 R. Wayne Reynolds
P. O. Box 28
Stevenson, MD 21153

445 Gotham Book Mart & Gallery
41 W. 47th St.
New York, NY 10036

446 The Antique Phonograph Shop
320 Jericho Turnpike
Floral Park, NY 11001

Clubs and Publications on Antiques and Collectibles

As editor of the WALLACE-HOMESTEAD PRICE GUIDE TO ANTIQUES AND PATTERN GLASS, Tenth Edition, there are a couple of requests I would like to make. First, when corresponding with anyone listed here, *always* enclose a self-addressed, stamped envelope (SASE). And when writing, please be patient. Some of the clubs listed here have moved without letting us know. Don't blame us if you cannot reach them. If you would like a particular club listed, let us know.

We are always glad to hear that you are making new friends, but, once again, please don't hold us responsible for any situation arising between you and anyone listed in this section.

The names of club publications and newsletters are indicated beneath the association's name in italic type.

Airplanes
Antique Airplane Assn.
Rt. 2, Box 172
Ottumwa, IA 52501

Akro Agate
Akro Agate Art Assn.
P. O. Box 758
Salem, NH 03079

Aladdin Lamps
Aladdin Knights
The Mystic Light of the Aladdin Knights
c/o J. W. Courter
Simpson, IL 62985

Horatio Alger
Horatio Alger Society
Newsboy
4907 Allison Dr.
Lansing, MI 48910

Alice in Wonderland
Lewis Carroll Society of North America
617 Rockford Rd.
Silver Spring, MD 20902

Amusement Parks
National Amusement Park Historical Assn.
National Amusement Park Historical News
P. O. Box 83
Mt. Prospect, IL 60056

Angels
Angel Collectors Club
Halo, Everybody!
11334 Earlywood Dr.
Dallas, TX 75218

Animal Licenses
International Society of Animal License
  Collectors
Paw Prints
4420 Wisconsin
Tampa, FL 33616

Antique Auto Racing
Antique Auto Racing Assn.
Rt. 1, Box 116
Ixonia, WI 53036

Antique Automobiles
Antique Automobile Club of America
Antique Automobile
501 W. Governor Rd.
Hershey, PA 17033

Horseless Carriage Club of America
9031 E. Florence Ave.
Downey, CA 90240

Veteran Motor Car Club of America
105 Elm St.
Andover, MA 01810

Antiques and Collectibles
Wallace-Homestead Book Co.
(catalog available on request)
1912 Grand Ave.
Des Moines, IA 50309

Autograph Collectors
Manuscript Society
350 N. Niagara St.
Burbank, CA 91505

Universal Autograph Collectors
Pen and Quill
P. O. Box 467
Rockville Centre, NY 11571

Autumn Leaf China
National Autumn Leaf Collectors
(publishes a newsletter)
4002 35th St.
Rock Island, IL 61201

Aviation
American Aviation Historical Society
P. O. Box 99
Garden Grove, CA 92642

Avon Bottles
Bud Hastin's National Avon Collectors'
  Club
The Avon Times
P. O. Box 12088
Overland Park, KS 66212

Western World Avon Club
Western World Avon Collectors Newsletter
P. O. Box 27587
San Francisco, CA 94127

Bands (Music)
Big Bands Collectors' Club
P. O. Box 3171
Pismo Beach, CA 93449

Banks
Mechanical Bank Collectors of America
P. O. Box 128
Allegan, MI 49010

Still Bank Collectors Club
Penny Bank Post
c/o Andrew Moore, Beverly Bank
1357 W. 103rd St.
Chicago, IL 60643

Barbed Wire
California Barbed Wire Collectors Assn.

California Barbs
1046 N. San Carlos St.
Porterville, CA 93257

International Barbed Wire Collectors
   Historical Society
International Barbed Wire Gazette
c/o Jack Glover
Sunset, TX 76270

New Mexico Barbed Wire Collectors Assn.
Wire Barb & Nail
2816 Camino Principe
Sante Fe, NM 87501

Barber Shop
Barber Shop Collectibles
c/o Robert E. Powell
P. O. Box 833
Hurst, TX 76053

Baseball
Society for American Baseball Research
The Baseball Research Journal
P. O. Box 323
Cooperstown, NY 13326

Beads
The Bead Society
The Bead Society Newsletter
P. O. Box 605
Venice, CA 90219

Bears
American Bear Club
(publishes a newsletter)
P. O. Box 179
Huntington, NY 11743

Good Bears of the World
Bear Tracks
P. O. Box 8236
Honolulu, HI 96815

Teddy Bear Boosters
P. O. Box 814
Redland, CA 92373

Beer Cans/Breweriana
Beer Can Collectors of America
Beer Can Collectors News Report
747 Merus Ct.
Fenton, MO 63026

Breweriana Openers Collectors Club
Just for Openers
63 October Lane
Trumbull, CT 06611

Eastern Coast Breweriana Assn.
961 Clintonville Rd.
Wallingford, CT 06492

National Assn. of Breweriana
Breweriana Collector
c/o Gordon B. Dean
Willson Memorial Dr.
Chassell, MI 49916

National Pop Can Collectors
National Pop Can Collectors
3014 September Dr.
Joliet, IL 60435

World Wide Beer Can Collectors
WWBCC Newsletter
P. O. Box 1852
Independence, MO 64055

Belleek
Belleek Collectors' Society
The Belleek Collector
P. O. Box 3179
Jupiter-Tequesta, FL 33458

Bells
American Bell Assn.
The Bell Tower
Rt. 1, Box 286
Natronia Heights, PA 15065

Bibles
International Society of Bible Collectors
The Bible Collector
P. O. Box 2485
El Cajon, CA 92021

Bicycles
Antique Bicycle Club
260 W. 260th St.
Bronx, New York, NY 10471

The Wheelmen
The Wheelmen Newsletter
1708 School House Lane
Ambler, PA 19002

Blotters
Blotter Collectors
c/o R.J. Romey
2222 S. Millwood
Wichita, KS 67213

Blue and White Pottery
Blue and White Pottery Club
P. O. Box 297
Center Point, IA 52213

Blue Willow China
Blue Willow Collectors Society
Willow Talk
4140 Lomo Alto, Highland Park
Dallas, TX 75219

(Blue) Willow Society
The Willow Notebook
6543 Indian Trail
Fallbrook, CA 92028

Boats
Antique and Classic Boat Society, Inc.
Rusty Rudder
P. O. Box 831
Lake George, NY 12845

Bottle Openers
Figural Bottle Opener Collectors Club
c/o Linda Weber
11 Mark Drive
Port Chester, NY 10573

Bottles
Antique Bottle Collecting (British)
Chapel House Farm, Newport Rd.
Albrighton, NR Wolverhampton
Staffordshire, England

Federation of Historical Bottle Clubs
The Federation Letter
10118 Schuessler
St. Louis, MO 63128

International Assn. of Jim Beam
   Bottle & Specialties Club
Beam Around the World
5120 Belmont Rd., Suite D
Downers Grove, IL 60515

National Ezra Brooks Bottle & Specialties
   Club
420 W. First St.
Kewanee, IL 61443

National Grenadier Bottle Club
3108A W. Meinecke Ave.
Milwaukee, WI 53210

National Ski Country Bottle Club
The Ski Country Collector
1224 Washington Ave.
Golden, CO 80410

Bricks
International Brick Collectors Assn.
c/o Dr. Ronald P. Anjard, Sr.
10942 Montego Dr.
San Diego, CA 92124

Buffalo Bill
Buffalo/Western Americana
P. O. Box 203
Pocahontas, IA 50574

Business Cards
Business Card Collectors International

P. O. Box 466
Hollywood, FL 33022

Buttonhooks
The Buttonhook Society
The Boutonneur
83 Loose Rd., Maidstone
Kent ME15 7DA, England

Buttons
National Button Society
The National Button Bulletin
2733 Juno Pl.
Akron, OH 44313

Cabs
American British Cab Society
P. O. Box 904
Stamford, CT 06904

Cambridge Glass
National Cambridge Glass Collectors
The Cambridge Crystal Ball
P. O. Box 416
Cambridge, OH 43725

Candlewick Crystal
Candlewick Crystal Collectors
17370 Battles Rd.
South Bend, IN 46614

Ohio Candlewick Collectors' Club
613 S. Patterson St.
Gibsonburg, OH 43431

Candy Containers
Candy Container Collectors of America
The Candy Gram
P. O. Box 184
Lucerne Mines, PA 15754

Carnival Glass
American Carnival Glass Assn.
American Carnival Glass News
P.O. Box 273
Gnadenhutten, OH 44629

Heart of America Carnival Glass Assn.
H.O.A.C.G.A. Bulletin
3048 Tamarak Dr.
Manhattan, KS 66502

International Carnival Glass Assn.
Carnival Town Pump
Rt. 1
Mentone, IN 46539

Carousels
American Carousel Society
(publishes newsletter and booklets at
   random)

1785 South Forest Rd.
Troy, OH 45373

National Carousel Roundtable
448 Riverside Dr.
Honesdale, PA 18431

Carriages, Horse-drawn
American Driving Society
The Whip
79 Southgate Ave.
Hastings-on-Hudson, NY 10706

Carriage Assn. of America
The Carriage Journal
P. O. Box 3788
Portland, ME 04104

Cars, Professional
The Professional Car Society
12505 Bennett Rd.
Herndon, VA 22070

Cats
Cat Collectors
(publishes a newsletter)
c/o Marilyn Dipboye
31311 Blair Dr.
Warren, MI 48092

Chess
The Verein Chess Society
P. O. Box 2066
Chapel Hill, NC 27514

Chrysler Cars
W. P. C. Club
P. O. Box 4705
N. Hollywood, CA 91607

Cigar Bands/Labels/Seals
International Seal, Label and Cigar Band
   Society
ISL & CBS News Bulletin
8915 E. Bellevue St.
Tucson, AZ 85715

Cigarette/Cigar Lighters
International Wristwatch and Cigarette
   Lighter Club
Old Flames and Old Timer
832 Lexington Ave.
New York, NY 10021

Lighter Collectors' International Society
829 Rockaway St.
Grover City, CA 93433

Cigarette Packs
Cigarette Pack Collectors' Club

c/o Richard Elliot
5 Governors Ave.
Winchester, MA 01890

Cigarette Pack Collectors of America
Brandstand
61 Searle St.
Georgetown, MA 01833

Circus Fans
Circus Fans Assn. of America
500 Kathy Dr.
Mesquite, TX 75149

Citrus Labels
The Citrus Label Society
16633 Ventura Blvd., #1011
Encino, CA 91436

Civil War
Civil War Token Society
6222 Little River Turnpike
Alexandria, VA 22312

Clocks/Watches
American Watch Assn.
39 Broadway
New York, NY 10016

Antiquarian Horological Society
Antiquarian Horology
New House, High Street, Ticehurst
Wadhurst, Sussex TN57AL, England

International Wristwatch and Cigarette
   Lighter Club
see **Cigarette/Cigar Lighters**

National Assn. of Watch and Clock
   Collectors
The Bulletin of the NAWCC
514 Poplar St.
Columbia, PA 17512

Cloisonné
Cloisonné Collectors Club
The Cloison
1631 Mimulus Way
La Jolla, CA 02037

Coats of Arms
Ship's Chandler
Wilmington, VT 05363

Coca-Cola
Coca-Cola Collectibles
P. O. Box 36M01
Los Angeles, CA 90036

The Cola Clan
The Cola Call

Cola Call Classified
3306 Yellowstone Dr.
Lawrence, KS 66044

Coin-Operated Games/Machines
For Amusement Only
1853 Ashby
Berkeley, CA 94703

Society for the Preservation of
  Coin-Operated Machines
100 North Central Ave.
Hartsdale, NY 10630

Coins
American Numismatic Assn.
P. O. Box 2366
Colorado Springs, CO 80901

American Numismatic Society
617 W. 155th St.
New York, NY 10032

Cookie Cutters
Cookie Cutter Collectors' Club
Cookie Cutters Collectors' Club Newsletter
5426 27th St. NW
Washington, DC 20015

Country Store
Country Store Collectibles Club
P. O. Box 521
Connersville, IN 47331

Bing Crosby
Bing Crosby Historical Society
P. O. Box 8013
Tacoma, WA 98408

Crosley Cars
Crosley Automobile Club
3323 Eaton Rd.
Williamson, NY 14589

Custard Glass
American Custard Glass Collectors
Partyline
P. O. Box 5421
Kansas City, MO 64131

Cut Glass
American Cut Glass Assn.
Hobstar
P. O. Box 7095
Shreveport, LA 71107

Depression Glass
International Depression Glass Club
2737 Wissemann Dr.
Sacramento, CA 95826

National Depression Glass Assn., Inc.
News and Views
8337 Santa Fe Lane
Shawnee Mission, KS 66212

Dionne Quints
Dionne Quint Collectors
The Quint News
P. O. Box 2527
Woburn, MA 01888

Disneyana
Disney Collectors Society
Sherman Turnpike
Danbury, CT 06816

The Mouse Club
The Mouse Club
13826 Ventura Blvd.
Sherman Oaks, CA 91432

Dolls
Doll Artisan Guild
The Doll Artisan
35 Main St.
Oneonta, NY 13820

Doll Collectors of America
14 Chestnut St.
Westford, MA 01886

Madame Alexander Fan Club
Madame Alexander Shopper
P. O. Box 146
New Lenox, IL 60451

United Federation of Doll Clubs
Doll News
2814 Herron Lane
Glenshaw, PA 15116

Doorknobs
Antique Doorknob Collectors of America
Doorknob Collector
P. O. Box 3088
Sedona, AZ 86340

Dorflinger Glass
Christian Dorflinger Glass Study Group
8701 Georgia Ave., Suite 406
Silver Spring, MD 20910

Duncan Glass
National Duncan Glass Society
The National Duncan Glass Journal
P. O. Box 965
Washington, PA 15301

Early American Decorations
The Historical Society of
    Early American Decoration, Inc.

The Decorator
19 Dove St.
Albany, NY 12210

Elephants
National Elephant Collectors Society
Box C-Y-7, 400 Commonwealth Ave.
Boston, MA 02215

Ephemera (Short-lived)
Ephemera Society
12 Fitzroy Grove
London, W1, England

The Ephemera Society
The Ephemerist
The Ephemera News
124 Elm St.
Bennington, VT 05201

Expositions
Expo Collectors and Historians
  Organization
Expo Info
1436 Killarney Ave.
Los Angeles, CA 90065

Fans
East Bay Fan Guild
East Bay Fan Guild Newsletter
P. O. Box 1054
El Cerrito, CA 94530

Fan Association of North America
Country Rd. 7
Clifton Springs, NY 14432

Fast-Food
Fast-Food Memorabilia
5000 Y St.
Sacramento, CA 95817

Fenton Glass
Fenton Art Glass Collectors of America,
  Inc.
Butterfly Net
P. O. Box 2441
Appleton, WI 54911

Fire Marks
Fire Mark Circle of the Americas
*The Fire Mark Circle of the Americas
  Newsletter/Journal*
10 Broadway, Suite 1645
St. Louis, MO 62102

Fishing Lures
National Fishing Lure Collectors Club
The N.F.L.C.C. Gazette
3907 Wedgewood Dr.
Portage, MI 49008

Flags
Flag Research Center
The Flag Bulletin
3 Edgehill Rd.
Winchester, MA 01890

Ford V-8s
Early Ford V-8 Club of America
P. O. Box 2122
San Leandro, CA 94577

Fostoria Glass
Fostoria Glass Society of America, Inc.
Facets of Fostoria
P. O. Box 826
Moundsville, WV 26041

Franklin Mint
The Franklin Mint Collectors Society
The Franklin Mint Almanac
Franklin Center, PA 19091

Gambling
Gamblers' Book Club
630 S. 11th St., Box 4115
Las Vegas, NV 89106

Gar Wood Boats
Gar Wood Society
P. O. Box 6003, Teal Station
Syracuse, NY 13217

Genealogy
Accelerated Indexing Systems
3346 S. Orchard Dr.
Bountiful, UT 84010

National Genealogical Society
1921 Sunderland Place NW
Washington, DC 20036

German Military
Imperial German Military Collectors
P. O. Box 651
Shawnee Mission, KS 66201

Glass, Early American
Antique & Historical Glass Assn.
P. O. Box 7413
Toledo, OH 43615

National Early American Glass Club
9 Commonwealth Ave., Apt. 4A
Boston, MA 02116

Golf
Golf Collectors' Society
Golf Collectors' Society Bulletin
638 Wagner Rd.
Lafayette Hill, PA 19444

Gone with the Wind
GWTW Collectors Club
6047 Oakland Mills Rd.
Sykesville, MD 21784

Graniteware
American Graniteware Assn.
Granitegram
P. O. Box 605
Downers Grove, IL 60515

Greentown Glass
National Greentown Glass Assn.
N.G.G.A. Newsletter
1807 W. Madison
Kokomo, IN 46901

Greeting Cards
Prank Mark Society
American Life Foundation
Watkins Glen, NY 14891

Guns
National Rifle Assn.
1600 Rhode Island Ave. NW
Washington, DC 20036

Handbags
The Costume Society of America
c/o Metropolitan Museum of Art
New York, NY 10028

Harmonicas
Society, Preservation and
    Advancement of the Harmonica
P. O. Box 865
Troy, MI 48099

Hatpins/Hatpin Holders
International Club for Collectors of
    Hatpins and Hatpin Holders
Points
H&H Pictorial Journal
15237 Chanera Ave.
Gardena, CA 90249

Heisey Glass
Heisey Collectors of America, Inc.
Heisey News
P. O. Box 27
Newark, OH 43055

Hubcaps
Hubcap Collectors Club
Hubcap Collector Newsletter
P. O. Box 54
Buckley, MI 49620

Hummel
Goebel (Hummel) Collectors' Club
Goebel Collectors' Club Insights

105 White Plains Rd.
Tarrytown, NY 10591
Hummel Collectors Club
Hummel Collectors Newsletter
P. O. Box 257
Yardley, PA 19067

Hymns
Hymn Society of America
The Hymn
Wittenberg University
Springfield, OH 45501

Ice Cream
Ice Cream Collectors
1042 Old Hickory Rd.
Lancaster, PA 17601

Imperial Glass
Imperial Glass Collectors Society
Imperial Collectors Glasszette
P. O. Box 4012
Silver Spring, MD 20904

Infant Feeders
American Collectors of Infant Feeders
Keeping Abreast
540 Croyden Rd.
Cheltenham, PA 19012

Inkwells
Society of Inkwell Collectors
The Stained Finger
5136 Thomas Dr. South
Minneapolis, MN 55410

Insulators
Glass Insulators
c/o A. L. Rash
Rt. 3, Box 669
Silsbee, TX 77656

National Insulator Assn.
3557 Nicklaus Dr.
Titusville, FL 32780

Yankee Pole Cat Insulator Club
5 Brownstone Rd.
E. Granby, CT 06026

Japanese Swords
Japanese Sword Society, U.S., Inc.
(publishes a newsletter and bulletin)
5907 Deerwood Dr.
St. Louis, MO 63123

Jazz
New Orleans Jazz Club of California
P. O. Box 1225
Kerrville, TX 78028

Jazz Records
International Assn. of Jazz Record
  Collectors
90 Prince George Dr.
Islongton, Ontario
M9B 2X8, Canada

Al Jolson
International Al Jolson Society
2981 Westmoor Dr.
Columbus, OH 43204

Keys
Key Collectors International
Key Collectors Journal
P. O. Box 9397
Phoenix, AZ 85068

Kitchen Equipment
Early American Industries Assn.
P. O. Box 2128
Empire State Plaza Station
Albany, NY 12220

Knives
American Blade Collectors
Edges
The American Blade
112 Lee Parkway Dr.
Stonewall Bldg.
Chattanooga, TN 37421

Ka-Bar Knife Collectors Club
The Collector
434 North 9th St.
Olean, NY 14760

Knife Collectors Club
1705 Highway 71 North
Springdale, AR 72764

National Knife Collectors Assn.
The National Knife Collector
P. O. Box 21070
Chattanooga, TN 37421

Lace
International Old Lacers
5206 Olley Lane
Burke, VA 22015

License Plates
Automobile License Plate Collectors Assn.
ALPCA Newsletter
P. O. Box 712
Weston, WV 26452

Michigan License Plate Collectors Assn.
601 Duchess Rd.
Milford, MI 48042

Charles A. Lindbergh
Charles A. Lindbergh Assn.
P. O. Box 63
Genevieve, MO 63670

Lithophanes
Lithophane Collectors' Club
Lithophane Collectors Club Bulletin
Blair Museum of Lithophanes
2032 Robinwood
Toledo, OH 43620

Locks
American Lock Collectors Assn.
(publishes a bimonthly newsletter)
14010 Cardwell St.
Livonia, MI 48154

Magic Lanterns
Magic Lantern Society
819 14th St. NE
Auburn, WA 98002

Manuscripts, Old
The Manuscript Society
Manuscripts
350 N. Niagara St.
Burbank, CA 91505

Marbles
Marble Collectors
c/o Gary Huxford
1114 Pine
Marengo, IA 52301

Marble Collectors Society of America
Marble Mania
P. O. Box 222
Trumbull, CT 06611

Matchcovers
Rathkamp Matchcover Society
Voice of the Hobby
1312 E. 215th Pl.
Carson, CA 90745

Medals/Tokens
American Numismatic Assn.
P. O. Box 2366
Colorado Springs, CO 80901

American Numismatic Society
617 W. 155th St.
New York, NY 10032

Token and Medal Society
611 Oakwood Way
El Cajon, CA 92021

Military
American Military Historical Society

1528 El Camino
San Carlos, CA 94070

American Society of Military Insignia Collectors
Trading Post
744 Warfield Ave.
Oakland, CA 94610

Military Vehicles Collectors Club
P. O. Box 33697
Thornton, CO 80233

Milk Bottles
MOO (Milkbottles Only Organization)
The Milking Parlor
P. O. Box 5456
Newport News, VA 23605

Mills
Society for Preservation of Old Mills
P. O. Box 435
Wiscasset, MA 04578

Miniature Figures
Miniature Figure Collectors of America
The Guidon
The Newsletter
102 St. Paul's Rd.
Ardmore, PA 19003

National Association of Miniature Enthusiasts
The Miniature Gazette
P. O. Box 2621
Brookhurst Center, CA 92804

Tom Mix
Tom Mix Straight Shooters Club
P. O. Box 15553
Belleville, IL 62224

Model A's
Model A Ford Club of America
250 S. Cypress St.
La Habra, CA 90631

Model A Restorers Club
24712 Michigan Ave.
Dearborn, MI 48124

Model Cars
Model Car Collectors Assn.
6434 Amherst Ave.
Columbia, MD 21046

Model T's
Model T Ford Club of America
P. O. Box 7400
Burbank, CA 91510

Model/Toy Soldiers, *see also* Miniature Figures

American Model Soldier Society/
American Military Historical Society
Dawk
1528 El Camino
San Carlos, CA 94070

National Capital Military Collectors
P. O. Box 166
Rockville, MD 20850

Motor Bikes/Motorcycles
Antique Motorcycle Club of America
2411 Middle Rd.
Davenport, IA 52803

Historic Motor Sports Assn.
Vintage Racer
P. O. Box 30628
Santa Barbara, CA 93105

Vintage Motor Bike Club
The Vintage Motor Bike Newsletter
330 E. North St.
Coldwater, OH 45828

Movies
Film Collector's World
Rapid City, IL 61278

Hollywood Studio Collectors Club
P. O. Box 5815
Sherman Oaks, CA 91403

Motion Picture Collectibles Assn.
Newsreel Magazine
P. O. Box 33433
Raleigh, NC 27606

Old Time Western Film Club
Western Film Newsletter
P. O. Box 142
Silver City, NC 27344

Studio Collectors Club
Hollywood Studio
P. O. Box 1566
Apple Valley, CA 92307

Music Boxes
Automatic Musical Instrument Collectors Assn.
The AMICA
P. O. Box 172
Columbia, SC 29202

Musical Box Society International
MBS News Bulletin
Music Box Society International Bulletin
Rt. 3, Box 202
Morgantown, IN 46160

Musical Instruments
American Musical Instrument Society

AMIS Newsletter
Journal of the AMIS
University of South Dakota, Box 194
Vermillion, SD 57069

Violin Society of America
Violin Society of America Journal
23 Helena Ave.
Larchmont, NY 10538

Nails
Texas Date Nail Collectors
Nailer News
501 W. Horton St.
Brenham, TX 77833

Needlework
Collector Circle
1313 S. Killian Dr.
Lake Park, FL 33403

Netsukes
International Netsuke Collectors Society
*Journal of the International Netsuke
    Collectors Society*
P. O. Box 10426
Honolulu, HA 96816

Netsuke Dealers Assn.
P. O. Box 714
New York, NY 10028

Netsuke Kenkyukai
Netsuke Kenkyukai Study Journal
P. O. Box 2445
Gaithersburg, MD 20879

Newspapers
International Newspaper Collectors Club
The Newes
P. O. Box 7271
Phoenix, AZ 85011

Nippon
International Nippon Collectors
Nippon Notebook
P. O. Box 102
Rexford, NY 12148

Occupied Japan
Occupied Japan Club
Old Heady Rd.
Louisville, KY 40299

The Occupied Japan Collectors Club
Occupied Japan Collectors Club Newsletter
18309 Faysmith
Torrance, CA 90504

Old Sleepy Eye Pottery
Old Sleepy Eye Collectors Club

Sleepy Eye Newsletter
P. O. Box 12
Monmouth, IL 61462

Olds, Curved Dash
Curved Dash Oldsmobile Club
3455 Florida Ave.
Minneapolis, MN 55427

Rose O'Neill
International Rose O'Neill Club
The Kewpiesta Kourior
309 Walnut St.
Branson, MO 65616

Owls
Owl Collectors Club
The Owl's Nest
Box 5491
Fresno, CA 93755

Russell's Owl Collectors Club
P. O. Box 1292
Bandon, OR 97411

Pairpoint
Pairpoint Cup Plate Collectors of America,
    Inc.
The Thistle
5906 Arbroath Dr.
Clinton, MD 20735

Paper/Advertising
National Assn. of Paper & Advertising
    Collectors
The Paper and Advertising Collector
P. O. Box 471
Columbia, PA 17512

Paper Money
Society of Paper Money Collectors
P. O. Box 4082
Harrisburg, PA 17111

Paperweights
American Paperweight Guild
312 N. Gladstone Ave.
Margate City, NJ 08402

Paperweight Collectors' Assn.
*Annual Bulletin of the Paperweight
    Collectors Association*
P. O. Box 11
Bellaire, TX 77401

Pencils
American Pencil Collectors Society
The Pencil Collector
603 E. 105th St.
Kansas City, MO 64131

Society for the Collection of Brand Name
  Pencils
The Branded Pencil
4601 W. 101st St.
Oak Lawn, IL 60453

Pens
The Pen Fancier's Club
The Pen Fancier's Newsletter
1169 Overcash Dr.
Dunedin, FL 33528

Pewter
Pewter Collectors Club of America
Pewter Bulletin
P. O. Box 239
Saugerties, NY 12477

Phonographs
Antique Phonograph Collectors Club
Antique Phonograph Monthly
650 Ocean Ave.
Brooklyn, NY 11226

Michigan Antique Phonograph Society
Lansing, MI 48909

Photographic
Photographic Historical Society
Photographic Historical Society Newsletter
P. O. Box 9563
Rochester, NY 14604

The Photographic Historical
  Society of New York, Inc.
Photographica
P. O. Box 1839, Radio City Station
New York, NY 10101

Western Photographic Collectors Assn.
The Photographist
P. O. Box 4294
Whittier, CA 90607

Pins
International Pin Collectors Club
P. O. Box 227
Marcy, NY 13403

Pipe Smokers
International Assn. of Pipe Smokers' Clubs
647 S. Saginaw St.
Flint, MI 48502

Universal Coterie of Pipe Smokers
The Pipe Smoker's Ephemeris
20-37 120th St.
College Point, NY 11356

Planters Peanuts
Peanut Pals

Peanut Papers
P. O. Box 4465
Huntsville, AL 35802

Plates
Collectible Resource Group, Inc.
6700 Griffin Rd.
Ft. Lauderdale, FL 33314

International Plate Collectors Guild
*International Plate Collectors Guild
  Newsletter*
5581 Sandoval Ave.
Riverside, CA 92509

The Plate Collector
P. O. Box 1041, ACC
Kermit, TX 79745

Plate Insider's Club
P. O. Box 981
Kermit, TX 79745

Playing Cards
Chicago Playing Card Collectors, Inc.
1559 W. Pratt Blvd.
Chicago, IL 60620

Playing Card Collectors Assn.
3612 Douglas Ave., Apt. 524
Racine, WI 53402

Police Insignia
Police Insignia Collectors' Assn.
135 Tate Ave.
Buchanan, NY 10511

Political Items
American Political Items Collectors
Keynoter
1054 Sharpsburg Dr.
Huntsville, AL 35803

The Political Collector
The Political Collector
444 Lincoln St.
York, PA 17404

Postcards
Angels Flight Postcard Club
2027 Appleton St., #5
Long Beach, CA 90803

Deltiologists of America
*Deltiology, A Journal for Postcard
  Collectors and Dealers*
10 Felton Ave.
Ridley, PA 19078

International Federation of Postcard
  Dealers
P. O. Box 1765
Manassas, CA 22110

Metropolitan Postcard Collectors' Club
c/o Ben Papell
146 - 17 Delaware Ave.
Flushing, NY 11355

The Organization for Collectors of Covered
　Bridge Postcards
The Bridge
603 E. 105th St.
Kansas City, MO 64131

Postcard History Society
(publishes a newsletter before shows)
P. O. Box 3610
Baltimore, MD 21214

Pre-Columbian Art
The Pre-Columbian Art Collectors of
　America
P. O. Box 11
Farmington, MI 55024

Prints, Historical
American Historical Print Collectors
　Society, Inc.
Imprint
555 Fifth Ave.
New York, NY 10017

Puppets
Puppeteers of America
2311 Connecticut Ave. NW #501
Washington, DC 20008

Radios/Phonographs
Antique Radio Club of America
The Antique Radio Gazette
1 Steeplechase Rd.
Devon, PA 19333

Antique Wireless Assn.
Old Timer's Bulletin
Main St.
Holcomb, NY 14469

Association for Recorded Sound Collections
ARSC Newsletter
P. O. Box 1643
Manassas, VA 22110

Association of North American Radio Clubs
ANARC Newsletter
557 N. Madison Ave.
Pasadena, CA 91101

Radio Club of America
P. O. Box 2112, Grand Central Station
New York, NY 10017

Vintage Radio & Phonograph Society, Inc.

Reproducer
P. O. Box 5345
Irving, TX 75062

Railroadiana
National Railway Society
P. O. Box 5181
Denver, CO 80217

Railroadiana Collectors Assn.
405 Byron Ave.
Mobile, AL 36609

Reamers
National Reamer Collectors Assn.
*National Reamer Collectors Association
　Quarterly Review*
277 Highland Ave.
Wadsworth, OH 44281

Red Wing Pottery
Red Wing Collectors
Red Wing Collectors Newsletter
c/o David A. Newkirk
Rt. 3, Box 146
Monticello, MN 55362

Norman Rockwell
Norman Rockwell Memorial Society
(publishes a newsletter)
12109 Wasatch St.
Tampa, FL 33624

The Rockwell Society of America
Rockwell Society News
Box BC
Stony Brook, NY 11790

Rogers Statuaries
The Rogers Group
The Newsletter of the Rogers Group
4932 Prince George Ave.
Beltsville, MD 20705

Royal Doulton
Royal Doulton International Collectors Club
*Royal Doulton International Collectors Club
　Newsletter*
U.S. Branch, P. O. Box 1815
Somerset, NJ 08873

Royal Souvenirs
Commemorative Collectors Society
25 Farndale Close
Long Eaton, NG10 3PA, England

Roycrofters
Roycrofters at Large Assn.
The Roycroft Campus Chronicle
Erie City
East Aurora, NY 14052

Salt Dishes
New England Society of Open Salts
c/o Otto W. Olson, Jr.
Olson's Way
East Greenwich, RI 02818

Scales
International Society, Antique Scale
  Collectors
Equilibrium
20 N. Wacker Dr.
Chicago, IL 60606

Seats
Cast Iron Seat Collectors
P. O. Box 14
Ionia, MO 65335

Sheet Music
National Sheet Music Society, Inc.
National Sheet Music Society Newsletter
1597 Fair Park Ave.
Los Angeles, CA 90041

Signs, Porcelain
Porcelain Advertising Collectors Club
P. O. Box 381
Marshfield Hills, MA 02051

Snuff Bottles
International Chinese Snuff Bottle Society
*International Chinese Snuff Bottle Society
  Journal*
2601 N. Charles St.
Baltimore, MD 21218

Spark Plugs
Spark Plug Collectors of America
The Ignitor
P. O. Box 2229
Ann Arbor, MI 48106

Spoons
American Spoon Collectors
Spooners Forum
P. O. Box 260
Warrensburg, MO 64093

The Scoop Club
Spoony Scoop Newsletter
84 Oak Ave.
Shelton, CT 06484

Souvenir Spoon Collectors of America
P. O. Box 814
Temple City, CA 91780

Stained Glass
Stained Glass Assn. of America

Stained Glass Magazine
1125 Wilmington Ave.
St. Louis, MO 63111

Stamps
American Philatelic Society
P. O. Box 800
State College, PA 16801

The Collectors Club
22 E. 35th St.
New York, NY 10016

International Stamp Collectors
P. O. Box 854
Van Nuys, CA 91408

The Philatelic Foundation
270 Madison Ave.
New York, NY 10016

Society of Philatelic Americans
P. O. Box 9041
Wilmington, DE 19809

Steamships
National Maritime Historical Society
Sea History
2 Fulton St.
Brooklyn, NY 11201

Oceanic Navigation Research Society, Inc.
Ship to Shore
P. O. Box 8005
Studio City, CA 91608

Steamship Historical Society of America,
  Inc.
Steamboat Bill
345 Blackstone Blvd.
Providence, RI 02906

Titanic Historical Society
The Titanic Commutator
P. O. Box 53
Indian Orchard, MA 01151

World Ocean and Cruise Liner Society
P. O. Box 92
Stamford, CT 06904

Steins
Stein Collectors International
Prosit
P. O. Box 463
Kingston, NJ 08528

Stereoscopics
National Stereoscopic Assn., Inc.
Stereo World
P. O. Box 14801
Columbus, OH 43214

Stevengraphs
Stevengraph Collectors Assn.
Daisy Lane
Irvington-on-Hudson, NY 10533
Sugar Packets
Sugar Packet Collectors Club
Sweet Collectibles
6033 105th St.
Kansas City, MO 64131
Swords
Assn. of American Sword Collectors
P. O. Box 341
Delmar, DE 19940
Tea Leaf Ironstone
Tea Leaf Club International
Tea Leaf Club International Bulletin
10747 Riverview
Kansas City, MO 66111
Telephones/Telegraphs
Antique Telephone Collectors Assn.
News and Views
P. O. Box 94
Abilene, KS 67410
Morse Telegraph Club, Inc.
Dots and Dashes
712 S. 49
Lincoln, NE 68510
Shirley Temple
Shirley Temple Collectors' Club
P. O. Box 524
Anchorage, AK 99510
Thimbles
Collector Circle
Collector Circle Gazette
1313 S. Killian Dr.
Lake Park, FL 33403
Thimble Collectors International
TCI Bulletin
P. O. Box 143
Intervale, NH 03845
The Thimble Guild
(publishes a newsletter)
315 Park End Dr.
Dayton, OH 45415
Thimble Society of London
(publishes a quarterly magazine)
Chenil Gallery, 181 King's Rd.
Chelsea, London SW3, England
Timetables
National Assn. of Timetable Collectors

The First Edition
199 Wayland St.
Hamden, CT 06518
Tin Containers
Historical Society of Early American
    Decoration, Inc.
The Decorator
19 Dove St.
Albany, NY 12210
Tin Container Collectors Assn.
Tin Type
P. O. Box 4555
Denver, CO 80204
Tobacco
Tobacco Collectors
713 Parrott Ave.
Kinston, NC 28501
Tokens/Medals
American Tax Token Society
American Tax Token Society Newsletter
P. O. Box 26523
Lakewood, CO 80226
American Vecturist Assn.
The Fare Box
P. O. Box 1204
Boston, MA 02104
Society of Ration Token Collectors
P. O. Box 1
Tecumseh, MI 49286
Token and Medal Society
P. O. Box 127
Scandinavia, WI 54977
Tools
Early American Industries Assn.
The Chronicle
The Shavings
P. O. Box 2128, Empire State Plaza Station
Albany, NY 12220
Toothpick Holders
National Toothpick Holder Collectors'
    Society
Toothpick Bulletin
P. O. Box 246
Saywer, MI 49125
Toy Trains
Lionel Collectors Club
Lion Roars
P. O. Box 11851
Lexington, KY 40578

The Toy Train Operating Society, Inc.
T.T.O.S. Bulletin
25 W. Walnut St., Room 306
Pasadena, CA 91103

Train Collectors Assn.
Train Collectors Newsletter
Train Collectors Quarterly
P. O. Box 248
Strasburg, PA 17579

Toys
Antique Toy Collectors of America
Rt. 2, Box 5A
Parkton, MD 21120

International Toy Buffs Assn.
25 W. Walnut St., Room 306
Pasadena, CA 91103

Matchbox Collectors Club
(publishes a newsletter)
141 W. Commercial Ave.
Moonachie, NJ 07075

Trades/Crafts
Trades & Crafts Society
605 Heathcliff Dr.
Seaford, NY 11783

Trucks
American Truck Historical Society
201 Office Park Dr.
Birmingham, AL 35223

Unique/Unusual
The Trivial Group
The Unique and Unusual Collection
603 E. 105th St.
Kansas City, MO 64131

Valentines
Antique Valentine Assn.
P. O. Box 178
Marlboro, NJ 07746

National Valentine Collectors Assn.
National Valentine Collectors Bulletin
111 E. Cubbon St.
Santa Ana, CA 92701

Wallace Nutting
Wallace Nutting Collectors Club
Wallace Nutting Collectors Newsletter
Kampfe Lake, East Shore Dr.
Bloomingdale, NJ 07403

Watch Fobs
International Watch Fob Assn.
5892 Stow Rd.
Hudson, OH 44236

Watches, *see* Clocks/Watches

Wedgwood
Wedgwood Collectors Society
(publishes a newsletter)
41 Madison Ave.
New York, NY 10010

Wedgwood Society
The American Wedgwoodian
55 Vandam St.
New York, NY 10013

Wedgwood Society of Philadelphia
246 N. Bowman Ave.
Merion, PA 19066

Whistles
Whistle Collectors
c/o Carlin N. Morton
121 Sea Horse Lane
Fort Myers Beach, FL 33931

Wild Turkey Whiskey
Wild Turkey Ceramic Society
P. O. Box 353
Lawrenceburg, KY 40342

Wine, French
Vin Mariani Wine Collectors
1724 20th St. NW
Washington, DC 20009

Wizard of Oz
International Wizard of Oz Club
The Baum Bugle
220 N. 11th St.
Escanaba, MI 49829

Woodcarvers
National Woodcarvers Assn.
Chip Chats
7424 Miami Ave.
Cincinnati, OH 45243

Wooden Desks
Wooden Desk Owners Society
9-20 166th St.
Whitestone, NY 11357

Wooden Money
American Wooden Money Guild
Old Woody Views
P. O. Box 3445
Tucson, AZ 85722

Dedicated Wooden Money Collectors
Timber Lines
5575 State Route 257
Radnor, OH 43066

International Organization of Wooden
    Money Collectors

Appraising, Insuring, and Protecting Your Antiques

Quality antiques are an appreciating investment, and because you should protect any investment, you should have your antiques appraised by a qualified appraiser. I'm a member of the Appraisers Association of America, Inc., 60 East 42nd Street, New York, N. Y. 10017. For $3.00 they will send you a list of all their members, nationwide. Another reputable organization is the American Society of Appraisers, Dulles International Airport, P. O. Box 17265, Washington, D. C. 20041.

Establish the cost *before* you allow an appraisal to be made. You will be quoted either an hourly rate or a flat fee. Keep in mind that there is no such thing as a licensed appraiser. Paying a fee to a city or county for a public service operator's license says absolutely nothing about the appraiser's qualifications. Ask for references. Then check those references before you avail yourself of the appraiser's services. Look for the appraiser who keeps up with current prices of antiques. Spend as much time finding the right appraiser as you did looking for quality antiques.

Because homeowners' and tenants' insurance policies in most states have built-in limits ($100 limit on coins and currency, $500 on jewelry and furs, $1,000 on firearms and related equipment), it's an excellent idea to have your antiques covered on a separate fine arts rider or a personal property floater. Too many Americans are underinsured. If

you think you're underinsured or that your antiques are not adequately covered on your homeowners' and tenants' policy, check with your insurance agent about increasing your coverage. Rates vary from state to state, according to the Insurance Information Institute. Remember, in case of loss, the insurance company can pay you only the amounts stipulated in your policy. In my opinion, insuring your antiques separately is a *very* wise investment. If you have jewelry or furs worth more than the $500 limit, you certainly need further coverage. This obviously holds true for your coins, firearms, silverware, and other collectibles.

The statistics aren't pleasant to think about, but every thirty-four seconds a fire breaks out in a home in America; a theft occurs every twenty seconds. What can you do about it? Well, stop thinking that because the doors and windows are locked, your possessions are safe. They aren't. Locks keep honest people out. What are your options? You could sell your antiques, but then you're right back to square one. Inflation dollars, taxes to be paid.

A lot of people think that if they receive an antique as a gift or inherit one they do not have to pay taxes if and when they sell it. Wrong! You pay capital gains taxes on any profit you make over the original purchase price or its value at the time you received it as a gift or by inheritance. Some very good advice: Don't get cute

43

with the Internal Revenue Service. You'd be surprised what they know about you, what they have stored in their computer banks. A few years ago I tried to sue the IRS and had a "really big" attorney. He filled me in on the facts of life. Simply stated, he said, "You haven't a chance in court, but you can whisper about them at cocktail parties!"

Always photograph each item. Use a camera with a good lens to get the details. If you're photographing a shiny surface or something behind glass, shoot it at a 45-degree angle. The fine features of a figurine, for instance, will show up better if photographed against a plain wall. Always group small items on a table, rug, or blanket, and get close enough to record good detail. You will not get detail with an inexpensive camera. Nor are instant-type printing cameras recommended for capturing close-up detail.

If you have a fire or a theft, immediately notify the nearest law enforcement agency and your insurance agent. Too few people know about C.I.C. and they should learn about it. C.I.C. stands for Crime Information Center, and 90 to 95 percent of all law enforcement agencies have this facility.

This nationwide system is usually a single computer, dual retriever system; a computer box tied into your state capital and also into the national C.I.C. system in Washington, D.C. If you have a theft of antiques, tell your local, county, or state police what specific items were stolen. They in turn put all pertinent information into the C.I.C. computer. It's recorded at your state capital and in Washington, D.C. But the great thing about it is that it also goes out to all fifty states. So, if some of your antiques show up in Maine or Texas or Oregon, *every* state knows what's been stolen. The dual response from your state capital and Washington could find your stolen antique instantly.

Security systems are fine if you can afford them. If not, use dead bolt locks—the bolt goes through the panel and cannot be opened with a plastic card or knife. Half the fun of owning antiques used to be displaying them for the benefit of yourself or your friends. If you insist on showing them off in a cabinet or on a table, install a security system. And *always* inform your local law enforcement agency when you're going to be away from home for an extended period.

Keep your small items—valuable coins and stamps—in a safety deposit box. That's like holding hands with a stainless steel female in Des Moines in February, but necessary.

Remember, two people can keep a secret if one of them is dead. You talk and friends who come to visit talk. Unfortunately, we're living with a generation of thieves. Today's burglars skip your $2,000 television-stereo set. They're after portable items such as your sterling silver place settings, your coin collection, your silver candelabra conveniently displayed on the dining room table.

No one can tell you how to avoid being robbed. Keep in mind that professional thieves are looking for antiques, especially the quality kind. It's difficult to outguess them. Just make sure you've taken every sensible precaution to prevent a break-in. With these actions and the security of an adequate insurance schedule, you can enjoy your antiques and collections in your own home with peace of mind for years to come.

About the Editor

Robert W. Miller is a member of the Appraisers Association of America, the National Trust for Historic Preservation, the Audubon Society, the National Geographic Society and the Smithsonian Institution.

He's a recognized authority on antiques and does consultant work for museums, worldwide. Former editor of The *Antique Trader Weekly,* former host of his own television program on PBS, Mr. Miller is also a contributor of articles on antiques and collectibles to the magazine, *Better Homes and Gardens.*

Eagle center, centennial, exposition	122-134
Elephant center	42- 50
Floral center, 6¼″	19- 29
Football center	53- 62
Franklin proverbs (Meakin)	74- 83
Gathering cotton	67- 77
Girl and boy, 6½″	34- 45
The Graces	56- 67
The Guardian (Meakin)	58- 67
Hen and chicks	33- 41
Horse racing, 7″	40- 50
Hunters and dogs, 7½″	42- 50
Importance of Punctuality, maxim verse	100-112
Little Bo-Peep	47- 57
Little Miss Muffet	42- 52
Mother and daughter, 6½″	43- 53
New Pony (Meakin)	44- 54
Nursery Tales, Cinderella	48- 59
Puss-in-Boots	44- 51
Rabbit, sign language around border	61- 70
Rooster	44- 50
Simple Simon	47- 52
Tired of Play, 6¼″	41- 51

Glass

Child's head, amber, 6¼″	43- 52
Clock, amber, 7¼″	42- 52
Clock, amethyst, 7¼″	66- 74
Daisy, 6¼″	41- 50
Dog's head, blue, 6¼″	44- 52
Ducks, two, amber, 6¼″	45- 53
Elephant center, 6″	35- 40
Hen and chicks, 6¼″	34- 41
Little Bo-Peep	49- 54
Star center	32- 39

Tin

Birds, animals, 8¼″	35- 45
Cock Robin	47- 56
Girl on a swing, 6½″	38- 47
Hey Diddle Diddle, 9¼″	45- 55
Jumbo, 6¼″	36- 46
Liberty, 5½″	66- 74
Mary Had a Little Lamb	45- 57
Numerals, 6½″	38- 47
Tom, Tom, the Piper's Son	44- 53
Victoria-Albert, 5½″	42- 51
Washington bust, 5½″	67- 76

Abacus

Used by the Chinese for centuries, it's simply a counting frame with movable wooden beads. The older ones are collectible.

Ebony frame and beads, brass rods (ill.)	$ 35- 43
Ornate teakwood frame inlaid with mother-of-pearl, beads, brass rods (ill.)	40- 50
Teakwood frame and beads, brass rods	36- 46

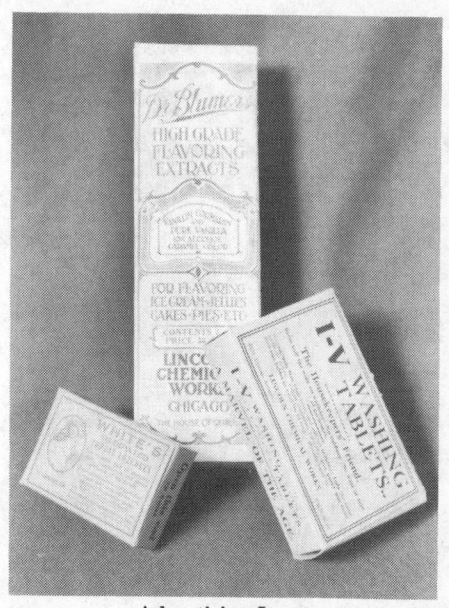

Advertising Items

All these, and more, created a new field for advertisers at the turn of the century. Most items listed here were given away free to customers. Today, all are collectible. Prices given are for items in good-to-fine condition, with small chips, dents, scratches, or tears taken into consideration. See **Clubs and Publications**, this Price Guide. There are many organizations to do with advertising items, such as **Bottle Openers, Breweriana, Knives, Paper/Advertising, Planters Peanuts, Tin Containers, Watch Fobs,** and many more. When you join or subscribe, tell them you found their names in this Tenth Edition, WALLACE-HOMESTEAD PRICE GUIDE TO ANTIQUES AND PATTERN GLASS.

Baseball Cards

There are several good books on baseball cards. Check your local bookstores or library.

American Motors Home Run Derby, 1959, ea.	$	7-10
Atlantic-Richfield Red Sox portraits, 1969, ea.		2- 4
Black Border Baseball Series, 1907-10, ea.		14-21
Buchner Tobacco, 1887, ea.		35-70
Dixie Cup Series "B," 1952, ea.		7- 9
Globe Clothes, 1916, ea.		10-16

Advertising Items

Holsum Bread, 1920, ea.	7-11
Milk Duds, 1971, ea.	1- 2
Peters Meats, 1961, ea.	4- 5
Stahl-Meyer Franks, 1953, ea.	87-99

(This series features the rare Mickey Mantle card, worth $600+.)

Breweriana

Beer bottle labels, before 1950, ea.	75¢ 1
Cardboard coasters, most brands, pre-World War II era, ea.	50¢ 1
Paper sign, Krantz Brewing Co., 25½"×37"	50- 65
Paper sign, Old Dutch Beer, 16¼"×22"	87- 99
Paper sign, Pabst Brewing Co., 28"×36½"	875-950
Paper sign, Rettig Brewing Co., 15"×18"	260-285
Tin sign, Burger Brewing Co., 15"×17"	77- 88
Tin sign, Falstaff Brewing Co., 24" dia. (being reproduced)	227-250
Tin sign, Felsenbrau Beer, 11½"×17½"	47- 55
Tray, Anheuser Busch, oval, 15½" wide	400-450
Tray, Elk Run Brewing Co., 12 dia.	137-162
Tray, Iroquois Brewery, 12" dia.	155-175
Tray, Rubsam & Horrmann, c. 1911, 12½" dia.	350-400

Buttons

Countless thousands were made, advertising almost every product in the world. Average price, 40¢-75¢ each.

Cigar Box Labels

H & H Specials, blue/white .	25¢-40¢
Happy Felix, green/red/ gold	25¢-40¢
Valley Cuba Cigarros, red/ blue/white	25¢-40¢

Cigarette Cards

Between the Acts, theater personalities, ea.	4- 5
Gypsy Queen, 1887, ea.	85-125
Helmar Turkish Cigarettes, 1916, ea.	2- 3
Old Judge, 1887, ea.	19- 28
Strollers, 1913, ea.	2- 3

Pepsi-Cola

Button, celluloid, "Drink Pepsi Today"	2- 3
Button, celluloid, Bigger, Better Pepsi-Cola	2- 3
Key chain, c. 1940	12- 16
Sign, wall, "Pepsi-Cola, 12 ounces, 5¢"	40- 50
Tray, 1906	170-205
Tray, 1925	44- 54
Watch fob, Jamestown Exposition, 1907	60- 70

Posters

Cardboard, wall, Clyde Beatty Circus, standard size	3- 4
Cardboard, wall, Golden Crescent Oranges, 14"×28"	17- 26
Cardboard, wall, Herkimer's Shoe Polish, 18"×37" . . .	19- 28
Paper, billboard size, Frank Buck Circus	170-210

Trade Cards

These were small, thin pieces of cardboard that advertised a manufacturer's product. From the late 1880s until the 1920s, about every company gave them away with every purchase. Those made in sets are harder to find than the individual cards. Few are dated. They come in all sizes and shapes. Prices given are for those in good condition.

Baking:

Babbitt's Baking Powder, girl with kitten	95¢ 1
Czar Baking Powder, black lady cook in kitchen	1- 2
Gold Mine Flour, miners panning for gold	1- 2

Clothing:

Boston & Meriden Clothing Co., small girl wearing glasses	1- 2
Gerber Hats, man playing accordion	1- 2
Hucklemyer Clothiers, man wearing top hat	1- 2
Myers-Cohen Haber- dashers, goat wearing brown derby	1- 2

Advertising Items

Orr's Pantaloon Overalls,
men, tug-of-war 1- 2
Rhostberg & Kline Men's
Suits, 3 men on bicycles .   1- 2
Union Clothing Co., young
lovers on bridge 1- 2
Coffee:
Arbuckle Bros., girl riding
goat 1- 2
Englehard Coffee, "The
Name Means Good
Coffee" 1- 2
Sarica Coffee, maid deliv-
ering note on tray 1- 2
Farm:
Ayreshires Milk, "You
Can't Go Wrong," cow . .   1- 2
Huber Tractors, "Econ-
omy, Durability, Safety,"
tractor 1- 2
McCormick Harvesting
Machine Co., farm scenes   1- 2
Princess Plow Co., "Queen
of the Turf" 1- 2
Vitality Feeds, rooster 1- 2
Food:
Dunham's Cocoanut, black
cook with cake 1- 2
Excelsior Cracker Works,
dancing couple 1- 2
Holmes & Coutts, fruit cake   1- 2
Woolson Spice Co., hunter
shooting bird 1- 2
Medical:
Brown's Iron Bitters, farm
girl with bucket 1- 2
Perry Davis Pain Killer,
professor at blackboard .   1- 2
Hunt's Remedy, boy in
sailor suit 1- 2
Kluckmyer's Soothing
Syrup, girl on swing 1- 2
Lash's Bitters, man on
horseback 1- 2
Miscellaneous:
Blue Ribbon Meat Meal,
hog wearing nightcap . . .   1- 2

Coney Island Amusement
Park, roller coaster ride .   1- 2
Heinz, girl in shape of pickle   1- 2
Keystone Jewelers, pocket
watch in keystone 1- 2
Soapine, the Dirt Killer,
whale on beach 1- 2
White Sewing Machines,
kitten making dress 1- 2
Shoes:
Drown Boots & Shoes, girl
with crow pie . . . .   75¢ 1
Chas. D. Griffith Shoe Co.,
shoe inside letter "G" . . .   1- 2
Star Brand Shoes, firm's
initials in large star . . . . .   75¢ 1
Tess and Ted School Shoes,
girl and boy dancing 1- 2
Stoves:
Andes Stoves & Ranges,
firm's name in shield . . . .   75¢ 1
Chicago Stove Works,
naked boy by fire in
woods 1- 2
Dixon's Stove Polish, black
man by stove, with black
kids 1- 2
New Tariff Ranges,
smelters in factory 1- 2
Tobacco:
Camel Cigars, Arab riding
camel 1- 2
Fast Mail Tobacco, railroad
engine pulling cars 1- 2
His Master's Choice Cigar,
dog looking at box of
cigars 1- 2
Ojibwa Chewing Tobacco,
Indian with tobacco leaf .   1- 2
Trays:
Change, Bromo-Seltzer,
"Cures all Headaches" . .   37- 45
Change, El Verso Havana
Cigars 28- 36
Change, Moxie, "Eat,
Sleep, Feel Better" 21- 30
Serving, Acadia Tea, "Yes,
It Is Excellent Tea" 60- 69
Serving, Elk Run Brewing,
large elk in field   138-160
Serving, Hampden Brewing
Co., "The Handsome
Waiter" 56- 65
Serving, Moxie, girl with
drink, c. 1905 . . . .   81- 95

Africana

Popular items are carved wooden statu-
ettes, animal hides, spears, masks, and
carved ivory.

Africana

Animal hide, zebra $200-300
Dog-face mask, 8½" high 72- 85
Grass face mask, 10" high 62- 78
Ivory carving, woman, 4¼" high
(ill.) 94-110
Jug, pottery, Sierra Leone, 9"
high..................... 52- 64
Shield, zebra hide, 5' high 182-225
Spear, all wood, 7½' long 78- 89

Agata Glass

Made in 1887 by the New England Glass Company, for less than a year. The glass item to be ornamented was first coated with a metallic stain or mineral color (of color desired) then spattered with alcohol, benzene, or naphtha. When this evaporated, it left a mottled surface on the glassware. Don't confuse the genuine with a marbled ware called Akro Agate.

Bowl, 3" high $1,900-2,300
Celery vase, pink 1,900-2,100
Cruet, multi-mottling 1,800-2,200
Sugar bowl, blue/green,
4½" high 2,300-2,500
Toothpick holder, four way .. 1,100-1,225
Tumbler, pink 900-1,000
Vase, lily, 11½" 1,800-2,100

Akro Agate Glass

The Akro Agate Glass Company didn't get around to making glass until 1932. Before that, in 1911, they were jobbers for a marble company in Ohio. In 1914 they moved to

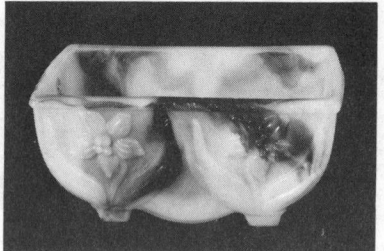

Akro Agate Glass

Clarksburg, West Virginia, and made their own marbles. They made various types of glass in several colors until they went out of business in the late 1940s.

Ashtray, leaf-shaped .... $ 16- 22
Bowl, green slag 17- 24
Cigarette holder 17- 22
Creamer, 3" high, blue 18- 28
Dish, shell-shaped, green 14- 19
Match holder, green, white, black 21- 30
Planter, blue/white (ill.) 24- 33
Powder jar, dog, white 35- 45
Tumbler, green/white.......... 21- 29
Vase, blue, 6" high 23- 33
Vase, green and white 25- 32
Vase, small, orange and white ... 24- 34

Alexandrite Glass

Thomas Webb & Sons, England, made this beautiful glass at the beginning of the 20th century. It shades from pale yellow to rose, then to blue. Stevens & Williams, England, also produced it, using the cut-through method to achieve their effect. A ware somewhat similar to the above also was made by Moser of Carlsbad, Czechoslovakia.

Goblet, amethyst, signed
Moser ....$ 190- 215
Match holder, 2½" dia.,
signed Webb 800- 850
Plate, 6", 7" dia., Webb 800- 850
Plate, 8" dia., signed Moser .. 160- 172
Rose bowl, 2" dia., fuchsia,
signed Webb 1,700-2,100
Toothpick holder, ITP, amber,
Webb.................. 1,800-2,100
Wine, 3½" high, Webb 275- 290
Wine, 4" high, Stevens &
Williams 266- 275

Almanacs

These small booklets forecast the weather as well as predicting many other daily activities.

Ayer's American Almanac, 1876,
published by Dr. J.C. Ayer &
Co. (ill) .... $ 18- 26

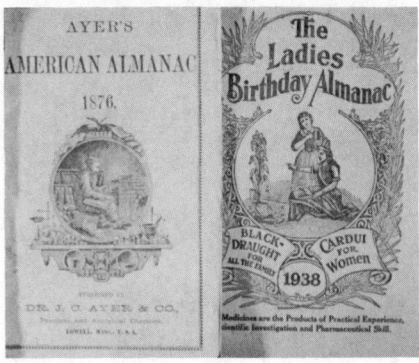

Almanacs

Amberina

Centaur Almanac, 1874, published by J.B. Rose, New York	14-	21
Farmer's Almanac, 1849, Boston	19-	24
The Gardener's Almanac, 1952, by Comstock, Ferre & Co., Conn.	20-	28
B.F. Goodrich Farmer's Handbook and Almanac, 1948	7-	11
The Ladies' Birthday Almanac, 1960 (ill.)	7-	10
Leavitt's Farmer's Almanac, 1893, Concord, N.H.	21-	30
Dr. Miles New Weather Almanac and Hand Book, Miles Laboratory, 1937	8-	11
Miner's Almanac, 1873, Pittsburgh	15-	23
Morning, Noon and Night, 1871-2, P.H. Drake & Co's Plantation Bitters	19-	24
New England Almanack, 1795, New London, Conn.	33-	40
Old Farmer's Almanac (no "k"), 1868, published by Brewer & Tileston	16-	25
Old Farmer's Almanack, 1853, published by Jenks, Hickling & Swan	30-	35
Pocket Almanac and Account Book, by Brown's Iron Bitters, 1889	12-	21
Poor Richard's Almanac, 1834, Tobias Ostrander	26-	40
Rawleigh's Good Health Guide Almanac Cook Book, 1927	7-	11
Tarrytown Argus Almanac, 1874	14-	20
Vinegar Bitters Almanac, 1879	14-	20
Watkins Almanac and Home Book, 1939	7-	12
Wright's Pictorial Family Almanac, 1891	9-	20

Amberina

Patented in 1883 for the Libbey brothers and their New England Glass Company,

Amberina was made by placing a small amount of gold in a transparent amber glass batch. The article was formed and allowed to cool below a glowing red heat; then specific parts were reheated at the glory hole. This caused the finished product to be shaded from amber to ruby red. Genuine Amberina is scarce today. "ITP" means Inverted Thumbprint. Lots of repros!

Art glass basket	$ 875-	925
Bowl, Diamond Optic, 4¼" dia.	220-	242
Bowl, Diamond Quilted, 4½" dia.	210-	245
Bowl, finger, ruffled, 4" dia.	250-	260
Bowl, fluted, applied handles, 4¾" dia.	310-	325
Candlesticks, pair, 14" high	242-	270
Caster, pickle, ITP, footed silver plateholder	610-	655
Celery, Daisy & Button, 5" high	345-	360
Celery, Diamond Quilted, 6" high	350-	362
Compote, Diamond Optic, 8" dia.	410-	435
Compote, wafer base, signed Libbey, 8" dia.	430-	445
Creamer, amber handle, 4½" high	275-	295
Creamer, Daisy & Button, 6" high (ill.)	235-	272
Creamer, ITP, clear handle, 4½" high	250-	270
Cruet, Diamond Quilted, c.g. stopper, 6¾" high	345-	362
Cruet, ITP, cut glass stopper, 7" high	270-	285
Cup, punch, Baby ITP	160-	170
Cup, punch, Herringbone, clear handle	165-	175
Cup, punch set 12, all signed Libbey	2,200-	2,450

51

Amberina

Cup/saucer, both signed Libbey	210-	225
Decanter, 14½" high, blown glass stopper	550-	570
Decanter, 12½" high, ITP, blown glass stopper	525-	555
Decanter, 12" high, cut glass stopper	525-	562
Mug, amber handle	162-	172
Mug, child's, clear handle	140-	160
Mug, swirled, Diamond, clear handle	168-	184
Parfait, ITP	181-	195
Pitcher, applied, twisted handle, Diamond Optic, 9" high	360-	375
Pitcher, Diamond Quilted, 9¾" high, clear handle	300-	320
Pitcher, milk, ITP, 10" high	275-	310
Pitcher, water, applied rope handle, 9" high	560-	580
Pitcher, water, clear handle, fuchsia, 9½" high	290-	320
Plate, 7½" dia.	150-	160
Plate, Diamond Quilted, 7¼" dia.	138-	143
Plate, fluted edge, signed Libbey in pontil	172-	192
Salt, master, 1½" high, Diamond Quilted	163-	173
Salt, master, 1½" high, ruffled edge	160-	180
Salt/pepper shakers, 4" high, pewter tops	252-	272
Salt/pepper shakers, 4½" high, ITP, pewter tops	262-	283
Salt/pepper shakers, 4" high, Expanded Diamond, p. tops	250-	270
Sauce, Daisy & Button, 4¼" dia., expanded diamond	188-	199
Sauce, Diamond Quilted, 4½" dia.	174-	184
Sauce, Diamond Optic, 4½" dia.	151-	167
Sugar bowl, 5" high, double handles, ITP	420-	440
Sugar bowl, 4¾" high, Diamond Quilted	362-	384
Sugar bowl, 4½" high, single handle	360-	390
Sugar bowl, 4½" high, double handles	355-	365
Toothpick holder, Daisy & Button, 3" high	229-	250
Toothpick holder, Diamond Quilted, 3¼" high	220-	240
Toothpick holder, ITP, 3½" high	250-	260
Toothpick holder, trefoil, 3½" high	252-	265
Tumbler, Baby ITP, 3¾" high	120-	133
Tumbler, Diamond Quilted, 4" high	152-	170
Tumbler, enameled flowers, 4¼" high	136-	154
Tumbler, Expanded Diamond, 4" high	119-	142
Tumbler, 4¼" high	122-	139
Vase, blown, with ribs, applied amber glass rigaree at neck (ill.)	232-	252
Vase, fuchsia, signed Libbey, 10" high	370-	390
Vase, Hobnail, 7¼" high	325-	345
Vase, ITP, 9" high	210-	228
Vase, Jack-in-the-Pulpit, signed Libbey, 14½" high	475-	550
Vase, lily-shaped, in silver plateholder, 7½" high	378-	392
Vase, ribbed, 10" high	371-	390

Amphora

A two-handled Greek vessel for holding wine, oil, etc. Originally made in 720 to 1200 in Rhineland villages as containers for wine which was exported to Britain and certain Baltic countries. What you find today in shops was made by Tillowitz in Germany in the late 1800s.

Basket, flowers in relief, 7½" high, signed	$260-280
Urn, 15" high, green/gold, blue trim, signed Amphora	315-340
Urn, applied flowers, gold handles, 9" high	220-235
Vase, applied flowers, gray/white, gold handles, 9" high	175-188
Vase, brown/green, jewel trim, 11¼" high	147-159
Vase, floral decor, 8½" high, signed Amphora with crown	250-270
Vase, gold/green, pink leaf decor, signed Amphora with crown	170-190
Vase, red/white/green, flowers, 10" high	132-142
Vase, yellow flowers, 7¾" high, signed	231-250

Andirons

Andirons

Dogs, as they were called in the earlier days, were usually made of wrought iron. Blacksmiths made them to personal order for the housewife. Brass andirons were known in America as early as 1740; even Paul Revere made a few.

Brass, finial top, 19th century,
    pr. (ill.) $400- 475
Brass, Georgian, pr., 17″ high 1,200-1,550
Brass, poodles, early 19th
    century, pr................. 510-530
Wrought iron, 15″ high, hand-
    forged, early 19th century, pr. . 198-225
Wrought iron, 17″ high, ring top,
    late 18th century 134-142

Animal Dishes (Covered)

Animal Dishes (Covered)

These covered dishes were made in clear, colored, and opal (milk) glass; also of pottery, usually from the Staffordshire District, England. They've been around for over 200 years and have been reproduced in every size and shape without exception. Prices shown are for the old and genuine. One of the finest collections in the United States is at the Houston Museum, Chattanooga, Tennessee.

Camel, 2 humps, white milk glass $130-140
Cat, white milk glass 140-150
Chick-in-egg-in-sleigh, white milk
    glass 92-110
Cow-shape cover, caramel slag
    (goes over butter) 210-230
Dog, purple slag 170-185
Ducks: clear glass, 6½″ 88- 93
    frosted glass, 6½″ 72- 82
    milk glass, white, 5″ 105-115
    multicolored 170-190
Eagle, milk glass 135-150
Fish on skiff, 7″ dia., milk glass .. 82- 92
Hens, colored glass:
    5″ and 6″, dark amber and
      light amber 160-170
    6½″ and 7″ dia., frosted 84- 95
Hens, milk glass:
    5″, white, Bakewell, Pears
      cross on bottom, wicker nest 80- 90
    5″, white with blue head 78- 88
    7″, white, lacy nest 205-215
    7″, white, lacy nest, caramel,
      flecked 205-225
Lamb, hexagon base, white 93-103
Pekinese dog, milk glass,
    4¾″ dia. (ill.) 70- 75
Quail, white milk glass 94-115
Rabbits; milk glass, 5½″
    same, mule-eared 108-118
Robin on nest, basketweave base,
    white milk glass 162-172
Swans:
    5″, blue 128-138
    6″, Staffordshire 325-365
    7″, Sandwich milk glass, pr. 400-420
Turkey, hen, 9″, Leeds 355-372

Apostle Pitchers

Embossed figures of the Apostles set within Gothic window frames were first made at Creussen, Germany, in the 17th century. Daniel Greatbach made one of Parian ware for the American Pottery Company, Jersey City. An Apostle cuspidor was made by the Congress Hill Pottery Company about the same time.

Apostle Pitchers

Cuspidor ....$ 475- 525
Pitcher, 18th century (ill.) 1,975-2,200
Pitcher, Parian ware,
    American 565- 585

Apothecary Collectibles

Apothecary Collectibles

Ammonia Jug, c. 1863,
    14″ high ....$ 5- 8
Apothecary funnel, copper,
    hanging ring, 9″ high 24- 33
Apothecary funnel, glass,
    7½″ high 13- 17
Baume stick w/case, 10½″ long .. 4- 7
Breast pump, rubber suction ball,
    4″ high 7- 11
Cachet kit (for making medicinal
    wafers), tin case, c. 1875,
    12″ long 35- 45
Cork press, lever type, 4 different
    sizes, 9″ long 64- 74
Counter scale, 2 large brass pans,
    full set of weights 165-180
Display case, tin/wood, 3 drawers 87- 97
Drug mill 75- 90
Hand scale, wooden box, full
    set of weights 55- 65

Hydrometer jar, hand-blown,
    12″ high 22- 30
Mentholatum lamp, brass, glass
    bowl, 6½″ high 25- 33
Microscope, brass, wooden case,
    6″ high 35- 45
Mortar and pestle, brass 100-120
Mortar and pestle, porcelain (ill.) . 33- 42
Nebulizer, #1, wooden box,
    7″ high 25- 33
Percolator, cylindrical, glass,
    hand-blown 7- 13
Pill machine, 16″ long 25- 33
Pill roller, wood, 3″ dia. 25- 33
Suppository machine, wooden
    case, c. 1880 .... 5- 9
Tablet mold, #10 (for making 50
    1-grain tablets), box 15- 23
Urinometer, glass, c. 1905,
    6″ long 4- 7
Vaporizer, steam, cardboard
    box, 6½″ high.............. 15- 23

Arequipa Pottery

This pottery was made by the patients at the Arequipa Sanitorium in Fairfax, California, from 1911 until 1918. The quality of the pottery ranges from poor to quite good. Six different marks were used. One of them is shown here.

Bowl, worker's initials, 7″ dia. ... $140-160
Bowl, matt brown, tan/white
    decoration, by Frederick
    Rhead, 5″ high 162-177
Vase, black glaze, 5″ high 98-107
Vase, blue ground, green/white
    decoration, 6½″ high 108-111
Vase, brown ground, blue/red
    decorations, director's initials
    (F.H.R.) on bottom, 9¼″ high 150-160
Vase, matt blue, tan/white
    decorations, 5¾″ high 105-118

Art Deco

Art Deco or Art Moderne was a style beginning after the Paris Exposition of 1925. It was the first modern design, Lincoln's Zephyr being a classic example. With its

Art Deco

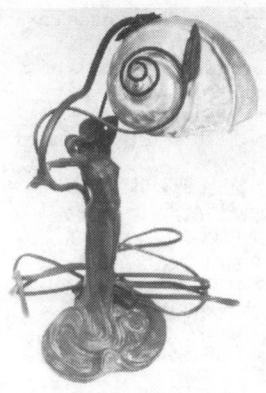

Art Nouveau

contrasting colors and wild lines, it was popular until World War II and is now back in vogue.

Cocktail shaker, aluminum	$ 30- 40
Compote, metal/glass, 19″ high . .	145-160
Cup, handled, green/blue, 3½″ high	42- 50
Desk clock, marble and cloisonne, luminous hands	67- 77
Dressing table set, cameo glass, inlaid silver, nudes, 1931	118-129
Elephant head incense burner . . .	36- 43
Figurine, ape in "thinking" pose, bronze, 12″ high	154-163
Figurine, dancing girl, partially nude, bronze, 10″ high	147-157
Figurine, lovers, bronze on marble pedestal, French	93-107
Flower holder, nude, porcelain, 7″ high (ill.)	48- 58
Lamp, Dutch silver (pot metal), kneeling black dancer, glass shade	110-128
Lamp, naked man holding nude woman overhead, bronze, glass ball shade	177-185
Mirror, hand, 11″ long, nude figure in relief on back	54- 64
Statuette, tubular metals, cubism design, dated 1934 on bottom .	72- 82
Vase, black glass, silver holder, Italian, 14″ high	156-166
Vase, blue, geometric design, 16½″ high, French	118-131
Vase, frosted lion over dead lamb, marble and glass, French, 1930s	116-141
Wall plaque, glass and cloisonne, nude figures, 8″×15″	118-140

Art Nouveau

Rebelling against the accepted forms of art, Art Nouveau was in vogue in the late 1800s, then until just before World War I. Tiffany collectors revived it and today it's highly collectible, in metal, wood, glass. Surface decoration is one of its identifying marks.

Bookends, nudes, sterling silver, pr.	$120-130
Bookmark, 2″ high	50- 60
Bowl, flower, Galle style, deep cut	158-190
Box, jewelry, footed, sterling silver, 4½″ square	89- 94
Brush, sterling silver	120-130
Buckle (also brooch), women's profile, silver	48- 57
Buttonhook, silver, entwining snake, 8″ long	40- 52
Buttonhook, sterling silver	68- 78
Cigarette case, chased copper, birds in relief, enamel-lined . . .	118-131
Clock, desk type, nude nymph, in metal case	69- 79
Figurine, dancing figure, bronze, 11″ high, marble pedestal	158-167
Figurine, nude male, Dresden porcelain, 14″ high	198-222
Flask, sterling silver, nude lovers on beach	320-350
Inkwell, devil's tail as penholder, bronze, 2½″ square	72- 84
Lamp, lady holding seashell shade, electrified, 14″ high (ill.)	650-700
Lamp, nudes holding 2 glass shades, 14″ high, electrified . . .	325-350
Lamp, young girl holding cigarette, cast iron base, 12″ high .	128-150
Match holder	48- 58
Nude, bronze, 8½″ dia.	720-745
Pin, angel, brass	22- 32
Pin, girl on horseback, brass	27- 37
Pin, profile of lovers, copper-on-brass	38- 48
Spoons, sterling silver, embossed figures, ea.	127-137

Tray, brass, reclining nude on beach, relief, 15" dia.	108-121
Tray, pin, reclining figures on couch, 14" dia.	62- 72
Tray, sterling silver, heart-shaped, initialed BHM, fluted rim	161-171
Vase, Amberina-type glass, in holder, 9" high	72- 82
Vase, pewter, autos racing, 13" high	141-151
Vase, pottery, flowers and butter-flies in relief, 10" high	60- 70
Vase, Tiffany type, iridescent, bronze holder, 14" high	142-158

Audubon Prints

Audubon Prints

Audubon originals, the engravings, are priceless today. The Havell edition, 1827-1838, the "Quadrupeds of America" series in 1844—all highly collectible. Many reproductions since 1915. Be careful. See **Clubs and Publications**, this Price Guide.

All prints listed here are from the Havell and Son Edition, London, completed in 1838.

65	Rathbone Warbler	970-1,150
74	Indigo Bunting	2,400-2,550
90	Black-and-White Creeper	920-1,100
101	Raven	3,250-3,450
115	Wood Pewee	925-1,100
133	Black Poll Warbler	1,200-1,400
139	Field Sparrow	1,100-1,400
148	Pine Swamp Warbler	975-1,100
155	Black-throated Blue Warbler	990-1,200
164	Tawny Thrush	990-1,250
179	Wood Wren	950-1,200
187	Boat-tailed Grackle	3,100-3,300
205	Virginia Rail	1,900-2,200
211	Great Blue Heron	4,400-4,800
232	Hooded Merganser	2,950-3,300
265	Buff-breasted Sandpiper	1,300-1,500

287	Ivory Gull	1,700-1,900
311	White Pelican	4,200-4,400
333	Green Heron	2,900-3,300
367	Band-tailed Pigeon	2,700-3,000
376	Trumpeter Swan (ill.)	4,500-4,750
382	Sharp-tailed Grouse	3,350-3,600
395	Audubon's Warbler	1,900-2,250
401	Red-breasted Merganser	4,200-4,400
409	Havell's Tern	1,350-1,550
432	Burrowing Owl	2,600-2,850

All prints listed here are from the Bien Edition, done in 1860 by Julius Bien in New York. All are full-sized plates.

18	Swallow-tailed Hawk	1,700-1,900
34	Barn Owl	2,250-2,500
57	Great Crested Flycatcher	390- 440
90	Yellow Redpoll	365- 428
124	Lesser Marsh Hen	395- 435
163	Henslow's Bunting	420- 455
189	Song Sparrow	410- 450
226	Fish Crow	1,700-1,950
244	Yellow-breasted Chat	1,100-1,350
293	Ruffed Grouse	2,400-2,550
358	Glossy Ibis	1,700-1,850
465	Great Auk	1,925-2,355

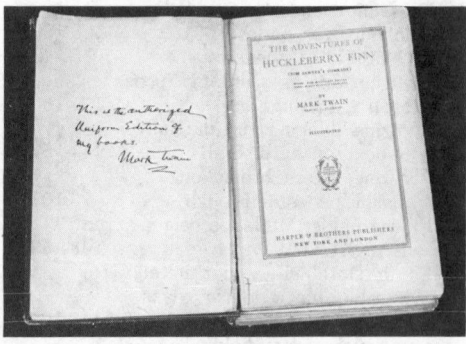

Autographs

Autographs (Philography)

The signatures of known people are always in demand by collectors. Keep in mind that governors, presidents, and the like seldom signed routine documents, leaving this menial task to clerks. Prices quoted here are for genuine signatures only. Holographs are letters written entirely by the hand of the signer of the letter. In the case of presidential letters, these are very valuable. A JFK holograph would bring upwards of $6,000. See **Clubs and Publications**, this Price Guide.

Arnold, Benedict (patriot/ traitor, Revolutionary War)	$ 4,800- 5,500

Caruso, Enrico, opera star of the 1920s	395-	420
Cody, "Buffalo Bill," program signature . . .	65-	80
Coolidge, Calvin, signed when campaigning through New England	195-	220
Davis, Jefferson, note declining invitation to supper party	440-	460
Eisenhower, Dwight D., note of thanks during World War II	245-	265
Grant, U.S., giving Sherman final approval to march to the sea . . .		8,400+
Grant, Ulysses S., letter of regrets for boy killed during war	750-	800
Hancock, John, Benedict Arnold's commission as Major General . . .		11,700+
Hitler, Adolph, signed document (careful of diaries here)		2,200+
Jackson, Andrew, inviting friend to horse race at Hermitage, Nashville	340-	360
Lincoln, Abraham, note to Union General		1,900+
Lincoln's Gettysburg Address, handwritten copy		110,000+
Lincoln, handwritten letters, 1846, poems to friend	2,600-	3,200
Lipton, Thomas, of tea fame, 1713	40-	50
Revere, Paul, handwritten signed document .		67,000+
Roosevelt, Franklin, presidential stationery, to senator, 1935 . .	220-	240
Roosevelt, Teddy, letter of regrets to banquet invitation	375-	420
Twain, Mark (if original) (ill.)		1,400+

Automobiles

Automobiles

In 1947 the Antique Automobile Club of America set up a system whereby buses, motorcycles, cars, fire engines, etc., made before 1930 would be classified as authentic antique vehicles. Generally, those cars from 1930 to 1948 are considered Classics. All prices listed here are for autos in restored condition. See **Clubs and Publications**, this Price Guide.

Apperson, Jack Rabbit runabout, 1914, 6-cylinder	$31,000-	34,500
Auburn, 4-cylinder touring, 1912	19,000-	25,000
Auburn, touring, 1917 . .	16,000-	19,000
Buick, 2-cylinder, chain drive, 1905	23,000-	27,000
Buick, Model E runabout, 1908	18,000-	21,000
Buick, Model 10 surrey, 1910	27,000-	32,000
Buick, roadster, 1914 . .	22,000-	27,000
Buick, 4-passenger coupe, 1922	16,000-	18,500
Buick, special cabriole, 1936	16,000-	19,000
Cadillac, roadster, 1904 .		27,000+
Cadillac, toy tonneau, 1910	34,000-	38,000
Cadillac, V-8, touring, 1916	27,000-	31,000
Cadillac, sport roadster, 1923		34,000+
Cadillac, Series 61 convertible sedan, 1939 .	34,000-	37,000
Chalmers, touring car, 1909	26,000-	28,500
Chandler, sport touring, 1921	24,000-	28,000
Chandler, 2-door sedan, 1926	19,000-	22,000
Chevrolet, Baby Grand roadster, 1913	23,000-	26,000
Chevrolet, roadster, 1913	20,000-	22,500
Chevrolet, touring car, 1916		17,000+
Chevrolet, 490 roadster, 1921	14,000-	16,000
Chevrolet, touring car, 1927	15,500-	16,500
Chevrolet, sport roadster, side mounts, 1929	19,000-	20,000
Chevrolet, standard sedan, 1935	12,000-	13,500
Chevrolet, standard coupe, 1937	9,000-	11,000
Chrysler, 6-cylinder sport phaeton, 1925 . .	20,000-	23,000

(continued)

Chrysler, Model 60
coupe, Royal 1926 ... 14,000- 15,500
Chrysler, 72 cabriolet,
1928 .... 18,500- 19,700
Chrysler, 6-cylinder
coupe, 1934 .... 13,800- 14,800
Cole, 5-passenger, V-8,
touring, 1916 .... 17,500- 19,600
Columbia Electric,
Victoria, 1904 ...... 15,000- 16,000
Columbia Electric,
Victoria, 1907 ...... 16,000- 17,000
Crane-Simplex, touring
car, 1912 .... 55,000- 60,000
Dodge, touring, 1915 ... 13,000- 13,800
Dodge, roadster, 1917 .. 9,900- 10,800
Dodge, touring car, 1922 9,300- 9,800
Dodge, coupe, 1937 .... 12,000- 12,750
Duesenberg, dual cowl
phaeton, 1921 ...... 175,000+
Duesenberg, phaeton,
1924 .... 195,000+
Durant, 6-cylinder
touring, 1923 .... 10,800- 11,400
Essex, 2-door coach,
1921 .... 6,000- 6,750
Essex, Boattail
Speedster, 1927 ..... 16,800- 17,900
Flanders, touring, 1911 . 16,000- 16,900
Franklin, roadster, 1910 25,000+
Franklin, touring, 1917 . 23,000- 24,500
Graham-Paige, 6-
cylinder coupe, 1929 . 10,000- 10,750
Hispano Suiza, touring
car, 1910 .... 43,000- 44,500
Hupmobile, coupe, 1910 12,000- 13,200
Hupmobile, roadster,
1913 .... 12,200- 12,950
Hupmobile, sedan, 1925 9,000- 10,000
International, high
wheel auto buggy,
1908 .... 11,000- 12,000
Isotta-Franschini,
tourer, 1914 .... 29,500- 34,000
Jordan, Playboy
roadster, 1920 ...... 18,500- 21,000
Jordan, 8-cylinder
sedan, 1927 .... 11,500- 13,500
Lafayette Nash, 2-door
sedan, 1936 .... 9,100- 9,875
LaSalle, rumble seat
coupe, 1935 .... 15,000- 17,000
LaSalle, opera coupe,
side mounts, 1936 ... 13,500- 14,800
Lincoln, LeLand
touring, 1922 .... 29,900- 34,500
Lincoln, limousine, 1924 13,700- 14,800
Lincoln-Zephyr, convert-
ible sedan, 1939 ..... 24,000- 27,000
Lincoln-Zephyr, convert-
ible coupe, 1941 ..... 25,500- 27,000
Locomobile, roadster,
1910 .... 25,500- 27,000

Locomobile, laundelette
coupe, 1915 .... 24,000- 25,500
Locomobile, sport
touring, 1922 .... 36,000- 38,000
Marmon, speedster,
1911 .... 28,500- 30,000
Marmon, Model 34
touring, 1916 .... 24,500- 27,500
Marmon, Model E 75
touring, 1924 .... 23,000- 24,000
Marmon, 8-70 convert-
ible coupe, 1931 ..... 21,000- 24,000
Maxwell, 2-cylinder
roadster, 1903 ...... 13,000+
Maxwell, roadster, 1912 14,900- 15,900
Mercedes, 2-passenger
racer, 4-cylinder, 1908
(ill.) .... 245,000+
Mercedes, touring car,
1912 .... 74,000- 79,000
Mercer, raceabout, 1913 250,000+
Mercer, sporting, 1915 . 55,000+
Moon, touring car, 1922 16,000- 18,000
Nash, touring car, 1921 . 15,000- 17,000
Nash, Special 6 sedan,
1926 .... 9,600- 10,500
Nash 400 touring,
1929 .... 9,900- 11,000
Oakland, 6-cylinder
touring, 1913 .... 24,500- 27,000
Oakland, touring, 1923 . 13,800- 15,900
Oldsmobile, roadster,
1901 .... 13,000- 15,000
Oldsmobile, touring,
1918 .... 15,000+
Oldsmobile, V-8 sport
touring, 1928 .... 12,200- 13,600
Overland, roadster, 1911 15,500- 16,700
Overland, Model 85
touring, 1917 .... 12,400- 13,200
Packard, 4-cylinder
roadster, 1909 ...... 58,000- 64,000
Packard, Twin-Six, 7-
passenger touring,
1915 .... 50,000+
Packard, 7-passenger
limousine, 1922 ..... 16,200- 17,200
Packard, 8-cylinder,
120C sedan, 1936 .... 15,000- 15,600
Pierce-Arrow, Great
Arrow, 1907 .... 58,500- 62,000
Pierce-Arrow, Model 38
touring, 1914 .... 59,000- 63,500
Pierce-Arrow, 7-
passenger touring,
1922 .... 48,000- 53,000
Rambler, 2-cylinder
touring, 1905 .... 16,600- 17,450
Regal, underslung
coupe, 1913 .... 24,500- 26,000
Reo, 1-cylinder
runabout, 1904 ..... 14,000- 16,000

Reo, 4-cylinder touring,
1910 . . . .   15,000+
Rolls-Royce, roadster
Silver Ghost, 1910 . . .   245,000+
Rolls-Royce, landaulet,
1914 110,000-118,000
Rolls-Royce, tourer,
1920 . . . .   82,000+
Rolls-Royce, Model 20
touring, 1923 . . . . 57,000- 64,000
Sears, motor buggy,
1907 . . . . 13,500- 14,800
Singer, LeMans
roadster, 1933 . . . . . . 11,000- 11,700
Stanley Steamer,
runabout, 1904 . . . . . 28,000- 31,000
Stanley Steamer,
touring car, 1908 . . . . 44,000- 46,000
Stevens-Duryea,
roadster, 1909 . . . . . . 47,000- 51,500
Studebaker, roadster,
1911 . . . . 14,700- 15,800
Studebaker, Model 25
touring, 1913 . . . . 17,200- 18,300
Studebaker, doctor's
coupe, 1924 . . . . 11,500- 12,600
Stutz, Bearcat roadster,
1914 . . . .   128,000+
Stutz, Bearcat
speedster, 1919 . . . . .   72,000+
Stutz, 6-cylinder
touring, 1924 . . . . 39,000- 44,500
Thomas, roadster, 1909 .   46,000+
Winton, touring car,
1917 . . . . 45,500- 47,500
Winton, 4-passenger
touring, 1921 . . . . 31,000- 33,500
Winton, 7-passenger
touring, 1923 . . . . 40,000- 42,500

Obviously, there are hundreds of other automobiles. Sorry if we've missed your model.

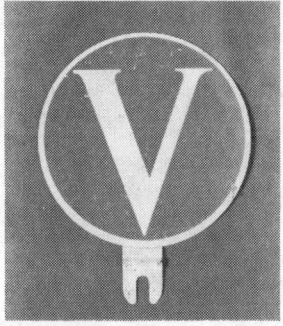

Automobiliana

Automobiliana

From 1900 until 1930 over 1,500 different makes of automobiles were manufactured in the United States. Practically every part of the car is collectible today, especially items such as radiator caps and emblems, dashboard clocks, brass headlamps, hubcaps.

Advertisement, Aerocar Motor
Co., "There's No Getting
Away," 1908 . . . .$ 39- 46
Advertisement, Dragon Touring
Car, "The motor that motes,"
1907 . . . .   48- 53
Advertisement, Goodrich Safety
Tread tires, 1914 . . . .   26- 36
Advertisement, Metz 22, $475,
The Gearless Car, 1913 . . .   34- 42
Advertisement, Midland Motor
Co., Moline, Ill., 1910 . . . .   34- 39
Advertisement, Murine (A tonic
for the auto eye), 1907 . . . . . .   36- 45
Auto Blue Books, 1909 through
1919, ea. 34- 42
Auto Green Books, 1915 through
1926, each 25- 32
Auto Wiring Manual, Abbot-
Detroit cars, 1910-1914 . . . . .   54- 62
Book, *Get Out and Get Under,*
1913, illustrated 47- 56
Book, *Salesman's Cadillac,* 1913 .   57- 66
Book, *The Open Road,* 1914 . . . . .   45- 55
Book, *The Easy Route to
California,* 1911   94-110
Bumper sign, "V" (ill.) 13- 21
Carbide tank for 1909 Ford
Model-T   177-185
Carbide tank for 1912 Cadillac . . .   231-240
Dashboard clock for 1914 Pierce
Arrow   94-108
Dashboard clock for 1916
Packard   94-107
Emblems: average price, each . . .   32- 41
Buick   Cadillac   McFarlan   Stutz
Oakland   Kleiber   DaVis   Overland
Franklin   Essex   DeLage
Bail handle light, brass, 1909
Hupmobile   370-440
Hood ornament, 1930s 25- 32
Horn, double twist, brass, bulb-
type, 1908 Maxwell   142-152
License plates, enamel-over-
metal, 1909-1916, average price   39- 62
Magazine *Car Life,* 1916, 12
issues, all   178-191
Motor meter (forerunner of the
speedometer), 1912 Marmon . .   110-128
Motor meter, 1913 Mercer   145-165
Motor meter, 1914 Columbia . . .   81- 91
Owner's manual, 1908 Rolls
Royce   245-281
Owner's manual, 1914 Stutz
Bearcat   179-191
Poster, 1913 Auto Show, Chicago,
15"×20", paper   178-210

Radiator cap ornament, knight
with lance 88- 97
Radiator cap ornament, Lady
Ascot, Rolls Royce, silver, 1911 394-425
Road map showing routes to
Chicago from New York City,
1909 .... 77- 88
Sales catalogs, General Motors
cars, 1916-1925, all 330-395
Signature of Ramsey E. Olds,
creator of the Reo and the
Oldsmobile, 1909 .... 40- 50
Spark coil for 1910 Model-T;
still works 88- 97
Spark plug for 1909 Saxon 24- 35
Vases, cut glass, used in back
seat of 1912 Locomobile limo .. 110-120
Vases, used in back seat of 1913
Cadillac limousine, pr., cut
glass 115-122

Autumn Leaf

Autumn Leaf (Jewel Tea Co.)

The Autumn Leaf line in early years was
referred to only as Hall, Jewel or Autumnal
design. It wasn't until the 1940s that the
pattern was given the name Autumn. In
1960 it got its name Autumn Leaf. Designed
by Arden Richards of the Hall China Company, East Liverpool, Ohio, for the Jewel Tea
Company in 1933, it quickly became a collectible. At least three other firms used the
Autumnal design, but Hall's was then and
still is the most famous and most sought
after. All pieces listed were made by Hall for
the Jewel Tea Company. See, **Clubs and
Publications**, this Price Guide.

Bowls, 6″, 6½″, 8½″, 9″ .... $ 10- 26
Butter dish, covered, ¼-lb....... 35- 45
Butter dish, covered, 1-lb. 77- 89
Cake plate, footed, metal base ... 16- 27
Cake safe 26- 41
Casserole (top is small pie plate) . 27- 35
Clock, electric, 9½″ dia. 228-261
Coffee dispenser, 10½″ high 39- 49
Cookie jar, covered, tab handles . 44- 52
Custard cup 9- 13

Gravy boat 17- 23
Pitcher, milk, water 15- 22
Platters, 11″, 11½″, 13″ 13½″ .. 12- 20
Salt/pepper set (ill.) 16- 24
Tablecloth, 54″×54″ and
54″×72″ 61- 70
Toaster cover, plastic 15- 22
Vegetable dish, oval 24- 32

Aventurine Glass

This yellowish glass has large numbers of
small crystals of copper. It is reasonably collectible, though Fostoria Glass Company,
Moundsville, West Virginia, has produced a
fair imitation in recent years.

Bowl, ruffled edges, 6″ dia. $138-150
Pitcher, clear applied handle, 6″
high 152-161
Rose bowl, 3″ high 140-150
Vase, flowers, 4″ high 185-195
Vase, flowers, ruffled lip, 11½″
high 228-240
Vase, fluted top, 10″ high 224-239

Baccarat Glass

Baccarat Glass

French, by La Compagnie Des Cristalleries
De Baccarat; they also had a factory in
Alsace-Lorraine. Factory started in 1765.
Famous for their cane and millefiori paperweights, 1860 to 1880. Careful! Excellent
fakes are coming into the U.S. Know your
dealer if you're after a genuine paperweight.

Bell, clear-cut .... $ 56- 66
Bird, frosted, 2-5/8″ long 48- 57
Bobeche, crystal, 3½″ dia., pr. 54- 65
Bobeche (wax catchers on
candlesticks), lacy, pr. 47- 57
Bottle, cologne, cut and
polished crystal.......... 45- 52

Eagle and Eaglets   Banks, Mechanical   Always Did 'Spise a Mule

Popeye knockout bank	400-	450
Preacher in pulpit	11,400-	11,650
Professor Pugfrog	2,600-	2,775
Pump and bucket	570-	640
Punch and Judy (iron and tin)	1,550-	1,700
* Punch and Judy, small or large letters	545-	610
Queen Victoria	5,200-	5,400
Rabbit in cabbage	310-	340
Rabbit, standing, on round base	345-	365
Red Riding Hood		5,000+
Rival		6,600+
Roller skating rink		4,400+
Rooster	245-	275
Saluting sailor (tin)	720-	740
Sambo	540-	580
* Santa Claus at chimney	450-	525
Scotsman (tin)	345-	375
Sentry bank (tin)	900-	975
Shoot the chute	6,400-	6,700
Signal cabin (tin)	365-	420
Speaking dog	340-	370
* Stump speaker	725-	775
Tabby bank	425-	455
Tammany	210-	240
Tank and cannon bank	460-	480
* Teddy and the bear	710-	760
Tiger (tin)		1,600+
Time is money	4,700-	4,975
Tower bank		2,900+
Trick pony	345-	365
Turtle	6,800-	7,300
Uncle Remus	1,500-	1,750
* Uncle Sam	610-	640
Watch bank	975-	1,100
* William Tell	420-	445
Wimbleton		2,800+
Windmill (tin)	180-	210
Wireless (tin)	260-	270
Woodpecker	1,800-	2,100

*Being reproduced.

Banks, Still

These banks don't have any moving parts. Usually cast in the shape of buildings, animal figures, etc., the same advice holds true for these as does for the mechanical. The General Pershing is being heavily reproduced, as are others.

Aunt Jemima with spoon	$ 72-	82
Bank building, 5″ high	73-	83
Baseball player	95-	115
Battleship Maine	175-	200
Bird on stump, 4¾″ high	81-	90
Black Beauty	120-	130
Blackamoor	73-	83
Boy Scout	105-	117
Buffalo, standing	94-	106
Buster and Tige	144-	154
Campbell Kids	220-	235
Captain Kidd, 5½″ high	172-	182
Cat, sitting	77-	85
Cat with ball, 2½″ high	75-	90
Deer with antlers	76-	87
Dog candy container, 3¾″ high	46-	54
Dog, 5″ long	40-	47
Dog with pack, 3¾″ high	72-	82
Donkey with saddle	155-	167
Duck	184-	194
Elephant on tub, 5¼″ high	110-	120
Elephant with howdah, 4¾″ high	70-	80
Empire State Building	84-	94
Feed My Sheep, pot metal, 3″ high	51-	62
Graf Zeppelin w/wheels, 8″ long	131-	140
Horseshoe	84-	94
Humpty Dumpty, tin, 5½″ high	51-	60

63

(continued)

Banks, Still

Indian head, maiden	88- 99
Jumbo savings bank, English, tin, 5¼" high	44- 51
Liberty Bell, Carnival glass	57- 67
Lion, large	110-115
Lion on wheels	109-118
Little Daisy	68- 78
Mailbox, green	56- 66
Mickey Mouse, aluminum, 8¾" high	160-185
Negro mammy	79- 89

Owl	160-172
Pig with bow tie, 3" high	84- 93
Poor tired Tim, tin, 5" high	75- 84
Prancing horse w/belly band, 4½" high	67- 74
Presto #426	77- 86
Rabbit, 5" high (ill.)	47- 54
Radio	79- 89
Rearing horse, Beauty, 5" high, on oval base	65- 75
Red Goose shoes, 3¾" high	74- 83
Resting camel, 2½" high	134-141
F. D. Roosevelt, die cast	61- 71
Rooster #187	101-118
Shell, WWI	53- 62
Soldier, WWI	110-120
Standing elephant	61- 71
Statue of Liberty	90-105
Teddy bear	77- 87
Thrifty pig	55- 65
Tiger	58- 67
Trolley car w/people, 3" high	141-158
Trolley car without people, 3" high	118-129
Turkey	75- 84
Two kids (goats), 4½" high	140-150
Uncle Sam, cash register	79- 89
Yellow Cab, 4" high	285-320

Banks, Still   Photograph: Louis S. Filles

Row 1

Taft and Sherman—political	$145-155
Sailor, small, 5½" high	82- 92
Golliwog (English)	135-160
Santa holding a tree, 5½" high	115-133
Capitalist	104-115
Owl on square base	81- 90

Bird on stump	74- 85
Bear stealing pig, 5½" high	195-220

Row 2

Independence Hall, 9" high	$151-162
Lighthouse	118-124
Panorama	75- 85
Bank building	70- 80

Row 3
Liberty Bell on base . . . . $ 84- 91
Liberty Bell 77- 87
Independence Hall (3 banks in
  one) 192-210

Row 4
Bank building, 3½″ high . . . . . . $ 49- 60

Bank building, 4½″ high 74- 83
Bank building, 5½″ high 72- 90
Horse on tub 70- 80
Small lion 62- 72
Lion on tub 79- 89
Tower bank 50- 60
Bank building, 11″ high 74- 84
Bank building, 7″ high 60- 70

Banks, Still

Banks, Still, Pottery

The crudest types were made centuries ago when someone wanted a container in which to bury valuables. They were usually made of fire-hardened clay and they remained popular until replaced by the iron banks in the mid-1800s.

Bear, sitting, 5½″ . . . . $ 56- 66
Bird 47- 55
Buffalo 54- 64
Corn 87- 95
Gourd 77- 85
Lion's head 56- 65
Pig, blue 56- 64
Teddy Roosevelt 150-163
Rooster, standing 62- 71
Tree stump 35- 44
Zeppelin 73- 82

Barbed Wire

Barbed Wire

First patented in the late 1800s, there were more than 600 kinds. It had a great effect on the cattle business in the West. It's very collectible today. Rare, one-of-a-kind pieces bring upwards of $100 for 18 inches. Also called devil's rope. See **Clubs and Publications,** this Price Guide.

Common variety, 18″ $1-2
Up to $350 for rare pieces.

Barometers, Chronometers

Used for indicating the weather, barometers go back to the 11th century. A great many of the older ones still work. If you find a Louis XVI, ormolu-mounted, $10,000 is about right!

Banjo, inlaid rosewood, 1860s . $240-260
Banjo, mahogany, John
  Berwinger 135-150
Banjo shape case, floral
  medallions, mahogany (ill.) . . 152-170
Banjo, silvered dial, rosewood,
  English 375-400

65

(continued)

Barometers

Chronometer, Whyte Thompson & Co., gimbled, double cased .... 1,950+

Desk style, brass case, German 90- 95

Desk style, brass dial, English, 8″ high 52- 60

Hygrometer, thermometer, spirit level, Joseph Alexander 240-260

Stick type, American, mid-19th century 525-610

Stick type, George III, Edinburgh, 40″ high, operating.. 355-368

Stick type, ivory register dial, rosewood, inlaid, London ... 250-260

Wall, circular, register dial, gilt, inlaid rosewood, 45″ high 420-440

Basalt

Wedgwood made this pottery in the late 18th century. It was also made in ancient times and is a black, vitreous pottery, shiny inside, glossy on the outside. It's rather expensive. Look for Wedgwood impressed in the bottom if you want the genuine.

Bowl, 9½″ dia., sterling silver rim $330-350

Bowl, 12″ dia., acanthus decor, marked Wedgwood 355-385

Bust, John Dryden, 14″ high .. 410-435

Bust, 9½″ high (ill.) 620-640

Bust, Shakespeare, c. 1800, marked Wedgwood 458-475

Candlesticks, 13¼″ high, pr. .. 340-352

Chalice, beaded pedestal base, marked Wedgwood 280-290

Basalt

Coffeepot, 9″ high 231-239

Creamer, black 101-118

Medallions, 2¼″×2¾″, marked Wedgwood and Bentley, George III and Queen Charlotte, pr. .. 1,100+

Pitcher, Flaxman figures in relief around base, leaves/grapes border at top, 6¾″ high 252-270

Sugar bowl, covered, black ... 237-254

Tea set, sugar, creamer, pot, tray, flower motif, all 440-470

Teapot, usual marking, classic design 272-310

Vase, 7″ high, c. 1890, marked Wedgwood England, pr. 333-375

Baseball Cards

Baseball Cards

The first baseball cards were issued in 1886 by Old Judge cigarets. Some of the rarest are Honus Wagner ($1,200+), Eddie Plank ($350-400), and Napoleon Lajoie ($300-350). Other companies, such as Glendale Meats, Signal Oil, and Tip Top Bread, put out these

Bavarian General

Bavarian, General

The small firms which produced ceramics in Bavaria have long since disappeared. Who made those pieces you find today, simply marked Bavaria on the bottom? Few records were kept, so we'll probably never know.

Berry set, hand-painted flowers, pink, green	$ 45-	55
Bowl, flower motif, 9″ dia.	20-	27
Bread plate, yellow roses, red border, 11″ long	39-	46
Candy dish, Dresden-type flowers, pink, blue	37-	45
Caster jug, vinegar/oil, red rose, green background	28-	35
Chocolate pot, roses, gilt trim, handled, with lid	52-	60
Hatpin holder, pink and yellow flowers, 8″ high	34-	40
Plate, flowers, garden scene, gilt edge, 7″ dia.	27-	33
Plate, white, gold (center left vacant for amateur painter)	29-	36
Plates, 4 fruit, pastoral scenes, signed PUNCH – Z. S. & Co., Bavaria, 9½″ dia., ea.	82-	92
Platter, pink roses around border, 10″ long	47-	56
Powder box, violets in blue and lavender, gilt edge	62-	72
Sugar bowl, multicolored flowers, handled lid	53-	59
Teapot, pink and green floral decorations, 5″ high, lid (ill.)	33-	43
Vase, gold and red roses, gilt lip, 6½″ high	36-	46

Bed (and Foot) Warmers

The earliest pans had iron handles. Usually what you find in shops have a wooden handle

Belleek, Irish

Made from feldspathic clay in County Fermanagh, Northern Ireland, Belleek was first made in 1857. The most characteristic productions are shell pieces and similar forms, supported by coral branches. Perhaps the loveliest are the openwork basket pieces. A real porcelain, the result of the simple vitrification of feldspar and china clay, it is extremely light and thin with a creamy, ivory surface and an iridescent luster. The typical Belleek mark consists of a hound, harp, tower, and shamrock, with the name Belleek on a ribbon underneath, printed in black, light and dark blue, brown, red, or green. Most original Belleek had this trademark. Look for marine plants, seashells, dolphins, coral designs, Echinus (sea urchin), Limpet (coneshaped shell of shellfish), Tridacna (clam); also shamrock decorations. A glittering iridescent glaze resembling mother-of-pearl is another way to identify this fine porcelain. Made continuously from 1857 to 1941, a black mark was used in conjunction with the hound, harp, etc. Production stopped in 1941, beginning again in 1946, when a green mark was instituted.

Animal, dog, black mark, 4½″ long	$137-	150
Animal, swan, black mark, 3″ high	166-	185
Basket, openwork, twisted handle, black mark, 8″	185-	192
Basket, openwork, woven bottom, black mark, 8½″ dia.	167-	177
Basket, openwork, woven bottom, 10½″ dia.	88-	95
Bowl, finger, green mark, 4¾″ dia.	78-	86
Bowl, round, openwork, woven bottom, black mark, 7″ dia.	232-	245
Creamer, Echinus pattern, black mark, 4½″ high	77-	84
Creamer, mermaid, black mark, 5″ high	67-	77
Creamer, Tridacna pattern, 4¾″ high	66-	76
Cup/saucer, Limpet pattern, black mark	138-	155
Cup/saucer, Shamrock, green mark	136-	147
Cup/saucer, Tridacna pattern, black mark (ill.)	125-	133
Dish, Dolphin pattern, green mark, 5½″ dia.	68-	75
Dish, openwork, applied roses, black mark, 5″ dia.	68-	75

(continued)

Hatpin holder, seashells, 6″ high, O. & B.	54- 62
Honey jar, beehive shape, green mark, 4½″ high	67- 73
Mug, Shamrock pattern, green mark, 6″ high	68- 74
Picture frame, black mark, 8″×10″	188-195
Pig, sitting, yellow/white, 3″ high, green mark	69- 74
Pitcher, Limpet pattern, 6¾″ high, green mark	98-108
Pitcher, swirling seaweed, black mark, 7½″ high	94-106
Plate, Limpet, black mark, 4½″ dia.	56- 66
Plate, mermaid, green mark, 6″ dia.	49- 58
Platter, Shamrock, 11″ long, green mark	88- 98
Salts, 6 individual, shell and coral, black mark, all	99-111
Vase, applied floral, green mark, 9½″ high	158-168
Vase, diamond-faceted tripod, dog-paw feet, black mark, 9″ high	310-325

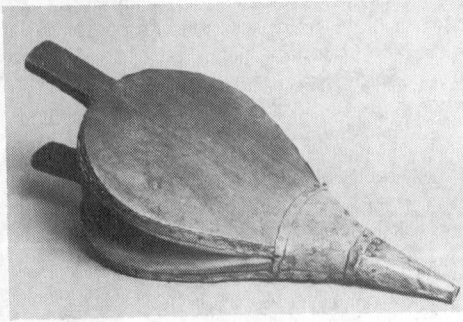

Bellows

Bellows

Usually made of wood with leather trim, they blew air on the smithy's coals or household fire. Some ornately carved, others painted. They go back into the dim shadows of time.

Brass covered wood, leather bellows, tavern scene in relief, mid-1880s	$170-180
Hand-carved, ornate wooden bellows, leather good, German, dated 1742	174-183
Ornately painted wooden bellows, Satan blowing on coals, dated 1735, East Hampton, Conn.	210-230
Smithy bellows, 5′ long, good leather, and all parts, mid-1800s	174-182

Wood body, leather bellows, brass tacks, carved, mid-1800s, works	120-130
Wooden bellows, leather good, brass tacks (ill.)	88- 98

Bells

Bells

Going back to ancient times, bells have been made in all sizes and shapes and have been used for calling to worship, alerting the town during Indian raids, and, of course, tolling in the New Year. Glass, brass, iron, wood, paper, just about every material has been used to make them. Some of the finest made in this country were and are still being made at the East Hampton (Conn.) Bell Factory. See **Clubs and Publications**, this Price Guide.

Brass, burnished, 14 on leather strap, 1″ dia.	$175-195
Brass calf bell on leather strap, 3″ dia.	69- 78
Brass, wooden handle, 8½″ high	66- 75
Chinese brass gong, dragon in relief	86- 98
Counter type (ill.)	10- 14
Cowbell, brass plated, 6″ long, original clapper	69- 78
Cowbell, leather collar, original clapper	66- 75
Same, brass	69- 80
Same, copper	65- 82
Dinner chimes, railroad-type, with mallet	82- 92
Dinner, sterling silver, handle, 4″ long	44- 53
Door, pull-type, brass	29- 39

Bennington Pottery

Cuspidor, enamel, flint, 1849,
7½″ dia. 148-168
Cuspidor, Shell pattern,
mottled brown glaze,
8½″ dia. 157-165
Doorknobs, 2 in set, mottled
brown glaze, pr. 83- 93
Flask, book-shaped, "Departed
Spirits," mottled brown
glaze 225-250
Flask, ½-qt., tavern scene,
mottled brown glaze 170-190
Foot warmer, holds 1 gal.,
mottled brown glaze 200-215
Frame, picture, blue/green/
brown, flint enamel 220-240
Inkwell, usual color, 4 quill
holes, raised design 240-250
Inkwell, dog's head, Rocking-
ham glaze 135-145
Jug, 2-gal., blue/green, flint
enamel 133-143
Jug, 1½-gal., mottled brown
glaze, 9½″ high 170-190
Mug, birds in relief 98-107
Mug, frog in bottom 195-220
Mug, Rockingham glaze, 6″
high 143-163
Pitcher, cherub and grapes,
Parian, 9″ high (ill.) 295-340
Pitcher, castle scene, 8¾″ high,
Rockingham glaze 420-460
Pitcher, Parian ware, paneled
vine and flower, rare . . . . . . 525+
Pitcher, tulip and heart, flint
enamel, 8¼″ high 170-180
Plates, 8¼″, 9″, 9¼″, 9¾″,
mottled brown glaze, av.
price, ea. 112-118
Pudding mold, tulip in bottom,
Rockingham glaze, 6½″ dia. 150-160
Teapot, 2-qt., mottled brown
glaze 138-148

Big Little Books
Photo courtesy Hake's Americana & Collectibles

Big Little Books

Although the Whitman Publishing Company published most of them, there were other companies competing for the reader market in the 1930s and 1940s. Most authorities agree that the modern comic book evolved from these chunky readables. Prices are for good-to-mint condition.

Ace Drummond . . . . $ 8-13
Alice in Wonderland 16-25
Alley Oop
  Alley Oop and Dinny 15-26
  Alley Oop in the Invasion
    of Moo 16-28
  Alley Oop in the Jungles
    of Moo 11-18
Andy Panda and Tiny Tom 8-12
Bandits at Bay 7-10
Betty Boop in "Miss Gulliver's
  Travels" 13-22
Betty Boop in "Snow White" 13-22
Billy the Kid's Pledge 9-12
Black Beauty 12-17
Blondie
  Blondie and Baby Dumpling,
    1937 15-27
  Blondie and Bouncing Baby
    Dumpling 15-26
  Blondie and Dagwood,
    Some Fun 17-26
  Blondie, No Dull Moments 15-23
Boss of the Chisholm Trail 10-14
Br'er Rabbit, 1945 31-40
Bringing Up Father 33-41
Buck Jones
  Buck Jones in Night Riders 21-28
  Buck Jones in Ride 'em
    Cowboy 21-30
  Buck Jones in the Fighting
    Code 20-28
  Buck Jones in the Roaring
    West 19-27
Buck Rogers
  Buck Rogers and the Doomed
    Comet 32-39

(continued)

Bing and Grondahl

Established at Copenhagen, Denmark, in 1853 by Harold Bing. Famous for their porcelain, stoneware, and earthenware, as well as their Christmas plates.

Bowl, boy kissing girl, 7½" dia.	$30- 38
Dish, flowers, blue, 4½" dia.	9- 15
Figurine, boxer, 5½" high	45- 54
Figurine, boy with horse, #2195, marked	300-318
Figurine, cat sitting, 4½" high	70- 78
Figurine, girl in blue dress, marked, 5½" high	65- 75
Figurine, girl with cat, 8" high	135-144
Figurine, Hans Christian Anderson, gray/blue, marked, 9" high	136-144
Figurine, lady holding umbrella, 7" high	68- 75
Figurine, Madonna, #2332, white, 9" high	47- 56
Figurine, mermaid, wreath on head, marked, 6½" high	63- 70
Figurine, merry sailor, marked, 6" high	90-110
Figurine, puppy, brown/white, 6½" high	80- 90
Figurine, springer spaniel, brown/white, marked, 8" high	75- 85
Figurine, waltzing couple, 8" high	235-245
Figurine, Youthful Boldness, #2162, marked, 7" high	118-126
Vase, grapevines, blue/white, marked, 6" high	85- 94
Vase, primroses, pink/white, 5¼" high	80- 90

Bisque

Bisque

Unglazed china describes it perfectly. Fired only a single time to harden to china, the pieces were then decorated with colors. Primarily a product of Europe, it was also made in the U.S. Some of the bisque-type figurines coming from Japan are of excellent craftsmanship and too many people are being fooled by unscrupulous dealers. Please know your dealer.

Box, candy, rose blossoms, blue/white	$ 34- 43
Candlesticks, bride and groom, 11½" high, pr.	75- 83
Figurine, baby in diaper swing	24- 33
Figurine, bathing beauty, 9" high	40- 48
Figurine, black baby on potty	37- 47
Figurine, boy and dog, 12" high	46- 56
Figurine, boy with shovel, 10½" high (ill.)	44- 53
Figurine, chicks on nest	38- 48
Figurine, Cupid shooting bow	38- 47
Figurine, Cupid sitting on boy's lap, 8½" high	35- 45
Figurine, dog with puppies	39- 44
Figurine, elephant, on hind legs	38- 47
Figurine, elves on mushroom, 6" high	46- 54
Figurine, girl holding kittens	45- 55
Figurine, girl on swing, dog in lap	45- 52
Figurine, kitten with drum	34- 40
Figurine, maiden standing by tree, 9½" high	46- 55
Figurine, monk with beer mug	54- 63
Figurine, nude lady, reclining, 8¼" high	139-152
Figurine, peasant boy, pipe in mouth	46- 52
Figurine, Russian dancer, 7" high	45- 54
Figurine, Santa Claus, 5" high	21- 28
Lamp, Cupids, 14" high, no shade	120-133
Match holder, in shape of dog's head	37- 44
Match holder, wall type, boy/girl kissing	34- 44
Match holder, wall type, cherubs	25- 35
Planter, sleigh-shaped	34- 45
Planter, Swiss chalet	46- 54
Slipper, blue/pink, roses	45- 53
Slipper, green/pink, flowers	44- 53
Toothpick holder, fluted edges, pink/brown, 2½" high	22- 29
Toothpick holder, in shape of boy's boot, 2" high	25- 34
Vase, boy with dog, 7¼" high	45- 55
Vase, Cupid, girl lid, 11" high	64- 74
Vase, girl in tree, 6¼" high	35- 45
Vase, tree trunk, brown/green, 9" high	44- 53

Black Amethyst Glass

When this black glass is held to a strong light, it appears to be a deep purple color. Sandwich, as well as others, made it.

Barber bottle, castle scene, pewter cap	$ 69- 79

(continued)

Black Amethyst Glass

Bowl, finger, rough pontil, 6″ dia.	32- 40
Candleholders, pair, 7″ high.....	38- 48
Compote, clear stem, 6½″ high ..	29- 38
Dish, bird decor, 5″ dia.........	27- 36
Flask, cornucopia/eagle, rough pontil, ½-pt., 5″ high	175-192
Lamp, kerosene-type, 8″ high, original brass collar	64- 73
Mug, child's, Little Bo-Peep, 4″ high, handled	44- 52
Paperweight, triangular, floral enamels, 5½″ long	27- 37
Pitcher, water, enameled flowers, ferns, 6″ high	42- 54
Plate, 6″ dia., Mary Gregory	118-134
Sauce, Millersburg, 2½″ deep ...	42- 52
Vase, enameled flowers, 5″ high, pair	67- 77
Vase, enameled design, possibly Sandwich	78- 84
Vase, etched flowers, 7″ high	46- 56
Wine, bell-shaped, clear stem, 3½″ high, set of 6	59- 68

Black Collectibles

Collectors are seeking anything to do with the Negro race.

Calendar, Bridal Party ....$	8- 11
Chalkware figurine, boy eating watermelon, 5″ high.........	28- 37
Figurine, bisque, black lady in evening dress, 9¼″ high	72- 81
Humidor, black boy smoking cigar, porcelain, 4½″ high	88- 98
Lamp, black man on donkey, pot metal, 11½″ high	84- 93
Painting, Washington, D.C., street scene, signed W. Paris. .	750-825
Print, lithograph, black boys playing cards, 10″×12½″	25- 34

Blanc de Chine

This porcelain was first made in the Chinese province of Fukien during the Ming Dynasty. The Kuan Yin (Goddess of Mercy) figurines are the most sought after. Most of the older pieces found today were made in the mid to late-19th century. This ware is still being produced today, and buyers are easily fooled into thinking a piece is older than it really is by scuffing on the base.

Figurine, dignitary seated on throne, c. 1750, 10″ high ...	$975-1,150
Figurine, Guanyin seated on rock, Kangxi period, 12″ high	1,700-1,900
Figurine, Putai (God of Happiness), holding scepter, 18th century, 5″ high	950-1,100
Figurines, Kuan Yin, 17″ high, pr. (ill.)	300- 350

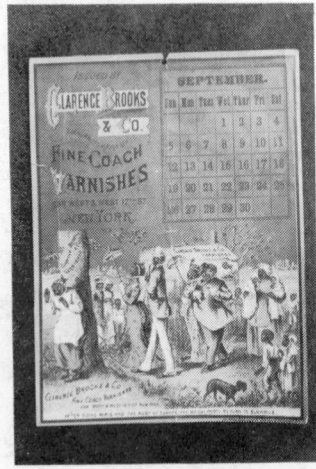

Black Collectibles

Blanc de Chine

Blue-and-White Ware, Chinese

Blue-and-White Ware, Chinese

This is currently a popular ware on the American market. The earliest pieces originated in the 14th century. A problem in buying and selling this ware is that very few dealers can distinguish the very old pieces from the copies produced during the late 1800s through the late 1930s. Most of the pieces are terribly overpriced.

Bowl, floral decor, 6″ dia.	$150- 175
Brush pot, old lady/ attendant, 5½″ high	225- 250
Dish, boats on lake, 5½″ dia.	55- 65
Ewer, pear-shaped body, dignitary/attendants, 7½″ high	375- 425
Jar, blue underglaze, scaly dragons, wood cover, 8¼″ high	325- 355
Jar, prunus blossoms, 5″ high (ill.)	550- 600
Jardiniere, riverscapes, foliated scroll, 15¼″ high	450- 500
Stands, baluster form, large lotus blossoms, pierced sides, 25″ high, pr.	1,775-2,225
Vase, Kangxi period, animal masks, yin and yang symbols, 8¾″ high	750- 800
Vase, Transitional period, formal lotus scroll throughout, 8″ high	750- 825

Blue Willow

See **Willow Ware.**

Bohemian Glass

Bohemian Glass

Ruby-colored, flashed, stained, in blue, yellow, green, other colors; 1870s until early 1900s, most sought after today. Originally made in Bohemia which is now part of Czechoslovakia. Hundreds of reproductions on the market. Careful!

Caster set, 4 bottles, ruby-colored, etched landscapes	$228-242
Compote, red, grapevine motif, 6½″ high, covered	150-160
Decanter	84- 92
Decanter, 6 small glasses, deer, forest, etched, yellow	236-258
Goblet, dog chasing deer, etched, yellow	59- 67
Goblet, footed, flower scene, yellow flashed, 7″ high	79- 82
Jar, covered, 5½″ high (ill.)	78- 82
Lustres, crystal prisms, 15″ high, pr.	192-207
Pitcher, deer and castle, 6 tumblers, ruby flashed	131-140
Pitcher, grape pattern, ruby flashed, 12½″ high	136-143
Rose petal jar, painted figure, ruby flashed, 8″ high	69- 78
Tumbler, deer, etched, green	68- 77
Vase, birds and flowers, red, etched, 11″ high	129-134
Vase, deer and castle, blue, 10″ high, pr.	110-121
Water set, leaf and grape motif, ruby, etched, 7 pieces	179-188

Book Matches

In the 1850s sheets of thin wooden matches appeared on the market. In 1897, the Diamond Match Company produced them in folder form with advertisements on the outside. Today, millions of advertisers

(continued)

use them to sell their products. Countless thousands of collectors are saving them. Any and all are collectible. If you begin a collection, it's a good idea to remove the matches before putting them in an album.

Common, usually purchased in bulk (per thousand)	$15-26
Early 1900s, usually purchased in bulk (per hundred)	26-35

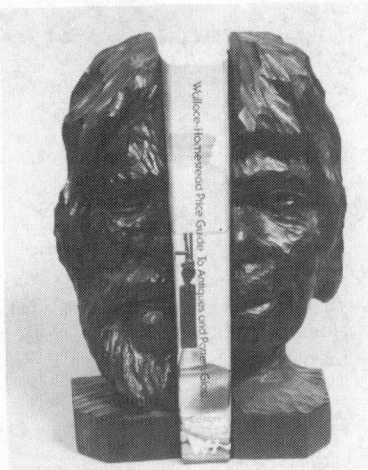

Bookends

Bookends

For years they were considered fashionable. Made from every type of material. All kinds are showing up at shops and shows—from the sublime to the ridiculous.

Bison, 6″×6″, late 1800s	$178-189
Bronze tigers on marble bases, 5″×2½″, late 1800s	143-162
Cast (pot metal) dog heads, 4″ sq., pre-WWI	31- 40
Copper ships, lead-weighted bases, 6″×3¼″, 1900s	47- 55
Elephants, rearing, bronze, 1890s, 8½″×6″	232-251
Indians, brass, on wood base, 6″×8″	182-193
Ivory elephants, teakwood bases, 6″ high, 1890s	161-174
Jade Foo dogs, ebony bases, 5″×3″, mid-1800s	1,750+
Lincoln, bust, copper, 1880s, 7″×9½″	181-192
Monkeys at play, carved wood, 6″×4″, early 1900s	44- 52
Owl on limb, brass, 7½″×9″	59- 68
Painted iron, flowers	35- 43
Pelicans, carved wood, 6½″×7″	47- 54

Porcelain, Japan, 5½″ high, 1930s	38- 47
Quartz birds, copper bases, 4½″×3½″, 1900s	88- 94
Reclining nudes, brass bases, 6½″×3″, 1900s	117-126
Roosters, painted, on wood base, 8″×7″	58- 65
Tigers, bronze, late 1800s, 6½″×9″	169-178
Wood, carved, Australia (ill.)	79- 89

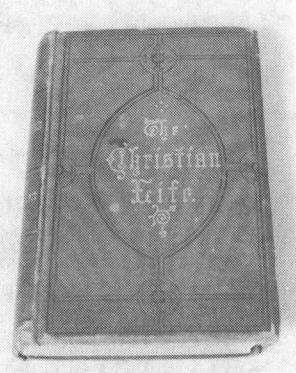

Books

Books

Soft clay cylinders, wax slates, papyrus scrolls, the degreased skins of cows and goats—a few ancient "books," going back before time immemorial. When Gutenberg (or Koster?) invented the printing press, things changed for the better in the book business. If you're looking for out-of-print books, Colonial "out-of-print" Book Service, Inc., 23 E. 4th St., New York, N.Y. 10003, is tops in its field.

Addison, Joseph, *The Free-Holder*, London, 1716	$ 89-107
Ade, George, *Fables in Slang*, Chicago, 1900	51- 62
Adeley, J., *The Christian Life*, New York, 1907 (ill.)	3- 6
Agee, James, *Permit Me Voyage*, New Haven, 1934	254-265
Alcott, Louisa M., *Little Men*, Boston	168-180
Alger, Horatio, Jr., *Do and Dare*, Philadelphia, no date	27- 36
Alger, Horatio, *Ragged Dick*, Boston, 1868, 1st ed.	525-542
Anderson, H.C., *Tales for Children*, London, 1891	22- 31

Obviously, there are millions of old books in every type of shop, at flea markets (see my *Flea Market Price Guide,* $6.95), in attics and basements, etc.

Boot Scrapers

Boot Scrapers

Usually set in the brick or cement of the front porch, the sharp blade was used to remove the mud or snow from the soles of the boots. Early 1800s to mid-1900s.

Antique car, brass	$135-148
Bristle brushes in metal frame ...	49- 59
Cast iron, bristle brush	29- 37
Cast iron, plain, still usable	29- 34
Horseshoes (ill.)	36- 45
Long-backed horse, iron	39- 48
Whale's belly, cast iron (rare)	99-110

Bootjacks

Apothecary Bottle

Bootjacks

Naughtie Nellie and the Beetle are two of the most collectible, though both are being reproduced. They were then and are still being used to remove tight boots. Usually in wood or cast iron.

American bulldog, folding pistol, brass	$ 82- 96
Same, except iron	59- 67
Beetle, brass	99-108
Beetle, harp-shaped, iron	59- 69
Beetle, iron	34- 43
Bull, cast iron	81- 90
Cap pistol, cast iron	49- 57
Cricket, cast iron, 10½"	28- 37
Naughty Nellie, brass	84- 93
Naughty Nellie, cast iron (ill.)	51- 62
Vine, cast iron, 11½"	29- 34
Wood, hand-carved cherry (ill.)	38- 47
Wood, hand-carved, lady's leg	42- 51

Being reproduced in Cricket, Naughty Nellie, and Pistol—probably others.

Bottles

See **Clubs and Publications,** this Price Guide.

Apothecary

Blown, Masson's Guaranteed on label, 14" high	$ 31- 37
Blown, Self Cure on label, 15" high	29- 36
Blown, squat green, 5" high (ill.)	27- 33
Brown, Extr. Strict on label, ground stopper, 15¼" high	29- 37
Brown, blown, gold label, 8½" high	28- 32
Brown porcelain, label, 7" high	26- 31
Bulbous, salesman's sample, fancy base, 11" high	29- 35
Capsicum on porcelain label, blown, 10½" high	27- 36
Clear, blown, stopper, 8" high	28- 37
Clear, blown, Tinc, Orsc on label, 12" high	26- 34

Ardos

Clock	45- 52
Green Duck	45- 52
Rocker	27- 37

Avon

Alpine flask, full and boxed	45- 54
Antique telephone, 1969	18- 27
Apothecary jar, 1965	20- 28
Bath, seasons, 1967	8- 12
Bath urn, clear	11- 16
Bath urn, milk glass, 1966	24- 32
Bay rum jug	14- 20
Bay rum keg, 1962	22- 27
Boot, gold top, label	8- 12
Boot, silver top, 1965	9- 16
Bud vase, 1962	15- 22
Bud vase, 1966	12- 21
Bud vase, 1968	14- 22
Candleholder, Christmas, frosted, apple, 1967	12- 19
Candlestick, Christmas, Charisma cologne, 4 oz., red/gold (ill.)	12- 16
Casey's lantern, amber, green, red	15- 27
Christmas ornaments—angel, balls, candle, icicle, sparkler, tree	14- 22
Daylight Shaving Time, 1968-70, 6 oz.	12- 15
Decanter, inkwell, owl	9- 13
Dollars and Scents, 1966	22- 27
Forever Spring, cologne, cream sachet, perfume, powder sachet	12- 21
Gavel, 1967, 6 oz.	16- 20
Gold Cadillac	12- 17
Greek goddess	12- 18
Keynote, label	12- 17
Kitten Little Cologne, 1973	4- 7
Nearness, body powder, toilet water	24- 29
Pony post, short, tall, label	11- 21
Quaintance, cologne, cream lotion, powder sachet, 1949	46- 52
Quaintance diary, 1949	95-107
Silver stein, 6 oz., 8 oz.	12- 18

Avon Bottle

Snail, boxed, label	12-	17
Stagecoach embossed, 2 oz., 4 oz.	12-	19
Topaze cream lotion, label	9-	16
Topaze Gem perfume, glass stopper	95-	107
Viking horn	19-	24
Warrior head, blue and silver, frosted label	15-	23
Western Choice (steer horns) pr.	22-	27
Wild Rose, cream lotion, cream sachet, toilet water	22-	28
Windjammer, printed label	9-	17

Ballantine (whiskey)

Duck	24-	34
Fisherman	24-	32
Golf bag	15-	24
Knight, silver	22-	30

Barber Bottles

Barber (clear, colored or milk glass)

Amber	77-	86
Amethyst	75-	85
Apple green, painted flowers (ill.)	52-	60
Bay rum, amethyst, etched, pewter spout	91-	98
Carnival, marigold, metal stopper	77-	87
Cobalt, pewter stopper	72-	82
Cranberry, Mary Gregory figure, pewter stopper	179-	190

Cut glass, sterling silver stopper, initialed	88-	98
Mary Gregory (ill.)	172-	179
Hobnail, honey amber, stopper	84-	94
Milk glass, octagon base, stopper	55-	65
Sandwich glass, amethyst, silver stopper	170-	180
Spanish Lace, blue, stopper	55-	62
Swirled Rib, ITP, amber	88-	94
Tiffany glass, sterling silver stopper, initialed BJM		475+

Jim Beam

Jim Beam bottles created quite a sensation in the bottle field. Several books are now available on these bottles. The Jim Beams listed here are for identification purposes.

Centennial Series:

Alaska Purchase (1966)	33-	40
Baseball	22-	31
Civil War: North, South, ea.	45-	55
Laramie	20-	30
Preakness	18-	28
St. Louis Arch, 1964	30-	40
Santa Fe, 1960	250-	275

Customer Specialties:

Cal-Neva	19-	25
First National Bank of Chicago, 1964 (recently counterfeited—be careful)		3,000+
Foremost, black and gold, gray and gold	170-	180
Foremost, pink speckled beauty		700+
Harold's Club: 12 bottles made so far, more to come, ea.	29-	35
Harold's Club, blue slot machine	30-	40
Harold's Club, man in a barrel, No. 1, 1957	500-	550
Harold's Club, VIP Executive, 1967, 1968, 1969, 1970, 1971	65-	75

Executive Series:

Royal porcelain, 1955	225-	250
Royal di Monte, 1957	80-	90
Blue cherub, 1960	80-	98
Royal rose, 1963	60-	68
Marbled fantasy, 1965	85-	95
Prestige, 1967	35-	45
Presidential, 1968	18-	27

Political Series:

Ashtrays, elephant and donkey, all years, pr.	35-	42
Boxers, pr.	35-	40
Clowns, pr.	20-	30

Regal China Series:

Arizona tombstone	22-	32
Black canasta, 1956	20-	30
Broadmoor Hotel	18-	25
Cable car, 1968	18-	22
Grand Canyon, 1969	20-	27
Kentucky Cardinal, 1973 trophy	35-	40

(continued)

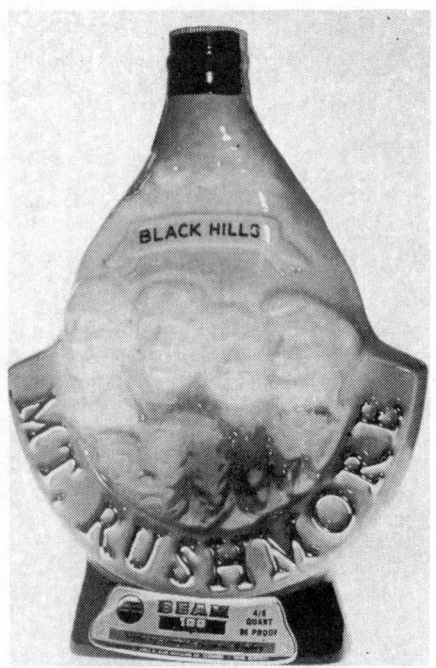

Jim Beam

Oatmeal jug	50-	58
Pony Express	12-	18
Scotch bell ringer	18-	20
Thailand	10-	12
Yosemite	10-	12
State Series:		
Alaska Star, 1958, 1964, 1965	70-	80
Hawaii, 1959, 1967	60-	65
Kentucky Derby, black head, 1967	18-	27
Nebraska	20-	30
North Dakota	80-	90
West Virginia Centennial	120-128	
Trophy Series:		
Dog, 1959	70-	75
Doe, 1963, 1967	30-	40
Fish, 1965	40-	50
Horses, three colors, ea.	40-	50
Ram	150-170	
Woodpecker	12-	18
Glass Specialties:		
Cannon	15-	22
Cleopatra, rust, 1962	20-	27
Dancing Scot, short, 1963	28-	38
Dancing Scot, tall, 1963	18-	27
Delft blue, Delft rose	18-	25
Mark Antony, 1962	20-	30
Pin: gold top, white top, wooden top	14-	22
Pyrex coffee warmers, 1954, four colors	18-	27
Royal Emperor	20-	27
Royal Reserve	20-	25
Smoked Crystal, 1964	18-	24

Beer Bottle

Beer

Cobalt, 9¾" high (ill.)	8-	11
Milk glass, 9" high	18-	22
Olive green, qt.	10-	14
Red, qt.	18-	21
Schmidt, original label, qt.	20-	27

Bischoff

Bell tower, 1959	50-	58
Boy, Chinese, Spanish	40-	50
Egyptian vase: single, double	40-	48
Fish bottle ashtray	25-	33
Grecian vase, decanter	18-	22
Nigerian mask	25-	35
Red clown	20-	30
Senorita	20-	30

Bitters Bottle

Bitters

From the 1860s until the early 1900s, various concoctions of herbs were mixed with alcohol (sometimes as much as 80%) and peddled as get-wells, feel-betters. More than one gal, fighting Demon Gin, got her pep, probably unknowingly, from sipping her husband's bitters.

Atwood's jaundice, screw
top, aqua 47- 57
Brown's iron, honey amber ... 50- 60
Clark's sherry wine, aqua 132-145
Cole Brothers 48- 54
Electric, embossed 59- 67
Goff's herb, embossed, aqua .. 32- 42
Kimball's jaundice (ill.) 138-160
Pinkerston's Wahoo and
Claisaya bitters, amber 69- 78
Prickly ash, amber, qt. 94-107
Tippecanoe, amber 157-165
Willards Golden Seal, aqua ... 92-107
Yerba Buena, amber, flask 141-150

Bols
Ballerina 26- 32
Cream de menthe, Delft 34- 44
Dutch: boy, girl 41- 50

Borghini
Dog 34- 42
Ford car, recent, old 22- 32
Horse's head 25- 34
Nubian girl 15- 21
Santa Maria 12- 19

Ezra Brooks
Antique cannon 32- 40
Bucket of blood 34- 40
Cable cars, 3 colors, ea. 22- 31
Churchill bust 24- 33
Clown on drum, short, tall 84- 88
Dueling pistol 24- 34
Grizzly bear 20- 28
Gun series (4) 37- 47
Harold's Club dice 26- 36
Kentucky gentleman 34- 41
Mr. Foremost 34- 41
Oil derrick (gusher) 29- 38
Potbelly stove 18- 25
Queen of hearts 24- 32
Reno arch 18- 26
Trout and fly 24- 33
Wheat shocker, Kansas 31- 40

J.W. Dant
Alamo (black) 25- 32
Bobwhite 36- 44
Crossing the Delaware 24- 32
Field birds (chukar partridge,
etc.), ea. 24- 30
Indianapolis 500 .... 36- 42
Patrick Henry 22- 32

George Dickel
Golf club, large 27- 35
Golf club, miniature 12- 21
Powderhorn 22- 30

Doctors

In the late 1800s many "doctors" promised
their products would cure everything from
falling hair to falling arches. (Alcohol was
the base, and some users touched every
one.)
Dr. Baker's Pain Relief, aqua,
pt. 24- 30

Dr. Baxter's Benevolent Pro-
tector, green, pt. 22- 27
Dr. Caldwell's Syrup Pepsin,
aqua 21- 25
Dr. Churchill's Hypophosphite
Pectoral 19- 23
Dr. Kennedy's Prairie Weed .. 35- 40
Dr. Kilmer's Swamp Root
Kidney Cure 19- 27
Dr. Miles Nervene 19- 28
Dr. Pepper's (indented letters) . 18- 24
Dr. Wistar's Balsam 47- 54
Dr. Woods Sarsaparilla and
Wild Cherry 89-101

Figural Bottle

Figurals
Black bear, Smirnoff vodka ... 25- 33
Brown owl 22- 29
Christmas tree, star stopper .. 140+
Crying baby, clear, 6½" high .. 55- 62
Elephant (used as bank) 16- 23
Face, 12" high (ill.) 57- 63
Fish, ashtray 34- 42
Guitar, brown 15- 24
Hunter, lady, pr. 45- 55
Lincoln (used as bank) 20- 30
Queen Elizabeth II 24- 33
River Queen boat 24- 33
Violin, blue 62- 72
George Washington bust,
miniature 34- 42
Watchtower bell 35- 44

Garnier
Bellows 32- 41
Bullfighter 34- 48
Cardinal 36- 50
Duck 25- 34
Indian 28- 37
Locomotive 34- 44
New Mexico road runner 24- 32
Parrot 39- 47

Pheasant 25- 32
Quail 22- 32
Ship scene 24- 34

Grenadier (Soldiers)
Colonial series, 5 so far,
  military in nature 32- 40

House of Koshu
Daughter 25- 30
Golden pagoda 22- 30
Pink geisha 70- 77
Princess 23- 27
Two lovers 21- 30
White pagoda 29- 38

Luxardo
Bacchus 21- 30
Clock 27- 37
Dolphin 67- 77
Gondola 21- 28
Miss Luxardo 29- 38
Santa Maria 31- 41
Tapa Print 22- 30
Zodiac 42- 51

Medicine
Bird's lung cure, aqua 26- 34
Davis vegetable compound . . . 35- 44
Hall's catarrh cure, aqua 21- 31
Lydia Pinkham (most famous) . 22- 30
Moxie Nerve, aqua 31- 38
River Swamp chill and fever
  cure 88- 92
Shiloh's consumption cure,
  aqua 18- 24

Mineral Waters
Buffalo Lithia water, green,
  qt. 25- 33
Clark and White, olive green,
  qt. 46- 51
Congress and Empire 'E', pt. . . 34- 42
Empire water, qt. 47- 52
Gettysburg, green, qt. 65- 71
Hathorn Spring, qt. 35- 43
John Ryan, cobalt, pt. 36- 44
Mississquoi Springs, brown,
  pt., qt. 47- 51
Saratoga Red Spring, pt. 60- 67

Miniatures
Ardo Paestum 17- 27
Borghini black cat 21- 26
Borghini candleholder 24- 30
Borghini candlelamp 21- 28
Borghini redbird 15- 24
Drioli cat 25- 30
Drioli dog 25- 32
Drioli duck 22- 30
Irish Mist soldier 16- 20
Larson's Viking ship, china . . . 26- 33
Larson's Viking ship, glass . . . 22- 31
Ryenbende: churn, cruet, oil
  lamp, shoe 15- 24

Old Fitzgerald Cabin Still
Candlelight, pr. 34- 40

California 22- 30
Fish 16- 19
Florentine 24- 30
Gold coaster 29- 38
Hillbilly, pt., fifth, 1969 (ill.) . . . 21- 30
Lexington 18- 27
Quail 16- 23
Sons of Erin, 1969 . . . . 24- 31
Tournament, 1963 . . . . 29- 38
Tree of Life 21- 31
Venetian 15- 24
Weller masterpiece 56- 66

Perfume
Black amethyst, marked
  Guerlain France 26- 33
Bulbous, sterling silver
  overlay, 7" high 93-105
Crystal, silver overlay, floral,
  birds 82- 92
Cut glass, Harvard cut, silver
  cap 50- 60
Diamonds, sunbursts, cut
  glass 58- 67
Hobnail pattern, clear 19- 28
Lalique, rectangular 57- 67
Pelican, Germany, porcelain . . 24- 32
Silver overlay, leaf decor, ball
  stopper 27- 37
Thousand-eye, bulbous 35- 47

Poison
Amber, 3-sided, riffled, marked
  Poison 26- 36
Cobalt, 3-sided, riffled, marked
  Poison 28- 37
Skull and Crossbones,
  embossed Poison on all
  sides 32- 42

Spirits

Soda and Sarsaparilla
Ayers compound extract
  sarsaparilla, aqua 16- 20
Babcock's sarsaparilla, aqua . . 70- 77
Bull's sarsaparilla, plain, aqua . 94-106
Coca-Cola, dated 1909,
  Knoxville, brown 26- 31

Dana's sarsaparilla, Bangor,
Me., aqua 34- 42
DeWitt's sarsaparilla, aqua . . . 36- 44
Dr. Green's sarsaparilla, clear . 26- 32
Joy's sarsaparilla, aqua 36- 45
Rodway's sarsaparilla, aqua . . 38- 47
Scoville's unembossed, aqua . . 24- 32
Verner's ginger ale, embossed
seal 24- 30

Whiskey and Other Spirits
Belle of Anderson, milk glass . . 137-144
Binninger's barrel-shaped
whiskey, amber 580-610
Binninger's peach brandy jug . . 350-400
Binninger's Regulator, clock
shape, amber 620-670
E. G. Booz Cabin whiskey—an
original would be worth upwards of $350, but the 1920s
reproduction was a perfect
duplication **except** the original has a period (.) after the
word Whiskey on the "roof"
of the bottle. The 1960s
reproduction is so obvious it
should fool no one.
Chestnut Grove whiskey, pt. . . 228-245
Deep Spring, Tenn., whiskey . . 35- 42
Golden Wedding, 1933 . . . . 27- 35
I.W. Harper barrel, 1976,
seal unbroken (ill.) 40- 48
Hart, John and Co., figural,
amber 41- 50
Hayner Distilling Co., Dayton,
St. Louis, clear 23- 30
Jo-Jo Monogram, labeled, pt.,
qt. 82- 90
Lady's Leg, amethyst, green or
amber 77- 85
Lighthouse figural, C.T.
Morris, amber, qt. 131-137
Mallard Distilling, Baltimore
and N.Y.C., violin-shaped . . 44- 51
Miller's Game Cock, Boston . . 26- 35
Jessie Moore's whiskey, amber,
fifth 80- 87
Old Charter pure rye 34- 44
Old Gray Mare, amber 165-185
Old Quaker, embossed anchor
bottom, clear, pt. 61- 70
Paul Jones (printed on bottom),
amber, pt. 34- 41
Pike's Peak, aqua, pt. 47- 58
Quaker Maid, amber 45- 55
Spring-winter, aqua, ½-pt. 240-260
Van Denebergh, gin 132-162
Whitney, 1800s 225-240
Wicker covered, 7¼" high (ill.) 23- 31

Miscellaneous
Anderson's Dermador 21- 31
Belt buckle, Civil War 21- 30
Binocular shaped, black, qt. . . . 27- 34

I.W. Harper/Seagrams

Buffalo lithia water 19- 24
Bunker Hill pickles, honey
amber 37- 42

Burnham's beef wine and iron . 12- 16
Camel saddle, hand-blown 55- 62
Champagne, magnum, green . . 35- 42
Extracts, bottle, blue 19- 26
Geisha Girl, purple 31- 38
Glover's Imperial mange
medicine, amber 12- 21
H.J. Heinz, patented 1890 . . . . 22- 25
Harden's Hand Grenade, star,
blue, still full 30- 35
Horlick's malted milk, tin lid . . 14- 19
Hudson's Bay, flat, miniature
(rare) 50- 54
Pickle barrel, emerald green . . . 38- 46

Spirits

Boy Scout Collectibles

The Boy Scouts of America were incorporated February 8, 1910.

(continued)

Boy Scout Collectibles

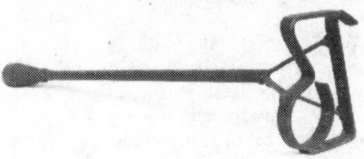

Branding Irons

Branding Irons

Used in the West for identifying a rancher's cattle, today they're collectible. Usually twisted iron on a long iron shaft with wooden handle, they were first used in the early 1800s in what is now California. Still being used on cattle and horses.

Wrought iron, letters (ill.) . . . . . . $ 35- 45

This is an average price, coast-to-coast.

Boy Scout Collectibles		
Bugle, brass	$ 45-	54
Old Scout manuals, 1920s and 1930s	14-	22
Scout and Cub Scout charters (ill.)	9-	12
Scoutmaster pins	11-	18
Uniform, complete, 1930s	34-	38

Bradley and Hubbard

This manufacturing company made lamps and other metal items at Meriden, Connecticut, at the turn of the 20th century.

Bookends, Art Deco, pr.	$ 72-	80
Box, cigarette, brass	32-	37
Box, stamp, 2 compartments, hinged cover	28-	38
Candleholder, bronze, 11' high . . .	110-121	
Candleholders, brass, 8¼" high, pr.	210-240	
Desk set, Art Deco, 7 pieces, all . .	300-325	
Desk set, embossed brass, glass inkwell, 3 pieces, all	88-	98
Lamp, banquet type, ornate base, 28" high, marked	158-164	
Lamp, pull down type, kerosene, brass front, blue shade, signed	420-470	
Lamp, table, brass, milk glass shade, 26" high	152-161	
Lamp, table, scrolled iron base brass front, signed, 25" high . .	255-270	
Planter, hanging type, brass, 6" high	28-	32
Stand, smoking, Art Deco, 27" high, marked	99-120	

Brass

Brass

A yellow alloy, usually consisting of copper and zinc, brass is an easily hammered metal which, when polished, takes on a beautiful hue. It's been in use since the days of the early Romans.

Ashtray, 5" dia., marked India	$ 14-	18
Ashtray, foliage, marked India . .	15-	20
Ashtray/match holder, embossed scrolls, dolphins	37-	44
Ashtray shaped like lock	22-	25
Bookends, rearing horses, 7" high, pr.	45-	52
Bowl, 6" dia., footed, marked India	19-	23
Bowl, 8" dia., marked China, dragon motif	34-	44
Bullet mold, hinged	45-	52

Candlestick, push-up ejector, 5″ high, pr.	64- 72
Candlesticks, English, marked Storrar's, Chester, 10″ high	75- 84
Candlesticks, turned stem, 8″ high, pr.,	70- 80
Cigarette box, yellow, green, red stones inlaid in lid	26- 34
Coal bucket, iron bail handle	65- 75
Coal hod	135-142
Coffeepot, 10″ high	38- 48
Dipper, 12½″ long	52- 60
Easel, probably held miniature painting, 4½″ high	57- 65
Ice tongs, heavy	65- 75
Incense burner, 2-part, marked China	18- 24
Incense burner, w/lid, 4″ dia., 1890s	18- 27
Jelly kettle, iron bail handle, 2-gal. capacity	73- 83
Kettles, 6, 8, 10, 12 qts.	71- 81
Keys, assorted sizes, ea.	12- 18
Letter opener, dragon, marked China, 13″ long	15- 24
Mortar and pestle, pewter-lined, Russian, Eagle mark	175-188
Pails, 4, 8 qts.	115-120
Paperweight, lion and cubs, 6″ dia.	55- 65
Scales, grocery, counter type	92- 98
Sundial, on 3′ high marble base	370-420
Teakettle, (ill.)	101-111
Tray, flower motif, 7½″ dia.	65- 70
Trivet, pierced fretwork, ball feet, 1920s	24- 33
Umbrella stand, flower ring handles	108-112
Whistle, factory, 16″ high	170-180

Bread Plates and Trays

Usually popularizing people, places and things from the mid-1800s on, they were made of glass, china and metal. The U.S. coin plate is considered scarce.

Barley, clear glass	$ 52- 62
Bible	65- 75
Bread Is the Staff of Life, clear glass	52- 62
Bunker Hill Monument	72- 80
Coin, Columbian, gold gilt, clear glass	132-140
Coin, U.S., dollar decoration, frosted glass coins	340-355
Constitution	140-160
Cupid and Venus	57- 67
Dancing Bears	78- 82
Virginia Dare (first white baby born in Virginia Colonies)	88- 98
Dog Cart	69- 78
Eureka	65- 75

Faith, Hope and Charity, clear glass	88- 92
Frosted Stork	66- 76
Garden of Eden	58- 70
Garfield Drape	77- 86
Give Us This Day Our Daily Bread (ill.)	55- 65
Gladstone	48- 58
Heroes of Bunker Hill	85- 94
Independence Hall	119-130
It Is Pleasant to Labor	69- 78
Last Supper	52- 62
Liberty Bell, blue glass	79- 89
Liberty Bell, 7″×11″	170-177
Little Miss Muffet	67- 77
Little Red Riding Hood	69- 77
McKinley Memorial, "It Is God's Way," bread platter	78- 88
Nellie Bly (She went around the world in 80 days!)	225-240
Niagara Falls, frosted glass	160-170
Old Statehouse	88- 98
Pacific Fleet	520-580
Philadelphia Centennial, 1876, clear glass	69- 79
Queen Victoria	68- 72
Rock of Ages	88- 92
Sheaf of Wheat	65- 75
Shell and Tassel, oblong, small	77- 86
Shield, star border	110-120
Teddy Roosevelt	120-130
Theodore Roosevelt, clear, frosted	118-121
Waste Not, Want Not	68- 78

Brides' Baskets

Brides' Baskets

These one-of-a-kind novelties, popular as wedding presents during the mid-1800s until the early 1900s, were made in American and European glass factories. A great many came in silver or silver-plated frames.

(continued)

Amberina, Quilted Diamond,
twisted handle, triple plate
frame . . . . $ 378- 420
Amethyst, clear ruffled edge,
quadruple plate frame,
11½" dia. 238- 250
Cased, apricot, quadruple
plate frame, 10" dia. 228- 260
Cased, pink and white, EPNS,
11¼" dia. 210- 231
Cased, pinks, ruffled edge,
EPNS frame, 10" dia. 200- 220
Cranberry, ITP (Inverted
Thumbprint), EPNS frame,
9½" dia. 210- 222
Cranberry, overlay, ruffled
edge, EPNS frame 210- 230
Cranberry, ruffled edge, sterling silver frame, 10" dia. . . 300- 320
Cranberry to pink, enameled
flowers, 11" dia. 210- 228
Cut, Diamond, Strawberry
and Fan, quadruple plate
frame, 9¼" dia. 228- 237
Hobnail, blue/white, EPNS
frame, 10¼" dia. 215- 230
Mt. Washington, Peachblow,
ruffled edge, quadruple
plate frame, 13" dia. . . . . . . 1,600+
New England Peachblow,
scalloped edge, quadruple
frame, 12½" dia. . . . . 1,500+
Opaque, blue enameled
cherubs, triple plate frame,
9¼" dia. 210- 230
Pink, swirl designs, EPNS
frame, 9½" dia. 188- 220
Satin glass, ruffled edge,
EPNS frame, 10" dia. 210- 220
Tiffany, gold iridescent, sterling silver frame . . . . 1,550+
Vasa Murrhina, brown, gold
flecks, triple plate frame,
10¼" dia. 238- 255
Wheeling Peachblow, quad-
ruple plate frame, 11½"
dia. . . . . 1,850+
White, cased blue, clear
fluted edge, EPNS frame,
9½" dia. 188- 192
Yellow to pink, blue enameled
flowers, EPNS frame, 10½
dia. 182- 192

Bridle Rosettes

Made of glass, those small buttons were
used to decorate the horse's bridle. They're
being reproduced. The originals are beautiful
when made into pins.

Blue/gray ground, floral, brass . . $ 22- 30
Double heart, brass background . 21- 32
Ducks, grass background . . . 28- 31

Bridle Rosettes

Eagle and flag, blue background,
brass 22- 29
Flowers, blue/green, birds, brass . 27- 30
Heart design, initials, brass
background 24- 34
Horse and buggy (ill.) 29- 35
Shield and 13 stars, brass
background 31- 40
U.S. Cavalry, brass, pr. 32- 41
Water birds, floral, brass
background 27- 36

Bristol Glass

Bristol Glass

Bristol, England, became a glass center in
the mid-1700s. Many of the glass vases

attributed to the Amelung Glass Company and other companies in the U.S. were actually made at Bristol. One way to identify them is to hold them to the light—they should look like an orange forest fire.

Apothecary jar, white, green/
  white, enameled, cover $115-135
Bottle, dresser, green/gold, blue
  enamel trim 68- 78
Bowl, cased blue over white,
  scalloped, floral, enameled 122-132
Box, powder, round, dome,
  hinged, children and birds,
  1840   94-103
Cookie jar, satin finish, floral and
  fauna designs 103-111
Epergne, twin tulips, cranberry,
  fluted edges 321-340
Hand vase, ruffled top, pink/
  clambroth, gilded, frosted   90-101
Lamp, blue, enameled yellow,
  blue, lilies, green leaves 132-140
Lamp, hanging, white, red/yellow
  color, floral, brass chain 132-142
Mug, blue, "Love You" 50- 60
Platter, raspberry color, bird-of-
  paradise color, matching dish .   48- 58
Rose bowl, blue, frosted, ruffled
  lip 111-121
Smokebell, white, applied green
  band, crimped rim 34- 44
Toothpick, blue, rectangular
  panels 30- 40
Tumbler, white, blue/yellow
  enameled flowers 34- 44
Vase, blue/green, enameled birds
  and flowers 74- 83
Vase, brown thistle, white satin,
  floral enameled decor 86- 94
Vase, castle scene, 10″ high 72- 82
Vase, enameled, blue/yellow,
  birds, flowers   92-102
Vase, insects, flowers, enameled
  decor, ruffled lip 180-190
Vase, orchids, 9″ high 58- 68
Vases, blue opalescent,
  enameled flowers, 10″ high, pr. 139-150
Vases, floral, separate fonts,
  11½″ high, pr. (ill.) 350-375
Vases, Little Girl, fluted lips,
  flower outline, pr. 168-173

Britannia Ware

In the simplest language, pewter is cast, Britannia is spun. Also, they don't look alike, though the chemical makeup is about the same. If anything Britannia is better than pewter. Usually identified by the small catalog numbers stamped on it. Much of it also carries the maker's name. When mass

Britannia Ware

production was started around 1825, the spinning process used less metal and made it harder. Unfortunately, it also brought about poorer designing and less individuality. Conseqently, pewter brings higher prices.

Basically, Britannia Ware today brings about 70 percent of pewter prices, possibly a little less.

British Patent Office Registration Marks

From 1842 until 1883 the wares of many British manufacturers were marked with the following diamond mark, which indicated that the design was registered with the British Patent Office. The topmost section of the mark indicated the class (in this case IV indicates earthenware and glass). This gave copyright protection for three years. Unfortunately, the manufacturers didn't take too much time incising or imprinting the mark, and a lot of pieces are unreadable.

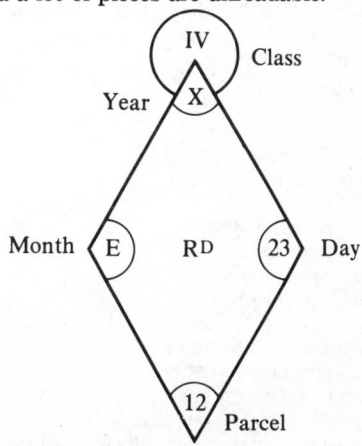

Example of earthenware design registered May 23, 1842

(continued)

Below is index to letters for each year and month from 1842 to 1867:

YEARS

1842 X, 1843 H, 1844 C, 1845 A, 1846 I,
1847 F, 1848 U, 1849 S, 1850 V, 1851 P,
1852 D, 1853 Y, 1854 J, 1855 E, 1856 L,
1857 K, 1858 B, 1859 M, 1860 Z, 1861 R,
1862 O, 1863 G, 1864 N, 1865 W, 1866 O,
1867 T.

MONTHS

January C, February G, March W, April H, May E, June M, July I, August R, September D, October B, November K, December A.

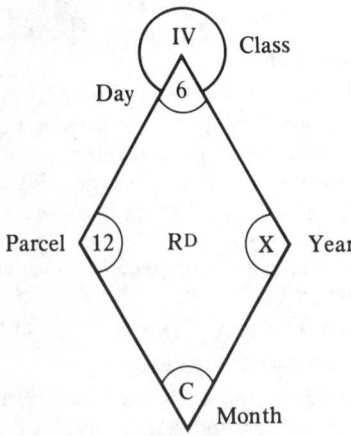

Example of earthenware design registered
January 6, 1868

Bronze, Chinese

Bronze, Chinese

Bell, clapperless, 6/5th century B.C., supported on 4 flattened pyramids, 20″ high .. $ 5,400- 5,900
Belt hook, silver inlaid, Han Dynasty, 5½″ long 275- 350
Bowl, Han Dynasty, 2 fish cast in linear relief in exterior, narrow ring foot, 15″ dia. 565- 660
Brazier, tripod type, Eastern Han/Six Dynasties, on tripod legs, shallow bowl, 7″ high 1,500-2,200
Buddhist, gilt bronze of a Bodhisattva, Northern Qi Dynasty, standing barefooted, approx. 7″ high 39,000-42,000

Cauldron, early Western Zhou Dynasty, supported on thick tripod legs, double loop handles, approx. 12½″ high 65,000-68,000
Food vessel, late 17th century B.C., bat head handles, 6″ high (ill.) 2,700-2,975
Food vessel, early Western Zhou Dynasty, upturned loop handles, approx. 7″ high . . . . 78,000+
Food vessel, Shang Dynasty, 2 loop handles, approx. 7½″ high 22,000-26,000
Knife, Shang Dynasty Dogtooth pattern handle in-laid with turquoise, approx. 9¼″ long 1,600- 1,800
Libation vessel, Shang Dynasty, helmet-shaped cup, 3 blade-shaped legs, approx. 8½″ high 950- 1,200
Libation vessel, Shang Dynasty, mushroom-capped lug handles, 3 blade-shaped legs, approx. 7½″ high . . . 1,400- 1,800
Mirror, "Star Cluster," 1st century B.C., approx. 7¼″ dia. 1,500- 1,700
Mirror, T'ang Dynasty, 2 phoenixes on clouds, approx. 8″ dia. 2,700- 2,900
Pouring vessel, c. 6th century B.C., horned *taotie* mask spout, approx. 9½″ long . . . 2,900- 3,200

Ritual beaker, Shang
Dynasty, flaring
trumpet neck, approx.
10″ high 2,600- 2,800
Ritual vessel, Shang
Dynasty, 6 full-length
dragons, approx.
12½″ dia. . . . .   47,000+
Sculpture, gilt-bronze
figure of Pratyeka
Buddha, Northern
Qi Sui Dynasty,
standing position,
approx. 7″ high . . . . .   37,000+
Vase, 5/4th century
B.C., 2 *taotie* masks,
approx. 13″ high 2,400- 2,500
Wine jar, Han Dynasty,
chain handle, pear-
shaped, approx. 17″
high 10,600-10,800
Wine vessel, 11/10th
century B.C., cylin-
drical form, concen-
tric bands, central
frieze of hooked
kui dragons, approx.
8″ high . . . .   98,000+
Wine vessel, late Shang
Dynasty, waisted
body, flared rim,
horned bovine head
strap handle, approx.
16″ high . . . .   68,000+
Wine vessel, Shang
Dynasty, U-shaped
body, 2 *taotie* masks,
approx. 9″ high 5,400- 5,600
Wine vessel, silver/gold
inlaid, Warring States
style, approx. 9″ high   10,500+

Bronze Figures

Bronze Figures

There are bronze figures and there are
"bronze" figures. Too many pot metal fakes
are around, so know your bronzes and your
dealer. A signed figure is worth more than an
unsigned. Don't worry about finding any
Frederic Remingtons.

Arab on camel, Austria, 6″
high . . . . $ 188- 197
Bird, signed Pautrot 650- 720
Bull, Charolais from
Burgundy, signed Rosa
Bonheur, 7″ high . . . . . .   3,700+
Cossack and girl on
horseback, Russia, 11″
high, signed Bonoguy . . . 1,400-1,600
Cow, 6″ long, signed R.
Bonheur 625- 750

Dachshund, 5″ high, self-
base 190- 210
Deer in forest 140- 160
Elephant, 7″ high, signed
Fratin 710- 800
Greyhound, signed Mene . . 1,200-1,450
Horse, Ch'ing (Manchu)
Dynasty 90- 100
Leopard stalking, 5″ high,
12″ long 210- 220
Lion roaring, 5″ high, 8″
long, signed Barye 320- 350
Panther, 7¾″ long, signed
Bayre . . . .   1,400+
Panther crouching, 17″
long, signed L. Bureau . . 255- 278
Pheasant, 7″ long, signed
Mene 895-1,200
Polar bear stalking seal,
Austria, 4″ high, 5″
long 240- 260
Retriever, signed Mene . . . .   1,500+
Running elephant, 5″ high,
7½″ long, signed Barye . 675- 730
Tiger on marble base, 6″
high, 7″ long 278- 289
Tiger on wood base, 5½″
high, 13″ long (ill.) 1,300-1,500
World War I Doughboy,
signed Roman Bronze
Works (same firm that
cast the Frederic
Remington bronzes) 198- 220

Keep in mind that if you do find a Frederic
Remington bronze (a Western scene—bucking
horse, Indian shooting buffalo, etc.), don't sell it.
One sold recently for $248,000!

Brownie Collectibles

Created by Palmer Cox, an artist-author, in
1888, these creatures of fantasy were popular
during that period. During the early 1900s
they were copied by other artists.

(continued)

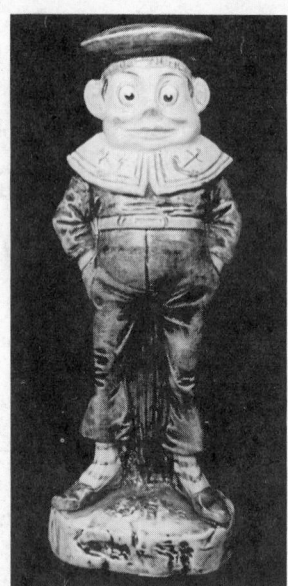

Brownie Collectibles

Book, *The Brownies*, Cox . . . . $ 40- 50
Book, *The Brownies*, More
    Nights 39- 52
Candlestick, Brownie, German,
    7½″ high, blue/brown/green
    (ill.) 44- 52
Cup/saucer, American Belleek . . . 56- 62
Mug, child's enameled Brownie
    figures, silver-plate 39- 44
Soda bottle, embossed, patented . 29- 38
Tile, Brownies, German-made . . . 36- 45

Buffalo Pottery

Buffalo Pottery

Established in 1901 in Buffalo, New York, the firm supplied pottery for the Larkin Company, which was in the soap business and later developed into a mail order firm specializing in premiums which helped to sell its goods. Best known and the most sought-after is the Deldare ware, first made in 1908. The firm continued until the 1940s. Most Deldare is done in old English tavern and hunting scenes.

Bowls
    Floral, 6½″ dia. . . . . $ 31- 40
    Roosevelt Bears, 6″ dia. 139-150
    Vegetable, covered, white/
        gold band, 8¼″ dia. 29- 37
Butter Tub
    Fern Rose pattern 47- 52
Creamers
    Cats, 4″ high 32- 39
    Cinderella, 3¼″ high 31- 40
Cups/Saucers
    Cinderella, child's 27- 32
    Puss 'n Boots 32- 40
    Teddy Bears 34- 41
Game Set
    15½″ platter, four 9″ plates,
        all signed Beck, all 210-220
Jugs
    Cinderella 210-225
    New Bedford 278-284
    George Washington 271-275
    Wild Duck 188-200
Mugs
    Arlington Club, 1915 . . . . 82- 91
    Vacation 77- 86
    Wildroot Hair Tonic 75- 85
Pitchers
    Deer Hunt 258-270
    Floral 240-260
    Landing of Roger Williams 320-328
    Robin Hood 288-296
    Roosevelt Bears 685-710
    Sailor 340-360
Plates
    Cinderella, 8″ dia. 172-182

Bullet Molds

Bullet Molds

During the days of the muzzle-loading rifle, hunters, soldiers, frontiersmen molded their own bullets from melted-down lead.

Brass, single, spattered iron, 3″
  long . . . . $ 67- 77
Brass, holds 12, 10″ long 79- 84
Brass, .41 caliber, holds 4, 6″
  long 65- 75
Iron, single, 2″ long 52- 61
Iron, single, 4½″ long (ill.) 61- 70

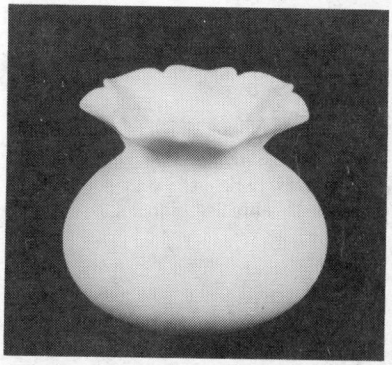

Burmese Glass

MT. W. G. CO.
BURMESE
PAT. APPLIED FOR

93

(continued)

Burmese Glass

This translucent, shaded ware, homogeneous in nature, was made at the Mt. Washington Glass Company in the late 1800s. Licensed to produce it in England, Thomas Webb & Sons called it Queen's Burmese. Burmese was a soft canary yellow shading to flesh pink. Unfortunately it's being reproduced skillfully enough to fool too many new collectors.

Bell, ivy motif, pink interior	$ 670- 710
Biscuit jar, Pairpoint silver frame	1,300-1,500
Bowl, triangular	260- 290
Bride's basket, silver holder, 9″ dia.	1,100-1,250
Condiment set, 3 pcs.	600- 650
Epergne, signed Webb	2,300-2,400
Fairy lamp, brass, Clarke holder	985-1,300
Glass, juice, satin finish, 4″	188- 199
Paperweight, egg shape	680- 750
Pitcher, bright pink-to-yellow, acid, 7″ high	2,400-2,700
Queen's Burmese, lamp, pyramid shape, salmon-to-yellow, 3¾″ high	470- 530
Queen's Burmese, lamp, same as above, 5¼″ high	590- 630
Rose bowl, 4¼″ dia.	565- 622
Salt/pepper shakers, ribbed, pr.	482- 492
Toothpick, decorated, signed Webb, 3¾″ high	456- 463
Toothpick, 4-sided, floral design	456- 460
Toothpick, glossy, 5-sided top	370- 382
Tumbler	482- 510
Vase, flared top, petal style, pr.	720- 735
Vase, glossy, signed Webb, 3¼″ high (ill.)	250- 260
Vase, lemon to pink, 8½″ high	344- 348
Vase, Mt. Washington, acid finish, 8″ high	765- 788
Vase, satin, pink, yellow, signed Webb, 24″ high	3,100-3,250

Buster Brown Collectibles

Buster Brown Collectibles

Dick Outcault created a comic strip in 1902 that was eventually syndicated. Buster Brown and his dog, Tige, appeared on the American market in the form of dolls and other objects. The most famous, of course, were shoes, which are still sold under the Buster Brown name.

Buster and Tige bank, cast iron, 5″ high	$172-188
Buster "to call dog" whistle	26- 34
Button, brass	15- 25
Button pin, Buster and Tige	29- 37
Camera, Ansco, in original box	47- 56
Cards, playing, c. 1907	48- 52
Clicker, advertising shoes	19- 27
Comb, brass	19- 28
Cup/saucer, Buster and girl (ill.)	32- 41
Dish, Buster and girl (ill.)	31- 41
Fork and spoon, silver metal, both	40- 50
Knife, pocket	92-101
Game, At the Zoo, deck of comic cards	27- 37
Hand puppet, Buster holding Tige, 1906	92-107
Mirror, advertising	19- 24
Mug, china, gold trim, 3″ high	69- 78
Pencil, advertising shoes	15- 22
Plaque, advertising	101-111
Plate, 5″ dia.	58- 61
Postcard, Buster at zoo with Tige and girl	11- 19
Scissors	44- 51
Shoe horn, advertising shoes	16- 22
Sign, Buster and Tige, advertising shoes, 21″×25″, tin	158-162
Toy, Buster and Tige cart	162-171
Whistle, advertising shoes	18- 27
Wrapping paper, Buster and girl, poems, complete roll	19- 28

Busts

1922, fruit, flowers, Newark, N.J.	29- 36
1923, Grant's Tomb	44- 46
1925, horse race, merchant	34- 39
1926, Kentucky Derby, Winner	56- 62
1927, merchant, Reading, Pa.	27- 32
1928, rose, trees, merchant	27- 32
1929, car, flags, Indy forever!	70- 80
1966, God Bless Our House	24- 29

Calendars

Calendars

The use of calendars goes back to the days of the Romans—probably even beyond. The Gregorian calendar is used by the western world as well as by the Republic of China, South Vietnam, etc. What you find in shops are from the late 1800s on. Year and condition dictate the price.

1876 Centennial Home Insurance Company, 12 months (ill.)	$ 21- 28
1896 Hartford Fire Insurance Co.	9- 17
1896 Root Beer	5- 8
1897 John Hancock	44- 54

Calendars

Vase, floral motif, standard glaze, 5″ high	77- 82
Vase, Oakwood, 11¼″ high	115-128
Vase, Otoe, 8¼″ high	85- 92

Cambridge Glass

Made in Cambridge, Ohio, by the Cambridge Glass Company, c. 1902, this pressed glass was usually marked with a C in a triangle; after 1906, the word near-cut was used. See **Clubs and Publications**, this Price Guide.

Amber (true amber brown)

Basket, footed, Jenny Lind pattern, 9″	$ 49- 52
Beverage set, 9-piece, ebony foot and base, all	222-231
Bonbon, 2-handled, gold-encrusted, "C" mark	37- 42
Bowl, apple or fruit, Ivy Cut pattern, 11″	115-129
Bowl, etched, w/figure flower holder, 11½″	147-152
Bowl, ram's head, Gadroon pattern, 9″	251-260
Bowl, rose, footed, Jenny Lind pattern	48- 54
Candlesticks, 9½″, pr.	222-231
Cologne, engraved, Tempo pattern	28- 31
Colognes, etched American Beauty Rose pattern, gold encrusted, pr.	55- 64
Cream and sugar w/tray, 3-piece, all	140-150
Ink bottle	34- 38
Letter holder	44- 52
Pen point holder	21- 32

Cambridge Glass

Plate, tomato, Decagon
pattern, "C" mark, 8" 162-167
Sweetmeat w/cover, 5" 39- 44
Tumbler, Georgian, 8-oz. 18- 21
Azurite (or azure blue—dark opaque blue)
Bowl, ebony foot, 6" 44- 52
Bowl, gold, encrusted
etching, 6" 57- 62
Bowl, rolled edge, gold-
encrusted etching, 10" 71- 82
Candlesticks, Hexagon pat-
tern, 7", pr. 77- 81
Dish, candy, w/cover, gold-
encrusted etching, 3-com-
partment, 6½" 73- 79
Mayonnaise set, 2-piece,
both 74- 81
Tray, sandwich, handled, 10" . 64- 71
Vase, crimped top, bud, 12" ... 52- 62
Vase, sweat pea, etched
gold-encrusted band, 7" 114-125
Carmen (clear brilliant ruby red)
Bowl, ram's head, Gadroon
pattern, 9" 440-462
Box, candy, w/cover, blown,
crystal foot, 5 3/8" 72- 80
Box, cigarette, w/cover,
crystal foot, 3"x3½" 60- 70
Cocktail, etched Portia pat-
tern, gold- encrusted, 3-oz. ... 24- 34
Cup, sherbet, Wild Rose
pattern, handled 32- 41
Flower center, w/crystal
foot, Seashell pattern, 8" ... 141-142
Ivy ball, w/crystal foot, 8½" .. 52- 61
Ivy ball, w/crystal foot, 7" 49- 57
Salt/pepper set, w/crystal
holder, 3-piece, all 42- 51
Sugar, Nautilus design,
crystal handles 64- 71
Wine set, 7-piece, all 120-130
Crown Tuscan (fleshlike opaque)
Ash tray, nude statue, 6½" ... 110-118
Ash tray, Seashell pattern,
"C" mark, 3-toed 31- 41
Bowl, Pristine pattern, 10" ... 70- 80
Bowl, salad, Seashell pat-
tern, 11" 110-118
Butter shell (or ice cream),
3-toed, 5" 44- 52
Candlesticks, nude statues,
9", pr. 210-218
Candlesticks, ram's head,
each side of top, 4", pr. 117-128
Candlesticks, 3-lite, 5", pr. 152-158
Celery/relish, Gadroon pat-
tern, 3-compartment,
3-toed, 10" 70- 80
Cocktail, nude statue, Gold
Krystol bowl, 3-oz. 75- 85
Cocktail, seafood, Seashell
pattern, 4½"-oz. 50- 60

Compote, nude statue,
flared, 7" 141-150
Cornucopia, miniature,
3", pr. 50- 60
Dish, nut, w/place card
holder, 3-toed, 3" 30- 40
Flower block, turtle, 3½" 90- 98
Ivy ball, footed, 7½" 62- 69
Jug, Doulton, 76-oz., 9¼" 240-247
Plate, Evergreen pattern,
8½" 58- 68
Plate, Gadroon pattern,
2-handled, round, 13" 60- 70
Plate, salad, Seashell pattern,
7" 50- 60
Relish, Seashell pattern,
3-compartment, 3-toed, 9" .. 75- 85
Slipper, 5" 61- 70
Swan, 3" 52- 62
Swan, 6" 88- 96
Vase, etched Portia pattern,
footed, 11" 141-150
Vase, Chintz pattern, black
enamel etching, globe
shape, 6½" 288-292
Vase, footed, etched Rose
Point pattern, 11" 262-269
Vases, cornucopia, etched
Portia pattern, gold-
encrusted, 9½", pr. 340-362
Ebony (black opaque)
Basket, handled, 11" 84- 92
Bowl, needle etched pea-
cocks, gold-encrusted, 12" .. 248-260
Bowl, punch, w/foot, Mar-
jorie pattern, early, 10½" .. 283-294
Candlesticks, Hexagon pat-
tern, 8½", pr. 54- 61
Console set: candlesticks, 7½",
pr.; bowl, footed, 7", all 128-132
Ewer and basin set,
Community pattern, 1-gal.
ewer, 15½" basin, both 394-420
Vase, urn, etched Rose
Point pattern, gold-en-
crusted, 10" 247-261
Vases, footed, etched Classic
pattern, gold-encrusted,
10", pr. 210-228
Heliotrope (purple opaque)
Bowl, ebony foot, gold-
encrusted etching, 10" 70- 80
Candlesticks, 8", pr. 128-134
Cheese and cracker set,
10", both 110-128
Cigarette box w/cover, 6" 62- 72
Cologne, gold-encrusted,
etched band, 7" 71- 81
Compote, 9" 77- 86
Console set, 3-piece: candle-
sticks, 10", pr.; bowl,
footed, 10", all 180-190

Cameos

A small carving in relief on glass, lava, stone, shell, or any other hard substance; usually done on agate or shell because these materials have layers of different colors necessary to the cameoist's work. Cameos were in vogue between 1840 and 1875. Too many repros are on the market today.

Bracelet, seven cameos, classic
 figures, silver links $150-160
Brooch, black-white, church,
 gold frame 124-132

(continued)

Cameos

Brooch, orange-white, lady's
head, gold frame 129-136
Brooch, pink-white, lady's
head, gold frame 138-154
Pin, black-white, woman's
profile, 14k gold 195-220
Pin, brown-white, woman and
child, 14k gold 182-191
Ring, girl, pink-white, 14k
mounting 68- 75
Tie pin, man's profile, 14k gold . 47- 52

Campbell Kids

Created in 1900 by Grace (Weiderseim)
Drayton, these comical figures have advertised a popular soup company for years.

Bowl, 6″ dia. (ill.) . . . . $ 14- 19
Bridge tallies 3- 6
Cutouts. 4- 7
Dolls, soft vinyl, 10″ tall, ea. . . . 9- 13
Spoons, ea. 7- 10

Campbell Kids

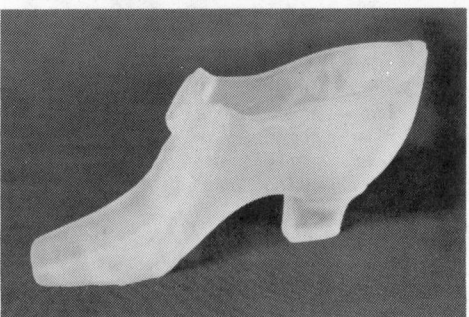

Camphor Glass

Camphor Glass

A cloudy white appearance identifies this
glass. After being blown or pressed, it was
treated with hydrofluoric acid vapor. Blue
camphor glass, attributed to the Sandwich
Glass Company of Cape Cod, is extremely
rare today.

Art glass basket, yellow flowers,
green leaves . . . . $ 87- 95
Ashtray, raised flowers 26- 34
Bowl, raised flowers 34- 41
Bowl, rose color, crimped top,
4″ high 44- 52
Box, powder, Cocker Spaniel
on lid 27- 36
Cologne bottle, gold gilt,
original stopper 45- 53
Compote, open, 6″ tall 44- 54
Compote, yellow, 7½″ tall 44- 57
Creamer, white, flower motif 28- 35
Dish, blue Sandwich glass
(authenticated) 238-244
Jar, powder, pink, silver lid 45- 52
Lamp, miniature, raised flowers . 77- 85
Match holder, pipe shape,
souvenir, 1906 . . . . 42- 51
Plate, 3 kittens 29- 37
Salt/pepper, Three Face,
2¾″ high, pr. 89- 92
Toothpick holder, shoe shape (ill.) 42- 51
Tray, oval scalloped border,
flowers in relief, 11″ long 37- 45
Vase, light blue, floral motif,
9″ high 46- 54
Vase, loop handles, 6½″ high 22- 31
Vase, raised flowers in silver-
plated stand 38- 47

Canary Lustreware

Generally attributed to the Staffordshire
District, England, early 1880s, the two jugs
shown are "American"—that is, made to attract the American market. Rare today!

Canary Lustreware

Jug, "Faith and Hope," large . $1,200-1,350
Jug, "Faith and Hope," small   875- 945
Large jug, bright canary-
    yellow ground, American
    Eagle, edged and divided
    into 3 cartouches with silver
    lustre lines. On each side,
    large American Eagle,
    names of 11 states,
    "Peace, Plenty and
    Independence" (ill.) . . . .   1,800+
Mug, "Thrift is spending
    wisely," 2½" high 525- 570
Small jug, basically same as
    large jug, "Success to the
    United States" (ill.) . . . .   1,850+

Candelabras

Candlesticks with arms is one way to
describe them. The more ornate ones are
called candelabrums, usually attached to a
vase. Silver, both sterling and plate, brass,
base metal, all were used to make the candelabras. Popular in the French and English

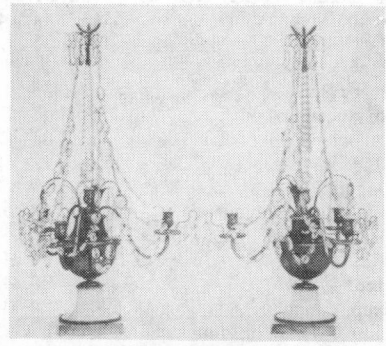

Candelabras

palaces as far back as the mid-1600s. What
you usually find today are early 19th century.

Brass, alabaster urn and
    base, pr. . . . . $ 540- 570
Brass, 12" high, 8-light, pr. . . .   135- 142
Cast pot metal, 17½" high,
    pr. 130- 150
Empire ormolu, 12-light, pr. . .   1,900+
English, cut glass, ormolu,
    18th century, 31" high
    (ill.), pr.   2,100-2,300
French ormolu figural, 5-light,
    early 19th century, pr. 670- 740
Gilt metal, George III type,
    cut glass prisms, pr. 750- 800
Sheffield silver (plate),
    English, early 19th century,
    pr. 535- 585
Sterling silver, mid-1800s,
    7-light, pr. 935- 965

Candle Molds

An early American laborsaving device,
they were usually made of tin, sheet iron, or
on occasion, pewter, in connected groups of
slender, tapered tubes. Melted wax was
poured into each tube. Twisted thread acted
as the wick. When the wax cooled or hard-
ened, the mold was dipped in hot water to
release the candles.

Tin, 4 hole . . . . $ 85-110
Tin, 8 hole   95-120
Tin, 12 hole (ill.)   125-140
Tin, 18 hole (ill.)   138-152
Pewter, same sizes as above,
    50% higher.
Sheet iron—same prices as tin.

(continued)

Candle Molds

Candlesticks

Shape is important, age-wise. The earliest were made from solid cast brass or wrought iron. Hollowstems with the sliding knob to raise or lower the candle were in use in the early 1700s; the sheet-iron type, early 1800s. 19th century types were larger and more ornate.

Beehive, push-up type, burnished, 9″, 10″, 11″, pr.	$118-132
Brass, 1840s, 11″ high, pr.	192-207
Brass, altar type, 22″ high	58- 67
Brass, dolphins, 7½″ high, pr. (ill.)	55- 63
Brass, India, 11″ high, pr.	44- 54
Brass, twisted stem, 8″ high	48- 58
Bull and beehive design, push-up type, 7″	54- 63
Crucifix, pr., Sandwich type	127-136
Glass, dolphin, Sandwich type	78- 88

Candlesticks

Heisey glass, glass prisms, 11½″ high, pr.	131-141
Hog scraper, push-up type, base metal, 6″ high	99-109
Porcelain, flower motif, pr., 10″ high	106-116
Saucer type, push-up snuffer included	64- 72
Winged dragon type, 8½″ high, pr.	61- 71
Wood, turned cherry, 8½″ high	27- 37
Wood, turned oak, 8″ high	28- 38

Candy Containers

These were used for holding tiny pellets of candy and came in the shape of guns, ships, fire engines, cars, boats, etc. Popular at the turn of the century, today they're much sought after. A metal screw cap kept the candy in, though a cork was used on the earlier ones. The Liberty Bell is popular today. See **Clubs and Publications**, this Price Guide.

Airplane, tin wings	$ 35- 42
Auto, Pierce Arrow	44- 52
Battleship	38- 42
Bear	30- 39
Betty Boop	36- 44
Bus, Greyhound	47- 54
Carpet sweeper	35- 42
Chicken-on-nest	22- 32
Dog (ill.)	19- 25
Donkey pulling barrel	42- 52
Duck, sitting	34- 43
Gun, 4″ long	34- 44
House	39- 47
Jeep	22- 31
Lantern, bail, original cap	37- 47
Lantern, tin top	42- 52

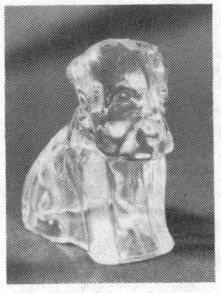

Candy Containers

Liberty Bell, blue, tin cap	64- 71
Locomotive	48- 54
Moon Mullins	48- 52
Motorboat	19- 24
Peter Rabbit	34- 42
Radio	27- 40
Revolver, clear	44- 52
Scottie dogs, J. Crosetti Co., pr.	60- 70
Submarine	44- 52
Suitcase	32- 42
Tank	29- 38
Telephone	33- 42
Train	39- 48
Turkey	38- 47
Van	19- 27
Victory bus	44- 52
Wheelbarrow	42- 51
Whistle	19- 27

Canton China

A product of Canton, China, for over two centuries, it was an inexpensive blue-and-white, hand-decorated ware made primarily for export to England and Europe. Those wares made in the late 1700s and early 1800s are more collectible than the 20th century ware.

Bowl, rice, early 1800s	$ 90-105
Butter patty, blue	31- 40
Charger, temple scene	148-157
Cup/saucer, blue/white, no handle	61- 70
Dish, shrimp, fish scene	90-107
Fish bowl, blue/white, on stand, 14" high	510-545
Fish dish, fish shape, blue/white	61- 71
Ginger jar, blue/white, double ring, 6" high	55- 64
Lamp, blue/white, shade not original	73- 82
Leaf, 7" wide (ill.)	81- 90
Milk pitcher, blue/white, mid-1880s	130-140
Plate, 8"	88- 97
Plate, 9"	87- 93
Plate, blue/white, open lattice edge, 8¼" diameter	86- 95
Platter, blue/white, cut corners, late 1700s	265-282
Platter, octagonal, blue/white, temple scene	192-199
Rose bowl, white poppy blossoms, cover	58- 68
Soup, blue/white, 8½" dia.	62- 72
Teapot, blue/white, straight spout, late	78- 87
Tile, 5" square, animal figures	69- 76
Tureen and stand, covered, blue/white	130-140
Warming dish, octagonal, 9" wide (ill.)	319-342

Canton China

Capo-di-Monte

Capo-di-Monte

Originally made in the factory of the same name in Italy in 1736, since then this ware has been reproduced many times. An N beneath a crown is the usual mark. That made by King Charles of Naples in 1743 is of museum quality and rare. The Doccia factory at Florence has made many reproductions. They're good and fool a lot of people. Just keep in mind that most of the originals are in museums.

Bell, N/Crown mark	$121-132
Box, garden scene, 2½"×3"×6½"	166-174
Dinner bell, cherubs, blue, Crown mark	139-154
Figurine, boy and girl with cow, N/Crown mark	191-210
Figurine, couple carrying water bucket, Crown mark	172-181
Lamp, swirled green/pink ribbing, usual cherubs	281-291
Plaque, classical figures, 8"×15" N/Crown mark	462-472
Plaque, figures in relief depict civilization, 20" dia. (ill.)	955-982
Stein, drinking scene, blue, Crown mark, 12" high	688-697
Tea set, teapot, creamer, sugar, unsigned	182-195
Urn, compote type, cherubs, blue, Crown mark	362-381
Urn, 15" high, cherubs playing, N/Crown mark	259-271
Vase, classical figures, N/Crown mark, 8½" high	188-198

Carlsbad

Wares from Carlsbad were exported to the U.S. in the 19th and 20th centuries. Later,

Carlsbad

when this area was a part of Czechoslovakia after World War I, some pieces were marked Karlsbad. Wares marked Victoria were made especially for Lazarus and Rosenfeldt, a firm in the U.S. that imported from this European country.

Cracker jar, white luster, pink/green flowers, marked Victoria	$ 58-	67
Pitcher, country scene, twisted snake handle, Karlsbad	82-	92
Plaque, in metal frame (ill.)	44-	54
Plate, cupids, floral border, gold decor, 10" dia.	52-	62
Plate, pink/green flowers, swirl and flute border, Victoria	54-	63
Platter, apple blossoms in pink, green flower border, Victoria	77-	86
Platter, poppies, birds around border, 12 matching soups, Karlsbad	127-138	
Tea set, flowers, birds, fluted border on saucers (set consists of teapot, creamer, sugar, waste pot)	132-141	
Tureen, blue/pink roses, floral edge, covered, Karlsbad	68-	77

Carnival Glass (Taffeta)

This originally low priced, iridized glass was made to compete with the expensive Art Glass (Tiffany, Steuben, Durand, Kew Blas, Quezal, etc.) of the early 1900s. It was originally called Taffeta glass and got its

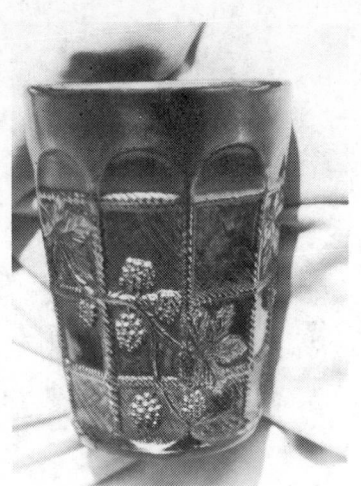

Carnival Glass

present name during the 1920s when circuses and carnivals gave it away as prizes. Grocery stores also gave it away with food purchases. It was dipped in vinegar to iridize it. When the sun came into contact with this "vinegar" glass, it left the glass looking as if it had the measles. Color of individual pieces determines value. Prices range upward from peach (lowest), to marigold to blue, green, or purple, to pastels (any color), to genuine *old* Red Carnival, the most valuable. Being reproduced. See **Clubs and Publications,** this Price Guide.

Banana Boat

Floral	$ 56- 64
Grape and Cable, green	183-192
Grape and Cable, marigold	170-180
Peach and Pear, marigold	78- 84
Thistle	98-107
Wreathed Cherry, purple	151-160
Wreathed Cherry, red	352-366
Wreathed Cherry, white	190-210

Bank

Bell, marigold	42- 52
Owl, marigold	66- 76

Basket

Basketweave, marigold	64- 71
Stippled Rays, 2 handles, purple	49- 58
Tree of Life, marigold	48- 54

Berry Set

Beaded Shell, 6 pcs., purple	279-288
Imperial's Grape, 7 pcs., green	159-167
Three Fruits, N mark, 6 pcs., purple	218-232

Bonbon

Persian Medallion, blue	88- 94
Pond Lily, blue	84- 93

Three Fruits, basketweave, marigold	67- 73

Bottle

Barber, marigold	66- 76
Horn of Plenty	68- 78
Raised Grape, purple	285-287
Toilet Water, marigold	68- 78
Whiskey, Golden Wedding, marigold	64- 73
Wine, New England Wine Co., marigold	62- 72

Bowl

Acorn pattern, marigold	71- 80
Apple Blossoms, 5½" dia., purple	78- 84
Berry, Acorn pattern, 7½" dia., blue	57- 66
Berry, Butterfly and Berry, marigold	69- 79
Berry, Lacy Edge, red	171-178
Berry, Peacock at the Fountain, amethyst	161-170
Berry, Vintage Grape, 5½" dia., purple	63- 73
Berry, Water Lily and Cattails, marigold	64- 74
Blackberry Wreath, 9" dia.	77- 82
Bouquet and Lattice, 6½" dia., cereal	51- 60
Candy, Fine Cut and Roses, N mark, purple	81- 90
Captive Rose, 8¾" dia., green	79- 89
Chrysanthemum, footed, 10" dia., blue	88- 98
Dogwood Sprays, marigold	77- 86
Dragon and Lotus, 8" dia.	77- 85
Embossed Grapes, 9½" dia., marigold	72- 81
Embossed Scroll, 8" dia., green	77- 86
Good Luck, 7¼" dia., blue	134-139
Grape and Cable, green	110-120
Grape and Cable, 6½" dia., marigold	62- 72
Grape and Cable, 7½" dia., purple	82- 91
Grape and Gothic Arches, marigold	55- 65
Heart and Vine, blue	78- 87
Heart and Vine, 8" dia., green	79- 89
Holly, 9" dia., blue	78- 88
Horse's Head Medallion, 6½" dia., marigold	81- 91
Imperial's Cherries, footed, 10" dia., marigold	77- 86
Imperial's Grape, 8¾" dia.	71- 82
Leaf pattern, 5½" dia., marigold	63- 73
Little Flowers, 10½" dia.	88- 93
Louisa, 8¼" dia., amethyst	64- 74
Millersburg's Cherry, marigold	78- 88
Millersburg's Cherry, 7" dia., green	74- 83

105

(continued)

Carnival, Pony

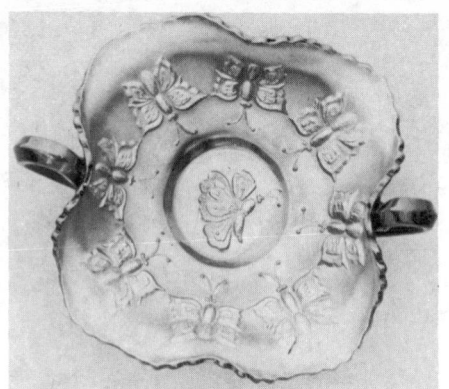

Carnival, Butterflies

(continued)

Carnival, Ragged Robin

Carousel

A German, Michael Dentzel, introduced the first carousel to America in 1867. We know the carousel in this country as the merry-go-round, a delightful ride for children of all ages, with a chance of grabbing the brass ring. An American, C.W. Parker, was known as the Amusement King in the late

(continued)

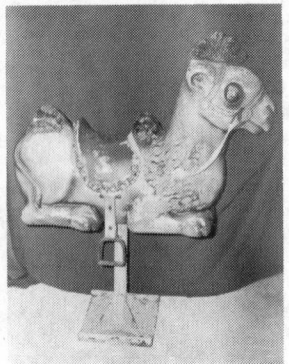

Carousel

1880s. Carousel animals that go up and down are known as "jumpers," and Mr. Parker invented and built them. His horses were things of beauty. See **Clubs and Publications,** this Price Guide.

Camel, 36″ high (ill.)	$ 225- 260
Jumper dog, 59″ long, made by Spillman	2,200-2,400
Jumper dog head, on front of saddle, jewels, 56″ long Parker	1,450-1,700
Jumper horse, lion hide saddle, jewels, made by Parker, 59″ long	1,500-1,700
Jumper Trojan horse, 60″ long, made by Spillman	1,500-1,900
Jumper zebra, 58″ long, made by Spillman	1,600-1,850

Cash Registers

A Dayton, Ohio, restaurateur, James Ritty, started it all. In 1883 John H. Patterson entered the picture and shortly after founded the National Manufacturing Company. His first model was called "The First Cash Register."

American Cash Register, 1880s	$ 875-	975
Federal Cash Register, 1890	850-	950
National Cash Register:		
Brass, nickel-plated, large	950-1,200	
No. 5, bronze	700-	800
No. 130, small	1,100-1,350	
No. 307 (ill.)	195-	225
No. 313, nickel-plated	650-	750
No. 425, 2-drawer	1,100-1,250	
No. 442, brass, oak base	950-1,100	
No. 711, c. 1920s	250-	295
St. Louis Cash Register Co., nickel over brass case	525-	575
St. Louis Cash Register Co., 1-drawer, brass	700-	780

Cash Registers

Caster Sets

Dating from the early 1700s, caster sets you find in shops today are of the Victorian era—3 to 7 condiment bottles in a metal frame, usually quadruple plate or pewter.

4-bottle, green/clear cut glass, quadruple plate holder, 7½″ high (ill.)	$365-385
4-bottle, quadruple plate frame, clear glass	182-192
4-bottle, Sheffield silver frame, Waterford glass, clear	210-250
5-bottle, quadruple plate frame etched flowers, clear glass	125-140
5-bottle, quadruple plate frame, amber Daisy and Button	210-240
6-bottle, quadruple plate frame, clear glass	88-105
6-bottle, quadruple plate frame, miniature, clear glass	101-115
6-bottle quadruple plate frame, Cranberry thumbprint	242-251

Caster Sets

110

6-bottle, quadruple plate frame, clear glass, patented 1857	200-220
7-bottle, sterling silver frame, Amberina type	610-655
8-bottle, clear glass, sterling silver caps	292-312
8-bottle, cut glass, sterling silver caps	395-420

Catalogs

Catalogs

Every company that could afford to issued a catalog extolling its products. The most collectible today are those that deal with the early automobile industry, jewelry and furniture makers and, of course, the now-expensive original Sears, Roebuck catalog from the early 1900s. Montgomery Ward's also brings brisk prices.

Franklin auto catalog, Syracuse, N.Y., 1907	$ 70- 80
Montgomery Ward catalog, early 1900s	182-195
Noritake china catalog, 1964 (ill.)	1.50- 3
Sears, Roebuck catalog, early 1900s	180-195
Singer sewing machine, parts catalog, 1920s	14- 21
Spode china catalog, 1964 (ill.)	5- 7

Cauldon China

This firm didn't make porcelain until the early 1900s. It's English and very collectible.

Cauldon China

Bonbon dish, floral decorations	$ 42- 51
Cup and saucer, Indian Tree pattern	55- 63
Egg cup	22- 31
Ewer, Indian Tree design	58- 67
Flower, "frog," floral decor, 10 holes	41- 51
Plate, hunting scene, 10½" dia.	44- 52
Plate, floral decor, roses-in-wreath, 10½" dia.	47- 56
Vase, Indian Tree pattern	66- 73
Vase, round form, roses (ill.)	52- 70

Ceiling Fans

Used in homes and stores after introduction of electricity. Being collected today by decorators and others.

Average price, good condition ... $180-240
Reproductions available—higher priced.

Ceiling Fans

Celadon

This is a rare type of highly fired porcelain from the Sung Dynasty. It's scarce and is only mentioned here because some of it has been brought in from Red China in recent years. It features a glaze that meanders from greens through tones of gray-blue, gray-white, etc. It was also made in Japan and Korea, and undoubtedly military personnel brought home original pieces without knowing their value.

Bowl, diamond shape panels, 11½" dia., Sung Dynasty	$3,200-3,400
Bowl, flower leaves, 6¼" dia., late	88- 97
Creamer, blue/white chrysanthemum leaves, late	95- 115

(continued)

Celadon

Dish (used as planters), blue/ white floral, early 19th century	325- 340
Ginger jar, floral decor, 5" high (ill.)	80- 90
Jar, birds in relief, 19th century	232- 342
Pitcher, green, flower, decor, "bamboo" handle	400- 425
Planter, birds in relief, 19th century	265- 280
Plate, scalloped rose pattern, birds, butterflies, enameled	178- 185
Teapot, floral motif, 6" high	112- 122
Vase, blue/gray, dragon motif, 9½" high	225- 245
Vase, grayish green, blue handles and figures, 16½" high	360- 375
Vase, on rosewood stand, bamboo motif, 19th century	420- 430

Celluloid (French Ivory)

Invented by John Hyatt around 1868, celluloid was considered a boon to men who had to wear collars. It was also used for hairbrush backs, combs, etc., but fell from style in the mid-1900s.

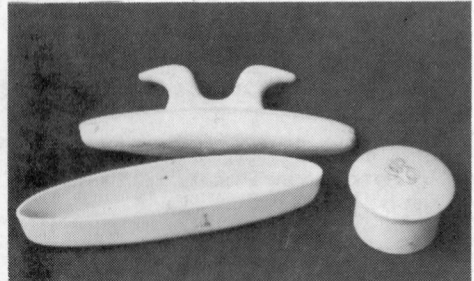

Celluloid

Collar box, velvet lined	$ 52- 60
Comb, lady's	19- 27
Cream jar w/cover, glass lining, 3" dia.	26- 32
Dresser set: tray, comb, mirror, hair receiver, powder box, etc., all.	77- 85
Dresser tray, 11¼" long	15- 22
Frame, 6"×9"	28- 37
Glove box, woman on lid	38- 41
Hair receiver and covered powder box	14- 18
Handled cuticle tool	11- 19
Lady's travel kit	37- 42
Manicure set, pink velvet case	37- 40
Napkin ring	11- 18
Opener, letter	18- 26
Pansy vase, 6" high	21- 32
Pin box, 1" high (ill.)	9- 14
Powder box, w/lid, 4½" dia.	20- 30
Nail buffer, chamois covered, 6" long	12- 19
Rattle, baby's	18- 25
Shoehorn	11- 21

Centennial Plates

Centennial plates obviously celebrate the 100th anniversary of cities, states, institutions.

Plate, Baltimore & Ohio, 1827- 1927, 10" dia.	$ 52- 60
Plate, Civil War, "North-South United," crossed flags, 10½" dia.	40- 50
Plate, Philadelphia, Declaration of Independence, 1776-1876, 8" dia.	51- 61
Plate, War of 1812, 9" dia.	44- 53

Ceramic Art Company

Founded in Trenton, New Jersey, by Jonathon Coxon, Sr., and Walter D. Lenox. Fine art wares in Belleek and other bodies were made from 1889. Undecorated pieces were marked with a painter's palette; Indian China, an undecorated ware, was marked with an Indian's head. A wreath enclosing the full name of the company was used to mark special decorative work. The firm is still in business. See also **Belleek, American**.

Cups, demitasse, 12 in set, Wreath mark, all	$320-330
Mug, floral decorations, 6½" high, Wreath mark	66- 74
Mug, monk, 7" high, Wreath mark	81- 90
Vase, floral scene, 6¼" high, Wreath mark	78- 88
Vase, undecorated, 8" high, palette mark	61- 71

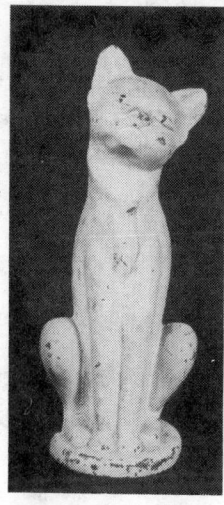

Chalkware

Chalkware

Contrary to popular belief, this was not made by the Dutch Germans in Pennsylvania in the mid-1800s. Italian immigrants in this country, 1820s to the Civil War, made the best—simply, plaster of paris decorated with water colors.

Bank, dog, black, glass eyes	$ 50- 60
Bank, rearing horse	27- 33
Bank, turkey, natural colors . . .	54- 62
Betty Boop, 14½″ high	188-197
Bookends, boy and girl reading, pr.	52- 61
Bookends, pirates, painted, pr. .	54- 63
Cat (ill.)	58- 68
Dog, 11½″ high, early	79- 85
Dove, green/blue wings	205-210
Figurine, bust of Indian	92-107
Figurine, cat sleeping	68- 78
Owl, 12″ high	183-190
Pigeon, green leaves, red berries	152-162
Sailor boy, 9″ high	22- 31
Snow White, 12½″ high	47- 53
Squirrel	174-178
Stag, on rectangular plinth	235-250

Character Collectibles

Character Collectibles

Though not antiques in the true sense of the word, there are many comic strip, movie, and television character items being collected today.

Andy Gump

Doll, chalkware	$ 17- 27

Beatles

Dolls, set of 4, in original box . . .	42- 51
Lunchbox, tin	35- 45
Pillow	43- 52

Betty Boop

Doll, celluloid windup, 7″ high . .	47- 54
Playing cards	54- 63
Tambourine, 6¼″	45- 55
Soap figure, in original box	77- 83

Buck Rogers

Disintegrator gun, 10″	220-230
Flash blast attack ship	54- 63
Liquid helium water pistol, red/yellow	70- 80
Puzzle, 1950s	45- 55
Pocket watch, by Ingraham	223-233

Charlie Chaplin

Glove box, wooden	52- 62

Donald Duck

Card game, 1950	18- 27
Cookie jar	41- 51
Doll, bisque, 3″ high	35- 45
Doll, celluloid, wearing Santa Claus suit	108-111
Doll, chalkware, 3½″ high	25- 32
Wristwatch	74- 79

Flash Gordon

Compass	46- 52
Compass, wrist	25- 32
Radio repeater space gun	165-180
Rocket fighter ship	56- 66
Signal pistol space gun	375-400
Space outfit: belt, glasses, watch, all	39- 49

Hopalong Cassidy

Belt and spurs, both	36- 45
Bowl, cup and plate, all	42- 52
Field glasses, in original box . . .	44- 56
Lunch pail and thermos, both . .	26- 36
Pennant, circus	12- 18
Radio, Arvin, black/silver	85- 93
Tumbler, 5″ high	17- 22

Howdy Doody

Beanie kit, leather	19- 27
Earmuffs	18- 27
Handkerchief	15- 24
Teaspoon, silver-plated	21- 31

Mickey Mouse

Bubble gum cards, 12, all	44- 52
Camera	30- 40
Charm, celluloid	19- 24
Crayon box, tin	19- 23
Doll, rubber, 5¼″ high	11- 17
Paint set	31- 42
Phonograph	52- 62

(continued)

Salt/pepper shakers (Minnie too)	19- 26	
Tea set, china, 15 pcs., all	81- 91	
Wristwatch, 1939	110-120	

Popeye

Bank, dime register, 1950s	18- 27
Game, Pipe Toss, in original box	52- 61
Harmonica, 1920s	70- 80
Pencil box, 1930	34- 42
Wallet, 1950s	30- 40

Roy Rogers

Boot tops, leatherette, pr.	18- 24
Cap gun, cast iron	26- 34
Clicker, tin	15- 19
Mug, plastic	12- 19
Wristwatch	51- 61

Shirley Temple

Book, *Rebecca of Sunnybrook Farm*	19- 25
Cereal set, bowl, creamer, mug, all (creamers, ill.)	108-111
Doll, soap	48- 56
Salt, 3″ high	19- 27
School bag	60- 70
Teapot, 2 cups, pink plastic, both	67- 72

Snow White

Wristwatch	34- 43

Superman

Brush, early	18- 25
Card game, by Ideal	19- 23
Club button, 3¼″	5- 9
Club member's certificate	30- 40
Game, in original box, early	101-111
Mug, 1960s	11- 16
Water gun	11- 19

Tarzan

Cardboard sign, advertising movie	28- 38

Tom Mix

Belt buckle	38- 47
Handkerchief	7- 9
Periscope ring	51- 60
Ralston ring, Straight Shooters	16- 24
Telescope, tin	57- 64

Cheese Dishes

Cheese Dishes

These wedge-shaped dishes-with-a-cover graced dinner tables for hundreds of years. Every country exported them to America and you'll find them still fairly inexpensive at shows, shops, and auctions.

Baccarat glass, mice engraved on lid (rare)	$375-410
English, Adams & Sons, green/ pink	265-280
English, hunting dogs, blue/ white, marked Clews	315-330
English, ironstone, birds/ flowers, blue/brown/white, marked Johnson Bros., England	155-170
English, ironstone, cottage scene, transfer design, brown/ white (ill.)	48- 56
English, ironstone, floral decor, blue/white, marked Meakin	230-245
English, Wedgwood, blue Jasperware, Greek maidens	295-335

Chelsea

This porcelain was made for the fashionable world of London society, from 1745 until 1784 only. Supposedly made to compete with Dresden, it never achieved Dresden's quality. Chelsea can be conveniently divided into four main classes: The first period of the incised triangle and the raised anchor marks, the 1740s; the period of (at first) the raised anchor and the red anchor marks, the 1750s; the period of the gold anchor marks, the 1760s; the Chelsea-Derby period, the 1770s. In 1770 the Chelsea factory was taken over by Derby and the period lasted until 1783. In the 1920s a great number of molds and models of figurines were found at the Spode-Copeland Works and many varied items were reproduced.

Bowl, 6¼″ dia., Red Anchor mark	$1,450-1,600	
Candlesticks, 11″ high, grape cor, Red Anchor mark, pr.	2,850-3100	
Cups/saucers, demitasse, c. 1770s, set of 6, all	130- 150	
Dish, floral design, Gold Anchor mark	81- 95	
Dish, Kakiemon decoration, Red Anchor mark	448- 465	
Dish, oval, scalloped edge, Red Anchor mark	147- 159	

114

Chelsea

Ewer, floral decor, 10″ high Red Anchor mark	565-	610
Figurine, dancing couple, Red Anchor mark	2,100-2,300	
Figurine, girl with lamb, Gold Anchor mark	220-	235
Figurine, woman with basket, c. 1770s	265-	285
Pitcher, sprig decor, 10½″ high, Gold Anchor mark	380-	395
Plate, grape decor, 8″ dia., 1770s	62-	70
Plate, hand-painted birds, Gold Anchor mark	375-	390
Plate, sprig decor, Red Anchor mark	1,250-1,400	
Sugar and creamer, grape decor, Gold Anchor mark, ea.	520-	560
Teapot, grape decor, 9″ high (ill.)	87-	97
Teapot, sprig decor, Gold Anchor mark	340-	365

Chess Sets

Also, see **Clubs and Publications**, this Price Guide.

Bone-carved, in wooden box, India, new (ill.)	$ 87-	96
Ivory-carved, in rosewood box, Chinese, 19th century	485-	540

Chess Sets

Irovy-carved, in walnut box, miniature set for children, old	395-	435
Jade-carved, in rosewood box, Chinese, early	1,975-2,500	
Jadeite-carved, in wooden box, Chinese, new	88-	92
Porcelain pieces, ½″ to 2″, Victorian dress, in wooden box	300-	340
Quartz pieces, 1″ to 3″, Chinese figures, 1890s	250-	270
Silver-plated figures, 2½″ to 5″, in silver-plated box, 1890s	420-	440

Children's Books

Children's Books

Subject, demand, author, condition—all are important when buying these books that were printed some 100 to 150 years ago.

Adventures of Famous Travellers in Many Lands, W.L. Allison, New York, c. 1880s	$ 23-	30
Baby's Lullaby Book, Charles Stuart Pratt, Boston, c. 1890s	31-	40
A Book of Nonsense, Edward Lear, New York, 1870	47-	52
The Boys of 1812, Prof. J. Russell Soley, Boston, 1887	32-	39
The Christmas Wreath, London, Pictorial Boards, 1877	19-	26
Cinderella, Dean & Son, London, 5 sets, 9 chromolithographed changes, c. 1880s	65-	72
The Jackdaw of Rheims, Thomas Ingoldsby, London, Paris, and New York, color cover, c. 1880s	32-	40
Life and Death of Cock Robin, Albany, N.Y., c. 1850s	35-	42
Little Greta of Denmark, Bernadine Bailey, 1920	6-	8

(continued)

The Merry Adventures of Robin
Hood, Howard Pyle, New York,
1883 .... 35- 47
Raggedy Andy Stories, Johnny
Gruelle, Boston, 1925,
(ill.) 25- 33
Watt's Songs of Early Religion,
McLoughlin Bros., 1860s 9- 14
Who Was the First Architect?,
The Busy-Bee Series, London,
Edinburgh, and New York,
1877 .... 26- 34
Wilson's Larger Speller, Marcius
Wilson, 1864.............. 18- 23

Children's Dishes

Toward the end of the 19th century the major glass and pottery firms produced tablewares specifically made for children. Little Lamb, Nursery Rhymes, and Bunnykins are just a few of the many pieces made. Don't confuse a miniature with items especially made for children.

Berry Sets
Pressed glass, Inverted Straw-
berry, large bowl, clear .... $ 38- 47
Pressed glass, Lacy Daisy, small
bowl, clear 15- 21
Pressed glass, Nursery Rhymes,
large bowl, milk glass 58- 62
Bowls
Porcelain, French, Limoges, 3"
dia., barnyard scene, set of 6 .. 115-121
Porcelain, "Germany," 5½" dia.,
fishing by the mill, set of 6 118-127
Pottery, Mexican, 5 sizes from
2" to 8", set of 5 .... 50- 60
Butter Dishes
Pressed glass, Amazon, clear 41- 51
Pressed glass, Children's
Colonial, clear 29- 38
Pressed glass, Heart Band, clear . 41- 51
Pressed glass, Liberty Bell, clear . 80- 90
Cake Stands
Pressed glass, Beautiful Lady,
clear 34- 39
Pressed glass, Hawaiian Lei, clear 38- 47
Candlesticks
Pressed glass, Swirl, clear, pr. 41- 50
Silver-plated, pr............... 33- 41
Canister Set
Tin, kitchen scenes, set of 6 ..... 60- 68
Creamers
Pressed glass, Arrowhead-in-Oval 22- 30
Pressed glass, Criss Cross 24- 28
Pressed glass, Jubilee 24- 30
Tin, children playing 12- 19
Cups and Saucers
Porcelain, French, Limoges,
kitchen scene 24- 33

Children's Dishes

Porcelain, "Made in Germany,"
Brownies 24- 33
Porcelain, "Made in Japan,"
nursery scene 24- 32
Feeding Dishes
Animals, 8" dia., (ill.) 19- 27
Porcelain, Campbell Kids, 7½"
dia., Buffalo pottery 62- 71
Porcelain, French, Limoges, 7½"
dia., Little Bo-Peep 51- 60
Porcelain, "Japan," 7¼" dia.,
little boys at play 42- 50
Feeding Sets
Porcelain, German, Three Bears,
3 pcs..................... 54- 63
Mugs
Bunnykins, English, 3" high 25- 35
Pottery, Mexican, 4" high 24- 33
Sterling silver, "BH", flowers ... 58- 62
Plates
Porcelain, 5" dia., Simple Simon . 15- 27
Porcelain, 5¼" dia., Mother
Goose center 17- 26
Tin, 5½" dia., Snow White center 31- 37
Tin, 5¼" dia., Little Bo-Peep
center 17- 26
Spooner
Porcelain, French, Limoges,
flower scene 27- 32
Table Set
Tin, 10 pcs., zoo animals, all 58- 64
Tea Sets
Porcelain, English, c. 1880s,
garden scenes, set of 10 ...... 70- 77
Porcelain, German, garden
scenes, set of 18 105-111
Porcelain, "Made in Japan,"
pagoda scenes, set of 15 ...... 83- 93
Tin, German, Snow White and
Seven Dwarfs, set of 22 132-141
Toilet Sets
Porcelain, German, animal
scenes, set of 9 .... 58- 68
Porcelain, "Made in Japan,"
flower scenes, set of 8 .... 52- 61

116

Children's Mugs

Children's Mugs

These 19th century items were usually given to children as gifts or as rewards for being good. Leeds, Ironstone, Gaudy Dutch, Liverpool, and Bristol are just a few of the many types made. Highly collectible.

Animals, 4″ high (ill.) . . . . $	8- 11
Boy with farm animals, ironstone	106-116
Ding Dong Bell, silver plated	54- 63
Franklin maxim, "The way to wealth"	107-117
Glass, ea.	8- 11
"The house that Jack built"	91-107
"Long may we live," Canary ware	173-179
"A new carriage for Ann," Canary ware	168-178
"A present for a good boy," Canary ware	180-190

Chocolate Glass

Often referred to as caramel slag, it was made by the Indiana Tumbler and Goblet Company, Greentown, Indiana, and also by Fenton. Popular patterns were Cactus and Leaf Bracket.

Berry bowl, Cactus, 4″ dia. . . . . . $	70- 80
Berry set, Leaf Bracket, 6 pcs., all	670-710
Compote, jelly, Cactus	140-160
Cracker jar, Cactus	228-252
Creamer, Austrian	122-131
Dish, butter, covered, Leaf Bracket	138-142
Lamp, 7 panel, fancy base and framework	231-241
Mug, Serenade	108-111
Nappie, handled (ill.)	91-108
Sugar, Leaf Bracket	101-112
Tumbler, Cactus	68- 78
Tumbler, 4¾″ high (ill.)	71- 80
Tumbler, Sawtooth	70- 79

Chocolate Glass

Chocolate Pot Sets

Chocolate Pot Sets

Just about every porcelain factory in Europe made these sets, popular in the 18th and 19th centuries. See also specific firms elsewhere in the Guide for prices.

Cream flowers, gold decor with 6 cups (ill.) $178-184
Lily decor, signed Germany, 6 cups/saucers 177-182
Oriental decor, Chinese garden scene, pot and 6 cups/saucers . 173-185
Rose decor, flower trim, signed Germany, 6 cups/saucers 154-162
Roses, cream ground, gold decor, 4 cups/saucers 180-190

Christmas Collectibles/ Ornaments

Old-fashioned Christmases are a thing of the past in this country. No stringing of popcorn to drape on the tree, no hiking through the snow to cut down a favorite tree. Older Christmas items are popular collectibles, but if you find old electric Christmas tree lights, be careful. Old wire can cause a fire in a matter of seconds.

Bulbs, Electric

Basket of fruit, green/red . . . . $	9- 13
Bell	17- 20
Bluebird, milk glass	11- 14
Clock	14- 17
Donald Duck	24- 28
Flower, rose	13- 17
Gingerbread man, brown	11- 15
House, Santa on roof	12- 16
Humpty Dumpty	31- 38
Kayo (comic strip character)	39- 44
Lantern, Japanese	8- 12
Mickey Mouse	14- 21
Minnie Mouse	10- 18

117

(continued)

Christmas Collectibles/Ornaments

Parrot, milk glass	11- 16
Pinocchio	25- 30
Santa, 5″, 6″, 6½″, 7″	11- 18
Santa, 8″, 8½″, 9″	50- 58
Snowman, 5½″, 6″, 7″	11- 20
Star, various sizes, 3″ to 6″	9- 19

Ornaments

Angel, carved wood, c. 1880s	44- 52
Angel, spun glass wings	10- 14
Basket of flowers	12- 14
Basket of flowers, carved wood, painted, c. 1880s	45- 52
Basket, pressed paper (holds candy)	24- 31
Beetle	13- 17
Bell, clip-on	9- 13
Bell, pressed paper	16- 21
Bell, red mercury glass	11- 20
Bird, cotton, clip-on	9- 14
Bird, spun glass tail	11- 17
Bugle, clip on	8- 12
Bugs Bunny	24- 32
Church, clip-on	12- 19
Church, mercury glass	9- 14
Clown head	9- 13
Crane, clip-on	8- 16
Fish, mercury glass	8- 14
Heart, red glass	9- 14
Horse, 5½″, 6½″, 8″	11- 16
Lion's head, pressed paper (holds candy)	27- 31
Owl, pressed paper	11- 15
Peacock, clip-on	12- 19
Pear, green glass	10- 12
Pipe, carved wood, painted, c. 1880s	44- 52
Pipe, painted glass	11- 14
Santa, basket on back (holds candy)	45- 52
Santa, mercury glass	13- 18
Santa, open bag, pressed paper (ill.)	40- 47
Santa, pressed paper (ill.)	44- 52
Snowman, mercury glass	12- 17

Snowman, pressed paper (holds candy), Germany, c. 1900s	112-119
Star, frosted glass	11- 17
Star, long shaft, for top of tree, 9½″ overall	31- 40
George Washington, mercury glass	43- 52
George Washington, pressed paper	51- 62

These are indicative prices. Countless thousands are waiting to adorn your tree.

CHRISTMAS Rörstrand PLATES SWEDEN

Christmas Plates

Bing and Grondahl and the Royal Copenhagen factories in Copenhagen, Denmark, make the best-known Christmas plates. Many American firms are now producing a plate.

Year	B&G	RC
1895	$ 4,000+	
1902	355-370	
1903	240-260	
1904	70- 80	
1905	95-110	
1906	133-150	
1907	150-162	
1908	100-115	$ 2,550+
1909	130-150	150-160
1910	105-112	143-153
1911	110-120	147-158
1912	110-120	140-150
1913	105-115	155-165
1914	90-100	137-142
1915	160-178	125-135
1916	110-120	130-138
1917-36	88- 98	110-120
1937	120-130	163-172
1938	128-138	278-290
1939	192-208	258-278
1940	175-190	520-540
1941	330-340	379-400
1942	170-190	438-470
1943	165-175	490-525
1944	100-115	235-244
1945	168-180	410-430
1946	90-110	228-242
1947	100-120	264-278
1948	68- 78	168-177
1949	78- 88	178-184
1950	110-115	178-186
1951	98-110	328-360
1952	78- 88	148-162
1953	108-112	120-135
1954	88- 98	148-158
1955	115-122	265-274
1956	128-138	177-187
1957	160-175	140-150

Christmas Plates

1958	138-148	153-163
1959	170-178	155-160
1960	168-180	168-178
1961	285-300	152-162
1962	80- 90	215-235
1963	127-140	63- 73
1964	90-100	62- 72
1965	77- 87	60- 70
1966 (ill.)	71- 79	70- 80
1967	73- 81	40- 50
1968	57- 67	35- 45
1969-79 (ill.)	44- 53	35- 45
Year	**Frankoma**	**Bayreuther**
1965	215-235	
1966	110-120	
1967	80- 88	110-118
1968	30- 40	44- 53
1970-79	30- 40	45- 52

Cigar Cutters, Pocket

When gentlemen wore vests and watch chains, the pocket-type cigar cutter was one of the attachments. Most were utilitarian but 14k gold and sterling silver models were much in vogue. A quality cigar always has to have the tip snipped off; a 5¢ stinker comes with the hole.

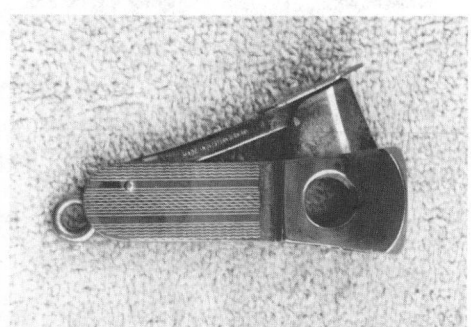

Combination cutter and knife
blade, 10k gold . . . . $ 45- 55
Combination cutter and watch
fob, 10k gold 47- 56
Combination cutter and small
scissors, stainless steel 28- 34
Cutter, stainless steel, Germany .   19- 25
Cutter, embossed, 14k gold 198-225
(Note: It *isn't* the cutter, it's the
price of the gold.)
Cutter, initialed, sterling silver . . 62- 72

Cigar Molds

Used to shape the cigar in the early days, today they make pleasant items to hang in the kitchen or on a den wall. See **Clubs and Publications**, this Price Guide.

Cigar molds, base metal, 2 pcs. . . $ 41- 50
Cigar molds, wood, 2 pcs. (ill.) . . .   44- 55
Cigar molds, wood, carved
"Havana's Best" on top lid . . .   52- 62

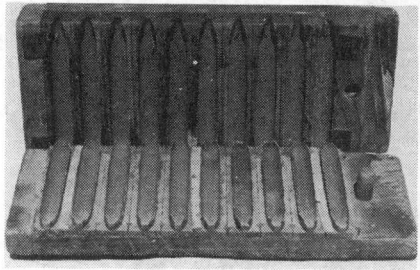

Cigar Molds

Cigar Store Figures

Cigar Store Figures

Used in America during the 19th century, almost life-size effigies of Indian braves and

119

(continued)

squaws were popular decorations outside tobacco shops. Other figures were also used. The practice comes from the Dutch who used this type figure to advertise tobacco in the 1600s. Also used in England in the 1600s.

Indian, 72" high	$7,500 +
Indian brave, 60" high (ill.)	6,900 +
Indian chief, painted, 5' high	7,400 +
Indian chief, small	6,750 +
Indian chief, wood painted, 6½" high	9,000 +
Indian chief, wood, painted 4' high	7,400 +
Indian maiden, 5' high	6,700 +
Indian squaw, wood, painted, half size	6,800 +
Turk, wood, painted	7,600 +

Cinnabar

Red lacquer built up slowly with layer after layer is called Cinnabar, the best coming from China in the late 17th century. It's made today any place in the Orient.

Bowl, red-brown, carved	$100-110
Box, red, carving on cover and sides, 4"×5"	88- 98
Button, lotus flower design, 4/5" dia.	37- 46
Plaque, red, carved, black and gold frame, 6"×7½"	58- 68
Snuff bottle, lacquer, floral, birds	142-152
Snuff bottle, red, white, jade top	189-210
Vase, brass rim, top and bottom, pr.	205-220
Vase, carved flowers on teakwood base, 8½" high, pr. (ill.)	385-425
Vase, carved overall floral and foliage design	165-180
Vase, trees, mountains, carved, 8" high	138-147

Cinnabar

Civil War Collectibles

Civil War Collectibles

Also called the War Between the States, depending upon which side you were on. CSA means Confederate States of America and GAR means Grand Army of the Republic. The Blue was the North and the Gray was the South. "Rebs" were Southerners, those who rebelled and joined Jeff Davis. "Blue Bellies" were Union troops, so named because the dye in their blue uniforms stained their bellies blue.

Album, regimental photos, 8"×11"	$385-450
Bayonet w/scabbard, CSA	75- 90
Belt buckle, CSA, brass	50- 60
Belt buckle, USA, brass (ill.)	58- 68
Bowie knife, bone handle, w/scabbard, marked "I*XL"	950+
Bowie knife, ivory handle, w/scabbard, no marking	750-850
Box, cartridges, CSA imprint	40- 50
Canteen, cloth-over-wood	92-110
Cap badge, GAR, enlisted man's	60- 70
Cartridge pouch, GAR, leather	87- 96
Diary, private's account, 150th Regiment	250-300
Discharge paper from 1st Ohio Volunteers, dated June 15, 1863	82- 92
Holster w/belt, Dragoon imprint	190-199
Horse's bit	35- 45
Knapsack, GAR	63- 73
Leather belt, brass buckle, GAR	71- 81
Lithograph, "General Sherman," 6½"×11"	22- 32
Naval cutlass, Confederate Navy, 26" serrated edges	210-240
Naval sword, dress, U.S. Navy, 35" long	300-320
Photograph, "Officers of Heavy Artillery"	60- 70
Poster, asking recruits to join Glennon's Brigade, GAR	78- 88

Poster offering reward for GAR
    deserters 78- 85
Saddle bags, CSA, Virginia 1st
    Cavalry, pr. 350-365
Saddle, McClellan-type,
    w/saddle bags 292-310
Slave document, 1846, purchase
    of Becky from Christopher
    Hutchins by I.W. Rawlings . . .   83- 92
Spurs, CSA, officer's 190-210
Telescope, U.S. Navy 430-455

Clambroth Glass

Its gray color, semi-opaque, supplies its
name. Popular during the Victorian era.

Barber bottle, Bay Rum, stopper $ 37- 47
Candlestick, Sandwich glass,
    1850s, 10″ high (ill.) 285-300
Cruet, applied blue twisted
    handle 77- 84
Dish, footed, 8″ dia. 37- 42
Egg cup, Diamond Point w/panels 143-152
Goblet, souvenir of Philadelphia,
    7″ high 37- 46
Toothpick holder, souvenir-type .   29- 39
Tumbler, souvenir-type 44- 53
Tumbler, whiskey 225-235
Vase, fluted top, 8½″ high 84- 92

Clambroth Glass

Clevenger Glass

Clevenger Glass

During the depression years of the 1930s,
this glass was freehand blown—sugar bowls,
vases, pitchers; in the 1940s it was mold
blown. The Clevenger brothers, Tom,
Lorenzo, and Allie, remained in business until
the early 1960s. A few years later the shop
was reopened and is still in business in
Clayton, New Jersey. Early pieces are
sought after by serious collectors.

Creamer, amethyst, Swirl
    pattern, 3½″ high (ill.) $122-131
Pitcher, aqua, Expanded
    Diamond pattern 138-144
Sugar bowl, amethyst, ribbed,
    3¾″ dia. (ill.) 105-111

Clewell Metal Art

Founded in 1906 in Canton, Ohio, by
Charles Walter Clewell. He completely
masked the ceramic body with a metal
coating. Clewell was a metalworker, not a
potter. Most pieces were marked Clewell,
Canton O.

Vase, copper finish, 8½″ high . . . $140-152
Vase, light blue-green, 7″ high . . . 152-162
Vase, silver metal finish,
    handled, 9¼″ high 172-180
Vase, velvety matt-green,
    11″ high 245-255

Clews, Ralph and James

Established in Cobridge, England, in 1814,
this pottery operated until around 1835 when
it was taken over by Wood and Brownfield.
Dr. Syntax and the Valentine were two of the
most popular subjects. Probably the most
popular series was the states.

Creamer, 5½″, eagle on urn $128-134
Cups/saucers, dark blue, Landing
    of Lafayette 137-144
Gravy boat with tray, Landing
    of General Lafayette at Castle
    Gardens, N.Y., August 16,
    1824 288-296
Pitcher, dark blue, 13 original
    states, series, 8″ high 325-345
Plate, 9″ dia., dark blue, states
    series 218-235
Plate, 7¼″ dia., dark blue, Dr.
    Syntax Turned Nurse 287-294
Plate, 10″ dia., dark blue, Dr.
    Syntax and the Bees 246-256
Plate, 10½″ dia., black,
    Pittsburgh, Pa. 218-224
Plate, 9″ dia., Dr. Syntax
    Reading His Tour 275-284

Clifton Art Pottery

CLIFTON POTTERY NEWARK. N.J.

William A. Long, an organizer of the Lonhuda Pottery Company, and Fred Tschirner, a chemist, founded this company in Newark, New Jersey, in 1905. Crystal Patina and Clifton Indian Ware were the two major lines produced until 1911. Then the company shifted to the production of porcelain-fired wall tile and vitrified floor tile, in all colors. By 1914 the firm's name had been changed to the Clifton Porcelain Tile Company. Most pieces were marked Clifton.

Vase, Clifton Indian Ware, 2¾" high	$178-184
Vase, Clifton, Tirrube, 8½" high	162-174
Vase, Crystal Patina, 9³/8" high	178-188
Vase, molded fish decoration, 3½" high	140-155
Vase, pink/white, mottled, 5⁷/8" high, dated 1905	152-162

Clocks, American

For a history of clocks, their current prices and a glossary of terms, see *Clock Guide, Identification with Prices*, Volumes I and II, Wallace-Homestead Book Co., Des Moines, Iowa, $8.95 and $9.95, each. All clocks listed here and many more can be seen there. See **Clubs and Publications**, this Price Guide.

Ansonia Clock Co., Ansonia, Connecticut, 1851-1878. Founded by Anson V. Phelps (located in Brooklyn, New York, 1879-1930s).

Automobile

Automobile #1, Arabic or Roman dial, black, nickel, 8-day	$ 57-	66
Automobile #2, black, 9-day	45-	55
Motor, Arabic or Roman dial, brass or nickel, 1-day, stem wind	58-	68

Calendar

Desk inkwell, 1-day, simple calendar	356-	372
Octagon long drop, wall, oak, 8-day, simple calendar	545-	575
Victorian kitchen, time, strike, 8-day, oak, barometer, thermometer	363-	390

Crystal Regulator

Claudius, polished brass, gold-plated, visible escapement, 8-day	295-	395
Coral, same as above	295-	395
Jupiter, polished brass, gold ornaments, hour and ½-hour gong strike, 8-day	1,775-	2,100
Oriel, polished brass, gold-plated, visible escapement, 8-day	485-	555
Rouen, same as above	295-	395
Wanda, same as above	295-	395

Japanese Bronze Alarm

Bronto, Arabic or Roman dial, 1-day	94-	110
Rattler, same as above	88-	104

Mantel (Black Enameled Iron)

B Assortment (Bangor, Batavia, Bath, Brandon, Butte), 8-day, hour, ½-hour gong strike, Arabic or Roman dial, Japanese bronze finish, choice of American sash, French sash, visible escapement, ea.	140-	163
C Assortment (Cambridge, Carlisle, Chatham, Compton, Coventry), same as above, ea.	132-	144
Paris Assortment (Chester, Palermo, Paris, Sorrento, Venice, Vienna), same as above, ea.	125-	138

Nickel Alarm

Bee, Arabic or Roman dial, 1-day (turn the back to wind)	70-	79
Clatter, Arabic or Roman dial, 1-day	34-	44
Luminous Pirate, Roman dial, 1-day	63-	72
Pirate, same as above	39-	52

Ansonia Regulator

Princess, Roman dial, 1-day .. | 53- | 64
Princess, Roman dial, 8-day .. | 73- | 83
Spark, Arabic or Roman dial,
1-day .... | 45- | 55
Spark, same as above except
8-day .... | 78- | 85

Novelty
Amigos, Arabic or Roman
porcelain dial, 8-day, gold
finish .... | 101- | 132
Breton, same as above except
bronze finish .... | 115- | 140
Elf, same as above except gold
finish .... | 101- | 132
Eveline, same as above ...... | 101- | 132
Good Morning #268, same as
above except bronze finish . | 115- | 140
Good Night #254, same as
above .... | 115- | 140
La Belle, same as above
except gold finish .... | 101- | 132
La Reine, same as above ..... | 101- | 132
La Rose, same as above ..... | 101- | 132
Normandie, same as above
except bronze finish ...... | 115- | 140

Office Regulator
Pacific No. 27, oak, 8-day,
time .... | 866- | 934
Pacific No. 29, same as above
except time and calendar .. | 965-1,250

Porcelain Regulator
Royal Bonn No. 2, decorated
top and base .... | 1,650-1,800

Regulator
Bagdad No. 108, Arabic or
Roman dial, spring, time,
black walnut, mahogany,
oak, or ash.............. | 925-1,000
Bagdad No. 109, same as
above except gong strike .. | 955-1,100
Capitol No. 102, Roman dial,
black walnut or ash finish .. | 1,375-2,445
Capitol No. 103, gong strike .. | 1,400-1,550
Santa Fe No. 100, Roman dial,
weight, time, black walnut,
mahogany, or oak .... | 1,575-1,750
Spring Time, Roman dial,
black walnut or ash finish .. | 1,375-2,445
Standard, Arabic or Roman
dial, weight, time, 8-day,
mahogany or oak, polished . | 765- | 795

Single Figure (Bronze)
Cincinnatus, Japanese bronze
finish .... | 650- | 785
Columbia, Syrian bronze
finish, cathedral gong,
½-hour strike, 8-day, porcelain, visible escapement,
dial .... | 1,875-2,250
Fantasy, Japanese bronze
finish .... | 650- | 785
Industry, same as above..... | 650- | 785

Lothario, Syrian or Japanese
bronze finish .... | 795- | 895
Opera, Japanese bronze
finish .... | 650- | 785
Pizarro, Syrian or Japanese
bronze finish .... | 850- | 975
Reubens, Japanese bronze
finish .... | 650- | 785
Tasso, Syrian or Japanese
bronze finish .... | 795- | 895
Troubadour, Japanese bronze
finish .... | 650- | 785

Swinging Ball
All clocks are 8-day with Arabic dial and real
bronze finish.
Arcadia .... | 1,900-2,200
Diana .... | 1,900-2,200
Double Figure .... | 2,975-3,400
Fortuna .... | 1,900-2,200
Gloria .... | 1,900-2,200
Hunter .... | 1,900-2,200
Juno .... | 1,900-2,200

Wm. L. Gilbert Clock Co., Winsted (Winchester),
Connecticut (Wm. L. Gilbert Co., 1850-1866.
Gilbert Mfg. Co., 1866-1871. Wm. L. Gilbert
Clock Co., 1871-1934. Wm. L. Gilbert Clock
Corp., 1934-1957). The business was sold to Spar-
tus Co., Chicago, in 1964.

Alarm
Bi-Nite, black dial, luminous,
nickel finish, 40-hour...... | 50- | 63
La Sallita, nickel-plated brass
case, 1-day............. | 53- | 66
San Toy, black dial, luminous,
nickel finish, 40-hour...... | 50- | 63
365 Nite, same as above ..... | 50- | 63
Tiger, nickel-plated brass case,
1-day .... | 53- | 66
Tornado, black dial, luminous,
nickel finish, 40-hour...... | 50- | 63

Calendar
Eclipse Regulator, oak, 8-day,
spring, simple calendar .... | 695- | 750
Eureka, oak, 8-day, time,
strike, spring, simple
calendar .... | 575- | 665
National, oak, 8-day, time,
strike, spring, simple
calendar, thermometer,
barometer .... | 850- | 975
Victorian kitchen, walnut,
8-day, time, strike, spring .. | 875- | 975

Crystal Regulator
All clocks are 8-day with ½-hour strike, ivory
porcelain dial, visible escapement, mercury pendulum.
Terese .... | 830-1,375
Tunis .... | 830-1,375
Tuscan .... | 830-1,375
Venice .... | 830-1,375

Mantel
Astoria, hand-rubbed
mahogany, 8-day, pendu-
lum, strike............. | 145- | 185

(continued)

Beckworth, same as above ... 145- 185
Big Premium, hand-rubbed
   mahogany, 40-hour, time .. 85- 109
Bloomfield, hand-rubbed
   mahogany, 8-day, pendu-
   lum, strike 145- 185
Cornell, same as above 145- 185
Debutante, same as above ... 145- 185
Exquisite, same as above 145- 185
Hatherly, same as above 145- 185
Junior, same as above....... 145- 185
Kimberley, same as above ... 145- 185
Ludlow, same as above 145- 185
Mobile, same as above 145- 185
Newark, same as above 145- 185
Orlando, same as above 145- 185
Osborne, same as above 145- 185
Pompton, same as above 145- 185
Refined, hand-rubbed
   mahogany, 40-hour, time .. 85- 109
Roscoe, hand-rubbed
   mahogany, 8-day, pendu-
   lum, strike 145- 185
Sheridan, same as above..... 145- 185
Two-Color, same as above ... 145- 185

Regulator
"A", walnut, standing, glass
   sides, 8-day, weight, time .. 675- 785
Leeds, 8-hour, spring, pendu-
   lum, mahogany flat finish .. 445- 565
No. 9, hanging, walnut,
   cherry, ash or oak, glass
   sides, 8-day, weight, time .. 2,975-3,400
No. 9, standing, walnut,
   cherry, ash or oak, glass
   sides, 8-day, weight, time .. 2,975-3,550
No. 10, same as above except
   hanging 1,100-1,375

Shelf
Abyla, 8-day, strike, cathedral
   gong, ash with walnut trim 295- 365
Calpe, same as above 295- 365
Cippango, same as above
   except walnut 265- 330
Crius, same as above except
   ash 250- 320
Dio, same as above except
   walnut 265- 330
Edina, same as above 265- 330
Eros, same as above 265- 330
Hestia, same as above 265- 330
Laurell, same as above 265- 330
Mahuta, same as above 265- 330
Peto, same as above 265- 330
Prince, same as above....... 265- 330
Werra, same as above except
   ash with walnut trim 295- 365

E. Ingraham & Co., Bristol, Connecticut. Elias Ingraham founded the firm in 1805 (E. Ingraham & Co., 1880-1884. The E. Ingraham & Co., 1884-1958. The E. Ingraham Co., 1958. The Ingraham Co., present).

Alarm
All clocks are 8-day with solid mahogany case.
Sancho 85- 105
Saturn 85- 105
Seville 85- 105
Sibl 85- 105

Banjo
Hyannis, circular finish, silver-
   plated dial, 8-day, marine
   movement, mahogany,
   colors 295- 410
Neptune, same as above 190- 245
Nile, same as above 190- 245
No. 1, same as above 190- 245
No. 2, same as above 190- 245
Nordic, same as above 190- 245
Norse, same as above 190- 245
Norway, same as above 190- 245
Treasure, same as above
   except hand-rubbed mahog-
   any, pendulum movement . 625- 750
Wellfleet, circular finish,
   silver-plated dial, 8-day,
   marine movement,
   mahogany 190- 245

Cabinet
Acme, 8-day, ½-hour strike,
   gong 195- 255
Dahlia, oak or walnut, 8-day,
   strike 250- 325
Era, 8-day, ½-hour strike,
   gong 195- 255
Globe, 1-day or 8-day 235- 295
Ingot, 1-day or 8-day 235- 295
Lilac, oak or walnut, 8-day,
   strike 250- 325
No. 7, 8-day, ½-hour strike,
   gong 195- 255
No. 8, same as above 195- 255
No. 9, same as above 195- 255
No. 10, same as above 195- 255
Pressed, 1-day or 8-day 235- 295
Puck, 1-day or 8-day 235- 295
Sun, 1-day or 8-day 235- 295
Tulip, oak or walnut, 8-day,
   strike 250- 325
Violet, same as above 250- 325
World, 1-day or 8-day 235- 295

Calendar
Drop Octagon, wall, solid oak,
   time and/or strike 485- 575
Figure Eight, wall, ash, 8-day,
   time, strike, B.B. Lewis
   movement 1,900-2,450
Gila, shelf, oak, 8-day, time,
   strike, spring, simple
   calendar, thermometer,
   barometer 450- 575
Globe Extra, shelf, oak or
   walnut, 8-day, strike,
   thermometer, barometer .. 375- 455
Parlor, shelf, walnut, spring,
   time, thermometer 1,800-2,375

Ingraham Kitchen (Shelf)

Pressed, shelf, walnut, 8-day,
strike 295- 355
Mantel
All clocks are 8-day with mahogany finish, hour
cathedral gong, ½-hour cup bell.
Belmont	135-	175
Berlin	135-	175
Burgundy	135-	175
Hammond	135-	175
Hampton	135-	175
Hather	135-	175
Hermes	135-	175
Howard	135-	175
Magic	135-	175
Magnet	135-	175
Nomad	135-	175

Office, Hanging
Dew Drop, oak, rosewood, or
walnut, 8-day 395- 475
Drop Octagon, solid oak, time,
strike, 8-day 365- 455
Misay, rosewood, 8-day 425- 510

Ithaca Calendar Clock Co., Ithaca, New York.
Founded in 1865 by H. B. Horton. The company
went out of business around World War I.
Alexis No. 1, walnut, 30-day,
time 695- 780
Alexis No. 2, walnut, 8-day,
time 625- 695
Alexis No. 3, walnut, 8-day,
strike 575- 640
Bank No. 0, wall, walnut,
8-day, weight, time 4,975-5,400
Bank No. 2, wall, walnut or
ash, 8-day, weight, time . . . 1,750-2,000
Belgrade No. 5½, wall, walnut
or ash, 30-day, double
spring, strike 2,775-3,455

Brisbane No. 2½, walnut or
ash, 8-day, ½-hour slow
strike, gong 2,975-3,665
Emerald No. 5, shelf, walnut,
8-day, spring, time, strike . . 2,700-3,375
Kildare No. 12, mahogany,
30-day or 8-day, spring,
strike 3,375-3,850
Library, wall, walnut, 8-day,
double spring, pendulum
movement 1,750-2,550
Melrose No. 15, cherry, 8-day,
strike 3,275-3,950
Office No. 4, wall, walnut or
rosewood, 8-day or 30-day,
double spring, time 2,100-2,875
Regulator No. 0, walnut,
8-day, double weight (also
a shelf model), ea. 3,475-5,000
Regulator No. 1, wall, walnut,
sweep second hand, 8-day,
weight, time 7,500-8,250
Mission Clocks. This is not a make, but a type of
clock popular from the early 1900s until about
World War I. These clocks were made of solid,
weathered oak, mahogany-finished oak, etc. Some
had brass hands and copper dials. Most were
8-day, ½-hour strike with cathedral gong.
Den, wall, dark oak, 8-day,
time 145- 185
Denmark, standing, solid oak,
wood dial, Arabic numerals,
pendulum movement 295- 365
Los Barrios, solid oak, wood
dial, Arabic numerals, pen-
dulum movement 140- 180
Madrid, wall, brass hands,
figures 108- 155
Mantel, solid oak, wood dial,
Arabic numerals, pendulum
movement 145- 190
San Martin, same as above . . . 140- 180
New Haven Clock & Watch Co., New Haven, Connecticut. Founded in 1853 by Hiram Camp, the
New Haven Clock & Watch Company originally
made movements for the Jerome Mfg. Co. The
firm enlarged and electric clocks were made for
the first time in 1920. The firm went out of
business in 1965.
Alarm
Alert, nickel, 1-day, alarm,
plush 52- 64
Beacon 44- 60
The Fly 44- 60
Junior Tattoo, 1-day, satin
silver, gold, gun metal
finishes 45- 63
Mauser 44- 63
Sprite 44- 63
Sting, nickel, 1-day, assorted
colors 44- 53
Sultana, nickel, 1-day, alarm,
strike 37- 45

(continued)

Decorated Porcelain

Fleetwood, 1-day, time, usual markings	70-	85
Gerald, 8-day, hour and ½-hour strike, cathedral gong, visible escapement	525-	595
Hamilton, same as above except no visible escapement	275-	345
Haverford, same as above with visible escapement	525-	595
Herbert, same as above except no visible escapement	275-	345
Holly, same as above with visible escapement	525-	595
Horican, same as above	525-	595
Lionel, 1-day, time, usual markings	70-	85
Mabel, 8-day, hour and ½-hour strike, cathedral gong	275-	345
Malabar, same as above	275-	345
Mortan, 1-day, time, usual markings	70-	85
Rosendale, 8-day, hour and ½-hour strike, cathedral gong	275-	345
Wakefield, 1-day, time, usual markings	70-	85

Enameled Iron

All clocks are 8-day with plain white gilt or pearl dial, ½-hour strike, cathedral gong, black, smoke, or malachite finish.

Carnival	235-	295
Chateau	235-	295
Chiselhurst	235-	295
Colonna	235-	295
Fairfield	235-	295
Fayette	235-	295
Ferncliff	235-	295
Galatea	235-	295
LeLand	235-	295
Mona	235-	295
Rosalind	235-	295
Scandia	235-	295
Thetis	235-	295
Titan	235-	295
Washington	235-	295

Mantel

Brazilian Line, oak, metal trim, 8-day, ½-hour strike, ½-hour strike alarm, or ½-hour strike gong	195-	255
Brazilian Line, same as above except walnut	245-	285
D Line, oak, 8-day, ½-hour strike, ½-hour strike alarm, or ½-hour strike gong	220-	265
D Line, same as above except walnut	265-	295
Felix, oak, metal trim, 8-day, ½-hour strike, ½-hour strike alarm, or ½-hour strike gong	195-	255

Felix, same as above except walnut	245-	285
Forum, oak, metal trim, 8-day, ½-hour strike, ½-hour strike alarm, or ½-hour strike gong	195-	255
Forum, same as above except walnut	245-	285
Maine Line, oak, 8-day, ½-hour strike, ½-hour strike alarm, or ½-hour strike gong	220-	265
Maine Line, same as above except walnut	265-	295
Merchant's Line, oak, metal trim, 8-day, ½-hour strike, ½-hour strike alarm, or ½-hour strike gong	195-	255
Merchant's Line, same as above except walnut	245-	285
Patrol Line, oak, 8-day, ½-day strike, ½-hour strike alarm, or ½-hour strike gong	220-	265
Patrol Line, same as above except walnut	265-	295
Picket Line, oak, 8-day, ½-hour strike, ½-hour strike alarm, or ½-hour strike gong	220-	265
Picket Line, same as above except walnut	265-	295

Office

Bank, oak, 8-day, time, strike	375-	455
Blake, wall, solid oak, 8-day, time, strike	340-	465
Braddock, same as above	340-	465
Regulator, wall, walnut veneer, solid walnut circle, 8-day, time, strike	455-	575

Single Figure (Gilt or Bronze Finish)

All clocks are 8-day with Roman, gong strike, visible escapement (finish does not affect clock's value).

Benvento Cellini	640-	765
Clotho	640-	765
Fame	640-	765
Flower Girl	640-	765
Flute Player	640-	765
Horse	640-	765
Ivanhoe	640-	765
Knight	640-	765
Norman	640-	765
Octavious	640-	765
Bernard Palissy	640-	765
Poetry	640-	765
Saxon	640-	765

Veneer

Cottage, 1-day or 8-day	195-	255
Guide, 1-day or 8-day	195-	255
Ogee (weight #2), 1-day with strike or 1-day with strike and alarm	315-	495
Round Gothic, 1-day, strike, spring	235-	295

Sharp Gothic "A," 1-day with strike or 1-day with strike and alarm 210- 240
Tuscan, visible pendulum, 1-day or 8-day, strike, spring . 195- 235

Sessions Clock Co., Forestville, Connecticut. Sessions took over the E. N. Welch Mfg. Co. in 1903.

Banjo
Gallery, wall, 8-day 255- 360
Halifax, mahogany case, 8-day, lever movement, eagle, brackets, c. 1932 .... 450- 565
Hyannis, old ivory finish case, 8-day, lever movement 365- 445
Provincetown, mahogany case, 8-day, lever movement, eagle, brackets, c. 1932 .... 450- 565
Regulator No. 2 .... 285- 400
Regulator No. 3 .... 625- 735
Salem, mahogany case, 8-day, lever movement, eagle, brackets, c. 1932 .... 450- 565
Star Pointer Regulator, quartered oak, 8-day, time 380- 465

Enameled Blackwood
Arcadia 255- 345
Ardmore 255- 345
Baldwin 255- 345
Elton 255- 345
Goldenrod 255- 345
Goldstar 255- 345
Ideal 255- 345
Manhattan 255- 345
Marbleized No. 1 .... 255- 345
Marbleized No. 2 .... 255- 345
Marigold 255- 345
Melrose 255- 345
Mozart 255- 345

Seth Thomas Clock Co., Thomaston, Connecticut. Founded by Seth Thomas in Plymouth Hollow, 1853. Plymouth Hollow was changed to Thomaston in 1866. Seth Thomas Clock Co. made Southern calendar movements in 1875 and watches from 1883 to 1914. The company became General Time Instruments Co., part of the General Time Corp., after 1949. The firm is still in business today.

Alarm
Echo, nickel-plated, 1-day, time 56- 74
Elk, same as above 56- 74
Nutmeg, nickel-plated, 1-day . 84- 95
Tocsin, same as above except with time 56- 74

Banjo
Brookfield, electric, time, hour, ½-hour strike 280- 365
Delaware, key wind, brass side ornaments, c. 1900s 275- 345

Calendar
Office No. 8, walnut, oak, 8-day, weight, time 3,875-4,400

Office No. 10, walnut, cherry, oak, 8-day, time, perpetual calendar 2,875-3,775
Office No. 12, same as above . 2,875-3,775
Parlor No. 3, walnut veneer, polished, 8-day, spring, strike 1,775-2,650
Parlor No. 6, walnut, oak, 8-day, spring, strike, cup bell, perpetual calendar 1,565-1,975

Eight Bell
All clocks are 1-day, brass or nickel-plated with metal case and strike.
Boat 485- 565
Cabin 485- 565
Ship 495- 575
Yacht 485- 565

Hall
All clocks are 8-day with weight, striking hour, ½-hour cathedral bell. The more expensive ones chime Westminster at the quarter hour on four cathedral bell and moon changes.
No. 22, mahogany, old oak or oak natural, chime, moon .. 6,475-7,850
No. 24, mahogany or old oak, weight, strike, chime, moon 6,450-7,375
No. 2272C, mahogany, old oak or oak natural, strike, moon 4,750-5,800
No. 2784, mahogany, golden oak, or old oak, cathedral chime, moon 8,500-9,750

Iron and Bronze
Egyptian No. 1, verde, bronze, 8-day, strike 475- 565
Egyptian No. 2, verde, light verde, French bronze, 15-day, hour and ½-hour strike 485- 578
Leisure, same as above 545- 565

Lever
Artist, nickel or gold gilt case or front 185- 235
Chronometer, 8-day 475- 550
Crystal, nickel or gold gilt case or front 185- 235
Engine, 1-day, time, nickel or gold gilt case 235- 375
Joker, nickel or gold gilt case or front 185- 235
Lodge, same as above 185- 235
Mikado, same as above 185- 235
Student, same as above 185- 235
Wood, mahogany or old oak veneer, polished, 8-day, time, strike 295- 345

Metal Case
All clocks are gold-plated and lacquered with beveled plate glass, front, and sides.
Empire No. 1, polished gold finish, 8-day, ½-hour strike, cathedral bell 455- 575

127

(continued)

Empire No. 4, bronze top,
base, 8-day, ½-hour strike,
cathedral bell 495- 585
Empire No. 9, gold finish,
8-day 675- 850

Metal Novelty
All clocks are 1-day with rich gold finish. The
more expensive models have Art Nouveau and/or
bronze tops and bases.

Ada	89-	109
Alice	145-	185
Beth	105-	129
Bona	89-	109
Bungalow	89-	109
Cherubs	89-	109
Cis	105-	129
Colonial	105-	129
Corinna	89-	109
Crispin	145-	185
Cyril	105-	129
Dido	89-	109
Dimple	105-	129
Floss	105-	129
Grapple	89-	109
Ivan	105-	129
Jess	145-	185
Joe	145-	185
Nan	105-	129
Piper	145-	185
Quaint	105-	129
Serenade	145-	185
Vanity	145-	185
Vera	105-	129

Office
Drop Octagon, 10″, rosewood,
walnut veneer, gilt lines,
8-day, spring, time (also an
8-day, spring, strike), ea. . . .   255- 435
Flora, walnut, oak, ebony,
mahogany, or cherry, hand-
carved case, 8-day, weight,
spring, cathedral bell 1,675-1,950
Globe, rosewood, walnut, or
old oak, 8-day, spring, time .   455- 565
Greek, walnut, ebony, oak, or
mahogany, 8-day, spring,
strike 435- 475
No. 3, rosewood or walnut
veneer, polished, 8-day,
spring, strike 425- 465
Queen Anne, walnut, cherry,
oak, or old oak, 8-day,
spring, strike, no second
hand 675- 775
Signet, walnut, 8-day, spring,
strike 435- 495

One-Day Novelty
All clocks have gold and/or bronze art finish.

Colin	94-	118
Dorrit	94-	118
Eagle	94-	118
Elephant	94-	118
Fountain	94-	118

Holly	94-	118
Natty	94-	118
Paddock	94-	118
School Days	94-	118
Tick Tock	94-	118

Regulator
All clocks are 8-day with weight, time and/or
strike.
No. 2, walnut, cherry or old
oak veneer, polished   995-1,450
No. 3, walnut, rosewood, or old
oak veneer, polished, strike   1,875-2,675
No. 8, walnut 2,450-2,875

Wood Case (Black Adamantine Finish)
All clocks have 8-day, ½-hour strike and/or hour
strike, cathedral bell. The more expensive ones
have gold-plated columns, ornaments, and adamantine onyx columns.

Adnaw	285-	355
Arno	285-	355
Bosnia	295-	385
Delos	295-	385
Domino	285-	355
Don	285-	355
Elba	285-	355
Harrison	295-	385
Hastings	285-	355
Hull	275-	365
Ideal	295-	385
Keswick	275-	365
Lyons	275-	365
Manchester	295-	385
Milo	295-	385
Niphon	295-	385
Pasha	285-	355
Pelham	285-	355
Pequod	285-	355
Petrol	295-	385
Ravenna	295-	385
Sparta	295-	385
Sussex	285-	355
Texel	295-	385
Toulan	285-	355
Tyro	295-	385
Viking	295-	385
Wanda	295-	385
Windsor	285-	355

Waterbury Clock Co., Waterbury, Connecticut.
Founded in 1857, Waterbury Clock Co. was originally a part of Benedict & Burnham. It became a
part of U. S. Time Corporation in 1944.

Crystal Regulator
All clocks are cast gilt bezel with beveled glass
front, sides, and back, ivory dial, visible escapement, mercury pendulum, 8-day, and ½-hour
gong strike. Also gold-plated.
Bordeaux, green onyx base
and top   995-1,450
Cantel 475- 535
Dieppe 475- 535
Gard, green onyx base and
top   995-1,450

Gers, same as above 995-1,450
Girande, same as above 995-1,450
Mogul, same as above 995-1,450
OstendBrest 475- 535
Rennes, green onyx base and
  top 995-1,450
Savoy 475- 535
Vannes 475- 535

Regulator
No. 3, walnut or mahogany,
  8-day, weight, time 1,875-2,450
No. 6, walnut, standing case,
  brass weights, 8-day, time . 2,975-3,450
No. 14, walnut, cabinet finish,
  brass weights, 8-day, time . 2,675-2,990
No. 66, quartered oak, 8-day,
  time 1,775-2,565

Wall
Antique Drop, antique oak,
  8-day, ½-hour strike,
  calendar 475- 560
Arion, 12″, oak or mahogany
  finish, 8-day, time 355- 415
Asbury, walnut, cabinet
  finish, 1-day, weight, strike
  (also with alarm) 645- 715
Cairo, oak, walnut, or
  mahogany, 8-day, spring,
  time 775- 845
Calendar No. 33, oak or
  walnut, 8-day, time, spring,
  ½-hour gong strike 2,475-2,775
Consort, oak or walnut, 8-day,
  time 455- 575
Drop Octagon, 12″, oak, 8-day,
  time 310- 375
Prescott, walnut, 8-day, time
  (also 8-day, ½-hour slow
  strike) 665- 745
Regent, rosewood veneered,
  8-day, time 475- 565
Study No. 4, oak, cabinet
  finish, glass sides, 8-day,
  weight, gong strike 1,300-1,575
Toronto, walnut, 8-day,
  spring, strike........... 1,300-1,600
Yarmouth, oak or mahogany,
  8-day, spring, time 695- 765

Welch, Spring & Co., Forestville, Connecticut.
Founded by Elish N. Welch and Soloman C.
Spring in 1868. Welch, Spring & Co. merged with
E. N. Welch in 1884.

Calendar
Gale, wall, walnut, 8-day,
  pendulum 5,750-6,800
Italian-type, shelf, rosewood,
  8-day, spring, V-calendar
  movement 1,775-2,650
Regulator No. 11, rosewood,
  8-day, spring, V-calendar
  movement 3,875-4,650
Wagner, mantel B.W., 8-day,

time, strike, V-calendar
  mechanism 2,975-3,675

E. N. Welch Mfg. Co., Bristol (Forestville), Connecticut. Formed by a merger with Welch, Spring
& Company in 1884. Stayed in business, and, in
1903, the firm's name was changed to Sessions
Clock Company.

Alarm
Fairy Queen, 8-day, lever 75- 105
Fairy Queen, 8-day, lever,
  calendar 150- 195
Fire Bug, 1-day, lever, nickel . 165- 245

Calendar
Victorian kitchen, shelf,
  walnut, 8-day, time, strike . 1,375-1,675

Mantel (Black Enameled Wood)
All clocks are 8-day with cup bell, American sash,
white, gilt, or fancy perforated dials.
Alberta 285- 325
Andree 285- 325
Belasco 285- 325
Burkhart................. 285- 325
Calve................... 285- 325
De Merode............... 285- 325
De Reszke 285- 325
Karina 285- 325
Leno 185- 256
Nansen 285- 325
Roosevelt 285- 325
Shafter 195- 235
Sorma 285- 325
Stagnor 285- 325
Ulmar 195- 235
Zella................... 195- 235

Regulator
"A," black walnut, mahogany
  or antique oak, 8-day,
  weight, 3-mercury
  pendulum 4,750-5,550
"E," walnut, ash, or mahog-
  any, hanging, 8-day, weight,
  time 2,650-3,200
Eclipse, walnut, 8-day, time,
  spring, simple calendar
  (Made by Welch for Metropolitan Mfg. Co., New York) 1,700-1,995
No. 7, polished black walnut,
  8-day, time, sweep second .. 2,975-3,550

Shelf
Assortments A-K, Nos. 1-65,
  8-day, ½-hour strike, with
  or without wire or cup bell,
  walnut, ea............... 235- 275
Dewey, oak, same movement
  as above 325- 385
Lee, same as above 325- 385
The Maine, same as above ... 325- 385
Sampson, same as above 325- 385
Schley, same as above 325- 385
Wheeler, same as above 325- 385

Many wholesale dealers, jewelers, and
mail-order houses sold clocks with

(continued)

German Miniature   **English Export or German Wall**   **German L.F.S.**

trademarks (such as "Buy at Bowl"), but without a maker's name. Thousands of these clocks were sold in America from the 1850s until World War II.

Alarm

Bell, 1-day . . . . $	39-	53
Black and Tan, 1-day	64-	74
Boom, 1-day	39-	53
Jumbo Watch Alarm Clock, nickel case	70-	78
Mandolin, 1-day	65-	75
New Echo, nickel-plated	45-	54
Parlor, walnut case, gold trim	62-	74
Queen, 1-day	39-	53
Sleigh bell, copper case, gold gilt	59-	70

Iron and Bronze

Arbor, 1-day, iron	177-	188
Dolphin, 8-day, bronze	235-	255
Dragon, 8-day, bronze	190-	210
Drummer, 8-day, bronze	190-	210
Eagle, 8-day, bronze	245-	265
Gleaner, 8-day, bronze	190-	210
Guardian, 8-day, bronze	190-	210
Horse, 8-day, bronze	255-	270
Juno, 8-day, bronze	190-	210
Lion head, 1-day, bronze	235-	275
Opera, 8-day, bronze	240-	265
Patchen, 8-day, bronze	240-	265
Sambo, 1-day, winker (eyes move), iron	985-	1,100
Vintner, 8-day, bronze	190-	210
Washington, 1-day, iron	170-	190
Wine Drinker, 8-day, bronze . .	190-	210

Novelty

Barge, silver finish	155-	174
Carriage, extra nickel, 1-day, ½-hour strike, alarm	255-	275

Castle, silver finish, 1-day, time	93-	110
Conductor, gold, silver, or oxide silver finish, 1-day, time, alarm	157-	167
Duke, nickel or gilt, 1-day, time	53-	66
Empire, rich gold or antique brass finish, 1-day, time . . .	69-	77
Little Corrine, nickel sides, glass top, 1-day, time	93-	110

Clocks, Foreign or European

Dutch, porcelain hanging wall clock, time only . . . . $	120-	140
English carriage clock, brass case, time and alarm	410-	475
English carriage clock, brass case, time and strike	250-	295
English export or German wall clock, box type, solid oak, time and strike, age and maker unknown (ill.) . . .	180-	210
English watchman's clock, punch type, fusee movement, walnut case	370-	425
Esberger Bros., Jeweler, Cincinnati, alarm clock made for their customers . .	80-	92
European case, American movement wall clock, walnut case, time and strike	285-	320
Chas. W. Fleichtinger, Sinking Spring, Pa., oak case, Victorian kitchen, shelf calendar clock, 8-day, time and strike	2,200-	2,600

Forestville Clock Manufactory, Bristol, Conn. (one of J.C. Brown's trade names), triple-decker, carved top, walnut case, painted tablets, 8-day brass movement, 1849-1853 1,900-2,400

French carriage clock, silver case, repeater with alarm .. 295- 345

French desk clock, brass case with finials, 8-day, time and strike 360- 420

French shelf clock, gold gilt with porcelain dial and cap, 1860-1870 .... 545- 610

French statue clock, brass, marble, time and strike 495- 540

French statue clock, bronze figure, porcelain inserts in cast brass base, time and strike 610- 650

French statue clock, bronze, on marble base, time and strike 645- 720

French statue clock, ormolu, gilt 620- 700

Galusha Maranville, Winsted, Conn., octagon drop wall, calendar, rosewood, time and strike, Pat. March 5, 1861 1,975-2,400

German game clock, cast metal, time only 145- 175

German L.F.S. make, oak wall clock, 8-day, time and strike, 1890-1900s (ill.) 260- 280

German mantel clock, time and strike 165- 198

German mantel set, 3-pc., bisque, time only 220- 255

German miniature carriage clock, time and strike 220- 255

German, miniature, 8-day, time and strike, oak case, 1880-1890 (ill.) 220- 260

German shelf clock, time and strike 245- 285

German wall clock, time only . 170- 195

Cloisonné Enamel

Developed during the 19th century, glass enamel was applied between small ribbon-like pieces of metal on a metal base. Supposedly from Japan, most of what is found in shops today is European and brought into the U.S. between 1870 and 1900.

Ashtray, dragon motif, China, 3½″ dia. .... $ 32- 43

Ashtray, enameled, matchbox holder attached, China, 5″ dia. 40- 50

Cloisonné Enamel

Bowl, brown ground, multi-colored floral design, chop mark 87- 95

Bowl, green/red, China, 4″ dia. 50- 60

Box, black ground, yellow/green/red, dragon, 3″ square, early 54- 63

Candlesticks, black/blue/green, dragon motif, 11″ high, pr. 137- 144

Cigarette case, 3½″ long 42- 51

Clock w/two yellow urns, other colors include blue, pink, green, clock 11″ to top of finial 2,400-2,600

Decanter, usual color 47- 57

Desk blotter, blue/green, roll type, China 45- 55

Dish, floral design, Oriental motif, chop mark 60- 70

Dish, yellow, dragon, 5″ dia., China 64- 73

Ginger jar, blue ground, red flowers, cover, chop mark .. 147- 152

Incense burner, Foo Dog, 10″ high, China 68- 78

Napkin ring, blue ground, birds, China 38- 42

Pitcher, black ground, butterflies, birds, floral, chop mark 205- 211

Plate, blue, flowers, 11″ dia., China 68- 74

Plate, Japanese, blue/red/green, 6½″ dia., chop mark . 88- 98

Snuff bottle, blue ground, Buddhist emblems, stopper, chop mark 170- 182

Teapot, brown ground, flowers, 7″ high, chop mark 150- 163

Teapot, yellow ground, cane handle, chop mark 105- 110

131

(continued)

Tray, Japanese, morning
giories, fruit, Bamboo
pattern, brass rim, 12″ dia.,
China 288- 292
Urn, Japanese, covered,
bronze finial, floral design,
2½″ high, 2¼″ dia., China . 85- 90
Vase, beige ground, turquoise/
gold, dragons, 11″ high 187- 194
Vase, blue ground, butterflies,
chop mark 200- 222
Vase, blue ground, floral/birds,
9¼″ high (ill.) 700- 800

Clothing

The nostalgia boom is in full swing and old
clothing is leading the parade. No longer
items to be found at the Salvation Army
stores, today fashionable boutiques feature
clothing from WWI to the 1940s.

Capes
Opera, black, red silk lined,
tassels, c. 1920s . . . . $ 100- 120
Sealskin, c. 1930s 46- 54
Coats
Army, WWI, olive drab, brass
buttons, full length 74- 83
Calfskin, half length, c. 1930s . 77- 83
Lady's long (or automobile),
c. 1915, all wool kersey 98- 107
Man's, moleskin, full length,
c. 1920s 74- 83
Raccoon, man's, full length . . 1,100-1,200
Collars
Mink, 8″ wide, c. 1930s 44- 52
Rabbit, c. 1940s 31- 40
Dresses
Lady's black silk peau de soie,
c. 1915 . . . . 65- 74
Lady's evening, blue silk,
full bustle, c. WWI 132- 142
Lady's taffeta, silk, c. WWI . . 52- 62

Clothing

Handbags
Alligator, chatelaine, chain
and belt attachment 53- 60
Beaded, cut steel, steel bead
fringe, chamois back, silver-
plated frame, chain, hook . . 35- 43
Beaded, red/black, tasseled
bottom, purse string top . . 28- 33
Leather, nickel-rivoted frame,
leather straps, belt hook . . . 32- 40
Metal, chatelaine, nickel, chain
and belt hook 28- 33
Opera shopping bag, black
moiré silk, silk cord handles 24- 33
Silk, embroidered bead ini-
tials, silver frame and chain 45- 54
Hats
Lady's Italian leghorn, pink/
white Japanese silk,
c. 1920s 48- 58
Lady's jaunty turban, silk
finished black mull, c. WWI 52- 61
Lady's mushroom brim, c.
WWI 42- 52
Man's derby (or stiff), c. 1920s 28- 32
Man's fedora, nutria fur
c. 1915 . . . . 38- 47
Man's Stetson, Dakota style,
c. 1910 . . . . 46- 52
Man's top hat, black silk,
collapsible type, c. 1920s . . 47- 51
Jackets
Lady's muskrat, half length,
c. 1920s 40- 50
Lady's sheared lamb, full
length, c. 1930s 83- 92
Man's buckskin, c. 1930s 73- 83
Man's cardigan, double
breasted, c. WWI 40- 50
Parasols/Umbrellas
Lady's all-silk, colored serge,
c. 1920s 38- 42
Lady's tight roll taffeta silk,
c. 1920s 39- 50
Lady's twilled silk, white pearl
handle, c. WWI 40- 50
Man's taffeta silk, weichsel
wood hook handle, c. WWI . 47- 52
Man's twilled silk, Prince of
Wales hook handle, c. 1915 . 45- 55
Petticoats
Fast-colored striped gingham,
c. WWI 23- 32
Mercerized percaline, black/
white stripes, c. 1915 . . . . . 27- 36
Sateen, flounce around
bottom, lined with black
glazed cloth 29- 37
Shawls
Lady's all wool split zephyr,
c. 1915 . . . . 36- 45
Lady's Shetland wool, 36″
dia., c. WWI 44- 52

Shoes

Lady's black cloth top, c. 1908	38-	48
Lady's patent leather, c. WWI (ill.)	55-	65
Lady's velour calf, Goodyear welt, c. 1915	40-	50
Man's box calf, c. WWI	38-	42
Man's coin toe stain calf, c. 1915	40-	50
Man's leather oxford, c. 1915	35-	44

Spats

Man's, pearl gray, M-O-P buttons, c. WWI	29-	37

Suits

Man's long roll frock, c. WWI	42-	52
Man's square cut single breasted sack, c. 1915	45-	53
Man's three button cutaway sack, c. WWI	46-	54

Coal Hods

Lugging coal from out-of-doors was a pain in the 1800s, but at least the hods were decorative. Usually black with bright flowers and birds, the coal hod stood out in every room.

Stamped iron, black, removable liner, flowers/birds, claw feet	$114-125
Tin/copper, painted with removable liner, flower motif, 17½" high	120-130

These are average prices.

Coalport

The factory operated at Coalport, England, from the late 1700s until 1926, since then at Stoke-on-Trent, making bone china.

Bowl, fruit, blue fluted and ruffled sides, castle scene	$ 92-105
Chocolate pot, Indian Tree, rose/ green foliage, 6 cups and saucers	200-220
Cup/saucer, black/orange floral on white	40- 50
Cup/saucer, Indian Tree	50- 60
Dish, floral decor, 1820, 9¼" square	118-123
Letter holder, 1820, rose/green	205-212
Mug, leaf design, white, 4½" high	122-138
Pitcher, Indian Tree, 5" high	100-115
Plate, Indian Tree, scalloped, 7½", set of 6	105-113
Platter, Indian Tree, 13"	80- 90
Salt/pepper, Indian Tree, beehive shape, pr.	78- 85

Tea service, blue banding, gilt, pink blossoms, approximately 30 pcs., all		595-625
Trivet, Indian Tree		70- 80
Vase, 6", cobalt, gold trim, handled		158-169

Coca-Cola Collectibles

Coca-Cola Collectibles

Anything with "Coke" or Coca-Cola on it is highly sought after today. The prices are high, too. See **Clubs and Publications**, this Price Guide.

Bingo board, 1930s	$ 28-	37
Binoculars, 1910	185-	210
Blotter, 1930	25-	35
Blotters, 1900s-1920s, ea.	88-	98
Book, *Know Your War Planes*, 1943	55-	65
Book, *Pause for Living*, 1960s	28-	34
Bottle openers, 1910-20s, ea.	55-	65
Buddy Lee doll, deliveryman, 1928, 12½" high	188-	195
Calendar, 1975	7-	12
Calendars, 1900-08, complete	700-	800
Calendars, 1909-15, complete	565-	640
Carrying tray, 1915	115-	130
Case, miniature, 28 bottles, gold finish	58-	68
Case, wooden, 24 bottles, c. 1920	24-	32
Cigarette case, 50th anniversary, 1936	188-	194
"Coke Can" radio, 1971	70-	80
Comb, "Drink Coca-Cola 5¢"	40-	50
Coupons, good for one free bottle of Coca-Cola, 1900	148-	154
Coupons, same deal, 1920s	68-	78
Cribbage board, 1930	55-	65
Dominoes, 1940	50-	60
Glass, drinking, 1900	218-	240
Glass, drinking, 1905 (ill.)	205-	212
Glass, drinking, 1921	70-	80
Glass, drinking, 1930s, pewter	77-	87
Glass holder, 1901 (ill.)	410-	455

133

(continued)

Key fob, bulldogs, 1½"×1", metal, 1925	128- 134
Key fob, 1½" dia., celluloid, 1900	348- 365
Key fob, oval, 1¾"×1¼", 1906	287- 299
Knife, switchblade type, 1909	118- 127
Leaded glass globe, hanging type, late 1920s	4,900-5,300
Mechanical pencil, 1930	47- 56
Menus, 1900-05, "Hilda Clark," ea.	180- 190
Milk glass shade, dome light, 10" dia., 1920s	575- 640
Miniature plastic bottle and case, 1970	20- 30
Mirror, "Girl in bonnet," 1914	170- 180
Needle cases (held sewing needles), 1920s, ea.	68- 78
Night light, "Courtesy of your C-C Bottler," 1945	30- 40
Pencil sharpeners, 1930s-60s, ea.	45- 55
Playing cards, 1909-27, ea. deck	81- 91
Playing cards, 1930-40s, ea. deck	40- 50
Postcard, "Coca-Cola Delivery Truck," 1915	105- 111
Pretzel dish, "Coke" bottles for legs, 1936	70- 80
Radio, shaped like drink box, 1949	182- 192
Radio, shaped like "Coke" bottle, 24" high, 1930	310- 325
Seltzer bottles, 1900-20s, ea.	78- 88
Sheet music, "Old Folks at Home," "The Palms," "Rock Me to Sleep, Mother," "Juanita," "My Old Kentucky Home," ea.	144- 152
Sign, 8" dia., glass, 1915	128- 132
Sign, 30"×7¾", tin, in shape of arrow, 1927	130- 140
Sign, tin, 15"×18½", "Hilda Clark," 1904	2,200-2,350
Syrup bottles, 1910-20s, ea.	175- 185
Take home carton, late 1930s	50- 60
Toy drink dispenser, 1960	130- 140
Toy stove, electrified, 1938	238- 260
Thermometers, 1930-50s, ea.	58- 68
Thimble, aluminum, 1920	55- 65
Tray, "bottle," 9¾" dia., 1900	1,200-1,400
Tray, girl in yellow bathing suit, 1937	60- 70
Tray, 8½"×19½", "Elaine," 1917	140- 150
Tray, oval, "Hilda Clark," 18½"×15", 1904	1,550-1,700
Tray, 10" dia., "Vienna Art," 1905	182- 188
Tray, 10½"×13¼", farm boy w/dog, 1931	92- 107

Coffee Grinders

Coffee Grinders

This product was made for the wall, the lap and the table, of glass, metal, or wood. When ready-made coffee came on the market in the 1920s, out went the grinder. The large wheel types are in demand today.

Arcade, iron and glass	$ 63- 72
Box type, Stobridge	84- 94
Dovetail, Arcade Manufacturing Co., wood and iron	80- 90
Drawer, wooden base	80- 90
Glass container, iron, Enterprise	48- 58
Iron base, patented July 12, 1898, Enterprise	172-190
Iron, early	75- 85
Lap type, handled, cherry	88- 98
Lap type, maple (ill.)	59- 69
Lap type, metal, 7½" high, 6" wide	80- 90
Lap type, wooden, iron dome top	78- 88
Pewter bin, dovetailed, brass knob, signed W. W. Weaver	108-115
Store type, signed Enterprise Manufacturing Co., 1873, 12" high	113-122
Table model, drawer, iron and wood, 6½" high	235-242
Turn crank, drawer, iron	96-107
Two wheels, red, Cole Manufacturing Co., Philadelphia	850-900

Repros all over the place!

Coin Spot Glass

Opalescent spots in the glass that look like coins. Light blue, clear, cranberry, amethyst. In mid-1800s, many firms made it.

Bowl, ruffled edges, 6" dia.	$ 47- 53
Bride's basket, opalescent spots	215-225
Cruet, light blue	108-112
Pitcher and 6 glasses, blue and white (pitcher, ill.)	259-263

1969—America the Beauti-		
ful, red Carnival	58-	67
1970—America the Beauti-		
ful, green Carnival	62-	72
1970—Christmas, Carnival	52-	62
1971—Christmas, Carnival	50-	60
1971—Christmas, Doeskin	47-	57
1971—Coin plate, Crystal	50-	60

Ispanky (limited edition)

The Hunt (decorated)	2,000-2,400	
Jessamy	675-	710
King Arthur	440-	460
Morning	645-	662
Orchids	2,000+	
Owl	1,000+	

Ispanky (non-limited edition)

Elizabeth	200-	218
Huck Finn	200-	216
Peter Pan	198-	216
Prudence	188-	230

Israel

1967—Tower of David	47-	56
1967—Wailing Wall	47-	54
1968—Masada	44-	52
1969—Rachel's Tomb	32-	42
1970—Lake of Galilee	42-	52
1973—Acre	47-	57

Jensen, Svend

1970—Mother's Day	98-	107
1971—Mother's Day	112-	118

Kaiser (Bavaria)

1970—Christmas, first		
edition	62-	72
1970—Passion Play	45-	55
1970—Royal Horse Show	52-	62
1971—Christmas	54-	64
1971—Mother's Day, first		
edition	54-	62
1972—Mother's Day	41-	50
1973—Yacht, "Cetonia"	100-	106

Kirk

1972—Mother's Day	248-	257
1972—Thanksgiving	166-	169
1972—Washington	235-	242
1973—Christmas	200-	210
1973—Mother's Day	187-	196

Lalique (France)

1965—Annual	2,300+	
1965—Crystal	1,600-1,785	
1967—Annual	220-	240
1968—Annual	165-	172
1969—Annual	152-	162
1970—Annual	142-	152
1971—Annual	128-	137
1972—Annual	99-	108
1973—Annual	118-	128

Lincoln Mint (sterling silver)

1971—Dali, Don Quixote	325-	345
1972—Dali, Dionysus	268-	277
1972—Easter, Dali, gold-on-		
silver	261-	281
1972—Madonna Della,		
sterling	325-	345

Lindner, Doris (limited edition)

Aberdeen Angus	1,200-1,300	
Charolais bull	1,100-1,250	
Dairy Shorthorn	1,250-1,400	
Hereford bull	1,200-1,300	
Jersey bull	1,100-1,250	
Jersey cow	1,400-1,500	
Quarter horse	1,100-1,250	
Shire stallion	2,400-2,450	

Lladro (Spain)

1971—Christmas	67-	77
1971—Mother's Day	152-	159
1972—Mother's Day	81-	91
1973-74—Mother's Day	92-	107

Marmot

1970—Christmas, Polar		
Bear	77-	87
1970—Father's Day, Stag	51-	64
1970—Stag Plaque	49-	58
1971—Christmas, Buffalo	52-	62
1971—Father's Day, Horse	51-	61
1971—President		
Washington	54-	64
1972—Mother's Day, Seals	60-	70
1973—Christmas,		
Snowman	62-	72
1974—Mother's Day	67-	77

Moser (Czechoslovakia)

1970—Annual	640-	730
1971—Mother's Day,		
Peacocks	338-	358
1972—Annual	192-	221
1972—Mother's Day,		
Butterflies	210-	222
1973—Mother's Day,		
Squirrels	224-	238

Noritake

1970—Easter Egg, first		
edition	72-	84
1971—Easter Egg	48-	58
1972—Easter Egg	43-	54
1973—Valentine Heart,		
first edition	62-	72

Orrefors

1970—Notre Dame		
Cathedral	90-	108
1971—Westminster Abbey	86-	98
1972-73—Mother's Day	82-	93
1973—Annual	92-	107

Pickard

1971—Game Birds, pr.	660-	710
1972—Truman plate	110-	120
1973—Lincoln	105-	111

Porsgrund

1968—Christmas, church		
scene	138-	142
1969—Christmas	44-	52
1970—Castle, Hamlet's	44-	52
1970—Christmas	59-	60
1970—Deluxe Christmas	88-	98
1970—Jubilee	50-	58
1970—Mug	34-	41

139

(continued)

1971—Christmas	40-	50
1971—Father's Day	29-	39
1971—Mother's Day	34-	44
1972—Easter	32-	42

Reed & Barton

1970—Christmas	575-	615
1971—Christmas	188-	192
1972—Silver & copper annual	170-	180
1972—Audubon plate, Sandpiper, silver & copper	200-	215
1973—Russell's Free Trapper	168-	178

Rorstrand

1968—Christmas	65-	72
1969—Christmas	40-	50
1970—Christmas	44-	52
1971—Christmas	47-	57
1971—Father's Day	48-	58
1971—Mother's Day	42-	52
1972—Mother's Day	48-	58
1973—Father's Day	44-	54

Rosenthal

1967—Christmas	163-	171
1971-3—Winblad Christmas	328-	344

Roskilde

1968—Church	47-	57
1969—Church	38-	47
1970—Christmas	38-	42
1971-2-3—Church	44-	52

Royal Copenhagen, RC

1969—Apollo II	67-	73
1969—Mermaid Summer ..	63-	68
1971—Mother's Day	161-	170
1971—Statue of Liberty ...	58-	64
1972—Mother's Day	65-	72
1972—Olympic	71-	81
1973—Mother's Day	62-	80

Royale

1971—Mother's Day	41-	48
1971—Father's Day	68-	78
1972—Mother's Day	51-	60
1972—Father's Day	50-	60
1972—Christmas	42-	52
1972—Game plate........	340-	350
1972—Crystal annual	500-	552
1973—Christmas	60-	70

St. Amand

1970—First edition	47-	52
1971—Second edition	39-	44
1971—Christmas	39-	46

Santa Clara

1970—Christmas	39-	49
1971—Mother's Day	51-	60
1972—Christmas	47-	56
1972—Mother's Day	50-	60

Schumann

1970—Beethoven	37-	45
1971—Christmas (Azburg) .	47-	57
1972-3 Christmas	52-	60

Seven Seas

1969—Astronaut	40-	50

1970—Christmas, New World	44-	50
1970—Mother's Day	45-	54
1970—History	56-	62
1971—Christmas Carol....	50-	60
1971—Mother's Day	45-	54
1972-3—Mother's Day	47-	57

Spode

1970—Christmas	52-	66
1970—Annual	68-	78
1970—Charles Dickens	160-	170
1970—Winston Churchill bust	192-	198
1971—Christmas	57-	66

Stanek

1968—First Moon Landing	2,000-2,200	
1972—Columbus.........	1,450-1,575	

Tirschenreuth

1969—Christmas	47-	57
1970—Christmas	42-	52
1971—Christmas	41-	51
1972-3—Christmas	39-	50

Val St. Lambert

1968—Rembrandt and Rubens, pr.	118-	127
1969—Pilgrims plate	199-	210
1969—Van Dyck and Van Gogh	92-	107
1970—Old Masters (set of 2)	82-	92
1970—Pilgrim Fathers	80-	90
1970—Rembrandt Crystal .	80-	88
1970—Rubens Crystal	70-	77
1970—Van Dyck Crystal ..	71-	81
1970—Zodiac	259-	266
1971—Washington	375-	395

Veneto Flair

1970—Madonna	1,150-1,300	
1971—Elephant	500-	540
1971—Three Kings	452-	470
1971—Wildlife, Stag	652-	670
1972—Last Supper, set of 5	2,000-2,250	
1972—Mother's Day	230-	240
1974—Cat	108-	115

Vernonware

1971—Christmas, Poppy-trail	70-	80
1972—Christmas, Poppy-trail	67-	74
1973—Christmas	60-	70

Washington Mint

1972—Mint Picasso	166-	174
1972—Mint Sawyer	168-	175

Wedgwood

1969—Astronaut (Apollo II)	258-	270
1969—Christmas	225-	242
1970—Christmas	81-	90
1971—Calendar plate	67-	78
1971—Christmas, Picca-dilly Circus	91-	106
1971—Mother's Day	82-	94
1973—Christmas	88-	94

Wyeth, Andrew

1971—The Kuerner Farm	114-	121
1971—Royal Tettau Pope Paul VI	150-	160
1972—Fourth of July annual	267-	278

Combs

Combs

Usually made of tortoiseshell, though some were made of silver, ivory or bone. They go back to the 16th century. Those you find in shops today cost from $5 to $13.

Average price	$ 14-	23
Barrette, carved (ill.)	16-	22
Ivory, inlaid, imitation diamonds	18-	32
Sterling silver, ornately carved	29-	40
Tortoiseshell, carved (ill.)	19-	25
Tortoiseshell, ornately carved	21-	30

Comic Books

There are countless thousands involved in this non-antique category. Prices given are for books in mint condition. See **Clubs and Publications**, this Price Guide.

A-1 Comics (Compix Magazine Enterprises), 139 Issue #s, 1944–1955

#18, Jimmy Durante	$ 27-	34
#41, Cowboys/Indians	5-	6
#62, Starr Flag Undercover Girl #5	50-	55

Ace Comics (David McKay Publications), 151 Issue #s, 1937-1950

#2	79-	89
#6-10	44-	54
#26, Prince Valiant	120-	140
#135, The Lone Ranger	7-	9

Action Comics (National Periodical Publications), more than 400 Issue #s, 1938-present

#1, Superman (1st appearance)	7,000+	
#4, Superman	1,500+	
#252, Supergirl (1st appearance)	140-	155

Adventures of Bob Hope (National Periodical Publications), 109 Issue #s, 1950-1968

#1	35-	41

#36-60	4-	5
#91-105	3-	4.50

Adventures of Pinky Lee (Atlas Comics), 5 Issue #s, 1955

#1	19-	27
#4-5	9-	13

Al Capp's Shmoo (Toby Press), 5 Issue #s, 1949

#1	31-	38
#4-5	10-	16

Boots and Her Buddies (Standard Comics/Sisual/ Argo Publishers), 9 Issue #s

#1-3 (reprints)	5.50-	7
#9	27-	34

Boy Explorers Comics (Harvey Publications)

#1, 1946	101-	121

Butch Cassidy (Skywald Comics), 3 Issue #s, 1971

#1-3	1.50-	2.50

Captain Tootsie and the Secret Legion (Toby Press), 2 Issue #s

#1	20-	27
#2	13-	16

Chamber of Darkness (Marvel Comics Group), 8 Issue #s, 1969-1970

#1-3	3.25-	5
#5-6	2.75-	3

Comics Revue (St. John Publishing Co.), 5 Issue #s, 1947-1948

#1, Ella Cinders and Blackie	13-	17
#4, Ella Cinders	7-	9

Daredevil Comics (Lev Gleason Publications), 134 Issue #s, 1941-1956

#1, Daredevil Battles, Hitler, Silver Streak	675-	775
#12, Claw	125-	145

Diary of Horror (Avon Periodicals)

#1, 1952	19-	27

Fight (Fiction House Magazines), 86 Issue #s, 1940-1954

#1, Spy Fighter	120-	130
#31-50	16-	19
#80-86, Tiger Man	8-	9

Funny Pages (Centaur Publications), 45 Issue #s, 1936-1942

#6, The Clock	35-	42
#7-20	26-	36

Green Giant Comics (Harvey Publications)

#1 Issue, 1940	675-	788

Human Torch (Marvel Comics Group), 8 Issue #s, 1974-1975

#1	2.50-	3.50
#2-8	1-	1.75

Monsters Unleashed (Marvel Group), 11 Issue #s, 1973-1975

#1	3.75-	5.25
#5, Man-Thing	4-	5
#10	3-	4

My Friend Irma (Marvel Comics Group/Atlas Comics), 46 Issue #s, 1950-1955

#4	28-	31
#6-10	6-	11

Namora (Marvel Comics Group), 3 Issue #s, 1948

#1	118-	127
#2-3	82-	91

(continued)

Commemorative/Historical/Souvenir Glass

Commemorative/Historical/ Souvenir Glass

People, places, and things of historical significance were commemorated in glass by firms, worldwide. A great many 1976 bicentennial items are being sold for old. Scuffing a piece of glass on cement will give it instant age.

Slippers
    Columbian World's Fair, Libbey,
      large, frosted 44- 54
    Philadelphia Centennial, 1876,
      Gillinder, clear 24- 33
Tumblers
    Buffalo, N.Y., 1907, ruby-flashed 16- 23
    Jacksonville, Fla., ruby-flashed .. 16- 21
    World's Fair, 1893, ruby-flashed . 15- 20

Commemorative/Souvenir Plates

Bread Plates and Trays
    Brooklyn Ferry, Thomas
      Goodwin, 8½" .... $ 66- 74
    City Hall, New York, soup,
      Charles Meigh, 10½" 37- 44
Clews
    Columbian World's Fair,
      Administration Building 29- 36
E Pluribus Unum
    Father's Day, 1969, Bareuther .. 184-220
    Fort Edward, Hudson River,
      Adams, 5¼" 90-101
    Fort Hamilton, New York,
      Mellor, Vennables, 8¼" 77- 87
Gladstone "For the Million"
    Gunton Hall, Norfolk, Hall, 8" .. 54- 62
    Harper's Ferry, U.S., platter,
      Adams, 15½" 72- 80
Mayer, T. J. and J.
    Mother's Day, 1971, Santa Clara
      porcelain 49- 54
    New York World's Fair,
      panorama, 10½" 22- 29
    Paul Revere's Ride, 1970, Val St.
      Lambert 170-185
Sunderland Lustre
    Tombs of Etaya, soup, Hall, 8" .. 40- 50
    Windsor Castle, Stevenson, 10½" 49- 52
World's Expositions and Fairs
    Washington Tomb, Mount
      Vernon, Mellor, Vennables,
      7½" 54- 62
    Water Works, Philadelphia,
      Jackson, 9" 141-147
    West Point, Hudson River,
      Clews, 8" 110-121
    White Sulphur Springs, Town of
      Delaware, Ohio, Jackson, 10" . 152-161
    Yale College, New Haven, Meigh,
      7¼" 91-101

Commemorative/Souvenir Spoons

Another people, places, and things category. Memento spoons have come back into popularity. During the 1880s and 1890s countless thousands were made, both here

Commemorative/Souvenir Spoons

and abroad. Differences in patents, copyrights, and trademarks cause a lot of confusion in this field of collecting. Rarity and type of metal dictate the price. The spoons listed here are .800 to .900 fine silver.

Battle of Plattsburg 25- 34
James G. Blaine 36- 45
Boston Tea Party 24- 32
Brooklyn Heights 25- 34
Commodore Perry 25- 34
Confederate Monument 28- 38
Devil 31- 42
Easter Chick................. 19- 27
Easter Lily 19- 25
El Camino Real.............. 20- 27
Fort Dearborn 27- 34
Fort Pitt 26- 33
General Sherman 39- 42
German coats-of-arms 12- 15
Grant's Tomb............... 24- 31
Lexington Minuteman 26- 34
Massachusets, sterling (ill.) 35- 45
Memphis, sterling (ill.) 35- 45
Merry Christmas 21- 29
Miner 19- 27
Minneapolis, Minnesota 22- 28
Nantucket Old Mill 34- 39
Pan-American Exposition 21- 37
William Penn, 2 styles 35- 90
Philadelphia 26- 34
Priscilla and John............ 27- 35
Rip Van Winkle 26- 36
Betsy Ross 38- 47
St. Augustine, designs 1
    through 4 .... 24- 42
Springfield Rifle 36- 47
Miles Standish 32- 43
Harriet Beecher Stowe 31- 42
Thanksgiving 29- 37
Uncle Sam, 3 sizes, ea. 38- 84
Washington, D.C............. 39- 49
White House (ill.) 17- 24
Yuletide 26- 34

Compasses

Instruments for indicating direction; those with a magnetic needle swinging freely on a

143

(continued)

Compasses

pivot and pointing to the magnetic north are highly sought after.

Boy Scout compass in canvas
case, 1920s . . . . $ 20- 25
Engineer's compass in mahogany
box, signed "W. & L.E. Gurley,
Troy, N.Y.," "E" and "W"
backward (ill.) 148-165
Ship's compass, in original box,
WWI destroyer 322-340

Confederate Provisional Stamps and Envelopes

June 1, 1861, the South stopped using stamps made by the federal government. The Confederacy set up provisional post offices throughout the South. Today, a stamp and/or envelope from one of these offices, dated October 14 (the first day the proper Confederate stamps were available for use), or after, would be worth a considerable amount. Some stamps from the following offices range in value from $1,200 to $16,000. A stamp's value depends on its rarity, condition, etc. Consequently, we give you only the locations of some of the Confederate post offices. If you think you have a rarity, check with a reputable stamp dealer.

Athens, Georgia
Autaugaville, Alabama
Baton Rouge, Louisiana
Beaumont, Texas
Bridgeville, Alabama
Danville and Emory, Virginia
Franklin, and Lenoir, North Carolina
Goliad, Texas, and Gonzales, Texas
Helena, Texas
Knoxville, Tennessee
Macon, Georgia
Spartanburg, South Carolina
Uniontown, Alabama

Not all are mentioned. There are probably 25 more. Any Southern stamp dated between June 1 and October 14, 1861, should be checked.

Cookbooks

Cookbooks

These cookbooks, especially those printed in the early 1900s, are collectible. Condition and age establish the price.

Agate Iron Ware, c. 1890s . . . . . . $ 7- 10
Arm & Hammer Valuable
Recipes, c. 1921 . . . .   6- 10
Baker's Chocolate Best Chocolate
Recipes, c. 1934 . . . .   5- 7
Cutco Cookbook, c. 1960 . . . .   4- 6
Denver Post Prize Recipes,
c. 1932. . . . .   7- 9
Fannie Farmer's Boston Cooking-
School Cook Book, c. 1920 (ill). .   7- 11
Fleischmann Yeast Recipe
Booklet, c. 1900s 6- 8
Granite Iron Ware, c. 1880s 7- 9
Hamilton Beach Blender Recipes,
c. 1949 . . . . 3-3.50
Jell-O Recipe Booklet, Jack
Benny promotion, c. 1930s . . .   11- 13
Kate Smith's Favorite Recipes,
c. 1940s 9- 12
Kellogg's Keep on the Sunny Side
of Life, c. 1933 . . . .   2- 5
Maxwell House Coffee Cookbook,
c. 1960s 6- 8
National Biscuit's Biscuits for
Salads, c. 1920s 2- 4
Pepsi-Cola Recipe Book, c. 1940 .   11- 15
Purefoy (Alabama) Cookbook,
c. 1930s 4- 6
Royal Baking Powder's Baker
and Pastry Book 5- 7
SnowDrift Secrets, c. 1913 . . . . . .   4- 6
Wesson Oil Recipes, c. 1913 . . . . .   4- 7
Wine in Cooking, France, c. 1920 .   9- 11

Cookie Molds

Hand-carved, these have been around for centuries. Most European countries export them into U.S. antiques shops. Those from

144

Cookie Molds

Holland are particularly collectible. They make great wall decorations! See **Clubs and Publications**, this Price Guide.

Depending on age and condition ... $39-63

Coors Pottery

In 1910, the Coors Porcelain Company began manufacturing pottery in Golden, Colorado, but what is found in shops today is the pottery and dinnerware made in the 1930s. There were about 35 vase styles and 4 lines of earthenware dishes. The pottery has a satiny texture; most pieces have a matt finish. Some colors are Delft blue, white, yellow, turquoise, brown-beige, peach-beige, pastel aqua and lilac pink.

Ashtray, white, "Coors" in
  center, raised signature $23- 34
Casserole, white 29- 37
Cookie jar, covered, Rosebud
  pattern, ink stamp "Coors
  USA" 27- 36
Honey pot, lilac pink, two-
  handled, ink stamp mark 34- 42
Jug, water, Rosebud pattern,
  turquoise, 7" high, ink stamp
  mark 41- 50
Mortar and pestle, 1¾" and 3"
  high, ink stamp "Coors
  Porcelain" 27- 37
Salt/peppers, Rosebud pattern,
  ink stamp mark "Coors USA" . 35- 45
Vase, rope-handled, 8" high,
  turquoise liner, 8" high 41- 50

Vase, white, 6" high, turquoise
  liner, ink stamp mark 38- 47
Vase, yellow, rope-handled, 12"
  high, ink stamp mark 42- 52

Copeland-Spode China

Josiah Spode established the Spode Works in Staffordshire, England, in 1770. Copeland and Garrett took over around 1840, and later, W. T. Copeland and Sons who marked their wares "Late Spode." Wares included Delft, Salt Glaze, and Jasperware; porcelain figurines and fine dinner services.

Chocolate pot, Indian Tree,
  6 cups and scalloped saucers . . $198-240
Creamer, shell shaped, c. 1860 . . . 130-150
Ewer, heavy beading, leaves,
  ring handle with mask, 1870 . . 128-132
Gravy boat, heron, palm tree,
  gilded grape leaves, 1847 . . . . . 77- 82
Jug, Jasper ground, applied
  grapevine and drinking scene . 172-181
Pickle, pink, embossed hunting
  scene, silver fork, 1897 . . . . 71- 81
Pitcher, blue/white, raised fig-
  ures, cherubs, floral decor 110-120
Plate, bird's nest, butterfly,
  rushes, daisies 58- 68
Plate, castle scene, blue/white,
  (ill.) 70- 80
Plate, plover, blue/white 69- 78
Sugar bowl, shell-shaped, c. 1860 . 124-132

Copeland-Spode China

145

(continued)

Copper

Copper

One of the world's most important metals,
it's been used for centuries in every shape,
size and object. Wire, cooking utensils,
jewelry, weathervanes, you-name-it.

Apple butter kettle, dovetail
bottom, mid-1800s, 25" dia. $ 475- 525
Basket, Art Nouveau, cherubs
in relief, 13" high 88- 99
Basket, double handle,
hammered bottom, 1920s,
10" dia. 52- 61
Candy kettle, mid-1800s,
19" dia. 250- 260
Chafing dish, complete, 1920s 122- 132
Coachman's horn, 38" long,
pewter mouthpiece,
mid-1800s 132- 141
Coffee set, French, 4-pc.,
1890s, all 142- 150
Cover pan, zinc handles,
1900s 66- 76
Desk set, 5-pc.—inkwell,
blotter holder, letter holder,
pen(s) holder, tray, 1920,
all 132- 150
Dippers, many types, all ages,
average price 36- 100
Foot warmer, brass bail
handle, early 1800s 79- 84
Milk pail, iron handle, late
1800s 107- 115
Planters, set of 6, brass
handles, pre-WWI, all 105- 118

Plaque, hand-tooled, Vikings-
in-ship, 3"×7", dated 1905 . 82- 91
Samovar, brass-footed, 15"
high 285- 300
Teapot, 9" high (ill.) 52- 62
Umbrella stand, brass
bottom, tooled scenes of
flowers, 1900s 150- 160
Vase, pewter base, tulip lip,
14" high, 1900s 74- 82
Vase, silver inlay of butter-
flies, flowers, 9½" high,
1900s 121- 130
Wash boiler w/lid, burnished,
early 1900s 152- 172
Weathervane, American eagle,
complete, mid-1800s 2,500-2,900
Weathervane, racing sulky,
complete, after Civil War . . 2,800-3,100

Copper

Copper Lustre

The use of a copper compound in the glaze
resulted in a metallic, copperlike surface.
Made in the Staffordshire District, England,
in the early 1800s. Most of what you find today was imported into the U.S. between 1835
and the late 1800s. Reproductions since the
1920s have caused this ware to fall from
popularity. The new is heavier and much
thicker than the old.

Bowl, floral on green bands . . . . . $ 92-107
Bowl, dark green, raised red
roses, 4" dia. 94-111
Chalice, beaded border, enameled
floral decor, 4½" high 85- 97
Compote, royal blue band, 3
raised groups, girl, cat, 1820 . . 92-107
Creamer, 3" high 40- 50

Copper Lustre

Flowerpot, beaded border,
  enameled decor, 4½" high 262-275
Goblet, pink and white floral,
  green leaves 108-118
Mug, blue band, greyhound,
  cow in relief, 3" high 99-109
Mustache cup and saucer, left-
  hand, 3 brothers, ship 111-118
Pitcher, blue band with pink
  roses, 6" high 120-130
Pitcher, bulbous, up-down ridges,
  Hawkes spout, 6" high 124-132
Pitcher, floral motif, 6¼" high
  (ill.) 79- 88
Pitcher, Wedgwood, brown,
  Fallow Deer, 4" high 88- 98
Salt, master, blue band, em-
  bossed pink roses, footed 64- 73
Sugar bowl, blue band,
  beaded, raised floral, children,
  footed 66- 75
Teapot, floral and leaf design,
  6½" high 188-192
Toby jug, early, high relief
  on hat and cheeks 425-460

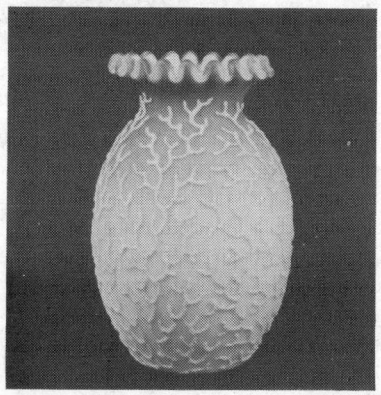

Coralene

Coralene

Glass with applied glass beading that looks
like natural coral. Made at the New England
Glass Company in the late 1800s, it's highly
collectible today. Don't be fooled by the
cheap type sold in stores during the same
period. Rub the surface; if the beads come
off, it's junk.

Pitcher, birds and leaves $475-525
Pitcher, ribbed, green opalescent,
  bird and flowers, 7½" high,
  signed Webb 552-572
Toothpick, satin glass, silvered,
  cased 420-440
Tumbler, graduated pink, cased,
  gold branches, 5" high 290-322
Tumbler, Seaweed pattern on
  yellow cased glass 301-318
Tumbler, white satin, brown oak
  leaves, Mt. Washington Glass
  Co. 298-340
Vase, blue/white, cream casing,
  yellow seaweed branches, 8½"
  high 310-340
Vase, coral branch beading, off-
  white casing, 4½" high 462-470
Vase, Mt. Washington
  Peachblow, 7¼" high (ill.) 540-558
Vase, pink overlay, ruffled top ... 500-518
Vase, red beads, garnet gems ... 518-521
Vase, satin, yellow and white,
  wheat sheaf, 5" high 370-395
Vase, yellow coral branch bead-
  ing, white casing, 5½" high ... 450-485

Poor imitations now available.

Cordey China

Cordey China

The Cordey China Company was founded
in 1942 by Boleslaw Cybis in Trenton, New
Jersey. Gift shop items and lamps were produced until 1950; then Cybis porcelains were
made.

(continued)

Box, powder, birds, 2½" sq..... $ 29- 37
Box, powder, floral, footed,
  2¼" sq................... 31- 36
Bust, woman, ribboned bonnet,
  7" high 42- 50
Figurine, colonial couple holding
  hands, 11¾" high.......... 69- 74
Figurine, Victorian lady,
  12½" high 66- 71
Lamp, bird in flower, 14½"
  high (ill.) 118-136
Vase, bird in tree, 8¼" high 54- 63
Vase, bird on flower stalk, 7" high 54- 63

Coronation Collectibles

After a coronation, items in china and glass appeared on the English market. Tin candy and cracker boxes are especially collectible. Elizabeth II paperweights are considered prizes by those who seek out coronation items.

Beaker, Edward VII, 1902, Royal
  Doulton .... $ 55- 62
Brandy snifter, King Edward
  VIII, coat of arms 44- 52
Cup, Garter emblem, 5" high 46- 56
Cup, King Edward VII 41- 52
Cup/saucer, Mary/George V 38- 50
Globe, Edward VIII, porcelain .. 42- 51
Handkerchief, Elizabeth II, 1953 14- 19
Humidor, Queen Elizabeth II,
  1953, silver plate 46- 56
Mug, George V and Mary, 1911,
  portraits, 3" high 56- 62
Paperweight, QE II, 1953,
  St. Louis 325-338
Pitcher, Victoria, 6" high (ill.) ... 37- 47
Plaque, Edward VII, Alexandra,
  1902, Royal Doulton 92-107
Plate, bread, George VI, 1937 ... 42- 52
Plate, Edward VII, 1902 ...... 51- 61
Spoon, George VI, 1911,
  demitasse 34- 44

Coronation Collectibles

Teapot, Elizabeth II, 1953, gold
  portrait, crest 51- 61
Toby mug, George V, Queen
  Mary, 1910, hand-painted, 6" . 52- 62
Tray, QE II, 1953 .... 28- 38
Tumbler, Elizabeth II, blue 37- 48

Country Store Collectibles

See Almanacs, Bed (and Foot) Warmers, Bellows, Boot Scrapers, Bootjacks, Brass, Candy Containers, Cash Registers, Clocks, Coffee Grinders, Dolls, Firearms, Fruit Jars, Kitchen Collectibles, Lamps, Lanterns, Locks, Marbles, Mortars and Pestles, Needlework, Phonographs, Postcards, Quilts, Sadirons, Shaving Mugs, and Washboards.

Coverlets

Coverlets

Made during the 18th and 19th centuries, they were the original do-it-yourself item. Women sheared the sheep, carded the wool, dyed it to the desired color, spun it on a wheel, wove it on a loom. There are four kinds of coverlets, each popular for a short time only: Double-woven, Jacquard, Summer/winter, Oversheet. Prices vary as to condition, location, and collector.

Bedspread, Popcorn pattern,
  crocheted, 90"×100" .....$ 360- 380

148

Bedspread, "United We Stand," Alcott	1,700-1,850	
Bonnet, hoop, 1790s	300-	350
Carpet, oblong panels, needle-work, 175"×90"	355-	375
Coverlet, blue/white, double-bed size, handloomed, 1840s (ill.)	255-	280
Dresser scarf, Battenberg, 4½" long, 16" wide	61-	71
Jacquard, signed, red, eagle motif	330-	350
Jacquard, unsigned, red, eagles at corners	272-	281
Lap robe, sleigh, horse head design, woolen, 50"×60"	165-	174
Quilt, Log Cabin pattern, patches, wool and cotton, 75"	160-	170
Robe, blue silk, gold thread, gold birds, China	270-	280
Rug, needlework, England, 85"×41"	470-	492
Sampler, alphabet, animals, child's age, dated 1828	92-	111
Shawl, black silk, embroid-ered, Spanish, 5' square	98-	112
Spread, Statue of Liberty, 100"×85"	560-	585
Tablecloth, homespun, cream color, crocheted edge, 68"×64"	88-	98

Cowan Pottery COWAN Pottery

Founded by R. Guy Cowan, Cleveland, Ohio, in 1913, it was called the Cleveland Pottery and Tile Company. Wayland Gregory was one of Cowan's leading artists. Lusterware and crackleware in a wide variety of colors were offered. Redware of the 1913-1917 period was incised with "Cowan Pottery." On later work the stylized semicircular Cowan mark was used. In 1931 Cowan closed his shops and moved to Syracuse, New York. He died in 1957.

Bowl, blue luster, footed, 12¼" high	$ 52-	61
Bowl, green luster, 7" high	50-	60
Candlesticks, blue luster, Art Deco, 6" high, pr.	50-	60
Candlesticks, pink/white, 6" high, pr.	41-	60
Flower frog, nude dancers, ivory glaze, 9½" dia.	41-	52
Vase, blue luster, 9" high	32-	52
Vase, orange luster, 5½" high	17-	21
Vase, redware, black glaze over orange ground, 12" high	178-188	
Vase, yellow luster, marine decor, 6½" high	47-	53

Cracker Jars

Cracker Jars

These are kissin' cousins to the cookie jar. In continuous use for the past 150 years, they come in pottery, wood, glass. Some had silver-plated lids.

Acid finish with enameling, Britannia handle and lid	$128-138
Bristol glass with enameled flowers/butterflies	120-140
China, blue/green, floral decor (ill.)	68- 79
Limoges, shell design, gold trim	72- 82
Satin glass, frosted, bead and grape design	220-240

Crackle (Craquelle) Glass

Crackle (Craquelle) Glass

Invented by the Venetians in the 16th century, it was made by plunging hot glass into cold water, then reheating and reblowing it.

149

(continued)

This process produced the crackled effect. It's also called frosted and iced glass. Some of the finest was made at Sandwich; also at Hobbs, Brockunier and Company, Wheeling, West Virginia, in the late 1800s. Being reproduced by Pilgrim Glass Corporation.

Bowl, Mt. Washington, gold
  iridescence, enameled lobster
  decor, 5½" high $182-199
Bowl, white, blue dots, 8" dia. . . . 295-342
Lemonade set, blue, 8 pcs. 88- 97
Pickle jar, hourglass shape, silver
  plated 75- 85
Pitcher, applied reeded handle,
  clear 74- 84
Sugar bowl, pink, enamel floral,
  silver cover 77- 86
Sweetmeat jar, sapphire blue,
  red strawberries, amber edge . . 481-520
Toothpick holder, marine green . . 52- 62
Toothpick holder, hat, green 60- 70
Vase, applied blue glass buttons,
  12½" high (ill.) 60- 70
Vase, Chinese decor, floral,
  13½" high 138-142
Vase, cranberry, 6½" high 88- 98
Vase, iridescent, signed
  Imperial 150-160

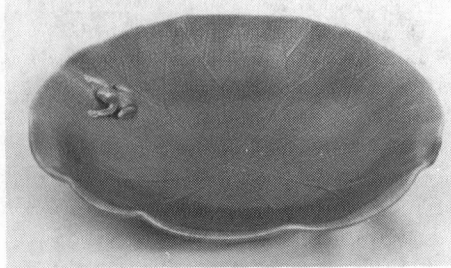
Crackleware, Chinese

Crackleware, Chinese

This well-known porcelain, called *Ko Yao*, originally came from the Ko kilns during the Sung Dynasty. The crackling is deliberate. Colors range from gray to gray-green. This ware is still being made today.

Beaker vase, slender form, 7"
  high $300-345
Bowl, flared feet, 7" high 285-320
Dish, flared rim, 6¾" dia. 420-470
Dish, frog motif, 12¼" dia. (ill.) . . 175-200
Jar, ovoid form, short-lipped rim,
  7½" high 375-420
Vase, 6⅜" high 375-410
Vase, 9½" high 275-245

Cranberry Glass

Cranberry Glass

Gold was added to the glass batch, which was then blown or molded. When reheated at a low temperature, the cranberry shade developed. It also was called Ruby glass. In later years, copper was substituted, creating a harsh amber-red tint. There are many Cranberry pieces represented in this Guide. Here are a few. Oh, those repros!

Bottle, barber, green/white
  flowers, 8" high . . . . $ 70- 80
Bowl, finger, Inverted Thumb-
  print (ITP), 5" dia. 112-121
Bowl, rose, pleated and fluted
  top, 4¾" dia. 120-130
Box, blue decorated flowers,
  4½" square 62- 72
Candlesticks, twisted stem, 10¼"
  high, pr 141-152
Compote, clear pedestal base,
  6¼" high 138-151
Creamer, fluted lip, clear
  handle, 3½" high 67- 73
Cruet, ITP, 8" high (ill.) 120-130
Knife rest, ball ends are cut,
  3¼" wide 92-102
Rose bowl, ribbed, applied clear
  rigaree, snail feet, berry prunts,
  signed Webb, 5" high 395-420
Wine set, 11" high decanter,
  10" wide tray, 6 glasses 188-195

Crazing

This word is included in this Guide because it confuses so many people. It's simply a fine network of cracks or fissures in the glaze caused by the unequal shrinkage of the body and glaze during the cooling. It does not mean the piece is cracked and/or damaged. Some pottery factories deliberately "crazed" certain pieces. Rookwood Pottery Company was one.

Crest China

Crest China

An inexpensive "fairing" (small souvenir) china made in England and the U.S. during the late 19th century—usually found in mugs, toothpick holders, shoes, or pin trays.

Creamer, miniature, green crown emblem, 2¼″ high (ill.)	$ 24- 32
Figurine, "The first to rise," man in bed, nightcap, Germany	47- 52
Mug, "Sip Slowly," 5½″ high	45- 50
Pin tray, floral design, France, 1880s	24- 31
Powder box, "Love's light never dims," Germany, 1887	39- 48
Shoe, applied flowers	24- 32
Toothpick holder, "Take one," Germany, 1890s	22- 34

Crown Derby

Crown Derby

An earlier factory of the same name operated in the early 1800s, but what we know as Crown Derby today was made in

England in the late 1870s until the late 1880s.

Coffeepot, Oriental decor, brown floral	$120-128
Creamer, flowers, oriental-type, Crown mark	58- 68
Cup/saucer, white/blue, floral decor	92-102
Ewer, turquoise ground, raised gold floral decor, 9″	181-191
Figurine, seated lady, white ground, 6½″ high	120-130
Pin, flowers, 2″ long, (ill.)	47- 57
Plate, dark blue/white, rust panels, 9″ dia.	62- 72
Plate, flower border, 8½″ dia.	71- 81
Toothpick, white ground, flowers	63- 73
Vase, red/gold, 6″ high	110-118

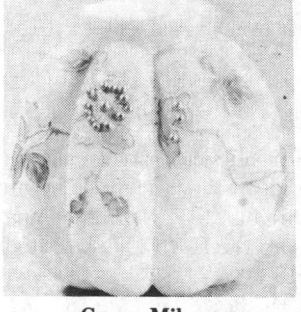

Crown Milano

Crown Milano

This fine glass was made in the late 19th century by the Mt. Washington Glass Company. It is often decorated with flowers and leaves overlaid with gold and silver. Quite a few pieces were marked with the letters C.M. in the pontil.

Bowl, melon rib, floral decor, 4½″ (ill.)	$ 675- 720
Bowl, tan, flowers, pewter top and handles	560- 580
Bride's basket, enameled pansy decor, tricorn, signed	2,900+
Cookie jar, signed	1,350-1,600
Cracker jar, apricot, apple blossom limbs and flowers, signed	790- 820
Cracker jar, jeweled, mottled background, applied gold threading, signed MT. W.G. Co., c. 1890	1,950+
Cracker jar, pansy, signed	925-1,100
Cracker jar, quadruple plate rim and lid, pansy decor, signed, c. 1894	885- 955

151

(continued)

Humidor, cream ground, pansies, silver-plated lid, signed M.W.	920-	960
Jewel box, original lining, Mt. Washington Glass Co.	670-	750
Shade, floral, gold, Burmese coloring	652-	718
Sugar bowl, covered, melon rib, floral decor	452-	484
Sugar shaker, Mt. Washington, pewter top	452-	510
Tumbler, gold decor, signed Crown	589-	622
Vase, cream ground, apple blossoms, signed, 6½" high	1,275-	1,450
Vase, white satin ground, pink shading, pansies, 6" high		1,400+
Vase, yellow to peach ground, Mt. Washington Glass Co.		1,400+

Cruets

These came in all sizes and usually were made of pressed or blown glass. The more expensive were cut. Every glass company made them, from the late 1700s on. Reproductions galore.

Amber, clear handle ....$	58-	67
Beveled Star, amber, clear stopper	52-	61
Blue, amber stopper and handle, 8" high	88-	94
Bohemian glass, deer scene	51-	60
Cobalt overlay cut to clear, Rose pattern	97-	105
Cranberry, enameled lilies of the valley (ill.)	105-	109
Cranberry, ITP, clear stopper	120-	130
Cut glass, signed Hawkes	140-	152
Depression glass, American Sweetheart	51-	60
Emerald green ground, white enamel lily of the valley	82-	90

Cruets

Frosted glass, green enamel decor, 7½" high	62-	72
Green cut to clear (ill.)	142-	152
Green ground, white and gold enamel, floral	67-	77
Mary Gregory glass, boy with hoop, blue/white	135-	145
Millefiori, canes, yellow/white, blue, cut glass stopper	245-	270
Opalescent, Stars and Stripes (ill.)	118-	125
Paneled Thistle, prism stoppers	70-	80
Peachblow, Wheeling, yellow, amber handle and stopper		1,400+
Pink swirl, blown	92-	107
Rayed Star base, notched handle, cut glass, 7½"	72-	82
Spatter glass, clear stopper	81-	91
Strawberry, Hobnail, clear applied handle and stopper	60-	70
Tiffany, blue, ribbed, signed	405-	418
Vasa Murrhina, clear stopper	92-	107
Vaseline to pink, Hobnail, 7" high	77-	86
Venetian glass, blue swirl	80-	90
Waterford, new mark	88-	98
Zipper edge on ribs and handles, 5½" high	50-	60

CT Germany   C.T.

Made by C. Tielsch & Company, Altwasser, Silesia, from 1845. The mark of this hard-paste porcelain is illustrated here.

Chocolate set, 8 cups and saucers, floral motif, all	$108-118
Cups and saucers, 8 each, flowers, demitasse, all	257-282
Plate, birds in tree, blue/green/red, gold trim, 8¼" dia.	42- 51
Plate, dancing ladies, red/blue, gold trim, 8" dia.	40- 50
Plate, game, partridge, cream/brown, gold trim, 9" dia.	39- 47
Vase, floral decor, blue/red, gold handles, 11" high	74- 83
Vase, pink/blue, fluted lip, gold handles, 10¼" high	73- 84

Cup Plates

During the mid-1800s, gentlemen drank their tea or coffee from the saucer. The plates that held the cup while he was slurping are collectible today, both in glass and in china. Sandwich made the most beautiful glass

Cup Plates

ones. They should ring when plinked. Reproductions were made in glass by Westmoreland Glass Company in the 1930s. They don't ring. Still being made.

Beaded hearts, Midwest, glass (ill.)	$ 42- 51
Benjamin Franklin, clear glass	44- 52
Blue/white, Clews china, 1819	45- 54
Brown, eagle and floral border, boat center, Clews, 1825	47- 57
Bunker Hill, Sandwich (ill.)	49- 58
Dark blue, scenic views, Clews, 1822, pr.	62- 72
Heart center, 13 hearts, clear glass	38- 41
Henry Clay, clear glass	38- 44
Log cabin, clear glass	135-162
Sailing ship, men in rowboat, ship border, brown, Staffordshire	37- 42
Sandwich, clear glass, 3⁵/16″ dia., eagle looking left	66- 76
Sandwich, clear glass, 3½″ dia., Henry Clay, star under bust (ill.)	62- 72
Sandwich, clear glass, 3⁷/16″ dia., U.S. Constitution (ill.)	66- 71
Valentine, blue	160-171
Wedding Day, 3 weeks after (reverse faces) (ill.)	41- 50

Currier and Ives

Nathaniel Currier worked for himself in 1834. In 1857, James Ives joined him in the firm that was to become one of the world's greatest producers of inexpensive lithographs. Scenic, political, disaster, nautical, sporting scenes, horses, animals, biblical scenes; no subject was ignored. Original C & I prints show up under magnification as a series of short lines; reproductions show up as a series of small dots. C & I prints were made in three sizes: small folio, 7.8″×12.8″; medium folio, 13″×20″; large folio, 18″×27″. Do beware of insurance company calendar prints and all those reproductions. C & I went out of business in 1907. See **Clubs and Publications (Prints)**, this Price Guide.

American Farm Scenes, #1, "Spring," large folio	$ 640-	672
American Farm Scenes, #2, "Summer," large folio	625-	638
American Farm Scenes, #3, "Autumn," large folio	645-	662
American Farm Scenes, #4, "Winter," large folio		1,700+
"American Girl," 1871, small folio	78-	88
"Arkansas Traveler," 1870, small	128-	138
"Autumn Fruits," small, medium	79-	88
"The Bad Husband," 1870, small	132-	142
"Battle of Gettysburg, Pa.," 1863, large	262-	290
"Beach Snipe Shooting," 1869, medium	1,200-	1,275
"The Beautiful Persian" (ill.)	60-	70
"Belle of the Winter," medium	272-	340
"The Best Horse," small	88-	92
"The Bible and Temperance," N. Currier, small	130-	140
"A Black Squall," 1879, small	65-	75
"The Boatswain," N. Currier, small	88-	94
"Bombardment of Fort Sumter," small	160-	170
"Boy and Dog," small	110-	128
"Brigham Young," medium	120-	129
"California Gold," N. Currier, small	475-	562

Currier and Ives

153

(continued)

"Canvasbacks," small 178- 228
"A Champion Race," 1889,
   small 240- 352
"Champions of the Union,"
   large 162- 172
"The City of Boston," 1873,
   large 358- 375
"City of New York," N.
   Currier, 1844, small 410- 450
"Clipper Ship *Flying
   Cloud*," N. Currier, 1853,
   large .... 5,400+
"Dartmouth College," small . 1,400+
"The Death Shot," small ... 162- 200
"A Fair Start," small 80- 90
"Farmyard Pets," small 105- 115
"Feast of Roses," 1873,
   small 132- 147
"Flying Fish," 1879, small .. 135- 180
"The Game Cock," N.
   Currier, small 185- 240
"General Grant," medium .. 110- 135
"General Robert E. Lee,"
   small 132- 152
"General Tom Thumb's
   Marriage," 1863, small ... 142- 162
"Going It Blind," N.
   Currier, small 132- 141
"The Golden Morning,"
   small 132- 141
"The Grand Drive, Central
   Park, New York," 1869,
   large 1,800-2,300
"Grant in Peace," small 80- 90
"Great Exhibition of 1860,"
   small 110- 132
"Hanover," 1887, small 138- 172
"Highland Fling," 1876,
   medium 130- 150
"Horace Greeley," medium . 121- 140
"The Hunter's Dog," N.
   Currier, small 242- 251
"In the Harbor," small 240- 260
"Indian Buffalo Hunt,"
   medium 470- 520
"Iroquois," 1882, large 555- 622
"The Jockey's Dream,"
   1880, small 92- 131
"Jolly Young Ducks," 1866,
   small 92- 115
"Quail," 1865, small 261- 295
"Rail Shooting," small 870- 955
"A Run of Luck," 1871,
   small 88- 94
"Rush for the Pole," 1887,
   small 138- 182
"St. Lawrence," small 152- 172
"Santa Claus," 1882, small .. 140- 160
"The Shoemaker," small 110- 132
"Starting Out on His
   Mettle," 1876, small 141- 170
"View on the Rondout,"
   small, medium 191- 242

"Warming Up," 1884, small . 128- 161
"The Water Jump," 1884,
   small 348- 372
"Wood Ducks," small 260- 280
"A Wreath of Flowers,"
   small 98- 121

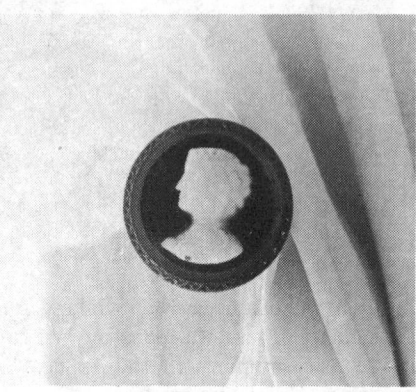

Curtain Tiebacks

Curtain Tiebacks

During the Victorian era, the day of floor-to-ceiling drapes, usually velvet, these tiebacks were used to hold the drapes open during the day. Sandwich Glass tiebacks are very rare today. Made of brass, cast iron, inlaid with porcelain medallions (illustrated), sometimes just a velvet cord with tassels.

Brass, stamped design, pr. ...... $ 44- 56
Medallion type, brass framing
   (ill.), pr. 69- 78
Porcelain head, iron spike, screw-
   type, pr. 41- 52
Sandwich glass (authentic),
   star-petal design, pr. 132-152
Sandwich type, blue or other
   colors, pr. 61- 70

Cuspidors

Usually made of brass, the early ones were

Cuspidors

made of pottery, also glass. When it was fashionable to chew tobacco, before cigarettes and cigars, every hotel lobby, barbershop, and beer parlor had at least one. They were also called spittoons. Heavily reproduced.

Brass, 10″ dia. . . . . $ 90-110
Glass, patent January 8, 1898 . . .   92-107
Porcelainized metal, 2 pcs. 40- 49
Rockingham pottery (ill.) 182-194
Rookwood, 11″ dia., 1914 255-300
Silver-plated, hotel-type 75- 90

Custard Glass

Harry Northwood is credited with bringing Custard Glass to this country from England. Utilitarian as well as decorative, large amounts were manufactured in the late 19th and early 20th centuries. See Argonaut Shell, Chrysanthemum Sprig, Drapery, Fluted Scrolls, Geneva, Heart with Thumbprint, Honeycomb with Flower Rim, Intaglio, Ivorina Verde, Louis XV, Maple Leaf, Maize, and Wild Bouquet in the Pattern Glass Section, this Price Guide.

Cut Glass

The Brilliant Period of this glass ranges, generally, from 1880 until 1915. How do you tell if it is cut or pressed? (1) **Ring**. Cut glass will ring like a bell when tapped lightly. (2) **Sparkle**. When held to the light, you can notice the refractions made by the cutting. Pressing destroys this quality. (3) **Sharpness**. If the edges are sharp, the glass is cut; smooth edges denote pressed glass. (4) **Weight**. Cut glass, because of a high lead content, is usually heavy. Cut and engraved glass are done on a wheel. Etched glass is not a type of cut glass—it's made by the application of a corroding acid. Cut glass is always hand-blown or blown-molded, never pressed. Since there are thousands of reproduction pieces on the market today, don't assume that (1) through (4) above distinguish the old from the new. Study, learn by feeling, but know from whom you buy. See **Clubs and Publications**, this Price Guide.

Baskets
Cornflowers, handled, 13½″
  high (ill.) . . . . $ 240- 255
Harvard pattern, intaglio
  floral, 12″ high 220- 240
Pinwheel pattern, 7″ high . . . 150- 165

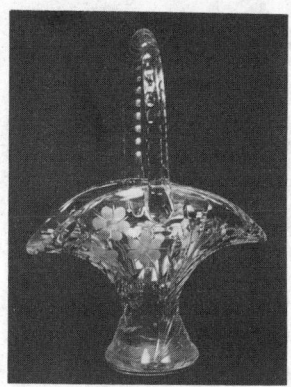

Cut Glass Basket

Bowls
Etched flowers, signed
  Clarke, 9″ dia. 240- 250
Flowers, deep cut, signed
  Irving, 8″ dia. (ill.) 150- 160
Green cut-to-clear, signed
  Dorflinger, 5″ high (ill.) . . . 320- 365
Hobstar, Pinwheel pattern,
  8″ dia. 170- 180
Russian pattern, panels of
  fans 130- 145

Boxes
Cigarette, signed Hawkes,
  late 77- 87
Collar, mirror inside for
  m'lady, silver bindings . . . 200- 220
Dresser, silver rim, 5¾″ dia.
  (ill.) 185- 195
Dresser, Venetian pattern,
  silver trim 140- 150

Butter Dishes
Hobstar, Strawberry,
  Diamond Point and Fan,
  signed Hawkes 275- 285
Pinwheel and Fan, cut knob
  finial 120- 140
Rosette flowers, cut knob
  finial 110- 120

Celery Dishes
Florence pattern, boat type,
  signed Libbey 250- 260
Grecian pattern, signed
  Hawkes 180- 189

Cut Glass Bowl

(continued)

Cut Glass Bowl

Cut Glass Punch Bowl

Strawberry, Diamond and
Fan, boat type, signed
Hawkes 225- 245

Champagne Tubs
Basketweave 220- 235
Chrysanthemum, jug, 2 qt.,
no stopper, signed
Hawkes 240- 247

Chandeliers
Empire Ormolu, 19th
century .... 4,900+
Five branch, cut glass
hurricane globes .... 4,400+
Gas fixture type, clear and
frosted glass, mid-1800s .. 1,200+
Hanging lantern with
smoke bell, early 1800s ... 1,500+

Cheese Dishes
Diamonds, fans, sterling
silver dome 285- 310
Hobstar, 5″ high, cut knob
finial 260- 275
Mitre Star, varied pattern,
7½″ high 255- 280

Isabella, 7″ high, short
stem, square top 180- 210
Seashells, 6″ high, short
stem, signed Clark 220- 240

Creamers
Flower design, 2¾″ high ... 150- 165
Harvard pattern, jug,
straight-sided, fluted top . 80- 90
Hobstar 82- 90
Pinwheel 75- 85

Cruets
Corinthian, 4-oz. oil, vinegar
to match, both 140- 150
Harvard, 8-oz., signed
J. Hoare 182- 192
Prism, 4, 5, 6-oz., short-
stemmed, signed Libbey,
ea. 150- 160

Decanters
Bull's Eye, pt., qt., 1½-qt.,
ea. 220- 240
Corinthian, pt. and qt., long
necks, some handled, ea. .. 210- 235
4 sherry glasses, match
Mitre Star decanter, all ... 90- 100

Cut Glass Box

Compotes
Flowers, 7¼″ high, signed
Hawkes, sits on plate of
same design, 16½″ dia. .... 1,100+

Cut Glass Pitcher

Cut Velvet Glass

Czechoslovakia

though some are artist/maker marked, indicating they were made before the country became independent. Most of what you find are in the $8 to $30 range.

Creamer (ill.) . . . . $ 8-11
Vase, handled, stenciled design
   under glaze, signed Erphila
   Art Pottery on paper label,
   7″ high 27-37

Daguerreotype Cases

Littlefield, Parsons and Company patented these cases on October 14, 1856. When you find them with the daguerreotypes missing,

they make fine holders for your favorite photos.

Average price $15-27

Daguerreotype Cases

Daguerreotypes

Daguerreotypes

The method is named for the Frenchman who discovered it—Louis Jacques Mande Daguerre—in 1837. He covered a bright copper plate with silver salts, then placed it between two pieces of glass to protect it. When exposed to light, the silver compound produced a picture. Civil War scenes are collectible and rare.

Civil War soldier, Union Army . . $ 85- 95
Daguerreotypes without case . . . 11- 18
Eagle on American Flag 50- 60
Girl with dog 47- 57
Lady (ill.) 35- 45
Volunteer fireman, Ambrotype* . 69- 78
Wedding photo 44- 52
*Ambrotypes are photographs on glass.

D'argental

Another of the cameo-type glasses produced in the last part of the 19th century, it

(continued)

was named for its originator who lived in France. Somewhat similar to Galle and Lalique. Scarce.

Bowl, yellow matt, red roses,
leaves, carved, 6″ high, signed . $510-552
Bowl, red matt, blue/white
flowers, carved cameo, 8½″
high 532-561
Vase, blue morning glories, yellow
ground, cameo, 8″ high 451-480
Vase, frosted blue ground, brown
and rust leaves, signed, 6″
high 475-510
Vase, 3-layer, amber-rose ground,
signed, 7″ high 610-632

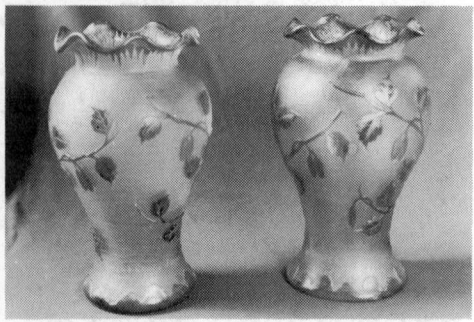

Daum Nancy

Daum Nancy

Auguste and Antonin Daum made and signed this beautiful cameo-type glass in the late 1800s. They also made fine enameled glass. Both are hard to find today.

Bottle, acid cut ground, man
and windmill, enameled,
stopper . . . . $ 610- 660
Bowl, blue iris cut through,
floral, 8″ high, signed 785- 920
Bowl, fruit decor, blue
ground 410- 440
Box, carved blue crocus, blue-
green ground, lid, signed . . 520- 540
Compote, amethyst, footed,
8½″ high, signed 285- 296
Compote, blue and brown
ground, sprigs, leaves,
footed, 8″ 478- 510
Jar, floral scene cut through,
acid finish, signed 520- 560
Lamp, enameled leaf decor,
mottled floral background,
signed . . . . 1,800+
Pitcher, frosted green, floral,
9½″ high, signed 585- 620

Plate, turned up sides, yellow/
orange 550- 700
Rose bowl, green, blue cut
through, 3½″ high 520- 620
Tumbler, barrel shape, gold
ground, flowers, 5″ high . . . 615- 710
Tumbler, white ground,
shaded red, blue, green,
signed 610- 710
Vase, birds in trees, green/
blue/brown/red, 8″ high,
signed 785- 885
Vase, enamel, floral, medal-
lion, 4½″ high, signed 570- 620
Vase, flowers, 28″ high . . . . . . 2,500+
Vase, mottled orange, yellow,
6½″ high, signed 510- 550
Vase, satin, orange/green,
enameled pseudo-cameo
technique, 8¾″ high 288- 320
Vase, serpentine shape, floral,
brown/green/blue, 7¼″
high, signed 620- 680
Vase, summer scene, 10″ high,
signed 575- 655
Vase, winter scene, 9″ high,
signed 620- 680
Vases, pink/gold flowers, 10″
high (ill.), pr. . . . . 1,600+

Davenport China

Davenport China

Made by John Davenport at Lonport, England, late 1700s, this china is light in weight, cream colored, and has a soft, velvety texture. It's marked with the name Davenport above an impressed anchor. The factory closed in the late 1800s.

Creamer, bulbous white with deep
blue decor $140-160
Cup/saucer, Derby colors, 1810 . . 95-110
Dish in plated holder, Imari
colors, 1875 150-170
Dish, vegetable, Berry pattern,
impressed signature and
anchor 82- 92
Ewer, white, blue marbling,
1815 170-190
Jug, bright blue decorations,
1800 235-265

Platter, blue/white Oriental, reticulated border, anchor mark . . . 150-160
Tea set (teapot, covered sugar),
Spring pattern in red/green,
anchor 350-370
Teapot, pink lustre decorations . . 342-371
Trivet, blue/red decor, no mark . . 135-142
Urn, blue/gold on white, 6″ high
(ill.) 310-340

De Latte

Another of the cameo types, it was usually opaque and was made by Andre De Latte in Nancy, France, in the 1920s. Light fixtures were also made there, but De Latte is best remembered for his cameo glass.

Box, pink ground, cut blue
flowers, signed, 3½″ high,
4″ sq. $575-620
Vase, aqua ground, birds, flowers,
blue/green decor, signed, 8¾″
high 555-575
Vase, blue ground, purple iris
decor, signed, 9½″ high 572-585
Vase, gold/red ground, yellow/
pink floral, signed, 11½″ high . 575-620
Vase, opaque ground, handled,
river scene, 14″ high 420-450
Vase, pink with mottled blue
ground, lavender-pink floral,
signed 395-420
Vase, yellow, trees, deer, brown
background, signed, 8½″ high . 540-580

De Vez

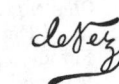

This glass was made in Pantin, France, and was similar in style to that made by Marinot, Rousseau, and others. It is another of the cameo types, late 1800s, and is scarce today.

Atomizer, birds, brown/yellow,
6″ high, signed $675-800

De Vez

Bowl, 3″ high, 5″ dia., flowers/
birds 385-440
Bowl, 4″ high, 4½″ dia., scenic,
blue/green, signed 475-520
Vase, acid cut, harbor scene, 8½″
high, signed 790-825
Vase, scenic, satin ground,
signed, 8½″ high 695-750
Vase, 7″ high, river scene,
mountains, signed 520-560
Vase, 7½″ high, house/trees,
pink, green, signed 562-592
Vase, translucent ground, castle
scene, signed, 10″ high 782-900
Vase, 11″ high, scenic, blue/red
iridescent, signed 600-682
Vase, 14″ high, clouds, blue/green
ground, signed 620-650

Decanters

Decanters

Used mainly by taprooms and inns to store their wines and liquors, they became stylish in homes in the mid-1700s. They first were crude in shape and material; later they were made of cut glass, Amberina, even Tiffany glass.

Amber, Inverted Thumbprint,
stopper, pedestal foot $150- 170
Brown, blown, fluted sides,
clear stopper, attributed to
Sandwich, 1850s, 14″ high . 250- 300
Clear, gold leaf design, 12″
high 350- 420
Clear, hand-painted eagles,
dated 1779, blown, clear
stoppers, pr. . . . . 1,100+
Clear, 4-part, stoppers, Sandwich type, late 1800s,
France, 12½″ high 265- 320
Clear, signed Libbey, silver
overlay, Riverboat type . . . 275- 320

(continued)

Cobalt, swirled body, clear
stopper, pontil mark, mid-
1800s 210- 250
½ pint, 3-mold (McKearin
G111-14) 260- 270
Engraved glass, floral/Cupid
designs in silver base, 6½"
high, pr. 675- 775
Ruby glass, clear twisted
handle, blown stopper, 6½"
high (ill.) 185- 220

Decoys

Imagine! A Lesser Yellowlegs by Elmer
Crowell bringing more than $12,000! And
other sales are following this example. These
carved wooden birds, used to lure live birds
into range for the hunter, are becoming scarce
and *very* expensive. The beginning collector
should consider: (1) reputation of the carver,
(2) species, and (3) condition — original paint,
repairs, alterations. Today's buyers are more
knowledgeable, but even they can be fooled
on occasion by the excellent fakes that
always appear when a particular item
becomes collectible.

Black Duck, Charles
Hart $4,400- 4,650
Black Duck, Gus Wilson   165- 180
Black Duck, Mason's
premier grade 190- 220
Black Duck, Thomas
Fitzpatrick, Delanco,
New Jersey 170- 185
Black Duck, Wild-Fowler
Decoys, Inc., Old
Saybrook, Connecticut   95- 110
Black-bellied Plover,
Mason Decoy Factory   1,400- 1,600
Black-breasted Plover . .   1,600- 1,875
Bluebills, Ward Bros., pr.   1,700- 1,900
Brant, hollow-carved,
Cobb Island, Virginia .   28,000-29,500
Brant, Mason's
Challenger grade 245- 275
Canada Goose, canvas-
covered, George Boyd   4,600 4,775

Decoys

Canvasback Drake,
balsa, Ward Bros.,
Crisfield, Maryland
(both Stephen W.
(1896-1976) and his
brother, Lemuel T., Jr.
(1896-   ) are world-
famous for their birds)   1,200- 1,400
Canvasback Drake and
Hen, balsa, Ward
Bros., pr. . . . .   3,500+
Cape Cod Black Duck . . .   105- 118
Chesapeake Bay Coot,
Madison R. Mitchell,
Havre de Grace,
Maryland 195- 255
Coot, Benjamin J.
Schmidt, Centerline,
Michigan 195- 230
Coot, maker unknown,
initials "D.G." carved
on bottom 70- 80
Coot, Singing River
Decoy Co., New
Orleans, Louisiana,
pre-1940 . . . .   90- 110
Coot, Xavier Bourg,
Larose, Louisiana 165- 180
Curlew, Elmer Crowell . .   9,000+
Eider Drake 225- 265
Gadwell Drake, John
English, repainted by
Robert White 510- 565
Goldeneye Drake and
Hen, Ward Bros., pr.   3,400- 3,600
Mallard Drake, Harry
Fennimore, Borden-
town, New Jersey 195- 240
Mallard Drake, Mason
Decoy Factory,
Challenger grade. 2,550- 2,700
Mallard Hen, Jester
Family, Chincoteague,
Virginia 145- 175
Massachusetts Black-
breasted Plover 495- 575
Massachusetts Lesser
Yellowlegs 1,600- 1,800
Merganser Drake,
Mason, Challenger
grade 2,800- 2,975
Mergansers, Mason,
Challenger grade, pr.   5,600- 5,950
Old Squaw Drake,
Milton Crowley, South
Addison, Maine,
c. 1920s 120- 150
Old Squaw Drake,
Norris E. Pratt 300- 355
Red-breasted Merganser,
Elmer Crowell 3,900- 4,500
Red-breasted Merganser,
Gus Wilson, Casco

Bay, Maine	395-	440
Red-breasted Merganser, Harry V. Shourds	460-	510
Red-breasted Merganser, Hurley Conklin	365-	435
Red-breasted Merganser Drake, Frank Dobbins	165-	235
Redhead Hen, H. Keyes Chadwick (carved in 1949 when he was 80)	325-	370
Redheads, Mason, Challenger grade, pr. . .	3,800-	3,975
Scaup Drake, hollow-carved, Harry V. Shourds	245-	275
Scaup Hen, hollow-carved, Capt. Jess Birdsall, Barnegate, New Jersey	150-	180
Sleeping Canvasback Hen, J. Corbin (Corb) Reed, 1962	280-	335
Snipe, metal, folding-type	50-	60
White-winged Scoter, Joe Lincoln	3,800-	4,350
White-winged Scoter, Warren Wass, Cape Split, Maine, c. 1905 . .	110-	145
Widgeon Drake, "Shang" Wheeler	7,200-	7,450
Wood Duck	150-	175

Dedham Pottery

Dedham Pottery

Alexander Robertson founded this company in Chelsea, Massachusetts, in the late 1860s. He changed the name from Chelsea Pottery to Chelsea Ceramic Art Works in 1872, and finally to Dedham Pottery around

1894. They specialized in crackleware in blue and high-fired colored pieces. The rabbit motif is what you see the most of on Dedham pottery. Most collectible today.

Bowl and plate, rabbits, signed . .	$152-170
Bowl, mushrooms, Chelsea Pottery mark	101-118
Candlesticks, rabbits, signed, pr..	228-245
Chocolate pot, rabbits, signed . . .	215-250
Creamer, elephants, 4½" high . . .	220-240
Creamer, rabbit, 3¾" high	178-192
Creamer, rabbit, 6¼" high	162-172
Cup/saucer, rabbits, elephant, polar bear	172-188
Dish, elephants, Chelsea Pottery mark	110-118
Egg cup, rabbits	182-195
Mayonnaise bowl, rabbits, 6¼" dia.	125-142
Mug, handled, rabbit border, 5½" high	250-265
Mug, handled, water lily, large . .	122-140
Plate, duck, 10" dia.	178-188
Plate, rabbit, 8"	152-162
Plate, rabbit, 10" (ill.)	110-120
Plate, swan, 8½" dia.	240-260
Plate, turkey, 8"	170-180
Platter, rabbit border	259-279
Salt/pepper shakers, rabbit, pr. . .	215-240
Saucedish, rabbits	120-130
Saucer, water lily, 4" dia.	88- 98
Sugar bowl, lid, 3"	210-220
Tile, 6" square, horse chestnut . .	135-160
Tray, elephant border, 7¼" long .	350-370
Vase, blue over green, 4½" high .	620-660
Vase, charcoal gray, raised floral decor, 6" high	125-150

Degenhart Glass

Mentioned here because so much new Degenhart glass is surfacing at flea markets and garage sales. Crystal Art Glass was founded at Cambridge, Ohio, in 1947 by John and Elizabeth Degenhart. When Island Mold Company purchased the molds in 1978 they removed the familiar trademark. Currently they are reproducing the original Degenhart glass without the "D" within the heart mark. A few molds were left intact to produce glass for a proposed Degenhart museum. The museum will emphasize that these pieces are current, not old. More than 200 colors were produced in numerous variations. John Degenhart was world famous for his paperweights. Bernard Boyd recently purchased the plant. His mark is a "B" inside a diamond.

(continued)

Animal Dishes, Covered
Amberina hen, 5″ . . . . $ 355-365
Amethyst hen, 5″ 183-192
Peachblow turkey, 5″ 110-120
Bicentennial Bells
Ivorine 44- 50
Pearl Gray 45- 53
Vaseline 28- 34
Candleholders, Bird
Basic colors, crystal 24- 33
Opaques 67- 74
Creamer and Sugar
Crystal Daisy and Button 85- 93
Crystal Texas 85- 93
Opaque Texas 132-141
Drawer Pulls, Sandwich-type
Crystal 15- 22
Milk blue 45- 53
Opalescent 65- 73
Owls
Champagne, 3″ high 184-193
Crystal, 3″ high 24- 29
Lemonade, 3″ high 34- 40
Paperweights
Bubbles with miniature
bird or other animal 240-255
Name 133-142
Novelty 133-142
Rose, footed, most colors 118-126
Pooch Dogs
Amber, 2½″ high 44- 52
April green, 2½″ high 34- 42
Blue, 2½″ high 107-114
Snow white, 2½″ high 50- 58
Portrait Plate (Elizabeth Degenhart)
Amberina crystal 82- 90
Canary crystal 55- 63
Smoky 110-118
Shoes
Crystal 24- 28
Opaque 38- 44
Slippers, Cat and Bow
Crystal 24- 32
Opaque 37- 44

Delft

Earthenware with a blue decoration on a white background. Tin compound was used to produce the glaze and a number of companies made it at Delft, Holland, at the beginning of the 17th century. It was also made in England. Most of what you find in shops today is from the late 1800s until World War I. Now being reproduced.

Ashtray, windmill scene . . . . $ 47- 52
Bottle, blue/white, 9½″ high,
1740s 275-285
Bottle, Dutch girl with dogcart,
windmill scene 68- 78

Delft

Clock, Dutch scene, 8-day
German movement 225-245
Coffee grinder, wall type, typical . 140-160
Cow, 6″ long, signed Delft 105-111
Creamer, flowers, Holland, 2¾″
high 32- 42
Creamer, sleeping cow, Germany,
1890 . . . . 72- 82
Cup/saucer, floral, Holland, 2″
high 26- 36
Cup/saucer, windmill scene 30- 40
Figurine, Dutch, girl and boy,
pr. 77- 88
Inkwell, stand, metal cap, blue/
white, no mark 66- 72
Jar, lid, Dutch boy, 13″ high 312-340
Plaque, sailing scene, 18th
century, 14½″ high 328-338
Plate, blue, Dutch canal in winter,
13½″ dia. 77- 85
Stein, drinking scene along canal,
dated 1723, 11″ high, pewter
cap 420-432
Tray, water scene, blue/white,
12″ wide 199-220
Vase, blue/white, scrolls, lovers,
16″ high, pr. 320-340
Vase, windmill, Holland, 7½″
high (ill.) 140-150
Wine bottle, Holland, Dutch boy,
7½″ high 58- 68

Depression Glass

The glass is confusing because collectors and those compiling books about it have given names to patterns unnamed by the makers. It was made during the depression years of the late 1920s and early 1930s and was considered inexpensive tableware. Hocking, Westmoreland Glass Company, and the Indiana Glass Company were three of many firms making it. Pink, green, milk-white, and amber were a few of the colors. Reproduced in a number of different patterns.

Adam or Adams
Jeannette Glass Co., Jeannette, Pa., 1930-1934. Crystal, green, pink. Prices are for all colors.

Ashtray, 4½"	$ 8-12
Bowl, casserole, covered, 9"	19-28
Bowl, salad, 7⅞"	11-17
Bowl, vegetable, 9¾"	12-18
Candlestick, 3⅞"	26-33
Plate, dinner, 8⅞"	7-15
Plate, salad, 7¾"	5-11
Pitcher, footed, square base, 8" high	21-30
Tumblers, 7-oz., 9-oz., ea.	11-19
Vase, flange rim, 7½"	24-33

Alternating Flue and Panel
Imperial Glass Co., Bellaire, Ohio, 1931. Crystal, ebony, green, rose.

	Cry'l Gr'n Rose	Eb'y
Bowls, 8" berry, 9" fruit, ea.	9-16	12-20
Bowls, shallow, deep, 9", ea.	7-15	11-19
Creamer, footed	5- 9	11-18
Sugar, footed, cone shape	5- 9	11-18

American Sweetheart
MacBeth-Evans Division, Corning Glass Co., Corning, N.Y., 1930-1936. Cherry red, monax, pink, ritz blue, smoke.

	Pink	M'x	Red Blue	Smoke
Bowl, soup	9-17	22-30		
Bowl, vegetable, 11"	17-25	35-44		
Creamer, footed, oval	7-12	9-13	126-144	32-39
Pitcher, ice guard, 60-oz.	70-78			
Plate, chop, 11"	8-12	10-16	148-156	
Plate, luncheon, 9"	7-11	9-13		10-16
Tumbler, juice, 3½"	17-21			

Anniversary
Jeannette Glass Co., late 1940s. Pink. Sprayed-on iridescent-type sold in 1969-1970.

Bowl, fruit, 9"	8-12
Bowl, soup (or cereal), 7⅜"	5- 9
Cake plate, 12½"	8-13
Pickle dish, 9"	7-12
Plate, sandwich server, 12½"	9-14
Sherbet, footed stem	5- 9
Vases, wall pin-up, 6½", ea.	10-18

Bee Hive (Prisma Line)
Hazel Atlas Glass Co., factories in Ohio, Pennsylvania, and West Virginia, 1939. Crystal, pink.

	Cry'l	Pink
Bowl, berry, tab handles	3- 7	4- 8
Bowl, fruit, tab handles	6-11	7-12
Butter dish, covered	10-15	14-21
Creamer	5-10	6-11
Plate, cake, covered	17-26	
Sugar, flat, covered	5-10	6-11

Blossoms and Bands
Jenkins Glass Co., Kokomo, Ind., 1927-1928. Crystal, clear green, clear pink, iridescent, marigold.

	Cry'l	Pink Gr'n	M'gd Irid't
Bowl, berry or salad, 7¼"	7-12	11-16	15- 24
Bowl, individual berry	5- 9	9-15	10- 15
Lamp, sewing	38-47	67-77	168-192

Cameo
Anchor-Hocking Glass Co., Lancaster, Ohio, 1930-1934. Crystal, green, topaz, with or without platinum trim; pink.

	Gr'n Topaz Cry'l Plat. Trim	Pink
Bowl, console, 3 legs, 11"	39-52	47-55
Bowl, master berry, 8¼"	11-19	
Bowl, salad, 7¼"	9-17	
Candlestick, 3¾"	21-30	
Cookie jar w/cover	25-31	
Creamer, footed, cone, 4¼"	8-13	32-41
Creamer, footed, round bowl, 3¼"	9-14	
Plate, dinner, 9½"	8-15	22-31
Plate, serving, 10"	13-21	
Sherbet, footed, 3⅛"	8-11	
Tumbler, juice, 5"	13-17	25-34
Tumbler, table, 9-oz.	12-19	32-41
Vase, swelled shape, 8"	18-27	
Vinegar bottle (ill.)	24-29	
Water bottle, cork stopper	21-29	

Cherry Blossom
Jeannette Glass Co., 1930-1939. Crystal, delphite, green, jadeite, pink, rose.

Depression Glass

165

(continued)

	Pink Rose	Gr'n	Delphite
Bowl, cereal, 5¾"	8-13	7- 13	14- 23
Bowl, salad, handled, 9"	15-24	17- 26	29- 31
Bowl, 3 legs, 10½"	26-33	115-132	114-133
(If jadeite, $230+; crystal $14-22)			
Creamer, 3¼"	8-14	9- 17	20- 29
Plate, cake, legs, 10¼"	12-20	18- 28	27- 38
Plate, dinner, 9"	8-12	9- 17	17- 24
Plate, oval, 11"	14-20	18-24	
Plate, sherbet, 6"	6-11	7- 12	12- 20
Sherbet, round foot	8-12	9- 14	15- 24
Tumbler, cone, round foot, 9-oz.	16-22	17- 25	27- 36
Tumbler, flat, banded, 5-oz. (Crystal $6-9) ..	10-14	12- 18	

Cloverleaf
Hazel Atlas Glass Co., 1930-1936. Black, crystal, green, topaz.

	Topaz	Black	Pink Gr'n Cry'l
Ashtray, 5¾"		72-78	
Bowl, cereal, 5"	7-11		7-11
Bowl, dessert (or berry), 4" .	7-11		17-24
Candy dish, covered	52-60		42-51
Creamer, footed, 3⅝"	8-12	11-19	8-13
Plate, grill, 10¼"			7-14
Plate, salad or luncheon, 8"	7-13	14-19	7-12
Salt/pepper shakers, pr. ...	71-79	53-62	28-38
Sherbet, footed stem, 3-oz. ..	8-13	18-25	6-11
Tumbler, flat, table, 8½-oz.	12-21		12-20
Tumbler, footed cone, 13-oz.	14-21		11-18

Colonial Petals
U.S. Glass Co., 1928-1931. Green, salmon pink. Prices are for both colors.

Creamer, 4½"	8-14
Salt/pepper shakers, silver-plated cone lids, 3¾", pr.....................	12-19
Sugar, 3½"	8-15
Tumbler, footed	13-17

Cube (Cubist)
Jeannette Glass Co., 1929-1933. Crystal, green, pink.

	Pink Cry'l	Gr'n
Bowl, salad, 6½"	7-13	8-14
Bowl, serving, 4½".............	5- 9	7-11
Butter dish, w/lid	42-51	53-62
Candy jar w/cover	15-22	15-25
Creamer, 3"	6-12	7-12
Cup	4- 7	6- 9
Plate, dessert or sherbet, 6"	3- 6	15-22
Plate, salad, 8"	5-10	7-11
Salt/pepper shakers, pr.	22-31	32-38
Sherbet, stemmed, footed, 5-oz.....	4- 9	5- 9
Tumbler, table, 4-oz., 9-oz., ea.	10-15	13-22

Diamond Point Columns
Hazel Atlas Glass Co. (?), 1920-1930s. Crystal, clear green, clear pink; also iridescent—listed in Carnival books.

	Gr'n Pink	Cry'l
Bowl, master berry, 7¼"	10-18	7-11
Bowl, salad, 6¼"	9-12	7-12
Butter dish w/cover, table, 6¾" ..	33-44	16-25
Creamer, 4"	8-12	6-11
Plate, sherbet liner, 5⅞"	5- 7	3- 7
Sherbet, footed stem	5- 7	4- 8
Sugar, cylinder	8-12	5-11
Tumbler, table, 9-oz.	9-13	5-11

Diana (Swirled Sharp Rib)
Federal Glass Co., Columbus, Ohio, 1937-1941. Crystal, golden glow, pink. Prices are for all colors.

Ashtray	6- 9
Bowl, cream soup, handled............	9-16
Bowl, salad, 9"	8-15
Child's set: rack w/6 each cups, saucers, plates (also called demitasse set), all	73-82
Plate, bread and butter, 6⅛"	5- 7
Plate, dinner, 9⅜"	5-10
Plate, sandwich, 11¾"	8-12
Salt/pepper shakers, pr.	28-37
Tumbler, table, 9-oz.	9-16

Floral
Jeannette Glass Co., 1931-1935. Crystal, emerald green, jadeite, pink, rose, other colors. Prices are for all colors except jadeite.

Bowl, salad, 7½"	13- 18
Bowl, vegetable, oval, 9"	16- 22
Bowl, vegetable, round, covered, 8" ...	17- 27
Candy jar, covered..............	28- 38
Coaster, 3¼"	6- 9
Creamer, flat bottom, cylinder	9- 13
Pitcher, lemonade, 10¼"	160-177
Pitcher, water, 8".............	32- 40
Plate, dinner, 8⅞"..............	8- 12
Plate, salad, 8"	7- 11
Refrigerator box, covered, 4¾" sq.....	17- 25
(Same in jadeite $15-22)	
Salt/pepper shakers, pr..............	27- 37
Tumbler, footed cone, 7-oz.	12- 19
Tumbler, footed cone, juice, 4"	10- 18

Heritage
Federal Glass Co., 1940s-1960s. Crystal, Madonna blue, pink, spring green.

	Cry'l	Pink, Spr'g Gr'n	Md'na Blue
Bowl, berry (or salad), 8½"..	8-15	12-18	16-25
Bowl, fruit, 10½"	10-13	12-18	17-25
Bowl, sauce, 5"	7-11	8-12	9-15
Creamer, footed	6- 9		
Cup, 3⅝"	6-10		
Plate, bread and butter	3- 8		
Plate, dinner, 9¼"	6- 8		
Plate, salad, 8"	3- 7		
Plate, server, 12"	6-13		

Hobstars Intaglio
Imperial Glass Co., late 1920s, early 1930s. Crystal, green, pink. Prices are for all colors.

Bowl, individual berry	7-12

Bowl, master berry 17-27
Creamer, scalloped edge 15-24
Plate, cake (or sandwich) 16-25
Plate, dessert, 7" 7-12
Sugar, scalloped edge 16-24

Lace Edge (Open Lace)
Hocking Glass Co., mid-1930s. Crystal, frosted, pink. Prices are for all colors.

Bowl, cereal, 6³⁄₈" 8-12
Bowl, flower, ribbed sides 21-29
Bowl, salad, 7³⁄₄" 9-14
Butter (or bonbon), covered 18-27
Candy jar, covered, ribbed sides 13-22
Compote, covered, footed 16-26
Compote, open, footed, 7" 28-36
Creamer, ribbed sides 10-17
Plate, dinner, grill, 10½", ea. 9-13
Plate, salad, 8³⁄₈" 7-11
Plate, serving, 3-partition, 13" 11-16
Sherbet, footed stem 21-27
Sugar, ribbed sides 11-18
Vase, 7" 21-29

Madrid
Federal Glass Co., 1932-1939. Crystal, golden glow, Madonna blue, rose glow, spring green.

	Cry'l Golden Glow Rose Glow	Spring Green	Madonna Blue
Bowl, individual berry, 5"	5- 9	7- 11	10- 15
Bowl, master berry, 8"	11-15	15- 22	18- 27
Bowl, vegetable, oval, 10"	11-17	13- 19	20- 28
Butter dish, covered	69-78	95-109	171-186
Candlesticks, 2¼", pr.	19-27		
Cracker jar, covered	34-42	61- 70	
Creamer, footed . . .	6-10	7- 11	16- 27
Pitcher, square, 60-oz.	37-45	88- 98	162-172
Pitcher, swelled, 80-oz.	55-70	148-164	
Plate, dinner, 10⁵⁄₈"	14-20	14- 21	19- 28
Plate, grill, 10⁵⁄₈"	9-12	11- 18	11- 18
Plate, salad, 7½"	6-11	8- 12	10- 16
Salt/pepper shakers, pr.	28-33	39- 49	108-126
Sherbet, cone shape, footed	7-11	8- 12	13- 18
Tumbler, blown, footed cone, 10-oz.	14-21	17- 28	
Tumbler, blown, iced tea, 12-oz.	14-19	17- 22	21- 31
Tumbler, blown, juice, 5-oz.	7-12	9- 13	13- 19

Miss America
Hocking Glass Co., early 1930s-1937. Crystal, apple green, green, honey amber, pink, cerise.

	Cry'l	Pink Cerise	H'y Amber	Gr'n Apple Gr'n
Bowl, cereal, 6¼"	7-11	8- 14		
Bowl, fruit, 7³⁄₄"	27-37	36- 45		
Bowl, sauce (or berry), 4½" .				8-12
Bowl, vegetable, oval, 10"	14-22	19- 26		
Butter dish, covered	57-67	248-270		
Celery tray, 10½"	11-16	14- 22		
Creamer, footed	11-15	12- 18		
Compote, 5"	10-17	14- 19		
Goblet, 4³⁄₄" high	9-12	12- 16	11-17	
Goblet, 10"	12-19	16- 22	17-27	
Pitcher, ice lip, 65-oz.	47-56	56- 64	62-70	
Pitcher, no ice lip, 65-oz. . . .	38-47	44- 52	47-56	
Plate, bread and butter, 6³⁄₄"	5-10	7- 11		
Plate, cake, footed, 12" .	19-27	21- 27		
Plate, dinner, 10¼"	9-14	12- 18		
Plate, salad, 8½"	7-12	10- 14		
Platter, oval, 12"	12-19	13- 19		
Salt/pepper shakers, footed, pr. . .	25-36	24- 34		
Sherbet, footed stem, 5-oz. . . .	8-11	9- 12		9-14
Tidbit server, 2-tier	16-22	20- 27		

New Century
Hazel Atlas Glass Co., late 1920s-1935. Amethyst, crystal, cobalt, green, pink.

	Am'st Cobalt	Gr'n Pink Cry'l
Bowl, individual berry, 4½"	7-11	5- 9
Bowl, master berry, 8"	13-17	9-12
Butter dish, covered, 6³⁄₄"	59-69	47-57
Creamer, footed, 3³⁄₄"	12-17	9-12
Cup, 2³⁄₄"	7- 9	6- 9
Decanter w/stopper	39-48	29-37
Pitcher, 60-oz.	32-41	27-37
Pitcher, ice guard, 80-oz.	43-51	28-37
Plate, dinner, grill, 10", ea.	9-12	8-12
Plate, salad, 8½"	8-10	7-11
Salt/pepper shakers, pr.	19-24	14-19
Saucer, 5³⁄₈"	5- 8	3- 6
Tumbler, highball, 10-oz.	12-17	8-12

(continued)

Tumbler, iced tea, 12-oz. 14-19 10-17
Tumbler, juice, 5-oz. 10-15   9-12
Tumbler, juice, footed 5-oz. 10-14   7-11
Wine, footed stem 14-19 10-14

No. 600 (Modern Art)
Indiana Glass Co., 1920s-1930s. Crystal, frosted on crystal, green, pink.

	Pink Gr'n Cry'l	Frosted on Cry'l
Banana split, footed, 7½"	8-12	
Bowl, finger	7-11	
Bowl, oval, 9½"	19-27	
Bowl, master berry, 8½"	10-17	
Candlestick, irregular rim	8-13	
Creamer, berry, large, footed, 4"	8-12	
Ice bucket, metal bail handle	17-27	
Plate, dessert, sundae or sherbet liner	4- 8	4- 7
Plate, salad, 8½"	8-12	8-12
Plate, sandwich tray, 10½"	11-17	
Sandwich server, center glass handle	19-27	
Sundae, low foot, 3¼"	6- 9	
Sugar jar, spout, metal cover	14-22	
Tumbler, flat bottom, 12-oz.	8-14	
Tumbler, footed, tapered, milk shake, 12-oz.	12-19	9-18
Tumbler, 6-oz.	5- 9	5- 9
Vase, bud, slender, 11"	12-19	
Vase, crimped rim, 11"	27-37	

Peacock and Rose
Paden City Glass Co., Paden City, W.Va., 1930s. Emerald green, rose-pink. Prices are for both colors.

Bowl, console, 11"	15-22
Bowl, footed, 8½"	12-19
Bowl, fruit, handles, 8½"	13-18
Candlestick, rolled top, 5"	6-12
Candy dish, covered, footed, 7" high.....	12-19
Compote, footed, 6"	11-19
Compote, mayonnaise, 3-pc. w/liner plate, ladle	24-32
Creamer, footed, 4"	7-10
Ice tub, tab handles, 5¾"	11-19
Plate, cake, footed, 11"	10-18
Relish dish, 3 compartments, covered, 6¼" dia.	11-19
Sandwich tray, center handle, 10½" dia. .	10-19
Sugar, footed, 4"	7-11

Pressed Hobnail and Diamond
Hocking Glass Co., 1930s. Green, rose, topaz.

	Gr'n	Rose	Topaz
Bowl, Hocking handles, 10"	11-18	9-14	8-12
Bowl, low centerpiece, 11" .	12-22	10-19	10-18
Bowl, salad, Hocking side handles, 9"	8-16	7-12	6-11
Plate, cake, 12"	10-17	8-12	8-12
Plate, salad, 8"	5- 8	4- 8	4- 8

Princess
Hocking Glass Co., 1931-1935. Apricots, crystal, green, pink, topaz.

	Topaz Apr't	Gr'n Pink Cry'l
Ashtray, 4½"	6-10	5-10
Bowl, individual berry, 4½" ...	5- 8	4- 8
Bowl, salad, octagon, tab handles, 9"	9-16	8-14
Bowl, vegetable, oval, 10"	10-16	8-15
Butter dish, covered, 7½" dia. ..		62-72
Cookie jar w/cover, 7" high	18-26	14-21
Creamer, oval, flange rim	7-12	6-11
Pitcher, juice, 37-oz.	32-41	20-28
Pitcher, 60-oz.	48-57	35-44
Plate, cake, 10"	12-17	10-14
Plate, dinner, grill, 9½", ea....	7-11	5-11
Plate, sandwich, handled, 11½"		8-12
Plate, sherbet liner, 5½"	4- 8	4- 8
Relish dish, 4-part, 7½"	12-17	8-12
Salt/pepper shakers, 4½", pr. ..	39-47	15-24
Salt/pepper shakers, 5½", pr. ..		24-30
Sherbet, footed, stem, blown ...	5- 7	5- 9
Tumbler, iced tea	12-19	12-18
Tumbler, juice, 5-oz.	9-15	10-16
Tumbler, juice, 9-oz.		10-16
Vase, 8"		14-21

Rosemary (Dutch Rose)
Federal Glass Co., 1935-1937. Crystal, golden glow, rose glow, spring green.

	Spr'g Gr'n	Rose Glow G'ldn Glow Cry'l
Bowl, cereal, 6"	7-11	4- 8
Bowl, cream soup, 5"	9-13	7-12
Bowl, vegetable, oval..........	11-20	10-17
Cup	8-14	4- 9
Creamer, footed, 4"	10-16	5-11
Plate, dinner, grill, 9½", ea......	7-11	5- 9
Plate, salad (or dessert), 6¾" ..	5- 9	4- 8
Saucer	4- 7	3- 5
Tumbler, table, 9-oz.	16-21	11-17

Royal Lace
Hazel Atlas Glass Co., 1934-1941. Amethyst (special orders only), cobalt, crystal, green, pink.

	C'blt	Gr'n	Cry'l Pink
Ashtray, 3½"		10- 13	9-12
Bowl, fruit, 3 legs, 10"	29- 34	27- 34	15-22
Bowl, individual berry, 5"	11- 15	9- 15	5- 9
Bowl, master berry, 10"	25- 32	21- 29	11-19
Butter dish and cover	228-245	228-245	75-85
Candlestick, flared edge	25- 32	20- 28	14-19
Candlestick, ruffled edge	24- 33	21- 29	14-19
Cracker jar w/glass cover	71- 77	47- 54	34-39
Cracker jar w/metal cover	73- 83		
(Amethyst .. $93-103)			

168

Creamer, footed 23- 29 26- 31 8-12
Pitcher, ice guard,
80-oz. 79- 94 120-131 41-50
Pitcher, no ice lip,
60-oz. 72- 85 97-108 40-51
Pitcher, no ice lip,
96-oz. 136-150 129-132 44-51
Plate, dinner, 9⅞" ... 18- 22 12- 16 7-11
Plate, grill, 9¾" 17- 22 13- 16 8-11
Plate, luncheon, 8⅜" . 14- 19 8- 11 6- 9
Sherbet, all glass,
footed 19- 27 12- 18 9-12
Sherbet, in metal
holder 24- 30
Sugar, footed 22- 29 25- 32 8-11
Tumbler, juice, 5-oz. . 16- 20 15- 22 10-14
Tumbler, table, 9-oz. . 22- 28 19- 25 12-17
Tumbler, either
height, 12-oz. 26- 31 19- 27 12-19

Tiered Semi-Optic

Paden Glass Co., 1927-1933. Amber, crystal, green, pink. Prices are for all colors.

Banana split dish, 8½" long 8-12
Bowl, console, 14" 14-23
Creamer, 6-oz. 5- 8
Goblet, footed, 8-oz. 4- 7
Goblet, footed, malted milk, 10-oz. ... 5-10
Goblet, iced tea, 12-oz. 7-11
Oyster cocktail, footed, 3½-oz. 5- 9
Parfait glass, 5-oz. 6-11
Pickle (or banana split) dish, 8¼" 7-11
Plate, coaster for tumblers, 6" 4- 8
Plate, sandwich (or salad), 8" 5- 9
Sundae, high footed, 5½-oz. 7-11
Sundae, low footed, 4½-oz. 5-10
Tumbler, cola, cupped rim, 6-oz. 4- 8
Tumbler, cupped rim, phosphate or water,
8-oz. 6- 9
Tumbler, iced tea, 12-oz. 7-12
Water jug, ½-gal. 21-27

Vitrock Kitchen Line

Hocking Glass Co., 1935-1936.
Ashtray, match holder, 2 rests, plain 6-11
Dripping jar w/cover 7-12
Bowls, mixing, 6½", 7½", 8½", ea. 4- 9
Bowls, mixing, 9½", 10½", 11½", ea. 6-12
Egg cups on standard 5- 9
Entire range set, 4 pcs. 26-36
Leftovers jar and cover 7-12
Orange reamer, table 9-15
Orange reamer, utility, for bowl or cup.... 6-11
Range set, shakers, ea. 6-10

Waffle (Waterford)

Hocking Glass Division of Anchor Hocking, 1938-1944. Crystal, forest green, pink.

	Cry'l	Pink
Ashtray, 4"	3- 6	3- 5
Bowl, cereal (or sauce), 5½"	3- 6	4- 9
Bowl, individual berry, 4¾"	3- 6	3- 7
Bowl, master berry, 8¼"	4- 6	5-10
Butter dish with cover	27-39	51-60
Creamer, oval	3- 6	4- 7

Pitcher, ice lip, 80-oz. 21-29 28-35
Pitcher, juice, ice guard, 42-oz......10-16
Plate, dinner, 9½" 4- 7 5- 9
Plates, salad, 7⅛"; liner, 6", ea..... 3- 6 4- 7
Salt/pepper shakers, pr. 6-11
Sherbet, footed stem, scalloped rim. 5- 9
Sherbet, footed stem, smooth rim .. 3- 6 4- 9
Tumbler, table, footed, 10-oz....... 5-10 7-12
Vase, 6¾" 5- 9 7-13
(Forest green $10-15)

Windsor

Hocking Glass Co., 1930s. Apple green, crystal, pink, ruby.

	Pink Ruby Apple Green	Cry'l
Pitcher, 85-oz.	27-35	12-20
Pitcher, 64-oz.	15-23	8-14
Tumbler, ice tea, flat bottom, 12-oz.	6-11	4- 9
Tumbler, juice, 5-oz.	3- 6	3- 6
Tumbler, juice, 9-oz.	4- 8	3- 6

Windsor Diamond

Jeannette Glass Co., 1936-1946. Crystal, green, wild rose.

	Cry'l	Wild Rose	Gr'n
Ashtray	3- 6	4- 9	4-10
Bowl, individual berry, 4¾"	3- 6	3- 5	4- 7
Butter dish with cover	29-36		
Compote, covered, tall	9-12		
Pitcher, juice	9-15	10-18	10-19
Pitcher, milk, 16-oz.	5-11	10-18	12-23
Pitcher, table, 52-oz.	12-21	22-32	24-32
Plate, salad, 7"	3- 5	3- 6	3- 6
Plate, sandwich, handles, 10¼"	6-10	6-11	7-14
Plates, chop, 13⅝"; serving, 13½", ea.	5- 9	6-11	6-11
Tray, 4" sq.	3- 7	4- 8	7-10
Tray, oblong, 4⅛"×9"	4- 8	7-12	8-13
Tumbler, iced tea, 12-oz.	6-10	8-11	8-13
Tumbler, juice, 3¼"	4- 8	6-12	8-12

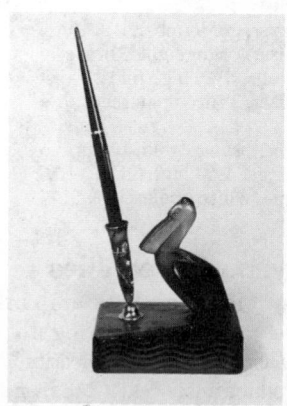

Desk Sets

(continued)

Desk Sets

Every type, from the lowliest to the most expensive, was in vogue until the invention of the ink-filled pen.

Brass desk set, French, mid-1800s, signed M. Bounel . . .	$ 460- 520
Desk set, brass, cut glass inkwells, early 1900s	108- 121
Desk set, iron, 2 inkwells, footed, mid-1800s	61- 70
Paperweight type, pelican, signed Davesen (ill.)	78- 82
Tiffany desk set, 5 pieces, signed Tiffany Studios, bronze/glass	975-1,250
Tiffany desk set, 6 pieces, Spider Web, signed and numbered	1,450-1,700

DeVilbiss

DeVilbiss

Steuben made both atomizers and cologne sets for this company. All pieces are signed DeVILBISS.

Atomizer, black satin glass, orange enamel floral, brass fittings, 5½″ high (ill.)	$ 55- 63
Atomizer, blue opalescent, 6″ high	52- 60
Atomizer, gold/amber, 4¼″ high .	51- 60
Atomizer, orange/gold, brass fittings, 5½″ high (ill.)	57- 64
Atomizer, white opalescent, 5¾″ high	48- 58
Cologne, orange/gold, brass fittings, 4½″ high (ill.)	57- 67
Cologne, white opalescent, 5½″ high	47- 57

Disneyana Collectibles

Mickey Mouse watches are out of sight, pricewise. Anything relating to the early days of Disney is highly collectible. Look out for reproductions! See **Clubs and Publications**, this Price Guide.

Disneyana Collectibles

Davey Crockett pocket knife . . .	$ 32- 42
Donald Duck bank, plastic	58- 68
Donald Duck watch, Ingersoll, 1939, marked WDP (ill.)	242-252
Dopey figurine, chalkware, 4″ high	39- 49
Dumbo creamer	28- 38
Mickey and Minnie Mouse figurines, painted, ea.	67- 73
Mickey Mouse alphabet bowl, cereal premium	58- 68
Mickey Mouse clock, Ingersoll, 1930s	520+
Mickey Mouse dishes, child's service for 6, Japan	130-150
Mickey Mouse watch, Ingersoll, metal band, running condition	282-298
Pluto mug, Japan	58- 68
Pluto pencil sharpener	24- 33
Snow White and 7 Dwarfs cottage cheese glass, milk company premium, set	172-182
Snow White fork	40- 50
Snow White watch, running condition	148-158

Doll Furniture

Doll Furniture and Accessories

See **Clubs and Publications**, this Price Guide.

Bed, complete with spread,
blue finish . . . . $ 42- 50
Bedroom set, 5-pc.: bed, tin
washstand, table, 2
chairs, oak, 1" scale, all 158-168
Birdcage with bird 54- 64
Bird's-eye maple bed, 4"×21",
slats, handmade quilt 252-270
Bookcases, balsa wood, pr. 35- 42
Booth table, 3 pcs., all 35- 46
Brass bed, 4"×19", springs,
pad, spread, all 221-241
Candelabra, pot metal, 2" high . . 20- 29
Chair, ladderback, 4" high 27- 34
Chair, wicker rocker, 2½" high . . 29- 39
Cradle, hand-carved, 12"×16" . . 49- 54
Cradle, hand-carved, walnut,
13½" high to hood, pre-Civil
War 128-142
Desk, dropfront, matching
chair, both 45- 55
Desk, wooden, brass pulls,
6¼" high (ill.) 93-104
Fireplace tools with stand,
6 pcs., all 19- 22
Knives and forks, service for
12, complete, all 55- 65
Living room suite, 6 pcs.,
complete, all 67- 77
Stove, 4-burner, 4" high 38- 47
Trunk for doll clothes 87- 94
Wicker porch set, 4 pcs.:
swing, settee, 2 chairs, all 124-132

Dolls

This category is one of the most popular and is getting more expensive every day. Just know your dolls or get a book and study. *The Price Guide to Dolls,* Wallace-Homestead Book Co., Des Moines, Iowa 50305, $10.95, is considered the best price guide by most of the knowledgeable doll collectors and dealers. See **Clubs and Publications,** this Price Guide.

All Bisque
German, brown bisque,
unmarked; socket head,
mohair wig, inset glass
eyes, open mouth, molded
teeth; jointed at shoulders
and hips, 4½" tall . . . . $ 155- 188
German, Cupid's sister,
marked 10414 Germany;
molded/painted hair and
features, upside-down bows;
jointed at shoulders and
hips, 5¼" tall 142- 172

German, Indian, mark on foot
not readable; molded/
painted hair and features,
loincloth and sandals,
2¼" tall 59- 70
German, marked 2/0; molded/
painted hair and features;
jointed at shoulders and
hips; molded/painted shoes
and socks, 3½" tall 128- 152
German, marked 5 D 3 1/2 10;
molded/painted hair and
features; jointed at
shoulders and hips; molded/
painted shoes and socks,
6" tall 147- 169
German, marked 83 N 100;
mohair wig, glass sleep
eyes, open mouth; jointed at
shoulders and hips; molded/
painted shoes and socks,
6½" tall 215- 246
German (?), marked 3701 1;
mohair wig, glass inset
eyes, open/closed mouth;
jointed at shoulders and
hips; molded/painted shoes
and socks, 4¾" tall 155- 170
German, marked Germany;
mohair wig, glass inset
eyes, closed mouth; jointed
at shoulders and hips;
molded/painted shoes and
socks, 3½" tall 126- 163
German, marked HEUBACH
(in a square) 9748 4; molded/
painted hair and features,
5" tall 218- 261
German (?), marked three leaf
clover P 23; molded/painted
boy-style hair and features,
shoes and socks; jointed at
shoulders and hips,
5½" tall 142- 170
German (?), molded/painted
hair and features; jointed
at shoulders and hips;
original clothing, 1¾" tall 49- 61
German, Nodder, marked
Germany; molded/painted
hair, features, hat, clothes,
shoes, and socks; swivel/
nodding head, 3" tall 49- 67
German, Snow Baby, marked
Germany (ink stamp);
molded/painted features;
molded snowsuit, 2½" tall . 49- 61
German, unmarked; mohair
wig, molded/painted fea-
tures; jointed at shoulders
and hips; molded/painted
shoes and socks, 3" tall 145- 172

(continued)

German (?), unmarked; molded/painted hair, features, stocking cap, clothes, shoes, and knee-length socks; jointed at shoulders, 8″ tall 162- 181

Japanese, bride and groom, stone bisque, marked JAPAN; molded/painted hair and features; jointed at shoulders, 3″ tall, pr. 71- 88

Japanese (?), fine quality stone bisque, marked SHINOOA (indistinguishable symbol); painted hair, molded/painted features; jointed at shoulders and hips; painted shoes, original costume, 4″ tall 48- 59

Japanese, marked JAPAN; molded/painted hair, features, clothes, shoes, and socks, 3½″ tall 27- 35

Japanese, marked JOLLIKID NIPPON (on a sticker); molded/painted hair, features, and clothes; jointed at shoulders, 3½″ tall 39- 47

Composition Dolls

Amberg, Louis & Son, Vanta Baby, shoulder head, marked VANTA BABY AMBERG; molded/painted hair, metal sleep eyes, open/closed mouth; cloth body, compo arms and legs, 14″ long, 10″ head circumference 150- 175

Arranbee Doll Company, swivel head, marked R & B; mohair wig, plastic sleep eyes, closed mouth; jointed at shoulders and hips, 18″ tall 155- 175

Cameo Doll Company, Kewpie, molded/painted hair and features; paper label on body reads KEWPIE Reg. U.S. Pat. Off.; sticker on bottom of feet reads ROSE O'NEILL (KEWPIES—REG-U-S-PAT.-OFF-III-4-1913); jointed at shoulders, 9″ tall 265- 320

Cameo Doll Company, Scootles, swivel head, molded/painted hair, painted eyes, closed mouth, jointed body, 14½″ tall 295- 330

Cameo Doll Company, swivel head, painted hair, painted eyes, closed mouth, compo body, wood jointed arms and legs; label reads BETTY BOOP, 12½″ tall 595- 650

Change-O-Doll Company, Family Doll, interchangeable compo heads, unmarked; head with smiling face has mohair wig and molded/painted features; head with crying face has molded/painted hair and features; brass screw coupling inside neck; cloth body, threaded neck plug, compo arms and legs, 16″ tall 595- 675

Doll Craft Novelty Corporation, Lone Ranger, compo flange head, molded/painted hair, painted eyes, closed mouth; cloth body, compo hands and feet. All original with tag, 16½″ tall 465- 550

Effanbee, Candy Kid, swivel head marked EFFANBEE; molded/painted hair, plastic sleep eyes, closed mouth; toddler body marked EFFANBEE; jointed at shoulders and hips, 12½″ tall 165- 190

Effanbee, swivel head marked EFFANBEE; lamb's wool wig, glass-like flirty eyes, closed mouth; compo jointed baby body, 20″ tall 162- 190

Freundlich, jointed at shoulders and hips; molded/painted hair, painted eyes, closed mouth; tag reads Gen. MacArthur, The Man of the Hour. All original, 18½″ tall 360- 420

Horsman, Baby Bumps, brown compo head marked E.I.H. c (in a circle); brown bald head, molded/painted features, flange neck; cloth body, compo hands, brown sateen legs; cloth label on body reads Copyright 1910 by E.I. HORSMAN, 12″ tall, 9″ head circumference 295- 335

Ideal, Flossie Flirt, head marked U.S. IDEAL (in a diamond) OF A.; saran wig, metal flirting sleep eyes, open mouth; cloth body, voice box, compo arms and legs, 20″ tall 165- 220

Dolls

Ideal, Pinocchio, swivel head
marked Cop W.D.P.
IDEAL DOLL; molded/
painted hair, painted eyes,
closed mouth; compo/wood
jointed body, molded/
painted clothes, 11″ tall ...   185- 240

Ideal, Shirley Temple, swivel
head marked SHIRLEY
TEMPLE C/OP (inside)
IDEAL N & T CO.; mohair
wig, plastic sleep eyes,
open mouth; body marked
SHIRLEY TEMPLE;
jointed at shoulders and
hips. All original, 19½″
tall   925-1,000

Ideal, swivel head marked
13 SHIRLEY TEMPLE
Copy IDEAL N & T Co.;
mohair wig, glass-like sleep
eyes, open mouth; compo
jointed body marked SHIR-
LEY TEMPLE. Original
trunk, all clothing, 13″
tall, complete (ill.) 795- 825

Lee, H.D. Company, Inc.,
jointed at shoulders;
molded/painted hair,
painted eyes, closed mouth;
label on pants reads Union
Made LEE Reg. U.S. Pat.
Off., 12½″ tall 158- 178

Reliable Toy Company, swivel
head, nylon wig, plastic
sleep eyes, open mouth,
compo jointed body; label
reads HER HIGHNESS
CORONATION DOLL. All
original, 15½″ tall 145- 170

Unmarked, American Wave,
jointed at shoulders and
hips; molded/painted cap
and hair, painted eyes,
closed mouth; tag reads
W.A.V.E.S. All original,
14½″ tall 110- 135

Unmarked, Snow White and
Seven Dwarfs, jointed at
shoulders and hips; molded/
painted hair, painted eyes,
closed mouth. Dwarfs, 8″
tall, ea. 56- 64
Snow White, 13½″ tall 120- 135

Creche Dolls

Terra-cotta shoulder head,
molded/painted hair, inset
glass eyes, closed mouth;
hemp body, detailed
wooden hands and feet.
All original, 20″ tall 810- 900

Wooden creche set, all hand-
carved by Tita Ling; carved/
painted hair and beard
(Mary has human hair wig);
glass inset eyes, hair upper
and lower lashes; closed
mouth, carved/painted
treasures and sandals;
animals are carved/painted
with painted eyes. Very
fine detail, 3½″ tall to
11½″ tall, 14 pcs., all   950-1,300

Foreign, in Native Costume

China, actor in Chinese opera,
plaster head, molded/
painted features, ornate
molded/painted paper head-
dress; Chinese symbols on

Dolls

(continued)

back of neck; paper-covered
straw-like wooden torso,
mache hands, wood/metal
legs, painted wooden shoes.
All original, 12″ tall 210- 252
China, General Kuan Yu,
plaster-type head, molded/
painted ornate hat; long
hair attached inside holes
on each side of head; long
beard inserted in slash
above mouth; molded rust-
painted face, painted features; paper-covered straw-
like wooden body, mache
hands, plaster-type shoes;
costume lined with paper
printed in Chinese. All
original, 10″ tall 245- 270
England (?), knight in armor,
wooden head, painted eyes,
closed mouth; cloth body,
woven metal armor, 8″
tall 52- 61
Greece, cloth head, mohair
wig, molded/painted fea-
tures; unjointed hard plastic body. All original,
7½″ tall 24- 33
Japan, girl in kimono, mache
head, human hair wig, inset
glass eyes, closed mouth;
cardboard body, mache
arms and legs, 14″ tall 132- 150
Japan, nobility dolls, mache
head, human hair wig, inset
glass eyes, closed mouth;
cardboard body, wooden
hands and feet, 3½″ tall . . . 98- 107
Japan, Samurai warriors,
mache head, inset glass
eyes, closed mouth; cloth
body, wooden hands and
feet, 8½″ tall 240- 265
Latvia, dancers, cloth head,
floss and yarn hair, yarn
face, embroidered features;
cloth and wire body,
crochet-covered wire hands,
crocheted clothes. All ori-
ginal, 7″ tall 72- 80
Norway, girl, molded cloth
head, hands, and feet;
mohair wig, painted eyes,
closed mouth; cloth body,
9″ tall 34- 44
Poland, celluloid head, silky
fine thread-type hair;
molded/painted features; all
cloth body. All original,
14″ tall 42- 52
Russia, all cloth, molded/
painted features, string

Dolls

wrapped around legs, straw
woven shoes. All original,
6″ tall (ill.) 34- 46
Russia, boy and girl, mache
head, mohair wig, painted
eyes, closed mouth, 4″
tall, ea. 28- 35
Russia, Cosaque boy and
Kazakh village girl, all
cloth, mohair wig, painted
eyes, closed mouth, 7″
tall, ea. 77- 88

French Bisque, Characters
Lanternier & Cie, Toto,
bisque socket head
marked DEPOSE TOTO
N3 Mialono SC A L & C
LIMOGES; human hair
wig, paperweight eyes,
open/closed mouth, two
molded teeth and tongue,
unusual expression;
mache/wood jointed body,
rare, 16″ tall 1,500- 1,800
S.F.B.J., bisque socket
head marked S.F.B.J.
250 PARIS 11; human
hair wig, glass sleep eyes,
open mouth; mache/wood
jointed body, very rare,
25″ tall 12,500-14,000
S.F.B.J., bisque socket
head marked UNIS
FRANCE (in an ellipse) 71
(below on left) 149 (below
on right) 251 8; human
hair wig, glass sleep
eyes, open/closed mouth,
two molded teeth and
tongue; mache/wood
jointed body, 17″ tall 1,800- 2,600

Dolls

S.F.B.J., Twirp, bisque
socket head marked
FRANCE S.F.B.J. 247
PARIS 4; human hair wig,
glass sleep eyes, open/
closed mouth; two molded
teeth and tongue; mache/
wood jointed body, 14″
tall 2,875- 3,650

French Bisque, Children
Bru Jne & Cie, bisque socket
head marked BRU Jne R
11; human hair wig,
paperweight eyes, open
mouth; mache/wood
jointed body, 24″ tall 2,975- 3,550
Company Unidentified,
Belton-type, bisque
socket head marked N or
W over 2; mache/wood
jointed body, 10½″ tall . . 830- 900
Fleischmann & Blodel,
bisque socket head
marked EDEN BEBE
PARIS 10 DEPOSE;
human hair wig, paper-
weight eyes, open mouth;
mache/wood jointed body,
23″ tall (ill.) 975- 1,200
Lanternier & Cie, bisque
socket head marked MON
CHERIE L. G. PARIS 6;
human hair wig, paper-
weight eyes, open/closed

mouth, molded porcelain
teeth; mache/wood jointed
body, mama pull cord,
16½″ tall 950- 1,200
Rabery & Delphieu, bisque
socket head marked R 4
D; human hair wig, paper-
weight eyes, closed
mouth; mache/wood
jointed body, 28½″
tall 2,700- 3,400
Rostal, M. (Henry), bisque
socket head marked 295
MON TRESOR 9; human
hair wig, paperweight
eyes, open mouth; mache/
wood jointed body, mama-
papa pull cords, 22″
tall 1,475- 1,875
Schmitt & Fils, bisque
socket head and torso
marked with crossed ham-
mers over SCH (inside
a shield); human hair
wig, paperweight eyes,
closed mouth; mache/
wood jointed body, rare,
14″ tall 7,300- 8,300
S.F.B.J., painted plaster-
bisque socket head
marked S F B J PARIS
3/0; mohair wig, glass
sleep eyes, closed mouth;
mache jointed body,
native costume; tag reads
Made in Martinique,
12½″ tall 340- 385
Steiner, Jules Nicholas, Bebe
Steiner, bisque socket
head marked J.
STEINER Bte S.D.G.D.
PARIS F.I. re A
7; human hair wig, paper-
weight eyes, closed
mouth; mache/wood
jointed body marked
LE PETIT PARI-
SIEN BEBE J.
STEINER MARQUE
DEPOSE MEDAILLE
D'OR PARIS L'
1889 (paper label),
15″ tall 3,500- 3,700
Steiner, Jules Nicholas,
bisque socket head
marked J. STEINER Bte
S.D.G.D. PARIS F.I. re A
7; human hair wig,
paperweight eyes, closed
mouth, all-metal jointed
body, 15½″ tall 3,650- 3,900

(continued)

French Bisque, Fashions

Unmarked, parian quality shoulder head, mohair wig, paperweight eyes, closed mouth; head bent forward looking down; kid body, individually wired and stitched fingers, 15″ tall 2,900- 3,400

Unmarked, swivel head on bisque shoulder plate, mohair wig, inset glass eyes, closed mouth; kid adult body, individually wired and stitched fingers, 11½″ tall 2,700- 3,300

Unmarked, swivel head on bisque shoulder plate, mohair wig, inset glass eyes, closed smiling mouth; kid adult body, individually stitched fingers, 16″ tall 3,100- 3,700

German Bisque, Babies

Alt, Beck & Gottschalck (?), Character, bisque socket head marked A.B. & G. 1322 (over) 55; human hair wig, glass sleep eyes, open mouth; mache/wood jointed body, 22″ long, 17″ head circumference 1,500-1,700

Averill, Madame Georgene, Character, bisque swivel head marked GEORGENE AVERILL 1005 3652 Germany; molded/painted hair, glass sleep eyes, open mouth, flange neck; cloth body, compo arms and legs, 22″ long, 14½″ head circumference 1,600-1,875

Kammer & Reinhardt, bisque socket head marked K STAR R S & H 122 32; human hair wig, glass sleep eyes, open mouth; mache/wood jointed body, 13½″ long, 10″ head circumference 550- 625

Kammer & Reinhardt, Character, bisque socket head marked K STAR 100 50; molded/painted hair, painted eyes, open/closed mouth; mache/wood jointed body, 19″ long, 14″ head circumference 975-1,550

Marseille, Armand, crying Dream Baby, bisque swivel head marked A M Germany 347/3; molded/painted hair, glass sleep eyes, open/ closed mouth; cloth body, compo hands, 12″ long, 10½″ head circumference .. 550- 650

Marseille, Armand, Oriental, olive color bisque socket head marked A ELLER (in a star) M Germany 4/K; painted hair, glass sleep eyes, closed mouth; olive color mache jointed body, 14½″ long, 12½″ head circumference 675- 725

Marseille, Armand, Rock-A-Bye, brown painted bisque head marked A.A. Germany 351/1 K; molded/painted hair, glass sleep eyes, open mouth; brown mache/wood jointed body, 13″ long, 10″ head circumference   ... 395- 450

Putnam, Grace Storey, Bye-Lo, bisque swivel head marked copr. BY GRACE S. PUTNAM MADE IN GERMANY; molded/painted hair, glass sleep eyes, closed mouth, flange neck; cloth body red ink stamped BY-LO-BABY Pat. Appl'd For, COPY BY GRACE STOREY PUTNAM; celluloid hands, 11″ long, 10″ head circumference. (Note: This doll has many fakes, right down to the tea stains on the dress front. The fakes have bisque hands.) 550- 675

Recknagel, Th., bisque socket head marked Germany 3 1/2 R. 138 A; molded/painted hair, glass sleep eyes, closed mouth; mache jointed body, 14″ long, 11″ head circumference 295- 365

Reinecke, Otto, Character, bisque socket head marked P.M. 23 Germany 4½; mohair wig, glass sleep eyes, open mouth; mache jointed body, 15″ long, 11½″ head circumference .. 450- 520

Schmidt, Franz & Company, Character, bisque socket head marked F.S. & Co. SIMON & HALBIG 1397 Made in Germany 52; mohair wig, glass sleep eyes, open mouth; mache/wood jointed body, 20″ long, 15″ head circumference 595- 675

Wolf, Louis & Company, Character, bisque socket head marked 152 L.W. & Co. (in a square) 7; mohair wig, glass sleep eyes, open mouth; mache jointed body, 15″ long, 12″ head circumference 395- 496

Wolf, Louis & Company, Character, bisque socket head marked 152 (over) 7; mohair wig, glass sleep eyes, open mouth; mache jointed body, 16″ long, 12½″ head circumference .. 395- 470

German Bisque, Characters

Bahr & Prochild, bisque socket head marked 678 B P (in a heart) Made in Germany; human hair wig, glass sleep eyes, open mouth; mache/wood jointed body, 19″ tall 775- 900

Heubach, Gebruder, bisque socket head marked 76 2 02 (GH sun segment mark) Germany; flocked hair, painted intaglio eyes, closed pouty mouth; mache jointed body, 12½″ tall 995-1,200

Heubach, Gebruder, bisque socket head marked 8192 Germany Gebruder Heubach G 1 H; mohair wig, glass sleep eyes, open mouth; mache/wood jointed body, 14½″ tall 675- 775

Heubach, Gebruder, bisque socket head marked 8192 Germany Gebruder Heubach (sun rays mark) G 2/0 1/2 H; mohair wig, glass sleep eyes, open mouth, 14″ tall 595- 685

Heubach, Gebruder, Whistling Jim, bisque flange head marked 5 57 74 HEUBACH (in a square) Germany; molded/painted hair, painted intaglio eyes, open whistling mouth; cloth excelsior-stuffed body, compo arms, squeaker in torso, 13½″ tall 1,600-1,900

Kammer & Reinhardt, bisque socket head marked 11 K (star) R SIMON HALBIG 115/A; mohair wig, glass sleep eyes, closed pouty mouth; mache/wood jointed body, 12½″ tall 2,900-3,350

German Bisque, Heubach Figurines

Black banjo player, sun seg-

ment mark on back, molded/painted hair, features, and clothes; intaglio eyes, open/closed mouth, upper and lower molded teeth, 5½″ tall 345- 425

Unmarked, boy with shovel, molded/painted hair and features, 9½″ tall 220- 245

Unmarked, molded/painted hair, features, and clothes, 8½″ tall 165- 195

German Bisque, Piano Babies

All bisque, sun segment mark on back; molded/painted hair, features, and clothes, intaglio eyes, 9″ long 245- 285

All bisque, sun segment mark on stomach; molded/painted hair, features, and clothes, intaglio eyes, 11″ long 250- 280

Marked, sun with rays; molded/painted hair, features, and clothes, intaglio eyes, 8″ long 250- 280

Unmarked, molded/painted hair, features, and clothes, intaglio eyes, 13½″ long ... 700-1,000

Miscellaneous Materials

Corn shuck, cornsilk hair, painted features, 9½″ tall 19- 27

Leather, Moroccan leather head, hands, and feet; molded/painted features; crude cloth body marked Tangier Africa 6-10-48; baby on shoulder. All original, 26″ tall 185- 220

Palmetto (?) fiber cloth, American Seminole Indian, stationary head, embroidered features; two babies cradled in arms, 10½″ tall 55- 70

Plaster-bisque, flange head, molded/painted hair and features; all cloth body, original clothes, 5¼″ tall .. 37- 46

Plaster W.P.A. project doll, molded plaster head, mohair wig, painted features, cotton wound, wire armature, plastic arms and legs. All original, 9½″ tall 95- 135

Papier-Mache Dolls

Greiner, Ludwig, mache shoulder head labeled Greiner's improved Patent

(continued)

Heads Pat. March 30th '58; molded/painted hair, painted eyes; cloth body, kid arms. All original 1,500-1,700

Ridley, R., mache shoulder head marked W.A.H. Nonpareil 3015; molded/painted hair and features, 6″ tall 275- 320

Superior, M & S, mache shoulder head labeled M & S SUPERIOR 2015; molded/painted hair, painted eyes; cloth body, mache arms, 20½″ tall 380- 425

Unmarked, black mache shoulder head, mohair wig, inset pupil-less glass eyes; cloth body, mache arms and legs, 9½″ tall 320- 370

Unmarked, jockey, mache head and body (one piece); molded/painted hair, molded and cloth bill cap; painted eyes, wooden hands on wire arms, kid legs, molded/painted mache boots. All original, 9½″ tall 365- 435

Unmarked, mache head in wooden cradle, squeak box. All original, 3″ long 235- 375

Unmarked, mache shoulder head, human hair wig, inset glass eyes; cloth body, kid arms, 29″ tall 425- 495

Pincushion Dolls

Bisque baby, marked 574; molded/painted hair, net costume, features, 3″ tall . . 89- 114

Bisque, marked 938C; molded/painted hair, features, and clothes, 2½″ tall 89- 103

China Frozen Charlotte, unmarked; molded/painted hair and features; paper tag reads TEMPERANCE. All original, 4¼″ tall 125- 144

China, marked 1509 Germany; molded/painted cap, spit curls, and features, 3¼″ tall 52- 63

China, marked Germany 16495; molded/painted hair, features, and clothes, 2½″ tall 44- 56

China, marked Germany; molded/painted hair, features, and clothes, 3½″ tall 43- 55

China, pincushion and powder box marked 5063 Germany; molded/painted hair, features, and clothes; box marked BRAMbilt Shoes Made in Germany, 4¼″ tall (overall) 54- 65

Painted bisque, marked S1684; molded/painted hair and features, 3½″ tall 44- 54

Papier-mache, marked W (in a diamond) Germany (ink stamp); mohair wig, painted features, 5¼″ tall 42- 53

Plastic and Vinyl Dolls

Arrow Novelty Company, Skookum Indian, hard plastic head, mohair wig, painted eyes, closed mouth; cloth body, plastic legs and feet, blanket-dressed, 7″ tall 25- 36

Deluxe Toys Company, all vinyl, swivel head marked DELUXE TOPPER 1968; rooted hair, plastic sleep eyes, closed mouth; jointed at shoulders and hips; battery operated; arms move and play tune on accordian, 18″ tall 67- 79

Duchess Doll Corporation, all hard plastic swivel head; mohair wig, plastic sleep eyes, closed mouth; body marked DUCHESS DOLL CORPORATION DESIGN COPYRIGHT 1948 (on back); molded/painted shoes, all original clothes, 7½″ tall 24- 33

Eegee Doll Mfg. Company, Walker, all hard plastic, swivel head, synthetic wig, plastic sleep eyes, open/closed mouth; body marked EEGEE (on back); jointed at shoulders and hips; legs move, head turns, 17″ tall 23- 33

Effanbee, Gum Drop, all vinyl, jointed at shoulders and hips; rooted hair, plastic sleep eyes, closed mouth; body marked EFFANBEE 1962, 15½″ tall 42- 54

France, Bella, vinyl head; rooted hair, plastic sleep eyes, closed mouth; plastic body jointed at shoulders and hips; marked Bella Made in France, 11½″ tall 45- 54

Furga, all vinyl, jointed at shoulders and hips; rooted hair, plastic sleep eyes, open mouth; head marked FURGA/ITALY, 14″ tall 69- 80

Furga, Rosetta, all soft vinyl, swivel head marked FURGA ITALY; rooted hair, plastic sleep eyes, open/closed mouth; body jointed at shoulders and hips. All original, 16″ tall 89- 98

Hasbro, G.I. Joe, all hard plastic with human joints, molded/painted features; body marked G.I. Joe YM copyright 1964 by Hasbro Patent Pending Made in USA, 11½″ tall 35- 45

Horsman, Poor Pitiful Pearl, all vinyl, jointed at shoulders and hips; rooted hair, plastic sleep eyes, closed mouth, 18″ tall 47- 58

Mary Hoyer Doll Mfg. Company, Mary Hoyer, all hard plastic, swivel head, saran wig, plastic sleep eyes, closed mouth; body marked ORIGINAL MARY HOYER DOLL (in a circle); jointed at shoulders and hips, 14″ tall 87- 109

Ideal, Pebbles, all vinyl, jointed at shoulders and hips; rooted hair, painted eyes, open/closed mouth; body marked Hanna-Barbera Prod., Inc. Ideal Toy Co. Corp. F.S. 11½, 12″ tall 28- 38

Ideal, Toni, all hard plastic; jointed at shoulders and hips; glued nylon wig, plastic sleep eyes, closed mouth; head marked P-90 IDEAL DOLL Made in USA; body marked IDEAL DOLL P-90, 14½″ tall 58- 69

Irwin Plastics Company, all plastic, jointed at shoulders, molded/painted hair, painted eyes, closed mouth, knitted wool costume; marked IRWIN Made in USA (in a circle), 6½″ tall 33- 42

Kathe Kruse, hard plastic head, synthetic wig, molded/painted features; cloth body, jointed at shoulders and hips; paper tag reads ORIGINAL KATHE KRUSE Stoffpuppe. All original, 14½″ tall 625- 675

Mattel, Chatty Baby, vinyl swivel head, rooted hair, plastic sleep eyes, open mouth; vinyl body, jointed at shoulders and hips; marked Mattel 1961, 17″ tall 49- 58

Mattel, Cheerful Tearful, raise left arm to change facial expression from happy to sad; vinyl head, rooted hair, painted eyes; mouth opens and closes; vinyl body, jointed at shoulders and hips; marked Mattel, Co., Inc., Hawthorne, Cal. U.S. Patent Pending 3036-014-4, 13″ tall 48- 57

McCall Corporation, Betsy McCall, hard plastic swivel head; rooted hair on skull cap, plastic sleep eyes, closed mouth; hard plastic body; jointed at shoulders, hips, and knees; marked McCall Corp., 8″ tall 142- 160

Sun Rubber Company, Mouseketeer, all soft vinyl, swivel head marked c (in a circle) WALT DISNEY PROD.; molded/painted hair, plastic inset eyes, molded/painted clothes, molded/painted Mickey Mouse Club pin; molded/painted shoes and socks, 12″ tall 62- 70

Vogue, Ginny, walker, all hard plastic, head marked VOGUE; mohair wig, plastic sleep eyes, closed mouth; body marked GINNY VOGUE DOLLS INC. PAT. NO. 2887594 MADE IN U.S.A.; jointed at shoulders and hips; head turns when legs move, 7½″ tall 96- 108

Vogue, Love Me Linda, vinyl swivel head marked Vogue Doll Co. 1965; rooted hair, painted eyes, closed mouth; vinyl body, jointed at shoulders and hips, 15″ tall 63- 69

Rubber Dolls
American Character Doll Company, Tiny Tears, hard

(continued)

plastic swivel head marked
AMERICAN CHARAC-
TER DOLL PAT. NO.
2.675.644; synthetic hair
rooted in skull cap, plastic
sleep eyes, open/closed
mouth with nursing hole;
all rubber jointed baby
body, 15½" long, 13" head
circumference 90- 108
Company Unidentified, all
latex compo, swivel head
marked STEHA (in an
elongated diamond) DRP
839466; synthetic wig, flirting sleep eyes, closed
mouth; jointed body, voice
box, 21" tall 71- 82
Seiberling Latex, Dopey,
marked DOPEY (on hat) c
(in a circle) WALT DISNEY
SEIBERLING LATEX
MADE IN AKRON, O.
U.S.A. (on back), 5½" tall . .   38- 48
Sun Rubber Company, all hol-
low rubber, molded/
painted hair, features, and
clothes; marked Ruth E.
Newton The Sun Co.,
8½" tall 27- 35
Unmarked, Early American
rubber doll (possibly gutta
percha mixture), rubber
shoulder head; molded/
painted hair, painted eyes,
closed mouth; cloth body,
leather arms, 18" tall 625- 675

Wax Dolls
Montanari-type, poured-wax
shoulder head; baby-fine
human hair inserted in
small tufts; glass inset eyes,
hair eyebrows and eye-
lashes, closed mouth; cloth
body, poured-wax arms and
legs, 30" long, 14" head
circumference   1,400-1,550
Vargas, all solid wax, molded
wax hair, inset bead eyes,
open/closed mouth, cotton
clothes wax dipped. All
original, 7" tall 175- 230
Vargas, poured-wax head,
mohair wig and beard,
painted eyes, closed mouth;
cloth body, detailed wax
hands. All original, 27"
tall 255- 275
Wooden Dolls
Carni, Orthopedist, all wood;
paper label on bottom of

base reads TORIART
ITALY 11801/6 ORTHO-
PEDIST ANATOMISTA
ANATOM 1958 by CARNI
INC. MASS.; molded/
painted hair, spectacles,
features, and clothes, 5½"
tall 54- 63
Company Unidentified, Pinoc-
chio, all wood, painted
features; jointed at
shoulders and hips; stickers
on feet read Made in
Poland/Pinocchio, 7½"
tall 77- 88
Ellis, Joel, wooden head (one
piece with torso); molded/
painted hair, painted eyes,
closed mouth; wooden body,
tenon joints, metal hands
and feet, partially restored,
15" tall 825- 900
Hennessey, Wm., Toby, all
wood, carved/painted fea-
tures and clothes; 1868
Wm. HENNESSEY carved
on front; Wm. HENNES-
SEY carved on back and
legs; TOBY carved on hat;
jointed at shoulders; tenon
joints at elbows, hips, and
knees, 12½" tall 565- 625
Unmarked, early peg-wooden
man, gesso head (one piece
with torso); molded/painted
hat, hair, and features;
wooden body peg-jointed
at shoulders, hips, elbows,
and knees. All original,
5½" tall 375- 445
Unmarked, English peg-
wooden doll, all wood,
painted hair and features;
jointed at shoulders, hips,
elbows, and knees, 12½"
tall 180- 220
Unmarked, wooden doll
dressed as peddler, all
wood, painted hair and
features; jointed at
shoulders, hips, elbows,
and knees, 13" tall 177- 192

Door Knockers
These have been around for hundreds of
years and are made of wood, metal, even
glass. Iron and brass were the most popular,
in animal heads and other forms.

Brass, American Eagle, 1800s . . . $340-380
Brass, dog's head, 7" high, old . . .   78- 88

Door Knockers

Brass, fox head, 8″ high	81- 94
Brass, hand holding ball	105-111
Brass, horse's head, flowing mane, dated 1845	205-218
Brass, jaguar growling, 8″ high	94-111
Brass, lion with ring in mouth, French, 1800s (ill.)	195-225
Grecian bust, head only, bronze, 4½″ high	121-131
Iron, cat's head, smiling, 4″ high	58- 68
Iron, gloved hand	74- 84
Iron, hammer	61- 71
Iron, hand, fist-shaped, 8″ high, old	60- 70
Iron, horseshoe	62- 72
Iron, horseshoe hitting hammer head, 1930s	62- 70
Iron, spur hits metal block on wooden board	61- 71
Pewter (?), hand holding ball, 1920s	54- 62
Spur	68- 79

Doorstops

Doorstops

Made of many materials. Metal stops in the shapes of animals or buildings were used for propping open doors. Particularly popular in the 1920s.

Cottage, iron, 5¾″ high	$ 42- 50
Dogs: Airedale, Bulldog, Chow, German Shepherd, etc.	51- 60
Fala, FDR on side, 10″ high	58- 67
Flower basket, cast iron, 7″ high (ill.)	39- 47
Flowerpot, cast iron, enameled, 7¼″ high	36- 46
Frog, iron, webbed feet, 15″ high	47- 54
Horse pulling cart, iron, 6½″ high	42- 52
Horse, rearing, lead base, 1930s	47- 57
Lady, cast iron, enameled	38- 47
Lion, painted, 15″ high	57- 66
Parrot, red/yellow/green, 10″ high	58- 64
Polo player on horse, 9″ high	47- 57
Rabbit, iron, 11″ high	58- 61
Ship, Mayflower, cast iron	63- 71
Sunbonnet girl, 6½″ high	60- 70
Squirrel, iron, 11″ high	57- 69
Wagon train, horse, 10″ high	65- 75
Wolf, on leash, iron	48- 58

Dorflinger Glass

Dorflinger Glass

Christian Dorflinger founded his first factory at White Mills, Pennsylvania, in 1865, having come from Alsace, France, in 1846 to learn the American glass trade. He also operated a factory in Brooklyn, New York, from 1852 until the late 1880s when J. S. Hibbler took over all the firm's interests. The Kalana Lyly pattern shown here is but one of the many fine examples of glass made by one of the greatest glassmakers in the world. It's of interest to know that Mr. Dorflinger brought the great Nicholas Lutz to America in 1860.

Doulton Pottery

DOULTON
LAMBETH
ENGLAND

SILCON DOULTON LAMBETH
ENGLAND

Doulton Pottery

In the mid-1850s Henry Doulton's partner, John Watts, retired and Mr. Doulton continued the firm as Doulton and Company. From the 1850s until just before 1900, his wares were marked Doulton Lambeth. After 1901, Royal was added to the firm's name, without the Lambeth. Salt-glazed stoneware was one of the many fine types of pottery made at Doulton.

Biscuit, jar, 1880s	$197-240
Bowl, flowers, gold trim, artist-signed	125-138
Ewer, blue scrolling, floral decor, 9" high	79- 84
Ewer, tapestry, Slaters Patent, 8½" high (ill.)	180-200
Ink bottle, slipware finish	61- 70
Mug, probably for ale, tan/brown, artist Hannah Barlow	82- 90
Mustard pot, blues, brown, 1883	110-121
Pitcher, Columbian Exposition, 1893	148-168
Pitcher, hunting scenes, tan/brown	88- 98
Plate, Dickensware, Tom Pinch	84- 94
Plate, Melrose, 9" dia.	72- 82
Plate, tavern scene, artist M. Aitken, 9" dia.	83- 93
Plate, varicolored flowers, 1884, 10" dia.	60- 70
Tray, Dickensware, signed Noke	134-148
Vase, hunting scene, 1870s	91-106
Vase, multicolored, 8" high	82- 90
Whiskey jug, marked JRD and Fine Old Scotch Whiskey	172-192

Dresden China

In the early 1700s, Johann Bottger produced the first porcelain in Europe that was considered quality. His factory was at the Royal Saxon Porcelain Works at Meissen, Germany. His work was finely decorated in exquisite shapes, often with raised enamel flowers. The famous crossed swords in blue are known throughout the world. Unfortunately the factory is now behind the Iron Curtain. Most of the Dresden in the U.S. was brought in by importers in the late 19th century.

Dresden China

Basket, floral decor, twisted handle, 7" high	$ 155-	170
Bowl, flowers, hand-painted, gold trim, 10"	132-	150
Box, open latticework, silver mounts	482-	535
Candelabra, 6-candle, 22" high, boy/girl, blue ground, flowers, pr.	1,500-	1,650
Candleholder, pink-applied roses, 14" high	132-	144
Chocolate pot, cobalt, gold border, miniature roses	284-	295
Compote, reticulated, 11" high, pr.	548-	610
Cup/saucer, floral designs overall	142-	150
Figurines, cupids, ladies, 8¼" high (ill.), pr.		1,600+
Lamp, applied flowers, square base, early	470-	520
Plate, deep, ribbed, blue/yellow decor, signed Villeroy and Boch	132-	141
Plate, pink floral decor, 9" dia., reticulated border	74-	84
Plate, reticulated border, cherubs	102-	114

Tea caddy, flowers/roses,
gold, blue Crown under
glaze 152- 170
Teapot, roses with thorns,
leaves, gold, blue Crown .   210- 222
Urn, battle scene, 16″ high,
old mark, pr. 188- 198
Vase, floral decor, white
ground, 8″ 284- 292
Vase, painted birds, signed,
6″ high 228- 240
Vase, portrait of gentleman,
overlay gold decor, 10″
high 250- 270

Durand Art Glass ~~DURAND~~

Durand Art Glass

Resembling Tiffany in some respects,
Durand was made by the Vineland Flint
Glass Works in Vineland, New Jersey,
around 1924. Victor Durand, founder, put
paper labels on some pieces while others were
signed with a V in the pontil. Victor Durand,
Jr., ran the factory until his untimely death in
1931. The factory was then taken over by
Kimble.

Bowl, blue, label, signed $520-565
Bowl, gold iridescent, signed
"V"   321-342
Candleholders, gold lustre, opal
and gold, 6″ high, signed   300-320
Compote, Blue Feather pattern,
amber base, 7″ high   570-610
Decanter, blue, iridescent, signed,
8″ high   452-470
Lamp, green, Pulled Feather
design, gold threading, bronze
cherub base, electrified   320-340
Perfume bottle, orange iridescent,
signed DeVilbiss   220-240
Plate, cobalt, Peacock Feather
pattern, cut flowers, 8″
dia.   362-382

Rose bowl, green/gold, original
paper label   262-290
Shade, gas, white ground, gold/
green, calcite interior   210-240
Vase, blue iridescent, orange trim,
8½″ high   482-510
Vase, blue, white, swirls from top
to bottom, 9″ high   375-410
Vase, green, gold, rose iridescent
threading, signed   445-480
Vase, orange, iridescent, blue
highlights, 8½″ high   470-495
Vase, peach iridescent, beehive
shape, 7½″ high   595-620
Vase, Pulled Feather, threading
8½″ high (ill.)   620-635
Wine glass, blue, white loops,
vaseline stem   210-242

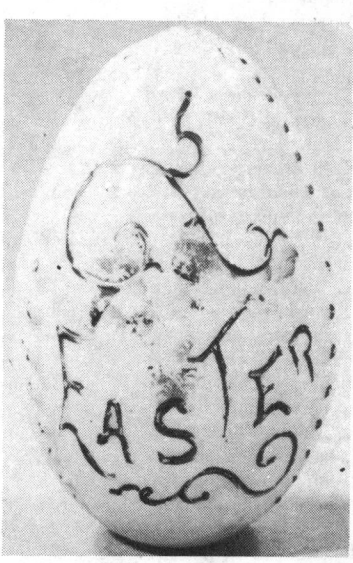

Easter Eggs

Easter Eggs

Usually of blown glass, they were favorites
with the children in the mid-1800s. The same
type is used to attract hens to a nest. The
older types were hand-painted, professionally
or otherwise.

Easter egg, 4″ high, handblown
(ill.) . . . . $ 50- 60
Easter egg, Polish eagle, dated
1809, flowers   152-170
Easter egg, Russian, 19th cen-
tury, religious subject   138-150

Edged Weapons

"On guard!" Two words that brought fear
to more than one man. Any and all are collectible and going up in price every day.

(continued)

Edged Weapons

American Indian pipe tomahawk, c. 1780, 19″ overall	$1,300-1,500
American Revolution horseman's saber, 36″, s.e. blade	720- 770
Arabian chieftain's Jambiya dagger w/sheath, 9½″ d.e. blade	168- 178
Australian knuckle-duster fighting knife, WWII, 6½″ long	192- 199
Austrian officer's sword w/sheath, WWI, 29″ s.e. blade	228- 250
British artillery, short sword, c. 1810, brass hilt, 22″ long	320- 340
British general officer's sword, silver hilt, c. 1825	1,400-1,550
British naval boarding ax, c. 1840-1860, 21″ handle, 10″ iron head	392- 420
British naval officer's sword, c. 1790, 30″ straight s.e. blade	320- 340
British prison guard's sword, c. 1850, 22″ curved s.e. blade	162- 172
British trench knife, WWI, marked Robbins-Dudley, 4¼″ long	265- 285
Ghurka knife (Kukri), WWII, 9″ incurved blade, has 2 miniature knives in leather-covered wooden case	90- 110
Indo-Persian fighting knife, c. 1820, 9″ d.e. reverse curved blade	121- 138
Italian cup hilt rapier, 17th century, 34″ long d.e. blade	342- 362
"Khyber" knife and sheath, pearl handled, 11″ long	228- 250
Knights of Columbus ceremonial sword, made by Pettis & Ranken, Troy, N.Y., c. 1925, 29″ long	130- 142
Revolutionary naval cutlass, 28″ straight s.e. blade	425- 455
Special Civil War contract cavalry saber and scabbard, marked Tiffany & Co., 36″ curved s.e. blade	530- 575

Tachi, child's, 17″ long (ill.)	332-	370
U.S. Civil War saber bayonet, probably for Merrill Navy rifle	260-	272

"Portrait of Jan Asselyn"

"Night in Ely Cathedral"

Engravings, Etchings

If horseracing once was considered the

sport of kings, this category is fast becoming a collectible of millionaires. The prices being realized at the better auctions are staggering. This category is for reference only. See **Clubs and Publications,** this Price Guide.

Marius A.J. Bauer, contemporary Dutch etcher, b. 1867, "Entrance to a Mosque," etching, signed proof.

Nicholas Bazin, French, c. 1636-1706, "Marie Therese, Queen of France," line engraving.

Jacques Firmin Beauvarlet, French, 1731-1797, "Pierre Mignard," line engraving.

Frank W. Benson, American, b. Salem, Mass., 1862, "The Punter," etching, proof, signed in pencil.

Arthur Brisco, English marine painter-etcher, "Three Bargers," etcher, proof, signed in ink.

Felix Buhot, French, b. Valognes, 1847, "La Place Breda," etching, signed in the plate.

David Young Cameron, painter-etcher, b. Glasgow, Scotland, 1865, "Hotel de Sens," etching, proof signed in pencil.

C. Chartran, "Leo XIII," etching, signed proof on vellum.

A.G.L. Desnoyers, France, 1779-1857, "St. Catherine of Alexander," line engraving, proof before all letters.

Albrecht Durer, 1471-1528, Germany, "Apollo and Diana," engraving, signed in the plate.

Cornelius Dusart, Dutch, 1660-1704, "The Violin Player," etching, signed in the plate.

Kerry Eby, American, 1890s, "Spring Freshets," etching.

Jean Louis Forain, French painter, etcher, lithographer, 1852-1931, "Lourdes—La Paralytique," etching, signed in pencil.

G. Garavaglia, "La Madonna Della Seggiola," line engraving, proof before letters.

Axel Herman Haig, Sweden, 1835-1921, "Burgos Cathedral: Interior," etching, signed proof.

Childe Hassam, American painter-etcher, b. 1859, "Walt Whitman's House," etching, proof, signed in pencil.

Philipp Kilian, German engraver, 1628-93, "Damian Hartard," line engraving.

Alphonse Legros, French etcher, 1837-1911, "Le Refectoire," etching, proof, in the second state.

James McBey, 1883-1959, "Night in Ely Cathedral," etching, signed in ink (ill.).

Rembrandt Van Rijn, Dutch painter-etcher, "Portrait of Jan Asselyn," etching, signed in the plate (ill.).

Pieter Van Schuppen, 1627-1702, "Louis, Dauphin de France," line engraving, dated 1684.

Levon West, "Blizzard Coming," etching, proof, signed in pencil.

Epergnes

Epergnes

These elaborate table centerpieces, designed to hold sweetmeats, fruits, or with vases to hold flowers, were in vogue in the early and mid-1800s. Many were attributed to the Sandwich Glass Company, Sandwich, Massachusetts, but as many come from Europe and few were signed. It's another case of knowing your dealer.

Blue, crimped top, bowl with trimming	$365-440
Cranberry, crimped top and lower bowl, 3 lily vases, 20" high	425-452
Crystal/blue, opalescent, 4 lilies, 25" high overall	295-310
Rose/pink, upper and lower edges ruffled, 4 lilies, 27" high	335-360
Ruffled bowl, 3 lilies, silver frame, 12½" high	320-340
Sandwich Glass overshot, mid-1800s (ill.)	840-875
Silver plate, 11" high, 4 lilies	245-275
Single lily, sterling silver base, 12" high	510-522
White satin glass, silver-plated standard, 3 glass lilies, 22" high	288-320

ES Germany

This fine porcelain was made by Erdmann Schlegelmilch in Suhl, Germany, from 1861 until the mid-1920s. The factory also sold blanks for people who chose to decorate their own. ES Germany prices are comparable to RS Germany.

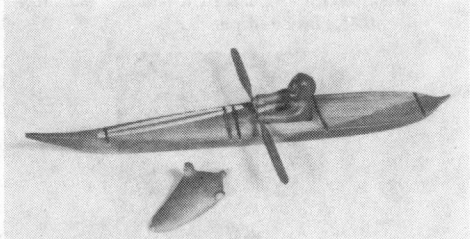

Eskimo Art

Eskimo Art

These natives of Canada, the Aleutian Islands, Alaska, Greenland, and Siberia have carved items from walrus tusks, whales' teeth, and wood. Their basketry is world-famous. The most sought after work today was made in the mid-1800s, although much of what you find in antiques shops was made to be sold at the trading posts.

Arctic fox, carved from walrus
  walrus tusk, 1¼"×5¼", c.
  1930s $350- 400
Basket, rye grass, yarn
  woven in, 11" high, c. 1900 .. 225- 285
Basket, utility type, designs
  aniline dyed, 7½" high, c.
  1930 .... 58- 72
Cribbage board, in shape of
  seal, 12½" long, c. 1880s ... 395- 420
Dominoes, complete set in box,
  c. 1930s.................. 192- 210
Eskimo, soapstone with ivory
  spears, 7" high, c. 1900s.... 340- 360
Fish dish, wooden, 6½"×8",
  c. 1930s................. 132- 142
Fish spear (called a leister),
  carved from walrus ivory ... 280- 320
Kayak, seal (ill.) 395- 420
Mask, carved cedar,
  10½"×7½", c. 1880s 1,100-1,250
Mortar, wooden, for grinding
  tobacco, 4½"×8½", c. early
  1800s 192- 220
Snow goggles, wooden,
  leather thongs, c. 1900s 130- 155
Trinket box, carved from
  walrus tusk, late 1880s 425- 470

European Art Glass

The uninformed collector buys this type of glass too often as Tiffany or Steuben on the basis that it's guaranteed. Many producers of good art glass didn't sign their pieces, thus creating more confusion. If the piece isn't signed, you should demand and get a written

European Art Glass

receipt when you buy. The American market was flooded with European art glass in the late 1800s. Just know from whom you're buying.

Bowl, 8" dia., green .... $ 60- 68
Inkwell, brass cap and sleeve,
  2¼" high (ill.) 120-135
Vase, blue, pink/blue flowers,
  6" high 59- 68
Vase, green, yellow flowers, 8"
  high 64- 73
Vase, orange, castle scene,
  fluted top, 7½" high......... 64- 73
Vase, ruffled lip, fine enameling, pink liner, 6" high 92-111
Vase, white satin glass, yellow
  liner, clear frosted feet, 4¾"
  high 168-174

Faberge   КФ

Peter Carl Faberge was jeweler to the Russian Imperial Court from the early 1870s

Faberge

186

until 1914. One of the largest collections in the world is the Matilda Geddings Gray Foundation Collection.

Ashtray, Art Nouveau, silver,
1900 . . . . $1,100-1,350
Bell push, in form of jade
elephant, ruby eyes, 2″ high 4,300-4,500
Cigarette case, rectangular,
silver gilt, green moss
agate, with cabochon ruby
thumbpiece 3,900-4,800
Clock, gilded silver, gold
overlay, translucent
enamel, 1914 4,200-4,400
Figure, Atlas, gilded, silver
mounted 4,500-4,700
Icon, Our Lady of the Sign . . . 4,200-4,700
Inkwell, hollowed-out cube of
onyx mounted in silver,
photograph of the
Czarevitch on front, 3½″
high 4,100-4,275
Letter opener, silver, gold,
diamond knob, 12″ long . . . 2,975-3,400
Penholder, silver 2,300-3,000
Shade, candle, silver-mounted,
1900 1,900-2,250

The illustrated Imperial Easter egg is similar to one that was presented to Czarina Marie Feodorovna by her husband, Czar Alexander III, around 1893. $125,000+!

Faience

A tin glaze earthenware, this "soft" pottery achieves its opaqueness by being treated with tin oxide. Delft and Majolica are made by the same process.

Bottle, white ground, flower
motif, 7½″ high $182-190
Dish, blue/white, Oriental, pr. . . . 171-182
Inkwell, French, yellow glaze,
signed VP (Veuve Perrin) (ill.) . 180-190
Jar, blue/white, landscape,
handles, Italy, 18″ high, pr. . . . 227-242
Jug, tulip, roses, tin glaze,
enamel, 1780s 159-172

Plate, floral, insects, Armorial,
Italy, pr. 188-198
Plate, tin glaze, red/blue, French,
1765 162-175
Platter, Delft type, 18″×15″ 192-199
Teapot, 11″ high, signed 320-325
Tureen, lettuce decor, French,
1770, pr. 520-532
Vase, 12″ high, tin glaze, signed . 110-121

Fairy Lamps

Fairy Lamps

Candle-burning night lamps consisting of two parts, base and shade, were first made by the Samuel Clarke Company, England, in the mid-1850s. Phoenix Glass Company, Monaca, Pennsylvania, was granted the exclusive right to make them in the U.S. Came electricity, out went the light in the fairy lamp. Lazarus and Rosenfeld, New York City, imported thousands of them from Bohemia in the 1880s. Made in every type of glass, from cheap to Tiffany and Amberina.

Amber Swirl and Cut pattern
base, acorn shade, signed
Clarke $175-185
Blue base, bulbous shade, raised
floral decor, signed Clarke 228-250
Bisque, Cocker 182-192
Camphor top, clear bottom,
blown glass wick holder 265-275
Cranberry glass shade, hobnail
base, signed Clarke 272-282
Green satin, ribbed, signed
Clarke 170-180
Green/white, swirls, thorn decor . 162-172
Lithophane, child scene, white
porcelain base, signed Clarke . . 452-472
Millefiori shade, glass base 310-320
Pink quilted satin glass, signed
Clarke (ill.) 210-221
Rose satin top, Diamond pattern,
clear base, signed Clarke 258-272
Satin glass, pink/blue 328-344
White, pink stripes 220-260
Yellow satin glass shade, ribbed
pattern base, signed Clarke . . . 185-210

Famille Rose

This Chinese export porcelain was made

(continued)

in the 18th and 19th centuries. Birds, insects, figures, and flowers are frequently used as decoration in opaque hues of blue, rose, and yellow. Considered highly collectible.

Bowl, 4 figures under flowering quince tree, 18th century, 4½″ dia. . . . .$ 135- 155
Bowl, garden scene, 3 panels, 18th century, 13″ dia. 1,375-1,550
Garden seat, birds/floral decor, 19th century 2,500-2,675
Plaque, peacocks, trees, 18th century, 10″ dia. 950-1,100
Plate, birds, flowers, 19th century, 8¾″ dia. 88- 98
Plate, floral decor, 18th century, 9¼″ dia. 260- 272
Vase, birds/garden motif, 19th century, 9¼″ high . . . 685- 750
Vase, floral decor, 18th century, 11¼″ high 1,100-1,350
Vase, garden scenes, 3 panels, 19th century, 12½″ high . . 775- 825

Fans

During the Victorian era young ladies gave many signals with the fan. One gesture could mean "Leave me alone!"; another, "Mother's watching!" Fans were made of every type of material. Paper and ivory seemed to be the most popular. Who invented the first fan is unknown. See **Clubs and Publications**, this Price Guide.

Advertising, Cafe Brightwood, Kingston, N.Y., 1908, paper . .$ 15- 20
Black lace sticks, floral on black satin, opens to 22″ 67- 76
Black lacquer, silver flower painting on back, 21″ 69- 78
Celluloid frame, white, carved flower, 7″ long 48- 54
Engraved and painted, blossoms, butterflies, 22″ 44- 52
Floral, vocalist, buildings, flowers, 24″ 39- 49

Fans

Ivory splats, chiffon, sequins, 9″ long 52- 61
Lace, sandalwood, painted, 8″ . . . 58- 68
M.O.P. frame, lace cloth, gold silk thread (ill.) 340-370
Paper and wood, matadors, bull fight, 18″ long 24- 32
Paper, Japanese, ea. 12- 18
Silk, black/green, 13″ long 69- 74
Tortoiseshell ribs, ostrich plumes, 9″ long 82- 92
Turkey feathers, hand-painted, 1870s opens to 19″ 79- 89
White lacquer, silver-plated handle, 1900s, opens to 22″ . . . 58- 69

Feather Work

Cut into the shape of flower petals and leaves, usually painted or dyed, this work is mainly found in a glass box-in-frame.

Bouquet of blue and green flowers, glass and frame in good condition . . . .$ 47- 55
Pansies, blue, yellow, green glass and frame in good condition . . . 51- 60
Roses, pink, yellow glass and frame in good condition 57- 64

Fenton Art Glass

Founded in 1905 by Frank Fenton, at Martins Ferry, Ohio. Soon afterward the company moved to its present location in Williamstown, West Virginia. Carnival glass, opalescent, custard, stretch, ruby, mandarin, dolphins are a few of the many types made there.

Apple Tree (cobalt)
Pitcher $335- 365
Tumbler 59- 68
Buttons and Braids
Pitcher 185- 220
Tumbler 39- 47
Celeste Blue (stretch)
Bonbon, covered 49- 58
Bowls
Flared, 7½″ dia. 49- 58
Lily, 5″ dia. 43- 52
Orange, crimped 104- 115
Butter ball, 7″ dia. 52- 62
Candlestick, 6″ high 44- 53
Cologne, w/drip stopper 101- 111
Compote, flared 37- 45
Fern dish, footed 39- 47
Night set (carafe and tumbler) . 59- 68
Cherry and Scale (custard)
Butter dish, covered 275- 284
Creamer 168- 174
Master berry 77- 84

Sauce	90-	101
Sugar bowl, covered	192-	201

Dolphins

Bonbon, Diamond Optic, crimped, 6″ sq.	52-	62
Bowls		
Cupped, 9″ dia.	84-	94
Oval, 10½″ dia.	158-	168
Candlestick	62-	72
Compote, round	152-	161
Sandwich tray, Diamond Optic, 10″ dia.	61-	70

Florentine Green (stretch)

Bowl, candy	118-	127
Candlestick	63-	70
Cigarette holder	77-	84
Creamer	32-	41
Pitcher	112-	122
Plate, salad, 8″ dia.	42-	51
Sugar, open	38-	47
Vase, fan, etched, 5″	45-	55

Jade Green

Basket, wicker handle, 10½″ dia.	69-	78
Bowl, flared, 11″ dia.	44-	52
Candlestick	12-	18
Candy jar w/lid	54-	63
Lemon tray	39-	49
Vase, 10″ high	45-	55

Mandarin Red

Ashtray, pipe	81-	91
Bowl, flared, 11″ dia.	146-	156
Cake stand, Mikado		370+
Candlestick, 10″ high	108-	119
Compote, Mikado		345+
Vase, flared, 8″ high	120-	132

Marigold

Candlestick, 6″ high	32-	42
Candy jars, ½ lb. and ¾ lb., ea.	51-	61
Cigarette holder	62-	72
Cologne	62-	70
Guest set (water glass "stopper" in pitcher)		350+

Milady (cobalt)

Pitcher	640-	725
Tumbler	77-	87

Rose

Ashtray, cut	49-	59
Compote, dolphin stem, oval	48-	59
Flower pot w/base	46-	54
Goblet, 9-oz.	44-	54
Plate, dolphin handles	54-	62
Sherbet, cut	47-	57

Velva Rose (stretch)

Bowl, crimped, 10″ dia.	147-	157
Candlestick, dolphins	52-	62
Candy jar, ½-lb.	54-	63
Cologne	92-	107
Guest set	137-	145
Vase, bud, 12″	45-	55
Vase, crimped top, 12″	68-	78

Water Lily and Cattails (chocolate)

Berry, 4″ dia.	82-	92

Butter, covered	925-	955
Creamer	365-	410
Pitcher	1,000-	1,350
Spooner	440-	470
Sugar, covered	565-	635
Tumbler	295-	325

Fiesta Ware

Fiesta Ware

Homer and Shakespear Laughlin founded the Homer Laughlin China Company in East Liverpool, Ohio, in 1871. At one time it was the world's largest single pottery plant. In March, 1937, Fiesta Ware was patented in red, blue, yellow, and green. Fiesta was a first in commercial pottery. Red was the most difficult color to control. A redesign took place in 1969 and the ware was discontinued in 1973. Most pieces are incised "FIESTA." Red pieces bring 45 to 80 percent more than other colors.

Ashtrays

Chartreuse, 1947	$ 27-	37
Green, 1959	26-	35
Red, 1959	32-	39
Turf green, 1972	18-	24

Bowls

Dessert, old ivory, 1936, 6″ dia.	10-	17
Fruit, turquoise, 1939, 11¾″ dia.	31-	47
Nested, 7 in set, 1943, 5″ to 11½″ dia., all		74-210
Salad, footed, red, 1941, 12″ dia.	52-	74
Salad, individual, green, yellow, 1959, 7 5/8″ dia., ea.	8-	13

Candleholders

Bulb-type, old ivory, turquoise, 1936-1945, ea.	35-	47
Tripod-type, red, 1936-1943	50-	67

Casseroles

Covered, turquoise, 1940	52-	77

189

(continued)

French, old ivory, 1939 . . . . 58- 77

Creamers
Regular, turquoise, 1938 . . . . 10- 17
Stick-handled, green 13- 21

Coffeepots
A.D., green, 1941 . . . . 35- 44
Regular, red, 1940 91-108

Cups
Egg, red, 1941 . . . . 19- 27
Cream soup, green, 1945 . . . . 17- 29
Onion soup, covered, turquoise,
1938 . . . . 71- 81
Jug, red, 1941, 2-pt. 24- 34

Marmalades
Regular, yellow, 1943 . . . . 32- 42
W/metal holder, green, 1943 . . . . 41- 50

Mug
Tom and Jerry, red, 1941 . . . . 37- 47

Mustard
Green, 1939 . . . . 29- 39

Pitchers
Disc, water, rose, 1947, 2-qt. 36- 44
Ice, green, 1944, 2-qt. 77- 84
Juice, yellow, 1941, 30-oz. 45- 58
Syrup, red, 1941 92-104

Plates
Chop, turquoise, 1941, 13",
15", ea. 9- 17
Compartments, various colors,
1937, 10½", 11 ⅝", ea. 18- 27
Deep, green, 1943, 8" 10- 17
Various colors, 1936-1968,
6", 7", 9", 10" (ill.), ea. 8- 18
Platter, oval, yellow, 1941, 12" 25- 35
Salt/pepper shakers, all colors,
1936-1973, set 9- 21
Sugar, creamer and tray,
turquoise, 1941, set 35- 47
Tumblers, green, 1943, 5-oz.,
10-oz., ea. 14- 21

Vases
Bud, yellow, 1939 . . . . 35- 46
Old ivory, yellow, blue,
1936-1941, 8", 10", 12", ea. . . . 39- 52

Finger Bowls

Always accompanied by a matching underplate, these small receptacles for cleansing
the fingers after eating were made of a
variety of glassware.

Amber, ITP . . . . $ 52- 63
Apple green, Depression glass
type 21- 29

Bohemian glass, blue, deer scene . 65- 72
Cobalt 54- 64
Cranberry, Lutz-type threading . 85- 92
Green, fluted lip 58- 68
Moser glass, green/blue 55- 64
Mother-of-Pearl, Diamond
Quilted satin glass (ill.) 450-520
New England Peachblow, satin
finish (ill.) 675-740
Pink, Depression glass type 28- 35
Threaded glass, pink/blue 49- 58
Tortoise glass, enameled florals
(ill.) 410-425

Fire-Fighting Collectibles

Another of the Americana series that's now
highly sought after. Call it a fire sale if you
will, but the amounts being paid certainly
aren't fire sale prices. See **Clubs and
Publications**, this Price Guide.

Bell, hand-cranked, East
Hampton Bell Factory . . . . $ 222- 242
Fire bucket, Elmira,
Engine 3 . . . . 410- 420
Fire bucket, English,
London Fire, paint worn
thin 315- 340
Fire bucket, Scarsdale's
Finest 435- 480
Fire lantern, Dietz King,
brass 120- 140
Helmet, brass eagle finial,
English, c. 1870 . . . . 342- 361
Helmet, leather, Phila-
delphia, c. 1860s 381- 410
Hose nozzle, brass, 14¾"
long, c. 1890 . . . . 195- 220
Parade belt, lettered P.R.
Abbit 101- 111
Presentation shield,
Tannersville, N.Y. 1,500-1,600
Silver-plated engine lamp,
King Neptune 1,475-1,650
Speaking trumpet, brass,
names of volunteers
engraved on lip 620- 640

Finger Bowls

Fire-Fighting Collectibles

Speaking trumpet, silver plate, dated 1872	528-	568
Speaking trumpet, sterling silver, Boston 1872	640-	652
Wooden chest, fire rescue scene painted on front	1,900+	

Firemarks

Firemarks

Associated Firemen's Insurance of Baltimore, Md., issued in 1848.

Citizen's Fire, Marine and Life Insurance Co., Wheeling W. Va., 1856.

City Insurance Company of Cincinnati, Ohio, about 1846.

Clay Fire and Marine Insurance Co., Newport, Ky., 1789.

Firemen's Insurance Co. of Pittsburgh, Pa., about 1851.

Franklin Insurance Co., St. Louis, Mo., 1855 (ill.)

Home Insurance Co., New Haven, Conn., 1859.

Insurance Co. of Florida, Jacksonville, Fla., 1841.

Insurance Co. of North America, extremely rare in copper, eagle rising from cloud.

Western Mutual Fire and Marine Insurance Co., St. Louis, Mo., 1857.

Each of these firemarks is worth at least $400 or more, some as much as $3,500.

Firemen's parade belts, various sizes and colors............. $195-260

If you're into fire fighting paraphernalia, visit the Home Insurance Co. Museum, 15th floor, 59 Maiden Lane, New York City, or the American Museum of Fire Fighting, Fireman's Home, Hudson, N.Y. There are other museums, of course, but these two, in particular, are great.

Firearms

This is a highly collectible (and expensive) category. Skillful repros are flooding the market, so do business with reliable people, please. Abbreviations used are as follows: cal—caliber; revol—revolver; CW—Civil War; perc—percussion; FL—flintlock; BL—breechloading; PG—pistol grip; SS—single shot; bbl—barrel; mkd—marked; oct—octagonal;

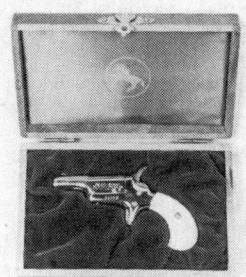

Firearms

SA—single action; DA—double action. Please Note: Federal Firearms Regulations: All firearms made in or before 1898 have been exempted from federal firearms regulations which means that unless your state or town has a special law preventing your purchase of such a gun, they can be freely sent and purchased interstate and mail order. On those guns made after 1898, there is a prohibition for sales to anyone except a federally licensed dealer. The federal law does not conflict or cancel any existing state or local laws that might be in effect in your area; hence, although weapons prior to 1898 are exempt under federal law, it is still necessary for you to sign a statement regarding permits or other requirements in your own local area if applicable. Don't get cute with the regulations. You're a candidate for a prison term if you do. See **Clubs and Publications,** this Price Guide.

American Hand Guns

Allen & Thurber 6-shot .31 cal perc Pepperbox, mkd Young & Smith—New York—Allen's Patent ...$	550-	625
Allen & Wheelock 5-shot .31 cal perc DA revol, 4″ oct bbl............	570-	610
American perc pocket (or belt size) pistol, c. 1840-50, carved stock, silver, gold inlay, 4″ large round bbl.................	2,475-	2,650
Cased Colt DA 1878 Frontier Model revol....	1,350-	1,475
Colt .36 cal 5-shot perc Pocket Model of Naval caliber	770-	840
Colt #3 Derringer .41 rim-fire.................	765-	845
Colt .44 cal perc Army revol	740-	770

(continued)

Colt 5-shot .31 cal perc
revol, 4″ oct bbl, 2-line
N.Y. address 1,600- 1,800
Colt Open Top 7-shot .22
cal spur trigger revol . . .   520-   580
Colt SA Frontier revol,
44/40 cal, mkd on side
Colt Frontier Six Shooter   1,350- 1,475
Colt 3rd model .44 cal
perc Dragoon revol,
8″ bbl . . . .   7,700+
Colt 5-shot .31 cal perc
revol, 4″ bbl   560-   590
Colt .36 cal perc Navy revol 1,600- 1,800
Colt .41 cal rimfire
(repro of original, cased)
(ill.)   82-   95
Cooper .36 cal perc Navy
DA revol, 4″ oct bbl,
Frankford, Philadelphia
address 1,150- 1,400
CW Rogers & Spencer .44
cal perc Army revol 1,875- 1,975
Derringer pistol, 2¾″ fluted
bbl swivels, mkd Double
Header—E.S. Renwick
Manuf'r—New York—
Pat. June 21, 1864 . . . . .   7,800+
FL martial pistol . . . .   1,700+
.41 cal rimfire Derringer,
mkd XL Derringer, spur
trigger   450-   525
Harpers Ferry FL martial
pistol, mkd Harpers
Ferry 1807 . . . .   3,500- 3,800
H. Aston .54 cal martial
pistol, 1848   650-   750
James Warner 6-shot .31 cal
perc pocket revol, 2½″
round bbl.   525-   625
Manhattan Arms Co. perc
SS .31 cal, mkd Hero,
14″ round bbl   350-   450
Merwin & Bray Firearms
Co., N.Y., 5-shot, .30 cal
cup-primed revol, 3½″
cot/ribbed bbl   650-   710
Metropolitan .36 cal perc
CW revol, fashioned
after an 1851 Colt 2,200- 2,550
Remington Beals .36 cal
perc Navy revol   620-   655
Savage .36 cal CW perc
ring trigger Navy revol. .   520-   610
Sharps 4-bbl .22 rimfire
Pepperbox.   625-   700
6-shot perc .31 cal Pepper-
box, 4½″ ribbed bbls,
mkd S. Baylis—1853
along rib, etc. . . . .   3,400+
6-shot .31 cal perc revol,
made by Wm. Marston,
New York, mkd The

Union Arms Co., known
as 7th model, 5¼″ bbl . . .   770-   785
Smith & Wesson Model L 1,
2nd, 3rd issue 7-shot .22
rimfire revol, ea. 1,900- 2,200
(Called Ladysmiths be-
cause the gals in the
West carried them in
their garters. Wesson
was highly religious—
when he learned of its
use, he stopped making
this pistol.)
Spalding & Fisher dbl bbl
(side-by-side) perc belt
size pistol, .36 cal 5″ bbls,
single trigger   525-   610
Starr SA .44 cal CW perc
Army revol, 8″ bbl 2,300- 2,500
.22 cal rimfire Derringer/
pocket pistol, mkd
Lombard & Co., Spring-
field, Mass.   540-   610
.35 cal perc pistol, mkd
Bacon & Co., Norwich,
Ct., oct/rnd bbl, 4″ long .   375-   395
.31 cal perc Pepperbox,
6-shot, mkd Allen &
Thurber, Norwich, Ct.,
3¼″ bbls   640-   680
U.S. Navy Boxlock perc
pistol, mkd Ames-
Springfield—U.S.N.—
1845 on lock   895-   945

American Shoulder Guns
Ballard sporting rifle, combination .44 rimfire and
perc, 27½″ rnd bbl   840-   950
Boy's Cadet size perc mili-
tary musket, 1840-1860,
45″ overall   710-   740
British cavalry officer's FL
pistol, c. 1760-1775, .69
cal . . . .   2,500+
British Modified Pattern of
1796 FL cavalry pistol,
.76 cal, 9″ bbl, mkgs of
17th Light Dragoons . . .   785-   820
British naval officer's FL
holster pistol, c. 1800,
.52 cal 1,200- 1,350
British perc holster pistol,
c. 1830-1840, 8″ oct. bbl,
14″ overall, mkd with
American eagle and
patriotic motifs . . . .   5,400+
Burnside CW perc BL
carbine   660-   720
Colt's Patent-Hartford
1863 CW .58 cal perc
musket 2,500- 2,750
Committee of Safety
FL Revolutionary
musket, 41″ bbl . . . .   3,500+

CW repeating .50 cal rim-
fire carbine, 30" bbl, mkd
Triplett & Scott   820-   850
Evans sporting rifle, .44 cal,
30" rnd bbl 910- 1,100
FL cavalry carbine, .64 cal,
Brown Bess type lock,
20" bbl   875-   950
FL Kentucky-style rifle, .54
cal, 36" oct bbl, mkd
Derringer Phila 4,800- 5,200
Henry lever action repeat-
ing .44 rimfire, Ser. No.
7055 . . . . 4,200- 4,500
Kentucky full stock perc
rifle, c. 1830, .38 cal, 41"
oct bbl . . . .   3,700+
Maine or Massachusetts
half stock Kentucky style
sporting rifle, c. 1820,
31½" oct bbl, .64 cal,
mkd Leland 1,500- 1,700
Parker DB 10 gauge
hammerless shotgun,
"D" grade, 29" bbls   710-   725
Plains-type rifle, .41 cal,
32" oct bbl, mkd J.H.
Johnston—Great
Western Gun Works,
Pittsburgh, Pa.   660-   720
1797 State of Pennsylvania
Contract FL musket,
mkd Miles/CP 2,900- 3,500
Sharps New Model 1859,
.52 cal perc carbine, used
by cavalry in CW   720-   780
Spencer CW cavalry
carbine, .50 cal rimfire,
22" bbl   860-   925
Spencer CW 7-shot repeat-
ing carbine, .52 cal rim-
fire, 22" bbl   775-   865
Springfield 1873 rifle, 45/70
cal   750-   920
U.S. FL common rifle, mkd
U.S.—N. Starr—Midd'n
—1826 . . . .   3,400+
U.S. FL musket, mkd
Harpers Ferry—1831 . . . 1,900- 2,250
U.S. Mississippi rifle, .54
cal, mkd E. Whitney—
U.S.—1848   875-   950
U.S. Springfield trap-door
45/70 cal rifle, dated 1890   650-   750
Winchester Hotchkiss 3rd
model, 45/70 cal . . . .   2,700+
Winchester saddle ring
carbine, 38/40 cal, 20"
bbl   520-   565
Foreign Hand Guns
Belgian perc belt pistol,
6½" oct bbl, .52 cal 1,400- 1,650

British cavalry officer's FL
pistol, c. 1760-1775, .69
cal 2,100- 2,500
British Modified Pattern of
1796 FL cavalry pistol,
.76 cal, 9" bbl, mkgs of
the 17th Light Dragoons   785-   850
British naval officer's FL
holster pistol, c. 1800, .52
cal 1,100- 1,350
British naval officer's FL
pistol, c. 1790, 9" brass
oct bbl 1,300- 1,550
British perc holster pistol,
c. 1830-1840, 8" oct bbl,
14" overall, mkd with
American and patriotic
motifs 4,700- 5,200
Dutch over/under pistol,
c. 1650, .46 cal, 13¾"
oct bbls . . . .   12,700+
English combination FL
pistol and sword, mkd
Clarke—London, .50 cal,
3" rnd screw bbl, 29½"
overall . . . .   3,500+
English FL Dragoon pistol,
Queen Anne period, 18"
overall, 11" rnd bbl, c.
1700-1710 . . . . 2,900- 3,400
European martial FL pistol,
c. 1840, .65 cal, 10" rnd
bbl   640-   685
European perc pistol, c.
1840, 9" rnd bbl, 15½"
overall, .67 cal   775-   820
FL boxlock English pocket
pistol, c. 1790, .41 cal,
mkd Brasher—London,
2½" rnd screw bbl   535-   590
French boxlock FL holster
pistol, c. 1760, .38 cal,
6" overall   490-   520
German FL holster pistol,
c. 1680, 21" overall, mkd
Herman Ghiot, 13½"
rnd bbl 4,800- 5,300
Italian FL holster pistol,
c. 1720, 16" overall, 9½"
rnd bbl 4,600- 5,400
Match pair, cased English
perc dueling pistols,
.44 cal, 16" overall, 10"
oct bbls, mkd J. Purdey
—Oxford St.—Gun Mfr—
London 9,700-10,375
Mid-Eastern FL holster
pistol, c. 1750, .60 cal,
19½" overall 5,700- 5,975
Miniature blunderbuss-
pistol, FL, mid-Eastern,
c. 1750, 11¾" overall,
5½" oct/rnd blunderbuss
bbl   925-   975

193

(continued)

Miniature FL pistol, c.
1720, 4¾" overall, .28 cal,
mkd Claude Niquet A
Liege 3,420- 3,600
Scottish Highland and
military style, 18th
century, FL belt pistol,
type used in Colonial
America, .62 cal 1,550- 1,750
Spanish Miquelet belt
pistol, c. 1810, 5½"
oct/rnd bbl. 1,100- 1,400

Foreign Shoulder Guns
Ancient matchlock wall
gun, India, 8" overall, 18
lbs., early 18th century
(or earlier) 950- 1,100
Ancient North African
(Berber) Snaphauce
camel gun, 5'3" overall,
49" oct/rnd bbl 625- 685
Austrian perc .58 cal rifle,
issued to U.S. troops at
beginning of CW, 37" bbl 790- 850
British Enfield .577 cal perc
musket, mkd 1858—
Tower with crown over
"VR" 1,350- 1,475
British FL swivel blunder-
buss, 24" brass bbl,
muzzle, 3" dia., 22 lbs.,
41" overall. 2,400- 2,700
British officer's FL fusil or
full stock fowling piece,
c. 1790, 38" oct/rnd bbl . . 1,200- 1,400
British 10 gauge side
hammer dbl bbl shotgun,
30" bbls 650- 675
CW British Enfield .577 cal
perc rifle musket, mkd
Barnett—London Tower 725- 785
Dutch FL military rifle,
used during American
Revolution, 36" oct/rnd
bbl, .67 cal mkd Thone &
Zoon—Amsterdam 2,400- 2,600
Dutch FL officer's fusil, 36"
bbl, .70 cal 1,600- 1,850
English perc dbl bbl side-
by-side shotgun, c. 1850,
28" bbls, 14 gauge 775- 850
French/Belgian DeLvigne
.69 cal perc musket,
imported for CW use by
Union Army, 40" bbl . . . 850- 925
French Charleville FL
musket, 1763, CP mkgs . 3,400- 3,575
French FL musket, used by
American in Revolution-
ary War 2,500- 2,675
French FL musket, mkd
Charlottesville on lock,

American Revolutionary
War 1,700- 1,900
German/Dutch FL musket,
43" bbl, type used in
American Revolution . . . 1,400- 1,550
German FL musket, 17th
century, military, 42"
oct/rnd bbl, .80 cal, mkd
Leopold I of Wiemer-
Neustadt 3,400- 3,700
Italian FL full stock fowling
piece, c. 1750, 5' overall,
.67 cal, mkd P. Bonafino . 3,750- 4,200
Italian Vetterli bolt action
rifle 265- 285
Japanese matchlock
musket, 42" oct bbl, .64
cal 850- 950
Japanese matchlock
musket, 40" oct bbl, .57
cal 825- 910
Japanese pill-lock short
hand cannon or carbine,
41" overall, 9 lbs., quite
ancient 775- 855
2nd model British Brown
Bess FL musket, 42" bbl,
used during French-
Indian and Revolution-
ary Wars 3,200- 3,500

Fireglow

When held to a light this glass, attributed
to the Mt. Washington Glass Company,
shows a fiery opalescence. It was made during the 1890s.

Creamer, ruffled top, pink/blue
flowers (ill.) . . . . $ 97-108
Sugar bowl, ruffled top, pink/
blue flowers (ill.) 120-130
Vase, autumn leaves, 7½" high . . 168-175
Vase, Bristol style, child's face,
button feet 180-190
Vase, brown/blue leaves, 7" high . 164-175

Fireglow

Fireplace Accessories

Our ancestors depended on the fireplace for
warmth and a place to cook their food. The
tools they used are collectible today. Brass

Fireplace Accessories

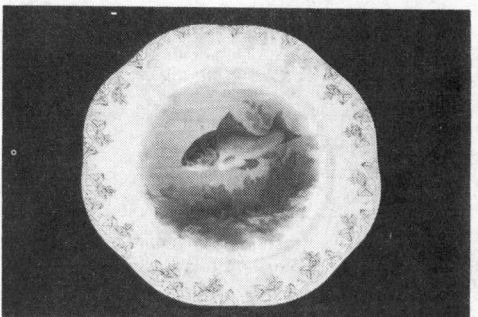

Fish Sets

and copper pieces are especially desirable; andirons (fire dogs), coal hods and fenders are among the most desired.

Coal box, English, tooled brass . . $162-180
Fender, brass, English, mid-1800s 720-775
Fender, brass, fan-type mid-1800s 785-850
Fire tending tools in rack, brass,
    mid-1800s, 4 pieces (ill.) 210-240
Grate, iron, on legs 110-122
Lighter, Cape Cod (ill.) 58- 68
Screen, hinged type, English 172-182
Screen, solid iron type used in
    summer to cover fireplace 118-124
Tools: shovel, poker, brush, in
    brass stand 88- 98

Fischer China

The firm was founded by Moritz Fischer in Herend, Hungary, in 1839. It was still operating in the 20th century just before World War II.

Egg cup, gilt trim $174-184
Figurine, sitting dog, white 77- 85
Vase, embossed flowers, reticu-
    lated handles, 12″ high 420-460
Vase, medallion front and back,
    yellow scrolls, hunting decor . . 390-452
Vase, pink/beige/green, 12½″
    high 392-420

Fish Sets

In vogue during the late Victorian era, they consisted of a large platter and 12 plates. Each piece was decorated with a fish. Havi-

land, Rosenthal, and most other china companies made these sets.

Hand-painted, embossed gold,
    sauceboat, 12 plates, blue/
    green $195-220
Haviland, green/pink flowers,
    fish in pond, 16 pcs., in
    leatherette case 395-440
Limoges, enameled branches,
    hand-painted, 23″ long 425-452
Limoges, seashells and fish,
    platter and 6 plates 182-192
Plate, 9½″ dia. (ill.) 49- 58
Platter, 12 plates, painted
    trout, bass, perch, carp, pike . . 268-282
Porcelain, seashells, lily pads,
    frogs, signed Germany, 12
    pcs. 291-310
Roses/vines, hand-painted,
    Austria, 1908, 8 pcs. 240-250

Flasks

Flasks

Chestnut, ½ pt., red brown,
    c. 1830s $280-299
Cut glass, sterling silver caps . . .   79- 89
Glass, ½ pt., pewter cup fits over
    bottom, 1930s 61- 70
Glass, ½ pt., pewter bottom and
    cap, 5¼″ high (ill.) 35- 42

195   (continued)

Grain, pt., aqua, maker unknown,
c. 1850s   240-260
Hip type, ½ pt., sterling silver,
1920s 77- 87
Ribbed, ½ pt., yellow amber,
c. 1840s   235-245
Sterling silver, monk, 4½" high . .   265-275
"Success To The Railroad," pt.,
olive green, large eagle on
reverse side, made by Kensing-
ton Glass Works, Philadelphia,
c. 1830   380-420
Violin, ½ pt., aqua, c. 1850s   172-182
Walking stick, ¼-pt. capacity,
glass rod fits inside, silver cap .   170-180
Washington and Taylor, qt.,
aqua   240-260

Florentine Art "Cameo"

Made in Bohemia, this glass has a satin
glass body and is heavily decorated with
enamel. Some think it's cameo glass but it
isn't. Late 18th, 19th century.

Vase, blue satin glass, white
flowers, 8" high $120-135
Vase, green satin glass, butter-
flies and flowers, 8½" high . . .   108-118
Whiskey glass, blue satin glass,
castle scene, set of 6   292-320

Flow Blue

Blue-and-white china on which the cobalt
blue glaze was caused to run during firing is
called Flow Blue. Mainly made in the Staffordshire District at various potteries, and
also produced in the United States, it was
popular during the mid to late 1800s. Highly
collectible today.

Bone dish, Ormonde pattern,
Meakin $35- 45

Flow Blue

Bone dishes, Johnson,
England, set of 6, ...   130-145
Bowl, soup, Rhone pattern 27- 36
Butter dish, Grindley   200-230
Butter pat, flowers (ill.) 19- 27
Butter patties, bluebirds, set
of 6   128-138
Cake stand, floral decor, 13"
high   140-155
Chocolate pot, blue/gold,
LaBelle   155-175
Compote, floral decoration,
molded leaf handles, cover 77- 86
Creamer, Haddon 74- 83
Creamer, Meakin 70- 79
Creamer, Ridgway 69- 77
Cup/saucer, Alberta pattern,
set 48- 56
Cup/saucer, Dahlia pattern,
set 58- 75
Cup/saucer, Japanese pattern,
Wood & Baggaley, set 50- 58
Cup/saucer, Jewel pattern,
Johnson, England, set 49- 56
Dish, Touraine pattern, Alcock,
England   153-165
Dish, vegetable, Imperial pat-
tern, Myatt, Son & Co.   95-130
Gravy boat, Astoria pattern,
Johnson Bros. 43- 53
Gravy boat, Begonia pattern,
Johnson Bros.   180-190
Gravy boat, Paisley pattern 59- 68
Jar, biscuit, barrel shape, elks,
c. 1890 . . . .   74- 83
Pitcher, English scene, 8" high . .   74- 83
Pitcher, gravy, Lonial pattern . . .   44- 54
Pitcher, Jenny Lind pattern,
England 57- 67
Pitcher, syrup, Warwick pat-
tern, Warwick China (USA) . . .   47- 56
Pitcher and bowl, floral decor,
Ridgway, both   215-235
Pitcher and bowl, LaBelle pat-
tern, both   195-235
Plate, Castro pattern, 14" dia. . . .   47- 55
Plate, flowers/leaves, 11" dia. . . .   57- 66
Plate, Marguerite pattern, scal-
loped edge, Grindley 46- 56
Plate, Melbourne pattern, 11"
dia. 40- 47
Platter, Blue Danube pattern,
oval, 10¼" dia. 66- 75
Platter, Jenny Lind pattern,
11" long   95-110
Platter, scalloped edge, Krona
pattern, Wood & Sons 76- 85
Punch bowl, flowers/leaves,
Ridgway, England   290-320
Ring tree 43- 51
Sauce, Touraine pattern,
Alcock 34- 44
Sugar bowl, Albany pattern 85- 95

Fluting Irons

Made of iron or brass, they rolled pleats in petticoats and cuffs. Early 1800s to early 1900s.

Fluting iron, marked Geneva,
    roller type (ill.) .... $ 82- 90
Iron handled tube, 3-legged
    stand, early 74- 83

Fluting Irons

Folk Art, American

Folk Art, American

Folk painting is the product of one un-trained in art; the effort of the painter to depict or portray scenes, persons or objects of interest to them. A lack of perspective, depth, and proportion, are a few of the chief characteristics of folk painting in America. Once again, prices change too quickly to give you an honest cost. A John Brewster, Jr., recently sold for $67,000; a J. Bradley, $43,000; a Nathaniel F. Wales, $12,000. Folk

Art, American, is here to stay.

"Brothers," done in crayon, Connecticut, c. 1860, 8"×11"
"The Country Church," c. 1855, 7"×11"
"Farm in West Cornwall, Connecticut," 1895, 8½"×18"
"Farm Scene," signed J.F. Gilman, dated 1871, charcoal, 19"×27"
"Fort Plain, New York," c. 1850, 23"×34"
"Home for Thanksgiving," New York State, c. 1850, 25"×30"
"Hunters," c. 1870, 14"×22"
"Landscape with Sawmill," G. Marston, 1863, 22"×30"
"The Mansion," charcoal c. 1850, 15"×23"
"Mississippi Farm by a River," c. 1875, 22"×27"
"Morning Chores in New Hampshire," c. 1840, 30"×36"
"Train on a Bridge," painted on tin, c. 1840, 10"×14"
"The Village Banker's Home in Winter," c. 1870, 22"×27" (ill.)
"Village Lake with Indians," c. 1850, 17"×23"
"Young Lady on a Balcony," c. 1820, 20"×36"

Much of this type of Americana is around. A lot of fakes are around also, so challenge the auctioneer if you don't think he's right (he probably is), question the antiques dealer, and know from whom you buy.

Fostoria Glass   FOSTORIA

Originally manufactured in Fostoria, Ohio, in 1887, the factory was moved a few years later to Moundsville, Virginia, where it continues to make a quality glassware. Discontinued patterns and early 20th century pieces are what collectors and dealers look for. Most pieces you find are in the $8, $20, and $65 range. It's lovely glass to collect, and here are a few of the many patterns: American, Baroque, Beverly, Amber and Green; Fairfax Ebony, Green, Pink, Rose, Topaz; Lafayette Clear; Mayfair Amber, Ebony, Green, Pink,

Fostoria Glass

197

(continued)

Rose, Optic Rose, Pink, Clear. Enjoy collecting a lovely glass. See **Clubs and Publications**, this Price Guide.

Bowl, pink opalescent	$ 50-	58
Bookends, dog heads, pr.	57-	67
Candleholders, Baroque, w/prisms, pr.	79-	84
Candleholders, Topaz, 2-light, pr.	75-	79
Cruet, Optic Rose, 5″ high	51-	58
Figurine, duck, Beverly	42-	52
Mugs, fish-shaped	24-	28
Platter, Ebony, open handles	45-	58
Vase, clear pedestal base, acid etched acorns and oak leaves (ill.)	84-	93

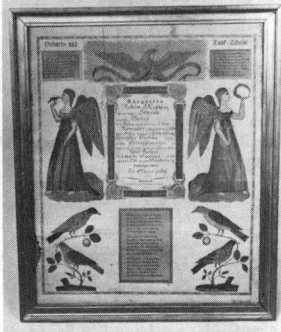

Frakturs

Frakturs

Simply put, a fraktur is a birth certificate that is ornately decorated. They were popular in the Pennsylvania German area in the early to late 1800s.

Birth certificate, framed, signed
W. Grofs, 1861. Printed in
Allentown, Pa., 16″×19″,
hand-colored birds, angels, and
an American eagle (ill.) $130-145

Francesware

Frosted with stained amber rims or tops, this glass made by Hobbs, Brockunier and Company was both pressed and blown-molded in the 1880s. A real collector's item today. Don't confuse the name with Francis Ware, which was japanned tinware made and decorated by Henry and Tom Francis in Philadelphia around 1830.

Bowl, clear, 7″ sq.	$ 77-	85
Match holder, frosted, amber top	88-	94
Pitcher, blown, 4 mold, amber stained top, frosted hobnail body, 8″ high (ill.)	320-340	

Francesware

Sauce, 4½″ sq., hobnail	58-	63
Tumbler, typical	71-	82
Water set, 6 pcs., frosted, amber tops, all	570-620	

Frankoma Pottery

John Frank began the pottery firm in Sapulpa, Oklahoma, in 1933. He combined his chemical knowledge with the pottery making traditions of the Indians of the Southwest. The mottled lines result from the use of colored earthenware clays. The pacing leopard was the original trademark, but it was discontinued because of difficulty encountered reproducing it in soft clay. FRANKOMA is the mark used today. In 1965 they began making commemorative Christmas plates.

Bowl, 11″ dia., mottled hues of brown and yellow, Leopard mark	$ 64-	73
Christmas plate, "Laid in a Manger," 1969	45-	52
Christmas plate, "Gifts for the Christ Child," 1967	70-	80
Cookie jar, mottled blue, FRANKOMA mark	62-	74
Cup/saucer, mottled brown and yellow, FRANKOMA mark (ill.)	45-	54
Vase, 11″ high, brown/green, Leopard mark	138-152	
Vase, 6″ high, blue/brown, FRANKOMA mark	41-	51

Frankoma Pottery

Fraternal Order Collectibles

Fraternal Order Collectibles

Elk, Moose, Lion, Eagle, Mason, Odd Fellow—all are fraternal organizations. What they wore or carried during the 18th and 19th centuries is collectible today.

A.O.F. parasol, 1908 convention .	$ 49-	54
BPOE ashtray, Cincinnati, 1904, Rookwood pottery (rare)	67-	74
BPOE handled mug, elk and clock	48-	54
F.O.E., watch fob	42-	52
Knights of Columbus match safe	47-	54
Masonic jug, Canary ware, English	382-	420
Masonic shaving mug	48-	58
Odd Fellow's jug, pink lustre, English, rare	410-	442
Plate, Masonic, 10¼″ dia.	37-	47
Ribbon, Modern Woodmen (ill.) . .	25-	32
Shrine goblet, Washington, D.C., 1902, red flashed glass	49-	58
Shrine, Omaha, 1918, mug	47-	57

Fruit Jars

Fruit Jars

In one word—Mason—John Landis Mason, that is. A tinsmith by trade, at the age of 26, in his shop in New York City, he designed his now-famous wide-mouth jar, the Mason's Pat. Nov. 30th 1858. He also invented the tin screw-on lids to fit the jars he farmed out to the various glassmakers in the area. **Important:** This explains why there are so many names on his jars, but always with Mason's name blown into the glass. Many pioneer firms are still in the business, such as Drey, Ball, Kerr, and Boyd. Mason's "Black" glass jars are priceless today.

Atlas, Cloverleaf, pt. or qt.	$ 27-	35
Atlas, E-Z Seal, amber, qt.	40-	50
Ball, Ideal, ¼-pt., ½-pt., clear or green	28-	36
Banner, patented February 9, 1864, aqua	44-	54
Clark's Peerless, pt. or qt.	34-	42
Crown emblem, ½-gal., amber . . .	49-	60
Dillon & Co. #4, emerald green (ill.)	120-	130
Eureka, qt., clear	42-	50
Gem, qt., clear	25-	34
Globe, pt., amber	76-	82
Hazel preserve, Atlas lightning seal, qt., aqua	27-	34
Lightning, qt., amber	47-	53
Mason, Maltese Cross emblem, patented November 30, 1858, ½-gal., amber	52-	60
Mason's 1872, patented, qt., aqua	38-	40
Smalley self sealer, qt., amethyst, ...	37-	47
Spencer, C.F., patented, qt., aqua	32-	41
Victory, qt. or ½-gal., clear	22-	31
Woodbury, qt., aqua	41-	51
Mason's Pat. Nov. 30th 1858	62-	72

Fry Glass

Fry Glass

Made by H.C. Fry Company, Rochester,

(continued)

Pennsylvania, 1900 to 1929. Fine cut glass for the first 15 years, then Foval glass was introduced after 1925. Some pieces are marked Fry. Gold was used in the batch to make Foval. Collectors are just beginning to appreciate Fry glass. Usually a combination of two colors in pastel shades of greens, pinks, blues. Foval is also known as Pearl Art.

Bowl, black, clear bell stem, 6" tall, marked Fry, dated	$255-272
Candlesticks, blue trim, 13" high, Foval	425-485
Cologne bottle, clear, green stopper, signed Fry	148-159
Creamer, opalescent, green trim under tray, signed	220-240
Cup and saucer, Foval, 2½" high	110-124
Custard cup, ovenware, 1919	62- 72
Epergne, intaglio cut, signed	240-250
Foval, barber bottle, milky white, fiery opalescent	88-100
Foval, candlestick, blue/white, 10" high	232-248
Foval coffeepot, opalescent, white handle, 10" high	325-350
Foval, compote, cream color base, blue standard, 9¼" dia.	220-232
Foval, cup/saucer, blue jade handle	122-140
Foval, pitcher, yellow iridescent, cobalt handle, 6 tumblers	260-270
Pitcher, craquelle, applied blue handle (ill.)	162-170
Pitcher, opalescent blue stripes over blue crystal, 4 tumblers	362-382
Sugar bowl, covered	280-290
Toothpick, ruffled, applied blue crystal handles	88- 98
Vase, craquelle, blue application (ill.)	123-140
Vase, cream, cobalt handles, 7½" high	210-242

Fulper Pottery

What you find today was made at Flemington, New Jersey, from around 1910 until the late 1920s when the factory burned. In 1930 the name was changed to Stangl.

Bowls

Flared rim, matt green finish, 10" dia.	$ 75- 86
Footed, copper glaze finish, 9" dia.	74- 84
Rolled edge, deep blue glaze, 8¼" dia.	70- 80
Two-handled, brown matt finish, 9½" dia.	64- 72

Lamps

Night, seated lady, 7¼" high	175-182
Perfume, ballerina, blue, pale pink, yellow, ea.	192-199
Perfume, young girl in skirt, 6" high	182-194
Perfume, young girl w/fan, purple, 7½" high	210-240

Miscellaneous

Bookends, Egyptian scribes, dark green matt finish, pr.	175-190
Candlesticks, browns/blues, 5½", pr.	52- 62
Flower frog, olive green matt finish, 4" high	61- 70

Pitchers

Bulbous, multi-brown glaze, 7¼" high	52- 62
Coiled style, turquoise glaze, 6¼" high	128-140

Vases

Bulbous, rose drip/blue matt finish, 7" high	62- 72
Bulbous, grey flecks, 8¼" high	94-108
Cornucopia, green/blue/green, 9¼" high	151-172
Flared rim, handled, Famille Rose glaze, 7" high	161-170
Squat, green matt finish, 5½" high	58- 68
Stick type, handled, blue/grey glaze	70- 80

Furniture, American

The prices quoted here have to be very general as antique furniture prices are climbing steadily, day by day. The better auction galleries are getting unbelievable prices for Chippendale, Queen Anne, Hepplewhite—both American and English—and there's no end in sight. Just know what you're doing, or pay a member of the Appraisers Association of America to assist you.

Pilgrim style, 1650-1690
William and Mary style, 1690-1720
Queen Anne style, 1720-1750
Chippendale style, 1750-1775
Shaker, 1776-1900
Hepplewhite style, 1785-1800

Fulper

Duncan Phyfe, 1795-1847
Sheraton style, 1800-1820
American Empire style, 1820-1840
Rococo style, 1840s to 1860s
Gothic style, 1840-1865
Belter furniture, 1844-1863
Cottage furniture, 1850-1880
Spool-turned style, 1850-1880
Renaissance style, 1860-1875
Louis XVI style, 1865-1875
Eastlake style, 1870-1880
New England style, 17th to mid-19th
centuries
Pennsylvania Dutch, 18th and 19th
centuries

Armchairs

Bentwood, c. 1860, caned,
set of 6 .... $ 378- 420
Ladder-back, maple, rush
seat, c. 1840, set of 4 ...... 495- 550
Ladder-back, sausage turned,
old green paint, rush seat ... 250- 285
Ladder-back, Shaker style,
4-slat, New England, rush
seat 375- 420
Massachusetts, c. 1730s 465- 510
Medallion back, open arms,
oak, upholstered, c. 1890s .. 185- 220
Platform type, open arms,
curved wooden frame,
upholstered 245- 285
Windsor, comb-back, serpen-
tine crest rail 2,500-2,775

Beds

Brass, double size, swellfoot
end, c. 1880s 1,700-1,875
Brass plated, double size, bow-
foot end, c. 1890s 975-1,100
Cabinet mantel type, elm,
beveled mirror, c. 1890s 420- 450
Child's, iron, white enamel,
drop sides, c. 1890s 325- 345
Half tester, walnut, recessed
veneer panels, c. 1850 ..... 2,600+
Jenny Lind spool, double
size 420- 480
Oak, double, raised paneling,
head and footboard,
c. 1890s 385- 425
Oak, twin, carved, head
and footboard, c. 1890s 295- 360
Rope, high posts, cherry,
corn-shuck mattress,
c. 1820 .... 1,500+
Spool, low posts, triangular
headboard, c. 1855 .... 950- 995
Walnut, single, molded foot
and head rail, carved
crest, c. 1850 .... 520- 545

Benches

Church pew, pine, unrestored,
New England, c. 1850s,
10' long 750- 800

Cobbler's, complete with all
tools, original condition,
c. 1840 .... 875- 990
Deacon's, original dark
finish, 10' long, New
Hampshire, c. 1820s 985-1,100
Deacon's, spindle back, 8-leg,
Connecticut, c. 1830 1,000-1,700
Mammy rocker, removable
guard rail, stenciled,
c. 1840 1,600-1,800
Mammy rocker, wooden cog
to operate butter churn,
etc., c. 1840 1,700-1,975
Porch, poplar, heeled
through seat, solid back 220- 250

Bookcases

Globe Werneke type, 5-
section, oak, top and
base, all 350- 420
Library type, 6' wide,
4 adjustable shelves,
3 glass doors 610- 675
Oak, 5 adjustable shelves,
open lattice-work in
top, glass door 395- 475
Oak, 6 shelves, glass doors,
c. 1880s 375- 455
Rosewood, wall type, 3
shelves, c. 1840s 420- 482

Bureaus

Bowfront, maple, carved
pulls, 4-drawer, c. 1860 ..... 950- 995
Cottage, 4-drawer, pine 380- 460
Hepplewhite, pine, bracket
feet, 4-drawer 985-1,150

Chests

Apothecary, oak, 60-drawer,
porcelain knobs, c. 1840 .. 1,400- 1,550
Blanket, bracket feet,
poplar, black brush and
comb decoration (ill.) 520- 585
Blanket, cherry, dovetail,
rattail hinges, c. 1730s ... 1,875- 2,400
Blanket, Pennsylvania
Dutch, green, dull red trim 2,800- 3,200
Blanket, pine, strap hinges,
2 drawers in base, c. 1830 . 1,500- 1,700
Chippendale, bowfront,
cherry, 6-drawer, c. 1760 . 6,700- 7,400
Chippendale type, mahog-
any, ogee feet, 6-drawer .. 820- 860
Dower, Pennsylvania, paint-
ed and decorated pine,
hinged top, animals,
fowls, c. 1773, 19¾" high,
50½" long (ill.) 5,400- 5,800
Dower, Pennsylvania Dutch,
painted green/red
w/flowers on front 4,200- 4,600
Dower, Pennsylvania Dutch,
tulip decor, original paint,
c. 1810 .... 4,875- 5,600

(continued)

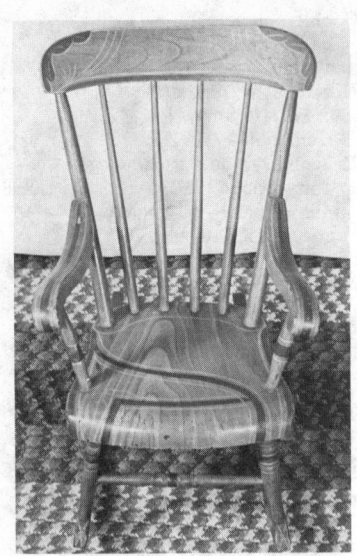

Furniture, American

Hepplewhite, pine, 4-drawer,
veneered mahogany front,
c. 1790 . . . . 1,800- 2,450

China Cabinets

Corner, swell front, 4 adjustable shelves, oak,
c. 1890s. 620- 680

Mahogany, carved crest,
beveled glass on 3 sides,
5 adjustable shelves 770- 850

Oak, glass on 3 sides, mirror
on top, lattice-work in
door, c. 1890 . . . . 640- 695

Oak, spiral fluted pillars,
beveled glass on 3 sides,
c. 1890s. 775- 840

Oak, swell-shaped glass in
ends, carved feet, 4
adjustable shelves 820- 860

Cradles

Hooded, hickory, hand holes,
c. 1820s. 670- 720

Hooded, pine, c. 1830s 520- 580

Open, walnut, spindle construction, c. 1850s 620- 680

Rocker type, cutout hearts,
maple (ill.) 575- 655

Rocker type, slat decorated,
cherry, c. 1830 . . . . 545- 640

Round rails, square posts,
knob finials, walnut,
c. 1840 . . . . 520- 580

Cupboards

Corner, cherry, 2 doors
above and below, 1 draw-
er, c. 1830 . . . . 4,700- 5,200

Corner, maple, solid doors
above and below, scroll
top, c. 1850 . . . . 3,700- 3,975

Corner, poplar and pine
paneled doors, c. early
1800s, 6' 7" high 1,200- 1,400

Corner, poplar, glass doors
above, solid below,
original paint, c. 1840s . . . 2,500- 2,700

Dutch, cherry, glass doors
above, solid below, cham-
fered corners, solid ends,
wooden knobs, c. 1760s . . 5,400- 5,850

Hanging, pine, single glass
door, 3 shelves, c. 1830s . . 770- 820

Linen, Pennsylvania, original green paint, solid
doors, c. 1830 . . . . 2,400- 2,700

Open, glass doors above,
solid below, 3 drawers in
middle, c. 1850 . . . . 2,850- 3,300

Open, recessed top, glass
doors above, solid below,
carved pulls, c. 1840 . . . . . 1,975- 2,450

Pantry, Pennsylvania
Dutch, red/green, white
flower decor, c. 1740 . . . . . 3,400- 3,700

Pewter, painted pine, New
England, 6 shelves, solid
doors below, c. 1750s 3,400- 3,800

Pewter, pine, hutch top, 3
shelves, solid doors below,
2 drawers, c. 1830 . . . . 3,400- 3,800

Pie safe, pine, pierced
geometric tin panels 900- 1,150

Desks

Bureau, fall front secretary
drawer, carved pulls on 3
drawers, c. 1860s 1,100- 1,400

Butler's, walnut, c. 1850 . . . 2,900- 3,400

Chippendale, shell-carved
mahogany yoke-front,
gadrooned base, New
England, 18th century,
42¾" high, 41¼" wide
(ill.) . . . . 65,000+

Chippendale style, cherry,
slant-front, Oxbow, Block
and Fan interior, original
pulls, ball/claw feet,
c. 1750 . . . . 4,200- 4,800

Chippendale style, mahog-
any slant-front, Colonial,
38" high, 36½" wide (ill.) . 8,400- 9,300

Cylinder front, walnut,
veneered cylinder panel,
machine lines and carving,
spindled gallery, 3 draw-
ers below, c. 1840s 2,900- 3,400

Drop front, table type,
walnut, beaded molding,
c. 1850s 1,400- 1,800

Hepplewhite, mahogany,
slant-front, original bail
handle pulls, c. 1790 . . . . . 4,200- 4,400

Furniture, American

Lady's, pine, 4 drawers
below writing surface,
c. 1820 . . . . 975- 1,100
Lady's, walnut, 3 drawers
below writing surface,
c. 1850 . . . . 875- 1,100
Lap, mahogany, brass trim
overall, ink bottles, etc.,
c. 1840 . . . . 525- 575
Plantation, walnut, glass
doors above lift-top
writing surface, c. 1830s . 2,900- 3,200
Rolltop, oak, c. 1880s 1,900- 2,200
Rolltop, oak, miniature,
child's, c. 1890s 750- 900
Rolltop, walnut, c. 1860s . . . 3,200- 3,450
Schoolmaster's, mahogany,
bookcase top, burned legs,
c. 1830s 850- 975
Schoolmaster's, oak, cub-
byholes below gallery rail,
c. 1850 . . . . 700- 800
Schoolmaster's, walnut,
turned legs, single drawer
below, c. 1840 . . . . 850- 975

Dough Troughs
Chestnut, lid, turned legs,
dovetailed box, c. 1860 . . . 660- 720
Pine, squared tapered legs,
original red paint, c. 1840s 750- 840
Pine, turned legs, dove-
tailed box, grained finish,
c. 1840s 720- 770
Poplar, dovetailed box, on
box frame, c. 1830 . . . . . . 585- 650

Dressers
Dressing case, marble top,
burl stiles, mirror frame,
applied molding around
lower drawers, c. 1830 . . . 1,400- 1,600
Marble top, molded burl
veneer panels on drawers,
c. 1840 . . . . 785- 855

Marble top, projecting front
ring, molding on drawers,
original pulls, c. 1860 . . . . 875- 950
Marble top, swing mirror, 2
boxes, applied molding on
drawers, c. 1840s 978- 1,150
Oak, beveled mirror,
4-drawer, c. 1870 . . . . 385- 430
Oak, German beveled mir-
ror, 2 small, 2 large
drawers, c. 1895 . . . . 345- 475
Oak, lyre frame mirror, 2
small, 2 large drawers, applied molding on mirror
frame and drawer fronts,
brass-plated pulls, c. 1890 295- 328
Oak, 4-drawer, wooden pulls,
c. 1870 . . . . 320- 360
Oak, 6-drawer, spindled
gallery on top, brass pulls,
c. 1860s 420- 485
Pine, 3-drawer, New
England, c. 1790 . . . . 3,400- 3,800
Wooden top, burl veneer
panels on drawers, tear-
drop pulls, c. 1850 . . . . . . 920- 980
Wooden top, maple swing
mirror, 2 hanky boxes,
marble insert, c. 1850 . . . . 940- 980

Dry Sinks
Cherry, splashboard back,
single door below, c. 1850 . 1,100- 1,400
Pine, high back, candle
drawer, single door below,
c. 1840 . . . . 895- 1,200
Pine, lift top, 2 drawers
below, c. 1850 . . . . 755- 875
Pine, single door below,
c. 1830 . . . . 795- 840

Footstools
Mahogany frame and legs,
upholstered, late 1800s . . 270- 320

203

(continued)

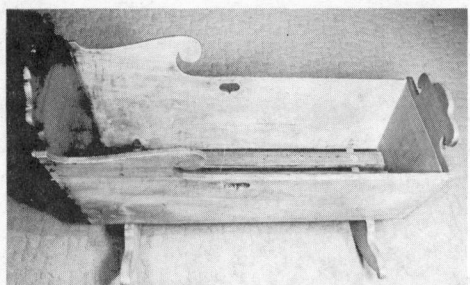

Furniture, American

Furniture, American

Mahogany veneer, cabriole legs, needlepoint cover, c. 1870s	360-	420
Maple, carved legs, c. 1840	320-	410
Scroll type, Louis XV, velvet upholstery, c. 1860	595-	685
Walnut, beaded edge, upholstered, bun feet, c. 1860	320-	360

Hall Trees

Oak, French beveled mirror, 6 iron hat holders, double umbrella holders, c. 1880	480-	510
Oak, German beveled mirror, 6 double hooks, iron, umbrella holder, seat w/lid, c. 1870s	485-	570
Walnut, burl veneer raised panels, molded, incised pediments, double umbrella holders, pierced back, marble shelf over drawer, c. 1840	1,750-	1,900
Walnut, German beveled mirror, veneer raised panels, brass double hat hooks, marble shelf over drawer, carved applied ornaments, c. 1840s	1,600-	1,850

Hat Racks

Accordion type, 7 wooden pegs, porcelain tips, chestnut, c. 1860	190-	210
Accordion type, 13 wooden pegs, porcelain tips, walnut, c. 1850	180-	220
Walnut, molded frame, 8 wooden pegs, c. 1850	260-	270

Love Seats

Hepplewhite, walnut, carved mirror back, c. 1790	1,900-	2,200
Medallion back, walnut frame, upholstered, Louis XV style	1,975-	2,450
Serpentine back, walnut frame, upholstered, c. 1850s	1,200-	1,400
Victorian, mirror back, New England, pineapple upholstery, c. 1850	1,900-	2,400
Wooden framed back, applied burl veneer panels, incised lines, c. 1830s	1,900-	2,200

Lowboys

Mahogany, drake feet, Penn-

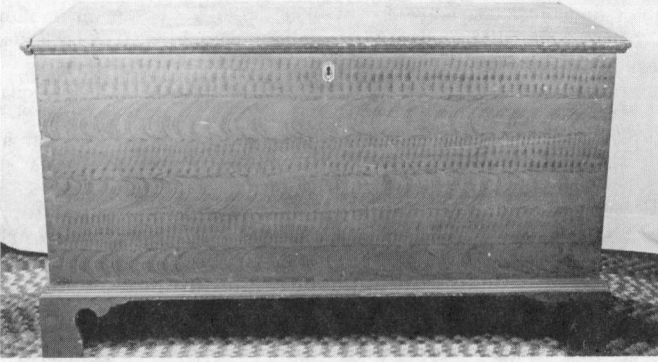

Furniture, American

sylvania, 18th century,
32" high, 34½" long (ill.) . 5,400- 5,750

Magazine Racks

Oak, spindle construction,
c. 1890s 180- 220

Wall type, reticulated, chest-
nut, c. 1880 . . . . 225- 245

Wall type, walnut, Eastlake
style, c. 1875 . . . . 192- 225

Mirrors

Courting, walnut,
11"×15½", c. 1800 . . . . . 1,400- 1,750

Mahogany, scrolled crest,
floor type, c. 1870 . . . . . . 595- 650

Shaving, 2-drawer, walnut,
c. 1850 . . . . 485- 545

Sheraton, maple frame,
carved, 21"×29", c. 1790 . 695- 750

Wall, Chippendale, carved
and parcel-gilded, walnut
(ill.) 5,600- 5,800

Wall, curly maple, New
England, c. 1830 . . . . 580- 695

Secretaries

American Empire, mahog-
any veneer, bookcase
top, c. 1830 . . . . 2,200- 2,700

Block front, mahogany,
Massachusetts, all origi-
nal, c. 1750 . . . .   87,000+

Chippendale, Philadelphia,
cherry, slant-front, c. 1765   96,000+

Sheraton, mahogany,
original pulls, c. 1815 . . . . 4,200- 4,700

Tambour, mahogany, late
18th century, bureaulike
base, 4 graduated draw-
ers, French splayed
bracket feet, 2 diamond-
glazed doors above 4,200- 4,900

Sideboards

American Empire, piecrust
molding, cherry top,
mahogany, c. 1830s 2,900- 3,400

Butler's, bird's-eye maple,
New England, c. 1800 . . . 3,800- 4,475

Hepplewhite, breakfront,
butler's, mahogany 9,100-10,000

Marble top, molded drawers,
veneer panels, chamfered
corner stiles w/applied
molding, projecting front,
c. 1840 . . . . 3,200- 3,700

Sheraton, mahogany, 4
doors, 3 drawers, c. 1810 . 7,000- 7,600

Sofas

Belter, laminated rosewood,
ornately carved back,
c. 1840 . . . .   22,000+

Double arch, molded frame,
button-tufted upholstery,
c. 1850 . . . . 2,200- 2,700

Furniture, American

Finger roll back, tufted
upholstery, walnut frame,
c. 1860 . . . . 2,200- 2,800

Serpentine back, walnut
frame, Louis XV style . . . 1,900- 2,200

Wicker, 5 feet wide 375- 420

Stands

Lamp, marble recessed in
molded rim, walnut,
tripod base, c. 1859 . . . . . 380- 420

Lamp, marble recessed in
molded rim, cherry,
carved bird ornament,
tripod base, c. 1840 . . . . . 475- 525

Night, curly maple,
2-drawer, turned legs, 28"
high (ill.) 520- 555

Furniture, American

Furniture, American

Night, 2-drawer, porcelain knobs, turned legs, walnut, c. 1850	420-	480
Parlor, marble top, squared corners, incised lines, c. 1855	420-	482
Parlor, rectangular marble top, veneer frieze, machine lines, c. 1850	520-	580
Parlor, round wooden top, walnut, tripod base, c. 1860	325-	385
Sheraton, night, cherry, 2-drawer, c. 1810	620-	680
Wig, mahogany, c. 1830	340-	350

Tables

Banquet, walnut dropleaf, 91" long, c. 1840	3,700-	4,200
Butterfly, dropleaf, cherry, c. 1750s	1,800-	2,400
Card, Hepplewhite, cherry, c. 1790	1,900-	2,400
Card, Sheraton, inlaid mahogany, serpentine-front, Boston, c. 1800 (ill.)	3,200-	3,700
Chippendale, card, lunet-ted corners, c. 1770		27,000+
Chippendale, piecrust tilt top, birdcage, carved base, claw feet	2,700-	2,975
Console, maple, lift top, 1-drawer, c. 1820s	1,400-	1,700
Dining, rectangular, dropleaf, cherry, c. 1840	1,600-	1,900
Dining, round extension w/5 leaves, cherry, c. 1830s		3,700+
Dining, round extension w/3 leaves, walnut, turned legs, c. 1850	1,400-	1,700
Dining, square extension w/4 leaves, pedestal base, c. 1860	1,100-	1,350
Kitchen, chestnut, rec-tangular top, turned legs, c. 1860s	550-	570
Kitchen, pine, dropleaf, drawer at one end, c. 1840s	720-	780
Library, lower shelf, 1-drawer, c. 1870s	362-	420
Library, poplar frame, mahogany veneer top, rectangular top	285-	300
Parlor, mahogany, French legs, c. 1890s	270-	295
Parlor, oak, half shelf, rectangular top, c. 1895	295-	320
Round, 48" dia., pedestal,		

Furniture, American

lion's paw feet, tiger
oak, c. 1890   820-   855
Round, oak, 54″ dia.,
pedestal, square feet, 3
extra leaves   645-   725
Round, oak, 36″ dia.,
round base, lion's paw
feet, 2 extra leaves,
c. 1890s   670-   740
Tavern, cherry, round,
single drawer, c. 1830 . . . .   1,600- 1,950
Tavern, maple, single
drawer, turned legs,
c. mid-1800s 1,800- 2,200
Tea, tray-top type, Chip-
pendale, carved mahog-
any, claw-and-ball
feet, New York, 18th
century (ill.) 4,200- 4,700

Washstands

Commode, marble top
and splashboard, burl
veneer panels on 3
drawers, molded pilas-
ters, projection front,
c. 1840   800-   900

Furniture, American

Commode, marble top
and splashboard,
single drawer, 2 doors
below   750-   855
Maple, 1 drawer, towel
racks at each end,
c. 1870   420-   460
Oak, single drawer, slop
jar compartment,
brass-plated handles   370-   420
Oak, 3 drawers, slop jar
compartment, c. 1890s . . .   350-   428
Pine, towel bars, opening
for basin, 1 drawer
below, c. 1850   545-   700

Whatnots

Corner, on cupboard base, 3
graduated shelves w/fret-
ted backs, c. 1860   620-   700
Corner, walnut, 5 graduated
shelves, turned finials,
c. 1850   710-   800
Hanging, glass doors above,
2 drawers below, applied
molding at top   510-   585
Hanging, walnut, leaf
carved, 4 graduated
shelves, c. 1850   620-   655
Side, 5 graduated shelves,
walnut, turned finials,
c. 1860   650-   720

Furniture, English

Furniture, English

The demand for the genuine far exceeds the genuine. Prices are staggering—and going, going higher! The prices listed here are already out-of-date.

William and Mary style, 1689-1702
Queen Anne style, 1702-1714
Early Georgian style, 1702-1745
Chippendale style, 1745-1765
Adam style, 1765-1790
Hepplewhite style, 1780-1800
Sheraton style, 1790-1810
Regency style, 1793-1820

Beds

Adam style walnut and
damask bedstead
w/round fluted pillar
legs . . . . $ 2,700- 3,200
Chippendale style carved
mahogany 4-post canopy
w/acanthus carved flar-
ing tester and shaggy
claw feet 6,700- 7,700

Cabinets

Chippendale style, book,
mahogany, 2 paneled
cupboard doors, bracket
feet 7,100- 7,800

207   (continued)

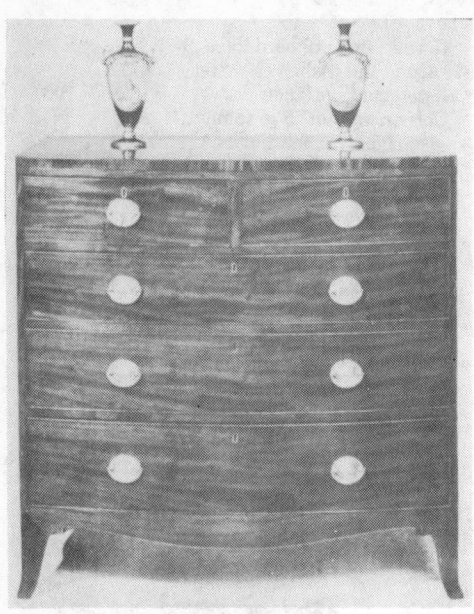

Furniture, English

Early Georgian breakfront,
carved and inlaid mahog-
any, plinth base 8,200- 9,000
Hepplewhite, bowfront, on
stand, inlaid mahogany,
in 2 sections, round
tapered legs........... 8,700- 9,400
Regency style, breakfront,
4 glazed doors, cupboard
below............... 7,000 +
Sheraton style, carved and
inlaid, butler's china,
w/secretary drawer,
double doors, single-
shelved cupboard 8,300- 8,500

Chairs

Adam-Hepplewhite, painted
and gilded, tapered legs . 3,700- 4,200
Chippendale style wing, on
mahogany molded square
legs 7,900- 8,700
Early Georgian, damask
upholstery, walnut, pad
feet 5,400- 6,200
Gilded, decorated, inlaid
M.O.P., papier-mache,
c. 1860 (ill.) 360- 370
Hepplewhite style, dining,
leather seat, balloon
back, set of 4 .... 5,400- 5,700
Queen Anne style, corner,
slip seat, shell-carved
front legs............. 4,400- 4,800
Queen Anne style, dining,
solid and burl walnut,

fiddle-shaped seat, leaf-
carved cabriole legs 3,800- 4,700
Regency style, library, rosewood, leather upholstery,
reeded seat rails, incur-
vate legs 4,200- 4,800
Sheraton style painted and
decorated armchair,
shield-shaped back
w/square tapering
splayed legs, crewel
embroidery 4,500- 4,700
William and Mary style,
side, walnut, needlepoint
seat and back 2,800- 3,200

Chests of Drawers

Early Georgian mule type,
mahogany, on ogival
scrolled bracket feet 6,200- 6,800
Hepplewhite, inlaid mahog-
any, serpentine front,
valance apron continuing
to splayed feet......... 5,100- 5,700
Hepplewhite, mahogany,
bowfront, splayed
bracket feet........... 5,400- 5,700
Queen Anne, inlaid burl
elm and walnut 6,600- 6,975
Sheraton, inlaid mahogany
bowfront, c. 1800, 41½"
high, 41" wide (ill.) 5,400- 5,900
William and Mary style, on
bun feet 4,900- 5,600

Chest-on-Chests

Chippendale, mahogany,
scrolled bracket feet .... 42,000 +
Queen Anne style, black
and gold, 3 drawers
below, 6 above, resting on
cabriole legs, club feet... 17,000-19,000

Desks

Early Georgian, walnut and
mahogany, counting-
house type............ 4,800- 5,200
Queen Anne, slant-front,
inlaid walnut, cartouche-
shaped brasses and bail
handles, molded base
w/bracket feet 9,000- 9,800
Sheraton, carved mahogany
cylinder, pullout slide,
tapering legs, castered,
c. 1800, 41½" high, 46"
long (ill.).............. 8,500- 9,400
Sheraton style, inlaid
mahogany and leather
kidney-shaped pedestal
desk, kneehole style 9,400- 9,800
Writing, Georgian, mahog-
any double-sided pedestal
type, red leather top,
18th century, 30½" high,
54" wide (ill.) 4,400- 4,975

Furniture, English

Furniture, English

Love Seats
  Early Georgian, walnut,
  loose seat cushion,
  acanthus-carved cabriole
  legs, claw-and-ball feet .. 7,500- 8,600
Secretaries
  Early Georgian, cabinet
  type, inlaid walnut and
  burl walnut, 2 mirrored
  doors, bracket feet 19,000-22,500
  Queen Anne, bookcase type,
  inlaid burl walnut, slant-
  front, double doors
  above, bracketed feet ... 27,000-29,000
Settees
  Queen Anne, 2-chair back,
  walnut, slipseat, slight
  cabriole legs, pad feet ... 7,400- 8,200
  William and Mary, walnut,
  needlepoint covering,
  loose seat............. 6,200- 6,700
Sideboards
  Hepplewhite, small bow-
  front, inlaid mahogany,
  tapering legs w/string
  lines, spade feet........ 10,200-11,100
  Regency style pedestal side-
  board, inlaid mahogany
  and satinwood, valanced
  gallery, on quadrangular
  pedestals, each w/shallow
  drawer and cupboard,
  short saber feet........ 9,900-10,250
  Sheraton style bowfront, inlaid mahogany and burl
  wood, bottle drawers,
  etc., square tapering legs
  inlaid w/panels of burl
  wood 10,400-11,300
Stools
  Early Georgian, mahogany
  and damask, fireside type,

  cabriole legs, club feet ... 2,900- 3,400
  Queen Anne, w/valanced
  frame and cabriole legs,
  club feet 3,900- 4,400
Tables
  Breakfast, Sheraton, mahogany, late 18th century,
  28½″ high, 50½″ long ... 4,400- 4,700
  Chippendale mahogany octagonal tripod, tilting top,
  tilting on a "birdcage"
  support, whorled feet.... 4,900- 5,400
  Chippendale, side, mahog-
  any and inlaid satinwood,
  on square tapered legs
  w/ormolu toes......... 6,200- 6,400
  Early Georgian 3-pedestal
  hunt table, mahogany,
  splayed tripods ending in
  snake feet 6,500- 7,200
  Hepplewhite style, card,
  cabriole legs crested
  w/shell motifs, slightly
  scrolled toes 4,400- 4,800
  Library, extension, drop leaf,
  mahogany, carved base,
  claw feet (ill.) 2,700- 2,975
  Sheraton style, inlaid satinwood, sewing, octagonal
  top, 2 drawers, sewing
  bag, tapered square legs . 3,900- 4,400
  Sheraton style, mahogany
  tilting-top breakfast, top
  on 4 reeded splayed supports terminating in con-
  forming brass toe caps ... 4,400- 4,850
Wine Cooler Stands
  Adam style, mahogany, 2
  brass handles, zinc-lined . 3,200- 3,800
  Early Georgian, mahogany,
  brass lion masks, loose
  ring handles 3,600- 4,200

(continued)

Regency style, mahogany,
fluted lower border and
square supports 2,900- 3,400

Furniture, French

Following its American and English neighbors, quality French furniture has gone out of sight, pricewise. Too much reproduction of the Louis XV and Louis XVI will eventually bring down the price of the original.

Louis XIV style, 1643-1715
Regence style, 1715-1723
Louis XV style, 1715-1774
Louis XVI style, 1774-1792
Directoire style, 1793-1804
Empire style, 1804-1814
French Provincial, made in provinces

Beds
Directoire style, alcove type,
carved fluted posts . . . . $ 3,200- 3,700
Directoire style, day type,
loose cushion and bolster .   3,100- 3,650

Chairs
Directoire style, armchair,
painted, upholstered loose
cushion 2,900- 3,400
Directoire style, ladder-back,
rush seat, fruitwood,
tapered legs 3,500- 3,800
Empire style, salon type . . .   2,200- 2,500
Louis XV style, carved
beechwood, sage green
satin, balloon-back, closed
arms, loose seat cushion
(ill.) 3,900- 4,200
Louis XV style, carved
beechwood, striped green
satin, modified wing back,
set of 6, all, (ill.) 4,900- 5,600

Louis XV style, walnut, dining, silk damask upholstery, cartouche-shaped
molded back, cabriole legs   4,400- 4,800
Louis XV style, wide armchair on cabriole supports,
sides, back and loose
cushion in floral damask
upholstery 4,400- 4,750
Louis XVI style, armchair,
carved and painted, loose
cushion 3,200- 3,800
Regence style, caned armchair, carved beechwood,
silk damask seat, X-scroll
stretcher, loose cushion . .   3,500- 3,900

Chaise Longues
Louis XV style, walnut,
canted back, molded rails,
cabriole legs, upholstered   4,950- 5,400

Cabinets
Louis XV style, inlaid
mahogany, inset w/Sevres
porcelain plaques, oblong
top, cabriole legs w/shelf
stretcher and shaped
front 16,000-18,000
Louis XV style, serpentine-
front encoignure, inlaid
tulipwood and kingwood,
marble top, 2 doors,
cabriole feet 10,500-11,700
Louis XVI upright type, inlaid w/tulipwood and
kingwood, marble plateau   7,800- 8,400

Candlestands
Louis XVI telescopic,
w/round statuary marble
top, on arched tripod
w/slender shoe feet 3,500- 4,400

Chests
Louis XVI style, commode

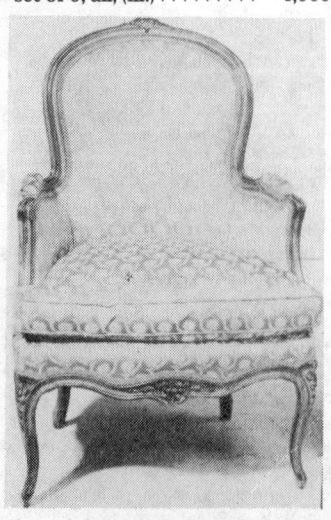

Furniture, French

Furniture, French

w/oblong marble top,
foliated cabriole legs 4,900- 5,400
Regence, serpentine com-
mode, inlaid woods, mar-
ble, 4-drawer 5,700- 5,900
Regence, walnut commode,
marble top, 4-drawer 5,600- 5,800

Desks

Directoire style, boudoir,
writing, mahogany, rec-
tangular 2-tier stand; rear
supports enclose a rising
silk screen 5,750- 6,200
Directoire style, fall-front,
mahogany, 4 long drawers
on square tapered sup-
ports, plinth feet . . . .   24,000+
Empire style, Bonheur-du-
jour (lady's desk), ormolu
mounts, mahogany   11,000-12,000
Louis XIV Boulle ebony and
brass marquetry, 7 small
drawers, 32″ high, 44½″
long (ill.) 9,200- 9,700
Louis XV style, Bureau Plat,
painted and decorated,
serpentine-contoured top,
3 working drawers, the
reverse w/mock drawers,
angular cabriole legs . . . .   28,000+
Louis XVI style, brass-
mounted Acajou Bureau a
Cylindre w/marble pla-
teau, fluted tapering legs .   6,500- 7,200
Provincial, Louis XV style,
slant-front, oblong top,
whorl feet 6,200- 6,800

Mirrors

Empire style, cheval glass,
mahogany, frame richly
inlaid, ormolu candela-
bras, urn mountings 4,700- 5,150
Louis XVI style, carved and
gilded, wall type, upright
frame w/paneled borders
around mirror, arched
cresting outlined w/carved
leaf scrolls 4,850- 5,400

Secretaries

Louis XVI style, brass-
mounted Acajou secre-
tary w/marble top, metal
gallery, 2 glazed doors, on
square tapering feet 7,400- 7,800

Sideboards

Louis XV style, buffet-
verrier, inlaid fruitwood
and ash, superstructure
has 4 open tiers, cabriole
legs 7,200- 7,550
Louis XV style, buffet base,
carved walnut, oblong
top, 2 frieze drawers and 2

fielded cupboard doors,
squat cabriole legs 12,000-13,500

Tables

Directoire style, mahogany
tric-trac w/removable
oblong top on square,
tapering legs 6,200- 6,900
Empire style, wall, mahog-
any, w/marble top, figural
supports, mirror panel . . .   6,700- 7,400
Louis XV inlaid tulipwood
and amaranth tric-trac
table w/oblong reversible
top, backgammon well, on
angular cabriole legs 8,900- 9,650
Louis XV small writing type,
oval top, tapered angular
cabriole legs 12,000-13,500
Louis XVI brass-mounted
Acajou Bouillotte table
w/drum top and pierced
gallery, 2 small drawers,
on fluted tapering legs . . .   7,300- 7,800
Louis XVI carved and gilded
petite console w/marble
top, a guilloche-carved
elongated S-scroll support   7,600- 8,400
Louis XVI mahogany exten-
sion dining table, on
square tapering legs 7,400- 7,700
Louis XVI walnut library
type, oblong top paneled
in leather 6,400- 6,700
Louis XVI yew wood table,
rectangular top, 2 small
drawers, on tapering legs .   6,800- 7,300

Galle Cameo Glass

Establishing his first factory at Nancy,
France, in 1883, Emile Galle developed a
fine cameo glass. Because so many assis-
tants made Galle glass, it is impossible to
know for sure which pieces Emile actually
made. After his death in 1904 a star (★)

Galle Cameo Glass

(continued)

was put in front of "Galle." This was done only for a short time, and today Star Galle is also quite collectible. All pieces were signed.

Atomizer, brown/green, frosted ground	$ 385- 450
Bowl, blue, floral, scenic lake and boats, 6" high, signed .	810- 885
Bowl, purple on frost, flowers, 5", signed	1,600-1,950
Box, covered, 6" dia., signed .	875- 995
Chandelier, 15" high, floral glass prisms, signed	3,200-3,800
Cruet, thistles, maroon, beige/ pink, applied handle, signed	900- 950
Inkstand, faience, 14" long, signed	750- 810
Jardiniere, yellow/black, acid etched, 8½" high	3,100-3,400
Lamp, glass, table, 23" high, signed	2,200-2,600
Pitcher, 9" high, signed	1,800-2,200
Rose bowl, flowers/birds, Star Galle	1,200-1,400
Toothpick, red/blue/yellow, signed	410- 450
Tray, rose/blue open handles, 18½" long	1,350-1,700
Tumbler, vaseline color, gold enamel border, 6" high, signed	510- 580
Urn, cherries/birds, acid etched, Star Galle	3,400-3,700
Vase, apricot/green, acid clear, 7" high	850- 950
Vase, bird scene, blue/ yellow/white, 7¼" high . . .	820- 850
Vase, dark green, red ground, Star signature . . .	820- 840
Vase, lotus blossoms, yellow/ pink/white, 5½" high, signed	1,500-1,700
Vase, miniature, frosted, pink/blue, Star Galle, 4" high (ill.)	425- 485
Vase, miniature, frosted, mauve to clear, floral, Star Galle	475- 520
Vase, water lilies, blue/ yellow/green, 6½" high, signed	820- 920

Game Plates

Plates decorated with fish, animals or birds fall into this category. They usually came in sets, 12 plates and a serving platter. Popular during the 1800s, most were made in Europe. Globe China Company in Ohio also made them in the late 1800s. Repros!

Bass on fly lure	$132-142

Game Plates

Birds in flight, blue/gold background, France, 8½" dia.	82- 92
Buck and doe, forest scene in various colors, 9" dia.	77- 87
Deer, Buffalo Pottery	75- 85
Deer grazing, Bavaria, 7½" dia. .	62- 72
Grouse, gold rim, Germany 11½" dia.	77- 87
Mallard duck, gold border, Staffordshire china, 7" dia.	81- 91
Pheasant, blue/gold background .	77- 87
Pheasants, signed Crown of Gold	44- 52
Quail, gold rim, pierced for handling	88- 98
Turkey, hunter, multicolors, Globe, 8" dia.	42- 52
Turkey on platter	61- 71
Wild boar in woods, Austria, 8" dia.	62- 72
Woodcock, 8" dia. (ill.)	38- 48

Games

Games

See also **Coin-Operated Machines**, this Price Guide.

Alley Oop	$ 15- 23
Authors, c. 1910	19- 24
Barney Google	73- 80
Checkered Game of Life	43- 53

Chinese Checkers, tin board, glass marbles		12- 16
Cribbage, inlaid board, ivory pegs, complete		18- 25
Dominos, wood, complete		11- 16
Eddie Cantor, all cards, original box		8- 14
Fish Pond		22- 28
Funny Faces, original box		38- 44
King Kong, early		15- 23
Lotto, c. 1935		9- 13
Mah-jongg, bone/bamboo pieces, leatherette box		30- 37
Mah-jongg, ivory pieces, sticks, original wood box		45- 53
Pick-Up-Sticks, c. 1940		8- 15
Puzzle, jigsaw, King Arthur's Court, 750 pieces, complete		45- 55
Puzzle, jigsaw, Map of the United States, c. 1925		18- 26
Puzzle, jigsaw, Peter Rabbit and Friends, c. 1932		13- 19
Tell It to the Judge, Eddie Cantor, original box		19- 27
Tiddlywinks, wooden cup, plastic pieces		14- 19
Two for Tennis, 12 metal pieces, complete		16- 24
West Point Cadet		18- 25
Wings, c. 1930		7- 10
Words & Sentences		23- 31
Zorro, c. 1967		10- 15

Garden Furniture

Most of what you find today in the better antiques shops is from the mid-to-late Victorian era up until World War I.

Armchairs, white-painted wrought iron, set of 6	$685-770
Center table, painted cast iron and white tile	320-355
Easy chairs, white-painted rattan, set of 4	370-420
Fountain figure, terra-cotta, winged Cupid, 31" high	410-450
Jardinieres, ochre-painted, set of 4	350-360

Occasional table, green-painted wrought iron, inlaid marble top	485-520
Side chairs, white-painted wrought iron, set of 6 (ill.)	540-580
Terrace chairs, white-painted wrought iron, set of 6	600-670
Terrace table, rattan, 27½" high	350-380

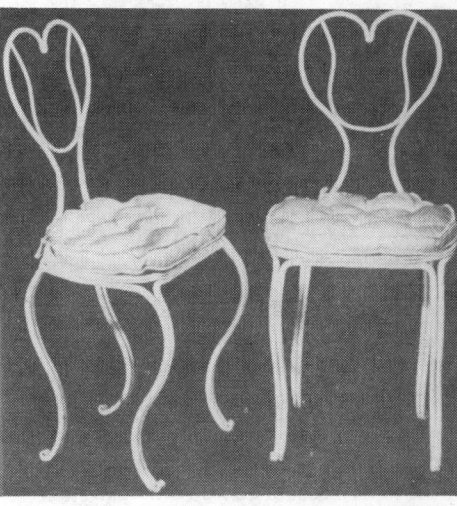

Garden Furniture

Gaudy Dutch

This highly-decorated lightweight china was made around 1825 in the Staffordshire District in England, reputedly for the Pennsylvania Dutch trade in the York, Lancaster, and Philadelphia areas. Today, the general collector confuses it with Gaudy Ironstone. The latter was made at a much later date and was marked. Gaudy Dutch was not. Some examples are impressed "Wood" and "Riley."

Bowl, King's Rose, 14" dia.	$320-340
Creamer, Dove pattern, 3½" high (ill.)	292-320

Gaudy Dutch

(continued)

Cup/saucer, handleless, signed,
1856 270-295
Cup/saucer, Single Rose (ill.) 345-385
Pitcher, Carnation pattern, 6"
high 510-520
Plate, Dove pattern, 9¾" dia. ... 770-790
Plate, Urn pattern, 7¼" dia.
(ill.) 420-450
Teapot, footed Daisy and Chain
pattern 265-380
Toddy, Carnation pattern 520-540
Waste bowl, Carnation pattern .. 185-220

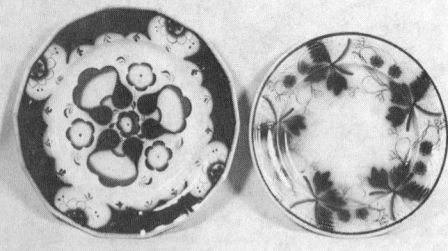

Gaudy Ironstone

Gaudy Ironstone

This was created in the early 1850s to stimulate more interest in the plain white ironstone. Decorated to some extent in the style of Japanese Imari, it is sometimes confused with Gaudy Dutch, but it really looks more like Gaudy Welsh. It never achieved popularity and was discontinued after a few years.

Cup/saucer, cobalt, orange/blue
flowers $200-230
Gravy boat and dish, red/blue/
green, floral decor 82- 94
Pitcher, blue/orange/green, 6"
high 187-194
Plate, Pinwheel design, cobalt/
burnt orange (ill.) 150-170
Plate, dinner, dark blue, 9¼"
dia. 132-142
Plate, Blackberry/Leaf design,
cobalt, impressed WALLEY
(ill.) 162-172
Platter, floral, signed Copeland,
10½" dia. 198-220

Gaudy Welsh

Gaudy Welsh

Made after 1850, this type of chinaware is cruder than Gaudy Dutch. Its bluish-purple coloring is one of its characteristics. General collectors confuse it with late Imari.

Cracker jar $142-157
Creamer, Daisy and Chain
pattern 90- 98
Creamer, Oyster pattern,
signed Allerton's (ill.) 77- 88
Cup/saucer, Tulip pattern (ill.) ... 120-130
Cup/saucer, Tulip pattern, no
handle 72- 82
Ewer, Tulip pattern, 4" high 81- 90
Mug, handled, Urn or Vase
pattern 72- 82
Pitcher, blue/red, reptile handle .. 142-152
Pitcher, Oyster pattern 120-140
Plate, Strawberry pattern, 8¼"
dia. 132-141
Platter, Wagon Wheel pattern ... 162-182
Tea set, complete 24 piece,
Tulip pattern 885-950
Teapot, Strawberry pattern..... 242-256
Sugar bowl, covered, Daisy and
Chain pattern 177-192

Geisha Girl China

Geisha Girl China

This once-expensive chinaware features standing and/or seated Bijin figures (Japanese beauties). It was made for export by the Japanese from the 1880s until just before WW II. Border colors include green, yellow, blue, brown and orange-red. Some colors were used in combination with gold. This ware is often reproduced, but the reproductions shouldn't fool too many folks.

Berry set, large bowl, 7" dia.,
6 smaller bowls, 3" dia., all .... $ 55- 65

Bowl, 8″ dia.	50- 60
Cake plate, 6½″ dia.	28- 34
Chocolate set, pot, 9″ high, 6 cups/saucers, all	70- 80
Coffee set, pot, 5½″ high, creamer, 4″ high, sugar, 4″ high, 6 cups/saucers, all	90-105
Creamer, 5½″ high	11- 16
Cup/saucer	15- 19
Plate, 9″ dia.	26- 34
Salt/pepper set, 3″ high, both (ill.)	19- 26
Tea set, pot, 8″ high, creamer, 4¼″ high, all	95-110
Toothpick holder, 2½″ high	12- 15

Gibson Girl Plates

The eminent American artist, Charles Dana Gibson, produced a series of 24 drawings entitled "The Widow and Her Friends." The Royal Doulton Works, Lambeth, England, reproduced the drawings on plates in the early 1900s. Price, each plate, $88-105.

And Here Winning New Friends
The Day After Arriving at Her Journey's End
Failing to Find Rest and Quiet in the Country,
She Decided to Return Home
A Message from the Outside World
Miss Babbles Brings a Copy of the Morning Paper
Miss Babbles, the Authoress, Calls and Reads Aloud
Mr. Waddles Arrives Late and Finds Her Card Filled
Mrs. Diggs Is Alarmed
A Quiet Dinner with Dr. Bottles
She Becomes a Trained Nurse
She Contemplates the Cloister
She Decides to Die in Spite of Dr. Bottles
She Finds Some Consolation in Her Mirror
She Finds That Exercise Does Not Increase Her Spirits
She Goes into Colors (ill.)
She Goes into Retreat
She Goes to the Fancy Dress Ball as Juliet
She Is Disturbed by a Vision
She Looks for Relief Amongst the Older Ones
Some Think She Had Remained in Retirement
They All Go Skating
They Go Fishing
They Take a Morning Run

Gillinder Glass

Gillinder Glass   GILLINDER

You'll find a lot of this fine glass in our Pattern Glass Section. Here are two indicative pieces.

Candlesticks, white milk glass, crucifixes, 6-sided bases, 9½″ high, pr. (ill.) $128-142
Goblets, 3-part mold, 1876 Centennial, 6½″ high, pr. (ill.) . 96-116

Girandoles

These are mantel garnitures, and a set consists of a centerpiece with a 3-branch candelabrum and 2 sidepieces for holding single candles. The bases were usually made of marble or alabaster and the main body cast in brass. Cut prisms, 4 to 6 inches long, hung from the

Girandoles

Gibson Girl Plates

(continued)

tops of the 3 pieces. They were expensive when they were in vogue, early 1800s to mid-1800s.

Brass mother, child, marble
base, etched prisms, pr. $135-165
Brass soldier and girl dancing,
cut prisms, pr. 300-345
Girl and boy, birds, gold leaf,
marble base, 16″ high, pr. 425-465
Girl and boy on marble base, 3
ornate brass arms, glass
prisms, pr. 565-630
Indian, full figure, spear, 3
branches 620-675
Lady and child, cast metal, marble base, bobeches, pr. 175-220
Man and woman, European
attire, double handle, brass,
prisms, pr. (ill.) 485-510
Three-piece set, 2-step marble/
brass base, star-cut prisms ... 550-625
Wandering gypsies, cast metal,
marble base, cut prisms, pr. ... 185-240
Young lovers, 3 branches, brass,
marble base, pr. 265-310

Girl Scouts

Girl Scouts

Juliette Low founded this marvelous organization at Savannah, Georgia, in 1912. Originally called Girl Guides. The older items are now collectible.

Camping kit, 1930s, 4 pcs. $10-16

Certificate of troop charter,
Scarsdale, N.Y. 7-11
Magnifying mirror, 1950s (ill.) ... 6- 8
Manuals, 1920s, 1930s 14-22
Mirror, 1950s (ill.) 6- 9
Uniform, complete, 1930s 32-42

Glass Mugs

Also see specific type and make in **Pattern Glass Section.**

Hobnail, blue (ill.) .... $ 24- 33
Little Orphan Annie mug 45- 54
Mephistopheles, blue opalescent,
3¼″ high (ill.) 58- 68
Mug, lemonade, cranberry (ill.) .. 67- 77
Postum mug, 1930s 42- 52
Shirley Temple, 3¾″ high 38- 48
Sterner's Clothing Store mug,
1920s 29- 39
Stump glass mug 37- 43

Glass Types
Cased Glass

Glass with layers of different colors—one color actually encases another. Usually two colors are used, three sometimes found. Four to five are rare.

Flashed and Overlay Glass

A gather of glass of one color is covered while hot with a thin layer of another color. This double gather is achieved by dipping the first quickly into the hot metal of the other. It's then worked out on a metal slab and blown, as if it were one piece; the thin layer being on the outside.

Luster-Stained Glass

A luster stain is applied much like varnish on the inside or the outside of the glass. After it's "painted," the glass is heated in the kiln to fix the color. Copper luster stains the outside red; green, blue, yellow or purple are also used. This is a cheap imitation of cased glass.

Glass Mugs

Goofus Glass

Goofus Glass

This is pressed glass painted by spraying before firing. What you find today usually has the paint chipped off in places.

Bowl, brown, red flowers, 10″ dia.	$ 37-	47
Bowl, Dogwood pattern, 8″ dia.	40-	46
Compote, red, gold over green, open, 7″ high	26-	34
Dish, ruffled, gold, shaded red, blues, 10″ dia.	35-	42
Jar, pickle, flowers, red/gold, 20″ high	28-	37
Lamp base, green, red, gold	42-	51
Plate, cake, red/gold, 8″ dia.	13-	18
Plate, ruffled edges, gold/red, 10″ dia. (ill.)	26-	34
Vase, grapes, 8″ high	22-	31
Vase, poppy, opalescent, 8″ high	38-	42
Vase, rose, 7″ high	36-	46

Goss-on-Trent

Goss-on-Trent

Considered a fairing, these ivory-tinted por-

celain pieces were made in the 19th century by William Goss at Stoke-on-Trent, England. Other factories imitated his wares.

Cup/saucer, Shakespeare crest	$ 21-	28
Elephant	27-	34
Hen-on-nest	27-	37
Pitcher, flowers, 4″ high (ill.)	28-	36
Plates, 4″ and 6″ dia.	24-	32
Vase, horseshoe, 3-leaf clover, 4″ high	31-	42

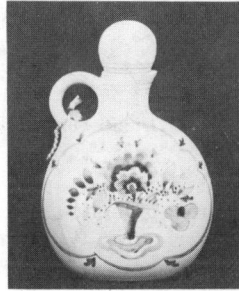
Gouda Pottery

Gouda Pottery

The land of the cheese—since the early 1700s the area around Gouda, Holland, has also been known as a pottery center. Clay pipes were one of the first products made. Art Nouveau type pottery came in around 1910. What we find today came from the 1910-1920 period.

Bowl, green/blue/yellow	$ 78-	84
Candlesticks, floral pattern, 5½″ high, pr.	99-	115
Compote, yellow/green, 11″ high	92-	99
Decanter, blue decoration on gray, 6″ high (ill.)	82-	92
Jug, matt finish, signed Canada	138-	142
Pitcher, orange/green/black, 6½″ high	162-	165
Plate, green/yellow pears, striped border, 6½″ dia.	57-	67
Tobacco jar, scroll/leaf decor, 7″ high	182-	192
Vase, multicolored glaze, paper label, 8″ high	118-	128

Granite Ware

This is a thick, heavy clay ware that too many people confuse with ironstone. Granite Ware was a product of the 1850s and was mass-produced for the people who couldn't afford anything better. It fell from grace in the late 1880s when the vogue shifted to European porcelains, Haviland in particular.

Graniteware

Graniteware

This name is given to all the enamelware made after the Civil War until the 1930s. Some called it agateware, others speckleware. Early pieces look like granite, and blue, gray, brown, yellow, and red are favorite colors of collectors. *Graniteware Collectors' Guide with Prices,* Wallace-Homestead, $12.95, is a beautiful book on the subject. See **Clubs and Publications,** this Price Guide.

Baby Accessories

Bathtub, decorated with nursery rhymes, 24″ dia.	$ 74- 85
Food, cup, tin lid, with tray	48- 52
Humpty Dumpty dish	24- 32
Mugs, various sizes and colors	18- 27
Plate, ABCs	24- 33

Bath Accessories

Comb case	18- 27
Basin, 10″ dia.	22- 31
Douche pan, strap handle	60- 70
Foot tub	30- 40
Pitcher and wash basin, both	48- 58
Potty, child's	24- 33

Breadmaking

Batter bucket, tin lid, handled	47- 53
Biscuit pan, 2 sizes	12- 19
Bread pan	16- 26
Measure, qt.	27- 35
Salt box, wooden lid	47- 52

Coffeepots

Percolator type	47- 57
Pt.	29- 39
Qt.	34- 42

Cups

Coffee	14- 19
Demitasse, w/saucer	11- 17
Mexican, fairly new	5- 8
Tea, w/saucer	14- 19

Funnels

Fruit jar (ill.)	16- 20
Elliptical	15- 19
Strap-handled	16- 19
Toy	35- 44

Graters

Cheese and vegetables, marked "Ideal"	35- 42
Table type, w/wooden pusher	46- 56
Toy, various sizes, ea.	16- 21

Invalid

Feeder	14- 19
Medicine cup	9- 14
Urinals, male, female, ea.	12- 19
Utility bucket	27- 34

Milk/Cream Can

Tin lid, ½-gal.	28- 32
Tin lid, qt.	24- 32
Tin lid, pt.	27- 32

Miscellaneous

Buckets, various sizes, ea.	17- 29
Candlesticks, various sizes, ea.	27- 34
Colanders, various sizes and shapes, ea.	18- 41
Cuspidors, various sizes and shapes, ea.	25- 34
Dippers, various sizes, ea.	14- 22
Lid racks, various sizes	16- 25
Measures, various sizes, ea.	14- 22
Pitchers, various sizes and shapes, ea.	22- 36
Skillets, various sizes and shapes, ea.	10- 28
Teakettles, various sizes, ea.	27- 42
Teapots, various sizes, ea.	12- 36

Molds

Barley design	28- 34
Corn design	25- 32
Gelatin	16- 26
Strawberry design	34- 39
Tube	17- 24

Muffin Pans

8-cup	16- 24
6-cup	28- 32
Turk's Head	34- 39

Picnic Sets

Coffee flask	38- 42
Water carrier	37- 44

Plates

Breakfast, various sizes, ea.	8- 13
Dinner, various sizes, ea.	11- 19
Luncheon, various sizes, ea.	11- 18

Pots/Pans

Double boilers, various sizes	18- 27
Roaster, self-basting, w/cover	21- 32
Vegetable dish, w/cover	28- 32

Scoops

Candy/ice	37- 47
Druggist's	54- 62
Grocer's, covered	27- 34
Utility	28- 38

Stoves

Electric burner	41- 50
Kerosene, 1-burner	194-250
"Mothers Oats Fireless Cooker"	82- 92

Toys

Dustpan	21-	31
Graters, various sizes, ea.	12-	19
Ladle	19-	28
Mold	14-	22
Pie pan	9-	14
Wash basin	19-	25

Greenaway, Kate

Greenaway, Kate

Daughter of an artist, Kate Greenway was born in England in 1846. As a young lady she illustrated Christmas cards and later many books. English and German potteries used her illustrations of children on their wares.

Buttons, brass, for child's dress, set of 6	$122-140	
Coffeepot, children under tree, 5½" high	142-162	
Cup/saucer, children playing with dog	58-	68
Fairy lamp, girl, Parian, 6" high	172-182	
Match holder, boy, bisque	82-	92
Mug, pink, children playing	84-	93
Plate, 2 girls playing ball, 5" dia.	80-	90
Plate, Copeland China, 8¼" dia. (ill.)	88-	92
Salt/pepper, pr. in wicker basket	89-110	
Teapot, children on cover and pot, 6" high	77-	86
Tray, boy with hoop, girls playing, silver frame	162-174	

Greentown Glass

Made by the Indiana Tumbler and Goblet Company, Greentown, Indiana, around 1894. See specific types in **Pattern Glass Section**.

Grueby Pottery

William Henry Grueby founded the Grueby-Faience Company in 1894, near Boston, Massachusetts. Many colors were produced, including yellow, blue, and brown, but Grueby cucumber green was the most famous. In 1907 the company was divided into the Grueby Pottery Company and the Grueby Faience & Tile Company. The Faience & Tile Company went into receivership in 1909, but continued under Grueby's direction until 1913. The pottery company closed in 1911. One of the seven marks used on the pottery is illustrated here.

Bowl, cucumber green, signed, 2" dia.	$210-240	
Candlesticks, blue matt, 6¼" high, pr.	320-360	
Tile, Bible scene, signed, 5" sq. . .	228-240	
Tile, cucumber green, 2"x6"	49-	59
Vase, bulbous, blue matt, signed, 5¼" high	452-472	
Vase, dark green matt, signed, 12" high	492-520	
Vase, 5 molded leaves and handles, green matt, signed, 10½" high	520-540	
Vase, green/mauve/oatmeal, signed, 6" high	515-532	
Vase, yellow matt, 3 handles, signed, 7¼" high	262-282	

Hair Work

In the late 1850s, *Godey's Lady's Book* printed directions for hair work, followed in 1864 by *Peterson's Magazine*. The craze lasted from then until the end of the 1800s. Brooches, lockets, woven chains, everything that could be made with human hair (also, cow's hair, though no one admitted to that), was produced. Most articles were made by braiding and interlacing hair over hollow forms. Hair wreaths, bouquets, and the like were made and framed for hanging on the wall. They're being collected today.

Bouquet of flowers, brown/black 6" high, in open frame	$ 35-	44
Wreath, brown/black, 10" dia., under glass in frame	37-	46

Hampshire Pottery

James Scollay Taft founded the firm in

219

Keene, New Hampshire, in 1871. Flowerpots were the first items made. Around 1878 the firm produced pottery with a Majolica finish, then a Royal Worcester type finish. Various marks were used, some of which were impressed on the base, while others were stamped on in color. "J.S.T. & Co., Keene, N.H." and "Hampshire Pottery" were just two of more than six marks used. Shapes and colors are similar to Majolica and Rookwood.

Bowl, fruit, Royal Worcester
finish, 13½" long, signed $240-260
Bowl, 6" high, matt green, leaf
motif, signed Hampshire
Pottery 82- 92
Chocolate pot, creamware,
goldenrod decoration, 9" high,
signed J. S. Taft, Hampshire
Pottery 162-178
Chocolate pot, dark green glaze,
embossed panel design, 9½"
high 121-132
Mug, Mt. Monadnock, tan, 4½"
high, signed Hampshire
Pottery 107-118
Pitcher, beige glaze, embossed
blackberries, both sides, 4¼"
high 92-107
Pitcher, souvenir type, Lake
Sunapee, 6½" high 94-107
Stein, Royal Worcester finish,
brown/green trim, impressed
Hampshire, 6" high 240-252
Stein, white, glazed, straight
handle, signed J.S.T. & Co.,
Keene, N.H., 5½" high 94-107
Teapot, dark green, highly glazed,
twig handle and finial, impressed Hampshire Pottery,
5" high 88- 98
Teapot, green, ribbed design, wire
handle, 3¾" high 101-112
Vase, matt green glaze,
embossed tulip design,
impressed Hampshire, also M
in circle, 8" high 84- 92
Vase, two-handled, mottled matt
blue finish, 5" high, impressed
Hampshire 91-107

Handel

This firm manufactured lamps, shades, other items such as tobacco jars, in Meriden, Connecticut, late 1890s until World War II.

Bowl, cased, brass collar,
signed, 6¼" dia. .... $ 150- 180
Box, verde finish, flowers
inside, signed Runge 290- 340
Humidor, brown ground,
Arabic scene, signed 395- 460
Humidor, tobacco, green/red
ground, hunter and dog 400- 485
Jar, cookie, blue/white,
flower, transfer 395- 420
Jar, tobacco, bird dogs,
brass trim, signed 410- 480
Lamp, blue, Arabic scene, 3
lights, 19" high 2,100-2,700
Lamp, desk, green art glass,
gold feather (Quezal?)
overlay, signed 1,300-1,500
Lamp, lily pond, frogs,
green/white shade, 3-
light, 22" high 1,650-1,900
Shade, yellow/opalescent
green, floral designs,
signed, 13" dia. 1,450-1,750
Vase, trees, signed and
numbered, 8" high 320- 350

Hatpins and Hatpin Holders

Hatpin Holders

Made of every type of material but usually glass, they were plain, decorated, even cut. Popular during the mid-1800s, they make fine flower holders. See **Clubs and Publications**, this Price Guide.

Blue/gold, birds, flowers, gilt
edge, Austria .... $ 42- 52
Carnival glass, Marigold, trunk-
shaped, N in bottom 61- 70
Fastened to porcelain tray, ring
tree each side, Austria 42- 52
Flowers and birds, gilt, Bavaria
(ill.) 29- 39
Sterling silver, initialed, signed
Tiffany and Company on side . 121-131
Tiffany glass, probably part of
dresser set 148-162

Heisey Glass

Ohio, purchased many of the Heisey molds and is reproducing Heisey today, sometimes without the Heisey trademark—an "H" inside a diamond. Paper labels were also used. See **Clubs and Publications,** this Price Guide.

Ashtrays

Crystolite, 3½″ sq.	$ 11- 15
Old Sandwich, individual	11- 16
Ridgeleigh, bride	9- 12
Ridgeleigh, round or square, ea.	10- 15
Whirlpool, 3″ sq.	9- 14

Baskets

Cake, Beaded Panel and Sunburst, 9″	129-134
Double Rib and Panel, Flamingo, 6″	77- 85
Raised Panel, 9″	118-127

Bonbons

Crystolite	10- 14
Ridgeleigh, 6″	11- 15

Bottles

Bitter, Crystolite, 4-oz.	38- 48
Cologne, Crystolite, 4-oz.	37- 46
Oil, Crystolite, 3-oz.	49- 54
Rye, 1-qt.	54- 59

Bowls

Finger, Old Sandwich	19- 24
Floral, Flamingo, 16″	45- 52
Floral, Moongleam, 16″	44- 52
Floral, oval, Ridgeleigh, 12″	34- 42
Floral, Queen Anne, 12½″	35- 42
Fruit, Fern, 13″	42- 49
Hollandaise sauce	31- 38
Salad, Tourjours, 10″	32- 41

Boxes

Cigarette, Colonial	25- 31
Cigarette, Crystolite, footed	28- 32
Cigarette, Crystolite, oval	19- 27
Cigarette, Ridgeleigh, 4″	24- 29

Candlesticks

Crystolite, 1-light	19- 26
Diamond Optic, Sahara, pr.	94-118
Horn of Plenty, Warwick, individual	24- 32
Queen Anne, 2-handled, pr.	38- 47
Ridgeleigh, 2-light, pr.	51- 60

Fancy Loop, 7½″	32- 46
Lariat, crimped lip	19- 27
Ridgeleigh, ball, 7″	32- 39
Ridgeleigh, candle, 6″	19- 29
Tourjours, centerpiece and vase, both	112-128

Heisey Glass Animals

Heisey Glass Animals

Some were made in the 1930s but the most famous were designed by Royal Hickman who worked for the Haeger Pottery Company. All were pressed in a mold. Some animals were marked with the Diamond H. Some were even marked twice, while others weren't marked at all. Most were made in crystal but some were made in deep amber, honey amber, and cobalt (blue). Some were frosted completely, others only partially. In 1962, Imperial Glass Company, which had purchased Heisey's molds in 1958, reproduced certain animals. Not all the reproductions are marked with the Diamond H. Those listed here have never been reproduced. See **Clubs and Publications,** this Price Guide.

Chick, 1″ high	$ 61- 72
Ducklings, floating or standing, 2¼″ and 2⅝″ high	64- 73
Elephant, 4½″ and 5⅞″ high	88- 94
Fish bookend, 6⅝″ high	122-132
Gazelle, 11″ high	101-114
Giraffe, 11″ high	92-108
Rearing horse bookends, 7⅞″ high, pr. (ill.)	195-225
Rooster, 5⅝″ high	101-112
Rooster vase, 6½″ high	102-118
Tropical fish piece, 12″ high	121-132

Others were goose (wings down), Clydesdale horses, filly horse (head forward), same (head backward), show horse, horse head bookends, piglets, bunnies, rabbit, cygnet, sparrow. Reproduced items, 1962-1968, were bull, hen,

(continued)

fighting rooster, dogs (Airedale, Scotty), donkey, ducks (3 mallards), medium elephant, geese (wings up, wings half-way), horses (flying mare, plug horse, ponies), pheasant, pigeon, rabbit, rabbit paperweight, and swan.

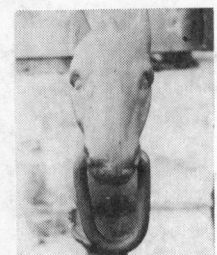

Hitching Posts

Hitching Posts

Used for years to keep the horse from wandering while its master visited or shopped. The Jockey is the most famous, also the one being reproduced the most.

Chimney sweeper, 32″ high $178-195
Hitching block, iron marked "Foundry, Toledo, 1885" (the portable kind you hitched to bridle) 59- 69
Hitching post, black bear on hind legs, ring in paw, 36″ high, European 440-462
Hitching post, Negro boy in jockey's clothing, ring in hand, 27″ high 388-420
Horse's head (ill.) 210-232

Holly Amber Glass

Holly Amber Glass

This glass is mentioned because it's so rare some classify it as art glass. It isn't.

Honesdale Glass

The factory that made this glass was originally established to decorate glass for Christian Dorflinger in White Mill, Pennsylvania, during the mid-1800s. The factory was purchased in 1916 by C.F. Prosch. He made one of the poorest imitations of cameo glass ever seen.

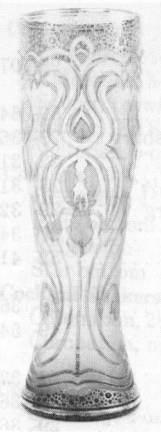

Honesdale Glass

Cameo vase, blue ground, red/yellow rose blossoms, 10½″ high, signed $295-330
Cameo vase, clear ground, green grapes, blue base, 12¾″ high, signed 242-260
Cameo vase, frosted iridescent, green/yellow flowers, 12″ high . 182-195
Vase, acid cut, blue/gold, frosted, signed, 7″ high (ill.) 281-291
Vase, Art Nouveau, floral decor, yellow-to-green, 11¼″ high, signed 181-220
Vase, iridescent, blue/green enameled flowers, 10″ high . . . 98-115

Hooked Rugs

Adam and Eve, fluctuating tan field, figures of boy and girl, 4′2″×2′10″ $118-128
Bundling, girl/mother, man in bed, 3′10″×3′ (ill.) 132-142
Children's Game, brown/gray ground, captioned verses on the joys of childhood, 4′2″×2′5″ 122-132
Cupid, blonde maiden, red costume, dog, young suitor, 4′2″×3′ 131-140
Old Maid, dark-haired maiden rejecting young man, brown/gray, 4′6″×2′5″ (ill.) 128-132
Samson and Delilah, maiden, scissors, reclining Samson, 4′4″×4′ 131-141
Why Hurry, white field, figures scurrying to and fro, 4′7″×2′9″ 110-120
Wife's Lament, man/cigar, wife, white ground, 4′2″×2′8″ 108-119
A Young Girl's Dream, kittens, girl sewing, 3′10″×2′9″ (ill.) . . . 132-142

Hooked Rugs

Horn

Horns from various animals have been used for centuries to hold liquids, gunpowder, food, you-name-it. Powder horns dating back into the 1800s bring high prices today. To bend the calf's horn, an iron ring was fastened at the base of the skull. It didn't hurt! Texas Longhorn cattle had magnificent horns, some measuring 7 feet across.

Hunting horn	$ 78- 84
Napkin ring	24- 33
Snuffbox, mid-1800s, American	51- 62
Texas Longhorns, velvet in center, ready for mounting	118-127
Tumbler	27- 36
Water carrier, Nepal, 22" long (ill.)	225-240

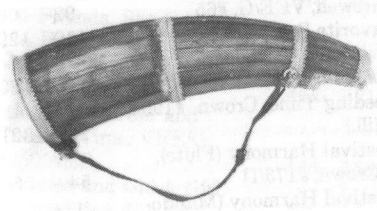

Horn

Hull Pottery

hull
Oven Proof
USA

This pottery was made in 1903 by Acme Pottery Company at Crooksville, Ohio. Hull

Soloist, Crown, #135	172-	195
Spring Dance, Stylized Bee, 353/I	299-	320
Stormy Weather, Full Bee, #71	399-	460
Surprise, Crown, #94/3/O	220-	250
Sweet Music, Stylized Bee, #186	110-	119
To Market, Crown, #49/O	320-	360
Umbrella Boy, Full Bee, #152/A/O	650-	750
Umbrella Girl, Full Bee, #152/B/II		2,400+
Visiting an Invalid, 3-line, #382	121-	132
Waiter, Full Bee, 154/O	188-	198
Wayside Devotion, 3-line, 28/III	220-	240
Wayside Harmony, Full Bee, 111/I	178-	188
We Congratulate, 3-line, #220	75-	85
Which Hand?, Stylized Bee, #258	92-	106

Madonnas

Flower Madonna, Full Bee, 10/I	800-	900
Madonna with Halo, Full Bee, #45/I	182-	192
Madonna without Halo, Full Bee, #46/I	99-	121

Music Boxes

Little Band, 3-line, #392/M	210-	240
Little Band (with candle), 3-line, #388/M	220-	240

Nativity Sets

Large set, 3-line, #260/A-R		3,400+
Small set, Stylized Bee, #214/A-O		1,400+

Plaques

Ba-Bee Ring, Crown, #30/A&B	225-	260
Child in Bed, Crown, #173/B	198-	240
Madonna, Full Bee, #48/II	240-	260
Mail Is Here, Full Bee, #140	280-	292
Merry Wanderer, Stylized Bee, #92	121-	138
Quartet, Full Bee, #134	363-	374
Retreat to Safety, Crown #126	352-	362
Vacation Time, 3-line, #125	99-	108

Annual Plates

1971, Heavenly Angel, 3-line, trade ed., #264		1,300+
1971, Heavenly Angel, 3-line, gift ed., #264		2,500+
1972, Hear Ye, Hear Ye, 3-line, #265	98-	107
1973, Globetrotter, VEE/G, #266	162-	172
1974, Goose Girl, VEE/G, #267	168-	172
1975, Ride into Christmas, VEE/G, #268	99-	127
1978, Happy Pastime, VEE/G, #271	152-	175
1980, School Girl, VEE/G, #273	162-	178

Icons

Icons

These are religious mementos, usually paintings with a brass encasement. Dating from the time of Christianity, what you find in shops today are usually from the mid-1800s on. A triptych is just a 3-panel icon.

Brass, Eastern Orthodox
church scene of Jesus,
5″×7½″ $1,585-1,850
Brass, Greek, on wooden
panel, 17th century,
13″×16″ 855- 960
Brass, Greek saints, enamel
background, 6″×6½″ dia. 485- 520
Bronze, Russian Orthodox
church scene, 18th cen-
tury, 14″×18″ 1,100-1,250
Painting on wood, brass en-
casement missing,
5½″×7″ (ill.) 245- 275
Triptych, cathedral scene,
Russian, 17th century,
ornate, 16″ high . . . . 2,200+
Triptych, 3-panel, Jesus and
Mary scene, 18th century,
15″ high 685- 740

Imari

A gaudy decorated type of chinaware imported into this country mainly from Japan in the last part of the 19th century. The original was made in Japan as early as 1600. During the 19th century, imitations were made in England. It's being reproduced today but it shouldn't fool anyone.

Bowl, blue/white, orange
flowers, 7″, not old $340- 362
Bowl, cobalt, scalloped rim,
6½″ dia. 71- 80
Bowl, panels alternating
blue and orange, 10″ dia.,
Japanese 340- 362
Creamer, orange/blue, old,
not Japanese 94- 106
Cup/saucer, handles, usual
colors, Japanese, 19th
century 91- 107
Dish, blue/white, fish shape,
8½″ long 99- 108
Jar, ginger, orange/blue,
original wood stopper, 6″
high, Japanese 172- 185
Jardiniere, plum trees, 14″
high . . . . 2,300+
Pitcher, Staffordshire,
usual Oriental colors,
1880s, 9″ high 220- 240
Plate, blue/white, 9½″
dia. (ill.) 75- 85
Plate, green/red/blue, tan-
gerine panels, 8½″ dia. . . . 97- 108
Platter, blue, red, cobalt
design, Oriental signa-
ture, old 192- 206
Platter, landscape, dragons,
temple, 14″ dia., old 198- 220
Teapot, peacocks, prunus,
blue/red, w/domed lid 98- 109
Vase, 4 panels, flowers, 7½″
high 188- 199

Imperial Glass

Founded in Bellaire, Ohio, in 1902, for manufacturing pressed tablewares, lighting fixtures, and shades. In 1910 they began production of an iridized glass that would

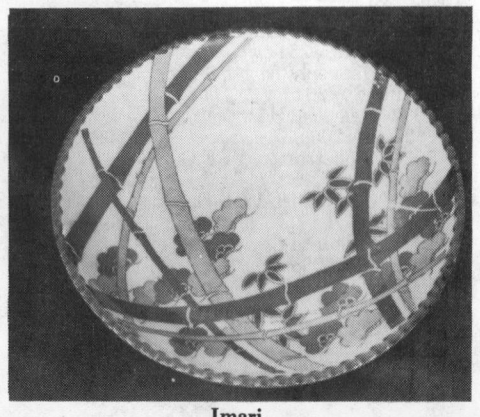

Imari

become famous as Carnival Glass. NUCUT and NUART are trade names used. Imperial Art Ware and Imperial Jewels were also names used to describe an inexpensive iridescent stretch glass, in imitation of Tiffany and Aurene; also Verre de Soie. Most of these pieces were marked with the Imperial-cross trademark. Imperial purchased molds from such companies as Heisey and Cambridge, and today there are thousands of reproductions on the market that tend to confuse the beginning collector.

Bowl, clear, signed NUCUT, 5½" wide	$ 30- 38
Bowl, Imperial Jewels, blue/gold, 6¼" high	78- 82
Bowl, Imperial Jewels, gold luster, Imperial cross mark, 6½" high	126-139
Bowl, scalloped top, signed NUCUT, 6¼" wide	29- 38
Candlestick, Candlewick, 3½" high	17- 26
Compote, Imperial Jewels, blue/gold, ribbed, signed, 6" high	81- 90
Vase, amethyst/ruby luster, 6¼" high	142-152
Vase, green/white looping, signed, 7" high	138-146
Vase, imitation cut glass, 7¼" high	44- 54
Vase, signed NUCUT, 6¼" high	22- 31

India Brass

India Brass

Most of what you find in shops was either brought home by soldiers serving in the China-Burma-India theater during World War II or is brand new. Usually "India" is stamped on the bottom. It was tooled brass, the items often being made from U.S. Army artillery shells. A form of enamel was rubbed into the tool crevices.

Dinner gong (ill.)	$ 32-	40
Ewer, handled, 13" high with 6 cups to match	38-	50
Incense burner, hanging type	34-	46
Kettle, matching tray	39-	48
Lamp, hanging-type, electrified	64-	72
Teapot, 11½" high, World War II	36-	42
Vase, 8" high	48-	52
Vase, 14" high, on teakwood stand	44-	52

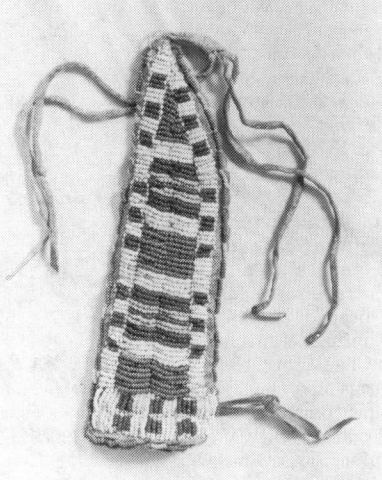

Indian (American) Artifacts

Indian (American) Artifacts

Even with all the fakes flooding the market, this is a hot collectible, nationwide. Just know your Indians! See **Clubs and Publications**, this Price Guide.

Apache Indian cradle board, c. 1860, 36" overall	$ 675-	750
Arrowheads, common type, ea.	.75-	1.50
Beaded belt, 42" long	155-	170
Beaded pouch, Oklahoma Indian	290-	320
Boots, buckskin, coin buttons	168-	178
Bow, wooden, Plains Indians, 47" long	79-	89
Breechcloth, Navajo, beaded, buckskin	325-	380

(continued)

Indian (American) Artifacts

Chief's wearing blanket, Three
  Hills Reservation, gray/
  white 1,400-1,600
Eastern Woodlands all beaded
  cap, possibly Iroquois,
  c. 1840 . . . . 585- 650
Fighting ax, Mohawk, 8″
  overall 170- 190
Halberd type spike-
  tomahawk, New England,
  c. 1720s, 7″ overall 342- 362
Hatchet, Western Plains,
  c. 1870s, 5″ overall 192- 225
Knife sheath, beaded,
  6″ long (ill.) 63- 73
Low bowl, pottery, Hopi,
  cream yellow slip, black/
  orange designs, 8″ dia. (ill.) . 172- 188
Moccasins, Arapaho, deerskin,
  beaded 142- 152
Painting, "Ignacio," signed
  Chas. Craig, 1889 . . . .   3,700+
Peace pipe, clay, Sioux 310- 340
Pipe, tomahawk, handmade
  pottery bowl, 9″ long 320- 350
Purse, Sioux, beaded, deer-
  skin, 4″×7″ 172- 190
Sioux bear claw necklace,
  c. 1850s, about 9½″, 21
  claws 1,800-2,400
Spike-tomahawk, Eastern
  Woodlands, c. 1750s, 8″
  overall 520- 610
Tomahawk, original handle
  and rawhide 138- 150
Trade beads, glass, amber,
  blue 182- 194
Vest, buckskin, beaded,
  tassels, Hopi 820- 850
War bonnet, eagle feathers,
  heavily beaded, Plains
  Indians 2,400-2,700
War club, Comanche 120- 132
Western Plains pipe-
  tomahawk, c. 1870s, 6½″
  overall 340- 380
Zia bowl, pottery, white slip,
  black/red design, 8″ high
  (ill.) 182- 220

Indian Tree Pattern

This pattern was popular from the 1850s until just before World War I. It takes its name from an Oriental, not an Indian, shrub. The colors were very soft—blue, pink, green—and it was made by various potters in England: Minton, Cauldron, Maddox, and others.

Berry set, Maddox, bowl, 10″
  dia., 6 sauces, 5″ dia. $210-240
Butter dish, covered, Burgess &
  Leigh 88- 92
Cake stand, Maddox 94-107
Compote, Copeland, 8″ high 63- 74
Creamer 69- 79
Plates, Cauldon, 9″, 10″, 11″ dia.. 52- 62
Plate, Noritake, 10″ dia. (ill.) 42- 58
Salt/pepper shakers, Minton, pr. . 67- 77
Sugar bowl, covered 73- 82
Sugar bowl, covered, Minton 71- 82
Teapot, 6 matching cups/saucers . 194-214
Vase, Cauldon, 8″ high 92-108
Vegetable dish, 10″ dia. 62- 72

Indian Tree Pattern

Inkwells and Bottles

These containers for holding ink usually were made of glass and have been around for centuries. Ink was made from chimney soot, dried berries, dried blood. The ballpoint pen rang the death knell for inkwells.

Blue, iridescent, pewter lid,
  Steuben type . . . . $ 69- 82
Brass, crab, glass liner 85- 96
Brass, glass liner, alabaster base . 49- 59
Cloisonne, 2 inkwells, on marble
  base 101-112
Covered container, 2 lovebirds,
  footed iron stand, 4″ high 61- 71
Cranberry, bronze, marked Ger-
  many 1875 on bottom 77- 88

Inkwells and Bottles

Crystal, two glass-lined, tray,
footed 63- 74
Cut, embossed silver hinged top,
3½" high 48- 58
Elk, 2 inkwells and rack 141-152
Glass, blown, c. 1820s (ill.) 52- 62
Green alabaster, dome top,
square base 61- 70
Ink stand, French porcelain, blue/
green/orange enamels, c. 1910,
3½" high 70- 80
Iron inkstand, horse, brass cap,
penholder on horse's back 52- 72
Milk glass, two cats, iron base ... 152-168
Ormolu, cherubs, red/gray marble
base, ormolu feet, France 210-222
Pen rack, iron and glass, dated
1877 .... 51- 61
Pewter, holes for quill pens,
England, 3" high 61- 71
Porcelain, flowers/cupids, 3 ink-
wells, on wood base 268-281
Red glass, round base, brass tray,
2 penholders 68- 78
School desk, black bakelite cap .. 38- 48
Swirl design, star base, brass
cover, footed.............. 52- 62

Insulators

Little did they think that when they strung
telephone and telegraph wires from coast to
coast, those glass insulators would create
such a furor in the antique business today.
Books, clubs, magazines, all having to do
with the insulator, are in great demand. See
Clubs and Publications, this Price Guide.

Armstrong, dome No. 2 .... $ 32- 41
B. T. C., Canada, ice blue 39- 47
Barclay, patent spiral groove ... 25- 35
Brookfield, green, 1865 .... 19- 28
C. C. T. and Company 35- 42
California, baby signal, smoky .. 24- 28
California, signal, gray 25- 34
Diamond pony, olive green 24- 32
Gayner, No. 48-400, aqua 28- 32
Green pottery 27- 37
H. G. Company, aqua, standard
signal, double petticoat 22- 30
Hawley, Pa., aqua, beehive 27- 31
Hemingray, double petticoat
beehive, aqua 27- 37
Hemingray, No. 14, vaseline 62- 72
Hemingray, No. 19, cobalt (ill.) .. 62- 74
Hemingray, No. 19, clear 17- 24
Knowles, No. 2, cable, green 25- 36
Locke, No. 21, green 48- 58
Lynchburg, No. 31 .... 18- 21
Maydwell, No. 20, milk glass 27- 37
McLaughlin No. 16, emerald
green 14- 29
Muncie, large, with stand 74- 77
No. 63, Carnival glass, Pyrex 36- 46
Opaline, No. E14-B 101-112
Peru-K. C. G. Company 62- 71
Postal beehive, pink 28- 34
San Francisco, pony, aqua 21- 29
W. E. Manufacturing Company,
aqua, Patented December 19,
1871 .... 32- 41
Whitall Tatum Company, No. 1,
purple (ill.) 26- 34

Insulators

Invalid Feeders

Invalid Feeders

During the 18th and 19th centuries many
potteries in the Staffordshire District in
England made these feeders. Adams, Clews,
Jackson, Mayer, Ridgway, and Stevenson—

231   (continued)

these are just a few of the many. Don't confuse with a Scuttle mug.

Invalid feeder, mid-1800s
  possibly Clews (ill.) $108-121
Invalid feeder, J. and J. Jackson,
  1830s   96-107
Invalid feeder, Ralph Stevenson,
  early 1800s, marked R.S.W. . . . 101-111

Iowa City Glass

Iowa City Glass

The Iowa City Flint Glass Manufacturing Company was incorporated in April of 1880. Iowa City factory was its general name. It is difficult to positively identify this glass, and the workmanship is on the crude side. Most pieces are quite thick, with mold lines much in evidence. Animal/bird motifs were very popular. Figures were often combined with mottoes such as "Be Gentle" (with lamb); "Be True" (with dog), etc.

Animal-motto plates, each . . . . . . $ 52- 62
Compote, etched birds, flowers,
  6" high (ill.) 62- 72
Creamer, Alhambra design 44- 52
Goblet, deer motif 48- 58
Mug, dog motif 52- 61
Platter, beehive motif, oval-and-
  bar border 70- 80
Platter, Elaine, oval-and-bar
  border 72- 82
Spooner, open handles 44- 52

Iron

Without it there would be no United States as we know it today. It rusts if not painted, but is durable and long-lasting, and helped to build our nation.

Andiron, girl/boy motif, 14"
  shank . . . . $ 62- 72

Iron

Anvil, blacksmith's size		1,700+
Apple peeler	44-	54
Bank, Battleship Oregon		
(still type)	58-	66
Bookends, horses, pr.	34-	48
Bootjack, beetle, 10"	29-	39
Buggy step (makes nice		
towel holder in kitchen)	24-	32
Candle trimmer, patented		
1854	49-	54
Cherry pitter	42-	52
Doorstop, flower basket	29-	32
Figurine, boy with flower,		
garden, 26" high	72-	78
Footscraper, Dachshund,		
15" long	48-	58
Grinder, for counter or table		
use	32-	39
Harpoon, toggle hook,		
original	220-	238
Ice tongs	34-	41
Ladle, long handle, 13"	35-	42
Mold, rabbit, 2-part, hinged,		
for ice cream	48-	58
Nutcracker, dog's tail closes		
jaw to crack nut	44-	57
Rack, hat, coat, 6 hooks,		
28" wide	42-	60
Sadiron	32-	41
Sadiron, French, mid-1800s . . .	45-	52
Stove, potbelly, old, ornate	107-	112
Stove, Sears, miniature,		
8½" high (ill.)	40-	50
Tongs, ironworker or		
blacksmith	47-	57

Irons

These are being reproduced but are still collectible. Children's sizes very popular.

232

Irons

Asbestos "Tourist Iron"	$ 32-	45
Bless & Drake, detachable		
handle (ill.)	28-	36
Children's flat iron	38-	47
Cross Hatch, original	41-	50
Curled handle, original	27-	37
Nickel-plated iron	24-	33
Rope handle, old variation	27-	36

Ironstone

Ironstone is an earthenware made from slag from the steel mills, with clay. Durable, it was first patented in 1813 by C. H. Mason. Later, many English firms made it, Meakin being famous for its lightweight ware. Other firms making it were Edwards, Johnson Brothers, Clemenston, Burgess, Podmore and Walker, Meller and Taylor, Wilkinson.

Bone dish, wheat motif	$ 28-	37
Bowl, covered, Meakin, 6½″ high	42-	52
Bowl, sugar, floral decor, gold		
lustre designs, Edwards	52-	61
Chocolate pot, 5½″ high (ill.)	27-	37
Coffeepot, Burslem, opaque		
granite china, 11″ high	192-221	

Jade

Usually associated with China, this cool, green, semiprecious stone has been around for years. Don't worry about finding any from the Ch'ien Lung dynasty or even finding an Imperial jade ring. But there are many interesting pieces in shops today. Know your dealer. It doesn't mean it's jade just because it feels cool against your face. So does an ice cube! Much alabaster passes for the real thing. Know about it.

Ashtray, 3″ dia.	$ 162-	172
Bottle, snuff, black/green,		
2¼″ high	385-	440
Box, light green-to-white,		
average color	365-	385
Butterfly, carved,		
white/green	220-	240
Cordial, green, set of 6	270-	290
Figurine, dragon, trees,		
brown/green	340-	370
Foo Dog on teakwood		
base, 16th century		4,400+
Grapes, bunch, 5″	270-	290
Incense burner, Foo Dog,		
5½″ high	550-	578
Letter opener, 8¼″ long	148-	162
Netsuke, dragons, 1¼″	155-	172
Pendant, white/green,		
2½″	108-	121
Statuette, lady w/fruit,		
9½″ high (ill.)	700-	775
Sword ornament, dragon,		
white/green	172-	190
Thumb ring	154-	162
Vase, carved, trees,		
flowers, 9½″ high		2,200+
Vase, green, carved birds,		
teakwood stand, late		
1800s	375-	410
Vase (rare), black, 8″ high,		
17th century		12,300+

Ironstone

Jade

Japanese War Items

Anything to do with wars is collectible. Japanese military items are no exception. Most are from World War II.

Cigarette pack, "From Island of Attu, May 13, 1943" (ill.) $	9-	16
Dagger, worn by Japanese officer, sharkskin handle	128-	138
Helmet, pith style, cork lined (ill.)	58-	67
Japanese battle flag, white with red ball, 14″×19″	107-	122
Mine detector in mahogany box	140-	160
Pilot's helmet, name on peak	68-	78
Samurai sword, military issue	140-	150
Samurai sword, name on blade, sharkskin hilt	1,300-	1,500
Wind indicator, used on aircraft carrier (ill.)	77-	88

Jewel Boxes

Popular in the late 1800s until the early 1900s. They were usually made of pot metal, then quadruple-plated, silver-plated

Jewel Boxes

or dipped in a cheap gold solution. Then they were stuffed with cotton, which was covered with velvet. Also made of wood, ivory, etc.

Gilded metal, Art Nouveau, pink lining $	58-	68
Gold-plated, blue velvet lining	42-	52
Gold-plated, porcelain painting in lid, 2½″ high (ill.)	72-	82
Quadruple-plated, velvet lined, on lid "Where's My"	34-	44
Silver-plated, velvet-lined, footed	42-	52
Sterling silver, velvet, initialed BHM	130-	140
Velvet ring box, 2″ square (ill.)	14-	24
Walnut box w/drawer, primitive (ill.)	68-	79
Wood, inlaid rosewood, tufted velvet lining, lock and key, French, mid-1800s	142-	152

Jewelry

In a word, antique jewelry is being bought to wear; expensive antique jewelry is being bought as an investment. Always get a receipt and know the seller. Obviously, you can't get a receipt from the Czar, but Cartier's will oblige if you purchase the Czar Alexander II of Russia necklace, consisting of emeralds and pearls, priced modestly at $1,250,000 or higher. Since the days of the Egyptians, women (and now men) have been fascinated by jewelry of all kinds. The age, content of gold or platinum, carat of the stone, quality—all enter into the price. Be careful.

Beads, agates, orange/white, graduated sizes, silver-plated clasp $	62-	71
Beads, amber, graduated sizes, 32″ overall, 14k clasp	132-	150
Beads, Art Deco, sterling silver, "lady" pendant, 19″ overall	72-	81
Beads, coral, hand-carved, graduated sizes, 27″ overall, 14k clasp	61-	72
Beads, coral, 6-strand, hand-carved, sterling silver clasp	410-	450
Bracelet, Art Nouveau, emeralds alternating with real pearls, 14k chain, 2 clasps	1,250-	1,400
Bracelet, baby, gold-filled, secret joint	42-	52
Bracelet, green jade, silver filigree and enamel (ill.)	250-	300

Jewelry

Bracelet, 14k gold, hand-
engraved, secret joint,
safety chain 570- 620
Bracelet, 14k gold, 1 diamond,
½c, 6 genuine sapphires . . . 1,975-2,300
Bracelet, 18k solid gold,
hand-engraved 795- 885
Bracelet, 10k solid gold,
machine-turned 84- 94
Bracelet, platinum, 36 cut
diamonds, 35 sapphires, all
genuine 1,100-1,400
Bracelet, watch chain type,
18k gold (ill.) 585- 640
Brooch, black mourning type,
6 styles, ea. 63- 73
Brooch, Bohemian garnets,
3 styles, ea. 88- 98
Brooch, brown/white cameo,
14k frame 420- 460
Brooch, Bull's Helmet cameo,
14k gold frame 520- 540
Brooch, 14k gold, carnelian
shell cameo 450- 485
Brooch, 14-point star, 108 real
seed pearls, 1 whole pearl,
14k frame 210- 220
Brooch, Jasperware,
Wedgwood medallion, blue,
14k frame 110- 128
Brooch, lady's face, hand-
painted on porcelain, 18k
frame 270- 290
Chain, attached picture
holder, 14k, 25″ 310- 340
Chain, belt, gold-filled, 3
initials 55- 62
Chain, rope, 3-strand, 14k,
religious medallion 585- 625
Chain, watch fob, 6 strands,
safety chain and charm,
gold-filled 52- 60
Chain, watch, 60″ long, 14k . .   422- 438
Chain, watch, slide inlaid with
seed pearls, 55″ long, 10k . .   172- 188
Chain, watch, ¼c diamond in
slide, 57″ long, 14k 550- 620

Collar button, 14k 38- 42
Cuff links, 14k 162- 172
Cuff links, sterling silver,
Art Deco 60- 70
Earrings, amethysts, sterling
silver mountings 92- 110
Earrings, Art Nouveau, nude
lady, sterling silver 50- 58
Earrings, Bohemian garnets,
10k gold settings 61- 72
Earrings, 14k gold, black
jet stones 55- 65
Earrings, ½c, 14k mountings .   345- 385
Lingerie clasp, 14k gold,
open work 67- 74
Lingerie clasp, 10k gold, hand-
engraved 42- 52
Locket, Art Nouveau, lady's
face, gold-filled, rose color . .   52- 62
Locket, 14k gold, tiny
diamond, front, 27″ 14k
gold chain 320- 340
Locket, rhinestones, gold-
filled 34- 42
Locket, sterling silver, hand-
engraved, 26″ sterling
silver chain 52- 67
Lorgnette, sterling silver,
45″ chain 385- 462
Necklace, 14k, amethyst stone
(ill.) 775- 825
Necklace, 14k gold chain,
2c Australian opal 410- 462
Necklace, green jade, 43
beads, graduated sizes,
14k gold clasp 520- 585
Necklace, moonstones 70- 84
Necklace, platinum chain,
2c diamond pendant,
Victorian 735- 842
Pin, Art Deco, sterling silver,
2″ long 82- 92
Pin, bar type, chip diamonds
in silver-plated frame 44- 54
Pin, 18k gold in shape of leaf,
w/diamonds and pearls 420- 482
Pin, 14k gold, amethyst
stone 148- 162
Pin porcelain painting 52- 62

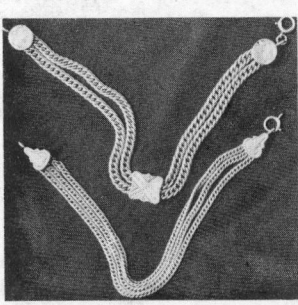

Jewelry

237

(continued)

Jewelry

Ring, amethyst, 4 stones,
2½c ea., 18k white gold
setting 620- 640
Ring, black onyx, 1 small
diamond, 18k gold setting .   152- 167
Ring, child's, ¼c diamond,
14k gold setting 99- 112
Ring, coat-of-arms crest, 18k
gold 895- 952
Ring, green emerald, 4c, 18k
gold setting . . . .   2,450+
Ring, pink shell cameo,
sterling silver setting 52- 62
Ring, sardonyx, 14k setting . .   160- 170
Ring, 6-star black sapphire,
38c, 18k gold setting . . . . . .   2,200+
Ring, topaz, 4c, 10k setting . .   68- 78
Ring, yellow sapphire, 62c,
18k gold setting . . . .   2,700+
Ring, zircon, 2c, 10k gold
setting 90- 110

Jugtown Pottery

Jugtown Pottery

Begun in Moore County, North Carolina, in
1920, by Jaques and Juliana Bushbee.

Orange was the predominant glaze used; a
Chinese blue glaze is the most sought after
today. The mark used is illustrated here.

Bowl, brown, signed Ben Owen,
5" high . . . . , ... $ 53- 62
Bowl, brown/orange, signed, 3½"
high 44- 53
Mug, Chinese blue, signed 39- 47
Plate, brown, signed, 5½" dia. . . .   27- 37
Plate, Chinese blue, signed Ben
Owen, 6" dia. 39- 47
Vase, brown, signed, 7" high 38- 47
Vase, Chinese blue, 3 handles,
signed, 6¼" high 46- 52
Vase, green, signed Ben Owen,
4¼" high 41- 50
Vase, green/tan, 2 handles,
signed, 4¼" high 40- 50
Vase, orange, signed, 6" high 29- 38

KPM

KPM

This mark was used at Meissen for two
years, c. 1723. In the 1830s it was adopted
by the Royal Factory in Berlin. Ten years
later the Prussian eagle was added to the
letters. Other factories adopted the KPM
letters in the late 19th century. There is no
proof that the factory using KPM was sanctioned by the royal families still ruling in
Germany at that time. There's obvious
confusion about the late KPM and eagle
today. Scarce, but know what you're finding.

Bowl, raised flowers inside,
blue, 8" dia. . . . . $ 74- 84
Chocolate pot, Silesia, Onion
pattern 83- 92
Creamer, sugar, violets,
green/pink ground, ea. 75- 84

238

Cup/saucer, demitasse, white ground, pink roses, 1830s	71-	82
Dish, raised leaves, cover, oval, 10" dia.	88-	99
Figurine, boy with goat, 9" high	110-	122
Picture, porcelain, family scene, 15"×20"	642-	710
Plaque, cupids, pink/blues, 6"×8"		1,400+
Plaque, 5½"×6¾", musicians	410-	450
Plate, cake, tulips, reticulated handles, rims, 9" dia.	77-	82
Plate, gypsy boy, 10" dia. (ill.)	92-	107
Teapot, creamer, sugar, tray, cups/saucers, flowers/ butterflies	510-	528
Vase, cherries and apples, 9½" high	267-	278

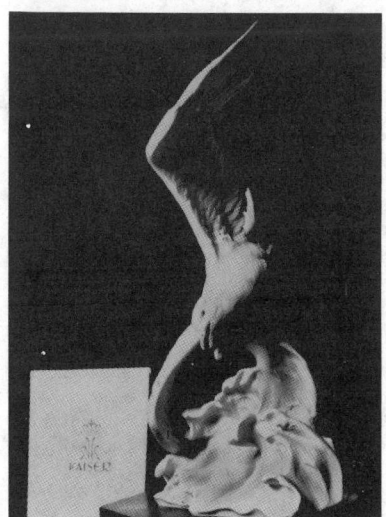

Kaiser Porcelain

Kaiser Porcelain

Bavaria, since 1872. Not antique but highly collectible. Cybis and Ispanky porcelains are also collectible. Prices listed are for Kaiser.

Flying Heron	$ 92-	107
Goose Girl	152-	170
Humming Bird	177-	192
Kingfisher, limit 2,000	292-	322
Pheasant, limit 1,500	388-	421
Pigeon group, limit 2,000	210-	240
Sea Gull, limit 1,000 (ill.)		2,600+

Kauffmann, Angelica

A native of Switzerland (1741-1807), she was a neoclassical painter and graphic artist, enjoying success in England as a portrait painter and decorator. Many porcelain pieces of the 19th century are attributed to her.

Bowl, classical scene, cobalt, gold trim, signed, 5½" high	$ 92-107
Bowl, maidens/cupid, blue, signed, 6¼" high	105-115
Box, classical scene, ladies in garden, signed	63- 73
Box, Greek scene, 2¼"×2½"	64- 84
Chocolate set: pot, 8 cups and saucers, classical scenes, gold trim on all pieces, all signed, set	620-640
Cup/saucer, demitasse, cobalt, gold border, signed	52- 62
Pitcher, maidens/cupid, blue, gold trim, signed, 7" high	112-123
Plate, classical scene, Austrian, signed, 9" dia.	67- 74
Plate, portrait center, gold trim, signed, 11¼" dia.	84- 92
Tray, 4 nymphs, maroon, gold trim, signed, 14½" long	152-160
Vase, portrait, gold handles, signed, 9" high	94-112
Vase, 3 maidens in garden, yellow, cobalt trim, signed, 8" high	108-118

Keramo Porcelain

This was from Karlovy Vary, the world-famous spa in Carlsbad, Czechoslovakia. The illustrated spa glass (porcelain) was filled with the health-giving waters, which were sipped through the top of the handle as illustrated here.

Keramo spa sipper (ill.)	$ 50- 60
Porcelain bottle to take home a sample for friends	49- 62
Souvenir plate marked Karlovy Vary, 1925	42- 52

Keramo Porcelain

239

Kew Blas Glass

Kew Blas Glass

Made at the Union Glass Works, Somerville, Massachusetts, in the 1890s, it was an iridescent glassware contemporary with Tiffany, Durand, Quezal, Steuben, and others. The name is not taken from Walter Blake's last name though he did work at the factory. Sometimes signed Kew Blas on the bottom, otherwise difficult to distinguish from other glasses named here.

Bowl, gold iridescent, signed
"Kew Blas A 500," 15″ dia.
(ill.) $365-410
Bowl, rose, gold iridescent/green
decor, Zipper pattern 358-375
Candlesticks, gold swirled,
signed, 9″ high, pr. 542-584
Creamer, Zipper pattern, 2½″
high 354-375
Plate, iridescent, blue, 6½″ dia. 372-392
Tumbler, blue iridescent, signed,
3½″ high 212-250
Tumbler, gold iridescent, signed,
4″ high 228-242
Vase, gold iridescent, signed,
5½″ high 528-562
Vase, green/brown iridescent,
signed, 9½″ high 710-732
Vase, pink/purple iridescent,
signed, 8″ high 615-635
Wine, gold iridescent, signed,
4¾″ high 198-224

Kewpies

Kewpies

Rose O'Neill drew pictures of these pixie-like figures for the *Ladies Home Journal* in the early 1900s. Around 1911 Kewpie dolls began to appear on the American market. The bisque dolls came from Germany, but the most common were the ones made of celluloid. Being reproduced.

Bank, glass, tin lid $122-142
Bowl, cereal, 6″ dia. 152-162
Candy container, 1915 142-150
Creamer, Kewpies playing in
yard 140-170
Cup/saucer, Germany, pink
lustre trim 133-152
Dish, feeding 72- 82
Doll, bisque, Japan, 4″ 65- 80
Doll, bisque, signed Rose
O'Neill 135-144
Doll, composition, Rose O'Neill
label, 12½″ 92-109
Doll, dressed, celluloid mark,
2½″ high 39- 47
Figurine, seated figure, 3″ high .. 252-272
Ice cream mold, hinged, pewter .. 91-108
Ice cream tray, signed Rose
O'Neill 72- 82
Lamp, chalkware, fringe shade .. 77- 87
Pitcher, 4 action Kewpies,
Royal Rudolstadt 298-320
Plate, Royal Rudolstadt,
signed Rose O'Neill 64- 74
Postcard, Christmas, "We love
you" 28- 38
Powder jar, signed 122-141
Teapot, creamer, sugar, signed
Rose O'Neill, porcelain 156-172
Thimble 27- 39
Toothpick, "Thinker," 5½″
high 81- 96
Tray, Kewpies picking berries,
signed 275-310
Vase, handled, Kewpies
playing, signed 157-182

Keys

Keys

Shown here because there are thousands of

different kinds. The old Spanish dungeon keys are quite collectible. Keys are a fun item to collect and decorate with. Too many to give specific prices.

Average price	$2-	3
Brass, early 1800s	8-	11
Folding type, nickel-plated	7-	11
Iron, jail type, large	14-	20

Kimble Glass

Kimble Glass

In the late 1800s, Colonel Ewan Kimble operated a factory at Vineland, New Jersey, for a relatively short time. The factory also operated jointly as Kimble and Durand. Not too much is known about this glass, but it is considered scarce today. After Durand's death in 1931, the factory was taken over by Kimble and today is part of Owens-Illinois. It is **not** spelled Kimball.

Bowl, Cluthra in white, rose, 4″
  high $274-292
Candlesticks, blue/green, iridized,
  14″ high, pr. 420-462
Vase, blue, white inside,
  scalloped, curved top, 7″ high . 162-180
Vase, Cluthra, blue/gray spirals,
  yellow iridescent, 6″ high 248-280
Vase, Cluthra, orange/white
  bubbles, dark handles, 11″
  high, signed "K-20144-11,
  Dec-7" (ill.) 292-325

King's Rose Pattern

Produced in the Staffordshire District, England, around 1820 to 1830, it's a soft-paste porcelain made especially for the Pennsylvania Dutch trade. The enamel decorations are usually in warm yellows, greens, pinks, and dark reds. Sometimes the colors flake off with use. It was good porcelain.

Coffeepot, 10¾″ high .... $ 1,550+
Cup/saucer, large size, King's
  Rose 280- 298

King's Rose Pattern

Cup/saucer, regular size	270-	288
Cup/saucer, regular size	260-	275
Plate, dinner, divided border, 9″ dia.	188-	196
Plate, dinner (ill.)	243-	262
Plate, toddy	220-	262

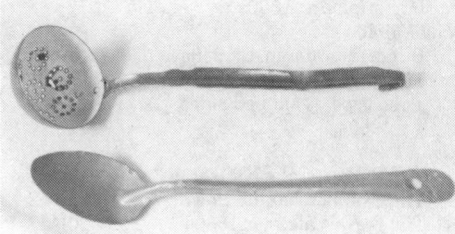

Kitchen Collectibles

Kitchen Collectibles

Anything to do with the kitchen—the older the better. 18th and 19th century items tend to be expensive, but mass-produced pieces are still readily available. Three eras are involved. 18th century kitchen—life revolved around the large fireplace; copper, brass, iron objects, all handwrought. Victorian kitchen—cast iron stoves, lots of tin, rugs on the floor, aluminum items. Early 20th century kitchen—electrical appliances, gadgets galore, refrigerators, cleanliness, orderliness.

Apple Corers
  All tin, 19th century .... $ 6- 9
Apple Parers
  Cast iron, F. A. Walker, c. 1870s 48- 57
  Rocking Table 44- 52

(contin

Tin, painted, "Matches," c. 1910 — 9- 16
Universal Stoves, cast iron, wall-type — 38- 47

Miscellaneous

Apple roaster, tin reflecting oven, c. 1850s — 88-101
Baller, nickel-plated, wooden handle — 8- 11
Bird nest fryer, tin/wire mesh, c. 1930 — 8- 15
Border mold, tin, fruit design — 11- 17
Bread board, maple, 19th century — 29- 37
Cabbage cutter, maple frame, steel blade — 57- 67
Carpet beater, woven wire, The Niagara — 26- 34
Cheese cutter, wire, c. 1920s — 8- 11
Egg glasses, F. A. Walker, c. 1870s — 51- 62
Egg scale, Acme, c. 1924 — 16- 23
Ice shaver, Logan and Strobridge — 11- 15
Ice tongs, handwrought, c. 1860s — 29- 36
Pie lifter, tin, c. 1900 — 15- 21
Pie stacker, 3-layer, c. 1920s — 17- 24
Raisin seeder, Pat. 1891 — 19- 27
Skillet, tin, mid-19th century — 47- 56
Slop urn, indurated fiber, c. 1898 — 25- 34
Vegetable skimmer, wood handle — 13- 18

Pans

Cake, cast iron — 32- 40
Corn stick, cast iron — 27- 36
Farina boiler, tin, 3-part, 4-qt. — 21- 29
Muffin, cast iron, 8-cup — 25- 34

Pot/Pan Scrapers

Babbitt's Cleanser — 16- 24
Better Butter, Fairmont Creamery — 24- 32
King Midas Flour — 19- 27
Sunshine Finishes — 20- 27

Push Handle Whippers

Galvanized, thumb handle on side — 13- 19
Push-handle type, wooden handle — 12- 18

Rolling Pins

Glass, screw-on tin cap — 17- 24
Maple, handmade, early — 27- 33
Meissen Onion pattern — 42- 51

Salt Boxes

Glass w/wooden lid — 34- 39
Pottery, wooden lid — 28- 38

Spice Boxes

Cabinet, wood, 8 drawers — 67- 77
Tin, jappaned designs, 7 round cans in large can w/lid — 68- 84
Tray, japanned tin, strap handle — 29- 38

Teakettles

Brass, early — 78- 98
Copper, early 19th century — 71- 81
Ironstone, English, c. 1870s — 48- 54

Tinware

Available in every gadget and utensil; all sizes, shapes, and prices.

Traps

Mouse, wheel-type, c. 1890s — 35- 45
Rat, cam, retinned, 6″×11″ — 29- 36

Waffle Irons

Crescent, wood handles — 47- 56
Griswold Mfg. Co., c. 1920s — 31- 40
Wrought iron, early 19th century — 79- 88

Washboards

M. C. Cable, hardwood frame — 24- 32
Glass Duke, glass board, hardwood frame — 32- 39
Sani-Steel, sheet steel — 26- 36

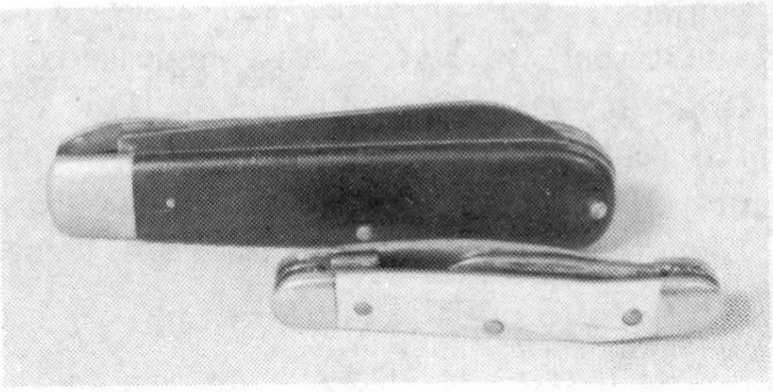

Knives

Knives

Remember Grandfather's advice, "Always cut away from your thumb!" All kinds of knives are collectible especially unusual pocket types.

Anvil, 3-blade (ill.) — $ 9- 13
Barlow, Blue Grass model — 92-107
Barlow, Remington, bone handle — 66- 74
Bowie, cased, 15″ overall blade, 1860s — 482-510
Camco, 2-blade (ill.) — 9- 13
Case, double X, stag handle, 3-blade — 77- 84
Case, double X, wood handle, 4-blade — 108-121
Gurkha, leather case and 2 skinning knives — 188-214
Hammer & Co., N.Y., pocket type, 2-blade — 42- 52
Jack, stag handle, 2-blades, old — 32- 41
Masonic, 14k gold, ornate enamel and initials — 57- 67
Pocket, Hopalong Cassidy, 3-blade — 48- 58
Pocket type, company advertising, fits on key chain, 2″ long — 47- 56
Remington, Babe Ruth emblem 2-blade, bone handle — 118-126
Remington, hunting type, 9″ blade, leather case — 94-109
Remington, pocket, 2-blade — 52- 63
Remington, R333, Boy Scout insignia, stag handle — 138-144
Sterling silver penknife, 2-blade nail cleaner — 55- 65
Winchester, Hawk bill, 1-blade, wood handle — 88- 97

(contin

Winchester, pocket type, 3-blade,
leather punch 77- 86
Winchester, 2-blade 84- 92

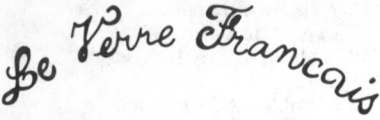

La Verre Francais Cameo Glass

Made in Paris, France, 1920s until 1930s,
usually only two layers with a single acid cutting. It was almost always mottled and
streaked or clouded with glass of varying colors. Most pieces were signed with the name
Charder occasionally appearing in cameo
relief.

Bowl, blue/orange, flowers,
signed, 11″ dia. . . . . $ 675- 750
Lamp, tortoiseshell color,
signed 1,200-1,400
Planter, yellow/orange, Art
Deco, 7″ high 325- 375
Vase, blue/orange, berries on
yellow ground 450- 525
Vase, blue/orange/yellow,
signed, 9¼″ high 430- 445
Vase, brown ground, blue
flowers, signed, 7″ high . . . 350- 410
Vase, floral, maroon/pink,
signed, 5¼″ high 240- 275
Vase, flying birds, blue/
yellow/orange, signed
Charder 425- 455
Vase, frosted yellow ground,
cut blue/orange, signed . . . 535- 560
Vase, orange flowers, brown/
green base, signed, 11″
high 420- 440
Vase, tortoiseshell color,
orange/blue, signed 510- 522
Vase, white base, red/blue
flowers, signed, 11″ high . . 385- 425

Lacquer

This is an Oriental form of art. Layer upon
layer of lacquer was applied to the item, then
designs were cut into the lacquer layers or
painted on in typical Oriental style.

Bowl, floral designs, painted . . . . $ 66- 75
Box, carved fish designs in red/
black, footed 67- 76
Box, Japanese, black/red, 5½″
sq. (ill.) 38- 43
Fireplace screen, carved in litho-
phane style 132-141

Lacquer

Jewelry box, 6-drawer, painted
designs 140-150
Sewing box, black, gold dragon
designs, painted 88- 98
Tea caddy, 2 compartments,
pewter lids 141-152
Tray, black, gilded Oriental
decor, 12¼″ wide 72- 80

Lalique Glass

Rene Lalique made this fine art glass in
France at the turn of the century. He was an
associate of Emile Galle, and their works are
similar in many respects. A combination of
blowing, pressing, frosting, and cutting
achieved the excellent effect Lalique gave to
his glass. "New" Lalique is being made in
France today. All listed pieces are signed "R.
Lalique."

Angel fish, blue, 2″ high $220-255
Bottle, frosted background,
dancing ladies, 6″ high 363-381
Bottle, heart-shaped, butterflies,
4½″ high 118-127

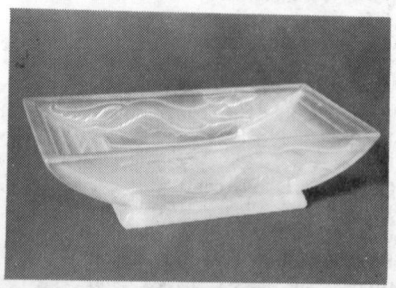

Lalique Glass

Miner's Lamp

Lamps

Gone With the Wind Lamp

(continue

Bristol Glass Type Lamp

Gone With the Wind lamp,
brass fittings, cast iron
base, 23½" high (ill.) 381-420
Gone With the Wind lamp,
green ground, pink/yellow
flowers 287-299
Gone With the Wind lamp,
hand-painted "cows
grazing," brass base......... 367-421
Gone With the Wind lamp,
red satin shade and base 310-341
Hand lamp, Coolidge Drape
shade, 9½" high, clear 148-158
Kitchen lamp, white shade,
brass font, 1880s 111-122
Log cabin lamp, clear glass 131-142
Millefiori, base and shade both
millefiori, 12½" high, 1880s
(ill.) 269-292
Oil lamp, Sandwich, Heart &
Waffle, mid-1850s (ill.) 238-245
Piano lamp, floor type, marble
top, porcelain-painted shade .. 261-281

Satin glass lamp, brass/wood
base 260-277
Pulpit lamp, spring base,
copper, 12" high 84- 93
Student lamp, single, milk
white shade, brass 298-320
Student lamp, double, green
shade, brass 820-920
Table lamp, green/blue ground,
flower decor, electrified,
1890s 392-418

Tiffany-type Lamp

Tiffany-type table lamp,
caramel slag glass shade,
brass base 985-1,150
Tiffany-type table lamp, tulips/
leaves glass, gilded cast iron
finial, 24½" high (ill.) 720- 820
Tiffany-type table lamp, metal
base, caramel slag glass
shade, 16½" high 452- 495
Wall lamp, iron ring type,
pressed glass bowl, white
shade, 1880s 92- 107
Wall lamp, tin bonnet 95- 118

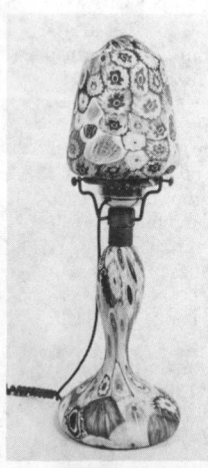

Millefiori Lamp

Lamps

Aladdin

This is one of the most popular lamps ever made. The Mantle Lamp Company of America, Inc., was founded in Chicago in 1908. These lamps are still being made in Nashville, Tenn. All lamps are priced with complete burners and shades. See **Clubs and Publications**, this Price Guide.

Practicus table lamp .... $	285-	310
Model No. 1 table lamp	182-	192
Model No. 1 parlor lamp	295-	320
Model No. 2 table lamp	252-	270
Model No. 2 parlor lamp	281-	295
Model No. 3 table lamp	194-	224
Model No. 3 parlor lamp	285-	288
Model No. 4 table lamp	198-	225
Model No. 5 table lamp	182-	192
Model No. 10 table lamp	340-	360
Model 1233 blue Venetian Art-Craft crystal vase lamp, 10¼″ tall	162-	182
Model No. 1241 variegated (two-tone) tan crystal vase lamp, 12″ tall	147-	158
Model No. 1242 Bengal red crystal vase lamp, 12″ tall .	281-	295
Model 1247 red Venetian Art-Craft crystal vase lamp, 10¼″ tall	269-	288
Style 99, Venetian, clear, Model A table lamp, 1932 .	358-	367
Style 101, Venetian, green, Model A table lamp, 1932 .	192-	220
Style B-25, Victoria, decorated china, Model B table lamp	410-	442
Style B-39, Washington Drape (round base), clear crystal, Model B	118-	127
Style B-62, Short Lincoln Drape, ruby crystal, Model B table lamp	530-	552
Style B-76, Tall Lincoln Drape, cobalt crystal, Model B table lamp (lamps with scallop design on the foot are worth much more)	562-	572
Style B-82, Beehive, amber crystal, light, Model B table lamp	120-	130
Style B-82, Beehive, amber crystal, dark, Model B table lamp	182-	192
Style B-86, Quilt, green moonstone, Model B table lamp	188-	210
Style B-100, Corinthian, clear crystal, Model B table lamp	106-	114
Style B-110, Cathedral, white moonstone, Model B table lamp	261-	281
Caboose lamp, Model B w/shade	188-	221
Caboose wall bracket lamp, alacite font	154-	164
Floor lamp, Model No. 12, w/shade, 1254 series	162-	172
Floor lamp, Model B, brass, w/shade	285-	295
Hanging lamp, Model No. 2 w/shade	333-	362
Hanging lamp, Model No. 3, double chandelier	1,200-	1,350
Hanging lamp, Practicus, w/shade	270-	290

Lamps, Miniature

Originally known as night lamps, today we

Lamps, Miniature

(continu⸺

call them miniature lamps. Every company made them in blown, blown-molded, pressed, every color, every price range. Most are collectible.

Blue glass, Inverted Thumbprint, 6½″ high . . . $	134-	143
Brass banquet lamp, purple shade, 8″ high	120-	128
Brass cabin lamp, 7″ high . . .	88-	99
Brass, saucer type, 4½″ high with chimney, patented 1873	94-	108
Bristol glass, pink, chimney-type shade	94-	108
Bristol glass, white, blue decor, 8″ high	88-	96
Cased glass, red over milk glass, matching half shade	132-	141
Clear glass, umbrella shade, flower decor	81-	91
Cobalt Little Duchess, 7½″ high	88-	98
Cosmos glass, white shade, 7½″ high	408-	418
Cranberry Beaded Swirl, 8″ high	132-	141
Cranberry, handled, 5½″ high	128-	134
End-of-Day (Spatter Glass), 7″ high	139-	148
Gold Eagle, orange body, gold trim (ill.)	184-	196
Milk glass, Columbus bust base (ill.)	232-	241
Milk glass, hand-painted, 5½″ high	60-	70
Milk glass, pink slag, Swan, shade, rare (ill.)	1,100-1,300	
Mt. Washington glass, blue flower decor, 7½″ high . . .	375-	450
Satin glass, blue, matching ball shade	128-	145
Satin glass, green 8″ high . . .	137-	152
Satin glass, pink, 8″ high . . .	142-	171
Satin glass, pink with flowers, frosted shade, 7″ high (ill.)	132-	154
Satin glass, red, 6½″ high . .	131-	151
Satin glass, white/pink diamond quilt, 7″ high	160-	185
Tiffany miniature mushroom lamp with shade, green/white, original bulb signed Edison Mazda; lamp signed LCT, 8″ high (rare) .	3,200-3,600	
Tulip lamp, flowers in green, 8½″ high	188-	220

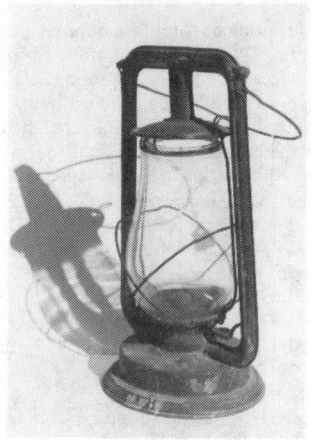

Lanterns

on, lanterns have been made in every size and shape to fit a particular need. Good repros are appearing at shows.

Buggy lantern, red bull's eye reflector . . . . $	128-142	
Candle lantern, tin and glass, early 1800s	61-	71
Candle lantern, tin, folding type	74-	84
Candle lantern, tin, 12″ high	94-108	
Carriage lanterns, beveled glass, red reflectors, pr.	342-362	
Construction-type, 11½″ high (ill.)	12-	17
Miner's lantern, iron, patented snuffer marked Hailwood	71-	81
Paul Revere type, pierced tin	88-101	
Police lantern, kerosene, bull's-eye lens, tin, 1880s	72-	82
Porch lantern, electrified	49-	59
Railroad lantern, hooded, inspector's	71-	81
Railroad lantern, red, squat globe, marked Southern RR . .	62-	72
Ship's lantern, captain's, copper reflector	288-320	
Ship's lantern, red globe, brass frame, 20″ high	645-675	
Skater's lantern, brass, with wire, kerosene	92-108	
Skater's lantern, silver-plated, mid-1800s, chain, kerosene . . .	72-108	
Skater's lantern, tin, wire handle	77-	86
Whale oil lantern, tapered glass globe, tin, early 1800s	169-184	

Lanterns

From the earliest pine splints during Colonial times to the first electrical types, 1870

Lap Desks

When traveling in the early days, one took along a portable desk. Usually it was made

Lap Desks

of wood, contained ink, quills, sealing wax. Most of the ink was in powder form—when mixed with water, it did the trick.

Rosewood, English, 18th century,
complete $240-270
Rosewood veneer box, brass
hinges, 4 compartments,
12" across 242-273
Walnut, English, hidden com-
partment under pen tray,
1800s 261-310
Yew wood, Staghorn covered,
15" wide (ill.) 300-328

Latticinio

Latticinio

Made by an ancient technique lost in time, this glass was produced by various glass houses in the mid-to-late 1800s. Uninformed collectors confuse it with Lutz-type glass.

Latticinio

Latticinio's crossed, curved lines beneath the decoration give it a peppermint cane effect. Actually it's a filigree glassware, first developed in the first or second century, B.C. Don't worry about finding any piece this old. Most of what you find in shops is in the $55-70 range. If it proves to be old, you've found a bargain. If not, you haven't paid attention when we say, "Know your antiques or know your antiques dealer!" Being reproduced—from the island of Murano, near Venice, Italy.

Plates, typical design, twisted
threads, gold/white (ill.), ea. . . . $ 80- 89

Lavender Pots

Lavender Pots

The dried flowers, leaves, and stalks of a European flower akin to the mint family, when dried, were used to fill sachets, perfume clothes and linens. The crushed plant was kept in a lavender pot, made by most European porcelain firms during the 1800s and until World War I.

Haviland lavender pot, rose
petals, pink border, 2 lids . . . . . $ 73- 82
Royal Worcester lavender pot,
2 lids, (ill.) 80- 88

Leeds Ware   LEEDS POTTEF

Begun in Yorkshire, England, about

Leeds Ware

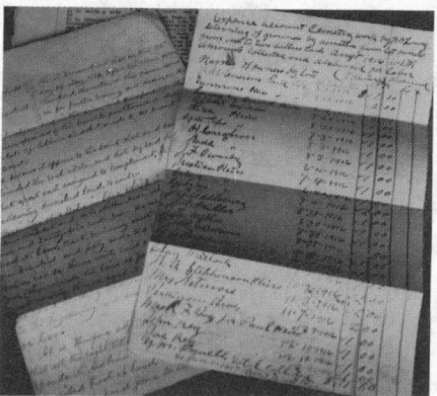

Legal Documents

this was a fine grade of creamware that competed with Wedgwood. A few years later reticulated and punched wares were made, with few pieces ever marked. Extremely rare and collectible.

Bowl, blue/white, twisted handles	$ 70-	80
Cream pitcher, yellow/blue/ green, 4½" high	168-	174
Cup/saucer, handleless, floral decor	98-	111
Jug, creamware, 1780, flowers in red	169-	174
Mug, Chinese decor, early 18th century	132-	152
Pitcher, farmer's coat-of-arms (rare)		1,400+
Pitcher, flower decor, 6" high (ill.)	218-	241
Plate, blue edge, marked, 12" dia.	108-	118
Plate, creamware, openwork, marked, 9" dia.	112-	131
Platter, cream, shell pattern, 16½" wide	178-	184
Sugar bowl w/lid, yellow/ green, 4½" high	121-	131
Teapot, red/green, shell pattern in body, 7½" high	265-	274
Tureen, white body, blue decor, 22" high, lid	262-	274

Legal Documents

Old handwritten deeds and wills, especially ~ose from England with the magnificent red ~ls and ribbons, are all being sought

...rance policy, 1875,
...ite paper . . . . $ 15- 19

English land deed on heavy parchment with ornate wax seal, early 1800s 63- 70
Framed cemetery plot receipt, "Woodlawn, Bronx, NY," 1892 18- 24
Handwritten deed, dated 1878 (ill.) 11- 17
Mortgage deed, Norfolk, N.Y., 1858, handwritten 14- 21
Quitclaim deed, 1849, Hunter, N.Y., handwritten 16- 22
Warranty deed, Westchester County, N.Y., 1866, "Certificate Magistracy" 19- 24

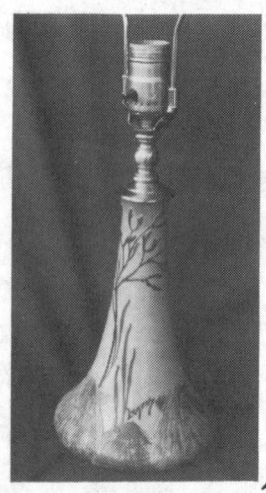

LeGras

LeGras

This gentleman was known for his unusually imaginative glassware and bottles. He discontinued operations just before World

War I. His scenic reproductions, also made in his factory at Saint-Dennis, were considered masterpieces. Being reproduced.

Bowl, beige, brown, green-
cased, signed 4½" high $685-742
Bowl, rose, enameled spring
scene, scalloped top, 7½"
high 252-280
Lamp, green, orange, trees,
electrified, signed, 7¼" high
(ill.) 587-638
Vase, Art Deco, autumn
leaves, 8½" high........... 475-532
Vase, brown, orange leaves,
enameled, 16" high.......... 482-520
Vase, cameo, cut back foliage,
green/blue, signed 710-715
Vase, cameo, green, yellow,
cobalt, acid cut to clear, 13"... 910-925
Vase, cameo, white apple
blossoms, green back-
ground, 8½" high.......... 420-432

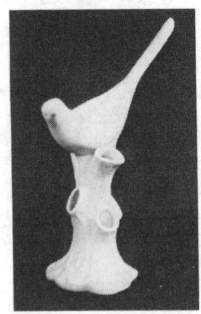

Lenox

Lenox

This firm started business in 1906 in Trenton, New Jersey. Among other wares, it made a good Belleek type.

Ashtray, shell-shaped .... $ 19- 26
Atomizer, perfume, penguin
shape, 4" high.............. 52- 62
Bottle, woman's head shape,
Hattie Carnegie cosmetics 84- 93
Bowl, oval, cream, gilt edge 70- 80
Candy box, cream, gold edge 88- 98
Coffee service, Ming pattern,
pot and bowl, large creamer ... 112-118
Cup/saucer, Ming pattern 34- 43
Jar, mustard, green, silver
overlay, lid 47- 56
Mug, gold scene, pr. (rare) 142-152
Plate, Ming pattern, 8¼" dia. ... 64- 74
Salt, swan-shape, master and 4
small, set 68- 78
Tray, pin, gold band, 6" dia...... 37- 47
Vase, Art Nouveau, 6½" high,

green, gold gilt 98-118
Vase, bird-shaped, flower 10"
high (ill.) 62- 72

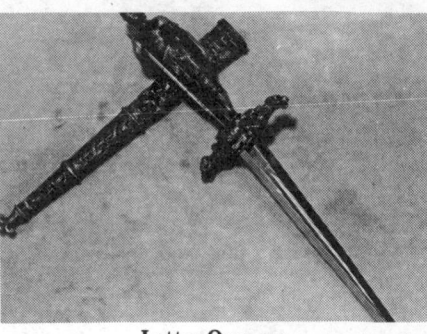

Letter Openers

Letter Openers

Made of bone, ivory, gold, silver, brass, wood, this item has been used for hundreds of years.

Alabaster, carved Chinese
designs, 8" long .... $ 32- 39
Brass, ornate case, African
figure, late 1800s (ill.) 62- 72
Gold, 14k, castle scene, French,
dated 1834, 7½" long 540-575
Ivory, carved figures on handle,
early 1800s 57- 67
Silver-plated, souvenir of Philadelphia Centennial, 1876 ..... 44- 53
Sterling silver, marked Tiffany,
6½" long................. 352-382
Wood, many types, souvenir, etc. 38- 47

License Plates

Since the early 1900s these have been collectible. The early plates, porcelain-on-metal, bring brisk prices today. All plates are in demand, from the 1900s until World War II. See **Clubs and Publications**, this Price Guide.

Porcelain, on metal, Pennsylvania, 1907 .... $ 45- 55
Tin, any state, 1900 to 1915 ..... 22- 31
Tin, any state, 1920s to 1940s ... 14- 24
1950s on 1- 2

License Plates

Lightning-Rod Balls

Lightning-Rod Balls

They were supposed to keep the house or barn from being struck by lightning, but they didn't. They appeared in the 1840s—glass, opaque, mirrored, or translucent. A hole at either end allowed one to be slipped over a lightning rod. The usual sizes are 3½" to 4½" in diameter. Green and orange, also ruby, are considered rare colors; white and blue, fairly common.

Ball, blue milk glass . . . . $ 18- 27
Ball, Electra, white, made in
 Albany, N.Y. (ill.) 14- 22
Ball, gold-toned mercury glass . . 22- 31
Ball, Hawkeye, white (ill.) 12- 18
Ball, W.C. Shinn, clear 14- 19

Limoges Porcelain

Limoges, France, is a village, not a maker of porcelain. The uninformed buyer purchases this as a particular brand. Haviland

Limoges Porcelain

was the most famous maker in this village Others were Ahrenfeldt and Son, A. Lanternier, R. Delinieres and Cie., Bernardaud and Cie., P.H. Leonard, Fontanille and Marraud, Raynaud and Cie., Union Limousine, and more. Prices are dependent on maker, year, type.

Atomizer, pearl lustre, hand-
 painted flowers . . . . $ 44- 53
Bowl, fruit decoration, 9" dia. . . . 52- 62
Bowl, orange poppies, 10" dia. . . . 48- 57
Box, enamel, farm scene 71- 80
Box, pill, floral scene, hinged 2½"
 square 72- 90
Butter pat, green floral, gold trim 17- 26
Candlesticks, pair, blue with
 white violets, 8½" high 82- 91
Chocolate set, pot and 8 cups/
 saucers, floral background,
 pink/white 137-146
Creamer, flowers, pink/green 34- 42
Cup/saucer, daisies, blue border . 44- 52
Cup/saucer, yellow and pink
 roses, gold trim 29- 38
Dish, bone, floral design, green/
 pink, set of 6 . . . . 64- 72
Fish set, yellow platter, different
 fish on each of 8 plates, set . . . 228-242
Mug, hand-painted, gold handle,
 drinking scene, 8" high 77- 87
Pitcher, cider, yellow/green
 flowers, gold handle, 14" high . 81- 91
Pitcher, tankard, grapes, green
 background, 12½" high 84- 94
Plate, cake, pink roses, gold
 border, set of 8 (ill.) 90-100
Plate, gold border, gold horse
 chestnuts, leaves outlined in
 gold, 9" dia. 77- 86
Plate, dinner, gold band, roses in
 center, set of 12 187-196
Platter, green/blue floral design,
 gold border, 16" dia. 82- 92
Tray, celery, blue and yellow,
 reticulated border 5½"×12" . . 77- 82
Tureen, soup, handles, yellow
 roses inside pink roses outside,
 15" dia. 84- 93
Vase, pink poppies, black back-
 ground, 11" high 90-101

Lithographs

Currier and Ives made them famous; other firms also. Most American lithographs weren't marked with the year and copyright until after 1848. Have fun, there are lots around. Just know your dealer.

Lithographs

"The Marquis de Sade Suite,"
signed twice and dated by
Salvador Dali, 1968, 58/160
(ill.) $675-752

Lithophanes

Highly translucent porcelains with impressed designs are formed by the difference in the thickness of the plaque. Thin parts let a lot of light through; thicker parts are usually shadows. First made in Berlin, Germany, around 1825; later other factories in France and England made them. Rarely signed. Extremely fragile. Highly collectible. See **Clubs and Publications,** this Price Guide.

Candle shield, 3 scenes, ornate
   wooden frame $242-261
Candle shield, woman seated,
   knitting, metal stand and
   frame 288-297
Farm family, 5"×7", metal
   frame and stand 205-215

Lithophanes

Hanging type, boy/girl in
   doorway, 6¼"×4½" (ill.) 132-142
Mother, child, puppy, 6"×5" 221-242
Mug, lithophane bottom, German
   soldier, WWI, 9½" high 175-194
Plaque, forest scene, 4"×5" 218-224
Plaque, lovers in boat, village
   scene, 4"×5" 210-221
Shade, leaded panels, children
   scenes, 4"×4" 420-442
Tea warmer, 4 German scenes,
   converted burner 265-285

Liverpool Pottery

Liverpool Pottery

Various potteries made this ware from the mid-1700s to the mid-1800s. From about 1788 to 1820 the leading pottery, Sadler and Green, decorated its wares with line drawings, usually in black and white or cream colored. The decorations were often designed for the American colonies, with famous people, eagles, and scenes from everyday life. Scarce.

Bowl, covered, blue/white
   Herculaneum $198-228
Creamer, strawberry lustre 187-194
Creamer, white/black transfer,
   Temperance 218-225
Cup/saucer, black transfer,
   castle scene, handleless 182-192
Cup/saucer, 1800, black
   transfer. 162-172
Jug, George Washington, ship,
   10" high (ill.) 690-720
Pitcher, large, English farm
   scene (ill.) 710-780
Plate, black, English ship 218-242
Plate, blue Chinese decor,
   1780s 218-222
Tea set, teapot, sugar and
   creamer, Queen Anne shape,
   strawberry lustre 581-589

Lobmeyer Glass

Lobmeyer Glass

Ludwig Lobmeyer opened his factory in Zlatno, Hungary, in the 1870s. He made the first commercial iridescent glass of the 19th century. No two pieces are alike in color. Typical pieces are in fine, clear glass, with transparent enamel washes, and/or flashed with red and yellow.

Candlesticks, gold rimmed, birds/
  flowers, pr. .... $ 82- 94
Cups/saucers, demitasse,
  transparent washes in floral
  patterns, flint glass, ground
  pontils, 2″ high (ill.), set 88-101
Vase, gilded, black enameling,
  chinoiserie decor 198-221

Lockets

These small hinged cases of silver, gold, or other metal, for holding a lock of hair or a photograph of a loved one, usually worn suspended from a necklace, have been collectible for years. The gold ones, often studded with diamonds, that hung from a man's watch chain are especially valuable.

Gold locket, studded with
  diamonds, late 1800s, 14k $465-542
Silver-plated locket, 1930s 27- 36

Locks

This is one of the fastest growing collectibles in the world. Some locks date back to the days of the early Egyptians. An Englishman invented the tumbler lock in the 1700s, and Lynus Yale invented the pin tumbler cylinder lock in the mid-1800s, thus changing the lock business forever. The best locks were made of brass, bronze, copper, steel, or a combination of two metals. For locks with original keys, add 20 percent to the prices listed; for railroad locks with original keys, add $6-7 more. Watch out for reproductions. See **Clubs and Publications**, this Price Guide.

Combination
  American Keyless Lock Co.,
    No-Key .... $ 34- 43
  Gougler, zinc alloy 5- 8
  Miller Lock Co., iron frame 24- 32
  Slaymaker, Barry Co. 8- 12
  Yale & Towne Mfg. Co., Yale 8- 14
Two Lever
  Corbin 11- 19
  Eagle 11- 20
  Fraim, E. T. Fraim Lock Co. 7- 11
  Master 7- 11
  U.S. Mail 12- 19
Three Lever
  Corbin 16- 22
  Eagle 9- 18
  Master 8- 12
  Miller, Protector 9- 16
  Russell & Irwin Co., Guardian ... 9- 15
  Yale, various sizes 8- 18
Four Lever
  Corbin 27- 36
  Eagle 19- 25
  Fraim, Western Union 34- 42
  Yale, various sizes 29- 48
Six Lever
  Corbin, Iron Clad 10- 16
  Edwards 9- 14
  Miller, New Champion 9- 17
  Quality (ill.) 22- 31
  Sargent & Co., Green Leaf 27- 37
  Slaymaker, Standard 9- 18
Eight Lever
  Blue Chief 11- 21
  Eagle, Mastadon 11- 20
  Sargent 10- 19
  Slaymaker 11- 20
Miscellaneous
  Jailhouse, iron, large key, c. 1880   86- 96
  Screw key, hand-forged, c. 1850 ..   47- 56
  Screw key, hand-forged, Mexican
    reproduction 10- 17
  Stateroom door, *Queen Mary* 44- 53
Pin Tumbler
  Corbin, various sizes 9- 21

Locks

Eagle, various sizes	9- 26
Mallory Wheeler & Co.	12- 19
Slaymaker, Steel State	11- 22
Yale, various sizes	7- 20

Railroad

Adlake, switch lock, steel	14- 19
Baltimore & Ohio, switch lock, brass	18- 27
New York Central, keyhole guard	48- 54
Penn, toolshed type	14- 21

Lotus Ware

Loetz Glass

Loetz Austria

Loetz Glass

Similar in appearance to Tiffany glass and made about the same time, it was produced in Austria and was considered a fine quality iridescent glass. The factory was also noted for its superior cameo effects produced on cased glassware. Sometimes marked Loetz in the pontil.

Atomizer, orange, cameo, cut, 5¾" high	$248-266
Bowl, green, hearts, signed, 3" high (ill.)	268-284
Bowl, green shading to gold, pinched sides	388-421
Bowl, ribbed with iridescence, folded down lip, green iridescent threading, 4½" high	287-299
Inkwell, green, iridescent purple/white in base, signed	268-284
Lamp, mushroom shade, turquoise iridescent, 20" high	342-362
Paperweight, blue, feather design, signed	288-294
Rose bowl, Art Deco, amber, iridescent, 4½" high	288-299
Tumbler, gold iridescent speckling, 3" high	162-172
Vase, blue iridescent, gold/pink threads, flower-form, signed	388-422
Vase, iridescent, turquoise, 9½" high, signed	385-395
Vase, rose, copper, green	420-442

Lotus Ware

Knowles, Taylor and Knowles Pottery Company, East Liverpool, Ohio, made this fine and delicate porcelain of warm whites and glossy greens in the late 1800s, and only for 10 years. First marks were KTK on the bottom; later they put the firm's name in a circle enclosing a crescent and star. Scarce.

Berry set, 3 pieces	$462-521
Bowl, green/gold, cream ground, KTK mark	187-210
Bowl, roses, turquoise medallions, signed KTK (ill.)	452-482
Creamer, pink flowers, fishscales, signed	291-320
Creamer, white, classic shape, KTK (ill.)	278-295
Pitcher, fishnet, enameled flowers, 4¼" high	487-498
Tea set, green/gold or cream, all	522-538
Vase, pink/blue floral, gold handles, signed KTK	900+
Vase, roses, fishscales, signed 8" high	328-376

Low Art Tile

Low Art Tile

John Gardner Low and his father, John, formed the J. and J. G. Low Art Tile Works in Chelsea, Massachusetts, in 1878. Around

(continued)

1904 firm operations closed.

Bonbon box, brown/green . . . . . $ 35- 44
Candlestick, blue/gray, 7″ high . .   38- 47
Clock case, chocolate glaze 47- 54
Flower holder, green glaze 22- 31
Tile, little girl, blue/green, 6″ sq.
(ill.) 43- 53

Lowestoft Porcelain

Lowestoft Porcelain

Made at Suffolk, England, from about 1757 to the early 1800s; it is also claimed that the porcelain pieces were imported from China and only decorated in England. If this is so, it should be designated as Chinese porcelain.

Basket, blue decoration, floral,
9″ dia. $332-361
Bowl, pink/yellow florals, medal-
lions, front and back, 10″ dia. .   480-498
Coffeepot, lighthouse, gold trim,
initial A   318-362
Cup/saucer, demitasse   142-160
Cup/saucer, Horn-of-Plenty,
demitasse   158-172
Cup/saucer, rose decor (ill.)   118-121
Platter, blue decoration, 12″ dia. .   222-242
Teapot, floral, Famille Rose
pattern, 6½″ high   495-525

Lustre Art Glass

Lustre Art Glass

Conrad Vahlsing made this glass in the

1920s. He was a son-in-law of Martin Bach Sr., who made the famous Quezal glass. Vahlsing's glass is most collectible today. Specific prices would be the same as Quezal.

Lustres

These vaselike vessels with hanging prisms were decorative devices for holding candles and were intended as mantel and tabletop pieces. They were made of every type of glass, but usually the glass was Bristol or Bristol type, in every color.

Blue/white enamel floral, cut
glass prisms, 10″, pr. $462-488
Bohemian glass, one row
crystal prisms, 1890, 14″
tall   510-522
Bristol, blue ground, yellow/
green decor, 11″ high, pr.   385-420
Cranberry, gold enameled
decor, cut glass prisms, 14″
high, pr.   770-795
Enameled decor, gold, ruby,
single row of prisms   432-442
Green, medallion, flowers,
prisms, 12″ high, pr. (ill.)   510-552
White-cut-to-cranberry,
prisms, pr.   520-610

Lustres

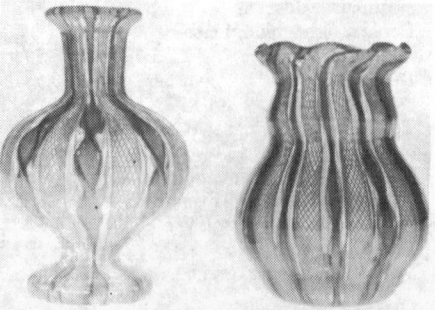

Lutz-type Glass

256

Lutz-type Glass

Nicholas Lutz came from St. Louis, France, in 1860 to work for Dorflinger at White Mills, Pennsylvania. It's really impossible to distinguish his articles of glass from those of other capable glassworkers of the same period. He also worked at Sandwich.

Basket, threaded, ruffled, 6¼″ dia.	$128-142
Bowl, berry, threaded, ruffled and crimped	163-178
Bowl, finger, apricot color	182-191
Compote, spiral striped, blue/ white, 13½″ high	675-740
Cup/saucer, demitasse, Latticinio, pink/white	220-250
Dish, bonbon, swirled candy cane, red/blue	210-242
Ewer, spiral striped, blue/ white, applied pedestal	398-422
Pitcher, blue/gold threading, 13½″ high	495-545
Plate, pale blue, gold twisted thread, pink ground	210-262
Tumbler, blue/gold, white, striped, flared lip	210-242
Vase, white clear, blue threads, 4″ (ill.)	275-295
Vase, white diagonal threads, 7½″ high	252-267
Vase, white frosted, embossed cranberry threads, 4″ high (ill.)	294-332

Lycett

The Lycett family decorated china for four generations. They came from England to the U.S. in the 19th century. President Lincoln commissioned them to decorate the dinner service for his second inauguration. Their formula for gold decoration was secret and has never been copied.

Maastricht Ware

This is a Dutch product made in Holland from the 1830s until the end of the 19th century. The English taught the Dutch how to make it. Petrus Regout and Company are again making this fine product. The sphynx with the firm's name is on all pieces.

Breakfast set, cup/saucer, plate, dike scene, all	$ 58- 72

Maastricht Ware

Cup/saucer, orange/black, dike scene	54-	63
Dish, blue/orange, deep, 9″ dia.	58-	68
Plate, blue, castle scene, signed Regout Company	52-	66
Plate, flow blue, 8½″ dia., pr.	49-	58
Plate, Liberation	67-	76
Platter, red/green flowers, yellow ground, 12½″ long	68-	78
Tea tile, Oriental scene, Regout Company	41-	50
Tureen, large, white, includes ladle	70-	77

Magazines

Magazines

Antique Magazine, April 1927	$ 18-	25
The Art Journal of America, 18 issues, 1875-1876, large engraving in each issue, all	152-	162
Colliers, 1939-1949	80-	90
The Cottage Hearth, Feb. 1883	16-	25
Country Gentleman, 1919-1926, all	71-	81
The Delineator, Oct. 1895, illustrations colored w/crayon	11-	17

(continued)

Godey's Lady's Book, 1840s,	
7 color plates	50- 60
Good Housekeeping, 1924-1940,	
all	158-165
House Beautiful, 1920-1925, all	72- 82
Ladies Home Journal, 1915	
through 1925, all	91-101
The Ladies World, 1914-1919	72- 82
Life, 1915-1919, all	80- 90
Life	9- 12
McCall's Magazine, 1920s	3- 4
McClures, Nov. 1904	11- 15
Modern Priscilla, Aug. 1924 (ill.)	3- 5
Needlecraft Magazine, Sept.	
1923	1- 2
The New Yorker, 1932-1942, all	121-130
Peterson's, 1867, 12 color plates	46- 52
Pictorial Review, 1921 through	
1924, all	44- 54
The Red Book, Jan. 1906	11- 16
Theater Magazine, 1911-1915, all	92-102
The Travel Companion, 3 issues,	
all	19- 24
The Youth's Companion, 1922, 6	
issues, all	52- 62

Generally, magazines are priced, depending on the year, condition, etc., at $2 to $5. If you're lucky, you'll find a Frank Leslie leather-bound with color fashion plates, $55-$70.

Magic Lanterns

These were the forerunners of home movie machines. They operated on kerosene or candles and probably caused more than one fire in their day. Most came from Germany during the late 1800s until the early 1900s.

5-slide, candle, tin, lens	$ 85-115
8-slide candle, reflector, lens	92-118
11-slide, kerosene, reflector, lens,	
tin	98-121
24-slide, electrified, 1920s	108-132
Average price, each slide	5- 8

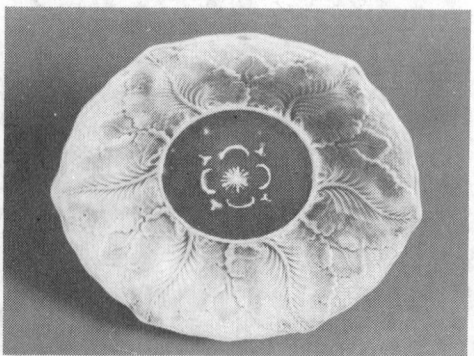

Majolica

Majolica

This is a soft pottery or faience covered with a glossy coating turned opaque by treating it with tin oxide. It was made as early as the 12th century, later in most European countries. Most of what you find today is from the mid-1800s. Griffin, Smith and Hill made it in the U.S. in the late 1800s and A & P stores gave it away as premiums at that time. They called it Etruscan and it was marked GSH in script on the bottom.

Cake stand, sunflowers,	
American, GSH	$108-118
Compote, Leaf Pattern, 5½" high	
(ill.)	94-107
Compote, sunflowers, American,	
GSH	92-102
Creamer, green/yellow, lovebirds,	
pink lining	108-118
Cup/saucer, cobalt/yellow, brown	
ground, handleless	109-122
Cuspidor, blue ground, fruit	
decor, 6½" high	89- 99
Dish, leaf, Etruscan mark,	
American, GSH	80- 90
Figurine, girl and boy playing,	
8" high, pr.	127-138
Humidor, Turk, 7" high	104-115
Jar, tobacco, floral decor, pink/	
green, pipe on lid, 6" high	88- 98
Jardiniere, flower design, stand,	
28" high	127-136
Jug, blue ground, dog, children,	
pewter lid, 7½" high	68- 78
Match holder, Negro boy, 6½"	
high	142-152
Pitcher, child with dog, 7" high	55- 65
Pitcher, fern pattern	61- 71
Plate, leaf pattern	68- 78
Plate, shell/seaweed, Etruscan	
Majolica, 7" dia.	118-122
Platter, leaf decor, 12" long	77- 87
Spooner, shell/seaweed, pink/	
green glazes. Etruscan	
Majolica	122-132
Sugar, cauliflower cover,	
Etruscan, GSH, American	70- 80
Syrup, pewter top	50- 60
Tea set, teapot, sugar, creamer,	
sunflowers, brown ground	262-271
Teapot, shell/seaweed, pink/	
green glazes, 6" high	238-242
Toothpick, 3-handle, brown/	
green	48- 58
Vase, two monkeys, green	
ground	97-108

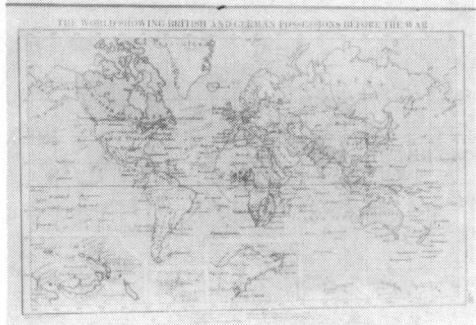

Maps

Maps

The older the better. A lot of guessing
went into making maps many years ago.
Today, examples of these maps are highly
collectible.

Africa $44-52
Arkansas, double folio, color,
  Bradley's Atlas, 1886,
  22"×15" 26-35
Balkan States, L.L. Poates
  Engraving Co., 1921,
  9¼"×11¼" 14-19
British/German, 10½"×7½" (ill.) . . 25-32
Central America, color,
  Worldwide Encyclopedia,
  10¼"×7½" 11-17
Florida/N. & S. Car./Ala. by
  George F. Cram, Chicago,
  1889 24-32
France, color, 1873, 8¾"×5⅝" 21-31
Holland and Belgium, color,
  9"×11¾" 19-26
Holy Land, from Bible Atlas,
  published by Newton Case,
  1832 16-32
State maps of Arizona, Wyoming/
  Idaho, North Dakota, Louisi-
  ana, Iowa/Minnesota, New
  Jersey, by C.S. Hammond &
  Co., New York, 1914,
  10½"×13", ea. 11-14

Marble

This is a hard, crystalline or granular meta-
morphic limestone, white or variously colored, sometimes streaked. It will take a high
polish. Don't confuse it with alabaster.

Chinese coolie, contemporary,
  6¾" high (ill.) $52-61
Collie dog, 9" long 42-52
Elephant bookends, 7½" high, pr. . . 47-56

Marble

Lion-on-pedestal, 8" high 41-50
Mother cat with kittens, 7" long . . . 60-70
Penguin bookends, 6" high, pr. 48-58
Rooster, 4½" high 28-38
Tiger, 8" high 42-52
Urn, flower motif, 12½" high 48-58
Vase, fluted lip, 11" high 42-52

Marblehead Pottery

In 1904 Dr. Herbert J. Hall founded the
pottery as part of a group of industries
known as the Handcraft Shops. Intended as
a rehabilitative program for patients at a
Marblehead, Massachusetts, sanitarium, it
lasted less than a year because of demands
upon the patients. About 1907 another pottery shop was in full swing; it closed in 1936.
Most of the wares were marked with the
familiar ship and "MP" cipher.

Bowl, blue glaze, 3½" dia. $107-117
Cereal set, light gray, 3 pcs., all . . 220-232
Luncheon set, cream, 4 pcs., all . . 260-268
Mug, green matt, 6" high 272-291
Teapot, mirror blue ground, 8"
  high 261-271
Vase, blue matt, 7¼" high 340-360
Vase, gray matt, tree design,
  12½" high 121-130
Vase, mirror blue ground, 8¼"
  high . . . . 134-14⁄
Vase, tobacco brown, 8½" high . . 295-3⁄

Marbles

Marbles

Glass companies in Pennsylvania and Ohio made the large glass marbles used by boys at the turn of the century. Some had colored stripes while others had animals inside. The larger are more collectible than the smaller. See **Clubs and Publications,** this Price Guide.

Agate, black/white, 1/2" dia.	$ 27- 32
Agate, brown/white, 7/8" dia.	26- 31
Agate, green/white, 3/4" dia.	22- 28
Bennington, mottled or fancy, 1¼" dia.	5- 8
China, bull's-eye, 5/8" dia.	10- 14
China, leaves, 1/2" dia.	12- 15
China, leaves, 7/8" dia.	14- 17
Goldstone, 5/8" dia.	32- 41
Kayo (comic strip), black/white	34- 40
Limestone, 5/8" dia.	7- 10
Multicolored swirl (ill.)	13- 17
Sandy (comic strip), blue/white	33- 42
Sulphide, baby (all positions)	118-121
Sulphide, boar	110-118
Sulphide, boy on stump	115-132
Sulphide, cat, lying down	117-128
Sulphide, cat, sitting	99-108
Sulphide, cow, grazing	112-121
Sulphide, frog	118-127
Sulphide, girl and dog	119-127
Sulphide, goat	90-101
Sulphide, lamb (ill.)	84- 93
Sulphide, owl, wings spread	141-152
Sulphide, ram	88- 98
Sulphide, rooster, running	88- 92
Sulphide, rooster, standing	74- 78
Swirls, Latticinio, onionskin, ea.	69- 74

Martinez Pottery

Maria Montoya Martinez was known as Maria, the potter of San Ildefonso. This talented woman was one of the best-known ceramists of the Americas and people came to Mexico from all over the world to see her work. Following the traditional om of learning the art of pottery began at the age of 14. She pass-

Martinez Pottery

ed away on July 20, 1980. With her husband, Julian, she brought world focus on the art of the Pueblos. Pieces signed Maria Martinez and Maria and Julian Martinez are extremely collectible, if authenticated. It is reported that signatures are being forged on certain pieces of the Feather design.

Bowl, black matt, Water Serpent design, signed Maria Martinez, 5½" high	$ 3,500+
Jar, black matt, signed Maria and Popovi, 9½" dia.	6,750+
Olla, fine black matt, Feather design, signed Maria Martinez, 7½" high (ill.)	3,800+
Olla, polychrome, signed Maria and Julian Martinez, 11" high	3,800+
Plate, black matt finish, Water Serpent design, signed Maria, 13¼" dia.	975-1,100
Plate, black matt, signed Maria and Julian Martinez, 13¼" dia.	775- 850
Vase, wedding type, black matt, signed Maria and Julian Martinez, 7½" high	950+

Mary Gregory

We know that she did exist and that she did work for the Boston & Sandwich Glass Company on Cape Cod. Obviously, she didn't decorate all those pieces attributed to her. She never tinted her fingers and/or costumes. They were always white. Look for children, 5 to 12. Tinted figures must be called Mary Gregory type and were made in Europe in the mid-1880s. No collector

Mary Gregory

should buy this glass as original before talking to an expert. Lots of repros.

Barber bottle, blue, boy playing with kite, all white figure	$ 210-	240
Biscuit jar, girl on swing, all white figure, blue glass	172-	182
Jewel box, black, girl in tree, all white figure	187-	196
Lamp, black, girl on the tree limb, all white figure	470-	510
Mug, cranberry, girl jumping rope, all white figure	210-	240
Perfume, cranberry, ITP, girl on swing, all white	192-	220
Pitcher, cranberry, boy with hoop, all white figure	340-	360
Pitcher, 6 tumblers, cranberry, ITP, girl and boy in tree, all white figure	430-	450
Rose bowl, girl, all white figure	232-	252
Tumble-up (carafe with tumbler), boy, all white figure	332-	345
Vase, clear, girl rolling hoop, all white figure	162-	172
Vase, girl on swing, all white figure	440-	470
Vase, green, boy with butterfly net, all white figure	121-	132
Vase, ruby, boy holding horn, ITP, 9″ high (ill.)	1,400-	1,600

Mason's Patent Ironstone

The Mason family first started making porcelain in 1802. It was 1813 before they made Ironstone, when Charles J. Mason took

Mason's Patent Ironstone

out his famous Ironstone patent. It was in a sense porcelain, as described in the patent. In reality it was a heavy, hard, opaque earthenware. G.M. and C.J. Mason, 1813-1829, was the first mark used; then C.J. Mason and Company, 1829-1844; and C.J. Mason, 1845-1848. The firm went bankrupt in 1848. Ashworth and Brothers, Hanley, England, produces a Mason-type ware today.

Bowl, red scene, early mark	$ 69-	79
Butter dish, Chinese decor	77-	87
Creamer, Chinese decor, 1819-1844 mark, 5½″ high	84-	93
Creamer, miniature, red flowers, blue underglaze, 2¾″ high (ill.)	92-	106
Jug, Chinese decor, 6¼″ high, early mark	62-	72
Pickle dish, Oriental pattern	51-	60
Pin tray, Oriental scene, 1829-1844 mark, 6″ long	66-	74
Plate, American naval scene, early mark	88-	95
Plate, Oriental pattern, 1829-1844 mark	56-	67
Platter, Japanese scene, 14″ long	59-	67
Teapot, red flowers, blue underglaze, 8½″ high	68-	74
Tureen, red/blue flowers	77-	86

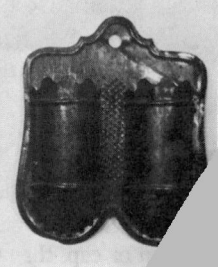

Match Holders

Match Holders

In the days of Lucifers or "house burners" (sulphur-headed matches), match holders were in vogue and were used to hold matches on the wall or the table. Used from mid-1800s until early 1930s. Many repros.

Bird, 4½" high, iron	$ 42- 50
Boots, china, green/yellow, 4½" high	44- 52
Bulldog's head, porcelain, Austria	42- 52
Butterfly, milk glass, 5" high	42- 51
Cast iron, c. 1880s	33- 42
Charlie Chaplin, clear glass (rare)	81- 91
Cricket, brass, hinged lid	50- 60
Dog, stump holds matches, iron	47- 57
Elephant, clear glass	45- 54
Flower basket, iron	48- 59
Grape leaf, 3" high, milk glass	46- 54
Indian head, 6" high, hangs on wall, milk glass	57- 62
Jenny Lind, clear glass	73- 83
Man with cane by tree stump, china, Germany	29- 38
"Matches" hangs on wall, tin, 5½" high (ill.)	32- 42
Rooster, hand-painted, Austria, china	39- 49
Two-compartment w/striker, tin, hanging type, 5" high (ill.)	21- 32

Brass, bulldog, hinged	$ 58- 68
Flower/leaves, Germany	21- 30
Papier-mache, painted figures	27- 32
Philadelphia Centennial, silver, 3" high, hinged	57- 68
Sterling silver, 3" high (ill.)	62- 72
Sterling silver, whiskey advertisement, bottle-shaped	42- 52
Tin, many types, average	18- 24

Matt Morgan Art Pottery

This short-lived firm was founded by Matthew Somerville Morgan at Cincinnati, Ohio, in 1883. It went out of business in 1884. Usually the mark is the impressed name of the company. Paper labels also were used; consequently, unmarked pieces are likely to be found.

Vase, dark blue glaze, gold decoration, 18½" high	$695-795
Vase, dragonflies, 4³/₈ high	462-510
Vase, terra-cotta, 19" high	520-542
Vase, turquoise ground, white flowers, 19" high	775-852

T.J. and J. Mayer Pottery

The year 1829 was the beginning of this fine china company. The coats-of-arms of the 13 original states are especially collectible. Stoke, Staffordshire, England.

Bowl, scalloped and embossed rim, 10½", Arms of Maryland	$900-1,100
Cup plate, 4½", South Carolina	362- 372
Plate, 8¾", Arms of Rhode Island	390- 420

Match Safes

Safes

that—kept the matches safe
ket. Usually metal with a
ey were inexpensive when

(continued)

T.J. and J. Mayer Pottery

262

Platter, 19″, New Jersey	810- 840
Soup plate, 9½″-10″, New York	232- 250
Vegetable dish, 8″, Massachusetts	862- 892

McCoy Pottery

McCoy Pottery

This pottery has been made in Roseville, Ohio, since 1910. In 1967 the firm was acquired by the Mt. Clemens (Michigan) Pottery Company. Early pieces are now becoming collectible. See **Clubs and Publications,** this Price Guide.

Blossomtime 700 Line
Jardiniere, ivory, sq., 4″ tall ..... $	22- 29
Planter, ivory	23- 32
Vase, ivory, McCoy, 6¼″	15- 24
Vase, yellow, concave sides, 8″ ..	22- 30

Butterfly Line
Planter, rose (leaf relief only), 8″ .	15- 24
Spoon rest, green, NM USA	22- 27

Cookie Jars
Bear #22	62- 70
Black antique stove	35- 42
Blue windmill	26- 34
Have a Happy Day (smile)	37- 47
Honey bear	40- 50
Mr. and Mrs. Owl	52- 62
Rocking horse	52- 61

Flowerpots
Dark green Double Beetle band ..	19- 24
Green basketweave #2, 3¼″	18- 24
Green, long leaves and dots, 3½″ dia.×3½″ tall, NM	17- 22
Green, long leaves, two, 3 and 3¾″ dia., 2¾″ tall, NW	18- 27
Orange Double Beetle band, 5″ ..	19- 24

Springwood Line
Bowl, 4-ftd., pink, 6⅝″ dia., McCoy USA	15- 24
Jardiniere, pink, 5⅜″, McCoy USA	24- 32

Vase, green, round bottom, sq. top, 7¼″, McCoy USA	16- 22

Swirl Line
Planter, orchid, ftd., 7″ long, McCoy USA	12- 16
Vase, orchid, ftd., 7″ tall, McCoy USA	14- 19

Tea Set Items
Creamer, pink/turquoise, matt, McCoy	11- 16
Leaf creamer, 2-tone green, #108 (ill.)	15- 24
Pinecone green/brown, 3-pc., McCoy	44- 52
Pinecone green creamer	19- 26
Pinecone green teapot and lid ...	28- 32
Pinecone teapot, no lid, light crazing in and out	30- 40
Tea set, 3-pc., green/brown	48- 58
Teapot lid, as above	16- 27

Vases
Butterfly vase, 7″, McCoy	24- 29
Cornucopia, cream, light crazing, 7″, McCoy	24- 32
Dark green vase, ftd., 10-sided, 7¼″×4½″, McCoy USA	22- 31
Flowers and Leaf Blades, green, handled, 8″	19- 27
Handled, ftd. vase, turquoise, Stylized Leaf and Twig, 9″ ...	26- 32
S&H/Peppers, pr.............	19- 24
Swan vase, pink, 9″, McCoy	20- 29

McKinley Act, 1891

Required that the name of the country of origin appear on all imports into the U.S.A.

Medals, U.S. and Foreign

Ever since the handmade silver medal was given by Congress to the three men responsible for the capture of a British officer connected with Benedict Arnold, the U.S. has been giving out medals for just about everything. The British, French, Italians, and Germans are also medal happy. It should be noted that any medal made of sterling silver has gone up in value, just for the silver content. See **Clubs and Publications,** this Price Guide.

British Burma Star .... $	15-	24
British Distinguished Service	132-	152
British Korea, 1950-53	27-	37
French Commemorative, WWI, sterling silver	242-	262

263

(continued)

Medals, U.S. and Foreign

Imperial German Iron Cross, 1870, 2nd Class	118-	132
Italian Fascist, Eastern Front Cross, 1941-42	70-	80
Officer's blue cloth plate, 1870s, 59th Regiment	107-	117
Officer's plate, Devonshire Regiment, 1878	138-	152
Officer's plate, 16th Bedford-shire Regiment	552-	575
Polish Independence Cross, WWII	37-	47
Polish Military Service Medal, 1918-21	45-	52
Polish Monte Casion Cross (serial numbered), WWII	38-	47
U.S. Air Medal	14-	19
U.S. Army, Good Conduct	7-	11
U.S. Army, Medal of Honor, 1862-1904		1,500+
U.S. Navy, Byrd Antarctic Expedition	232-	242
U.S. Navy, Civil War	32-	41
U.S. Navy, Medal of Honor	895-	975
V.F.W. (ill.), ea.	14-	19
Victoria Cross, English		8,500+

Medical Items

Old instruments, bottles, prescriptions, books—all are of special interest today, especially to one allied with the field of medicine.

Amputating saw, mfgd. by Charrier's, wide blade, 10 oz., c. 1915	$ 28-	44
Appendectomy rectractor, mfgd. by Mayo, 12 oz., c. 1915	14-	19
Arrow extractor, Bill's Arrow Forceps, mfgd. by Tiemann Co., c. 1895	52-	61

Betz stool, can be raised or lowered, white enamel, c. 1915	68-	77
Bullet extractors: Bullet Seeker, Bullet Screw, American Bullet Forceps, Sayre's Vertebrated Bullet Probe, all mfgd. by Tiemann Co., 1880s to 1915, ea.	54-	64
Dental forceps, Nos. 29, 31, 32, 33, 40, mfgd. by C. Ash & Sons, London, 1920, ea.	11-	17
Dentist's tooth key (or "turn key"), Spring Bolt, Rotating Fulcrum, mfgd. by Tiemann Co., c. 1888, ea.	66-	76
Doctor's bag, Pacific saddle bag, all original bottles, c. 1915	110-	121
Doctor's bag, Long Drive Combination, complete	78-	88
Doctor's bag, Country Doctor, complete	70-	80
Hearing aids: Currier's Duplex Conversation Tube, Ear of Dionysus, Corrugated Ear Trumpet, ea.	115-	140
Hearing aids: Dipper Trumpet, London Hearing Horn, Conversation Tube, Dome Trumpet, ea.	62-	72
Letter opener (ill.)	10-	14
Retractor, Fritch's, mfgd. by Tiemann Co., c. 1890	6-	9
Stethoscopes: Barclay's, Burrow's, Hawksley's, Short Cedar, all mfgd. by Tiemann Co., 1880s, ea.	48-	58

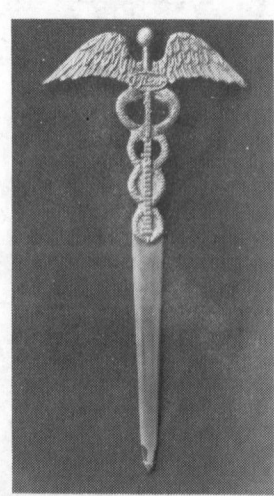

Medical Items

Meissen, Onion Pattern

Originally known as Bulb pattern, it's more commonly called Onion pattern today. A

264

 MEISSEN   **Meissen, Onion Pattern**

whiteware with cobalt decorations, it was made in the latter part of the 19th century. Reproductions from Europe are causing havoc for the uninformed collector.

Baby feeder, 6¾" long (ill.)	$ 39- 47,
Bowl, 6" dia.	58- 68
Bowls, 7", 8" square, pierced edges, ea.	70- 80
Breadboard	51- 60
Butter dish, covered	140-150
Candleholders, 4¼" high (ill.), pr.	70- 80
Creamer, individual and porridge, 3½" to 5½" high	70- 80
Cheese dish, covered	141-151
Cup/saucer, coffee (ill.)	38- 48
Cup/saucer, demitasse	40- 50
Cup/saucer, tea	40- 47
Egg cup	38- 50
Plate, 8" dia.	42- 52
Plate, chop, 14" long	110-121
Plate, soup, 9" dia.	55- 65
Platter, 12" long	132-142
Rolling pin	60- 70
Salt, master, footed 3¼" dia.	66- 76
Sauce, 4¾" dia.	28- 38
Teapot with matching tile	152-162
Tureen, soup, Crossed Swords	188-196
Vase, scroll feet, 6½" high	82- 92
Vegetable dish, covered, 10" square	148-158

Many other pieces are made in the Onion pattern.

Mercury Glass

Silver nitrate was sloshed around inside double-walled objects of glass, then the entrance hole was sealed. As air seeped in, the "mercury" flaked off, leaving an unpleasant-looking object. Made in England and the U.S., late 1800s.

Bowl, gilt interior, 5" high	$ 60- 70
Bowl, 6" dia.	62- 72
Bowl, painted flowers, 6" dia., 6" high	77- 82
Candleholder, signed Perdue, 8" high	54- 63
Creamer, clear handle, quadruple plate spout, 8½" high (ill.)	90-107
Dish, sweetmeats, sectioned	30- 40
Ornament, Christmas, grapes, 2½" dia.	14- 19
Pitcher, clear handle, 12½" high	112-127
Salt, footed	51- 61
Spooner	72- 82
Sugar shaker, metal cup	71- 80
Tieback, curtain, flower decor, pr.	45- 55
Vase, blue/clear, painted flowers on front, 8" high, pr.	52- 62
Vase, floral bands, castle scene painted on front, 9½" high pr.	87-102
Wig stand, pedestal base, 10" high (ill.)	110-121

Mercury Glass

Mettlach

(con'

Mettlach

Jean Francois Boch founded the Mettlach pottery in 1809 in an old abbey named Abbey Mediolacum ("Between the Lakes") from which the name Mettlach was derived. In 1841, the Nicholas Villeroy family joined the Boch family. V & B developed the technique of overglaze painting—firing a particular piece at 2400 degrees, then low firing other colors at lower temperatures; thus allowing the use of many colors and holding the same true color in stein after stein. V & B introduced many other techniques, pioneering the way for many of the world's famous potters. The main factory at Mettlach burned in 1921 and was never rebuilt. All attempts at reproducing this great pottery have failed; what is on the market today should fool absolutely no one. The Black Forest stein is considered the choicest collector's item, bringing over $5,000 when found and authenticated. Baskets, beakers, bowls, flagons, jugs, mugs, pitchers, plaques, tumblers, and urns were also made, but the stein made V & B world-famous. Serious Mettlach collectors collect by the number. Stein Collectors International is a great club to join. See **Clubs and Publications (Steins)**, this Price Guide.

Plaques

#1044—a large series— most plaques with this number sell	$ 385- 420
#1384	1,300-1,500
#1920	975-1,100
#2195	820- 840
#2442, 2443, 2445, ea.	860- 875
#3131	245- 290
#3163, 3164, ea.	1,350-1,475
#7025, signed "Stahl"	3,900+
#7040, 7041, 7043, 7045, ea.	3,500+
#7066	585- 620

Steins

#368, ½ L (liter—1.0567 liquid quarts)	570- 625
#406, ½ L	425- 465
#485, 1 L	470- 520
#675, ¼ L	295- 325
#675, ½ L	370- 430
#1052, ½ L	562- 620
#1069	1,100-1,300
#1095, ½ L	475- 525
#100, ¼ L	362- 420
1½ L	420- 442
	465- 535
	520- 580
	210- 250

#1286, 5½" high (V & B)	560- 660
#1498, 5 L	3,500-3,850
#1526—a large series— ½, 1, 3 L	410- 440
#1536, ½ L	482- 525
#1655, ½ L	590- 620
#1786, 1 L	1,475-1,675
#1863, ½ L	660- 720
#1909, 3/10 L	285- 320
#1932, ½ L	850- 920
#1941, 3 L	2,700-3,200
#2027, ½ L	850- 925
#2035, ½ L	770- 840
#2044, ½ L	750- 785
#2086, ½ L	552- 620
#2089, ½ L	720- 770
#2122, 5 L	3,650-4,100
#2181, ¼ L	355- 375
#2184, 3/10 L	725- 775
#2391, ½ L	780- 820
#2441, ½ L (ill.)	792- 842
#2479, ½ L	1,100-1,300
#2500, ½ L	1,100-1,250
#2556, 1 L	775- 825
#2582, ½ L	685- 745
#2768, ½ L	550- 620
#2802, ½ L	2,500-2,700
#2878, 1 L	775- 845
#2912, ½ L	452- 492
#2938, 1 L	725- 765
#2950, ½ L	850- 950
#2958, 3 L	2,200-2,500
#3091, ½ L	720- 745
#3099, 5 L	7,400-7,500
#3168, ½ L	850- 925

Obviously, hundreds and hundreds more. You're mixing with the professionals when you collect Mettlach steins, so read up and save up.

Military Collectibles

Military Collectibles

Items from the Revolutionary War on have long been popular. Nazi items are now collectible, as well as items from the Korean and

Vietnam conflicts. See Clubs and Publications, this Price Guide.

Armband, English firefighter,
World War II . . . . $ 28- 40
Bayonet and scabbard for
Enfield rifle, World War II . . .   52- 60
Bayonet with leather sheath,
Civil War, Union Army 72- 80
Belt buckle, brass CSA 54- 63
Canteen, clay (throwaway type),
Union Army stamp, brown . . .   132-150
Canteen, U.S. Cavalry, Civil War   101-111
Flag, Union Jack, English, World
War I, 40"×28" 62- 72
Helmet, English, World War I . . .   52- 62
Helmet, English, World War II . .   51- 61
Saddle, McClellan type, Union
Army, Civil War   180-190
Window marker (ill.) 5- 9

Milk Glass

Milk Glass

Milk glass was so named because of its opaque white appearance. It was made in England in the 18th century and attained its greatest U.S. popularity in the 1870s. Prices for a few selected items are given here.

Battleship Maine, white milk
glass $158-168
Dolphin condiment dish, opalescent, 3¾" high, scroll bead-
work   88-101
Drum and cannon, covered dish .   110-121
Eagle on nest, covered dish,
white opalescence, 4½" high
(ill.)   107-118
Fish, covered dish   92-107
Hand and dove, covered dish   121-131
Uncle Sam, covered dish   132-142

A huge collection of milk glass can be seen at the Houston Museum, Chattanooga, Tenn. Reproductions have ruined this as a serious collector's item.

Millefiori Glass

Millefiori Glass

This ornamental glass was made by fusing together slender canes or rods of glass, then cutting across them in small sections. These sections then were imbedded in the glass object being made. Lots of companies made it, here and abroad, mid-1800s on. General collectors will have a difficult time telling the old from the new. The paperweights are especially hard to distinguish. Watch out! Still being made on the island of Murano, Italy.

Basket, blues/greens, small $220-240
Bowl, 2 handles, 2" high   141-150
Box, covered, 3" high   198-220
Chocolate pot, 9" high, no cups . .   210-240
Creamer, red flower spray,
striped handle   218-227
Cup/saucer, demitasse   210-241
Cruet, cut glass stopper, 6" high .   460-472
Inkwell, paperweight base   348-362
Goblet, clear stem   252-272
Globe, lamp, 4" dia.   218-222
Lamp, has matching shade, 14"
high   278-284
Rose bowl, fluted lip, 6½" high . .   162-172
Salt, open, master, 6 small   340-350
Tumbler, 4" high (ill.)   122-132
Vase, 4" high   181-192
Vase, 4" high, scalloped top   188-197
Vases, handled (ill.), ea.   108-117

Miniatures

In the mid-1800s salesmen carried miniatures of their products: furniture, carriages, any bulky item. Anything miniature is collectible today: dollhouse furniture, pressed glass dollhouse dishes, and other items.

Bowl, blue porcelain, 1½" dia. . . . $ 32- 40
Bucket, pressed glass, metal bail
handle, 2" high 31- 39
Candlestick, brass, 1½" high, pr.   34- 42
Coal hod, brass 36- 46
Cowbell, brass, ⅞" 42- 52
Cranberry picker, 3" high (ill.) . . .   17- 24
Flatiron, on trivet (rare), 2½"
long   60-

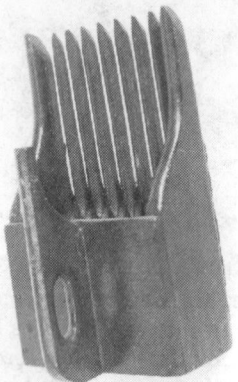

Miniatures

Furniture, cabinet, rosewood,
   German, 19th century 118-127
Jug, water, brass, ¾″ high 28- 38
Kettle, handle, brass, 1½″ high . . 24- 37
Lamp, clear, Thistle Panel, with
   chimney, 3½″ high 46- 56
Toby jug 11- 14

Minton

Minton

This factory, established in England around 1793, continues today under the same name. Early pieces were incised with the firm's name and are highly collectible now. Their Yearly Marks are shown here.

Bowl and pitcher, blue, leaves,
   flowers, marked $365-392
Bowl, lapis blue, wild vines/
   leaves, 9″ dia. 178-184
    dish, covered, floral motif . 172-182
     pot, white, etched/gold
      ed 170-180
      blue/white, 1887
       a. (ill.) 230-255

(continued)

MINTON
YEARLY MARKS

Impressed in the clay to show year of manufactu
42—1942 inclusive. The figures 43 etc. have been us
1943 onwards.

Minton Yearly Marks

Compote, enameled roses, signed,
   8″ high 182-192
Cup/saucer, demitasse, blue decor
   panels in gold rims 122-132
Egg cup, floral motif 41- 51
Jug, blue/white Jasper, 4½″ high 88- 98
Pitcher, water, grapes, gold
   decor, 11″ high, marked 174-182
Plate, Tree of Life pattern, 6½″
   dia. 77- 87
Teapot, sugar, creamer, white/
   gold trim, red roses, marked . . 152-162
Tile, blue/white, 6″ sq. 61- 71
Vase, birds and flowers, 7½″
   high 188-198
Vase, brown/green/turquoise,
   10″ high 240-260
Vase, farm scene, blue, 5½″
   high, impressed mark 266-277

Mocha Ware

Similar to Leeds Ware, Mocha is usually cream colored and decorated with seaweed, worms, or other such "lovely" items, in various colors on bands of blue, tan, red. It

Mocha Ware

was first made in Tunstall, England, in the late 1700s to the 1800s by William Adams, later by his son. Apparently it was never marked.

Bowl, Earthworm, blue/red,
7" dia. $294-299
Bowl, Seaweed band, blue,
8½" dia. 520-580
Bowl, tan/blue/white, feather
bands, 5" wide 352-361
Chamber pot, creamware, blue/
green, brown bands 371-390
Dish, master salt, green bands,
leaf handle 182-207
Jug, Seaweed design, 5" high . . . 229-262
Mug, large, blue and gray bands,
Seaweed design, 6" high (ill.) . . 241-260
Mug, multicolored, 3¾" high (ill.) 238-257
Mug, red ground, black/blue/
cream mottling, green-
threaded top 252-262
Mug, Tree pattern, 5" high 210-230
Mug, white ground, blue bands,
5" high 271-285
Pitcher, syrup, ferns/leaves,
8½" high 345-365
Pitcher, water, tan/black/white,
4" high 352-370
Salt shaker, Earthworm design . . 132-142
Sugar bowl, trees, green band,
5½" high 320-340

Molds, Food

See **Clubs and Publications**, this Price Guide.

Butter
Acorn and leaf, round . . . . $ 90-108
Cow, glass, round 82- 92
Cow, maple, round (ill.) 88- 98
Double 5-point star, maple, round . 42- 52
Eagle, maple, round (ill.) 210-220
Maple leaves, maple, rectangular . 78- 88
Pineapple, maple, box type (ill.) . . . 85- 95
Three leaf fern, maple, 4½" dia. . . 62- 72
Tulip, cherry, round 118-124
Wheat, maple, rectangular 52- 62
Wheat, maple, round 62- 72
Candy
Chicken on basket, tin 42- 52
Clown, pewter 77- 82
Easter egg, pewter (ill.) 52- 62
Frog, pewter 40- 50
Humpty Dumpty, tin 51- 61
Lion, tin 52- 62
Man in the Moon, tin 44- 54
Rabbits, 6½", 7¼", 11", ea. 52- 62
Santa Claus, pewter (ill.) 64- 74
Two hearts, tin 39- 52
Ice Cream
Apple, iron 24- 32
Automobile, iron 61- 70
Battleship, pewter 62- 72
Bell, pewter 40- 50
Chick, iron or pewter 35- 52
Eagle, American, pewter 82- 92
Fire engine, pewter 51- 60
Football, 2-part, pewter 44- 52
Heart and Cupid, iron 44- 54
Hobby horse, pewter 52- 61
Lincoln, pewter 77- 83
Locomotive, iron 74- 82
Pumpkin, iron 43- 52
Sailboat, pewter 70- 80
Santa Claus, pewter (ill.) 70- 78
Teddy bear, pewter 56- 66
Turkey, pewter 42- 52

Food Molds

269

(continued)

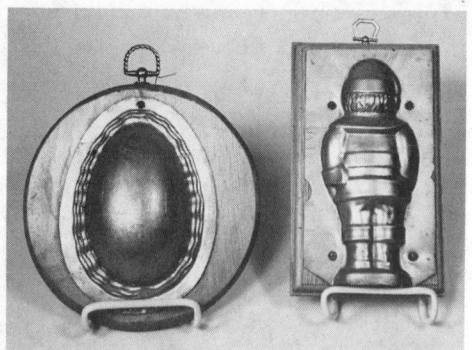

Food Molds

Uncle Sam, pewter	50- 60
Washington, bust, pewter	68- 72
Wishbone, pewter	32- 38

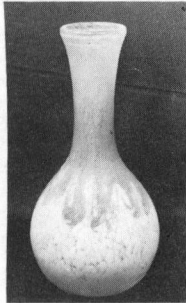

Monart Glass

Monart Glass

This glass was made in Scotland after World War I. Its style is considered Art Deco. Small pieces of embedded colored glass show through the heavy body.

Bowl, 4″ dia., pink/blue/green,
dark green swirls $162-180
Vase, 5½″ high, red to mottled
brown, green rim 175-210
Vase, 10¾″ high, Cluthra type,
green to mottled light blue,
ground pontil (ill.) 565-632

Mont Joy

This is cameo and enameled glass made at Pantin, France, by the same firm that produced De Vez.

Bowl, frosted body with
enameled flowers, signed,
3¾″ dia. $362-382
Rose bowl, ruffled lip, cameo cut
back, enameled lavender

Mont Joy

violets, gold leaves, 5″ high,
signed Mont Joy 238-247
Vase, bud, carved, red poppies,
purple ground, 20″ high 425-510
Vase, cobalt iris, green leaves,
11¾″ high (ill.) 362-382
Vase, enameled iris, buds, gold
leaves, acid-etched ground,
6″ high 358-388
Vase, flowers, gilded, frosted
green, signed, 11″ high 540-562
Vase, mottled orange/black
ground, signed, 11½″ high . . . 480-520

Moorcroft Pottery

Moorcroft Pottery

This is a modern English pottery which, for some unexplainable reason, is highly collectible. Factory established in 1913 by William Moorcroft at Cobridge. Script signature.

Ashtray, red/yellow flowers,
script signature . . . . $ 52- 61
Basket, metal holder, 6″ dia.,
green flowers 84- 93

Bowl, blue/white decor, fruit	....	92-107
Bowl, pewter foot, 6¼" dia., fruit decor, lavender/yellow/red/ green (ill.)	....	84- 93
Box, covered, orange/maroon, 4½" dia.	....	86- 94
Compote, green ground, purple flowers, 4½" high	....	99-107
Cup/saucer, fruit decor, green script	....	72- 81
Inkwell, blue background, signed	....	89-102
Tea set: pot, sugar bowl, creamer, blue ground. All have pewter lids	....	315-362
Vase, bud, light/dark green, trees, 8" high, script signature		232-261

Moriage

Not a specific company but a definition that applies to Japanese ceramics that have applied clay (slip) decorations. This type of decoration has been used for more than 200 years and is quite predominant on export wares produced since the Nippon era (1891-1921). Designs include lacy effects, border trimmings, birds, animals, floral decor, and landscapes. The most popular is the jewel-eyed slip trailed dragon. Workmanship dictates the value.

Cup/saucer, butterflies, green M in wreath, Nippon	....	$ 60- 70
Hatpin holder, 6" high, floral panels	....	66- 74
Pitcher, 12½" high, jewel-eyed dragon	....	242-261
Plate, 8" dia., green/yellow flowers	....	69- 78
Teapot, blue/yellow/brown, M in wreath, Nippon, 3" high (ill.)	..	69- 76
Teapot, dragon motif, Blue Maple Leaf, Nippon	....	94-107

Vase, flowers, gold trim, 10½" high, green M in wreath, Nippon	....	171-181
Vase, 14½" high, jewel-eyed dragon, green M in wreath	....	292-310
Vase, peacock, floral decor, 11½" high, Double T Diamond mark	....	247-265

Mortars and Pestles

Mortars and Pestles

The Egyptians used a crude form to grind sacred potions. Usually made of brass or a hardwood such as lignum vitae or bird's-eye maple, larger ones served for grinding grain, smaller ones for pulverizing salt, spices, and drugs.

Brass, early 1800s	....	$120-130
Iron, late 19th century	....	60- 70
Ironstone bowl (mortar), wooden pestle, mid-1800s	....	72- 81
Wood, bird's-eye maple, early	...	77- 85
Wood, cherry (ill.)	....	48- 53

Mosaic Tile

The Mosaic Tile Company was organized at Zanesville, Ohio, in 1893, by Herman C. Mueller and Karl Langenbeck to manufacture mosaic tiles. The company also made other pieces such as boxes and figurines. All pieces were marked with the monogram of the firm.

Tile, deer's head, tan/black	.....	$ 53- 64
Tile, German Shepherd, hexagonal, tan/brown	....	47- 57
Tile, Lincoln, profile, blue/white .		55- 66
Tile, George Washington, blue/white	....	57- 68

Moser Glass

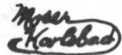

Moser Glass

This Art Nouveau glass as well as other types, some highly enameled, was made by Ludvig Moser at his factory in Carlsbad, Austria, at the turn of the century. Most collectible today.

Bottle, perfume, blue cut to clear, 7¼" high, signed	$167-182
Bowl, vintage decor, cranberry, footed, 7", signed	96-107
Candlesticks, Alexandrite, cube type, signed, 10", pr.	325-360
Compote, amethyst, gold border, 7" high	342-361
Compote, cranberry, cut overlay, signed, 9" high	290-320
Cruet, amethyst to clear, mushroom stopper, gold band, 5" high	185-210
Decanter, panel cut, signed	172-188
Dresser set, 2 perfumes, hair holder, tray, jewel box, gold enameled, all pieces signed	552-620
Goblet, cobalt, jeweled/enameled, signed	320-340
Jar, tobacco, panels/florals, leaves, rayed star base	182-192
Toothpick, clear, crystal	110-121
Vase, amber, gold band of Amazon women and centaurs, gold stripes, signed Moser Karlsbad (ill.)	319-347
Vase, amethyst, clear/intaglio cut floral, 11" high	472-492
Vase, clear to yellow, top to bottom decor	188-194
Vase, opalescent blue and white, enameled leaves and insects, applied red cherries, 6½" high (ill.)	582-625

Moss Rose Pattern China

In the mid-1800s, the English potters used this garden flower to decorate certain wares. It was used on Ironstone Ware for almost 50 years.

Bone dishes, set of 6, all	$106-118
Box, covered, rectangular, 2½"×6"	42- 51
Coffeepot, Johnson Bros., 8½" high	88- 99
Creamer, 4½" high	52- 61
Cup/saucer, Haviland	54- 63
Cup/saucer, Meakin	40- 50
Dresser set, 4 covered boxes, pr. candlesticks, pin tray, large tray, all	170-180
Dresser set, 3 covered boxes, candlestick, large tray	132-142
Pitcher, Bavaria, 8½" high	62- 72
Pitcher, Haviland, 8" high	77- 87
Pitcher, Ironstone, 9¼" high	65- 75
Plate, Bavaria, 7" dia.	48- 58
Plate, cake, pierced handles, 8¼" dia.	42- 52
Plate, Johnson Bros., 5½" dia.	36- 46
Platter, 14"×19", Meakin	62- 72
Platter, 13½"×18¼", American-made	52- 61
Saucedish, Johnson Bros.	52- 61
Shaving mug, Austria	60- 70
Shaving mug, Johnson Bros.	50- 60
Soup tureen, 8" high (ill.)	70- 78
Sugar bowl, Ironstone	60- 70
Tea set: teapot, sugar, creamer, 8 cups/saucers, tray, all	265-285
Teapot, American-made	54- 64
Teapot, Meakin, 7¾" high	72- 82
Water set: large bowl, large pitcher, small pitcher, soap dish, toothbrush holder, slop jar, chamber pot (thunder mug), all	685-772

Moss Rose Pattern China

272

Mother-of-Pearl

Mother-of-Pearl

This beautiful material comes from the abalone, the pearl oyster, and other marine shells. The hard, pearly internal layer is used in the arts and in the making of pearl buttons.

Checkerboard, inlaid abalone, 16"
   square . . . . $ 74- 83
Dresser set: brush, comb, hair
   holder, nail buffer, all 132-152
Frame, sterling silver trim,
   11"×9½" 71- 80
Knife set, 8 pcs., sterling silver
   trim, all 152-166
Madonna, 6" high (ill.) 68- 77
Pen, 14k gold nib 17- 22

Motorcycles

The Indian 'cycle once had a self-starter— a Hendee Special; before that, a hand crank. Remember "Cannonball" Baker? He made a fortune in the early days riding motorcycles across the U.S.A., attempting to set records. In 1911, in England the front wheel brake was first introduced—a Wilkinson. Old motorcycles are highly collectible.

1905 Clement (French),
   running condition,
   4-cylinder . . . .$ 2,900+
1908 Hendee (later, Indian),
   still runs 4,400-4,700
1909 N.S.U., 7 H.P., poor
   condition . . . . 2,700+

1910 Excelsior Auto-Cycle,
   excellent condition . . . . . . 3,900+
1911 Henderson, 4-cylinder,
   good condition . . . . 5,200+
1911 Thor, poor condition . . . . 3,400+
1912 Emblem, needs work . . . 2,400-2,750
1912 Marvel, good condition . 3,500+
1912 Pierce, 4-cylinder,
   running . . . . 3,700+
1913 Merkel, runs 3,400-3,700
1914 Harley-Davidson, good
   condition 3,900-4,400
1914 Yale, 2-cylinder, poor
   running condition . . . . 3,400+
1922 Cleveland, modified for
   racing, good condition 3,500-3,850
1923 Evans Power-Cycle,
   running . . . . 2,900+

Movie Memorabilia

Anything relating to Hollywood is being collected. See **Clubs and Publications**, this Price Guide.

Autograph, Wallace Berry $128-135
Autograph, Ann Blyth 15- 20
Autograph, Charlie Chaplin in
   "City Lights" 138-147
Autograph, Paul Newman 37- 47
Lobby card, "Deadline USA"
   with Humphrey Bogart 32- 42
Lobby card, "Giant" with James
   Dean 32- 42
Lobby card, "Niagara" with
   Marilyn Monroe 46- 56
One sheet poster, "Belle of New
   York" with Fred Astaire 44- 52
One sheet poster, "Woman of
   the Year" with Tracy and
   Hepburn 210-224
Script, "The History of the
   World," signed by Mel Brooks 34- 42
Sheet music from "Gone With
   the Wind" 62- 72
Transparency from "Bus Stop"
   with Marilyn Monroe 19- 27

Muffineers

Usually made of glass or silver, these containers were used for sifting sugar or cinnamon on muffins. Much larger than a salt shaker, they were popular in England in the late 1800s.

China, cobalt, floral decor, 5¼"
   high . . . .$ 47-
China, green/gold, decorated,
   silver cap . . . .
Cranberry glass, 5" high . . . . . .

Muffineers

Glass, cut, clear, sterling silver
   top, 7¼" high 88-100
Opalescent, lid, 6" high (ill.) 48- 59
Porcelain, silver cap, England,
   Meakin 46- 57
Spanish Lace, raspberry/satin,
   plated cap, 6" high 84- 93
Sterling silver, 6" high, beaded,
   3 curved feet 58- 70

Muller Freres

The Muller Brothers made a fine grade of
glass, including cameo, at Luneville and then
at Croismare, France, from early 1900s until
World War II.

Cameo vase, acid cut and
   enamel scenes in brown/
   yellow/ lavender, 4" high,
   signed . . . . $ 525- 610

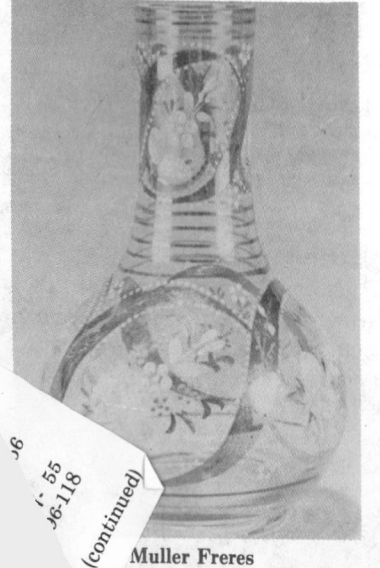

Muller Freres

Cameo vase, birds, enameled,
   multicolored, signed 585- 665
Lamp, hanging, Art Deco,
   wrought iron frame 642- 684
Lamp, table, 2 hanging
   shades, cameo cut leaves . .   1,150-1,400
Vase, ringed neck, enameled,
   flower decor (ill.) 275- 320

Music Boxes

Music Boxes

The Swiss and Germans were skilled
makers of music boxes. Many European
countries produced them but the movements
usually came from Switzerland. Made from
the 17th century on. See **Clubs and Publications**, this Price Guide.

Artison disc organ $1,800- 1,950
Birdcage type, bird moves
   and sings   785-   875
Bremond, 6" cylinder 2,500- 2,775
Capital style A "Cuff" box,
   w/6 "cuffs", c. 1896 . . . . .   5,100- 5,600
Columbia, 6 selections 1,200- 1,400
Coset Calliope, manual, 45
   pipes, brass . . . .   16,000+
Dawkins, 6 tunes, 6"
   cylinders 3,400- 3,700
Double comb, Polyphon,
   coin-operated 3,500- 3,800
Kalliope disc box, 7 discs . .   3,100- 3,375
Lochmann, winding rod,
   gold leaf decor, 21½"
   disc 4,100- 4,400
Mandolin, cylinder, No. Co
   12 . . . .   2,300- 2,550
Orchestral cylinder w/drum
   and 5 bells, plays 12
   tunes 3,350- 3,500
Paillard piccolo zither, 2
   combs, plays 12 tunes . . .   3,400- 3,700
Regina, automatic, No. 33,
   12 39" dia. discs 6,800- 7,400

Regina coin-operated, 12
records 5,900- 6,300
Rivenc interchangeable
cylinder box, plays 8
tunes on 1 cylinder 3,300- 3,550
Seeburg, Style K, piano,
mandolin, xylophone,
nickelodeon, 62″ high . . .   7,800+
Stella upright disc box, 10
bells, coin-operated 8,400- 8,800
Swiss, 9-bell cylinder 3,400- 3,900
Swiss, 4-tune, 5″ cylinders,
double comb 3,100- 3,700
Swiss, 8-tune cylinder, bells,
c. 1900 . . . .   4,300- 4,600
Swiss, 8-tune cylinder,
outside crank, 2 extra
cylinders 3,175- 3,600
Swiss, 10-tune cylinder,
bells 4,200- 4,600
Swiss, 12-tune cylinder,
5 bells 5,400- 5,700
Swiss, wooden grained case,
plays 10 hymns, 22″
across (ill.) 2,300- 3,700
Symphonion disc box, 22
discs 5,200- 5,400
Symphonion, 5 bells 5,600- 5,975
Symphonion, single comb . .   2,700- 2,950
Universal cylinder box, 10
cylinders, Pat. 1891 . . . .   4,200- 4,400

Music Stands

Music Stands

Just that—a rack on legs to hold sheet
music. They've been around for years and

collectors use them to hold the family Bible or
dictionary.

Ornate ironwork, cherry board,
1890s (ill.) $165-220
Ornate ironwork, double board,
poplar, 1890s   160-180

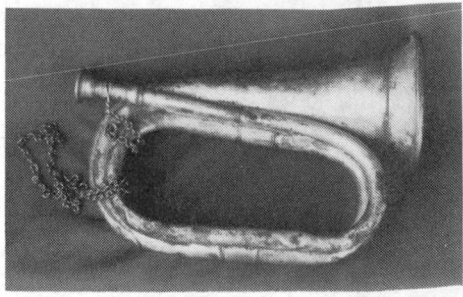

Musical Instruments

Musical Instruments

See **Clubs and Publications**, this Price
Guide.

Accordion, Adolphus
Special . . . . $ 185- 220
Accordion, Concertone, 10
keys, enameled,
mahogany finish 172- 195
Accordion, Kalbe Imperial,
twin bellows, nickel-
plated clasps and keys,
2 stops, 2 sets of reeds 472- 520
Accordion Pitzschier,
mahogany panels, 19
nickel keys, made in
Germany, sold in U.S.,
c. 1890s 675- 740
Bagpipes, Scotland, mid-
1800s   2,900-3,200
Bagpipes, Scotland,
pre-WWI   1,150-1,350
Banjo, calfskin head, 25
nickel-plated brackets,
maple neck, fingerboard
inlaid with M.O.P., c.
1890s 650- 725
Banjo, maple shell, nickel
band, 6 screw brackets,
11″ calfskin head,
c. 1890s 265- 280
Banjo, shell covered in
calfskin, hardwood neck,
40″, c. 1860 . . . .   545- 620
Bugle, artillery, brass,
c. 1890 . . . .   210- 23′
Bugle, Boy Scout, brass,
c. 1920 (ill.)   62-
Bugle, Civil War   445-

Bugle, officer's, nickel-
plated, c. 1890 . . . .   195- 220
Castinets, Mexican, c. 1920 .   72-   82
Castinets, Spanish, c. 1890s .   112- 118
Cello, American-made, sold
by Sears, c. 1910 . . . .   455- 475
Cello, American-made,
4-string bass, c. 1890s 840- 890
Cello, ¾ size, 4 strings, iron
head, c. 1890s, American-
made   965-1,200
Clarinet, Laube style, A,
low pitch, c. 1890 . . . .   442- 452
Clarinet, Laube style,
B-flat, low pitch, 1900s . . .   362- 382
Clarinet, Laube style, C,
low pitch, c. 1890s 345- 365
Concertina, French, c.
1850s 482- 492
Concertina, mahogany, 20
keys, English, bone
buttons, c. 1880 . . . .   392- 420
Cornet, Artists', B-flat,
nickel-plated, c. 1890s 375- 395
Cornet, Concertone, 1 water
key, M.O.P. buttons,
silver-plated mouthpiece,
brass, c. 1900 . . . .   225- 245
Cornet, Dupont, C, polished
brass, M.O.P. buttons,
c. 1890 . . . .   320- 340
Cymbals, American, 10",
11", 12", 12½", 13",
leather handles, c. 1890s,
ea. 210- 222
Cymbals, English, c. 1850s . .   252- 272
Cymbals, French, c. 1890s . .   225- 245
Drum, Acme Professional
bass, 24" dia., 26" dia.,
28" dia., 30" dia., c. 1890s .   262- 285
Drum, Acme Professional
bass, 14" dia., 16" dia.,
c. 1890s 262- 272
Drum, band instrument,
American, c. 1860s   1,400-1,600
Drum, Revolutionary War
field type, American   2,700-2,900
Drum, toy, tin, twisted rope
strap, painted, c. 1880s . . .   192- 222
Flute, American, 8-keyed,
c. 1900 . . . .   182- 192
Flute, French, 1-keyed,
c. 1850s, ivory (rare) . . . . .   5,400+
Flute, Italian, c. 1880s   2,900-3,200
Flute, ivory, 4-keyed, c.
1850s   2,900-3,200
American, Civil
. . . .   2,850-3,300
, The
. . . .   192- 221
1750s . . .   16,500+
ore, c.
. . . .   195- 230

72
465
(continued)

Guitar, The Richard,
concert size, c. 1900 . . . . . .   352- 372
Harmonica, Doerful's Inter-
national, celluloid, 10
double holes, 40 reeds   77-   87
Harmonica, Duss Band
Tremelo, 3-in-1, 32 double
holes, etc.   45-   65
Harmonica, Hohner, con-
cert, c. 1890s, 20 double
holes, 80 reeds 285- 320
Harp, English, maple base,
5'7", c. 1850s   1,900-2,200
Harp, Italian, carved rose-
wood, 5'6", c. mid-1700s . .   7,400-7,850
Jews' Harp, 2", 2¼", 2½",
2¾", 3¼", 3½" frame,
c. 1900s, ea.   15-   26
Lap harp, late 1890s (ill.) 275- 295
Lute, Flemish, c. 1750   2,200-2,400
Lute, French, early 17th
century . . . .   18,500+
Lute, Spanish, c. early 17th
century . . . .   17,000+
Mandolin, American, rose-
wood, c. 1860s 252- 262
Mandolin, English, late
17th century . . . .   14,200+
Mandolin, French, early
17th century . . . .   19,500+
Mandolin, French, c. 1790s .   2,900-3,400
Oboe, English, c. 1890s   4,100-4,400
Oboe, German, c. 1890s   5,000-5,700
Saxophone, Bantone, bell
front, 3 valves, upright
bell   1,700-1,900
Saxophone, DuPont, alto,
bell front, polished brass . .   252- 272
Saxophone, DuPont, B-flat
tenor, B-flat baritone,
polished brass 348- 388

Musical Instruments

276

Saxophone, Tourville & Co., alto, silver, polished	262- 272
Trombone, DuPont, B-flat, baritone valve, polished brass	410- 420
Trombone, DuPont, B-flat, tenor valve, E-flat alto slide, brass	650- 720
Trumpet, Concertone, B-flat, 1 water key, brass	218- 227
Trumpet, Holton, B-flat, "The King," lacquer bore	398- 442
Violin, Amati model, c. 1920s	260- 285
Violin, Concert Strad	200- 285
Violin, "genuine" Stradivarius Model, European	148- 167
Violin, Guarnerius model, c. 1900	172- 182
Violin, Stainer model	182- 192

Mustache Cups

Mustache Cups

They were popular in the 1800s. The partition in the cup supposedly kept the mustache out of the beverage. The majority were made in Germany using the transfer method—a method similar to our decals of today. Left-handed cups are rare. Lots of repros here.

Cup, blue floral, "Love Is Eternal" in gold	$ 65- 74
Cup, brown matt glaze, left-handed, 1890s	77- 87
Cup, diamond/shell pattern (ill.)	49- 57
Cup, gold band	54- 63
Cup, horses	34- 42
Cup, lavender, flower decor, man's name in gold	72- 82
Cup, "Love the Giver," blue/yellow background	77- 87
Cup, "Papa" in gold	82- 92
Cup, pink/orange, "WJM" in gold	77- 87

Cup/saucer, beaded leaf cluster, gold initials	74- 82
Cup/saucer, blue, white, scrolled medallions, Germany	73- 83
Cup/saucer, bright blue/green, gold initials, 1860s	78- 86
Cup/saucer, floral spray, German inscription, gold letters	68- 78
Cup/saucer, quadruple plate, revised initials, birds	77- 85

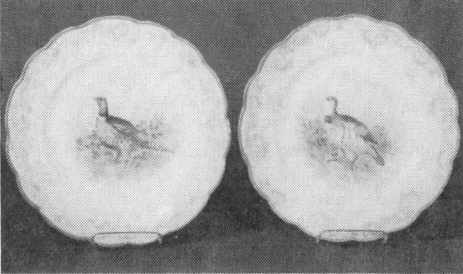

MZ Austria

MZ Austria

This porcelain was made by Moritz Zdekauer in the village of Alt-Rohlau, Austria, around 1900. Double eagle mark was used until 1920; then a 2-handled vase/MZ.

Bowl, flower, decor, fluted, 7" high	$ 64- 73
Bowl, pink roses, gold band inside lip, 4½" high	62- 72
Dish, vegetable, tab handles, blues/greens, 9½" wide	42- 52
Fish set, 12 plates, platter, gold rims, all	450-520
Plate, butterflies, blue/yellow, gold rim, 7½" dia.	42- 52
Plate, game, signed, 8½" dia. (ill.), ea.	51- 61
Tray, dresser, pink roses, green leaves, 9" long	52- 62
Tureen, soup, flower decor, 10¼" wide	61- 71

Nailsea Glass

This glass was produced at Nailsea, England, beginning in 1788. The loops and swirlings of the colored glass, combined with clear or opal glass, identify it. The more common color combinations are red/white and green/white. More repros!

277

(continued)

Nailsea Glass

Atomizer, clear, white loops, 7¼"
  high $147-156
Bottle, blue, white looping, blown
  stopper, 11¼" high with
  stopper 188-197
Carafe, matching late, dark
  blue/white typical looping 172-190
Caster set, 4 bottles, blue/white
  loopings, cut stoppers 184-194
Cookie jar, blue loopings,
  Britannia lid and bale, 6½"
  high 182-192
Cruet, blue, white loops, 6¼"
  high 210-228
Cruet, dark red, white loopings,
  blown stopper, 6½" high 97-107
Cup/saucer, blue swirl, 19th
  century 77- 87
Epergne, flower base, blue/white
  loopings around base, brass
  fittings 268-288
Fairy lamp, satin to clear, signed
  Clarke in base 320-340
Flask, red swirls, 5½" high,
  no cap 210-232
Gas shade, white loopings, 3"
  filter 121-131
Pitcher, blue, white loops, clear
  handle, 10½" high 368-392
Rolling pin, cranberry swirl, 16"
  long 284-294
Rose bowl, blue looping, 4" dia. .. 272-310
Tumbler, white/blue loops 110-122
Vase, green satin, fluted top,
  19th century 188-222
Vase, white with blue loopings,
  black handles and base, 9½"
  high (ill.) 162-180

Napkin Rings

These were in vogue for less than 50 years, beginning in the late 1870s. They were made of every type of material, including cut glass.

Most common are those from pot metal or quadruple plate.

Cherubs, silver plate, Derby
  Silver Co. .... $ 45- 54
Child's name engraved around
  chicks scratching, silver 60- 70
Porcelain, hand-painted, flowers
  and bees, Germany 47- 55
Silver plate, boy fishing on rock . 58- 64
Silver plate, boy with hoop 48- 58
Silver plate, butterfly (ill.) 55- 66
Silver plate, cherub, child's
  initials 42- 52
Silver plate, fireman's helmet,
  Pairpoint 81- 90
Silver plate, large boot 44- 54
Silver plate, rooster (ill.) 41- 52
Silver plate, souvenir, Niagara
  Falls 48- 57
Silver plate, wild boar, barrel
  type, Pairpoint 85- 95
Sterling silver, dog chasing cat,
  initialed 183-193
Sterling silver, Georgie, beaded
  edge 181-191
Sterling silver, owl on branch,
  child's name 170-180

Napkin Rings

Nash Glass

185 AD NASH

Nash Glass

A former employee of the Tiffany Glass Company, Douglas Nash purchased Tiffany's Long Island factory around 1929. His glass was flamboyant in color and most of it was signed Nash on the bottom.

Bowl, gold, stretched edge, 8"
dia. signed $452-473
Candlestick, gold, water base,
5" high 155-170
Decanter, pair, green/shaded
gold, 15" high 410-440
Plate, chintz, alternating greens
and pinks, signed Nash, 6¾"
dia. (ill.) 184-195
Plate, yellow, orange chintz,
signed, 8" dia. 185-220
Vase, chintz/orange decor, 7½"
high, signed 355-410
Vase, flower form, ruffled top,
pedestal base, peacock blue,
5½" high (ill.) 510-572
Vase, green, fluted top, 8½"
high, signed 640-665
Vase, iridescent, gold, impressed
veins circling vase, 6" high,
signed 620-652
Vase, Tiffany blue, 8" high,
signed 452-472

Nautical

Nautical

"Where away?" was the cry from the deck
when a sailor in the crow's nest spotted a
whale, an enemy ship or land. The English
and the Germans made the best telescopes,
from the early 1700s on. A real gem when
found in original condition. See **Clubs and
Publications**, this Price Guide.

Telescopes
Ship captain's, 13" when
closed; 2 large sections,
opened to 30" . . . .$ 575- 650
Ship captain's, c. 1820,
wooden barrel, brass
mounts, 35" overall,
marked "Gardner & Sons-
Glasgow-Day or Night" . . .   450- 520

Ship captain's, 36" overall,
original leather covering, c.
1850 . . . .   675- 720
Ship captain's, made by a
woman, Janet Taylor-
Minories, London 650- 720
Ship captain's, walnut tube,
brass, 26" overall 395- 420

Other Nautical Items
Bilge pump, 38" high 190- 235
Blubber or "boat" spade, 17"
overall 188- 240
British East Indiaman's
logbook, 9½"×15",
1799-1802 . . . .   720- 770
*The British Mariner's Direc-
tory & Guide to the Trade &
Navigation of the Indian &
China Seas,* by Elmore,
342 pages 538- 572
British midshipman's journal,
1929-1932, 8"×13" 368- 382
Clipper Ship card, 3½"×6½",
colorful, used to advertise
for cargo 364- 382
Copper ship's oil lamp, 18"
high, oil font intact 288- 324
Greener percussion, muzzle-
loading harpoon gun,
English 2,500-2,700
Harpoon for Greener gun, c.
1850, 51" overall, iron shaft   375- 410
History of Nantucket by Obed
Macy, Mansfield, Mass.,
1880, 313 pages   84-   94
Lamp, A. Ward Hendrickson,
20" high (ill.)   75-   85
"Lead," used for determining
depth of water, 30" overall,
in pin box 278- 295
Letter from Commodore Perry
to his wife, handwritten,
4 pages, 1852 . . . .   420- 460
Logbook from the ship
Urchin, 10½"×12½",
1838-1839 . . . .   610- 700
Notes on torpedo fuses, by a
Lt. Converse, U.S.A., 1875,
published by U.S. Torpedo
Station, Newport, R.I.,
31 pages 120- 130
Ordnance Instructions for the
U.S. Navy, Navy Dept.,
Washington, 1866 . . . .   120- 140
Sailing ship's stick-type
barometer, on gimbal
mount, English, 1820 2,300-2,500
Sailor's valentine, octagon-
shaped, hinged case,
seashells, etc. 570- 620
Ship captain's telescope, 30"
overall, covered with
leather, twined rope   410-

Ship's boat horn, 16" overall	342-	362
Ship's medicine chest, c. 1830, mahogany, 8"×10"×9", c. 1840s	710-	722
Ship's running lights, pair, brass, 14" high, 1930s	542-	563
Ship's sextant, brass, 9" wide, 8½" high, 6 swivel filters, etc.	885-	920
U.S. Navy ship's Battle-rattle used to sound General Quarters	495-	522
Whale-killing lance, c. 1840s, 59" overall	462-	485
Whaling bomb lance gun, c. 1860s, breech-loading, American	2,300-	2,450

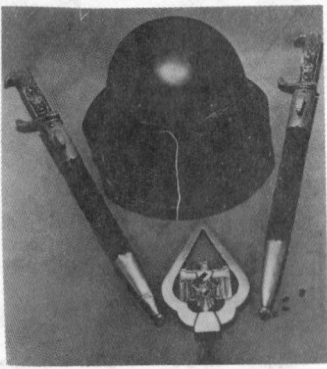

Nazi Items

Nazi Items

Hitler may have lost the war but collectors of his military items are growing every day. They are so popular, in fact, that reproductions are beginning to appear on the market. See **Clubs and Publications (Military)**, this Price Guide.

Afrika Corps Service Medal	$110-	122
Armband, German Armed Forces ("Deutsch Wehrmacht"), black/yellow	72-	85
Armband, H.J. (Hitler Youth), bevo weave	81-	91
Army mess kit	88-	96
Bayonet, Nazi police eagle's head, bone-type grips (ill.)	192-	220
Bayonet, police, eagle's head, etc. (ill.)	182-	195
'+ buckle, swastika insignia	135-	150
Army, w/eagle and ...ss guard	288-	320
...y the Brown ...rips, eagle,	320-	352

440 (continued)

Dagger, Hitler Youth, "Blut Und Ehre" on blade	332-	362
Dagger, Luftwaffe, 1937 model, flying eagle on cross guard	370-	410
Doll, Storm Trooper, 11" high, painted composition head	250-	272
Flag, 4'×7', swastika and German Cross	172-	183
Helmet, Afrika Corps, tan camouflage	292-	320
Helmet, Luftschultz w/wings (ill.)	112-	118
Helmet, Nazi police, chin strap, etc.	252-	272
Helmet, "R.L.B." (Air Defense League), parade type	462-	520
Iron Cross, 2nd class	99-	109
"Kreta" cuff title—awarded to participants in battle for Crete	320-	352
Luftwaffe badge, pilot, marked "Imme"	472-	542
Luftwaffe badge, "Webr. Schneider A wien"	628-	688
Mountain troops rucksack	108-	118
Peaked cap, Army infantry officer, silver cord, red piping	320-	342
Peaked cap, Artillery officer, silver cord, red piping	320-	342
Peaked cap, Luftwaffe officer	362-	382
Peaked cap, Navy captain, gold bullion wreath	384-	395
Photograph of Hitler and friends, signed by Hitler	420-	442
Pith helmet, Afrika Corps, green felt body, both metal badges	162-	182
Tunic, Luftwaffe, officer's summer white, complete	925-	1,100
Uniform, chaplain's Reichswehr tunic	542-	562
Uniform, medical officer's	385-	420
Uniform, Panzer Grenadier	372-	391

Needlework

Patterns were first engraved and hand-painted on paper; later they were stamped in color on canvas. If done in wool stitches this was called Berlin work. In addition to personal items, popular patterns were done in the form of bookmarks, mottos such as Home Sweet Home, Welcome, and religious sentiments. *Godey's* was just one of many magazines that printed patterns for this type of work.

Daily, "God Is Good," early 19th century	$ 50-	60

Handkerchief flowers, blue/gold,
19th century (frame not
included) 54- 63
Sampler, "Friends Forever,"
early 19th century 72- 81
Scarf, flowers, 36" long 52- 62

Netsukes

Netsukes

Usually carved of ivory, they're used as
fasteners, such as buttons for garments. The
old are highly collectible and they're being
skillfully reproduced in Japan. Careful! It's
pronounced "Netski." See **Clubs and Publications**, this Price Guide.

Apple vendor, woman	$ 84- 93
Boar	88-100
Cat	78- 87
Child with dog	91-106
Crab, stained dark brown (soaking in strong tea achieves this)	105-111
Devil's mask	108-112
Dog playing with fish	124-132
Elephant, two blind men	137-142
Frogs on lily pad	131-142
Happy/sad face (head revolves) . .	152-162
Hare on tortoise's back	99-108
Houseboat	121-131
Kangaroo rat	61- 70
Man carrying basket of fish	99-109
Man carrying boat net	98-115
Man carrying bundle of straw . . .	92-107
Man carrying donkey	132-142
Man holding cup (ill.)	120-130
Man holding tortoise	88- 99
Mouse, stained brown	98-107
Owl	108-118
Pearl diver	89-107
Rabbit	67- 77
Running boar	108-121
Smiling man with bread	107-117

Sumo wrestlers (look out for repros)	117-128
Tiger	121-132
Two women, one holding fish	106-118

Newcomb Pottery

It was opened in 1896 by Ellsworth and
William Woodward as a workshop extension
of the art school of Sophie Newcomb Memorial College for Women, New Orleans. By 1897
it was producing on a large scale. Most of the
pottery was turned on the wheel by Joseph
Fortune Meyer. It's highly collectible today.

Bowl, blue/green/pink tie-vine motif, matt glaze, Newcomb	$ 200- 209
Bowl, 3⅞" high, blue/green/pink/yellow narcissus motif	280- 292
Bowl, plain glaze, undecorated, 2⅛" high, Newcomb mark	238- 261
Bowl-vase, 4¾" high, blue/green, Spanish bayonet motif, matt glaze, decorator Julia Michel	328- 364
Inkstand, with liner and lid, blue/green/brown, glossy glaze, decorator Joseph Meyer	182- 198
Mug, florals, blue underglaze, signed Joseph Meyer	1,375-1,450
Pot, Ali Baba type, plain green semi-matt, 3⅛" high	178- 210

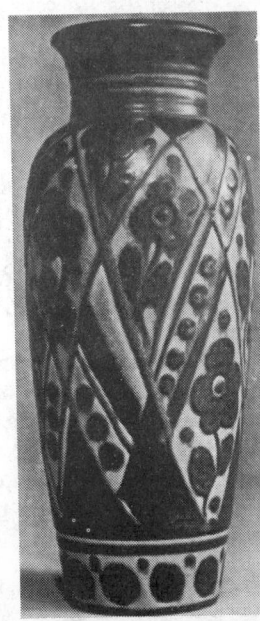

Newcomb Pottery

281

(continued)

Vase, green/blue, oak tree motif, matt glaze, 5¼″ high	290-	310
Vase, misty blue, massed flowers, blue/yellow	425-	462
Vase, 7¾″ high, blue/green conventionalized motif, glossy glaze (ill.)	310-	342

Newhall China

Newhall China

Some say this was the first true English china. It was made at Newhall in the Staffordshire District, England, around 1781. At first they specialized in hard-paste porcelain, later they produced bone china.

Creamer, enameled flowers, 4″ high (ill.)	$187-220	
Creamer, Pink Lustre decorations	142-152	
Cup/saucer, Blossom Band decor	88- 98	
Mug, Oriental scene, 3″ high	106-116	
Plate, rose decor, 7¼″ dia., early	111-121	
Plate, rose decor, 8″ dia.	98-109	
Sugar bowl, Pink Lustre decorations	172-182	
Teapot, creamer, sugar, Oriental decor	246-254	
Teapot, Oriental decor, 7½″ high	282-294	

Niloak Pottery 𝒩𝐼𝐿𝒪𝒜𝒦

This multicolored pottery was made at Benton, Arkansas, from the late 19th century until 1946. Glazed on the inside, it had a dull finish on the outside. Most desirable colors are rust and chocolate brown. "Niloak" is always stamped in bottom. It is beginning to be collectible. These are indicative prices.

Bowl w/flower frog	$ 68- 78	
Bud vase, 8″ high	72- 81	
Candlesticks, 7½″ high, pr.	110-121	
Chamber stick, 5″ high	70- 80	

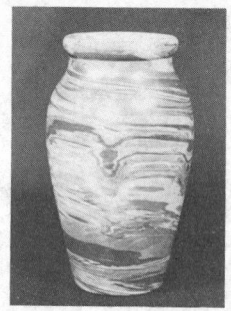

Niloak Pottery

Cigarette box	48- 52
Elephant, 1″ high	71- 82
Humidor, 6½″ high	91-108
Jigger, 2¼″ high	47- 57
Match holder, 1½″ high	42- 52
Tile, 4½″ square	50- 60
Vase, brown/tan/yellow, 6½″ high, the usual colors (ill.)	44- 52
Vase, 6½″ high	47- 57
Vase, 9″ high	58- 68

Nippon

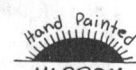

Hand Painted NIPPON

Nippon

Hand-decorated, generally it's defined as porcelain made in Japan between 1891 and 1921 for export. It was **not** a specific type of porcelain. The name used on the back of each piece denoted the country of origin. After 1891 the U.S. required that imported items from all foreign countries be marked with the name of the exporting country. Nippon is the Japanese word for Japan, but in 1921 the U.S.A. stated that the word Nippon was no longer acceptable as a country of origin marking. Thus ended the Nippon era. See **Clubs and Publications,** this Price Guide.

Ashtray, Persian design, signed . $ 53- 62

(continued)

Salt/pepper, green ground, gold
dots, pr. 24- 32
Sugar bowl, bluebird in tree,
signed 42- 52
Sugar bowl, yellow roses, Green
Wreath mark 40- 50
Tankard, bear on stump, 11½"
high   152-161
Tankard, Indian on horse, 12"
high, RC Nippon mark   161-171
Tea set, gold dragons, blue
ground, 17 pieces   162-172
Tea set, red/yellow flowers, 13
pieces, all   151-166
Teapot, garden scene, 8" high,
Green Wreath mark 44- 52
Teapot, hand-painted roses, gold
trim, 7" high, signed 39- 48
Teapot, lake scene, gold trim,
7¾" high 42- 52
Tray, dragon motif, 8½" high . . .   58- 68
Tray, farm scene, gold trim, 9"
dia. 62- 72
Vase, Art Nouveau scene, gold
handles, 9¼" high 63- 73
Vase, bathing scene, beaded
handles, 8" high 49- 58
Vase, twisted vines, red ground,
11" high 64- 73

Chinese boy in rickshaw, head
and hands move, bisque type . .   77- 87
Farm couple, green/yellow/
orange, 6¾" high (ill.) 86- 94
Girl and boy kissing, heads nod,
porcelain 52- 61
Hindu, turbaned, holding basket,
snake moves too, bisque 68- 78
Old lady in chair, sleeping head
nods, bisque 51- 61

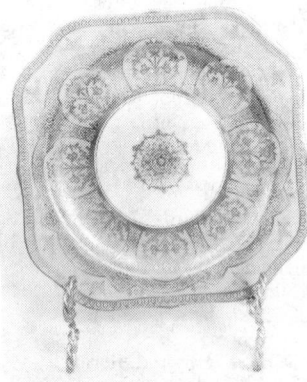

Noritake China

Noritake China

Produced by the Nihon Toki Kaisha firm in
Nagoya, Japan, after 1904, for export only.
Azalea is the best-known pattern. It was
given away as a premium by the Larkin Tea
and Coffee Company in the early 1900s. More
Noritake is on the market than any other
mark. Look for Noritake Nippon, Noritake M
in Wreath Nippon, and Noritake RC Nippon
marks. They're the earliest. Modern Noritake is marked Noritake China, Japan, with
the familiar "M" in the wreath above.

Basket, Azalea pattern, 5" long . . $110-122
Berry set, 6-pc., floral scene,
Green M in Wreath mark, set .   91- 98
Berry set, 7-pc., Azalea pattern,
all   112-122
Bowl, Azalea pattern, 10½" dia. . .   47- 58
Cake plate, Azalea pattern,
7" dia. 74- 83
Cake plate, green/gold,
M Mark (ill.) 39- 45
Celery dish, Azalea pattern,
12¼" long 64- 72
Celery dish, crimson roses, 9"
long, RC mark 47- 56
Chocolate set: pot, 8 cups, floral
scenes, Green M mark, all   92-107

Nodding Figures

Nodding Figures

Sometimes called pagods, these porcelain
figures have heads and hands that are attached to the body with wires. Any movement causes the figure to move up and down.
18th and 19th centuries, considered quite collectible today.

Bird in tree, trunk sways, bisque . $ 57- 67
Boy holding dog, dog's head
moves, porcelain, 18th century   72- 81

Compote, Azalea pattern, 6½" dia.	72- 78
Condiment set, Azalea pattern, 6-pc.	65- 75
Creamer, Azalea pattern, 4½" high	52- 62
Cup/saucer, Sedalia pattern, set of 12, Green M mark, all	101-112
Cup/saucer, Swans, gold rim, RC mark	35- 44
Dish, Azalea pattern, sauce type	13- 19
Dresser set, 7-pc., blue flowers, gold border, new mark, all	72- 82
Egg cup, Azalea pattern	40- 50
Figurine, boy fishing, green/ yellow, RC mark, 6" high	67- 77
Mayonnaise set, 3-pc., Azalea pattern, all	119-128
Plates, Azalea pattern, 7", 8½", 9¾" dia.	21- 30
Platter, Azalea pattern, 14" long	52- 62
Salt/pepper, Azalea pattern, pr.	34- 42
Salt/pepper, owl motif, Green M mark, pr.	40- 50
Shallow bowl, cherry blossom scene, 3-handled, Green M mark	52- 61
Tea set, garden scene, varied colors, RC mark	70- 80
Tea set, 17-pc., floral scenes, gold rims, Green M mark, all	162-180
Tile, Azalea pattern	44- 54
Tobacco jar, horse's head, blue/ red, Green M mark	68- 78
Vase, Azalea pattern, 8¾" high	88- 99
Vase, floral scenes, 7¼" high	44- 52
Vase, salmon/pink, 8" high	50- 60

North Dakota School of Mines

Pottery was made by this group at the University of North Dakota in the 1890s. Most items were signed.

Candlestick, green matt, 6¼" high	$118-127
Tile, Indian head, 5½" sq.	79- 82
Vase, black matt, 5½" high	67- 77
Vase, blue/gray matt, 4¼" high	52- 62
Vase, cobalt, 6¾" high	64- 74
Vase, prairie hen, 6" high	73- 83
Vase, tan/blue, handled, 5¼" high	66- 76

Nutcrackers

Teeth, stones, factory-made devices—they were all used for opening nuts. A popular

Nutcrackers

type in the early 1900s was an animal whose tail opened its mouth, into which the nut was inserted.

Alligator, brass, 13" long	$ 71- 81
Bear's head, wood, 8" long	70- 80
Cat, seated, iron, 11" high, tail opens mouth	42- 52
Dog, iron, 11" long, same operation (ill.)	44- 52
Dragon, brass	58- 68
Squirrel, brass, 8½" long, same operation	54- 62
Tiger, bronze	80- 90
Turtle, iron, 8½" long, same operation	42- 52
Wolf's head, iron, marked Renz, 9" high, same operation	48- 58

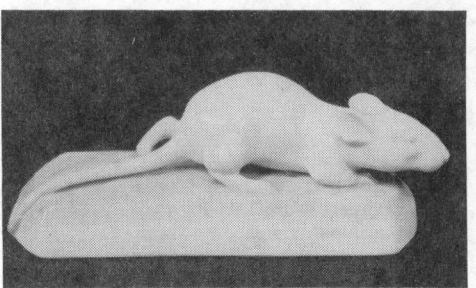

Nymphenburg Porcelain

Nymphenburg Porcelain

Established at Neudeck, Bavaria, in 1753, the factory was moved to Nymphenburg in 1761. Cane handles, toys, figurines, and animal groups are a few of the fine porcelain objects made. Figurines were reproduced from the mid-1850s on.

| Candlesticks, cream/green/ yellow, shield mark, 9" high, pr. | $ 117- 128 |
| Cane handle, blue/cream, animal figure | 62- 72 |

285

(continued)

Figurine, apple wife, cream/ green/red, signed, 6" high .	1,475+
Figurine, cheese monger, black/white/red, signed, 6¾" high	1,450+
Figurine, Italian comedy character, shield mark, 7" high	520- 542
Figurine, white rat, shield mark, 4½" long, (ill.)	121- 132

Occupied Japan Items

Occupied Japan Items

The United States occupied Japan for 7 years, from August, 1945, until April, 1952. "Made in Occupied Japan" and "Occupied Japan" are the most common marks found on items manufactured for export during that 7-year period. See **Clubs and Publications**, this Price Guide.

Animals
Dog, 4½" long	$ 13- 17
Easter rabbit pulling egg, 4" long	9- 14
Frog playing drum, 2½" high . . .	10- 16
Monkey playing violin, 3¼" high	9- 15
Mother and baby swan, 2" wide .	9- 13

Ashtrays
Cherubs	9- 14
Dog and fire hydrant, 4" high . . .	12- 18
Elf sitting on leaf, 4" wide	15- 21
Frog with open mouth, 3½" high	11- 16

Bisque
Boy with dog, 6" high	17- 22
Bud vase, 6" high	17- 24
Colonial couple, pr.	29- 39
Cupids on pedestals, 7½" high, pr.	24- 35
Peasant couple, 5½" high, pr. . . .	28- 35

Cups/Saucers
Black, Trimont china	19- 29
Blue Willow style	19- 29
Gray, Orion china	19- 29
Green, Trimont china	19- 29
White bone	19- 27

Figurines
Court jester, 6½" high	15- 22
Dancers, 1930s style, 2¼" high, pr.	23- 32
Farm couple, 7" high	21- 22
Fisherman and mate, 5" high, pr.	34- 42
Shelf sitter, 3" high	12- 17
Victorian couple, 8" high (ill.) . . .	32- 40
Warrior, 5" high	16- 22

Figurines, Children
Boy, Hummel type, 5½" high, "American Children, I bring you greetings," on bottom	54- 64
Boy playing horn, 3½" high	14- 22
Girl, Hummel type, 5½" high, same inscription on bottom (The Hummel types are good enough to fool many collectors of the real thing.)	55- 64
Peasant girl with lamb, 5" high . .	17- 22
Pigeon-toed girl, 4½" high	14- 21

Glassware and Lacquerware
Coasters, lacquerware, set of 6 . .	35- 45
Cracker server, scalloped edges, w/glass cheese dip dish and lacquer lid, 13½" dia.	49- 59
Lighthouse, battery-operated, souvenir of Coney Island	34- 44
Niagara Falls hanging plate, lacquerware	21- 29

Planters
Angel pulling cart, 4" wide	18- 24
Donald Duck and basket, 2" wide	21- 32
Donkey and packs, 3" wide	18- 29
Elf and basket, 5¾" wide	21- 29
Owl on limb, 3½" wide	22- 27
Panda climbing tree, 4" wide	16- 29

Salt/Pepper Shakers
Chicken in nest, 3-pc., all	17- 23
Dog and chair, 2-pc.	21- 28
Elephants, 1-pc.	14- 24
Mexican boys, pr.	17- 25
Roses with butterflies, 3-pc., all . .	17- 25

Toby Mugs
Captain Patches, 2¾" high	18- 22
Devil's face, 2" high (rare)	29- 38
Gent and dogs, 7" high	48- 58
Jail bailiff, 7" high	54- 64
Street peddler, 7" high	49- 57

Toothpicks
Cowboy, 4¼" high	22- 30
Pixie, 3" high	19- 26
Satsuma, vase type, 2¼", 2½", 11" high, ea.	15- 21

Vases
Angel, bud type, 2¾" high	9- 15
Boy blowing horn, 2" high	9- 15
Girl on stump, 3" high	17- 22
Miniature	14- 18

Ohr Pottery

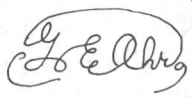

Ohr Pottery

George E. Ohr made his pottery at Biloxi, Mississippi, from 1883 until just after World War I. It was made from local clay and fired at low temperature. An extremely thin pottery, a contorted shape was one of its characteristics as were the many glaze colors Ohr used. Some referred to him as the mad potter of Biloxi but few denied his genius. He signed his pieces "G.E. Ohr, Biloxi" and "Geo. E. Ohr, Biloxi, Mississippi" in block letters or "G.E. Ohr" in script.

Bowl, folded lip, dark green/
  brown glaze, 2" high $140-170
Bowl, one side folded halfway
  over, mustard glaze, 2¾" high . 152-175
Candlestick, dark maroon, rough
  texture (ill.) 248-285
Candlestick, handled, mottled
  green glaze, 3¾" high 178-225
Mug, handleless, dark brown
  glaze, 3¾" high 225-245
Mug, puzzle, green glaze,
  decorated handle, pierced
  sides, 3½" high 248-278
Pitcher, folded neck, blood red
  glaze, 6½" high 485-520
Teapot, applied snake, pink
  "raku" glaze, 5¼" high 750-900
Vase, dark brown glaze, 2½" high 162-181
Vase, folded neck, dark lead
  glaze, 4¾" high 168-179
Vase, folded waist, green
  speckled glaze, 2½" high 172-182
Vase, 4-petal top, pinched,
  pewter-gunmetal bowl (ill.) 268-292
Vase, pinched sides, ruffled edge,
  3¾" high 268-290
Vase, squat, matt pewter finish,
  dented side (ill.) 330-345

Old Hall Porcelain

Old Hall Porcelain

Originally from Job Meigh and Son, Old Hall Works, Hanley, England, 1790. Name changed to Old Hall Earthenware Company in 1861; changed again in 1887 to Old Hall Porcelain Works. The firm ceased production in 1902. It was an opaque earthenware of the Staffordshire type. Generally, Staffordshire-type earthenware pieces are in the same price range as Old Hall. See specific Staffordshire types for prices. An indicative piece is shown.

Pitcher, cream brown transfer
  leaves and flowers, 4" high,
  signed "Old Hall Earthenware
  Co." (ill.) $52-62

OLD IVORY
84

Old Ivory China

The ground color of this ware gives it its name. Made in Silesia, Germany, in the last part of the 1800s, the marked pieces bear the crown Silesia mark, and/or pattern stock numbers.

287

(continued

Old Ivory China

Berry bowl, numbered .... $ 62- 71
Berry set, bowl and 6 small
  bowls 400-462
Cake plate, Silesia, open handles,
  numbered 92-107
Cake plate, 10″ dia., numbered .. 105-111
Celery bowl, Silesia, numbered .. 74- 82
Chocolate pot, peach color/rose,
  numbered 230-250
Comb and brush tray, pattern
  #16, 11½″ 72- 82
Creamer and sugar, numbered ... 94-103
Cup/saucer, numbered, orange
  poppies, green leaves 72-102
Platter, peach color, numbered
  (ill.) 160-170
Relish, dish, numbered 63- 73
Saucedish, numbered, 5″ dia..... 44- 52
Teapot, floral, peach, numbered . 225-260
Toothpick, numbered, 2″ high ... 91-107
Tray, numbered, Silesia, 2″ 82- 92

Old Paris China

Old Paris China

During the 18th and 19th centuries a number of pottery and porcelain factories were located in Paris. The better products were known as Old Paris, although few pieces were ever marked as such.

Cake plate, white, gold trim ..... $ 73- 82
Compote, 5¼″ high (ill.) 88- 98
Creamer, numbered, white, gold
  trim 65- 75
Cup/saucer, white, gold trim 107-117
Figurines, children with pets,
  pastel colored, pr. 162-172
Pitcher, water, white, gold trim .. 132-152
Plates, fruit, floral decor, 10″ dia. 70- 80
Tea set, pot, creamer, sugar,
  flower motif, gold trim 372-425
Teapot, white with gold trim 152-162
Vases, handled, gold trim, early
  1850s, pr. 432-442

Old Sleepy Eye Collectibles

In 1906 the Western Stoneware Company of Monmouth, Illinois, was formed to produce premium pottery for Sleepy Eye Milling Company in Sleepy Eye, Minnesota. The town and the mill were named for a Sioux Indian. His likeness, in profile, is on most of the pottery you find today. Other premiums were also given away by the mill. All are highly sought after now. The pottery is being reproduced in mugs, sugar bowls, small pitchers, salt/pepper shakers, and steins. Other reproductions are a glass jar, a large tumbler, a small advertising mirror, and the paper barrel labels. Be careful. See **Clubs and Publications**, this Price Guide.

Advertising cards, 10 in set,
  5½″×9″, all $452-481
Advertising postcards, 9 in set,
  3⅜″×5½″, all 470-492
Cookbook, Old Sleepy Eye on
  cover 132-150
Cookbook, shaped like the end of
  a bread loaf 132-151
Letter opener, bronze 101-111
Paperweight bust, bronze 152-162
Pitcher, blue-on-gray, 4″ high ... 152-161
Pitcher, blue-on-white, 4″ high .. 101-109
Pitcher, green 128-132
Stein, blue-on-gray, 7″ high 292-325
Stein, yellow, 7¼″ high 300-320
Vase, blue-on-gray 362-382
Vase, multicolor, bullrushes, 8¼″
  high 190-222

Onyx Glass

Characterized by its raised, 8-petal and leaf design, this decorative glass was made in 1889 by Dalzell, Gilmore and Leighton Com-

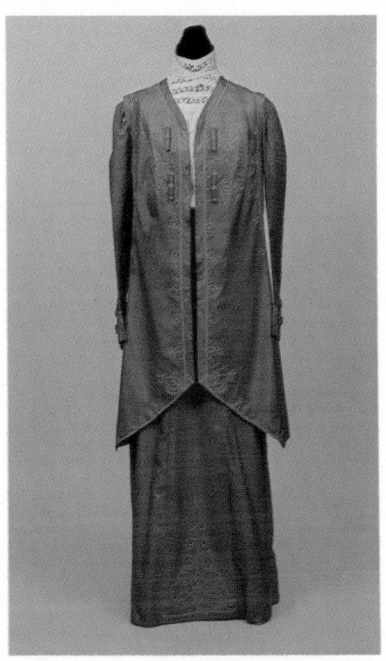

Walking suit in wine-colored silk with self-colored piping embroidery was worn with ivory silk, high-necked waist. C. 1885–1900. $275–300.

Blue silk velvet dress features hand-applied design in white glass beads. C. 1920–1930. $80–90.

Blue silk chiffon dress in bubble print has ecru lace inset in bodice. C. 1925–1935. $70–90.

Yellow silk crepe de chine and ruby silk velvet ball gown came with built-in corset. C. 1885–1900. $300–350.

Photographs from *Collectible Clothing with Prices* by Sheila Malouff.

Norwegian pine secretary shows traces of old red paint, has exceptional scalloping and drawer front decoration. $800–1,000.

Swedish, folk-painted hanging cupboard is a key safe. $600–800.

Norwegian trunk decorated in Telemark-style rosemaling dates from the golden age of such decoration. $800–1,000.

Photographs from *Antique Ethnic Furniture* by Lyndon C. Viel.

Provincial (country) German open dish dresser in Biedermeier style was found in northern Wisconsin. Possibly one-of-a-kind. $6,000–7,500.

Norwegian, folk-painted, closed dish dresser, signed and dated. Property of the Minneapolis Art Institute. $15,000.

Norwegian signed and dated pull-out couch bed is probably one-of-a-kind. Valued primarily as a fine folk art example. $1,500–2,000.

Photographs from *Antique Ethnic Furniture* by Lyndon C. Viel.

Steiff wooden toy vehicles. $200–300, each.

Early model teddy bear by Richard Steiff, designer credited with originating the ever-popular teddy bear. $400–600.

Sailor doll by Steiff with pressed felt face. $450–550.

Elegant doll couple made by Steiff. $650–750, pair.

Photographs from *Steiff Teddy Bears, Dolls, and Toys* by Jean Wilson and Shirley Conway.

1978—$75-80   1979—$50-60   1980—$35-50

1981—$20-30   1982—$20-30   1983—$11 (issue price)

Carousel Collectible Series Keepsake Ornaments issued by Hallmark Card Co. All prices are for mint items for sale in secondary market complete with original boxes.

Photographs from *Hallmark Keepsake Ornaments: A Collector's Guide* by Clara Johnson Scroggins.

293

Hilda Clark celluloid desk clock, 7¾″×5½″, issued in 1901. $3,000.

Photograph from the *Wallace-Homestead Price Guide to Coca-Cola Collectibles* by Deborah Goldstein.

December, 1941, issue of *Motion Picture* magazine is collectible because of Claudette Colbert likeness on cover. $15.

Lobby card for *Duck Soup* is rare in that it pictures all four Marx Brothers. $400.

Photographs from *Collecting Movie Memorabilia* by Anthony Slide.

Pine jelly cupboard, 41½ " wide, 15 " deep, 51 " high, $300. Diamond Dye cabinet, 21 " wide, 10 " deep 30 " high, $300. "The Improved Union Churn No. 1, Pat April 27, 1875," 17 " wide, 14 " deep, 31 " high, $325.

Brides' boxes, 11½ " × 19 " × 7½ " deep. $1,050, each.

Photographs from *Country Furniture and Accessories with Prices* by Robert and Harriett Swedberg.

Onyx Glass

Opaline Glass

pany, Findlay, Ohio. It was only made for six months. Colors were silver, amber, orange, raspberry, orchid, and purple. Considered scarce today, it was referred to as Oriental Ware by the people who made it.

Cream pitcher, silver $382-410
Lamp, 2-post base, silver 895-932
Salt shaker, amber 172-192
Sugar bowl, covered 366-390
Syrup, silver floral design, silver-
    plated cap, 6¾" high, applied
    opalescent handle (ill.) 452-480
Tumbler, raspberry 275-285

Opalescent Glass

Opalescent Glass

Clear or colored with a milky white opalescence, it's usually blown or mold blown. Seldom were pieces made as a set. It was made by Sandwich in their early days. Many other companies also made it, and many other pieces were made.

Vase, white opalescent-to-clear,
    tree bark design, 11" high (ill.) . $ 64- 74
Vase, yellow opalescent with
    Spanish Lace design, frilled
    top, 6½" high (ill.) 92-107

Opaline Glass

This glass looks like the opal when held to a light—milky iridescence with a fiery orange background. Don't confuse it with the cheaper milk glass, also made in the late 1800s. Being reproduced.

Barber bottle, 11" high . . . . $ 72- 81
Bowl, birds, cherries, 10" dia. . . . 54- 65
Box, blue, pink/white flowers,
    hinged top (ill.) 272-320
Butter pats, rose, beaded, set
    of 6 . . . . 54- 63
Inkwell, blue, silver deposit,
    gold, fluted 77- 87
Lamp, apple green, 13½" high
    overall, French 110-120
Match holder, pipe-shaped,
    souvenir 27- 37
Perfume, opaque white/gold
    enamel, 1850s, England 162-172
Sugar bowl, rose/opaque white,
    covered, 4" high 88- 92
Tumbler, raised rose/flower
    pattern 84- 93
Vase, blue overlay, pink ground,
    6½" high 120-140
Vase, gray, classic lines, ruffled
    top, 4½" high 162-172
Vase, rose, floral, leaves, rose
    motif, 5½" high 138-144

Opera Glasses

Simply, these are small binocular telescopes, used at the opera, theater, etc. From the plainest type to the glasses illustrated here, they came in all sizes and shapes. The French and Germans made the best. Some were inlaid with precious gems. They're turning up in shops today as old estates are emptying their attics and basements.

American, leather covered, in
    leather case, Bosch and Lomb,
    1900s . . . . $ 52- 62

(continued

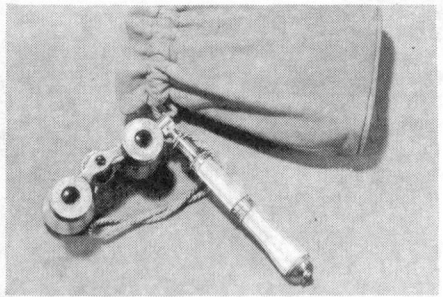

Opera Glasses

J. & E. Dickinson & Co.,
  Buffalo, N.Y. 60- 70
French, mother-of-pearl inlaid,
  early 1900s, removable handle
  (ill.) 78- 85
German, polished brass, Zeiss-
  Ikon lenses, velvet case, early
  1900s 64- 74

Optical Items

Optical Items

During the 1800s peddlers traveled from
farm to farm selling spectacles. Our ancestors bought the pair they could see best with,
a far cry from the practices in optometry
today.

Brass frames, adjustable in
  leather case (ill.) . . . . $ 47- 58
14k gold frames, adjustable,
  in leather case 84- 96
Metal frames, bifocals pasted on .   51- 62
Metal frames, no case 30- 41

Organs

No Victorian parlor was complete without
an organ. The cheaper models were made of
oak, while cherry, walnut and maple were
used in the more expensive models. Most
piano tuners can repair the bellows and
broken pedal straps. Tuning the pitch keys
requires only a musical ear and a wire coat
hanger. Type of wood, age, and condition
dictate the price.

Acme Queen parlor model, 5
  octaves, 11 stops, 2 octave
  coupler $1,150-1,350

Organs

Bilhorn telescope organ,
  portable 525- 650
Chestnut, complete with
  adjustable 3-legged stool,
  c. 1860   1,400-1,700
The Grand Sterling, walnut,
  c. 1880s   1,400-1,700
Happy Home, oak, c. 1904 . . .   1,100-1,300
Home Favorite piano-organ,
  made for Sears, Roebuck,
  c. 1903   1,100-1,250
Miller Organ Co. (ill.)   1,550-1,850
Oak, swing-out candleholders,
  display rack, c. 1880s   1,150-1,400

Overlay Glass

Overlay Glass

Too much of this type of glass is attributed
to the Sandwich Glass Company. Most of

what you find today is from the Sturbridge District in England, mid-1800s. Reproductions that should fool no one are sold in this country by a St. Louis, Missouri, firm.

Basket, opalescent, thorn handle,
yellow feet, green leaves,
amethyst stems (ill.) $462-485
Ewer, lavender, white opalescent
design, pink flowers (ill.) 292-325
Ewer, serrated top, blue to white,
pink/yellow/blue flowers, amber
handle, Mt. Washington (ill.) . . 432-442
Genuine Sandwich pieces start
at 375-420
Sturbridge-type pieces, slightly
less 362-384

Owens Pottery

OWENS FEROZA

Owens Pottery

The J.B. Owens Pottery Company produced this pottery in Ohio from the mid-1800s until 1933. It is comparable to Roseville and Weller.

Candleholder, Utopian, berry/leaf
decor, brown glaze . . . . $ 77- 88
Letter holder, floral decor, 3½"
high 62- 73
Mug, Utopian, fruit on vine,
5½" high 115-132
Pitcher, flowers, green leaves,
green ground, 10" high 108-121
Pitcher, orange/brown/yellow
floral leaves, Utopian 120-130
Pitcher, tankard-type, berries/
leaves, artist-signed 108-121
Vase, green leaves, green-to-pink
flowers, 5½" high 118-127
Vase, Lincoln, brown, tan, identical to an earlier Weller vase
(ill.) 95-107
Vase, Utopian, orange pansies,
6" high 92-107
Vase, Utopian, pansy decor,
6½" high 99-108

Paintings

Oil paintings, water colors, and pastels from the 17th, 18th, and 19th centuries, American or European, are highly collectible. American folk art is especially popular.

"The Ambush," signed F.
Remington, gouache
monotone . . . . $ 27,000+
"Autumn in the Catskills,"
signed Thomas Cole, oil,
c. 1817 2,700-3,200
"Autumn Landscape,"
signed Guy C. Wiggins,
oil, c. 1910 1,400-1,650
"Coast Scene," unsigned,
possibly Ben Foster,
c. 1890, oil 975-1,200
"A Country Stream," signed
Henry Pember Smith, oil,
c. 1875 1,100-1,400
"Fighting Meat," signed
C. M. Russell w/buffalo
skull remarque . . . . 7,500+
"Forest Opening," signed
Roswell Morse Shurtleff,
oil, c. 1879 1,200-1,400
"Italian Landscape," attrib-
uted to Richard Wilson,
R.A., c. 1750 . . . . 1,400+
"Ocean Wave at Twilight,"
signed A. Eugenie,
pastel 385- 450
"An Old Courtyard,"
signed Mark Anthony,
oil, c. 1855 1,400-1,700
"Seashore in Algiers,"
signed Frederic A. Bridg-
man, oil, c. 1912 1,200-1,400
"Smiling Countryside,"
signed W. H. Hilliard, oil,
c. 19th century 1,300-1,550
American Folk Paintings
"Civil War Generals," un-
signed, oil, c. 1865 1,500-1,700
"The Dayan Family,"
signed H. Pudor, oil,
c. 1858 1,400-1,800
"Gentlemen at a Fireplace,"
signed W. Twatman, oil,
c. 1843 1,350-1,600
"Landscape with Sawmill,"
signed G. Marston, oil,
c. 1863 1,200-1,400
"Mill by a Stream," signed
Virtue Howard, oil, c. 1853 . 900-1,400
"Thompson's Mill, Bowery
Bay, Astoria," signed E.
Doolittle, oil, c. 1877 . . . . . . 875- 950
"Village Election," un-
signed, c. 1860, oil 1,500-1,700
"Wife of a New England

(continued)

Sea Captain," signed
William LaFarge, oil,
c. 1860 1,500-1,700

Paintings, Miniature

Paintings, Miniature

These were usually painted on ivory; children and women in small oval metal or ivory frames. This type of painting has been done for centuries.

Children in garden, hand-
painted, ivory frame,
1800s $270- 295
Court lady, plumes in hair,
signed, in ivory frame 292- 343
Duchess of Devonshire,
hand-painted on ivory,
ivory frame 370- 410
Gentleman, American,
1860s, hand-painted,
ivory frame 392- 422
Lady, pink dress, pearls,
signed Davis, ivory
frame 432- 463
Man, ivory frame, signed
James Peale, 2" . . . . 5,500+
Officer, Continental Army,
1775, ivory frame 288- 320

silver and silver-plated wares, in addition to good blown glass objects such as candlesticks.

Barber bottle, chased silver,
plated, signed $228- 270
Bell, cut crystal, 5½" high 82- 92
Box, hinged silver inlay top, cut
glass 178- 185
Candlesticks, wheel cut, silver
leaves base, pr. 252- 272
Caster set in silver frame,
handled, 11" high 166- 172
Centerpiece, footed bowl, flint,
5¼" high, 12¼" dia. (ill.) . . . 210- 252
Compote, Old Colony pattern,
10" high 247- 262
Cracker jar, grape decor, blue,
shell feet 275- 310
Decanter, orange, ribbed inside,
5" high 118- 132
Lamp, blown red flowers,
signed base, 14" high
overall 750- 770
Mustache cup and saucer 178- 188
Paperweight, blue center,
bubble design, 3¼" dia. 1,100-1,320
Perfume, paperweight base,
flower finial on stopper, pr. . . 540- 550
Pitcher, cut crystal, 11½" high 221- 251
Plate, flowers/birds, 10" dia. . . 118- 132
Vase, overlay, cobalt, 6½" high 108- 121

Paper Money, American/Foreign

Find a reliable dealer. See **Clubs and Publications**, this Price Guide.

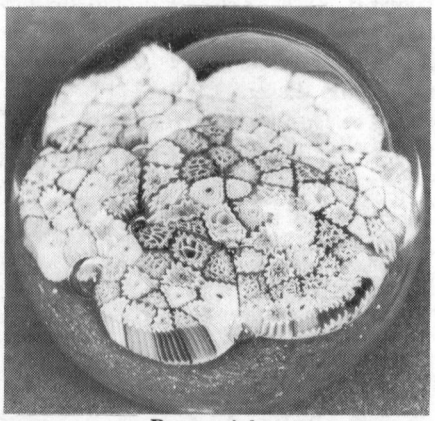

Paperweights

Paperweights

These small objects of glass were used to hold down paper on desks and tables. The Baccarats, Clichys, Gillilands, and Millefioris bring tremendous prices today when found

Pairpoint

Pairpoint

Successor to the Mt. Washington Glass Company, from 1880, these people made and authenticated. Scuffing a new one on cement or with sandpaper doesn't mean it's old. Look out for repros!

Baccarat, faceted white dahlia, 2½″ dia.	$4,200-4,700
Baccarat "flower" doorknobs, 2½″ dia., pr.	9,700+
Baccarat, flowers, salmon/ pink/white/rose, 2½″ dia.	4,200-4,600
Baccarat, Liberty Bell, contemporary	320- 365
Baccarat, millefiori, w/4 concentric rings of multicolor canes, 2½″ dia.	4,200-4,500
Baccarat, periwinkle bouquet, 3″ dia.	6,100-6,500
Baccarat, single rose, 2⅝″ dia.	4,300-4,550
Bohemian "Apple," speckled w/gilded "jewels," 3½″ dia.	420- 445
Bristol, engraved lacy filigree, 5-rosetted cluster, 3¼″ dia.	1,100-1,400
Brooklyn, millefiori, base cut in the form of a star, 3½″ dia.	775- 860
Clichy, millefiori, marked with "c" beneath, 2½″ dia.	4,200-4,450
Dorflinger, open flower design	275- 320
Glass, cardboard photo	36- 46
Jersey, lily, on stand, yellow/ rose flower, 9½″ high	1,100-1,350
Latticinio, 4″ high	120- 140
Millefiori, 4″ dia. (ill.)	175- 200
Millville, rose, half-open, green leaves, 4″ dia.	775- 850
New England sulphide portrait, w/portraits of Victoria and Albert, cameo profile, 2⅝″ dia.	985-1,100
Pairpoint, air bubbles, not signed	260- 280
St. Louis, fruits/pears/ cherries, 3⅛″ dia.	3,400-3,700
Sandwich, poinsettia, salmon/ pink petals, green leaves, 2⅝″ dia.	650- 720
Scottish, millefiori, by Pierre Ysart, hexagonal blossoms w/maker's initials, 3″ dia.	620- 640
Somverville, Five Little Pigs, on a grassy mound, 5″ dia.	2,800-3,200
Val Saint Lambert, thin overlay, faceted and cut, 2½″ dia.	2,400-2,900
Whitefriars, millefiori, on amber gold ground, 2⅜″ dia., c. 1848	440- 492
Zanesville, millefiori, 2⅝″ dia.	1,250-1,375

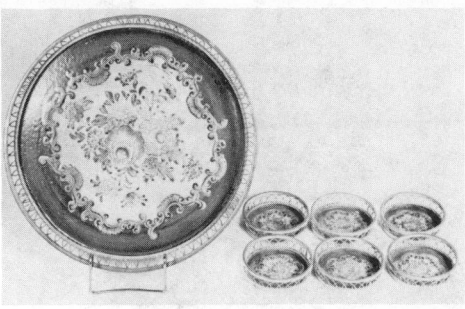

Papier-Mache

Papier-Mache

Chewed paper is a better word for it. Paper is soaked in water, ground up, molded into forms, japanned and dried at a high heat, around 300 degrees. The finished product is extremely tough and durable. A lot of so-called Chippendale trays were made by this method, then decorated.

Basket, MOP inlay, butterflies/ flowers, 11″ dia.	$150-160
Box, pearl inlay, 4″ square	52- 62
Box, snuff, pewter inlay in top, hinged	47- 57
Easter egg, red, chick and mama	48- 52
Figurine, bird, glass eyes, 4″ high	50- 61
Inkstand, birds, floral leaves, 3″ square	71- 80
Inkwell, MOP inlay, 8½″ wide	77- 87
Lap desk, black, brass fittings, MOP floral decor	181-191
Lap desk, pearl inlay, floral decor, slant-top cover	88- 92
Stationery rack, Oriental gilt, 7″ wide	77- 86
Tray, gold Chinese decor	52- 62
Tray, Japanese, embossed and painted, 12″ dia., with 6 coasters (ill.)	40- 50
Tray, lacquered, black ground, birds, flowers	192-210
Wine tray, recesses for decanters, pearl inlay	144-153

Parian Ware

First made by Copeland in England in 1842, by Fenton at Bennington, Vermont, in 1847, and by the U.S. Pottery Company, same town, 1853-1858. It was also made by Morrison and Carr, New York City, and by the Southern Porcelain Company, Kaolin,

(continued)

Parian Ware

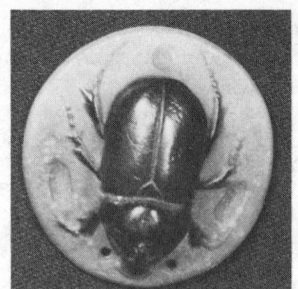

Pâte de Verre

South Carolina. The best American made is attributed to Fenton and U.S. Pottery Company.

Bowl, lilies, 5" dia. . . . . $ 79- 89
Box, embossed flowers, white,
   cover, 3½" dia. 88-108
Bust of Dante, 5" high 123-142
Bust of Dickens, 6¼" high 110-124
Bust of Shakespeare, 8" high 132-142
Candleholder, Cupid, grapes,
   tinted leaves, 7" high 140-150
Creamer, miniature, wheat
   sheafs, blue-tint 110-118
Cup/saucer, pond lily 92-109
Ewer, ring handle, Copeland,
   1850s, 8" high 180-210
Figure, bust of Venus, signed,
   9" high 132-142
Figure, dog chewing bone 99-108
Pitcher, calla lilies and basket-
   weave design, 10" high 380-398
Pitcher, hanging game, 10" high . 368-392
Pitcher, lavender, white, babes
   in woods 192-224
Pitcher, Niagara Falls design,
   U.S. Pottery Co. 670-699
Plaque, Greek goddess, floral
   border, 11" square 232-242
Sugar bowl, pond lily 152-162
Tray, Bennington type 142-168
Tumbler, classic figures, 4¼"
   high 70- 80
Vase, blue/white, Bennington
   type 168-174
Vase, corn decor, 6½" high 180-190
Vase, Grape pattern, 8" high (ill.) 142-152

Pate de Verre

Translated, Pate de Verre means paste of glass. This is a molded glass which is formed from ground lead glass. The resulting powder or crystals are made into a paste by a complicated formula. The glass paste is then molded, fired, and carved. As early as 1400 B.C. this formula was known and the French seem to have revived it, with the Daum Brothers leading the way. It's been discovered as a medium for sculpting by contemporary artists in the past few years.

Atomizer, blue/brown, pine
   cones . . . . $ 950-1,100
Bowl, cream/yellow, orange
   sunflowers, signed A.
   Walter, Nancy 580- 650
Figurine, monkey reading
   book, signed 1,350-1,500
Lamp, leaves/berries, gold/
   white, 5" high, signed A.
   Walter, Nancy 1,475-1,675
Medallion, scarab beetle,
   sienna coloration, 2¾" dia.
   (ill.) 485- 562
Pendant, brown/black beetle
   on gray ground, signed A.
   Walter, Nancy 470- 540

Pâte Sur Pâte

This means paste on paste. Its wares were designs in relief, this being achieved by adding layer on layer of thin pottery paste to the design. Solon was the most famous of the Frenchmen making it, but the best known comes from the Minton factory in England. An original, signed M. Solon, would be quite valuable today.

Bowl, cameo center, seraph,
   green ground, Germany . . $ 262- 282
Candy dish, handles, pedes-
   tal, signed, 5" high 1,350-1,500
Picture, cherubs, black/blue/
   white, velvet mat framed . 575- 650

Plaque, muse, blue ground,
signed, 4″×8″ 475- 565
Plate, blue/gold/white, clas-
sical figures, 9″ dia. 245- 272
Plate, blue/white medallions,
gold edge, signed, 9″ dia. . .   352- 382
Vase, light green ground,
white flowers, signed, 9″
high 372- 410
Vase, white/blue medallions,
green floral, signed Birk,
7″ high 542- 620

Peachblow, Gunderson

Peachblow, Gunderson

The Gunderson Glass Company, succes-
sors to the Pairpoint Company, which was
formerly the Mt. Washington Glass Company, all at New Bedford, Massachusetts,
made this "new" Peachblow from 1952 until
1957. It was heavier and not as well colored
as the earlier Peachblows.

Cup/saucer, reeded, opal handle . . $142-153
Decanter 260-270
Goblet 225-245
Pitcher, water 275-295
Toothpick, pink/white, 2½″ high
(ill.) 92-107
Toothpick holder, 1¾″ high 142-152
Tumbler 152-162
Vase 275-320

Peachblow, Mt. Washington

New Bedford, Massachusetts, 1886. It
shades from rose color at top to pale blue in
lower portion. Don't buy it if you don't know
it. Too many repros.

Basket, bride's, 10½″×
4¼″, in quadruple-plated
frame . . . . $ 840- 885
Biscuit jar, cameo, sterling
silver ring, lid, bail 1,400-1,575

Peachblow, Mt. Washington

Biscuit jar, enameled decor,
sterling silver ring, lid,
bail 752- 772
Bowl, bride's, footed, glossy
finish, 6½″ dia. 542- 572
Bowl, finger, fluted edge,
acid finish 525- 610
Bowl, rose, fluted lip, 4¼″
high, acid finish 525- 610
Butter dish, glossy finish,
ITP, glossy finish   1,500-1,750
Creamer, acid finish,
applied "rope" handle,
4¼″ high   1,450-1,700
Cruet, blown glass stopper,
ITP, 6″ high (scarce)   3,450-3,700
Cup, punch 575- 670
Cup/saucer, glossy finish . . .   720- 780
Darner, pear-shaped, glossy
finish 410- 450
Decanter, ITP, 8½″ high . . .   2,800-3,200
Muffineer, triple-plated cap,
5½″ high   1,500-1,800
Pitcher, applied clear
handle, ITP, 9¼″ high   2,300-2,400
Pitcher, decorated with
flowers, acid finish,
James Montgomery's
poem on side (ill.)   2,500-2,750
Plate, acid finish, 5½″ dia. . .   310- 330
Plates, set of 6, 5″ dia.,
all   2,400-2,500
Salt/pepper shakers,
tomato-shaped, floral
decor, pr. 685- 742
Toothpick holder, glossy
finish, 4¾″ high 650- 677
Toothpick holder, glossy
finish, ITP 645- 720
Tumbler, water, glossy
finish, ITP 685- 740
Tumbler, whiskey, glossy
finish 625- 685

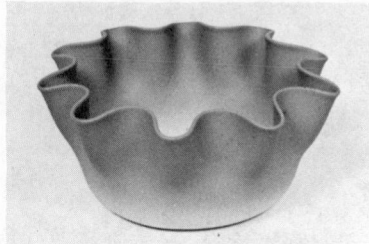

Peachblow, New England

Peachblow, New Martinsville

Peachblow, New England

Also called Wild Rose, it shades from rose at top to white in lower portion. Edward Libbey patented it in 1886 under the Wild Rose name. Being reproduced.

Bottle, perfume, 4" high . . . . . $	652-	682
Bowl, bride's, acid finish	452-	472
Bowl, finger, fluted lip, 4½" dia.	280-	295
Bowl, finger, satin finish, 5" dia. (ill.)	681-	695
Bowl, rose, crimped top	778-	792
Bowl, tricornered, 5¼" dia. . .	452-	510
Butter dish, glossy finish	1,700-	1,800
Creamer, applied clear handle, 4½" high	1,400-	1,500
Creamer, applied reeded handle, 4¼" high	1,400-	1,550
Cruet, clear stopper	1,250-	1,450
Cup, punch	492-	520
Darner, apple, acid finish	372-	452
Darner, pear, glossy finish . . .	420-	442
Decanter, blown glass stopper, applied reeded handle, 9½" high	3,300-	3,700
Lamp base, font only, glossy finish	875-	950
Pitcher, applied clear handle, glossy finish, 10¼" high . . .	2,200-	2,475
Pitcher, applied twisted "rope" handle, satin finish, 11" high	2,200-	2,400
Salt/peppers, triple-plated caps, acid finish, pr.	595-	645
Shade, lamp, 10½" dia.	685-	775
Sugar bowl, applied clear handles, 4½" high	750-	762
Toothpick holder, 3½" high . .	520-	542
Tumbler, glossy finish, 5" high	620-	670
Vase, crimped top, satin finish, 6¾" high	1,100-	1,200
Vase, fluted lip, acid finish, 7½" high	920-	985

Peachblow, New Martinsville

Its factory name was Muranese. Made at the New Martinsville, West Virginia, factory in the late 1800s and until 1907, Joseph Webb of the famous Sturbridge, England, family invented it. It got its name, Peachblow, in the early 1940s when antiques dealers tried to unload large amounts of it, following the success of the famous Wheeling Peachblow. It is good glass but doesn't compare to any of the three famous Peachblows—Mt. Washington, New England, and Wheeling.

Bowl, fluted edges, 8½" dia., Sunburst	$220-240
Bride's basket w/frame, 6" dia., Sunglow	210-235
Bride's basket w/frame, 8" dia., Sunburst	260-270
Bride's basket w/frame, 10" dia., Sunburst	262-275
Lamp shade, Frosted Salmon, 3½" high	158-167
Large berry bowl, Sunburst (ill.) .	242-252
Small berry bowl, Sunglow	182-192
Sugar shaker, original cap, Sunrise	142-152
Syrup jug, metal cap, 6" high . . .	144-158
Vase, floral panels, fluted lip, Salmon, 8" high	172-182
Vase, ruffled lip, Sunray, 7½" high	210-240

Peachblow, Wheeling

Peachblow, Wheeling

Hobbs, Brockunier and Company, Wheeling, West Virginia, made this fine ware, simulating the coloring of the original Morgan Peach Blow vase which was supposedly sold at auction (the original from the collection of a Chinese gentleman named Wang Ye) for some $18,000 in the late 1800s. The Wheeling type is red-rose at the top, shading to a bright yellow at the bottom. The rare vases, glossy or acid finish, on a gargoyle stand, are priceless today. Being reproduced.

Butter dish	$2,200-2,400
Cruet, glossy, with stopper, 6¾" high	1,350-1,475
Morgan vase on gargoyle stand, glossy finish 15½"	2,500-2,700
Pitcher, acid finish	2,400-2,600
Pitcher, rose to yellow, white liner, 5" high (ill.)	1,700-1,850
Rose bowl	1,500-1,700
Tumbler, glossy finish, rose to yellow, 3½" high (ill.)	485- 645
Water set, glossy finish, pitcher/6 tumblers	5,600+

Peanut Collectibles
Photo courtesy Planters Peanuts

Peanut Collectibles

It all began in 1906, in Wilkes-Barre, Pennsylvania, when Amedeo Obici and Mario Peruzzi decided to go into the peanut business. But it wasn't until 1916, when a local schoolboy drew Mister Peanuts, that the world suddenly became aware of goobers and how great they tasted. See **Clubs and Publications, (Planters)**, this Price Guide.

Barrel jar, glass, peanut finial on 8" lid (ill.)	$295-330
Mr. Peanut alarm clock	28- 34
Mr. Peanut ashtray, gold	28- 39

Mr. Peanut ashtray, silver, anniversary issue, 1906-1956	62- 71
Mr. Peanut "Bic" lighter	24- 32
Mr. Peanut drink stirrers, 6 in set, all	3- 6
Mr. Peanut jointed wooden doll (rare)	142-152
Mr. Peanut measuring spoon	3- 4
Mr. Peanut peanut butter spreader	3- 4
Mr. Peanut serving spoon	3- 4
Mr. Peanut tin store sign, 14"×20"	25- 35
Mr. Peanut watch	30- 40
Planters nut chopper, fits 8-oz. Planters cans	19- 29
Planters paintbook, presidents of U.S.	17- 30
Planter Peanut belt buckle	11- 20
Planters Peanut greeting card	18- 23
Planters Peanut lapel pin	14- 18
Planters Peanut wall clock (rare)	162-172
Planters ski cap	9- 12
Planters 12-month coloring book	16- 25

Peking Glass

Peking Glass

Chinese cameo glass, 18th and 19th centuries. Scarce today. Some of the finest comes from the Ch'ing Dynasty (Tung Chih period, 1862-1874).

Beaker, bronze-form, painted enamel figures	$ 720- 775
Bowl, blue, blown, 4½" dia.	2,400+
Bowl, cameo yellow raised flowers, 6½" high	475- 530
Box, green, enamel, lid inlaid with pearl	1,100-1,300

Plate, jade green, 9" dia.	1,200-1,400
Snuff bottle, amber color, quartz stopper	1,200-1,400
Snuff bottle, black/white	925-1,100
Tumbler, gray/green, 4¼" high	540- 620
Vase, cameo yellow raised floral decor, 4½" high	925-1,100
Vase, emerald green, Mei P'ing form, 8" high	375- 400
Vase, white ground, carved red flowers, 8½" high, on box stand	850- 900

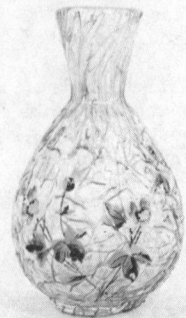

Peloton Glass

Peloton Glass

This glass was first made in Bohemia in 1880. Small threads of colored glass were rolled into the surface as the hot glass was removed from the furnace. Sometimes the pieces were dipped in an acid bath to give them a satin finish. Another item being reproduced.

Cracker jar, pink/red, blue ground, silver lid	$124-132
Cruet, multicolors on clear overshot	470-520
Pitcher, pink/blue, enameled decor, white opaque filaments	162-180
Pitcher, pink and blue threads, clear background, pink handle	172-182
Rose bowl, pink/blue miniature (rare)	262-268
Tumbler, blue filaments, 6" high	158-163
Vase, green red, yellow threads, ruffled lip, 5" high	182-192
Vase, miniature, pink threads on clear glass, enameled white flowers, 4" high, green leaves (ill.)	232-252
Vase, yellow, blue, red threads, clear background, 8" high	255-267

Pennsylvania Dutch Items

Pennsylvania Dutch Items

The Lord's hand helped these gracious people and today many of us are fortunate to know them and to appreciate their work.

Cabbage slicer, 22" long	$ 120- 140
Chest, miniature, handmade lock, domed lid, russet background, yellow borders, yellow tulips, 8¼" wide (ill.)	650- 740
Coverlet, blue/green/red/ white, "Mount Joy, Lancaster County"	2,175-2,450
Jewel chest, Dutch graining, "Corelia Brunning" on lid	362- 372
Whatnot, hanging type, green ground, red decorations, 11½" high (ill.)	210- 242

Pens and Pencils

Pens and Pencils

The steel pen was invented in 1870 by Samuel Harrison, but Richard Esterbrook first produced it commercially in the 1880s. Holders were made of fine materials such as gold, silver, and mother-of-pearl. George Parker and L. E. Waterman were both fountain pen pioneers, although Waterman is credited with its invention in 1884. W. A. Sheaffer invented the lever-filling fountain pen in 1913. Wahl (later, Wahl-Eversharp) made pens after WW I. In 1929, more than 34 million dollars' worth of fountain pens were produced in this country. Mechanical pencils have been around for years, and there are thousands of "advertising" pencils available.

Pens

Conklin

Dunn, 1922, black/red, gold-filled trim	$ 7- 9
1923, hard rubber case, gold-filled trim	12- 17
1923, Model 25R, lady's, ribbon on cap	33- 40
1925, Endura, ring top, spatter green	27- 33

Esterbrook

1928, green, gold-filled trim	12- 15
1934, red, gold-filled trim	11- 14

Eversharp

1933, Doric, Gold Seal, lady's	19- 26
1933, Doric, Gold Seal, man's	78- 84
1935, Midget, spatter green, gold-filled trim	9- 15
1944, Skyline, gold-filled trim	14- 22
Lady Webster, miniature	23- 28

Moore

1896, non-leakable, black case (ill.)	13- 19
1903, non-leakable, hard rubber case	43- 50
1907, lady's, black, hard rubber case, gold rings	13- 18
1916, red/rose, etched band on cap, 14K nib	14- 22

Mother-of-Pearl

Black rubber case	12- 16
Onyx handle, 14K nib	33- 42

Parker

1895, black rubber case, 14K gold trim	43- 52
1899, Model 20, hard rubber case	28- 34
1923, Big Red, Duofold point	87- 97
1929, Duofold deluxe, black/pearl, gold bands on cap	133-140
1942, Blue Diamond, blue/black, gold-filled trim	23- 31

Sheaffer

1923, White Dot, green, gold-plated trim	55- 63
1925, White Dot, ring top, black, gold-filled trim	18- 25
1932, spatter green, gold-plated trim	18- 25

Wahl

1918, silver overlay case	28- 34
1922, gold-plated	13- 19
1928, ball clip, gold-plated	27- 35

Waterman

1886, Model 12, spatter brown, 14K gold bands	39- 46
1913, Model 54, hard rubber case, silver-plated trim	34- 42
1918, Model 55, hard rubber case, silver-plated trim	70- 78
1925, Model 71, red, hard rubber case, gold-plated trim	69- 77
1928, Lady Patricia, sterling silver case	47- 56
1933, Model 5, black, gold-plated trim	35- 43
1943, Commando	13- 19
1947, spatter gray, silver-plated trim	7- 11

Pencils

Eversharp

1915, silver	15- 21
1920, silver-plated	6- 10
1931, silver-plated	6- 10

Mechanical, Advertising

Budweiser, whistle on end	9- 13
Castle Beer	6- 10
Dodge Autos	10- 14
Grand Canyon Route	8- 11
Heidlicker Beer	6- 9
Kitchenware Products	6- 8
Pure Oil Company	6- 9
Quaff-A-Kola	5- 8
Whirlpool	5- 8

Parker

1923, Duofold senior, blue, usual mechanism	44- 52
1929, Duofold deluxe, black/pearl, gold bands	46- 53
1936, Ronson, penciliter, spatter green, rodium-plated	27- 35
1948, Model 51, gold-plated	20- 26

Sheaffer

1917, gold-filled case, usual mechanism	17- 25
1921, ring top, gold-filled case, usual mechanism	10- 14
1926, White Dot, gold-filled	14- 18
1936, White Dot, black, gold-plated trim	13- 19

Wahl-Eversharp

1924, ring top, gold-filled case	9- 14

(continued)

Waterman

1918, Model 454, sterling silver
case 60- 68
1926, sterling silver case 36- 42
1933, Model 5, black, gold-plated
trim 13- 19

Perfume Bottles

Perfume Bottles

These have been around for centuries in all sizes and shapes. Made of glass, silver, pure gold, carved from jade, inlaid with precious stones, even "Avon calling!"

Chinese jade, dragon motif,
mid-1800s $120-132
Cornucopia, 2″ long 48- 58
Cut glass, sterling silver cap with
applicator attached, early
1900s   110-122
DeVilbiss atomizer, iridescent,
gold trim, flower motif   128-138
English lavender bottle 16- 27
Moser perfume bottle, multi-
colored enamel, Czechoslova-
kia, 6½″ high   232-242
Peking glass, 3″ high (ill.) 70- 80
St. Louis, paper label, acid etched,
10¾″ high   262-272
Sterling silver/glass, 2″ long (ill.) .   70- 80
Tiffany glass, signed LCT
Favrile   222-252

Peters and Reed Pottery

Though established by John Peters and Adam Reed in 1898, it wasn't until 1912, when Moss Aztec was developed, that the first of the art lines was introduced. Other art lines were Pereco, Landsun, Chromal, Persian, and Montene. These finishes were semi-matt in various colors, blended colors, designs, and iridescent variegated finishes.

Frog, Landsun, 4″ long . . . . $ 30- 39
Pitcher, Cavalier design, 7½″
high   172-190
Pitcher, wreath design, 11″ high .   120-132
Vase, Chromal, Art Deco scene,
blue/green, 4¾″ high   108-118
Vase, Moss Aztec, leaf design,
13″ high   92-107
Vase, Pereco, teal blue on Land-
sun blank, 9½″ high 78- 88

Pewabic Pottery

Mary Chase Perry founded this pottery at Detroit, Michigan, in 1903. She married William Buck Stratton in 1918. The business closed in 1961. Pewabic PP Detroit and PP Detroit are the marks usually found. Paper labels were also used.

Inkstand, green . . . . $ 62- 72
Lamp, brown luster glaze, 11″
high   188-220
Lamp, leaf stem, puffball, 12¼″
high   178-198
Tile, biblical symbol 52- 62
Vase, copper colored, 7″ high   172-182
Vase, dark iridescence, 10″ high .   170-180
Vase, green matt glaze, 7½″ high   188-192

Pewter

Pewter

An alloy of tin with lead, brass or copper, Colonial pieces are rare because the early settlers were not permitted to bring much of the raw material with them when they settled in America. Also, many pieces were melted down to make bullets during our Revolution. Pieces marked pewter generally were made after WWI. Older pieces have English or American touchmarks. **Never** polish old pewter. See **Clubs and Publications**, this Price Guide.

Basins

American, 7″ or 8″ dia.	$ 145-	160
English, 19th century, 11½″ dia.	210-	245
Incised mark of Daniel Curtis, c. 1830	470-	520

Beakers

American, 3¼″ high	60-	70
American, 3½/8″ high	78-	90
English, 19th century, 3″ high	84-	93

Bowls

American, 5″ dia.	72-	81
American, 11″ dia.	162-	180
Baptismal, broad-scooped rim, footed, 19th century .	120-	135
English, crescent, footed, 19th century, 7″ dia.	168-	179
English, hammered, footed, 9¼″ dia.	110-	122

Boxes

Match/pencils, ribboned incised cover	108-	121
Storage, indented corners, 19th century	84-	93

Candlesticks

American, beaded base, gadrooned edges, pr.	170-	190
American, fluted edge, boubeches, pr.	172-	184
American, plain, beaded edge, 9″ high, pr.	162-	172
English, baluster, domed foot, 19th century, pr.	310-	340
English, baluster, push-up, 7½″ high, pr.	222-	242

Caster Stand

5-bottle, 19th century	88-	98

Chalices

American, pedestal, 19th century	352-	372
English, knobbed stem on molded foot, pr.	440-	475
English, molded rim, circular foot, 19th century	410-	420
Incised William Calder, 6″ dia.	520-	532

Chargers

American, 14″ dia.	358-	375
American, 18″ dia.	420-	429
English, incised Samuel Duncombe, 18″ dia.	452-	500

English, 19th century, 14″ dia.	360-	382
English, touchmark, 14″ dia.	391-	420

Coffeepots

American, baluster body, scrolled handle, 12¼″ high .	210-	227
American, lighthouse shape, 11½″ high	245-	272
American, touchmark, 11¼″ high	178-	192
English, touchmark, 19th century	262-	288
Reed & Barton, 13″ high	170-	190

Creamers

American, marked Genuine Pewter, 20th century	42-	52
American, 19th century, 3¼″ high	110-	120
American, touchmark, 4½″ high	124-	132
English, incised tower, 19th century	92-	108
English, touchmark, 19th century	88-	98

Cups

American, baby's name on side, 3½″ high	72-	90
American, marked Genuine Pewter, 4″ high	35-	60
English, loving, 19th century	82-	94
English, 19th century, 4″ high	72-	84
English, touchmark, 3¼″ high	77-	85
English, wedding, 3-handled, 19th century	142-	152

Flagons

English, incised Pemberton, 10″ high	420-	452
English, touchmark, 19th century, 12¼″ high	462-	492
English, touchmark, 10″ high	422-	441

Flasks

American, Civil War, eagle motif	128-	135
American, marked Genuine Pewter	47-	57
English, regimental, 19th century	142-	152
English, touchmark, 19th century	112-	122

Humidor

American, cork-lined, 7″ high	60-	70

Inkstands

American, blue glass liner, holds 6 pens, 19th century .	121-	132
American, touchmark, 19th century	141-	152
English, touchmark, 18th century	162-	172
English, touchmark, 19th century	132-	142

(continued)

American, touchmark, 19th
century, 10¼" high 154- 162
American, trumpet shape, 9"
high 98- 107
English, touchmark, 19th
century 210- 221

Phoenix Glass

Phoenix Glass

This firm, located in Beaver County, Pennsylvania, made a fabricated Pearl Satin glass in the late 1800s. It also produced other glass, some rather good for the period. Don't confuse it with Lalique.

Basket, dogwood, 5" wide . . . . . $ 72- 84
Bowl, girl in bathing suit, satin
finish, pink/green 158-172
Box, covered, green, floral decor,
6" square 88- 99
Candlestick, blue, swirl stem,
4½" high 52- 70
Ginger jar, birds, cover, 9½"
high 92-107
Lamp, fruit decor, brown leaves,
vines (ill.) 150-160
Plate, cherry, 4" dia. 77- 84
Teapot, gold/wine color, 7" high . 62- 72
Vase, blue ground, birds in flight,
8" high 120-130
Vase, pillow, white geese in relief
on blue ground, 8½" high 158-168
Vase, pinecone decor, purple,
7" high 98-107
Vase, pink ground, sculptured
trumpet vines, original label . . 114-126
Vase, yellow ground, dancing
girls, blue/ivory 120-130

Phonographs

Thomas Edison invented the phonograph in 1877 and for years it was known as the talking machine. Many firms manufactured their own versions. Old Edisons are particularly collectible. See **Clubs and Publications,** this Price Guide.

Columbia AG Grand $1,900-2,200
Columbia BI 440- 470
Columbia BK, 14" brass belled
horn 395- 420
Columbia, cylinder 520- 545
Columbia Grafonala, 1911,
Regent model 380- 420
Columbia Gramaphone, 1886,
12 cylinders 770- 820
Columbia Grand Graphophone, 1905 . . . . 285- 320
Columbia, keywind 520- 562
Edison Amberola 422- 465
Edison, inside horn,
Amberola, 30 cylinder
records 462- 520
Edison Maroon Gem, original
K reproducer 910- 972
Edison, Model C, 12 cylinder
records 620- 650
Edison Suitcase Home 480- 520
Gem Graphophone Talking
Machine, 1902 . . . . 375- 420
Graphophone Grand, 1903 . . . 381- 410
Grand Peerless Talking
Machine, 24 cylinder
records 600- 675
Modernola, walnut case, complete with lampshade 1,900-2,200
Regina Graphophone, disc-
type, 1902 . . . . 365- 420
Sear's Cecelian, 1924 . . . . 320- 345
Victor, Gold Medal, 1905, dog
trademark 540- 575
Victor, Model E, horn, table
model 352- 372
Victor, Model VV-IV, oak
case, 1906 . . . . 440- 470
Victor, Royal, 1905, "dog" . . . 482- 492
Victrola, VV-S-215 (Thompson
neutrodyne radio on left
side) 520- 535
Vitanola, 1925 . . . . 380- 420

Phonograph Records

The 78 rpm market generally breaks down into four major groups: Popular—dance bands, combos, instrumental units; Classical—the "straights," strictly defined, operatic companies; Jazz-Blues—intimate, one-to-one, a small club, etc.; Country-Western—collect anything you can get your hands on. H-O-T!

311

(continued)

Ajax, Banner, Blue Disc, Brunswick, Capitol, Comet, Decca, Emerson, HMV (His Master's Voice), Melotone, Oriole, Regal, Varsity, and Victor are a few of the many record companies who, struggling and failing, brought music to what it is today.

Photography

Photography

Mathew B. Brady, best known for his photographs of Lincoln and the Civil War, created the public's interest in photography. Today, millions enjoy this fascinating hobby. See **Clubs and Publications**, this Price Guide.

QRS Kamra, bakelite box, for
    35mm film, late 1920s   61-   71
Ray box, for 30½"×30½"
    plates   77-   87
Reflex folding focal, for plates,
    postcard size, c. 1912 . . . . .   162- 172
Rex magazine, for 4"×5"
    plates, c. late 1890s 152- 162
Scovill folding view, for
    5"×8" plates, Waterbury
    lens, c. late 1880s 235- 255
Seneca box, for 4"×5" plates .   32-   44
Trio No. 1A folding, for 120
    film   34-   43
Univex plastic box, for No. 00
    film, model A, c. 1936   19-   22
Vive No. 1 box, for plates,
    c. 1890s, made by Vive
    Camera Co. 108- 111
Vokar I rangefinder, for 35mm
    film, c. 1940 . . . .   120- 130
Welta folding, for 35mm film,
    c. 1930   42-   52
Wirgin Stereo, for 35mm film,
    Steinheil Cassar lenses   72-   82

HO roll—used on small pipe organs.
XP roll—used on style X expression piano,
    also style Phono-Grand.

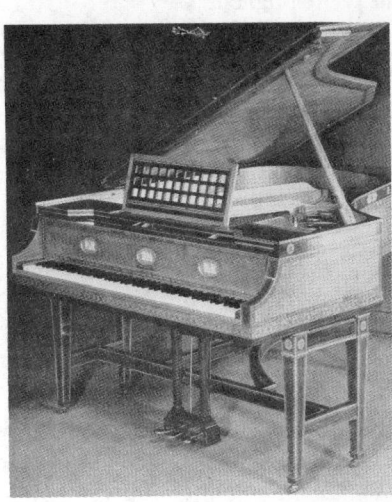

Pianos

Pianos

Maker, condition, year made—these dictate
price.

American Home upright,
    maple, full size, c. 1903 . . . .$ 462- 490
Baldwin Baby Grand, c. late
    1890s 680- 740
Beckwith Cabinet Grand,
    upright, c. 1890s   1,600-1,700
Broadwood Grand   3,400-3,600
Chickering Ampico-A Grand .   5,500-5,700
Cranisch & Bach, rosewood,
    c. 1890s   4,750-5,220
Emerson Oak Grand   5,600-5,800
Kimball Grand   4,550-4,750
Schiller, c. 1890s, upright   1,975-2,400
Sears, Roebuck Home Favor-
    ite, mahogany, c. 1890s . . .   940-1,100
Steinway & Sons Grand, 7'
    rosewood case, c. 1876 . . . .   18,000+
Steinway & Sons Grand,
    inlaid satinwood/
    mahogany w/Wedgwood
    porcelain medallions (ill.) . .   8,500-9,400

Piano and Organ Rolls

Piano and Organ Rolls

Now that player pianos are making a come-
back, here's a simplified guide to tell you
which piano rolls work on which type player
piano and/or organ.

Average price, in working condition . . $7-9
    (Certain Ampico rolls bring $55
    or more.)

Piano Roll Guide

A roll—basic coin piano roll of nickelodeon
    industry.
G roll—later 4X rolls. Keyboard style L, G,
    KT, KT special.
H roll—Styles J, H and most Seeburg
    photoplayers.
MSR roll—Styles MO, celeste and most
    Seeburg photoplayers, interchangeable
    with H rolls.

Pianos, Player

A self-playing piano uses suction which is
controlled by a paper roll passing over a
tracker bar. When the valves are actuated,
the pneumatics (tiny bellows), which operate
on the piano action, cause the notes to play.

313

(continue'

Although this type of mechanism was made by many companies, three firms dominated the field into the 1930s: Ampico, Duo-Art, and Welte-Mignon.

Alder Manufacturing Co.,
Amphion player
mechanism $1,650-1,900
Autotone Piano Co., Hard-
man Peck player
mechanism 1,800-2,000
Beckwith Pianos, sold only
by Sears, Roebuck;
Beckwith's, Simplex, and
Standard Player
mechanisms 1,600-1,900
Boudoir Piano Co., Amphion
mechanism 1,800-2,100
Cable Co. Pianos, used their
own mechanisms 1,700-1,975
Chickering and Sons, Gul-
bransen mechanism, also
Ampico Reproducing
player mechanism 2,100-2,500
Clarendon Piano Co.,
Amphion and Pratt &
Read player mechanisms . 1,600-1,750
Emerson Piano Co.,
Amphion, Angelus, Sim-
plex, and Standard playing
mechanisms 1,800-2,200
Grinnell Brothers, Aeolian
and Lester player
mechanisms 1,800-2,200
Harrison Piano, Kimball
Regular player mechanism 1,900-2,200
Knight-Brinkerhoff, Stan-
dard player mechanism . . . 2,000-2,250
Laffargue Piano Co.,
Amphion player
mechanism 1,875-1,985
Lindemann and Sons,
Angelus player mechanism 2,200-2,400
Melbourne Piano, Baldwin
player mechanism 2,100-2,350
Modello Player Piano, made
by Baldwin, Manualo
player mechanism 2,000-2,300
Norris and Hyde, National
Air-O-Player mechanism . . 2,200-2,450
Pianola, trademark name
used by Aeolian for their
player pianos 2,400-2,600
Regal Pianos, Standard
player mechanism 2,200-2,475
Sohmer and Co., Welte-
Mignon player mechanism 2,400-2,600
Straube Piano Co., made
their own player mecha-
nisms, also used Standard
mechanism 2,100-2,500
Stuyvesant Pianos, Aeolian
player mechanism 1,875-2,200

Weber & Co., Aeolian and
Duo-Art player
mechanisms 2,500-2,800
Wheelock Piano Co., Aeolian
and Duo-Art player
mechanisms 2,475-2,800

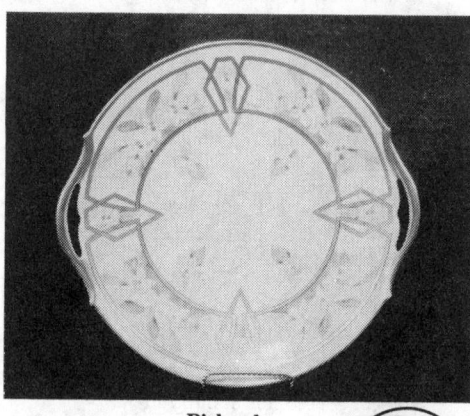

Pickard

Pickard

Wilder Pickard founded his company in Illinois around 1894. They're still in business. Once buying their pottery blanks from other firms, they now make their own.

Bowl, flowers and leaves, gold,
signed . . . . $ 92-108
Bowl, fruit, leaves, gold fluted
top, 8″ high 84- 94
Box, powder, with lid, Art Deco
flowers, gold/black/cream,
signed 190-220
Cake plate, hand-painted, artist-
signed, 10¾″ dia. (ill.) 72- 82
Candlesticks, etched gold, 4″
high, pr. 90-108
Chocolate pot, pearlized ground,
white, orchids, green leaves . . . 275-285
Compote, violet/gold, artist
signed, 8″ high 252-272
Creamer and sugar, forest scene,
gold handles and rim, pr. 141-151
Dish, open handles, 8″ dia. 40- 50
Pitcher, cider, gold color, blue
trim 77- 87
Pitcher, orange poppies, signed
Fuchs 82- 92
Plate, gold center, flowers,
signed, 7″ dia. 42- 52
Relish dish, pink/blue, floral,
signed 40- 50
Salt/pepper, all gold, 4″ high,
pr. 50- 60

Teapot, gold colors, 5″ high,
cover 67- 77
Tray, garden scene, signed E.
Challinor   425-460
Vase, floral, gold, signed,
12″ high 77- 87
Vase, peacock, multicolored,
paper label, signed E.
Challinor   775-845
Vase, scenic, signed Marke   101-112

Pickle Casters

Pickle Casters

Consisting of a glass jar sitting in a metal frame, with tongs and/or fork, usually made of quadruple plate, sometimes sterling silver. Considered a novelty of the late 1800s, they were more decorative than functional.

Amber, Cane pattern $200-225
Amberina, ITP, spoonholder and
tongs   495-535
Amethyst, enameled flowers   310-342
Birds/flowers, enameled, blue/
white, silver fork, frame   142-152
Blue looping, white threaded
glass, silver fork, frame   128-140
Blue/white, Spanish Lace, silver
fork, frame   130-140
Chain and Shield pattern, silver
fork, frame 82- 92
Clear, Cane (ill.)   94-107
Cranberry, silver fork, frame   161-171
Cranberry, ITP, silver fork, frame   262-275
Cupid and Psyche, silver fork,
frame   172-185
Daisy and Button, amber, silver
fork frame   140-152
Dark green glass, Thistle pattern
down side, silver fork, frame . .   133-148

Fine Cut pattern, clear, silver
fork, frame, footed   172-188
Herringbone pattern, green,
silver fork, tongs, frame   162-178

Picture Frames

Picture Frames

There are so many composition frames around today that a word of caution is necessary. Never clean gold gilt or gold leaf with water—**always** use alcohol. It won't dissolve the gold and/or plaster of paris molding. Use spackle to fill in broken areas, using fingernail cleaning tools to finish the design just before the spackle is hard. Then regilt. If too shiny, use cigarette ash moistened with water to dull the gold finish.

Black, gold leaf liner, 16″×26″,
c. 1875 . . . . $210-222
Black/gold leaf, open network
cylinder composition,
18″×26″   225-252
Gold leaf, 9″×16″, c. 1880s   210-225
Oak, gold liner, 14″×17″,
c. 1860s   158-166
Oak, silver liner, 8″×10″,
c. 1880s   124-129
Oval, applied composition pieces,
16″×20″, c. 1890   138-142
Oval, applied gold composition
pieces, 10″×12″, c. 1870s   142-152
Oval, simulated wood grain,
14″×18″, c. 1900   121-131
Oval, walnut, 9″×12″, c. 1880s . .   152-162
Simulated wood grain, burnished
gold liner, 10″×14″, c. 1870s
(ill.)   129-138

315

(continue

Toned wood, cylinder composition, 16″×20″, c. 1860s 170-180
Tortoise, gold gilt liner, 10″×12″,
c. 1860s 172-177
Walnut cross, carved leaf corners,
burnished gold liner 90-108
4-frame, 10″×12″, gold gilt,
c. 1870s 160-170
4-frame, 20″×24″, gold leaf,
c. 1887 152-170
3-frame, 16″×20″, walnut outer
frame, gold composition liner,
c. 1890s 142-153

Pink Lustre China

Pigeon's Blood Glass

Pigeon's Blood Glass

This red glass was made near the end of the 1800s. Today, some dealers sell any dark red glass as Pigeon's Blood. The original is an orange-red.

Bottle, cologne, 5″ high $230-250
Bowl, beaded top, fluted sides,
9″ dia. 240-260
Butter dish, covered, 8″ wide 232-245
Candlesticks, footed, twisted
stem, 9¼″ high, pr. 245-260
Candy dish, overlay, 8″ dia. 107-117
Caster set, 5-bottle, silver caps .. 280-290
Child's mug, "For a Good Boy,"
5½″ high, handled 150-160
Compote, 7″ high 249-268
Compote, scalloped edge, 8″ high 270-277
Creamer, metal top, clear applied
handle 188-192
Pitcher, clear applied handle,
11″ high 320-342
Salt, hexagonal, red/orange (ill.) .. 47- 57
Syrup jug, metal top 182-192
Tumbler, 4½″ high 120-130
Vase, pedestal base, scalloped
edge, 8½″ high 162-180
Vase, pink/white flowers, green
leaves, 12½″ high 610-630
Vase, slender neck, flat base,
enameled, 7″ high, France 205-209

Pink Lustre China

Made in the Staffordshire District, England, in the early 1800s, it gets its name from pink decorations used on the ware. Houses and fernlike trees were popular decorations. It is comparatively scarce today.

Biscuit barrel, 5½″ high, houses/
trees $179-187
Bowl, houses/trees, 4″ dia. 120-130
Bowl, trees, 6¼″ dia. 115-121
Box, covered, 2½″×2¼″×3¾″ . 120-132
Butter dish, covered, houses/
trees 108-114
Cup (handless)/saucer, floral
pattern (ill.) 72- 82
Cup/saucer, schoolhouse pattern . 74- 84
Mug, child's house/trees, c. 1850,
3½″ high 90- 94
Pitcher, floral pattern, 8¼″ high . 142-152
Pitcher, house/trees, 7½″ high .. 143-152
Plate, child with lamb, 7¾″ dia... 68- 78
Plate, floral pattern, 8¼″ dia. ... 70- 77
Plate, floral pattern, 7½″ dia.
(ill.) 66- 73
Plate, houses/trees, 8″ dia. 67- 74
Slipper, souvenir, Chicago
World's Fair 45- 55
Sugar bowl, floral pattern 98-107
Sugar bowl, houses/trees 132-143
Teapot, floral pattern, 6½″ high . 140-150
Teapot, houses/trees, 6¼″ high .. 141-151

Pink Slag

This rare glass is surrounded in mystery as to where it was made and by whom. Possibly Challinor, Taylor and Company made some at Tarentum, Pennsylvania. They made the purple (marble) glass. Miniature lamps in the shape of swans bring huge prices.

Berry bowl, 6½″ dia. $778- 795
Butter dish, covered, 6″ dia. .... 1,450+

Creamer, 3½" high, handled . . . 710- 775
Lamp, miniature, in shape
of swan (one at Houston
Museum) 985-1,100
Punch cup 642- 652
Sugar bowl, covered, 4" high . . 778- 842
Tumbler, ITP or Inverted
Feather and Fan, 4" high . . . 452- 462

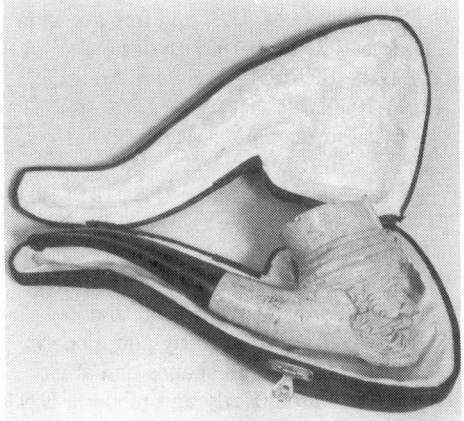

Pipes

Pisgah Forest Pottery

Pipes

Pipe bowls were carved from briar roots, meerschaum, or molded in porcelain and clay. When or who lit up the first one is lost to history. See **Clubs and Publications**, this Price Guide.

Alpine, porcelain bowl, 21"
long, marked "Holland" . . . . . $ 84- 93
Beethoven, briar, carved 75- 85
Briar, carved, sea captain 77- 87
Deer's head carved into bowl,
curved 10" stem 118-125
Elk's head bowl, B.P.O.E. and
date, straight 6" stem 81- 91
Face of monk in bowl, curved 7"
stem, clay 62- 72
Lion devouring prey, curved
stem, 11", briar 88- 98
Meerschaum, bearded Turk,
case 65- 75
Meerschaum, deer pursued by
dog, 9" curved stem 70- 80
Meerschaum, horse's head, trees,
9½" curved stem 80- 90
Opium pipe, Chinese figures, 14"
long, old 88- 98
Panther's head, glass eyes, 10"
straight stem 72- 82
Porcelain bowl, painted decor . . . 71- 88
Satyr, briar, carved 75- 84

Pisgah Forest Pottery

Walter B. Stephen founded this firm near Mt. Pisgah, North Carolina, in 1914. With his mother he produced a pâte-sur-pâte decorating technique, using as themes American scenes such as log cabins, buffalos, and covered wagons. Stephens also developed a high gloss glaze in several colors. He passed away in 1961, but the pottery is still in operation. Early pieces would be quite collectible today.

Vase, 5½" high, crackle glaze,
turquoise color, pink lined (ill.) . $ 74- 86

Pitchers, Glass

Every company made them in every size and shape. The Houston Museum's collection of over 15,000 pitchers is said to be the largest in the world. Any challengers?

Amethyst, clear applied handle,
9" high . . . . $ 73- 83
Blue basketweave, 10" high 80- 90
Clear glass, shades to blue/green
at top, blown, 11" high 134-142
Cut, Strawberry and Fan, clear
applied handle, signed Libbey . 210-227
Daisy and Button, V ornament,
12½" high 147-152
End-of-Day (Spatter glass), multi-
colored, 9½" high 138-152
Pomona first grind, 7½" high . . . 778-825
Royal Vienna, painting of church,
village background, 9" high . . . 168-178
Sapphire blue, clear applied
handle, blown, 8" high 158-172

Plated Amberina

This extremely rare art glass was made by

317

(continu~

Plated Amberina

the New England Glass Company in 1886. Opalescent glass was plated with a gold-ruby mixture, then reheated to develop a deeper color of certain portions which would then blend into the lighter part of the glass. Being reproduced.

Bowl, 8″ dia., 4″ high . . . . $6,500+
Cup, punch . . . . 3,450+
Pitcher, 7″ high (ill.) . . . . 5,400+
Syrup jug . . . . 4,500+
Tumbler . . . . 3,400+
Vase, 6½″ high, in silver holder . . . . 6,700+

These and others can be seen at the Houston Museum.

Playing Cards

Playing Cards

Most authorities agree that playing cards probably are an adaptation of chess which originated in India or China around 450 A.D. They are also mentioned in the annals of a German burg in 1361. The English copied from the French; we copied from the English. The Spanish never have had a queen in their deck; the French do. *Hobbies*—the Magazine for Collectors published the various classifications of playing cards in its October 1961 issue. Here is a brief summary:

I—Early Issues: Rare museum items, U.S. and foreign, prior to 1875.

II—Special Issues: U.S. and foreign, wide and narrow, from 1837 to date.

III—Wide Pictorials: U.S. and foreign, 1875-1930.

IV—Old Flower Cards: Wide and narrow, U.S., 1910-1921.

V—Narrow Named Cards: U.S., 1913-1925.

VI—Unnamed Narrow Cards: U.S., 1925-1935.

VII—Advertising Cards: U.S. and foreign, wide and narrow, from 1885 to date.

VIII—Novelty Cards: Early and modern, U.S. and foreign, all shapes and sizes.

IX—Game Cards: Early and modern, U.S. and foreign.

X—Modern: U.S. and foreign, wide and narrow, since 1925.

Most playing cards found today were made after 1920. If you're interested in joining a playing card collectors club, see **Clubs and Publications**, this Price Guide.

Advertising
Alleghany & Western Railroad,
complete, c. 1930s . . . . $ 8- 12
Chicago & Alton Railroad, in
original box, early 1900s 17- 24
Delta Air Lines, "Delta is ready
when you are," complete 1- 2
Delta Air Lines, seal unbroken,
1929-1979 . . . . 2- 3
Hilton, Las Vegas, complete, in
original box 1- 2
Marina Hotel, Las Vegas, seal
unbroken 1- 2
United Airlines, made in Hong
Kong, seal unbroken 1- 2

Civil War
Army and Navy, New York,
c. 1865 . . . . 74- 83
Confederate, Picture Playing
Cards, c. 1863 . . . . 77- 87
Union, New York, c. 1862 . . . . . . 69- 79

Clans
Anderson, Buchanan, Gordon,
MacDonald; any of these
decks, complete, c. 1920s, ea. . . 6- 8

Comic Strips/Characters

the mold lines.

Pomona Glass

Porcelains, Miniature

Pomona Glass

Joseph Locke invented it in 1884, first producing it at the New England Glass Company. It's a frosted ground on clear glass and decorated with mineral stains. Two types were made—first and second grind. First grind was etched by acid; second grind, the cheaper of the two methods, consisted of rolling the glass piece in particles of acid-resisting materials which were picked up by it. The piece was then etched. It's always blown. Don't confuse it with Midwest Pomona, a pressed glass in which you can see

Porcelains, Miniature

It was popular in the 18th and 19th centuries to paint faces on tiny pieces of porcelain which were then put in lockets or inside watches. Church scenes and landscapes were also popular.

French, church scene, 1"×1½", 18th century	$152-170
French, little boy, 1½"×2"	171-190
French, young man, 3"×2" (ill.)..	168-177
American, 19th century, Miss Lillian Russell	192-220

Porto Bello Ware

Porto Bello Ware

Made at Portobello Pottery, Midlothian, Scotland, late 18th century to commemorate Admiral Vernon's victory over the Spanish at Puerto Bello, Panama, on November 23, 1739. Usually it is a brownish-red pottery, glazed, with figures of ships, fortifications or other scenes. Designs on the first pieces made were in white. It remained popular until the 1860s and can be found in shops today.

Bowl, 4" dia.	$245-280
Jug, 7" high	272-290
Pitcher, large (ill.)	345-362
Pitcher, small	288-310
Plate, English coat-of-arms, 7" dia.	192-210
Platter, view of Puerto Bello, 11½" long	188-198
Tray, octagonal, signed	395-420

Probably many other pieces.

Portrait Plates

Portrait Plates

Considered fashionable in the late 1800s, these plates featured portraits, usually female, and were produced commercially for several years.

Blonde woman, copyright, 1909, Dresden, 11" dia. (ill.)	$310-342
Garfield, 13 stars around border, 10" dia.	48- 57
Girl's head, date 1884, France, 10" dia.	54- 63
His Majesty, Meakin, 11" dia.	52- 62
Lady's bust, blue, pink flowers, 8" dia.	52- 62
Abraham Lincoln and wife, 10" dia.	111-119
Louis XV, Sevres, blue/gold trim, 10" dia.	171-192
Man holding bird, forest scene, 8" dia.	52- 62
Peasant girl in wheatfield, 10" dia.	64- 74
Queen Elizabeth II, Johnson Brothers, 10½" dia.	67- 77
Three ladies at fountain, Germany, 11" dia.	68- 78
George/Martha Washington, reticulated edges, Germany, 8" dia.	82- 92
Martha Washington, white ground, pink roses, Germany	68- 77

Postcards

Postcards

Austria originated the postcard in 1869; the first one was mailed in this country in 1898. Many things dictate the price in this field of collectibles: rarity, subject matter, condition (most important), age (circa), artist, and how much you want it for your collection. See **Clubs and Publications**, this Price Guide.

Actors/actresses, pre-WW I	$ 2- 3
Advertising, early	1- 2
Animals	.50- 1

320

Automobiles, pre-1925	2- 3
Automobiles, post-1925	1- 2
Buses, trucks, farm equipment	.75- 1
Christmas, New Years (ill.)	.50- 1
Capitols, U.S., world	1- 2
Disasters, pre-1925	2- 3
Easter, embossed, pre-WW I	3- 6
Easter, general	.50- 1
Expositions/fairs	1- 4
Fire engines, pre-1930	2- 5
Fraternal	1- 2
Girls	1- 3
Greetings, general, pre-1925	1- 2
Halloween, pre-WW I	1- 2
Horse-drawn vehicles	1- 2
Humorous	1- 3
Indians, early	3- 7
Korea-Vietnam	.25- 1
Leather	.75- 1
Military, pre-WW I	3- 5
Military, pre-WW II	.50- 1
Negroes	1- 2
Novelties	.50- 1
Patriotic (ill.)	.50- 1
People (famous persons)	1- 2
Political	1- 2
Presidents, pre-WW I	2- 3
Presidents, to present	1- 2
Religious, early	2- 3
Royalty	1- 2
St. Patrick's Day, pre-WW I	2- 3
Santa Claus, early	5- 8
Santa Claus, pre-WW I	2- 3
Santa Claus, to present	.50- 1
Ships/nautical, early	2- 4
Ships/nautical, to present	1- 2
Souvenir folders, pre-1925	2- 4
Sports, early	5- 9
Sports, Roaring 20s	4- 6
States, early	1- 3
States, pre-WW II	2- 3
Thanksgiving	.50- 1
Thanksgiving, early	1- 3
Trains/trolley cars, early	3- 5
Valentines, early	3.50-16
Valentines, general	1- 3
Washington, D.C., pre-WW I	2- 3
Western/cowboys, early	2- 3
World War I	2- 4
World War II	1- 3

Pot Lids

Pot Lids

The Pratt Works at Fenton, England, made most of them. Used for holding shaving soaps, hair oil, etc., they were popular in the mid-to-late 1800s. Designs were placed under the glaze by a multicolor transfer method similar to decals of today.

Checker Game	$115-122
Contrast	120-130
Garibaldi	127-135
Hide and Seek	124-132
Lovers on the Bridge	118-127
Low Life	121-131
A Pair	111-120
Racing Scene	120-128
The Shrimpers	112-120
Village Wedding	118-127
Warming at the Fire	120-130

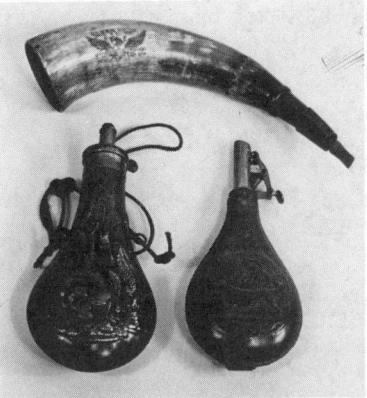

Powder Horns and Flasks

Powder Horns and Flasks

With the invention of the muzzle-loader rifle and pistol, these items were a necessity. From the crudest type, a cow's horn, to the ornately engraved brass and copper models, all are most collectible today.

Brass and pewter, 8½" long, c. 1830	$132-142
Brass, fluted sides, patent dispenser, c. early 1800s	170-180
Brass, hunter and dog, patent dispenser, 5" long	188-197
Brass, 6" long, hanging game on both sides (ill.)	135-142
Brass, small, 4½" long, type found in cased Colts	152-170
Calf's horn, wooden plug type, early 1800s, hand-carved	88-100

(continued)

Carved powder horn, New Hampshire, 14" long, c. 1846 415-470

Civil War, CSA, base metal, 8" long 88- 98

Civil War, pewter, brass cap and tip, 7½" long, marked U.S. . . . 89- 99

Copper, eagle, dated 1804, 7" long 178-182

Cow's horn, 8" long, brass cap and tip, c. 1845 . . . . 79- 89

Cow's horn, scrimshaw-carved eagle and name, signed Herman B. Seaborn, c. 1840 (ill.) 220-225

Japanese flask, for matchlock musket, 8" long, c. 1780 152-162

Leather flask, brass trimmings, 9" long, c. 1845 . . . . 74- 82

Persian flask, brass, 10¼" long, c. mid-18th century 149-162

Pistol, Colt's patent, 4½" long, brass, zinc, c. 1855 152-170

Pistol, 3½" long, brass, c. 1835 . . 92-108

Plate, horse race, blue, gold trim, 9" dia. 94-107

Pomade jar, signed, 3" high 106-116

Snuff jar, blue/tan/black, animal scene 60- 70

Sugar, matches creamer above . . 165-178

Teapot, large, Greek maidens, 6" to spout (ill.) 260-280

Teapot, pastoral scenes, 7" to spout 258-274

Urn, hunt scene, 4½" high 102-109

Vase, red/black, deer in forest, 8" high 142-152

Presidential Collectibles

Presidential Collectibles

These are items such as autographs or menus from the White House. Matchbooks marked "Stolen from the White House" were presidential favorites. Also photographs, lithographs, anything relating to United States presidents.

Ashtray, FDR, England, 4" x 4" . . . . $ 12- 16

Ashtray, FDR, souvenir of Warm Springs, 5" dia. 9- 13

Ballot, "Let Us Have Peace," Grant/Colfax, 1860, 7¾" x 4" 32- 40

Bandanna, jugate, Garfield/Arthur, 1880 . . . . 108- 116

Bank, metal, Ike, 5" high 14- 17

Bank, milk glass, red, white, blue, Taft/Sherman, 2½" high 69- 78

Bank, pottery, "Do as Coolidge Does — Save," 5" high 100- 115

Belt buckle, star-studded "C & H", Cleveland/Hendricks, 3¼" x 2¼" 25- 34

Bottle stopper, JFK's head, 5" high 10- 14

Button, brass, Garfield/Arthur, 1880, ¾" dia. 19- 25

Pratt Ware

PRATT
FENTON

Pratt Ware

The Fenton factory in the Staffordshire District, England, made this pottery from 1775 to 1805. Raised figures and decorations highly colored in green, purple, black, and orange are qualities of Pratt. Transfer pictures were also used.

Box, green/purple, naval battle, covered $107-118

Candleholder, black/orange, pr., 11" high 94-103

Compote, church scene, 4" high . . 188-194

Creamer, gray/green, cottage scene, 4" high 162-172

Cup/saucer, scenic transfer 64- 74

Pitcher, Doves of Peace, 5" high, purple/orange/green 320-340

Plate, fuchsia/purple/green, 10" dia. 90-108

Cane, jugate, McKinley/
Roosevelt, 1900 . . . . 100- 115
Cane, U. S. Grant 100- 115
Cardboard portrait, metal-
framed, Cleveland/
Hendricks 24- 32
Clicker, blue/white, "Click with
Dick" (Nixon), 2½" long 9- 11
Creamer, china, JFK/Jackie,
3¾" high 9- 12
Doll, compo head, JFK, 20"
high 55- 63
Donkey, ceramic, Carter/
Mondale, 4" high 8- 11
Game, Teddy Roosevelt, white
balls, 2¼" dia. 133- 140
Gravy boat, china, Lincoln's
Gettysburg Address, 8½"
long 65- 74
Lamp, metal, "The Man of the
Hour," FDR at the helm,
16" high 38- 46
Lithograph, Jefferson Davis,
president of the confederate
states (ill.) 50- 60
Match holder, transfer picture
of Woodrow Wilson, 2" high . 45- 53
Mug, china, Gerald Ford, 3¾"
high 24- 33
Mug, glass, Liberty Bell, Hayes/
Wheeler, 2" high 93- 102
Mug, John Adams, 2½" high . . 1,300+
Mug, Stangl Pottery, Al Smith
w/cigar, 4" high 41- 50
Mug, Stangl Pottery, FDR,
"Happy Days Are Here
Again," 4" high 41- 50
Necktie, Ike, 1952 . . . . 18- 25
Paperweight, Millard Fillmore,
New England Glass Co., 3½"
wide, 1" high 325- 350
Pitcher, Bennington-type,

Presidential Collectibles

James
A. Garfield, 1881, 7½" high . 215- 235
Postcard, decorated w/cloth,
Teddy Roosevelt/Taft 54- 63
Purse, leather, Warren G.
Harding, 3½" wide 43- 52
Ribbon, jugate, Cleveland/
Hendricks, 1884 . . . . 100- 110
Ribbon, jugate, Garfield/Ar-
thur,
1880 . . . . 85- 94
Sewing box, paper/wood, John
Quincy Adams inside lid,
1824 . . . . 1,100+
Stickpin, FDR (ill.) 1- 2
Stickpin, Loyal Democrat
(ill.) 1- 2
Tumbler, glass, U. S. Grant,
intaglio image on bottom . . . 50- 60
Train schedule, William
Jennings Bryan, 1896 . . . . . 7- 11
Watch, pocket-type, Carter/
Mondale 25- 33

Primitives

If you like primitives, buy *American Primitives* by Robert W. Miller, Wallace-
Homestead Book Co., Des Moines, Iowa
50309, or from your local bookstore.

Adjustable candleholder, tin,
1840s, 6" high . . . . $ 77- 84
Andirons, brass, ball type,
1840s 265-280
Andirons, claw feet, hand-forged
1840s 152-170
Battling stick, used for washing
clothes, early 1800s 62- 72
Bed warmer, copper, maple
handle, 1830s 269-280
Beeswax mold, used to make
blocks of beeswax, 2-pc.,
1820s 138-142
Bellows, wood, leather, crude,
1820s 77- 85
Betty lamp, wrought iron, twisted
rod on hook, 1820s 281-310
Block plane, #4 size, maple,
Kingston, N.Y., 1840 . . . . 74- 84
Branding iron, initials, "T.Y."
mid-1800s 89-105
Brass kettle, 6-gal., w/iron bail
handle, 1840s 358-372
Broad ax, mid-1800s 362-380
Broom press, used to make crude
brooms, early 1800s 82- 92
Buttress, used for trimming
hooves of oxen, early 1800s . . . 81- 90
Cabbage cutter, 1830s 62- 72
Cabbage cutter, early 19th
century 70- 80

323

(continued)

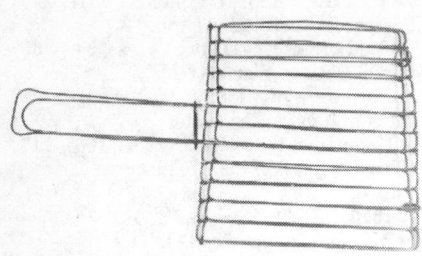

Primitives

Prints

Prints

Signed; signed and numbered; signed, numbered and remarqued; limited edition —all these affect the value, assuming the print has not been altered to fit a frame and is in good condition. Remarques are the artist's marks placed on a plate or on the original painting, such as C.M. Russell's buffalo skull.

John James Audubon, the
original edition engraved
by Havell & Son called
"The Birds of America";
there were 435 plates in all:

Plate #6, Hen Turkey .... $	10,000+
Plate #14, Prairie Warbler .	2,200+
Plate #27, Red-Headed Woodpecker	4,500+
Plate #82, Whip-Poor-Will .	4,100+
Plate #158, American Swift	1,700+
"The Battle of Lake Erie," line engraving, drawn by Sully, engraved by Murray, Draper, Fairman & Co., published in Philadelphia	470- 540
"Battle of New Orleans," print, aquatint by Debucourt, litho by Case & Green, 1815	215- 227
"Bonaparte in Trouble," line engraving, A. Doolittle . . .	242- 262
"Chesapeake and Shannan," colored aquatint, painted by Robert Dodd, published in August 1813	285- 340
"Fishing Along the Seine," pencil, lithograph, signed Charles Mondin	90- 110
"In the Garden," engraved and printed (ill.)	14- 19

"Le Serapis et le Bon-Homme Richard," line engraving, without artist's or engraver's name, framed	205- 212
"The Mediator and Alexander," line engraving, colored, Robert Dodd, published in London, 1783, by John Harris	380- 398
"Naval Battles of the Civil War," 4 lithographs, C & I	1,400-1,750

Of the different series—The Havell Prints; The Brien Edition; The Octavo Edition; The Audubon Quadrupeds; Audubon Prints on Fabric—the Octavo Edition is the most valuable.

"The Bathers," by Winslow Homer, 1872, wood engraving	320- 395
"Gathering Berries," by Winslow Homer, 1874, wood engraving	200- 242
"High Tide," by Winslow Homer, 1871, wood engraving	210- 262

If you're interested in buying and/or selling old prints, first establish contacts with reputable dealers who specialize in old prints. Also, read the periodicals that specialize in this field.

American Artist, 1 Astor Plaza, New York, N.Y. 10036

Art Investment Report, 54 Wall St., New York, N.Y. 10005

Print Trader, 6762 79 St., Middle Village, N.Y. 11379

Other things to remember: If marked "Published According to Act of Parliament," it's English, after 1735. If marked "Entered According to Act of Congress in the year —," it's American, after 1802. The first copyright laws passed by our government were in May, 1790.

Prints, Japanese

Prints, Japanese

The buyer should be aware that there are a

(continued)

great many 20th century reproductions flooding the market. When buying at auction, SPB is a name you can rely on. All measurements are approximate.

"Arhats," framed, ink on paper, unsigned, 41″×18″ $1,100-1,400

"Bamboo," hanging scroll, ink on paper, unsigned, 49″×11″ 2,300-2,400

"Calligraphy," hanging scroll, ink on paper, signed Sekiho, 53″×26″ 675- 775

"Chinese Children in Garden," small 6-fold screen, ink, colors on paper, 18th century, 34″×15″ 755- 820

"Cockerels and Peonies," hanging scroll, ink, colors on paper, signed Kokuhan, 1 seal, 66″×34″ 1,100-1,250

"Crouching Cat," hanging scroll, ink on colored paper, 19″×30″ 3,700-3,875

"Dragons," 6-fold screen, ink on paper, signed Tansaku, 67″×24″ 4,300-4,450

"Falcons and Pine Branches," 6-fold screen, ink and colors, 18th century, 62″×22″ 9,200-9,400

"Fishnets and Boats, Dawn," framed, colors on paper, signed Y. Ito, c. 1930s, 12″×19″ 385- 420

"Flowering Cherries," hanging scroll, ink, white/green colors, on silk, signed Taikan, 1 seal, 15″×20″ .. 570- 640

"Flowers and Grasses," 2-fold screen, ink, colors, gold paper, unsigned, 19th century, 55″×27″ 1,875-1,975

"Fuji and Pine," hanging scroll, ink and color on silk, signed Norinobu, 1 seal, 15″×24″ 420- 450

"Ghost With Bloodied Mouth," hanging scroll, ink, color on paper, signed, 62″×8″ 1,250-1,400

"Gorge Through Mountains," hanging scroll, ink, color on silk, signed, c. 1900s, 50″×20″ 1,900-2,200

"Monk, Woman at Gate," hanging scroll, ink, colors on silk, signed, 51″×23″ .. 2,400-2,600

"Moonlit Bridge," painting, framed, colors on paper, signed Y. Ito, c. 1930s, 12″×20″ 420- 465

"Nobleman in Palanquin,"

6-fold screen, ink, colors on gold paper, unsigned, 19th century, 150″×68″ 9,400-9,800

"Paragons," 6-fold screen, ink, colors on gold paper, 18th century, 47″×100″ .. 4,975-5,550

"Pheasant Beside River," hanging scroll, ink, color on silk, signed, 40″×16″ 5,975-6,375

"Rocky Landscape," hanging scroll, ink on paper, signed, 2 seals, 47″×10″ .. 1,400-1,600

"Sage and Attendant," hanging scroll, ink on paper, signed, 50″×25″ 995-1,400

"Spring Landscape," hanging scroll, ink, color on paper, signed, 51″×12″ .. 980-1,200

"Tiger and Bamboo," hanging scroll, ink on silk, signed, 19th century, 37″×13″ 745- 850

"Warriors," ink on paper, signed, 10″×18″ (ill.) 160- 195

"Warriors Attacking Palace," 6-fold screen, ink, colors on paper, signed, 19th century, 68″×24″ ... 3,450-3,650

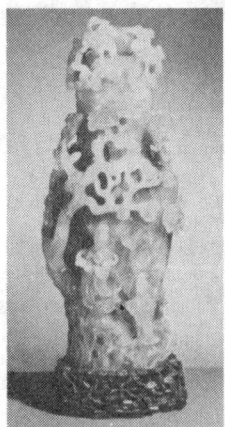
Quartz

Quartz

Figure, Kuan Yin, holding lotus blossom, 5½″ high .... $ 68- 78

Figurine, elephant group, trunks up, 4″ to 7″ high 175-195

Figurine, tiger, green, 7″ high, teakwood base 178-182

Snuff bottle, blossoms and leaves, carved, 3½″ high, ivory stopper 110-125

Vase, dancing figures, 22¾″ high (ill.) 658-685

Vase, dragons, birds, fruit motif, teakwood stand, 8″ high .. 320-340

Vase, fruit scene, rose-colored, 13″ high 170-180

Queen's Rose

Queen's Rose

English, soft-paste porcelain, maker unknown, probably early 1800s.

Creamer $110-122
Cup and saucer 135-155
Sugar bowl, covered 140-162
Teapot (ill.) 168-178

Quezal Glass

Quezal

Quezal Glass

Martin Bach, Sr., made this glass from 1901 to 1920. Formerly associated with Tiffany, Bach somewhat copied his former employer's work. Most pieces are signed Quezal. His son-in-law, Conrad Vahlsing, opened a shop after Bach's death, calling his wares Lustre Art Glass, which is also collectible today.

Bowl, ruffled top, signed,
  4" high .... $ 410- 430
Candlesticks, pr., blue
  iridescence 925- 985
Compote, blue iridescence,
  8½" high 520- 540
Finger bowl, gold iridescent,
  ribbed, signed, 4" dia. 192- 210
Goblet, footed, iridescent
  gold, signed, 5½" high 221- 231
Lamp, hanging, 4 iridescent
  shades, brass fixtures 820- 880
Lampshade, iridescent gold,
  feather design, signed,
  5" high (ill.) 220- 240

Nut dish, blue/rose, iridescent bronze, signed, 2½"
  dia. 172- 182
Perfume bottle, gold, signed,
  8" high 340- 362
Plate, blue iridescent, 11½"
  dia. 695- 770
Rose bowl, gold, purple/red
  iridescent, signed 352- 380
Salt, master and 6 individual,
  ribbed, iridescent gold,
  all signed 420- 430
Toothpick holder, iridescent
  gold, Feather design,
  signed, 3" high 122- 132
Vase, Feather pattern, red/
  purple, swirled base, 10"
  high, signed 1,400-1,700
Vase, Feather pattern,
  white/green/gold, signed,
  9" high .... 1,650+
Vase, green/gold feathers,
  white opalescent ground,
  8" high 1,200-1,550
Vase, peacock, blue, signed .. 900- 985
Vase, silver overlay, iridescent, signed, 9½" high .... 1,900+
Vase, trumpet, iridescent
  gold, signed, 8½" high 640- 675

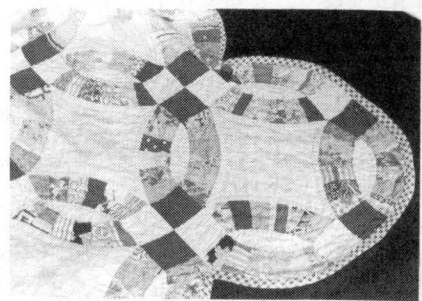

Quilts

Quilts

Most pieced quilts are formed by simple arrangements of diamonds, squares, right-angled triangles, stitched into a geometric design. Many are more than 150 years old. Today, all old quilts are collectible. Crib quilts are especially sought after. Some of the more popular patterns are Aeroplane, Basket, Flowerpot, Variable Star, Pansy, Fool's Puzzle, Log Cabin (I and II), Tennessee Tulip—to mention a few. Be prepared to pay anywhere from $50 to $600, depending on condition and scarcity. Some don't have a name. See quilt illustrated ($30-50).

Arkansas Traveler $120-133
Autumn Leaf 175-192

327

(continued)

Bear's Paw	182-194
Blazing Sun	170-192
Brown Goose	282-292
Butterflies	92-110
Caesar's Crown	168-180
Cats and Mice	85-200
Double Irish Chain	270-310
Dutch Tulip	210-220
Fanny's Fan	299-342
Festoon	210-222
Flying Dutchman	245-275
Golgotha	320-350
Henry of the West	370-390
Jacob's Ladder	240-270
Lost Ship	210-220
Melon Patch	225-232
Nine-Patch	310-325
Old Maid's Ramble	420-442
Pierrot's Pom-Pom	320-360
Puss in the Corner	432-442
Rambling Rose	285-300
Rocky Glen	292-325
Setting Sun	299-325
Storm at Sea	299-340
Swing in the Center	335-420
Tangled Tares	325-345
Texas Tears	375-410
Tic-Tac-Toe	162-182
Tippecanoe and Tyler Too	590-620
Tobacco Leaf	362-380
Travel Star	225-239
Turkey Tracks	245-262
Underground Railroad	620-660
Wagon Tracks	360-380
Water Wheel	199-220
Wild Goose Chase	310-340
Yankee Puzzle	265-295
Young Man's Fancy	295-340
Zigzag	295-360

Quimper

Quimper (Kam-pair)

Made in Finistere, France, from the end of the 17th century, its early products were in the style of Rouen. Pierre-Paul Caussy worked the factory from 1743 until 1782 when it was acquired by Antoine de la Hubaudiere. The Breton figures and floral sprays which most people recognize today as Quimper were originated by Julies Henriot who, more than likely, copied them from a potter named Fougeray. The familiar HB mark is that of Hubaudiere.

Ashtray, bone, dish-shaped, Breton figures, 6" dia.	$ 39- 47
Bowl, signed, 6" dia.	40- 50
Butter pat, set of 6, peasants in field	58- 68
Coffeepot, Breton figures, 11" high, signed	62- 72
Cup/saucer, flower and leaf	55- 65
Dish, flower motif, miniature, salesman's sample (ill.)	15- 21
Flower holder, birds, flowers, 7" high, signed	62- 72
Knife rest, women, flowers	50- 60
Mug	39- 48
Pitcher, milk, signed	59- 69
Plate, flowers, peasant woman, 8" dia. (ill.)	52- 62
Platter, peasant man, 12½" long	80- 90
Porringer, 2 handles, peasants, signed	57- 67
Salt, peasants, oval	41- 51
Salts, flower motif (ill.), ea.	39- 49
Teapot, 2-cup size, Breton peasants	105-112
Tray, man, woman in field, signed, 10" long	92-107
Vase, peasant man, flowers, 6½" high	58- 68

RADFORD

Radford Pottery   JASPER

Albert Radford, an Englishman, founded the A. Radford Pottery Company at Tiffin, Ohio, in 1896. In 1903 he moved his works to Zanesville, Ohio, and later in the same year moved to Clarksburg, West Virginia. The firm closed in 1912. Body colors of his pottery were usually pink, light or dark blue, gray, or tan, and often applied decorative outercoatings were used. Ruko, Radura, and Thera were three of the lines. Among the many items made were ewers, basins, toilet sets, mixing bowls, umbrella stands, art jars. Jasperware-type pottery made at Tiffin is highly collectible.

Jug, Lincoln/eagle, Jasperware-type, 7" high	$540-600
Jug, George Washington/eagle, Jasperware-type, 7" high	535-575
Umbrella stand, Ruko, 23" high	140-160
Vase, dark blue, 5½" high	120-130
Vase, green matt glaze, 7¼" high	122-141
Vase, Radura, 6" high	108-127
Vase, tan, 7¼" high	111-129

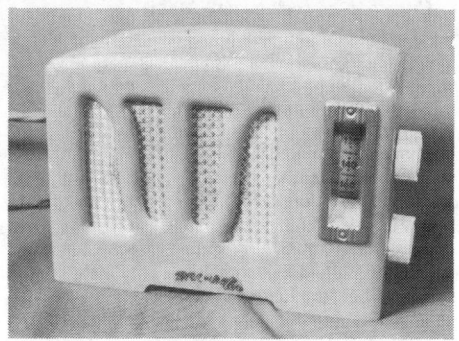

Radios

Radios

Guglielmo Marconi and Heinrich Rudolph Hertz get much credit for having invented the radio. But it took a lot of different men and a lot of time. Joseph Henry would get my vote. No matter, the influence of radio on the world is known and obvious. Those wireless sets of the 1920s are now highly sought after. See **Clubs and Publications**, this Price Guide.

Acme Apparatus, "Acmephone," 1924	$142-	162
Ajax, crystal set, 1924	120-	150
Atwater Kent, #5, 1921	1,650-	1,800
Atwater Kent, #10 (kit)	620-	710
Blue Seal, "Cincodyne," 1925	450-	475
Crosley, #5-38, 1926	275-	295
Crosley, "Radak HR," 1922	320-	350
Freed-Eiseman, #FE-15, 1924	270-	295
Kellog, "One Tube," 1922	195-	220
Magnavox, #TRF-5, 1925	320-	340
Mission Bell, "Mantle," 1930	272-	292
Q.T., Radio, "Little Giant," 1925	265-	295
RCA, "Radioal Senior," 1923	250-	280
RCA Victor, table model (ill.)	120-	130
Stromberg-Carlson, "Treasure Chest," 1928	350-	410
Western Air Patrol, #100, 1926	192-	222
Wurlitzer, #9A, 1929	235-	260
Zenith, "Super Portable," 1924	575-	640
Zenith, #40A, 1929	182-	195

Railroad China

Like so many other things, relating to the almost-extinct dining car, the china is now being eagerly sought after. Look for the line's name or initials on the front. Some of the firms who manufactured this china are Lenox, Maddock, Minton, Syracuse, and Warwick. Several factories in Limoges, France, also made it. Prices are for pieces in mint condition.

Ashtrays

Canadian Pacific, Banff National Park, 6½" dia.	$ 42-	52
Chesapeake & Ohio, Washington's bust, 7" dia.	77-	87
New York Central, Hudson River scene, 6¼" dia.	47-	52

Butter Patties

Baltimore & Ohio (ill.)	23-	32
Denver & Rio Grande	20-	27
Great Northern	22-	27
New York Central	21-	30

Celeries

Erie, floral designs, Erie, diamond logo, 10" wide	60-	70
Santa Fe, Flow Blue type, 12½" wide	77-	87

Creamers

Baltimore & Ohio, 1930s	42-	52
New York Central, 1940s	40-	50
Union Pacific	41-	50

Cups and Saucers

Coffee, Denver & Rio Grand	21-	29
Coffee, Florida East Coast	27-	33
Demitasse, Atlantic Coast Line	17-	27
Demitasse, Chesapeake & Ohio	16-	24

Egg Cups

Double, New York Central	14-	19
Double, Union Pacific	16-	24
Single, Baltimore & Ohio	11-	15

Miscellaneous

Cereal bowl, Erie, pinstripe border, diamond logo, 6" dia.	60-	70
Compote, Boston & Albany, double logo, 4" high	188-	225
Gravy boat, New York Central	62-	72
Ice cream dish, Canadian Pacific	29-	39

Plates

Dinner, Baltimore & Ohio	50-	60
Dinner, Great Northern	42-	52
Dinner, Penn Central	42-	52
Serving, New York Central	50-	60

Railroad China

329

(continued)

Serving, Santa Fe	50- 60
Salad, Chicago, Burlington & Quincy	39- 49
Platters	
Santa Fe	61- 71
Southern Pacific	62- 72
Wabash	58- 68

Railroad Collectibles

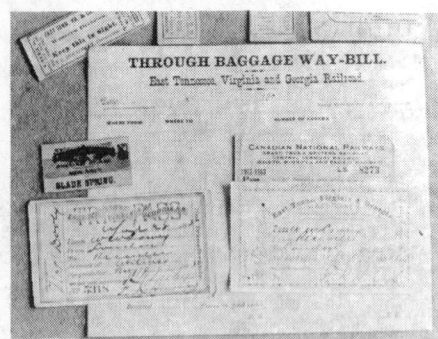

Railroad Collectibles

Railroad Collectibles

Anything relating to the Iron Horse is sought after today. Railroad silver, really just a silver-soldered product—lots of it made by Reed and Barton—is especially collectible. See **Clubs and Publications**, this Price Guide.

Attendants and waiters badges, most lines, ea.	$ 9- 15
Bonds, all railroads issued them, average price	9- 19
Breast badges, ea.	14- 19
Caboose lamp	54- 62
Cab badges, any railroad, average price, ea.	21- 29
Conductor's ticket punch, American brand	12- 19

Cuspidor, porcelainized, Maine Central	27- 34
Hand lantern, clear, Rock Island Line (ill.)	42- 52
Hand lantern, red, Southern Pacific	52- 62
Inspector's lantern, Bangor & Aroostock	88- 98
Journal box oil can, N.Y.N.H. & H.	38- 47
Knife, fork, spoon, napkin holder, Louisville & Southern R.R.	54- 63
Menu holder, Rock Island Line R.R.	24- 35
Passes: issued to conductors, officers of the company, average	10- 13
Postcards, depicting various R.R. scenes, ea.	1- 2
Pullman step	68- 74
Railroad employees' collar insignia, ea.	8- 14
Railway Express sign, 18"×18", reversible	44- 52
Tamping bar, 16 to 25 lbs.	18- 27
Track maul, 5 to 10 lbs.	18- 23
Tickets: Norfolk and Western, E. Tennessee, Virginia and Georgia R.R. (ill.), average price, ea.	8- 10
Timetables, most railroads, c. 1900s, average price, ea.	4- 6

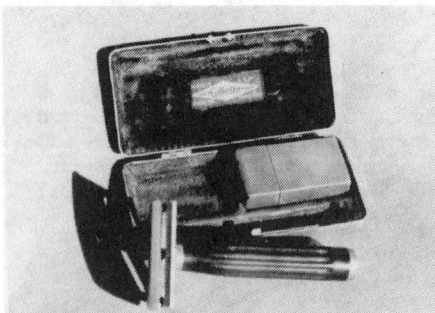

Razors

Razors

For years, Grandfather Pushbutton took his life in hand every time he shaved. Sailors prided themselves on being able to shave with a straight razor while the ship rolled from side to side. King Gillette ended it all when he invented the safety razor. The old straight razors are collectible and bringing good prices, depending on age and condition.

Gillette, early (ill.)	$ 19- 24
Ivory handled, polished Sheffield steel, original case	39- 52
King razor	16- 27

Others, average price	15-	24
Safety razors, early 1900s, average	8-	11
Solingar	25-	37
Star	34-	47

Reading Artistic Glass Works

Reading Artistic Glass Works

Founded by Lewis Kremp in Reading, Berks County, Pennsylvania, the firm operated from 1884 to 1886. The usual objects were made, including spittoons and whimsical canes. Opalescent colors included violet, canary, green, pink, white, and sapphire. Flint colors included green, light blue, amber, gold, and white. Specialty types had either mottling, overshot or craquelle finishes. Beginning to show up in shops in the Northeast.

Pitcher, 9½" high, pink with white mottling, thumbprint design, unusual 2-pc. opalescent, reeded handle (ill.)	$310-340
Vase, 14" high, baluster shape, black, applied neck ring (ill.)	310-325
Vase, 14" high, baluster shape, frilled top, black with white mottling (ill.)	282-292

Red Wing Pottery

1878-1967; Red Wing, Minnesota. Produced art pottery in the 1920s. Comparable to Roseville and Weller. Usually marked Red Wing USA, Red Wing Pottery, Inc., or RW USA. See **Clubs and Publications**, this Price Guide.

Bowl, deco relief, 8½" dia., marked Red Wing Pottery, Inc.	$ 37- 47

Bowl, white/brown trim, 8" dia.	22-	31
Candlestick, red maroon, 3" high, signed	15-	27
Cookie jar, Dutch scene, RW USA	36-	47
Cornucopia vase, ribbed and scalloped, 7¾" long, RW USA	25-	35
Creamer, waffle weave, 5⅜" high, RW USA	19-	27
Crock, blue/gray, 7½" high	44-	52
Marmalade jar w/lid, Red Wing USA	17-	24
Pitcher, ice guard, green swirled design, 7" high, marked Red Wing	52-	62
Vase, brown, mottled, Redwing USA	29-	38
Vase, chartreuse, flowers, bird of paradise, Red Wing USA B2000	37-	44
Vase, leaf-shaped, 9" high, blue/pink, Red Wing USA 1239	36-	45
Vase, white, flowers in relief, green, RW USA	29-	37
Vase, white, 7½" high, Red Wing, USA, Pat. Pending	19-	29

Redware

Redware

This is an unglazed red pottery, often with applied relief motifs, a Staffordshire type. Few pieces were signed with maker's name. Most of what you find today was made after 1850.

Pudding mold, swirl design	$ 89- 97
Teapot, dragon design (ill.)	103-121
Teapot, Oriental decor	118-128

Remington, Frederic

Lived 1861-1909; painter, sculptor, illustrator; best known for his sketches and bronzes depicting the Wild West as it really

(continued)

Remington, Frederic

was. His bronze statues were cast by the Roman Bronze Works, New York; also by Henry-Bonnard Bronze Company, New York. They were marked "Copyright by Frederic Remington." His sketches bring high prices. You can't buy a bronze for under $200,000. "The Bronco Buster," Cast No. 272, Trooper of the Plains, $227,000, is illustrated here.

Paul Revere Pottery

Paul Revere pottery was first made in 1908 in Boston. Its production was an outgrowth of a club known as the Saturday Evening Girls—SEG for short. Immigrant girls met on Saturday evenings for reading and craft activities. In 1915 another shop was built at Brighton. Children's dishes and tiles were popular items; paperweights, inkwells, and bookends also were made. Paul Revere on horseback was impressed or imprinted on the pieces, and sometimes PRP or SEG was painted on the base.

Children's breakfast set, Revere
    mark, 3-pc., all $142-152
Tea set, SEG mark, 3-pc., all 138-142
Tiles, depicting Revere's ride,
    PRP mark, 13 in set, all 475-525
Vase, flower motif, SEG mark,
    8³⁄₈" high 162-172
Vase, pine tree, Revere mark,
    9" high 88- 98

Reverse Paintings on Glass

This type of painting was done on the back

of the glass in reverse so the writing could be read. Popular during the early and mid-1800s, some of the English and Scotch paintings are considered rare today. Just about every subject was used: women, children, and prominent people the most popular. Average price $60-160.

Castle (ill.) $95-117
"White House on the Potomac,"
    gilded frame, 12¼"×10¾",
    c. early 1800s $84- 93

Reverse Paintings on Glass

Rhead Pottery

Founded in 1913, it was originally called the Pottery of the Camarata. The shop closed in 1917. Usual mark is Rhead Pottery/ Santa Barbara. Paper labels were also used.

Jardiniere, Chinese mirror glaze,
    signed, 34" high $395-462
Tile, inlaid process, signed 72- 82
Vase, floral, blue/green glaze,
    signed, 9¼" high 225-262
Vase, inlaid process, multicol-
    ored, signed, 7¾" high 298-342
Vase, matt green, pink/blue glaze,
    signed, 2¼" high 198-240

Richard Cameo Glass

A multilayered, acid-cut cameo glass, with scenic or floral designs. Made near Lorraine, France, after World War I. It is found in a great variety of shapes and colors. All pieces are signed in script.

Bowl, footed, yellow/green,
    orchids, 3" high . . . . $ 370- 420

Bowl, green/lavender, wild
  rosebuds, 4½″ high 450- 455
Bowl, village scene, oval,
  5″ high 440- 490
Lamp, blue/gray, wild
  orchids, 8½″ high 860- 925
Lamp, mountain lake, yellow/
  green, 11½″ high   2,600-2,850
Vase, blue/green, iris decor,
  7½″ high 650- 720
Vase, blue/yellow, swans on
  pond, 7″ high 750- 825
Vase, brown/orange, grape-
  vines, 13½″ tall 775- 845
Vase, brown/yellow, birds in
  flight, 6¼″ high 640- 655
Vase, orange/yellow, tiger
  lilies, 9¾″ high 920- 985

Ridgway Pottery

Ridgway Pottery

John and William Ridgway operated their pottery at Hanley, England, from 1814 until 1830. The Beauties of America series is world-famous. William Ridgway operated at Hanley from 1830 until 1854. Ridgway Potteries, Limited is still in business. It uses scenes and borders of another potter.

Bowl, 10″, Capitol, Washington . $152-162
Bowl, 10″, Pennsylvania
  Hospital, Philadelphia 165-175
Bowl, Racing the Mail, 8½″ dia. .   80- 90
Gravy, tureen, Bank, Savannah . 172-182
Mug, Eloping, 5″ high 62- 72
Plate, 8″, Library, Philadelphia . . 210-240
Plate, 6¼″, Athenaeum, Boston . 210-262
Platter, Maidenhair Fern,
  8½″ long 60- 70
Soup tureen tray, Deaf and
  Dumb Asylum, Hartford 162-172
Vegetable dish, 11″, Hospital,
  Boston 158-172

Ring Trees

Made of glass, metal, or porcelain, these

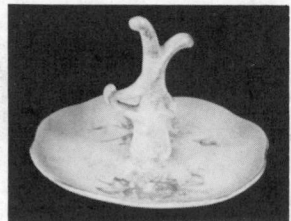

Ring Trees

small, treelike objects held one's rings for safekeeping while one bathed or slept. They were popular during the mid-Victorian era.

Cut glass, clear base, blue stem . . $ 59- 68
Parian ware, in shape of upraised
  hand 66- 72
Porcelain, decorated, American,
  2½″ high (ill.) 21- 28
Porcelain, 3-branch, Germany . . .   22- 29
Sterling silver in shape of 4-
  branched tree, 3″ high 41- 52
Just about every porcelain maker, here and abroad, made them.

Roblin Art Pottery

From 1898 until 1906, Alexander W. Robertson and Linna Irelan made this pottery in San Francisco, California. The primary product was vases, although, they also made some domestic wares such as mugs and bowls. The most familiar mark is illustrated here.

Vase, bisque ground, glossy
  interior, signed by Robertson,
  3½″ high $285-310
Vase, buff, signed, 6″ high 198-222
Vase, red ground, signed,
  5¼″ high 198-210
Vase, white bisque ground, glossy
  interior, signed, 4½″ high 221-242

Rockingham-Bennington Pottery

This is sometimes called Bennington Ware because it was made there in the mid-1800s. The original was made in the Staffordshire District before 1800. It was heavy, with a brown glaze. Actually, it was made by many potteries in the Ohio River Valley, and theirs was considered as good as that made in Bennington.

Bedpan . . . . $ 87-103

(continued)

Rockingham-Bennington Pottery

Bottle, monk	162-172
Bowl, chocolate glaze, tan ground, 9″ dia. (ill.)	92-120
Coffeepot, brown glaze, 10″ dia.	80- 90
Compote, blue flower decor	121-131
Creamer, cow, black, gold, glazed, 6¼″ long	120-130
Cup/saucer, green/gold, flowers	88- 92
Cuspidor, brown glaze, flower decor	97-108
Flask, brown glaze, acorns, leaves, 7½″ high	92-106
Footwarmer	128-142
Inkwell, monk's head, 3″ high	121-131
Pitcher, birds in swamp, 1850s, England, brown glaze	146-156
Plate, light brown, 9¼″ dia.	72- 89
Spill holder, brown glaze	77- 87
Teapot, white, orange, gold, glazed, 7″ high	138-142
Toby jug, brown glaze, England, 1850s	142-158
Tureen, covered, brown glaze, acorn finial on cover	262-272
Vase, white, multicolored flowers, 8″ high	70- 80

Norman Rockwell

Norman Rockwell

Severe art critics do not recognize his work as art, but for more than 60 years Norman Percevel Rockwell captured the hearts of the people, worldwide. Original oil paintings and the like are extremely expensive today. Limited editions are worthy collectibles; the unlimited or mass circulation items are just that. See **Clubs and Publications**, this Price Guide.

Bottle, Beam's 1976 bicentennial, 6 in series, ea.	$ 14- 19
Bowl, Ben Franklin, Danbury Mint, 1976, 5½″ high	120-138
Christmas gift wrap, C.P.S. Industries	.50-3.50
Cup set, Four Seasons, Gorham Fine China, 4 in set, all	120-133
Dolls, bisque porcelain, Rumbleseat Press, 20 in series, ea.	129-142
Figurine ornaments, porcelain, Grossman, 1978, 3″ to 3½″ tall, ea.	25- 42
Paperweight, sulphide crystal, Roger Brown, 1980	262-272
Plate, A Family Tree, Gorham, 10½″ dia. (ill.)	252-272
Puzzle, jigsaw, 40-50 different designs, ea.	4- 18
Spoons, souvenir, pewter, Grossman, 6¾″ long, ea.	38- 47
Thimbles, Danbury Mint, set of 6, ea.	8- 10
Thimbles, Nature Friends, 1979, set of 6, ea.	17- 19
Tray, Coca-Cola, American Art Works, 1931	210-220

Rogers Statuary

Rogers Statuary

John Rogers, an American born in 1829, studied sculpting in Europe and worked in plaster of paris to achieve some of his finest works. He put on the market more than 80 different subjects during the mid and late Victorian period, his pieces being reproduced more than 100,000 times! Highly collectible. See **Clubs and Publications**, this Price Guide.

Balcony	$ 560-	700
Bath	561-	572
Henry Ward Beecher	450-	500
Bubbles	545-	585
Bushwacker	470-	490
Camp Life	548-	600
Campfire	542-	585
Charity Patient	570-	620
Checker Players	625-	650
Chess	672-	682
Coming to the Parson	688-	725
Council of War (hands in any of 3 positions)	960-	982
Elder's Daughter	540-	552
Favored Scholar	620-	630
Fetching the Doctor	742-	752
First Love	488-	520
Fugitive Story	710-	740
Going for the Cows (ill.)	552-	582
Hide and Seek	680-	699
Home Guard	720-	740
John Alden and Priscilla	665-	685
Mail Day	692-	720
Miles Standish	452-	482
Matter of Opinion	570-	620
Mock Trial	720-	740
One More Shot	665-	710
Referee	710-	725
School Days	762-	782
Taking the Oath—Drawing Rations	752-	820
Traveling Magician	552-	592
Washington	1,400-	1,500
We Boys (head up or down)	542-	572
Weighing the Baby	820-	852
Wounded Scout	1,100-	1,400
Wrestler	1,500-	1,750

Rookwood

Rookwood

Founded in Cincinnati, Ohio, in 1880 by Mrs. Maria Longworth Storer, it was America's first art pottery. Tiger Eye, Iris, Vellum, and Ombroso matt glazes are some of the various glazes used over the 80-year period. The famous reversed R and P, uniformly adopted in 1886, appears on every piece. In 1887 a flame point was placed above the monogram and one point was added each year until 1900. In 1901 Roman numerals showed each ensuing year. Any similarity between the Rookwood produced in Ohio and that produced in Starkville, Mississippi, is purely coincidental. Kataro Shirayamadani, Albert R. Valentien, Matt A. Daly, Laura F. Fry, William Purcell McDonald, and Artus Van Briggle are some of the many famous artists who worked for Rookwood. Rookwood was Mrs. Storer's father's estate outside Cincinnati, so named because of the many rooks (crows) in the area.

Ashtray, blue "rooks," 4" dia., 1915	$ 65-	75
Ashtray, brown "rooks," 4½" dia., 1912	74-	83
Ashtray, elk's head, B.P.O.E., 6" dia., 1917	82-	93
Basket, pink/green matt finish, 11" high, dated 1911	101-	117
Bookends, ships at sea, signed McDonald, dated 1925	225-	232
Bookends, white horses, 7¼"×6", 1919, pr.	181-	192
Bowl, cherry blossoms, 3" high, 1907, Iris ware	172-	190
Bowl, green matt finish, dated 1920	77-	87
Candleholder, pink, 10" high, dated 1914	105-	111
Candlestick, tulip shape, 8¾" high, matt glaze, signed C.S.	172-	182
Cigar humidor, Indian head, 9" high, unsigned, 1932	192-	210
Chocolate pot, water lily motif, 9" high, 1904, initialed M.M.	215-	224
Creamer, daisies, initialed C.S., 1898	252-	272
Electrolier, tulip shape, 14" high, 1905, unsigned, matt glaze	310-	325
Ewer, brown/tan, flowers, vellum finish, signed Kataro Shirayamadani (he was Japanese, probably Rookwood's		

(continued)

greatest decorator),
dated 1897 . . . .   4,400+

Ewer, Japanese flower, 5½"
high, unsigned, 1904 . . . . .   325- 342

Flower frog, green/blue,
1925, unsigned 97- 108

Jug, handled, grape design,
6" high, 1905, initialed
M.M. 450- 510

Lamp, pinecone decoration,
Iris ware, 24" high, 1904,
unsigned 500- 525

Mug, grape design, 4¾"
high, 1905 . . . .   245- 262

Pitcher, green, floral, signed
Reed, dated 1893 . . . .   785- 825

Plate, 9½" dia., dragonflies,
1904, matt glaze,
unsigned 225- 260

Sugar bowl, clover design,
4" high, unsigned, matt
glaze 235- 262

Tea caddy, poppy design,
5¼" high, unsigned, Iris
ware 241- 251

Teapot, 7½" high, Tiger
Eye glaze, initialed
O.G.R., 1893 . . . .   378- 420

Vase, blue, vellum finish,
original store label,
signed LNL, 1918 . . . .   540- 567

Vase, brown/tan, 7" high,
initialed C.S., 1897 . . . .   675- 728

Vase, brown, vellum finish,
signed Carrie Steinle,
dated 1901 . . . .   560- 620

Vase, fern fronds, 6½" high,
1893, Tiger Eye glaze,
unsigned 428- 468

Vase, green, matt finish,
1932 (ill.) 132- 147

Vase, Japanese iris, 10"
high, 1907 . . . .   520- 540

Vase, light green, 7" high,
1924, unsigned 188- 210

Vase, matt glaze, green/
blue, 1935, 6" high,
unsigned (ill.) 108- 114

Vase, night-blooming
cereus, 13" high, initialed
S.S. 528- 562

Vase, pinecone design, on
teakwood base, 12" high,
1908 . . . .   524- 591

Vase, wild carrot, 6¼" high,
1904 . . . .   472- 512

Rorstrand Faience

in the early 1900s took on an Art Nouveau
style. The firm is still in business. It's mentioned here because it's beginning to show up
in the better shops. It's expensive and you
should know what you're doing if you decide
to collect it.

Vase (ill.) $750-840

Rose Bowls

These are crimped and pinched-edge bowls
used for holding dried rose petals. Decorative only, their rose-scented aroma helped
freshen the air in the parlor or dining room.
Mid-1800s, of every type glass. Being reproduced.

Amberina, Honeycomb pat-
tern, 6" dia. $372-395

Amethyst glass, enameled
flowers   188-220

Bristol glass, enameled flowers . .   152-172

Cranberry, white enamel decor . .   140-160

Mt. Washington and Wheeling
Peachblow   582-640

New England Peachblow, acid
finish   775-798

Overshot, fan design   250-262

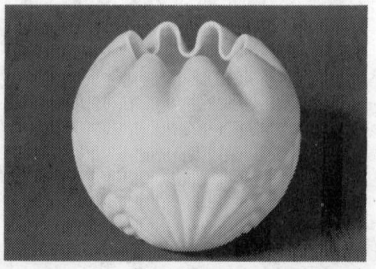

Rose Bowls

Rorstrand Faience

The company was founded in 1726 at Great
Rorstrand, near Stockholm, Sweden. Designs

Satin glass, flower decor, gold trim	250-270	
Satin glass, Shell and Seaweed, 5″ high (ill.)	220-240	
Spanish Lace, blue, 4½″ dia.	92-108	
Tiffin glass, black, poppies	77- 92	
Vasa Murrhina, pink, red, flecks of mica	172-182	
Vaseline, 3″ dia.	109-118	

Rose Medallion China

Rose Medallion China

A product of China, it was decorated in Canton and exported to every country in the world. It gets its name from the glazed pieces having figures of people alternating with panels of pink flowers, butterflies, and birds. If all the panels are filled with flowers only, it's called Rose Canton. This ware has been produced and reproduced for hundreds of years. Watch out!

Basket, people, roses, butterflies, 4½″ dia.	$ 730-	770
Bowl, people, roses, birds, butterflies	330-	370
Box, covered, usual design, 2½″ high	162-	190
Bulb or crocus pot		2,400+
Candleholders, people, flowers, 11½″ high, pr.	910-1,100	
Canister, set of 3, 3″, 4″, 5″, signed "China"	320-	332
Compote, typical design of birds, flowers, etc., 8″ high	197-	225
Creamer and sugar, covered	210-	240
Cup/saucer, thorn handle	122-	142
Cuspidor, typical scenes	542-	588
Dish, flowers, figures, 10″ dia.	220-	242
Jardinieres, teakwood stand, 8¾″ high, pr.	1,200-1,400	
Mug, rose floral band, birds, flowers, etc.	210-	240
Plate, 7″ dia. (ill.)	135-	142
Plate, 12″ dia.	233-	260
Platter, 19th century, typical scenes, 16″ dia.	355-	375
Powder box, roses, people, green ground	172-	182

Shaving mug	99-	110
Sugar bowl, berry handles, people and flowers	355-	375
Tea set, in lined wicker caddy for traveling, 2 cups	572-	620
Tea set: teapot, creamer, sugar, all	910-	940
Teapot, usual scenery, China	360-	392
Tureen, typical scenes, 11½″ long	420-	462
(Tureen of early 1800s, on stand, would be worth $1,600.)		
Urn, typical decorations, 16″ high	488-	521
Vase, 9¾″ high, on teakwood stands, 19th century, pr.	461-	482
Vase, roses, scenes, people, birds, etc.	372-	392
Washstand set, Chinese enameled, mid-1800s, usual design	640-	695

Rosenthal China

Rosenthal China

Established in Selb, Bavaria, by P. Rosenthal in the 1880s, the firm specialized in figure groups, dinner sets and other pieces. It was considered a fine hard-paste porcelain, and it's expensive when found today.

Bowl, berry, pink flowers, gold rim, scalloped, footed	$ 92-	101
Box, lady's face on lid, gold border on cover, 5″ high	95-	121
Candlesticks, white, gold trim, pr.	94-	116
Centerpiece with female figure, white, beige, gray, signed "K. Himmelstoss" and Rosenthal, 17″ high		2,400+
Chocolate pot, 6 cups/saucers, pinecones, trees, beige ground	262-	272
Chocolate set, demitasse, blue and gold, service for 6	342-	361
Compote, white ground, flowers, handles, gold trim, 8″ high	75-	85
Creamer, blue/pink, 5¼″ high (ill.)	77-	87

(continued)

Roseville Pottery

Roseville Pottery

Roseville, Ohio, 1892, this pottery firm was making stoneware jars, cuspidors and flowerpots. In 1898 the firm moved to Zanesville but didn't make art pottery until 1900. No art pottery was ever made at Roseville. Their first art line was called Rozane. Some of the marks used were "RPCo."; "Rozane—RPCo" beneath; "Rozane Ware Royal"; "Rozane Ware Mara"; paper "Roseville Pottery Co." labels were also used. This pottery was comparable to Weller. It never reached the quality level of Rookwood.

Vase, 8" high, Florentine line,
"R" containing small "v" 58- 67
Vase, 14" high, Indian chief
brown/red, Rozane Ware inside
circle 148-162
Vase, 13" high, metallic lustre
line, Rozane Ware Mara 152-161
Vase, 9" high, Woodland,
"Fujiyama" rubber stamped
on bottom 98-108
Vase, 11½" high, Woodland line,
floral designs, Rozane Ware... 88- 98
Vase, Rozane Ware, 12" high
(ill.) 142-162
Wall pocket, 10" high, Donatello
line 67- 77

Royal Bayreuth

Royal Bayreuth

This type of novelty ware was made in Germany for many years. The tapestry type porcelain is collectible today.

Ashtray, clown $142-166
Ashtray, monkeys playing cards,
black mark 82- 92
Berry set, dish, 6 saucers, grapes,
leaves 154-170
Bowl, Little Jack Horner, 5¾"
dia. 71- 80
Bowl, lobster-claw handles, pink/
red/purple 162-180
Box, Jack Be Nimble on lid,
colors 81- 92
Candlesticks, devil playing cards,
pr. 109-119
Chamberstick, green, musicians,
4¾" high, considered rare 310-325
Creamer and sugar, Fishermen
pattern 91-107
Creamer, bear 152-170
Creamer, clown 184-194
Creamer, crab 95-107
Creamer, tomato (ill.) 38- 47
Cup, demitasse, devil and dice ... 82- 92

Cup/saucer, demitasse, poppy
decor 169-180
Dresser dish, pink florals, greens,
7" long 64- 73
Gravy boat, tomato, leaf
underplate 177-185
Hair receiver, Little Bo-Peep,
light blue 84- 93
Humidor, tomato color, lidded,
7" high 127-132
Inkwell, boy in tree, 4" dia. 121-131
Match holder, clown, black mark . 147-152
Mug, Little Miss Muffet, 3¼"
high 130-140
Mustard jar, devil and cards 106-116
Pin tray, Santa Claus decor 155-170
Pitcher, animal decor, blue mark,
4" high 131-142
Plate, feeding, Sunbonnet Baby . 168-178
Plate, flower basket, pink/blue,
set of 8 148-157
Powder jar, pink/blue 118-127
Salt, open, lobster motif 57- 67
String holder, hanging, poppy
decor 185-195
Sugar/creamer/pitcher, devil and
cards 248-262
Tea set, strawberry, 3-pc. 310-320
Teapot, creamer, sugar, tomato
color 182-192
Toothpick holder, deer head 110-119
Tray, dresser, flower decor,
8" wide 105-111
Vase, Dutch scene, 6" high 103-115
Vase, peasants, blue 118-127

Royal Bayreuth Tapestry

This type porcelain, made about 1890, was created by covering porcelain with a piece of fabric tightly stretched over the surface. It was then decorated and glazed. Royal Bayreuth specialized in this in the late 19th century. Prices of this porcelain would be about 75 percent higher than similar pieces in previously listed **Royal Bayreuth**.

Royal Bonn

(continued)

Royal Bonn

Established in Bonn, Germany, in the last half of 18th century by Clemers August, most of what you find today is ornately decorated with flowers, sometimes with portraits. It was a fine-paste porcelain. Some pieces were marked with a castle.

Bowl, brown glaze, flowers, 10" dia.	$ 78-	83
Celery tray, flower motif	83-	93
Clock, colored flowers, 11½" high	410-	428
Cologne bottle, tapestry-like surface, flowers, handled	98-	111
Compote, ships at sea, 8" high	92-	107
Cracker jar, floral, gold trim	179-	188
Plate, pink flowers, green ground, 12" dia.	81-	90
Plate, guardsman, leaf rim (ill.)	105-	121
Vase, Delft blue, white, windmill scene, 8" high	115-	126
Vase, floral, blue ground, handles, 12½" high	111-	121
Vase, green ground, rose/yellow flowers, pr.	210-	230
Vase, peasant girl, 8" high (ill.)	90-	108

Royal Copenhagen Porcelain

Established in 1772, this firm has been in business ever since, manufacturing fine porcelain. Their Christmas plates are world-famous.

Bottle, wine, castle scene	$ 58-	70
Bowl, sculptured figure of mermaid, 6"	124-	133
Coffeepot, blue/white	231-	250
Cruet, blue/white, stopper	142-	152
Cup/saucer, blue/white, basketweave, 1924 mark, set of 8	105-	112
Dinner service, six 8-pc. place settings	1,250-	1,450
Figurine, bear, 7" high, deep blue, 1928	118-	124
Inkwell	88-	98
Mug, large, 1968	94-	106
Plate, brown/blue, Iris pattern	70-	80
Plate, mermaid in wintertime, pr.	75-	88
Platter, blue and white, 10" long	97-	106
Rooster, 1925, 6" high, pr.	192-	201
Toby jug, John Peel	84-	94

Tray, green and gold, 11" long	67-	77
Vase, bluebirds and flowers	136-	144
Vase, blue/white, 1934, slender neck	147-	152
Vase, flowers, blue/white, dated	119-	132

Royal Doulton

Royal Doulton

The art director at Royal Doulton, Charles J. Noke, developed a series of figurines, animal and bird models, and character jugs around 1913. The miniature (M) series was begun during the depression years of the 1930s. The K series is bird and animal miniatures. All pieces are marked Royal Doulton and bear the RD number, the registration number at the British Patent Office. Numbers for all figures are preceded by the initials HN. The numbers on the figurines are not chronological as some numbers were skipped, while others were held in reserve for future pieces. The letters A and D appear on jugs. For some reason, those bearing the letter A bring more money than those with the letter D. Watch out for repros!

Animal and Bird Models

Alsatian, 106	$ 310-	342
American Foxhound, large, 2524	262-	281
American Great Dane, large, 2601	328-	360
Baltimore Oriole, 2542	262-	281
Bulldog, brindle, large, 1042	220-	242
Bulldog, brown and white, medium, 1046	162-	172

Cairn, black, medium,
1105 . . . . 170- 180
Cat, Persian, white, 2539 . 158- 166
Cat, Siamese, sitting, 2665 78- 88
Cock Pheasant, 2632 . . . . 520- 540
Cocker Spaniel and Pheas-
ant, medium, 1028 . . . . 148- 172
Collie, silver gray, 975 . . . 320- 340
Drake, mallard, large, 956 210- 240
Fox, on rock, 147 . . . . . . 162- 172
Gordon Setter, small, 1081 148- 168
Hare, lying, small, 2594 . . 56- 66
Kingfisher, small, 2573 . . . 108- 121
Mallard, 2556 . . . . 240- 270
Peacock, 2577 . . . . 155- 166
Pekingese, sitting, large,
1039 . . . . 252- 275
Pig, asleep, 2545 . . . . 271- 282
Puppy, 128 . . . . 188- 199
River Hog, 2663 . . . . 152- 162
Sealyham, lying, large,
1041 . . . . 278- 320
Teal Duck, 229 . . . . 187- 196
Tiger, 2646 . . . . 887- 952

Character Jugs (all Ds)
Anne Boleyn, small, 6650,
1975 . . . . 67- 77
Apothecary, large, 6567,
1963 . . . . 89- 104
'Ard of 'Earing, small,
6591, 1964-67 . . . . 672- 720
Athos, large, 6439, 1960 . . 94- 106
Bacchus, small, 6505, 1959 67- 74
Blacksmith, small, 6578,
1963 . . . . 64- 76
Captain Ahab, miniature,
6522, 1960 . . . . 39- 49
Captain Hook, large, 6597,
1965-71 . . . . 332- 342
Catherine Howard, large,
6645, 1978 . . . . 108- 119
Churchill, large, 6170,
1940 . . . . 11,000+
Dick Turpin, small, 5618,
1935-60 . . . . 74- 83
Don Quixote, small, 6460,
1957 . . . . 62- 72
Falconer, miniature, 6547,
1960 . . . . 39- 48
Fat Boy, miniature, 6139,
1940-60 . . . . 77- 87
Golfer, large, 6623, 1971 . . 89- 99
Gone Away, small, 6538,
1960 . . . . 64- 73
Gulliver, large, 6560,
1962-67 . . . . 496- 552
Izaak Walton, large, 6404,
1953 . . . . 88- 101
Jockey, large, 6625,
1971-75 . . . . 174- 182
Johnny Appleseed, large,
6372, 1935-69 . . . . 282- 324
Long John Silver, small,
6386, 1952 . . . . 67- 77

Mark Twain, large, 6654,
1980 . . . . 88- 98
The Midado, small, 6507,
1959-69 . . . . 272- 299
Mr. Micawber, miniature,
6138, 1940-60 . . . . 61- 71
Neptune, large, 6548,
1961 . . . . 89- 99
Old King Cole, small,
6037, 1939-60 . . . . 108- 118
Parson Brown, small,
5529, 1935-60 . . . . 77- 87
Porthos, miniature, 6516,
1960 . . . . 40- 50
Robinson Crusoe, small,
6539, 1960 . . . . 62- 72
Sairey Gamp, small, 5528,
1935 . . . . 61- 71
Scaramouche, miniature,
6564, 1962-67 . . . . 352- 382
Smuggler, large, 6616,
1968-80 . . . . 88- 98
Toby Philpots, large,
5736, 1937-69 . . . . 124- 137
The Trapper, large, 6609,
1967 . . . . 82- 97
Vicar of Bray, large, 5615,
1936-60 . . . . 192- 221
Walrus and Carpenter,
small, 6604, 1965-79 . . . 77- 87

Figurines
Adrienne—purple gown,
yellow scarf, 2152,
1964-76 . . . . 188- 229
blue gown, light green
scarf, 2304, 1964 . . . . . . 173- 188
The Afternoon Call, 82,
1918-38 . . . . 2,500- 2,775
A La Mode, 2544, 1964-79 198- 232
Alexandre, 2398, 1970-76 . 167- 187
Annabella—orange skirt,
green bodice, 1871,
1938-49 . . . . 520- 570
green skirt, blue bodice,
1872, 1938-49 . . . . 525- 570
red dress, 1875, 1938-49 552- 561
Anthea, 1526, 1932-38 . . . 820- 856
Apple Maid, 2160, 1957-62 468- 492
Artful Dodger, 546, 1922 . 320- 344
At Ease, 2473, 1973-79 . . . 220- 242
The Awakening, 1927,
1927-28 . . . . 2,225- 2,520
Baby, 12, 1913-38 . . . . . . 2,295- 2,450
Balloon Man, 1954, 1940 . 210- 222
Balloon Seller, 548,
1922-38 . . . . 895- 970
Bather, 773, 1925-38 . . . . . 1,450- 1,650
Beachcomber, 2487,
1973-76 . . . . 220- 240
Belle, 754, 1925-38 . . . . . . 1,400- 1,600
Betsy, 2111, 1953-59 . . . . 392- 452
Biddy, 1843, 1938 . . . . . . 220- 240
Blithe Morning—pink

341

(continued)

skirt, blue bodice, 2021,
1949-71 .... 195- 242
red dress, green/yel-
low, 2065, 1950-73 ..... 235- 252
Bluebeard, 1528, 1932-49 . 1,400- 1,475
Bonnie Lassie, 1626,
1934-53 .... 338- 392
Boudoir, 2542, 1974-79 ... 344- 359
Boy on Pig, 1369, 1930-38 995- 1,270
Bride, 1st version, 1841,
1938-49 .... 925- 955
Bridget, 2070, 1951-73 ... 310- 340
Bunny, 2214, 1960-75 .... 162- 182
Buz Fuz, 538, 1922 ...... 325- 355
Camellia, 2222, 1960-71 .. 320- 345
Captain Hook, 2889, 1980 415- 452
Carolyn, 2112, 1953-59 ... 345- 362
Carrie, 2800, 1976 .... 142- 156
Charley's Aunt, 1st ver-
sion, 640, 1924-38 ..... 1,100- 1,275
Chelsea Pensioner, 689,
1924-38 .... 1,600- 1,800
Child and Crab, 32,
1913-38 .... 1,450- 1,550
Choir Boy, 2141, 1954-75 . 128- 142
Christmas Parcels, 2851,
1978 .... 248- 282
Cicely, 1516, 1932-49 .... 1,500- 1,650
Clockmaker, 2279,
1961-75 .... 410- 432
Coachman, 2282, 1963-71 . 575- 620
Colinette, 1998, 1947-49 .. 542- 562
Cookie, 2218, 1958-75 .... 110- 128
Country Lass, 1991, 1975 . 188- 198
A Courting, 2004, 1947-53 752- 772
Curly Locks, 2049, 1949-53 325- 365
Debbie, 2385, 1969 ...... 141- 152
The Detective, 2359, 1977 196- 221
The Diligent Scholar, 26,
1913-28 .... 1,400- 1,475
Double Jester, 365,
1920-38 .... 2,495- 2,720
Drummer Boy, 2679, 1976 410- 432
Easter Day, 1976, 1945-51 528- 588
Eleanor of Provence, 2009,
1948-53 .... 720- 790
Elyse, 2429, 1972 .... 232- 245
Enchantment, 2178,
1957 .... 182- 192
Evening, 2814, 1977 ..... 187- 242
Faraway, 2133, 1958-62 .. 220- 240
The Fiddler, 2171, 1956-62 1,100- 1,250
Flora, 2349, 1966-73 ..... 225- 245
Folly, 1335, 1929-38 ..... 1,875- 1,980
Friar Tuck, 2143, 1954-65 . 462- 485
Genevieve, 1962, 1941-75 . 252- 281
A Good Catch, 2258, 1966 190- 210
Grand Manner, 2723, 1975 278- 322
Guy Fawkes, 347, 1919-38 1,985- 2,375
Heart-to-Heart, 2276,
1961-71 .... 475- 525
He Loves Me, 2046,
1949-62 .... 162- 182

Iona, 1346, 1929-38 ...... 2,800- 3,000
Innocence, 2842, 1979 ... 175- 185
Jack, 2060, 1950-71 ...... 162- 192
Janet, 1537, 1932 (ill.) ... 130- 140
Janine, 2461, 1971 .... 195- 222
Jill, 2061, 1950-71 .... 188- 229
Judge and Jury, 1264,
1927-38 .... 3,450- 3,675
Kate, 2789, 1978 .... 178- 196
Katrina, 2327, 1965-69 ... 320- 352
Lady Betty, 1967, 1941-51 375- 395
Lambing Time, 1890,
1938-80 .... 180- 220
Long John Silver, 2204,
1957-65 .... 425- 456
Lucy Ann, 1502, 1932-50 . 370- 390
Mantilla, 2712, 1974-79 .. 362- 392
Masque, 2554, 1973 ..... 221- 241
Milady, 1970, 1941-49 .... 962- 992
Newsboy, 2244, 1959-65 .. 765- 795
Nina, 2347, 1969-76 ..... 168- 189
Orange Seller, 1325,
1929-49 .... 920- 945
Past Glory, 2484, 1973-79 265- 295
Pauline, 1444, 1931-38 ... 452- 482
Pedlar Wolf, 7, 1913-38 ... 2,475- 2,695
Picnic, 2308, 1965 .... 125- 142
Pirate King, 2901, 1981 .. 810- 880
The Potter, 1493, 1932 ... 362- 382
A Princess, 392, 1920-38 . 3,200- 3,400
Professor, 2281, 1965-80 . 210- 227
Prue, 1996, 1947-55 ..... 392- 422
Quality Street, 1211,
1926-38 .... 1,375- 1,475
Rendezvous, 2212, 1962-71 420- 460
Rhapsody, 2267, 1961-73 . 262- 292
Rosabelle, 1620, 1934-38 . 1,100- 1,300
Rosemary, 2091, 1952-59 . 522- 562
Salome, 1828, 1937-49 ... 4,900- 5,400
Seafarer, 2455, 1972-76 .. 220- 248
Sea Sprite, 1261, 1927-38 . 670- 690
She Loves Me Not, 2045,
1949-62 .... 185- 220
Shore Leave, 2254,
1965-79 .... 230- 262
Siesta, 1305, 1928-38 .... 2,200- 2,400
Simone, 2378, 1971 ...... 210- 242
Spirit of the Wind, 1825,
1937-49 .... 3,900- 4,400
Spooks, 372, 1920-36 .... 1,850- 2,100
Stiggins, 536, 1922 ...... 322- 351
Summer's Day, 2181,
1957-62 .... 462- 479
Suzette, 1487, 1933-38 ... 590- 638
Sweet Lavender, 1373,
1930-49 .... 740- 760
Sylvia, 1478, 1931-38 .... 820- 862
Thanksgiving, 2446,
1972-76 .... 199- 242
Tootles, 1680, 1935-75 ... 152- 172
Two A Penny, 1359,
1929-38 .... 1,100- 1,350
Veneta, 2722, 1974-80 .... 182- 192

Victoria, 2471, 1973	228-	310
Vivienne, 2073, 1951-67 ..	310-	362
A Wandering Minstrel, 1224, 1927-38	1,600-	1,850
Wayfarer, 2362, 1970-76..	175-	235
The Welsh Girl, 456, 1921-38	2,700-	2,950
West Wind, 1826, 1937-49	4,850-	5,450
The Winner, 1407, 1930-38	3,570-	3,690
Wistful, 2396, 1979	385-	420
Wood Nymph, 2192, 1958-62	285-	310
The Young Knight, 94, 1918-36	3,200-	3,500
Young Master, 2872, 1980	362-	422
Young Widow, 1399, 1930	1,500-	1,650

Royal Doulton Pottery

Royal Doulton Pottery

This is the same Doulton Pottery mentioned earlier in this Guide. After 1901 the word Royal was added. Scenes from daily English life identify this pottery. It's still being made. See **Clubs and Publications**, this Price Guide.

Biscuit jar, horses, white body, applied flowers, Lambeth .... $	510-	562
Bottle, Dewars Scotch	88-	98
Bowl and pitcher, cobalt, gold trim	182-	192
Bowl, Robin Hood..........	84-	94
Candlestick, castles, Crown and Lion mark...........	61-	71
Cheese dish, blue/yellow, white ground, 6½″ high ...	92-	109
Cup/saucer, demitasse	45-	56
Humidor, barrel-headed, green, fruit decor	80-	90
Jug, grapes, brown glaze, marked	54-	63
Mug, blue medallions, cobalt .	78-	88
Pitcher, 6″ high, "Morrisian".	62-	72
Plate, 10¼″ dia. (ill.)	54-	64
Plate, Admiral Nelson, fleet at Spithead	73-	83
Toby mug, 6″ high	90-	108

Vase, blue, Dutch Girl, 5″ high	54-	62
Vase, cobalt, Arabian heads form handles, 8½″ high ...	108-	121
Vase, dog and horse, blue/ olive/green glazes, 14″ high, Hannah Barlow's sgraffito decoration	2,200-	2,700
Vase, mottled blue/pink, birds	72-	81

Just about all the jugs have been reproduced, so be careful.

Royal Dux

C.N.

Royal Dux

Made in Bohemia, this porcelain was imported into the U.S. around 1900, mostly for sale in gift shops. It was considered inexpensive then, not so today.

Basket, blue basketweave pattern, satin ground, 4½″ dia. ...	$175-192
Bowl, girl with long hair, green/ orchid flowers, handles	168-174
Figurine, camel, rider, 17½″ high	452-472
Figurine, flapper, white/blue, gold decoration, 13½″ high, c. 1920 (ill.)	582-599
Figurine, hound in lying position gold matt, 14″ long	160-172
Figurine, lady holding water jug, Austria, 18″ high, pr.	187-196
Planter, boy playing flute, 7″ high	264-284
Planter, Grecian woman, ivory, on gold base, 11½″ high	268-288
Vase, applied flowers, Austria, 15″ high	136-142
Vase, applied flowers, peaches, apples, 12½″ high	228-252
Vase, floral, leaves, pink ground, 17¼″ high	168-174
Vase, pink/green, 19½″ high	182-194

Royal Flemish Glass

A product of the Mt. Washington Glass Company, 1889, it's identified by the heavy gold enameled lines dividing the surface of the glass into separate sections. Various decorations are found on the matt finish body. The pieces were colored in shades of gold, beige, and brown.

Bowl, tan/pink/light green,
  mustard panels, alternating
  w/frosted and gilted, raised
  coin and rampant lion
  motifs, 6″ across $2,575-2,775
Cookie jar, gold coin medal-
  lions, silver top and
  handles 2,675-2,850
Pitcher, satin glass finish,
  russet tan, enameled gold
  decor 2,700-2,900
Planter, opaque enamel in
  russet, tan/brown, gold
  decor, gold lion in
  medallion. . . . . 2,200+
Rose jar, green medallions,
  steeple top 2,150-2,250
Vase, russet, tan and brown,
  enameled gold decor . . . . . 2,400+
Vase, stick type, medallion
  design, 11″ high, initialed
  R.F. on bottom . . . . 2,700+

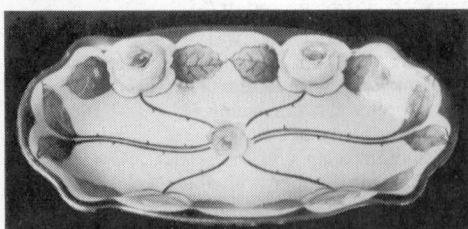

Royal Rudolstadt

Royal Rudolstadt

Established in 1720 at Thuringia, Germany. Later the factory was moved to Rudolstadt. Most of what you find in shops today is of the late 19th century. The marks are R for the early years, RW with crown on top for the later years. Pieces marked Germany were made after 1890. It's beautiful china with a Dresden-like coloring, often delicately decorated with flowers, sometimes

faces of famous people such as Beethoven.

Basket, floral decor, gold handle,
  old mark $128-142
Bowl, tiger lilies, footed 185-195
Bowl, winter scene, horse, sleigh . 180-190
Butter dish, burnt orange/green,
  covered 171-181
Cheese dish, bridal roses, floral . . 118-126
Compote, enameled flowers, gold
  trim 100-108
Dish, shell-shaped beige ground,
  daisies and violets, multi-
  colored, 8½″ dia. 109-119
Hatpin holder, bluebird decor . . . 92-107
Nappie, leaf-shaped 84- 94
Pitcher, flower decor, serpentine
  handle 103-116
Plate, fruit, gold band, 8½″ dia. . . 92-107
Plate, green ground, white roses,
  8″ dia. 94-109
Tray, pin, oval, pink flowers,
  6″ long (ill.) 45- 55
Vase, multicolor floral, claw feet
  and handles in gold, 6″ high . . . 178-188
Vase, Psyche, open handles, tan/
  brown ground, ruby neck 252-270

Royal Vienna

Royal Vienna

The factory was founded in 1719 and thrived when taken under royal patronage. This was a Meissen-type ware noted for its brilliant colors and artistic excellence. It was most collectible even in the 1800s. One of its distinguishing marks is the Beehive. What you find in shops today has been produced by other factories, some of which are still making it.

Basket, blue body, handles,
  applied leaves and fruit . . .$ 267- 278

Compote, red, cobalt, Beehive
mark 182- 191
Cracker jar, dancing girls,
floral decor 290- 310
Ewer, cream ground, floral
sprays, 10″ high 168- 174
Jar, lady dancing, cupids,
cranberry, Beehive mark in
red 161- 171
Plate, rose, gold, Palette mark,
8″ dia. 176- 184
Plate, portrait, gold border,
signed Wagner, Beehive
mark in red 238- 265
Plate, white/black, signed
Riener, 1750 mark, set of
12 .... 2,900+
Salt dip, ornate feet, beaded
gold, Beehive mark 71- 81
Statuette, 8½″ high (ill) 528- 540
Stein, monk, brown ground,
Beehive mark 620- 640
Teapot, white, fruit decor,
hand-painted, Beehive
mark 162- 172
Tray, green, gold trim 190- 199
Urn, Queen Louise, ormolu
finial, 14″ high, pr. 410- 428
Vase, medallion center, blue,
red, Beehive mark, pr...... 332- 344
Vase, pink ground, painted
scene, figure in center, 12″
high 438- 452
Vase, handled, Queen Louise,
wife of Frederick Wilhelm
III, King of Prussia, 13″
high .... 1,850+

Royal Worcester Porcelain

Royal Worcester Porcelain

This was a company within a company.
The Royal Worcester Porcelain Company,
Limited, was formed in 1862 and is still in
business. Important to know your marks or

you'll end up buying new for old.

Basket, beige, green leaves, 6½″
dia. $200-228
Bone dish, flower decor 68- 78
Bottle, perfume, roses, flowers .. 112-132
Cake stand, flowers, gold trim,
8½″ high 236-246
Candle snuffer, nun, 6½″ 132-142
Chocolate mug, floral enameled .. 58- 68
Chocolate pot, cream back-
ground, after 1891 311-329
Creamer, floral decor, large
leaf in relief near handle 188-199
Cup, boullion, 4½″ dia. (ill.) 26- 34
Ewer, green/gold lion, 10½″ high 220-240
Figurine, Sunday's Child, F.
Doughty, 4¾″ high 118-126
Flower holder, horn-shaped,
early 1900s 129-138
Mug, blue/white, Dr. Wall,
Crescent mark 372-384
Pitcher, 9″ high, horn-shaped,
cream background 210-218
Plate, floral scene, raised shell
edge, 8¼″ dia. 88- 99
Plate, floral center, leaf border,
9″ dia. 162-172
Sugar shaker, signed 120-140
Tea caddy, gold/blue spatter 188-199
Tea set (teapot, sugar and
creamer), floral decor 478-496
Thimble, flowers, signed 81- 91
Vase, floral decor, applied
handles 384-422
Vase, shell design, gilting, 8½″
high 318-340

Roycroft Items

Roycroft Items

The Roycroft community, founded by
Elbert Hubbard at East Aurora, New York,
in 1893, produced furniture, books, metal-
ware, jewelry, leatherwork, and lamps until
1938. Hubbard is famous for his small essay
entitled "A Message to Garcia." Periodicals

345

(continued)

printed by the Roycrofters included *The Roy-crofter*, *The Fra*, and *The Philistine*. Most items were marked with the R in circle/double cross.

Ashtray, copper, signed, 5″ dia.	$ 34- 46
Bookends, hammered copper, florals, owls, ropes, ea.	42- 51
Candlesticks, hammered brass, signed, pr.	47- 56
Desk set, hammered copper, signed, 4-pc., all	84- 93
Lamp, mica inserts, hammered copper, 15″ high	158-167
Lamp, oak/copper/leaded glass, designed by Dard Hunter, 26″ high	222-242
Scrapbook, leather bound (ill.)	29- 38
Trays, hammered copper, 10″, 15″ long, ea.	88- 98
Vase, bud, copper, 5″ high	74- 84
Vase, fluted top, hammered brass, 7″ high	94-103

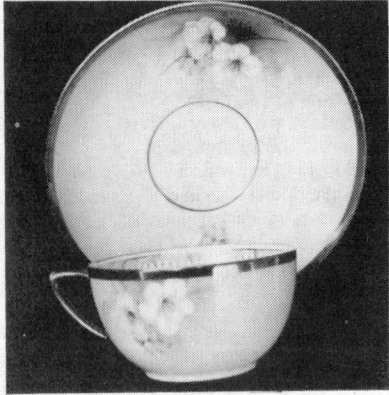

RS Germany

RS Germany

This is the same porcelain as RS Prussia. The name Germany was simply substituted for Prussia in 1891. Because of the demand for RS Prussia, especially the red star, dishonest dealers are removing the RS Germany and replacing it with the RS Prussia mark. It's a decal, 140 to the sheet, but the lettering is too modernistic. If in doubt, scrape vigorously with your fingernail.

Basket, roses, handles	$ 60- 70
Bowl, brown/green ground, flowers, 9¼″ dia.	78- 94
Bowl, floral decor, 9½″ across	88- 98
Box, covered, roses, green mark	60- 70
Candlestick, flared top, green lilies, 6″ high	77- 87
Celery vase, pink roses, gold, open handles	78- 86

Cheese dish, flowers, bisque finish	124-132
Chocolate pot, white ground, brown at top, roses, 6 cups	232-252
Creamer and sugar, pink roses	122-134
Cup/saucer (ill.)	78- 88
Dish, yellow, hand-painted, artist signed	67- 77
Hatpin holder, yellow floral, gold, marked	60- 70
Hatpin holder, white lilies	58- 68
Inkwell, covered, hand-painted	41- 51
Jam jar, lidded, flowers, green mark	66- 78
Nappie (dish with a handle), beige, apples, green mark	123-134
Plate, roses, gold edge, 8½″ dia.	67- 77
Relish dish, green ground, flowers	34- 45
Salt dip, rose decor, footed, marked	30- 40
Sauce, has tray, apricot roses, gold border, blue mark	64- 74
Sugar, covered, blue/pastel, flower decor	70- 80
Teapot, poppies, gold trim, green mark	58- 68
Toothpick holder, flowers, gold trim	60- 70
Tray, orange poppy, marked, 3¾″ dia.	55- 65
Vase, green, pink roses, 6″ high	61- 71
Vase, iris, 5″ high	67- 78

RS Prussia

RS Prussia

Similar to Haviland, it was made in Prussia during the last half of the 19th century. Rheinhold Schlegemilch operated the factory with his brother, Erdmann. The familiar mark, RS in a wreath and a red (or green) star, easily identifies it. Because it's so highly collectible, a sheet of decals, 140 to the sheet, has been on the market for several years, complete with firing instructions. Dishonest dealers are placing the decals on soft-paste porcelain pieces. Unless you're an authority, it will fool you. As always, if you don't know your antiques, know your antiques dealer. Red star is more collectible than green star.

Berry Sets

Blue/red flowers, gold trim, green mark, 7 pcs., all . . . . $ 620- 680

Roses, red mark, 8 pcs., all . . 740- 820

Water lilies, red mark, 7 pcs., all 742- 778

Bowls

Apple blossoms, ruffled edge, red mark, 8½″ dia. 200- 221

Berry, green ground, blue/white roses, red mark (ill.) . 318- 337

Fruit decor, yellow/green/white, green mark, 10″ dia. 240- 270

Pink roses, gold trim, handled, green mark, 8¼″ dia. 200- 222

White floral on green ground, red mark, 9″ dia. 263- 281

Chocolate Pots/Sets

Cottage scene, red mark, 6 cups/saucers, all 1,600-1,750

Floral decor, roses, white/red, red mark, 6 cups/saucers, all 528- 562

Rose sprays, gold trim, green mark, 3 cups/saucers, all . . 360- 375

Compotes

Blue/red roses, white ground, 7¼″ high 347- 366

Floral decor, red mark, 6½″ high 332- 370

Lilies, blue/yellow, red mark, 7″ high 345- 372

Red flowers, gold trim, 6¼″ high 320- 362

Cracker Jars

Floral decor, handled, red mark 300- 362

Large roses, blue ground, red mark 305- 325

Pink roses, footed, green mark 274- 279

Pink roses, scalloped base, red mark 281- 288

Creamers

Cottage scene, red mark 159- 168

Pastel flowers, red mark 164- 174

Pink roses, blue/white ground, green mark 142- 152

Wild lilies, scalloped feet, red mark 163- 172

Cups/Saucers

Blue/red flowers, green mark 54- 64

Dogwood blossoms, red mark 60- 70

Large roses, green/white ground, red mark 62- 72

Pink roses, white ground, red mark 63- 73

Demitasse Set

Pink roses, white/blue ground, 6 cups/saucers, all 652- 671

Dishes

Cake, lilies, reticulated handles, red mark 78- 84

Candy, pink roses, 3 legs, reticulated handles, red mark 84- 106

Ice cream, pink flowers, red mark, 6 in set, all 462- 483

Relish, dogwood blossoms, reticulated handles, green mark 54- 67

Relish, pink roses, reticulated handles, red mark 64- 72

Hair Receivers

Pink/blue flowers, round, red mark 84- 94

Pink flowers, scalloped base, green mark 77- 88

Roses, diamond-shaped, pearlized, red mark 96- 118

White flowers, green ground, red mark 81- 97

Wild roses, white ground, diamond-shaped, red mark 92- 108

Hatpin Holders

Blue flowers, scalloped base, red mark 130- 140

Bluebirds, scalloped base, red mark 152- 162

Leaf decoration, red mark . . . 93- 108

Wild roses, attached base, red mark 132- 142

Muffineers

Blue floral decor, handled, red star 168- 172

Poppies, handled, green star . 122- 132

Small roses, handled, red star 147- 156

Wild plums, handled, red star 152- 170

Mugs

Drinking, blue/red flowers, red mark 137- 156

Drinking, pink roses, red mark 146- 166

Shaving, dogwood blossoms, red mark 173- 182

Shaving, pink flowers, "Father" in gold script, red mark 210- 242

Shaving, small roses, yellow ground, red mark 184- 193

Mustache Cups

Dogwood blossoms, left-handed, red mark 147- 156

Pink flowers, red mark 140- 160

Wild roses, footed, green mark 125- 142

Mustard Pots

Blue flowers, handled, has ladle, red mark 118- 126

Cream floral, handled, green mark 111- 127

(continued)

Poppies, handled, has ladle,
gold trim, red mark 136- 145

Pitchers

Dogwood blossoms, red mark 292- 321
Floral decor, bulbous, red
mark 318- 344
Pink poppies, red mark, 11"
high 319- 341
Pink roses, tankard-shaped,
red mark 342- 366

Planters

Blue floral decor, footed, red
mark 234- 244
Dogwood blossoms, gold
trim, red mark 262- 281
Wild roses, white ground,
footed, green mark 235- 246

Plates

Cake, blue roses, handled,
red mark 142- 152
Cake, pink poppies, reticu-
lated handles, red mark . . . 146- 156
Roses, gold trim, reticulated
handles, red mark 152- 162
Scalloped roses, reticulated
handles, red mark 139- 149
Sunflowers, handles, green
mark 127- 137
Violets, reticulated handles,
red mark 121- 131
Wild plums, gold trim,
handled, green mark 130- 140

Sugar Bowls

Christmas holly, footed,
green mark 134- 144
Floral decor, footed, red mark 188- 199
Pink roses, footed, green
mark 162- 172
Water lilies, red mark 172- 182

Syrups

Dogwood blossoms, red mark 227- 234
Pink flowers, red mark 242- 252
Pink roses, white ground, red
mark 231- 248

Tankards

Daisies/rose, blue ground, red
mark, 14" high 573- 585
Floral decor, red mark, 15"
high 554- 566
Pink poppies, red mark, 16½"
high 684- 727
Pink roses, gold trim, red
mark, 15¼" high 563- 574

Tea Sets

Blue flowers, red mark, 3 pcs.,
all 378- 392
Pink roses, green mark, 6
pcs., all 642- 666
Poppies, red mark, 9 pcs., all . 1,200-1,450

Trays

Dresser, bluebirds, green
mark, 11¾" 143- 156
Dresser, dogwood blossoms,

red mark, 12½" 168- 178
Dresser, pink roses, handled,
red mark, 13½" 162- 172

Vases

Cottage scene, yellow/green
ground, red mark, 7" 462- 478
Pink flowers, gold trim, red
mark, 10½" 520- 532
Pink poppies, handles, green
mark, 11" 365- 384
Roses, flower form, red mark,
8¼" 420- 432
White/yellow flowers, bul-
bous form, red mark, 7" . . 362- 372
Wild plums, handled, red
mark, 9¼" 540- 562

Rubena Verde Glass

Rubena Verde Glass

Hobbs, Brockunier and Company, Wheeling, West Virginia, around 1890. Shading
from yellow-green to cranberry, it's now considered Art Glass and brings a good price
when found. Alas, being reproduced.

Bowl, crimped top, enameled,
ITP pattern, 3" high, c. 1880s
(ill.) $130-140
Bowl, Vine pattern, applied shell
feet 168-178
Cologne bottle, red shading,
clear stopper, 4½" high 138-148
Celery, 6¼" 148-152
Creamer, melon-ribbed, 9" high . . 262-272
Cruet, daisy, fern, opalescent,
stopper, clear handle 310-325
Decanter, cut, cranberry, 9" high 208-218
Epergne, clear to opalescent,
2-pc., 12" high 275-292
Perfume, swirl, matching
stopper, 6½" high 120-132
Pitcher, Diamond Quilted, reeded
handle, 6" high 308-321
Tumbler, ITP, flowers, enameled . 123-146
Tumbler, Quilted, 4" high 218-228
Vase, double tree trunk, 7" high . 92-109
Vase, Hobnail, red shading to
green, scalloped top, 7½" high 266-272
Vase, white enamel daisies,
gold leaves, pr. 432-452

Ruby Glass

Ruby Glass

This was a flashed glass, usually of the souvenir type. Deep red in color, it was made from the late 1880s until World War II. Some people confuse it with red Carnival.

Berry bowl, Saxon pattern, 12 smaller bowls	$ 66- 76
Butter dish, covered, Button Arches	94-103
Celery, Dakota (Baby Thumbprint)	62- 73
Cologne bottle, threaded stopper, 8″ high	77- 86
Compote, Thumbprint pattern, 7½″ high	56- 66
Cordial, Iowa State Fair	52- 77
Creamer, sugar, butter, spoonholder, gold intaglio carnations	120-130
Decanter, clear stopper	52- 62
Goblet, Diamond design, set of 12, all	178-188
Ice bucket, metal bail handle	45- 55
Lamp, signed Glow Lamp, Inc.	42- 52
Mug, souvenir, St. Louis Exposition, 1904, "Saddie"	51- 61
Pitcher, Atlantic City, 1908, To the Fairest	52- 62
Spoonholder, cherubs, 5½″ high	50- 60
Toothpick holder, Bettie	49- 58
Toothpick holder, Button Arches	51- 60
Tumbler, JHS, King's Crown	52- 62
Tumbler, Reading, Pa.	35- 45
Tumbler, Thumbprint pattern, 4″ high	44- 52
Vase, floral sprays, urn shape, 14″ high (ill.)	82- 92
Vase, fluted, disc stem, 8″ high	71- 81

Rugs, Oriental, and Others

Baktiari, varicolored panels, red border, ivory guard borders, approx. 9′9″×7′3″	$ 1,700+
Bidjar, corridor-type, Persia, early 20th century, ivory field w/vine tendril lattice pattern, approx. 18′4″×7½′	13,950+
Beshire prayer, Afghanistan, early 20th century, twin niches woven w/narrow polychrome stripes, approx. 4′6″×2′9″	2,700+
Caucasian, 3 hooked contiguous medallions, blue field, sawtooth guard border, approx. 3′4″×5′	550+
Chinese, room size, dark blue ground/birds/butterflies, approx. 9′6″×8′	1,700+
Chinese, sculptured beige floral ground, salmon/ black borders, approx. 11′6″×9′	1,700+
Daghestan, ivory field, flowers/zoommorphic figures, approx. 4′2″×6′3″	3,600+
Daghestan, ivory field, trellis work, flowers/ figures, approx. 4′3″×3′4″	3,550+
Doroosh prayer, Persia, 20th century, red ground, persimmon spandrels, Herati motif, approx. 4′5″×3′2″	8,900+
Gashgai, Persia, late 19th century, animal forms, midnight blue ground, approx. 9′2″×4′2″	4,800+
Gendje runner, late 19th century, red ground, rows of scorpion diamond medallions, approx. 3′9″×12′9″	2,975+
Gorevan, Iran, mid-20th century, Herez pattern, red/blue/brown colors, approx. 9′3″×12′5″	1,400+
Gorevan, large medallion, red/blue/cream, approx. 9′×6½′	1,450+
Hamadan runner, dark blue field, Herati motifs, floral borders, approx. 5′4″×17′	2,475+
Hamadan runner, dark blue field, Jerati motifs overall, approx. 5′4″×16′	2,800+
Ispahan, Persia, 20th century, cream ground, palmettes/leaves, sunburst medallion, approx. 6′×3′8″	8,900+

(continued)

Karabagh runner, dark blue
field, flower heads,
approx. 3'9"×18" ...... 2,575+

Kashan, room size, wine
central ground, animals,
central cartouche-shape
medallion, approx.
10'2"×19'8" .... 11,650+

Kashan, vine/flower field,
blue medallions, approx.
7'2"×10'3" .... 32,000+

Kazak, Caucasian, early
20th century, sky blue
field, ladder design, gold/
ivory, approx. 3'×5'4" .. 2,500+

Kazak, geometric center
medallions, camel hair,
approx. 7'×4' .... 1,500+

Khorossan, room size, blue
central ground, floral pattern, approx.
11'10"×17'9" .... 4,100+

Kirman, central carpet,
ivory ground, petal-
formed medallion,
approx. 13'6"×27' .... 6,700+

Kirman, ivory field, dia-
mond medallions,
approx. 16'2"×9'5" .... 2,975+

Kuba, blue field, overall
stylized geometric
ground, approx.
42"×61" .... 995+

Kuba, Caucasus, early 20th
century, tumeric field,
lattice pattern of stylized
flowers, approx.
6'3"×4' .... 3,100+

Kuba, Caucasus, late 19th
century, mustard field,
ivory border, rows of
bracketed rosettes,
approx. 4'2"×3'4" .... 5,975+

Lesghi, Caucasus, early
20th century, midnight
blue field, central ivory
Lesghi star, multiple
rosette borders, approx.
4'4"×3'7" .... 2,700+

Luri, Persia, mid-20th century, rose field, alternate
rows of 3 and 4 botehs .. 2,700+

Mahal, dark blue field, rose
border, scroll design,
approx. 12'5"×9'6" .... 2,900+

Melas, Turkey, early 20th
century, burnt red field,
pair of square form
medallions, approx.
4'9"×3'7" .... 14,800+

Nain, Persia, 20th century,
blue field, trees/flowers/
animals surrounded by

flower blossom/vine
border, approx.
8'5"×5'2" .... 5,200+

Sarouk, rose ground, mid-
night blue border,
approx. 11'8"×9' ...... 1,675+

Seichur, Caucasus, early
20th century, cream field,
twin Georgian crosses, 2
running dog borders,
approx. 6'×3'6" ...... 3,700+

Shirvan, ivory mihrab
woven in trellis designs,
starflower border,
approx. 3'9"×4'7" .... 5,600+

Ruskin Pottery

Established in 1898 at West Smethwick,
near Birmingham, England, the firm remained in business until 1935. All pieces
were signed and dated.

Vase, high-fired glaze, pear-
shaped, signed, 1923, 5½"
high $365-420

Vase, lavender/mauve glaze,
signed, 1905, 8" high 392-428

Vase, mottled purple/blue glaze,
signed, 1924 378-418

Vase, plum/mauve glaze,
signed, 1912, 4¼" high 272-293

Vase, red/blue glaze, signed,
1911, 7¾" high 169-188

Sabino Glass

They called him The Sculptor in Crystal,
and this creator of opalescent glass in the Art
Deco manner made his products in Paris,
France, in the 1920s and the 1930s. Vases,
lamps, nudes, and animals were some of the
many items he produced.

Ashtray, shell motif, 3½"×5½" $ 37- 47
Ashtray, swallows, 3¼" square . 32- 50
Bowl, snail 37- 46
Figurine, Kingfisher, 4¼" high . 72- 81
Figurine, nudes in circle, 6" high 162-172
Madonnas, 3", 5" 68- 77
Stork, 7½" 142-152
Turkey, 2¼" 44- 54
Venus de Milo, 2½", 4½" 54- 63

Sadirons

The old handle types were heated on a
stove. They're used as doorstops or bookends today.

Average price ....$ 24- 35
Gasoline iron (ill.), early 1900s ... 25- 34

Sadirons

Salopian Ware

Salopian Ware   SALOPIAN

Made in England at Salop in 1772, this decorated pottery was by Thomas Turner who took over the works in that year. In 1780 he opened a warehouse in London and marked his wares with an S or Salopian impressed or painted under the glaze. His Willow pattern is highly collectible. After he retired in 1799, the firm was sold and moved across the river by the new owners, John Rose and Company. The factory still operates, under a new name—Coalport.

Bowl, blue/white, 11″ dia. . . .	$405- 418
Creamer, House pattern	488- 535
Cup/saucer, blue/white, Deer pattern, handleless . .	375- 420
Cup/saucer, Early Cow pattern (ill.)	362- 382
Cup/saucer, late, Bird pattern (ill.)	366- 378
Jug, mask spout, 12½″ high	1,150-1,400
Plate, farm scene, 6½″ dia. . .	378- 420
Saucer, birds, cottage motif, 5″ dia.	188- 198
Saucer, fowl, fishing scene, 5″ dia.	220- 240
Tea set, blue/white, 6 cups and saucers, covered teapot, sugar and creamer, some pieces marked Caughley	2,450+
Teapot, House pattern	600- 675

Salt Glaze

Though the Staffordshire District, England, was considered the center of salt glazed pottery, some of the finest was made by the United States Pottery Company, Bennington, Vermont, 1853-1858.

Butter, covered	$285-	320
Creamer, hand thrown, red clay, 5″ high (ill.)	69-	79
Crock, hand thrown, cobalt leaves, signed "R.C.R.–Philadelphia" (ill.)	143-	164
Jug, wide-necked, bulbous, pewter lid	252-	263
Mug, blue, applied handle, stoneware	120-	132
Pitcher, 4 countries of Great Britain, pewter lid, registry mark	228-	237
Pitcher, Niagara Falls design, U.S. Pottery Co. . .	258-	275
Platter, white, 8½″ long	161-	181
Tea set, apostle figure, 3-pc., American	1,100-1,250	
Teapot, wild roses, U.S. Pottery Co.	192-	221

Salt Glaze

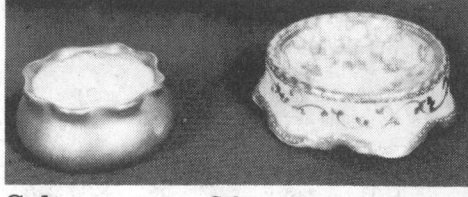

Salts   Salts

Open salts, popular from the 18th century on in America, stayed in vogue until the shaker type appeared on the market in the 1860s. Novelties in pressed glass are collectible today, such as those in the shape of birds and animals. You'll find prices for specific types listed in this Guide. See **Clubs and Publications,** this Price Guide

Bird salt, apple green glass	$ 99-122
Bird salt, clear glass	60- 72

(continued)

Bird salt, pattern glass 31- 44
Bird salt, vaseline glass 81- 92
Gold, white, Austrian (ill.) 15- 21
Noritake (ill.).................. 16- 27
Swan salt, cut glass bowl,
   sterling silver body and wings
   (wings fold back when not in
   use) 85- 98

Samplers

Samplers

Made from the mid-1700s until they fell from style in the early 1900s, samplers were made of cloth, usually, and contained homey messages such as Love Thy Neighbor, the alphabet, etc. Dates are given in listing.

Early 1800s, Jane Foulis
   Standrews, alphabet, bird/
   flowers, blue/green/black (ill.) .. $182-194
1806, alphabet, 9″×12″, framed . 178-189
1812, Love Thy Neighbor,
   alphabet around border,
   frame 221-248
1815, alphabet and numbers,
   Hannah L. Maywood, framed . 221-262
1818, religious verses, birds in
   corners, walnut frame 240-272
1819, memorial to War of 1812,
   child's name, frame 255-268
1847, church, flower border, Ruth
   Ann Mills, framed 251-272
1866, name of soldier killed at
   Atlanta, framed 218-227
1869, Home Is Where the Heart
   Is, flowers, etc., no frame 199-224
1873, Child's poem, on linen,
   birds, flowers, walnut frame .. 198-220

Sandwich Glass

The Boston and Sandwich Glass Company was founded by Deming Jarves in 1825 at Sandwich, Massachusetts, and operated until around 1888. Many fine types of glass were made there, including pressed, cut, and blown. Look out for reproductions.

Basket, cranberry, clear handle,
   6½″ dia. $400-462
Candlesticks, miniature 160-172

Cologne, jade green to white,
   Moorish overlay design, 7″
   high 185-220
Dish, lacy, Hearts design 88-102
Ewer, pink/white, clear thorn
   handle, 13″ high 365-395
Lamp, amethyst, 9″ high 520-540
Lamp, whale oil, Star and Buckle,
   8½″ high 328-358
Plate, Beehive, 9¾″ dia......... 152-162
Plate, Leaf and Scroll, 6″ dia..... 80- 90
Pitcher, bladder, (hole in side for
   ice to cool liquid), frosted
   cranberry 462-473
Pitcher, icicle, cranberry overlay . 505-518
Pitcher, overshot 278-292
Salt, eagle, opalescent 223-232
Salt, Fleur-de-lis 178-210
Vase, amethyst glass, Three
   Prunty, 9½″ high (ill.) 385-420

Sandwich Glass

Sarreguemines China

Sarreguemines China

First established in 1770 in Lorraine, France, it was under the direction of Utzcheider and Fabry. It's a faience type; that is, a tin-glazed earthenware. Most of what you find today is from the 19th century; 20th century pieces are impressed "Sarreguemines" and "Germany".

Bowl, fruit, fruit decor, 10″ dia... $ 73- 84
Creamer, green glaze, man's
   head, 7″ high, signed (ill.) 107-118
Ewer, butterflies, gold decor 72- 82

Jam jar, covered, dark yellow,
molded apple on cover 65- 75
Pitcher, cream, green/yellow,
5″ high marked   90-100
Pitcher, hunting scenes, 10″ high   118-126
Pitcher, roses, leaves in relief,
green/rose, 8½″ high   118-127
Plate, flower decor, reticulated
edge, marked, 4½″ dia. 52- 62
Toby jug, 6½″ high, typical   148-159
Vase, blue, green/yellow
geometric designs, 12″ high . . .   121-132
Wine jug, cherubs, trees, 11″
high   106-116

Satin Glass   Satin Glass

Frederick Shirley of the Mt. Washington Glass Company was issued the first patent to make this beautiful glass on June 29, 1886. Seven days later, Joseph Webb of the Phoenix Glass Company was issued his patent on July 6. It would seem both gentlemen had gotten their ideas from one Benjamin Richardson who outlined the method of making Satin Glass in 1858. In any event, this is a satin-finished glass, first blown into a mold, then treated in various ways to achieve the beautiful satin finish. It's been heavily reproduced since World War II, with thousands of pieces flooding the country. Do know your dealer of this glass.

Basket, swirl ribbed, peach/white,
thorn handle $300-325
Bottle, cologne, deep blue, MOP,
6″ high   190-218
Bowl, raised Poppies and Leaves,
blue/black, 5″ dia.   192-207
Box, 6″ square, pink/blue floral
decor   227-242
Candleholder, black/green,
quilted base, 9″ high 77- 86
Cologne bottle, blue, enamel
decor, cut stopper, 7″ high   172-196

Compote, green, MOP, floral
decor   381-420
Cracker jar, Swirled Rose
pattern, MOP, 4½″ dia.   188-211
Cracker jar, 7½″ high, Venetian
Swag, quadruple-plate lid,
enameled floral, signed M.W. . .   192-210
Rose bowl, blue and white stripes,
Stevens and Williams   258-278
Salt/peppers, enameled floral
decor   162-172
Sugar shaker, pink/white   168-177
Tumbler, Diamond Quilted,
raspberry   162-172
Tumbler, Herringbone pattern,
white lining, 4″ high   170-180
Vase, Diamond Quilted, white
to pink, 7″ high   320-340
Vase, tri-cornered, Diamond
Quilted, enameled flowers and
leaves, MOP, 6″ high (ill.)   288-299

Satsuma Ware

Satsuma Ware

Glazed pottery (faience), cream ground, Japanese, decorated with raised enamel figures, scenes, flowers, etc. A feudal lord brought Korean potters to Japan around 1600, settling them on the Island of Kysuhu. Their wares were undecorated until around 1750. By early 1800, the repetitive and geometric patterns were introduced. Figural Satsuma Ware was made primarily for export, around 1850. There are four important periods: Edo, c. 1615-1868; Meiji, c. 1869 to 1912-14; Taisho, 1912-14 to 1926-28; Showa, 1926-28 to present. Satsuma-style Ware, from around 1900 on, was mass-produced. It's what you find the most of in shops today.

Bottle, Edo period, yellow
ground, cherry blossoms,
8½″ high $1,275-1,375
Bottle, Meiji period, Phoenix
birds, dragons, 9¼″ high .   258- 272
Bowl, Showa period, Arhats
(elderly men) and Phoenix
birds 268- 288

(continued)

Bowl, Taisho period, square,
floral motif 185- 220
Box, Taisho period, dragon,
Diaper (repetitive) pattern,
3″×5″ 122- 138
Box, Taisho period, Ebisu
(abundance-of-food god),
2½″×4″ 132- 142
Brush pot, Showa period,
Fukurokuju (longevity
god), 2½″ high 118- 127
Buttons, Taisho period,
dragon on each, ¾″ dia.,
6 in set, all 115- 138
Camel, 8½″ high (ill.) 225- 245
Cup/saucer, Meiji period,
Arhats and clouds 110- 122
Cup/saucer, Taisho period,
Hotei (contentment god),
garden scene 80- 90
Cup/saucer, Showa period,
Kame (tortoise), Diaper
pattern 70- 88
Cup/saucer, Showa period,
Phoenix birds, yellow
ground 74- 85
Figurine, Jurojin (longevity
god), 3½″ high 46- 56
Figurine, Showa period,
Bishamon (glory god), 3½″
high 47- 57
Figurine, Showa period,
Ebisu, 3½″ high 44- 60
Figurine, Showa period,
Fukurokuju, 3½″ high . . . 47- 57
Figurine, Showa period,
Hotei, 3½″ high 46- 56
Figurine, Showa period,
elephant, 3″ high 36- 47
Jar, covered, Edo period,
Phoenix birds, dragons,
7″ high 480- 520
Jar, covered, Taisho period,
Arhats, black ground, 6″
high 172- 190
Juice set, Taisho period,
Arhats; elephant juice
pitcher w/Mahoot finial, 6
matching tumblers, all . . . 182- 192
Pitcher, Meiji period, Arhats,
garden motif, 7¼″ high . . . 525- 562
Pitcher, Taisho period,
Phoenix birds, clouds, 6¼″
high 240- 260
Pitcher, Showa period, ladies
in garden, blue ground, 7″
high 88- 98
Planter, Taisho period,
elephant, sitting, multi-
colors, 6″ high 70- 80
Tea set, Taisho period, 21
pcs. (6 cups, 6 saucers, 3
teapots, 6 cookie plates),

Arhats, clouds, dragon
finials, all 415- 422
Tea set, Showa period, 33
pcs., Arhats and Kwannon,
dragon finials, usual
Satsuma-style decorations
overall 725- 762
Teapot, Taisho period,
elephant-shaped, pagoda
finial, 7½″ high 110- 128
Teapot, Showa period,
elephant-shaped, Kwannon
finial, 6¼″ high 62- 75
Vase, Edo period, Arhats,
clouds, 15″ high . . . . 1,600+
Vase, Meiji period, Awata
(gray-cream), Kannon,
8¼″ high 860- 890
Vase, Meiji period, Kara Shi
Shi-with-Tama (pear or
jewel ball) finial, dragon
handles, 19¼″ high 842- 866
Vase, Meiji period, Phoenix
birds/dragons, yellow
ground, 9″ high 782- 795
Vase, Taisho period, Kabuki
dancers, 16¼″ high 340- 360
Vase, Taisho period, peonies,
lavender ground, Kara Shi
Shi (lion-dog) handles,
11½″ high 262- 272
Vase, Taisho period, warrior
motif, figural dragon
handles, 23″ high 645- 662
Vase, Showa period, Phoenix
birds, clouds, blue/green
ground, 16″ high 198- 225

Scales and Weights

Scales and Weights

Scales have been around for centuries.
Before the 20th century, the balance scale
was the most common, and it was used to
weigh everything from meat to cotton.
Weights usually come with the scales. Brass
or iron weights often have been melted down
for making military items. The scales you
find now come in a variety of types.

Apothecary

Brass pans, iron weights $166-175
Porcelain, iron base, brass
  weights 182-192

Balance

Lady holding arm, hanging brass
  trays 66- 74
Wrought iron hooks, 26" high ... 88- 98

Candy

Brass pans, weighs up to 4 lbs. ... 132-141
Cast iron, brass pans, stenciled,
  gilt paint 85- 95
Toledo, white porcelain, 1920s ... 66- 76

Chemist

Wood case, glass windows, brass
  weights 178-188

Coin

Brass, 2 pans, portable for
  carrying in pocket, 1850s 79- 89
Fairbanks, coin slots, late 19th
  century 105-118

Counter

American Cutlery (ill.) 75- 85
Double round tray, brass scoop,
  cast iron base 172-182

Gold

Brass, in wood/glass box, complete w/testing kit 365-410
Brass pans and weights, in
  walnut box 121-140
Wooden box, for traveling, all 9
  weights 132-152

Hanging

Brass face, 3 chains, mid-19th
  century 88-100
Brass, 2 pans, 12 weights 96-108

Miscellaneous

Egg, fits in pocket 52- 62
Grain, slot in side, 1-lb. to 5-lb.,
  set of 6 weights, all 65- 78
Ice, big dial face, brass hand,
  30" top to bottom 77- 87

Postage

Fairbanks, brass, iron base 56- 67
Hanging, standard-type, brass
  pan 75- 85

Store

Drug store, ornate mechanism,
  mahogany box, drawer for
  weights 242-272
Druggist's, mahogany box, set of
  12 weights, brass 58- 74
Grocer's, set of 8 weights, ¼-oz.
  to 2-lbs., iron, all 38- 54

Schneider

Schneider

This is a French glass, identified by its mottled colors and fine craftsmanship. Mid-1800s until just before World War I.

Bowl, topaz, acid cut, signed,
  14" high $237- 252

Bowl-vase, colors fused in
  glass, 7" high, signed 258- 272
Compote, orange/blue glass,
  9½" high, signed 325- 352
Finger bowl and plate, Art
  Deco, smoked glass 199- 228
Lamp, wall, red/white shading,
  5½" wide signed 210- 261
Pitcher, varicolored roses,
  twisted handle, signed 320- 352
Tazza, orange, amethyst,
  bubble effect, 7" dia., signed 199- 221
Urn, apricot to clear, 10 ribs,
  15" high 920-1,100
Vase, black blotches, 8" high,
  signed, also marked Oving-
  tons, France 272- 292
Vase, blue/red mottled, 10"
  high, signed 342- 352
Vase, yellow ground, lacy
  enamel, pinchbottle shape,
  signed 351- 362

Schoenhut Toys

Schoenhut Toys

Albert Schoenhut established his firm in Philadelphia in 1872 to make toys and pianos. His biggest success was his Humpty-Dumpty Circus, introduced in 1903. His multijointed animals in vivid colors are much sought after today. The firm is still in business.

Animals

Alligator, glass eyes ....$ 245- 260
Bear, brown, glass eyes 162- 188
Bear, brown, smaller, painted
  eyes 132- 146
Buffalo, carved ruff 242- 262
Buffalo, cloth ruff, glass eyes . 262- 278
Camel, double hump, large ... 199- 225
Camel, double hump, small ... 168- 188
Camel, single hump, decal
  eyes 240- 270
Camel, single hump, glass
  eyes 262- 272
Deer, glass eyes 290- 320
Donkey, large, glass eyes 140- 160
Elephant, large, blanket, glass
  eyes 208- 228
Elephant, large, painted
  eyes .... 127-'136
Giraffe, large, painted
  eyes 252- 272
Giraffe, smaller, painted eyes . 210- 242

(continued)

Goat, glass eyes	122-	133
Goose, painted eyes	225-	252
Hippo, painted eyes	210-	228
Lamb, glass eyes	162-	177
Leopard, glass eyes, open mouth, painted teeth	240-	260
Poodle, carved ruff	127-	138
Poodle, cloth ruff, glass eyes	200-	222
Tiger, painted eyes	167-	178

Blocks

Auto Build, 5-in-1	160-	170
Little Tots, original box	120-	130

Circus

Humpty Dumpty, original box and poster, introduced in 1902; items made until 1926; complete circus, including booklet "Illustrations of Schoenhut's Marvelous Toy Circus. Copyright 1902," 18″×44″ tent, many animals and performers, all in good to very good condition, 54 pcs., all 5,400-5,700

(Note: Animals w/glass eyes, performers w/bisque heads bring much higher prices.)

Circus Personnel

Acrobat, gent	170-	190
Acrobat, lady, bisque head	240-	262
Clown, large, cotton suit	110-	122
Clown, large, silk suit	132-	141
Delvan Humpty Dumpty figures, ea.	34-	94

(The Delvan Company reproduced the original circus c. 1950.)

Lion tamer, bisque head	210-	225
Lion tamer, wooden head	179-	210
Ringmaster, bisque head	300-	342
Ringmaster, wooden head	142-	162
Strong man, bisque head	290-	320

Comic Characters

Barney Google & Spark Plug	650-	680
Felix the Cat, large	220-	232
Felix the Cat, small	128-	142

Games

Elfy Blocks, 9 pcs.	90-	108
Locomotive, Modlwood	152-	162
Metalophone (ill.)	120-	130
Naval War, original box	148-	157
"Ole" Million Face	157-	177
Spirit of Hollywood camera	108-	121

Pianos/Stools

Baby Grand	210-	232
Stool, double	170-	190
Stool, single	88-	98
Upright, large	192-	220
Upright, medium	170-	182
Upright, small	160-	170

Rolly Dollys

Baby, large	245-	262
Clown	182-	199
Clown and donkey	225-	234
Drummer Boy, small	162-	172
Negro Billikin, small	171-	190

Sconces

Sconces

Lighting devices that fastened on the wall, they came in all shapes, usually made of ornate brass and primarily made to hold candles. Many people have them electrified.

Brass, 4-arm, French, flowers in glass, pr.	$388-	425
Brass, 2-arm, French, figural design, pr.	352-	372
Brass, 2-arm, eagle design, outstretched wings hold candles	362-	378
Glass, 4-arm, cut, hanging prisms, American	341-	361
Iron, 3-arm, painted, floral designs	168-	178
"Pear Tree," wrought iron, 17″ high (ill.)	320-	340
Tin (Toleware), candle type, early 1800s, pr.	270-	292
Wood and gesso eagle, carved and gilded, late 18th century, American	925-1,100	

Scrimshaw

Scrimshaw

These are objects carved from the teeth of whales or the tusks of walrus. This type of carving was a popular pastime among sailors during the 19th century. They rubbed ink in the carving to make it stand out. Extremely collectible today, they're being reproduced in New England (see illustration).

Beaver, 4¼" long	$ 175-	188
Bust of man, 3" high	188-	197
Cane, 38" high, brass tip at bottom	221-	240
Carpenter's square, teakwood handle, 1850s	288-	297
Corset stays, 8, home scenes, 1840s	224-	234
Crochet hook, floral design ...	78-	88
Mother, child on swing, walrus tusk carved, 11" long	340-	360
Napkin ring, striped cat	152-	162
Naval battle scenes, square rigged ship, 1840s	882-	899
Naval scene, Union and Rebel flags	384-	399
Powder horn, man's name, date 1793, Boston Harbor .	1,475-	1,550
Punch, lady's name	81-	91
Sailing ship, cuff links, early 20th century	178-	198
Walrus tusk cribbage board, 1800s, 14" long		2,700+
Whale tooth, eagle and flag, 5½" long	760-	778
Whale tooth, new, 5½" long (ill.)	60-	70
Whale tooth, whaling scene, 18th century, 5"	958-	977
Yardstick	218-	232

Scroddled Ware

Manufactured in Bennington, Vermont, at the Fenton Pottery, it was made by varying the amounts of a coloring agent in each batch of clay. It was all stirred together, this time with a larger amount of the usual cream-colored clay. The finished mixture was then pressed into a mold. After being fired, a clear coat of glaze was applied. Considered rare, you can still find it if you know what to look for.

Cuspidor, Diamond pattern, feldspar glaze, gray/blue	$247-262
Pitcher, Diamond pattern, 11" high, reddish-brown	352-366
Teapot, brown/tan, feldspar glaze	347-362
Washbowl and pitcher, dark brown, both	555-572

Probably other pieces.

Scuttle Mugs

The scuttle mug is just another shaving mug, but the shape is different. Age group is the same as shaving mugs. Many repros.

Cream-colored, floral decor, Germany	$ 57- 70
Floral and gold flowers, Thomas in script, Austria	54- 63

Pink roses, Haviland	62-	74
Union, Patent September 20, 1870	59-	68
White ironstone, country scene, Germany	47-	54

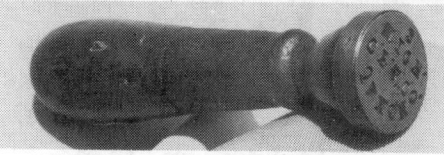

Sealing Wax Seals

Sealing Wax Seals

They've been used for centuries to seal letters, documents, etc. Solid gold 17th century French seals are especially collectible. Look for signet rings and seals that fastened onto gold watch chains.

Gold watch chain type seal, 1800s	$ 78- 87
Hand seal (ill.)	35- 44
Signet ring seal (usually coat-of-arms in 14k gold)	342-362

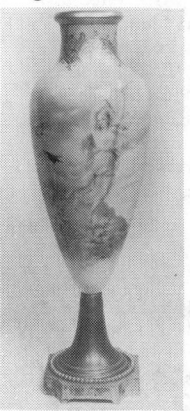

Sevres

Sevres

Madame Pompadour persuaded the factory to move from Vincennes to Sevres, France, around 1750. King Louis XV sanctioned the works, and some of the finest china the world has ever seen was made during that period. Biscuit and soft-paste porcelain were also made. Early pieces are scarce and expensive. Please, know your dealer.

Basket, blue/white, 13½" oval, signed	$1,375-1,450
Bowl, flower decor, ormolu handles and feet, 7½" high .	628- 642
Centerpiece, Art Nouveau, 8"×4"	375- 390

Clock, 2 urns to match, signed

(continued)

and dated 1756	2,975+
Coffee jar and saucer, blue/ gold, 18th century	447- 462
Creamer and sugar, yellow/ red roses, gold trim, signed Bavaria	218- 228
Cup/saucer, heavily enameled, 19th century	298- 320
Figurine, Bacchus under tree .	246- 256
Fruit cooler, roses, flowers, gold, metal liner, 1780s	2,500-2,700
Lamp, dated 1754, rare (demand receipt when you buy), pr.	3,500-3,900
Mirror, portrait, plaque of Sarah Bernhardt, brass frame, beveled glass, 6¼" long	188- 197
Pitcher, red rose, gold trim, marked Bavaria	220- 232
Plate, blue, gold trim decor, scalloped edges, 6" dia.	252- 263
Plate, blue/lavender ground, hand-painted, 1890s	198- 220
Statuette mantlepiece set of 4, bisque, cherub dancers	362- 371
Tea service, 4-pc., dated 1769 .	662- 678
Teapot, light blue, portrait medallion, gold handle	242- 256
Urn, enameled top, multi- colors, 12" high, pr.	720- 742
Vase, landscape, castle scene, 43" high, signed	1,985-2,220
Vase, pink/lavender/blue, on brass base, 15" high (ill.) . . .	328- 352

Darning eggs, ea.	4- 6
Dog-shaped "bird" (rare)	166-172
Iron buttonhole cutter, c. 1820 .	61- 71
Ivory/cloth tape measure, English, 3" high, c. 1750	70- 80
Ivory beeswax holder, to wax thread, c. 1830s	54- 64
Ivory fish, 1½" long, for winding thread, English, c. 1750	28- 38
Moroccan leather sewing box, brass feet, hinges, pulls, English, satin cushions, 3 compartments, c. 1730	795-950
Leather needle box, "By Appointment to her Majesty—"	51- 61
Sewing bird, brass, 1 cushion . . .	128-158
Sewing bird, brass, 2 cushion . . .	132-166
Sewing bird, silver plate, dated 1853, cushion missing (ill.)	125-150
Thimble, Acanthus design, silver, c. 1850	54- 63
Thimble, ½" high, Meissen, made by the Herold work- shop, early 18th century, sold at auction in London by Christie's in 1969	5,350+
Thimble, porcelain, Meissen, hand-painted, c. 1840s	128-132

Sewing Accessories

Sewing Accessories

The delicate art of sewing by hand is almost a thing of the past. Those items used in the 18th, 19th, and early 20th centuries are now collectible.

Cardboard thread winder, 8- pointed star, c. 1820	$ 34- 43
Chintz sewing bag, complete w/needles, c. 1840	48- 59

Shaker Collectibles

Shaker Collectibles

Ann Lee, daughter of a Manchester, England, blacksmith, founded the Shaker movement. The initial American settlement was established at Niskeyuna (now Watervliet), New York, in 1776. Originally the Shakers stemmed from Protestant peasants, the Camisards, who were persecuted by the Catholic

Louis XIV of France. Fleeing to England, they became known as French Prophets, and there they united with dissenting Quakers. The nickname, Shaking Quakers, refers to their habit of shaking or trembling with religious fervor at meetings, at the same time speaking in unknown tongues. Community spirit dominated everything they did. The finest Shaker furniture was produced between 1800 and 1860, and their handiwork had purity of form and simplicity. By the mid-1950s there were more than 6,000 Shakers living in 19 communities. Today, less than a dozen persons survive.

(continued)

Shaving Mugs

Shaving Mugs

Popular around the time of the Civil War,
they came into their own when a rash, called
Barber's Itch, swept this country in the late
1800s. After that, men demanded their own
mugs, usually with their names and/or occu-
pations painted on them. They were made of
porcelain, glass, silver plate. Scuttle mugs
were also a fad of the day.

Silver **Silver** **Silver**

Caster Sets

Beefsteak pattern, chased caster,
6 bottles, c. 1888 . . . . 70- 78

Befitting pattern, plain caster,
5 bottles, c. 1888 . . . . 80- 92

Decide pattern, chased caster,
5 bottles, c. 1889 118-121

Decipher pattern, plain caster,
5 bottles, c. 1888 132-142

Wince pattern, fancy gilt, 6
bottles, Derby Silver Co.,
c. 1885 120-132

Windlass pattern, w/bell handle,
6 bottles, Derby Silver Co.,
c. 1885 162-180

Celery Stands

Grecian chased, w/white glass,
Meriden Silver Plate Co.,
c. 1870 . . . . 52- 67

Medallion and chased, w/white
glass, Meriden Silver Plate
Co., c. 1875 . . . . 60- 70

Cups

Engine, plated or gilt, Meriden
Silver Plate Co., c. 1869 . . . . . . 19- 27

Grecian or damask, engraved or
plain, Meriden Silver Plate
Co., c. 1869 . . . . 18- 27

Goblets

Engine, plated or gilt, Meriden
Silver Plate Co., c. 1874 . . . . . . 24- 32

Plain, plated or gilt, Meriden
Silver Plate Co., c. 1867,
ea. 32- 42

Ice Pitchers

Grecian pattern, engine turned,
Meriden Silver Plate Co., c.
1887 . . . . 62- 71

Medallion pattern, Meriden Silver
Plate Co., c. 1885 . . . . 52- 62

Paneled chased, Meriden Silver
Plate Co., c. 1887 . . . . 62- 72

Syrup Cups and Plates

Damask chased, with plate,
Meriden Silver Plate Co.,
c. 1869 . . . . 40- 50

Grecian chased, without plate,
Meriden Silver Plate Co.,
c. 1875 . . . . 42- 52

Plain, with plate, Meriden Silver
Plate Co., c. 1868 . . . . 33- 42

Teapots

Flowers, signed "Meriden,"
8½" high 62- 72

Quadruple Plate

Cake Baskets

Debris pattern, etched, dated
1800s 72- 82

Decade pattern, satin chased,
c. 1889 . . . . 81- 91

Decamp, chased, 1880 . . . . 62- 72

Cups

Crumb brush, satin engraved,
c. 1889 . . . . 17- 24

Crumb tray, satin engraved,
c. 1889 . . . . 27- 38

Elfin pattern, hand-chased,
c. 1888 . . . . 29- 32

Florentine pattern, gold-lined,
c. 1887 . . . . 22- 31

Pied Piper of Hamelin, gold-
lined, c. 1889 . . . . 21- 30

Rose pattern, engraved handle,
c. 1895 . . . . 27- 32

Napkin Rings

Barefoot boy, 3" high, hand-
engraved, c. 1900 . . . . 24- 32

"Best Wishes," chick and
wishbone, c. 1880 . . . . 21- 30

Carved man and dog, 3" high,
satin finish, engraved, 1905 . . . 24- 34

Deficit pattern, hammered and
applied gilt, c. 1889 . . . . 27- 32

"Father," hand-engraved, 3" dia.,
c. 1890 . . . . 25- 32

Roses, repousse (ill.) 38- 47

Peppers

Decorous pattern, c. 1888 . . . . . . 12- 21

Decorum pattern, c. 1892 . . . . . . 19- 27

Decoy, c. 1889 . . . . 14- 19

Decree, gold-lined, c. 1889 . . . . . 15- 19

Pickle Casters

Behave pattern, blue, red or
canary bottle, c. 1889 . . . . 39- 47

Deduce pattern, red bottle, c.
1890 . . . . 34- 42

Napkin ring and pepper, Defence
pattern, c. 1890 . . . . 41- 51

(continued)

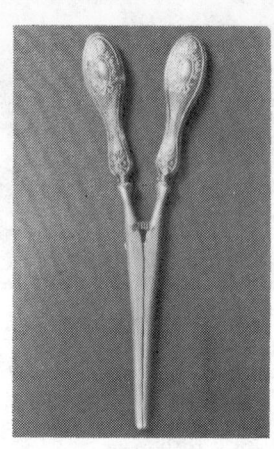

Silver

Mug, late 1800s 226-242
Napkin ring, etched flower
   decor 88- 99
Swedish
Creamer, flowers and foliage
   decor, early 1800s 64- 73
Tea set (pot, creamer, sugar,
   waste bowl, tray), 1800s, all . . . 1,475+

Silver Lustre Ware

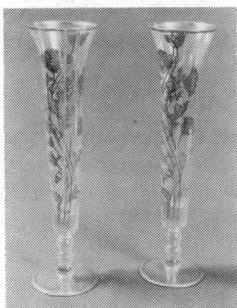

Silver Deposit Glass

Silver Deposit Glass

Popular since the late 1800s, it's simply silver deposited on the glass, usually by electro-depositing, a method involving electricity, flux, and silver anodes. It is still being made.

Bonbon dish, footed, 6½″ dia. . . . $ 82- 92
Bottle, cologne, green, 4″ high . . . 84-103
Bowl, 7″, 8″, 9″, clear glass 137-162
Bowl, 10″ dia., cobalt 162-172
Bud vase, 6½″ high, marked
   sterling 268-288
Cologne bottle with stopper, 4″
   high, marked sterling 352-372
Compote, green, 7½″ high 78- 88
Cruet, 7″ high, cut glass stopper,
   marked sterling 241-260
Decanter, 9½″ high, cut glass
   stopper, EPNS 159-172
Mustard jar, 4″ high 79- 89
Perfume bottle, 4″ high, cut glass
   stopper, marked sterling 244-271
Plate, green, sterling silver 99-119
Toothpick holders, 2″, 3″ high . . . 68- 78
Vase, bud, flared top, 8″ high
   (ill.), ea. 72- 82
Vase, 6″, 8″ high 79- 89
Vase, 9½″ high, marked sterling . 256-273

Silver Lustre Ware

Produced in large quantities between the early 1800s and 1840, in Staffordshire,

England, it went out of style in the 1850s when electroplating of metal items came into vogue.

Bowl, festoon and shell decor $137-148
Candleholder, ribbed design,
   11½″ high 118-127
Coffeepot, 10½″ high 420-442
Creamer, dolphin handle 168-177
Creamer, fine ribbed design,
   4½″ high to top of handle 182-192
Goblet, 4″ high 110-121
Goblet, 5″ high 88- 99
Pitcher, Leaf pattern, 4½″ high
   (ill.) 92-107
Pitcher, white quilted body,
   silver lustre at top 337-352
Sugar bowl, ribbed design 172-182
Teapot, 5½″ high 296-322
Teapot, footed, 8½″ high 342-362
Toby jug 351-371

Silver Resist Ware

Silver Resist Ware

This ware gets its name from the fact that the drawings or patterns resist the lustering solutions, and when fired in the kiln the entire surface of the piece, except for the pattern, is glazed. Similar to Silver Lustre except the pattern appears on the surface.

Creamer $192-201
Cup/saucer, Berry and Leaf 121-138
Jug, 5″ high 196-220
Pitcher, 6¼″ high 278-296

(continued)

Pitcher, canary ground, floral
  motif, 7″ high 294-322
Teapot, 5½″ high 269-289
Teapot, 6″ high (ill.) 252-272

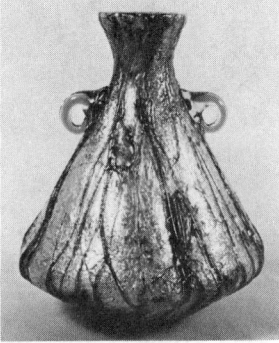

Silveria

SᵗⱱW

Silveria

This glass was produced by Stevens and Williams, Brierly Hills, England, about 1900. Its inventor, John Northwood II, gave it its name, and it was made by sandwiching silver foil between two layers of transparent crystal or colored glass. Drippings of transparent glass cover the outer layer of the glass. Two Frenchmen arrived at the formula in the late 1870s, but Northwood is generally credited with the manufacture of the glass. It's interesting to note that Northwood's son came to America and is given credit for creating Taffeta glass, better known, worldwide, as Carnival glass. Some pieces of Silveria are signed "England" while others may have the familiar "S & W" in script, with or without a fleur-de-lis on a ground pontil. Scarce, but a treasure when found.

Vase, applied green handles,
  pink/yellow/green drip-
  pings, 5″ high, c. 1900,
  signed "S & W" (ill.) $1,775-1,975

Slag Glass

Slag Glass

Mosaic was the original name for this glass, but it's been called marble or slag glass for many years.

Bowl, footed, purple, embossed
  design, 4″ high (ill.) $88-99
Salt, fish-shaped, purple (ill.) 76-86

Slides, Chain

These objects helped adjust the length of the watch chain hanging around the lady's neck. Gold or gold-plated, sometimes ornately set with precious stones, they're hard to find today because so many have been made into bracelets.

18k gold, small ruby, initials $130-140
14k gold, inlaid pearl on each
  side, late 1800s 180-190
10k gold, imitation diamond 30- 40
Keep in mind that 10k gold or less was usually used with imitation stones. The same applies to gold-plated.

Slipware

Made in Europe and the U.S. for many years, it's a ceramic decorated by applying slip (clay reduced to a liquid batter) to the surface of the piece being made.

Bowl, gray, 7″ dia. . . . . $ 92-107
Jug, figures in brown, 6″ high . . . 94-111
Pitcher, lustre striping, floral
  band, Staffordshire, 13″ high . 129-137
Plate brown/cream color, 10″
  dia. 172-188
Plate, red/brown, Pennsylvania
  Dutch motif, 9″ dia. 69- 82
Platter, brown, cream color,
  ornate decor, oval, 14″ dia. . . . 172-181
Pot, bean, red, glazed inside,
  9″ high 126-132

Smith Brothers

Alfred and Harry Smith established the decorating department at the Mt. Washington Glass Company in 1871. They were known for their excellence in enameling on bisque or opal glass. They established their own firm in 1875 in New Bedford, Massachusetts, and made the famous Smith vase in the late 1800s until it was cheaply copied and sold in dime stores by the hundreds.

Box, cigar, mahogany, brass
  fittings, 14″×11″ (ill.) 75- 84
Stand, smoking, brass, 27″ high,
  glass, ashtray, matchbox
  holder 69- 82

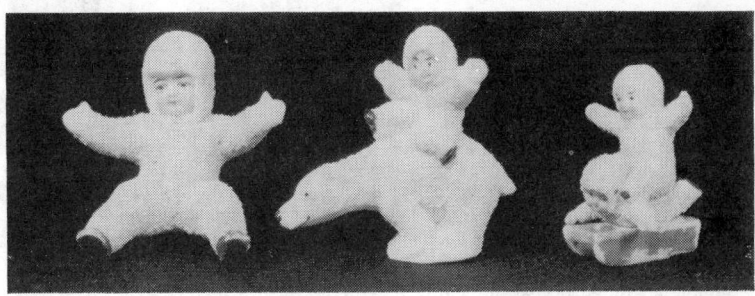

Snow Babies

Biscuit jar, daisies, blue shading,
  silver top, signed $385-425
Bowl, covered, signed   281-320
Cream bowl, white daisies,
  beaded top   275-325
Creamer/sugar, blue flowers,
  silver collar, white   251-271
Cracker jar, Burmese color, gold
  florals, silver bail   540-625
Plate, Santa Maria, 1880s,
  signed, 10″ dia.   620-688
Sugar shaker, ribbed, opaque,
  white, flowers, silver top,
  9″ high   137-146
Toothpick, flower decor, signed,
  3″ high   152-162
Vase, bird decor, enameled,
  signed   299-324
Vase, Burmese pink, yellow,
  fruits, acid cut   372-388

Snow Babies

These small bisque figurines originated in Germany in the late 1800s. Were they named for for Admiral Peary's daughter, born in Greenland, 1893, called the Snow Baby by the Eskimos; or were they Christmas candies, copied by German dollmakers? They are being reproduced.

Hiking, 3¼″ high . . . .$ 68- 82
Hugging, 2 girls, 3½″ high 73- 84
Lying on tummy, 3½″ long 108-126
Playing accordion 64- 73
Riding polar bear, 3½″ high (ill.) . 136-144
Riding sled, 3″ wide (ill.) 142-162
Sitting, 3″ high (ill.) 112-132

Smoking Accessories

Smoking Accessories

Box, cigar, inlaid M.O.P. top,
  rosewood, 12″×10½″ . . . .$ 54- 66

Snuff Bottles

Snuff Bottles

Usually intricately carved on the outer sur-

(continued)

face, they were made of glass, porcelain, jade, coral, etc. They were carried originally by Orientals in the 18th century. The habit of taking snuff, thought to be a medical cure-all, spread to Europe in the mid-1800s, probably even earlier. Snuff bottles were usually carried by women. See **Clubs and Publications,** this Price Guide.

Agate, carved, woman on
bridge, stopper, Ch'ien Lung
mark . . . . $ 710+
Cameo cut, pink/clear, jade top,
2¾" high 220-240
Cloisonne, 2½" high (ill.) 35- 40
Glass, blue painting on inside,
2¼" high 62- 72
Jade, stopper 325-360
Lapis lazuli, garden scene, coral
stopper 218-227
Mother-of-pearl, 19th century . . . 132-142
Opal, fish scene, coral stopper . . . 520-570
Peking enamel, women in
garden 242-252
Porcelain, horses, 2³/₈"
high (ill.) 35- 40
Rock crystal, quartz stopper 227-234

Snuffboxes

Snuffboxes

Made from metal, usually gold or silver, intricately carved, sometimes inlaid with precious gems; carried by men during the same period as snuff bottles.

Chinese, gold-on-steel, hinged
lid, footed $275-320
Cloisonne, blue enamel, flowers,
with lid 242-262
Glass, green/blue enamel, floral
decor 124-138
Louis XVI, gold/amber enamel,
3¼" long (ill.) 710-762
Sterling silver, initialed, lid 190-220
Tortoiseshell, primitive figures,
Chinese, early 1800s 425-462
Wood, inlaid silver, 4-leaf clover
on lid 79- 89

Soapstone

Soapstone

Soapstone is actually a mineral called steatite. It was used to make a variety of items during the 19th and early 20th centuries.

Bed warmer, wire handle $34- 43
Bookends, footed urns, reddish
brown, pr. 40- 48
Figurine, elephant, 4" high 42- 50
Figurine, Hoti, 6" high 54- 64
Figurine, man w/fish, 4¼"
high 44- 50
Flower holder, floral motif,
5" high 55- 63
Incense burner, dragon motif,
3¼" high 35- 42
Paperweight, 3 monkeys 40- 47
Rooster, 4" high (ill.) 60- 70
Toothpick holder, dragon's head,
3½" high 23- 30
Vase, floral decor, 8" high 63- 70
Vase, Kuan Yin figure, 7¾"
high 65- 73

Spangle Glass

Mica or other metallic flakes were imbedded between two layers of glass. Many firms made it in the late 1800s. Don't confuse it with Spatter (End-of-Day) glass. Poor repros being made.

Basket, blue/pink, mica, fluted
rim, clear handle $106-116
Basket, green/yellow, mica, thorn
handle, 7¼" dia. 138-158
Bowl, blue, mica, 7" dia. 74- 83

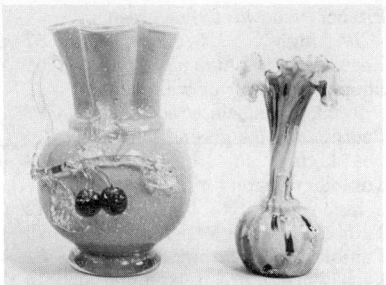

Spangle Glass

Bowl, cased pink/yellow, 6½"
dia. 54- 64
Cookie jar, usual marking, silver-
plated top and holder, 6" high . 71- 81
Paperweight, blue flowers, gold
mica flakes 132-143
Pitcher, blue, mica, cased,
miniature, 4½" high 132-142
Sugar/creamer, green, cased,
mica flakes 74- 84
Vase, cream lined, white/pink,
spangles, 8" high 57- 67
Vase, pink, silver flecks, red
cherries, applied clear handle,
"Stevens and Williams" (ill.) . . 74- 84
Vase, ruffled, spatter and
spangle, 6½" high (ill.) 73- 83
Vase, yellow ground, peach, mica,
cased pair, 6" high 75- 85

Spanish Lace Glass

Spanish Lace Glass

The opalescent designs of flowers and foliage identify this glass, popular in the late 1800s.

Barber bottle, cranberry, 9"
high . . . . $ 60- 70
Basket, blue/pink, ruffled,
scalloped, silver holder 80- 90
Bowl, blue/pink, ruffled lip 120-139
Bride's basket, blue, ruffled 140-150
Epergne, cranberry, 14" high . . . 220-240
Finger bowl, opalescent swirls . . . 58- 62
Lamp, cranberry, Fenton Glass
Works 140-150
Pitcher, blue opalescent, 9"
high (ill.) 160-170
Pitcher, vaseline, original tin
top 120-130
Rose bowl, vaseline glass 60- 70
Salt shaker, opalescent ruby,
4" high 40- 48
Spooner, vaseline 60- 70
Syrup, cranberry, tin lid 120-130
Toothpick, blue swirls, 3" high . . 52- 72
Vase, blue opalescent, 8½"
high 50- 60
Vase, blue opalescent, ruffled
top, 6½" high 60- 70

Spatter

Spatter

This is not a ware but a type of decoration used by potters worldwide. That made by Staffordshire potters, 1820-1850, interest collectors most. Much of it is ironston Adams made a lot in both the regular St fordshire, 1830s, and in ironstone in t 1840s. Most platters are octagonal. Pla are smooth rim or sided. The most pop pattern is Schoolhouse; Peacock is sec The most colorful is called Rainbow. ! popular colors were yellow, green, p pink, and blue. G. Adams and Son, A Cotton and Barlow, Davenport, J

(c

Heath, Powell and Bishop, Wedgwood (blue rim type) are just a few of the many firms who used this type decoration.

Bowl, blue, Peacock pattern, 6½"
dia. $236-247
Creamer, blue, Schoolhouse
pattern, 6" high 228-252
Cup and saucer, blue, Peafowl
pattern 242-271
Cup/saucer, Peafowl (ill.) 269-283
Pitcher, red and blue, School-
house pattern, 7" high 268-288
Plate, red, Peacock pattern, 9"
dia. 342-352
Plate, red/green background,
Schoolhouse pattern, 9½" dia. . 352-372
Plate, Star pattern, 8¼" dia.
(ill.) 262-281

Spatter Glass

Spatter Glass

It's doubtful that this glass was ever formally called End-of-Day. Legend has it that at nightfall the glassblowers used what was left over to make whimsies for friends and family. There's too much of it on the market. Though it was commercially made, it never achieved any great popularity when many firms made it in the late 1800s. Being reproduced.

Basket, multicolored, clear
handled . . . . $ 62- 80
Bowl, cased, typical spatter
colors, rigaree feet 42- 62
Creamer, 4" high 34- 44
Cup/saucer, blue ground, usual
colors 52- 60
Ewer, tortoise/opalescent
background, 8" high 58- 68
Jug, milk, yellow/blue spatter,
6" high 38- 48
Pitcher, blue/yellow/brown, clear
handle, 3" high 71- 80

Pitcher, yellow/red/blue/green,
7½" high 82- 89
Rose bowl, 3½" high (ill.) 58- 67
Slipper (souvenir or whimsey
item), green, white/red 27- 36
Toothpick, pink/green/brown,
4" high 44- 52
Tumbler, diagonal ribbing, 4¾"
high 42- 52
Tumbler, 5" high 29- 39
Tumbler, yellow/brown/green . . . 31- 41
Vase, blue/red/green, 11" high . . . 44- 52
Vase, red/bronze/green, 7½" high 47- 57
Vase, yellow, green 30- 40

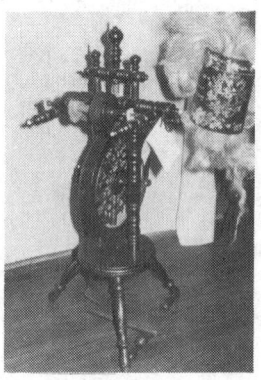

Spinning Wheels

Spinning Wheels

Who made and used the first one is not really known. We do know that there are two basic types of wheels, the flax wheel and the wool wheel. Basically, the spinning mechanism on a wool wheel is a metal spike, usually called a spindle. The spinning mechanism on the flax wheel is the bobbin and flyer.

American two-handed flax wheel,
c. 1850s $352-420
Appalachian area wool wheel,
c. 1840s 340-372
Connecticut double flyer wheel,
c. 1840s 320-361
European flax wheel, c. 1840s
(ill.) 352-362
New England wool wheel,
c. 1840s 382-420
New York two-handed wheel,
stamped A. Webster, c. early
19th century 360-385
Pennsylvania wool wheel,
c. 1830s 410-422
Shaker "SR AL" wool wheel,
c. 1830s 462-472
Shaker wool wheel, stamped
F.W., c. 1840s 441-452

Spongeware

Spongeware

Similar to Spatter, the designs were applied to the ware by daubing the color. Dealers call it Spatterware, or lump the two together. Any knowledgeable person can tell the two apart.

Bowl and pitcher, American made	$332-340
Bowl, blue, 8″ diameter	80- 90
Bowl, green or cream ground, 10″ dia. (ill.)	65- 76
Butter crock, covered, blue, 18″ high	172-182
Cup/saucer, multicolored, marked Adams	88- 98
Cuspidor, blue, blue bands	61- 71
Pitcher, blue decoration on buff ground, 6½″ high (ill.)	67- 77
Pitcher, blue, New England, 8″ high	106-116
Plate, blue, 8½″ dia.	66- 76
Spittoon, blue, 3″ high	74- 83
Vegetable dish, blue, 5″ dia.	77- 84

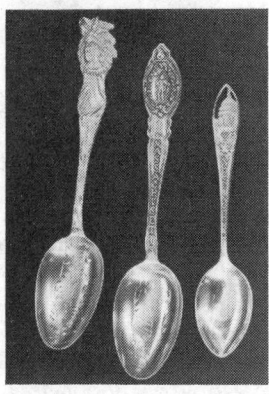

Spoons, Sterling

Sterling silver spoons are especially collectible. The maker and year decide the price. Prices given are for sterling only. Spoons are classified by maker, with pattern and type specified. Keep in mind what sterling silver

has done in 1981. See **Clubs and Publications**, this Price Guide.

Durgin
Bead, fruit spoon, gold bowl	$50-60
Bead, table or teaspoon, 5½″	40-50

Gorham
Blithe Spirit, sugar spoon	34-42
Cambridge, soup, teaspoon	24-31
Celeste, sugar, teaspoon	32-42
Etruscan, tablespoon	34-42

International
Blossom Time, dessert spoon	35-46
Charles II, teaspoon	42-52
Edgewood, sugar spoon	42-51
Moonbeam, tablespoon	44-53

Reed and Barton
Century, iced tea spoon	47-57
Columbia, teaspoon	32-42
Majestic, tablespoon	36-46
Tapestry, teaspoon	35-45

Tiffany
Wave Edge, serving spoon, gold bowl	45-55
Wave Edge, teaspoon	67-77

Towle
Contour, sugar spoon	68-78
Lady Diana, dessert, dinner spoon	34-43
Old Colonial, teaspoon	28-38

Wallace
Dawn Star, teaspoon	40-50
Eton, soup spoon	34-47
Rose, ice cream spoon	34-43
Waverly, teaspoon	36-46

Hundreds of other makers and patterns. Find a reliable dealer if you're interested in collecting silver, especially sterling.

Staffordshire

Staffordshire

Figurines and Figures
Boy and girl under tree, 5½″ high	$128-142
Cinderella, marked, 4″ high	69- 78
Dog, miniature, glazed white, 3″ high	49- 54

(continued)

Staffordshire

Dog, white lustre, seated, 14"
  high 99-109
Greyhound chasing rabbit, 11"
  high 69- 78
Horse, rider, groom holding
  bridle, 1785, 11" high 94-114
Lion slayer, 17" high (ill.) 261-280
Lover in a bower, 15" high 77- 84
Man and lion, 8" high 82- 92
Old woman and pipe, 1770,
  4½" high 510-542
Red Riding Hood, wolf, etc.,
  7½" high 132-140
William Tell, 18" high (ill.) 232-241
White cow, boy herder, 7" high .. 241-251
Miscellaneous
Box, boy riding Newfound-
  land dog, cover 52- 62
Cheese dish, blue/white,
  Fenton, England 61- 71
Creamer and sugar, Stag
  pattern, blue, white 52- 62
Cup/saucer, light blue,
  Challinor, handleless 47- 57
Hen dish, white bisque top,
  colored head, basket-
  weave base 128-142
Ice pail, ribbed, lion mask
  handles, cylindrical, pr. 344-362
Inkwell, masks on side, claw
  feet, cobalt bands 158-178
Jug, brown/yellow, willow,
  Pagoda, Porto Bello,
  5" high 92-108
Match holder, boots,
  striker, pr. 42- 52
Mug, Bacchus head, beard,
  pointed ears, 1800 152-162
Needle case, enamel, blue/
  green, red garlands 137-144
Pitcher, apple green, 12"
  high 62- 72
Plate, Avon cottage, blue,
  set of 6, 10" dia. 41- 51
Plate, Mayflower, 10" dia.
  (ill.) 54- 63

Platter, Lambton Hall,
  castle scene, blue 92-107
Quill holder, tree trunk, 2
  white dogs 73- 83
Tea service, strawberry
  lustre, 1825, 24 pcs., all ..... 1,250+
Toby jug, black/green,
  lustre trim, 10" high 199-224
Urn, Nottingham stone-
  ware, 1775, 6" high, pr. 222-231
Thousands of reproductions.

Stained Glass Windows

Louis Comfort Tiffany made some of the most beautiful. The more valuable come from Europe, but be on the lookout for old churches, old houses, even old railroad stations being torn down.

Church window, all glass perfect,
  3'×6' $742-762
Railroad station window,
  Southern, 2½'×6' 453-466
Window, green/blue, glass prisms,
  beveled glass, 6'×4' 524-538
Windows, each side front door,
  Victorian house, late 1800s,
  pr. 462-481

Stangl Pottery

Stangl Pottery

J. Martin Stangl was superintendent of the technical division of the Fulper Pottery Company as early as 1911. In 1930, Stangl acquired the Fulper firm. After 1935 emphasis was shifted from artware to dinnerware, produced under the Stangl name. In late 1955 the corporate title was formally changed to the Stangl Pottery Company. The pottery was made as late as 1972, the year of Stangl's death. "MS" is sometimes found on certain pieces though not all were signed. The Stangl birds are the most collectible.

Bird of Paradise .... $ 80- 90
Bluebird, signed 52- 61
Bowl, white, flower shape, 8" dia. 28- 37

Cardinal on stump	61- 71
Cockatoo, marked Jacobs	230-240
Double bluebirds	130-150
Double cockatoos	83- 93
Double hummingbirds	260-272
Gray cardinal	45- 53
Hummingbird, signed "STANGL POTTERY COMPANY" (ill.) .	65- 75
Oriole, signed as above	61- 71
Parrot eating worm	120-130
Rooster, signed as above	70- 80

Steins

Steins

The Westerwald area of Germany in the 17th century made the finest steins ever made. Mettlach also made fine steins, as did Dresden at Meissen, Germany. See **Clubs and Publications**, this Price Guide.

½ liter, flower motif, forest scene, pewter lid	$405-432
½ liter, green/buff, Liberal Arts Palace, St. Louis Exposition, 1904	400-421
½ liter, roses, castle scene, porcelain, pewter lid	388-421
1 liter, etched decor, porcelain lined, pewter lid	442-470
1 liter, musicians, barmaid, drinking scene, pewter lid	410-425
2 liter, blue and buff, pewter cap, 17" high	510-522
3 liter, brewery wagon and horse, advertising item, 1890s	232-248
Bardolph and Falstaff, #614, Germany, 9½" high, pewter cap, 1½ liter	218-227
Character steins, plain	192-210
Crystal deer, forest, hunters, pewter cap, 11½" high	320-332
Etched and art glass	268-278
Family crest, pewter lid, dated 1863, Germany	275-320

Fraternal, glass or pottery	210-232
Geschut, #1102, ½ liter	321-348
HR, etched	267-278
Hand-painted glass	198-232
Hunt scene, wild boars, pewter lid, 3 liter, 16" high	320-342
Lithophane bottom, nude, pewter top, Germany, 10" high, new . .	167-182
Merkelback & Wick, 7" high (ill.) .	177-192
Musterschutz, Bismarck, multi-colored	385-420
Musterschutz characters	292-321
Occupational porcelains	232-345
Pewter, scene in relief	269-310
Plain crystal	221-240
Pottery, scene in relief	188-196
Schultz and Dooley, Utica club beer, advertising item, 1900s . .	184-193
Stoneware, 3 liter, pewter cap, 16" high	210-228

Stereoscopes and Cards

Stereoscopes and Cards

These viewers came into use in the U.S. around 1850. They were invented in England a few years before. The picture is taken with a dual lens camera, then reproduced as two pictures. Seen through the viewer, the pictures blend into one 3-dimensional view. Every subject known to man was put on the cards. See **Clubs and Publications (Magic Lanterns)**, this Price Guide.

Single cards, any subject, average (rare)	$ 3- 7
Stereoscope and 12 cards	152-172
Stereoscope and 300 cards	475+
Stereoscope card, Philadelphia actress (ill.)	3- 4
Stereoscope, hand viewer, brass-mounted, 1896, 24 cards	172-188
Stereoscope, sliding adjuster, wooden, 36 cards	178-192
Stereoscope, sliding adjuster, Civil War scenes, 75 cards in box	388-425

373

(continued)

Stereoscope, table model,
walnut stand, Saturnscope,
1892, 12 cards 258-275

Steuben Glass

Steuben Glass

Frederick Carder founded the firm at Corning, New York, in 1903. In the field of decorative arts few men contributed more. In 1918 the huge Corning Glass Works assumed control of the Steuben Glass Company. Mr. Carder stayed with Steuben until 1933, acting as art director. He continued working in his own laboratory until he closed it in 1953 at the age of 90. He passed away in 1963 at the age of 100. Few men of his genius will pass this way again.

Ashtrays

Aurene, square, signed ..... $	352-	370
Verre de Soie, 3-cornered, signed	210-	228

Baskets

Blue Aurene on calcite......	675-	725
Blue jade	682-	725
Gold Aurene on calcite, signed	595-	640
Rosaline and alabaster, signed	950-1,100	

Bottles

Cluthra	940-	962
Cologne, blue Aurene, signed	552-	582
Green and amethyst, signed .	410-	432
Perfume, colored crystal	420-	435

Bowls

Blue Aurene.............	520-	540
Gold Aurene on calcite, signed	345-	370
Ivorine.................	162-	182
Jade green and alabaster ...	420-	432
Verre de Soie	421-	442

Candlesticks

Blue Aurene on calcite......	248-	270
Blue Aurene, tulip-shaped ...	192-	221

Cerise, signed, pr.	428-	442
Green jade and alabaster ...	172-	190

Compotes

Acid-etched, amethyst to clear, signed	342-	378
Blue Aurene, twisted stem, signed	310-	350
Gold Aurene and calcite, signed	395-	452
Green jade and alabaster, signed	548-	562
Rosaline and alabaster, signed	268-	277

Decanters

Gold Aurene	378-	422
Pomona green and amethyst	479-	492
Verre de Soie	262-	290

Darner

Stocking, blue Aurene......	392-	421

Dishes

Blue Aurene, salt..........	118-	142
Candy, blue Aurene, signed .	252-	270
Desserts, blue Aurene, 6 in set, all	520-	560

Figurines

Elephant, crystal, signed ...	532-	562
Leaping trout, signed	682-	741
Owl, signed	310-	342

Goblets

Blue Aurene and alabaster, signed, set of 6, all	492-	561
Gold Aurene and Venetian ..	172-	190
Green and amethyst	133-	143
Lavender and crystal	77-	87
Pastel blue and alabaster, signed	89-	92
Selenium red	268-	282

Lamps

Decorated gold Aurene	520-	540
Rosaline, bronze mountings, hanging type	532-	541

Plates

Green jade	88-	98
Ivorine, 7¼"	68-	78
Selenium red, 9"	88-	97
Verre de Soie, 6½", set of 6, all	265-	310

Rose Bowls

Green jade, signed	187-	196
Rosaline, signed..........	252-	272
Verre de Soie, signed	167-	182

Shaker

Verre de Soie	272-	290

Shades

Decorated Aurene, barrel shape	171-	191
Decorated brown Aurene ...	166-	174
Gold Aurene and calcite	184-	194
Gold Aurene, feather	152-	162

Sherbets

Blue Aurene, underplate	274-	281
Green jade, alabaster stem, underplate	163-	173

Vases

Aurene, 6″ (ill.)	385-	420
Blue Aurene and calcite	495-	532
Blue Aurene, Jack-in-the-Pulpit, signed	495-	542
Chartreuse	1,150-1,400	
Gold Aurene and calcite	420-	460
Ivorene, signed	452-	462
Jade green, 6″	152-	162
Moss Agate	2,100-2,400	
Rose Cluthra, signed	710-	742
Verre de Soie, 6¼″	262-	282

Stevengraphs

Stevengraphs

Thomas Stevens established his firm in 1854 at Coventry, England. He produced his first bookmarks in 1862, his first Stevengraph in 1874. He originated the name Stevengraph; his bookmarks should be called Stevens Bookmarks. The bookmarks were originally sold pinned to a paper backing bearing his name and trademark. Longer than wide, they are mitered at one end and finished with a tassel. His Stevengraphs are miniature silk pictures and matted. His name was never woven into the Stevengraph. It is woven into the bookmarks at a mitered corner. See **Clubs and Publications,** this Price Guide.

Bookmarks

Birthday Blessings (ill.)	$ 98-118
Centennial, George Washington .	210-232
Home Sweet Home	200-217
The Lady Godiva Procession	206-218
Many Happy Returns of the Day	121-132

Stevengraphs

Clifton Suspension Bridge, Stg. 140	450-482

The Death of Nelson, Stg. 152 . . .	350-385
Iroquois, Stg. 162	725+
The Lady Godiva Procession, Stg. 150	348-362
The Last Lap, Stg. 176	342-352
Madonna and Child, Stg. 87	900+
The Old Tyne Bridge, Stg. 144 . .	975+
Triumph, 1879	172-182

Stevens and Williams

Their factory has been at Brierley Hill, Staffordshire, England, for years. Some of the world's finest glass has been made by this firm.

Basket, clear to green, floral, crystal motif, 6″ dia.	$420-432
Bowl, swirls, camphor to cranberry, metal holder	562-582
Ewer, blue satin, enameled bird, coralene stem	382-420
Jam dishes, Rubena, pr. set in footed silver holder	328-368
Rose bowl, cranberry threading, blue interior, footed	462-491
Tazza, Rosaline baluster stem, 9″ across	575-620
Vase, enameled iris, acid-cut green ground, cameo type, 9″ high	520-540
Vase, peach color, enameled floral, blown	380-420
Vase, white satin, enameled floral, rainbow lining, 9″ high	442-481

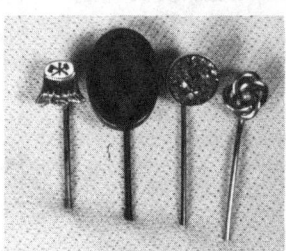

Stickpins

Stickpins

Stickpens are collectible because they are back in style. Diamond Jim Brady wore one set with diamonds worth $5,000. The Tennessee River pearl is worth $50 to $500. In general, prices are $6 to $10 for gold filled, $20 to $25 for 14k; with authenticated dia-

(continued)

monds, rubies, etc., they're much more. Get it in writing.

Anthracite diamond, 10k stem
(ill.) $25-32
Australian opal, 14k white gold 84-90
Brass-plated, initial (ill.) 11-16
Emerald, 18k gold 88-92
Pearl, genuine, 14k mounting 75-80
Pearls, seed type, 10k stems 16-20
Ruby, genuine, 18k.............. 84-91
Ruby, imitation, 10k setting 17-20
Sapphire, genuine, 14k 73-80
Sapphire, imitation, 10k......... 18-27
Silver-plated, initial (ill.) 11-16
Sterling silver, initials 24-34
Turquoise, coin silver stem 34-42

Stiegel-type Glass

Stiegel-type Glass

"Baron" Henry Stiegel made what is referred to as Stiegel glass at the American Flint Glass Works, Manheim, Pennsylvania, around 1765. Few authorities will positively identify it.

Case bottled, etched designs, pr. . $242-262
Flip glass, painted decorations .. 192-220
Glass, 2 etched birds in sunburst
(ill.) 138-147
Glass, 2 lovebirds and a heart
(ill.) 220-240
Glass, fluted sides (ill.) 127-142
Ink bottles, clear etched designs,
pewter cap 148-158
Mug, strap handle, etched tulip,
6½" high (ill.) 152-162
Tumbler, floral designs 150-160
Wine, etched designs, 4½" high . 166-172

Stocks and Bonds

After the crash of the stock market in 1929, countless millions of stock certificates weren't worth the paper they were printed on. Today—a new hot collectible. If the certificate hasn't been perforated, to cancel it, you may have a winner. Ask your friendly banker

how to trace old certificates. Average price, each, $2-7.

Allied Stores, Delaware, 1950s
Alma Lincoln Mines, Idaho Springs,
Colo., 1930s
American Telephone and Telegraph,
1960s
Basic Resources, Utah
Canada General Funds, 1950s
Cambridge Garage Co., Massachusetts
Centennial Mines, Washington
Dayco Corp., Ohio
Dahl Uranium Mines, 1950s
Dison Chemical Co., New Jersey, 1950s
Erleme Corp., early 1900s
Golden Cycle Mines, Colorado, 1920s
Great Northern Railway
Gulf Mobile and Ohio Railroad, 1940s
Louis Rothenblum, Inc., New York
Plastic and Fibers, Inc.
Publicker Industries, 1970s
Southern Railroad, 1960s
Spokane National Mines, Washington
Woodward Iron Co., Alabama
WS Lockman Construction Co.

Stoneware Pottery

Stoneware Pottery

A true form of early American art, decorated stoneware has come into its own from the collector's point of view. Slip-cup decoration is less common than brush-decorated pieces, but only the serious collector can tell the difference.

Crocks
1½-gal., butter, original lid,
floral spray in cobalt ...... $ 125- 160
2-gal., impressed Sam'l
Irvine, Newville, Pa.,
wreath decor in cobalt,
13" high 265- 310
2-gal., impressed Whites,
Utica, bird decor in
cobalt 242- 282

2-gal., not signed, bird in
tree in cobalt 118- 129

2-gal., straight-sided,
impressed FLACK &
VAN ARSDALE/
CORNWALL, ONT,
cobalt parrotlike bird 520- 580

3-gal., impressed New York
State Stoneware Co.,
winged bird landing on
stump in cobalt 970-1,175

3-gal., not signed, hen
pecking at corn in cobalt,
10½" high 250- 272

4-gal., impressed E. Norton
and Co., large flower in
cobalt, 11" high 262- 272

4-gal., impressed NEW
YORK STONEWARE
CO., floral spray in cobalt . . 152- 162

4-gal., straight-sided,
impressed Haxton &
Co./Fort Edward, N.Y.,
bird on branch in cobalt . . . 462- 492

5-gal., impressed Evan B.
Jones, bird on stump in
cobalt 362- 374

5-gal., impressed F.B.
Norton & Co./Worcester,
Mass., stylized bird on
leaf in cobalt 521- 542

5-gal., not signed, floral
spray in cobalt (ill.) 68- 78

5-gal., straight-sided,
impressed Hamilton &
Jones, running deer in
cobalt 428- 442

6-gal., impressed N. A.
White & Son, Utica, N.Y.,
floral spray in cobalt, 13"
high 320- 340

Jars

1-gal., impressed Warner,
West Troy, N.Y., cobalt
swirl, 11" high 168- 178

2-gal., covered, impressed
W. H. Farrar/Geddes,
New York, ovoid shape,
floral decor in cobalt 352- 372

3-gal., impressed T. Reed,
brushed tulip in cobalt,
11½" high 277- 292

3-gal., semi-ovoid, marked
ORRMAN BRO'S & CO/
FORT EDWARD, N.Y.,
crossed double birds in
cobalt 820- 870

4-gal., stenciled Hamilton &
Jones, Greensboro, PA,
14½" high 142- 152

4-gal., stenciled William &
Reppert, Greensboro,
PA, 14" high 47- 57

6-gal., double-handled,
signed in cobalt,
Lampert, Wenport 72- 82

Applied handles, brushed
blue floral band in cobalt,
13" high 172- 180

Simple leaf in cobalt, not
signed, 10¼" high 49- 58

Jugs

½-gal., impressed F.
Gordon, two small birds
in cobalt 77- 86

1-gal., impressed
Harrisburg 75- 85

1-gal., impressed N. White
& Co., flying bird in
cobalt, 11½" high 420- 440

1-gal., marked Camden &
Wilcox, Harrisburg, tulip
decor in cobalt 152- 162

2-gal., impressed New York
Stoneware Company,
Fort Edward, N.Y., quill
work flourish in cobalt 110- 132

2-gal., impressed T. F.
Connely, New
Brunswick, N.J., floral
spray in cobalt 115- 148

2-gal., marked Roberts,
Binghamton, New York,
large bird on front in
cobalt, 14½" high 410- 430

2-gal., marked W. A. Lewis,
large bird in cobalt, 13¼"
high 425- 485

2-gal., not signed, brushed
tulip in cobalt, 15" high . . . 220- 260

3-gal., impressed Julius
Norton, Bennington, VT,
running deer in cobalt 520- 540

3-gal., marked C. Hart,
flower/stem in cobalt,
14½" high 177- 192

3-gal., marked E. Norton,
flower in cobalt, 16" high . . 230- 240

Impressed New York
Stoneware Company, leaf
design in cobalt, 14" high . . 77- 86

Stretch Glass

An iridescent glass whose surface looks like
onionskin. Unknowing collectors buy it for
Steuben's Verre de Soie or Tiffany. Made in
the 1930s by Imperial.

Ashtray, blue iridescence,
Imperial . . . . $ 42- 51

Bowl, 8½" dia., light blue 52- 66

Bowl, reticulated 9¼" dia.,
pedestal base, light green 46- 57

(continued)

Stretch Glass

Candlesticks, pair, amethyst,
9½" high (ill.) 41- 51
Compote, 7½" dia., pedestal
type, blue 48- 58
Plate, 9" dia., white 34- 43
Vase, peacock blue, 8¼" high . . . 40- 50
Being reproduced.

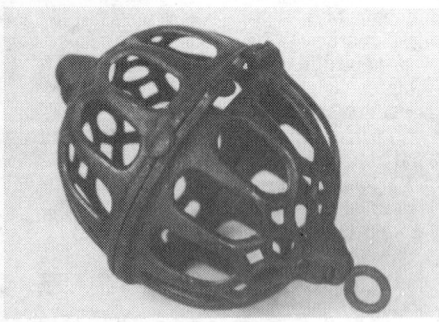

String Holders

String Holders

The hanging type and the beehive type were the most common. Used in grocery stores and homes, 1800s to 1900s. Near-perfect reproductions on the market today.

Counter type, pyramid cone . . . . . $ 47- 57
Glass beehive (scarce) 208-221
Iron beehive 47- 57
Iron, hanging-type, 4½" high
(ill.) 39- 49
Pottery, many shapes, cone-
shaped 32- 52
Sandwich Glass, overlay, red/
white 133-142

Sunbonnet Babies

Sunbonnet Babies

Bertha Louise Corbett, an artist, originated them. Unable to draw faces, she covered their faces with a bonnet. Early drawings conveyed Christmas and Valentine greetings. In 1902, Rand McNally published *The Sunbonnet Babies Primer*, the first school primer to be printed in four colors. Royal Bayreuth made a full line of china items, and others were made in Japan. Royal Bayreuth came out with porcelain plates in 1973 and porcelain bells in 1976.

Books
ABC Book, 1929 . . . . $ 52- 60
In Holland, dedicated to Princess
Juliana, 1915 99-108
In Mother Goose Land, 1927 . . . . 87- 97
Little Susie Sunbonnet, 1907 106-116
Miscellaneous
Baby blanket 108-118
Bookends, iron . . . . ʼ 72- 82
Cup and saucer, Candy for My
Mandy 181-191
Dish towels, for each day of the
week, all 128-142
Doll bedspread, 14"×20" 72- 82
Doorstop, iron 71- 80
Feeding dish, Getting
Acquainted, 8" dia. 242-262
Laundry bag, made from a
pattern 67- 74
Tea set, child's; washing, ironing,
6 pcs. 510-525
Trinklet box, Fishing on Pier,
4½"×2½" 77- 87
Pitchers
Cleaning House 108-118
Doing Wash 142-152
Fishing on Pier 132-142
Postcards
Days of the week, 7 (2 ill.), all . . . 172-190
Fourth of July (ill.) 29- 39
Months of the year, 12, all 238-242
You're Always Welcome 27- 37

Sunderland Lustre

Sunderland Lustre

Marbled or spotted decorations shading from pink to purple describes this fine ware. Gold compound applied over a white body created many shades of pink lustering. Many potteries made it, the better known firms being Wedgwood, Enoch Wood, and Adams.

Bowl, Sailor's Departure, 10″
  dia. $462-484
Box, black transfer, Old English
  scene, unattached lid 146-157
Button jar, purple lustre, pin-
  cushion on lid, 1820s 148-157
Cake plate, cottage scene 184-207
Creamer, raised floral figures 144-166
Cup/saucer, c. 1880 132-144
Jug, coat-of-arms, scenic, 6″ high 288-311
Mug, bridge over river, late 1700s 218-221
Pitcher, ship scene, ocean, 5½″
  high 284-293
Plaque, For man dieth, 6½″×8″
  (ill.) 178-192
Plaque, Prepare to Meet Thy
  God, 9″×8″ 178-188
Shaving mug, soldiers in bar-
  racks, late 1800s 177-186
Salt shaker, 4″ high 121-132
Teapot, black/pink, 6¼″ high ... 242-263

Swansea Porcelain

This pottery/porcelain was made at Swansea, Glamorganshire, Wales, about 1764, until the late 1800s. The wicker-bordered Swansea plates—birds, flowers, landscapes—are especially collectible today. The most reliable mark is an impressed SWANSEA, with or without crossed tridents. Know your dealer, please.

Cup and saucer, Willow pattern . . $107-117
Plate, wicker bordered, 8″ 132-152
Platter, Willow pattern, 22″ 162-177
Saucer, Willow pattern, 3½″ 121-131

Tapestries

Tapestries

There are tapestries and there are "tapestries." Some hanging in the Louvre, the ancient royal palace now converted into a museum in Paris, France, are worth a king's ransom. Most of what you find in shops today are late 18th or mid-19th century. A great many dealers are stripping "tapestry" drapes; that is, removing lining and selling them as genuine tapestries. Watch out!

Castle scene, pond, fish, birds,
  French, 80″×90″ .... $ 2,750+
Court of Louis XIV, France ... 328- 355
Court scene, French, 4′×6′ 338- 362
Deer and birds, scarlet on
  ivory, c. 1910 (ill.)   84-   94
English court, pastoral scene,
  3′×3½′ 242- 261
Ladies on horseback, gentle-
  men companions, French,
  3′×6′ 287- 306
Shepherd, shepherdess, sheep,
  original, France, 70″×95″ ..   3,875+
Troubadour serenading ladies .   92- 108

Tea Leaf Ironstone

In earlier years it was known as Lustre Band and Sprig, Lustre Band and Spray, and Edge Line and Sprig, among others. A gold lustre decoration on ironstone china with an oriental tea leaf best describes it. Nearly 30 English firms made it, including

(continued)

Adams, Alcock, Bishop & Stonier, Davenport, Maddock, Meakin, Shaw, and Wedgwood. About 20 American firms made it, including Buffalo Pottery, Hall China Company, Homer Laughlin, Knowles, Taylor & Knowles, and Wick China Company.

American
Bone Dishes
Meakin	$ 78- 88
Mellor-Taylor	82- 92
Powell & Bishop	64- 73

Creamers
East End Pottery	108-120
Red Cliff	54- 63

Cups and Saucers
Cumbow	51- 61
Knowles, Taylor & Knowles	34- 43
J. & E. Mayer	54- 63
Red Cliff (Hall)	31- 41
Walker	20- 30

Jugs
J. & E. Mayer	148-157
Sebring	128-142
Wick	81- 91

Miscellaneous
Berry set, Wick: bowl, 10″ dia.; 6 bowls, 6″ dia., all	118-127
Butter chips, most firms, ea.	13- 26
Butter dish, Wick, complete	81- 91
Waste jar, J. & E. Mayer	352-382

Nappies
Red Cliff	9- 12
Wheeling	27- 37

Plates
Homer Laughlin, pie	22- 32
J. & E. Mayer, sq.	54- 63
Red Cliff, large	7- 12

Platters
Buffalo Pottery	44- 53
East End Pottery	31- 42
J. & E. Mayer	31- 44

Sugar Bowls
J. & E. Mayer	77- 86
Red Cliff	43- 54
Wick	52- 62

Teapots
Goodwin Bros.	109-122
Red Cliff	79- 86

English
Bowls
Elsmore & Forster, waste, 4″	61- 71
Meakin, round, 9¼″	82- 92
Meakin, waste, 5½″	62- 72
Shaw, round, 6″	61- 71

Brush Holders
Furnival, 5″ high	162-172
Meakin, 5½″ high	177-184
Shaw, 5¼″ high	175-184

Butter Dishes
Grindley, 4½″ sq.	152-162
Johnson, 7″ dia.	142-153
Meakin, 4½″×6″	136-142

Casseroles
Furnival, 7½″ sq.	152-162
Powell & Bishop, 7″ sq.	87- 97
Shaw, 9″ long	152-166

Chamber Pots
Grindley	248-272
Meakin	256-269
Powell & Bishop	137-144
Shaw	229-252

Compotes
Meakin, 6″ high	187-197
Shaw, 9″ dia.	322-342
Shaw, scalloped edge, 9″ dia.	218-226

Creamers
Burgess, 4½″ high	121-131
Clementson, hotel type, 7¼″ high	108-118
Elsmore & Forster, 6¼″ high	109-122

Cups and Saucers
Davenport	87- 97
Edge, Malkin	81- 91
Elsmore & Forster	62- 72
Meakin	112-132

Dishes
Shaw, relish, 9¼″ long	47- 57
Wedgwood, square, covered, 8½″×6″	161-170

Milk Jugs
Burgess, 12″ high	158-168
Clementson, 8½″ high	162-177
Corn, 9ʺ high	147-162
Furnival, 9½″ high	157-166

Nappies
Furnival, 5″ sq.	31- 41
Maddock, 5¼″	35- 45
Meakin, 5″ dia.	38- 48

Plates
Adams, 10″ dia.	21- 31
Davenport, 10″ dia.	34- 44
Furnival, 10″ dia.	56- 66
Meakin, 10¼″	62- 72
Shaw, 10″ dia.	32- 42
Wedgwood, 6½″ dia.	12- 17

Platters
Mellor, Taylor, 12¼″ dia.	51- 61
Walley, 14¼″ dia.	74- 84
Wedgwood, 16¼″ dia.	72- 82

Shaving Mugs
Powell & Bishop	77- 87
Shaw	146-156

Soap Dishes
Grindley, 4″ high	152-162
Maddock	77- 88
Meakin, 4½″ high	158-172
Powell & Bishop	79- 89
Shaw, 5″ high	152-162
Wilkinson	166-172

Sugar Bowls
Clementson	68- 78
Davenport	71- 81
Edwards	82- 92
Meakin	86- 96

Teddy Bears

Teddy Bears

Supposedly, Teddy Roosevelt refused to shoot a bear cub while on a hunting trip in Mississippi, c. 1902. Actually, a political cartoon in *The Washington Post* on November 16, 1902, started the American craze for these cuddly toys. Rose and Morris Michtom made the first (c. 1907), calling their company the Ideal Novelty and Toy Company. Margaret Steiff, Germany, also made some of the originals in 1902-1903. Teddy bears are highly collectible and bring brisk prices.

5″, mohair, straw stuffed, button eyes and nose, Germany (ill.)	$ 28- 35
5½″, gold mohair, straw stuffed, black sewn mouth and nose, jointed limbs, Steiff, early 1900s	118-127
5½″, white mohair, shoe button eyes, Steiff, early 1900s	108-121
6″, brown mohair, straw stuffed, jointed limbs, head swivels, sewn nose and mouth, Steiff	127-142
8½″, brown mohair, roller skating windup, Made in U.S. Zone— Germany	299-340
9″, gold mohair, black sewn nose and mouth, jointed limbs, original ruffled collar and clown hat, Steiff, early 1900s	262-272
9½″, original felt jacket and pants, windup arms, bear somersaults, German, c. 1920s	368-382
11″, mohair, shoe button eyes, jointed limbs, red felt jacket and hat, dressed as bellhop; tail movement moves head	396-422
12″, brown plush, jointed limbs, swivel head, English	88-107
12″, mohair, shoe button eyes, black sewn mouth and nose, swivel head, Ideal, early 1900s	440-470
13″, soft brown mohair, glass eyes, black sewn mouth and nose, jointed limbs, swivel head, stomach squeaker, early 1900s	228-242
14″, brown plush, shoe button eyes, black sewn mouth and nose, felt paws, jointed limbs, swivel head, c. 1930s	162-177
15″, orange mohair, straw stuffed, glass stickpin eyes, black sewn mouth and nose, pink felt paws, stomach squeaker, c. 1940s	118-126
15″, white mohair, straw stuffed, glass stickpin eyes, linen paws, jointed, swivel head, early 1900s	168-182
16″, brown plush, special edition box, original tag, 75th anniversary	35- 45
18″, Beefeater outfit, English, modern	77- 87
19″, gold mohair, glass stickpin eyes, sewn mouth and nose, swivel head, hump, jointed limbs, early 1900s	328-348
20″, brown mohair, glass eyes, velvet paws, jointed limbs, Knickerbocker, c. 1938	142-152
22″, mohair, glass eyes, felt paws, tail moves head up and down, side to side, Roddy on tag, English	462-482
24″, white mohair, soft stuffed, glass eyes, felt paws, jointed limbs, swivel head, stomach squeaker, c. 1930s	236-246
Jewelry	
Charm, ruby eyes, 14 k gold	318-347

(continued)

Child's coffee set: pot, 2 cups/
  saucers, tray, c. 1920, all 112-127
China vase, green/white, 2 bears
  inside, c. 1900 91-107
Paper doll, E. I. Horsman, 5 out-
  fits, complete, early 1900s,
  10½" 410-446
Stickpin, sterling silver 42- 52

Miscellaneous

4-wheeler, brown mohair, glass
  eyes, growler operates when
  wire pulled, Steiff, modern, 20"
  high 328-372
4-wheeler, mohair, glass eyes,
  swivel head, squeaker, Steiff,
  8" high 162-177
Kellogg bears, printed fabric, soft
  stuffed, company premium, 3
  in set, c. 1920s, all 142-152
Muff, gray mohair, glass eyes,
  black sewn nose, felt paws,
  early 1900s, 15" 328-347
Perfume holder, mohair, jointed
  limbs, hinged body w/mirror,
  early 1900s, 3¾" high 187-196

Telephones

Telephones

The first patent for a telephone was
granted to Alexander Graham Bell in 1876.
Since then more than 300 types have been
made. See **Clubs and Publications**, this Price
Guide.

American Electric, 1905	$ 875-	950
Baird Mfg. Co., 1902	650-	730
Chicago, 1906	425-	585
Churchill, 1906............	295-	365
Columbia, 1902	550-	610
Corwin, 1916	650-	710
Couch-Sealy, 1900	875-	965
Dean, 1906-1914	495-	550
Electric Goods Mfg. Co.,		
1905	495-	570

Eureka, 1902	975-	1,300
Faar, 1906	425-	495
Julius Andrea, 1907	410-	465
Kellogg, 1910.............	375-	435
Stromberg-Carlson,		
1906-1908	420-	485
Sun, 1901...............	395-	445
Swedish-American, 1901	1,400-	1,650
Varney, 1902	625-	675
Voight-Berger, 1905	465-	535
Wall-type, 1916 (ill.)	275-	325
Wesco, 1907.............	435-	495
Williams, Abbott, 1901	465-	535
Wotton, 1907	365-	435

Teplitz

Teplitz

This porcelain was mass-produced in the
late 1800s in Germany, usually in vase form.
Originally priced in shops from 25¢ to $3.00,
prices have soared.

Basket, floral decor, twisted	
handle, 6½" high	$137-146
Bowl, 5-legged pedestal, black/	
green mottling	85- 95
Ewer, cream background, gilded	
Art Nouveau lizard handle,	
gold sunrise, bird, raised gold	
feathers (ill.)	122-132
Jardiniere, 4-handled, cream/	
maroon banding	162-172
Mug, Indian chief, blue back-	
ground, 4½" high	68- 79
Vases, all types and colors,	
typical price	88- 98
Wall plaque	232-247

Terra-Cotta

Used for making pottery, figurines, and
other ornamental objects, it's a brown-red
clay usually found in river banks. The
Chinese have been using it for thousands of
years.

Terra-Cotta

Chinese farmer, 7" high . . . . $ 72- 82
Chinese merchant at counting
   table, 8" high, 10½" dia. 79- 92
German tea set, 4-pc. 188-199
Italian jewelry box, 4" wide 79- 92
Italian peasant on donkey, 6¼"
   high (ill.) 88- 98

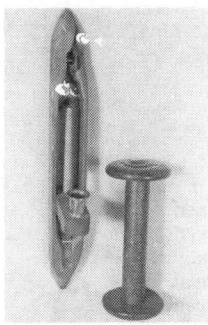

Textile Collectibles

Textile Collectibles

Various items relating to the textile industry are showing up in shops as mills put in
new equipment or go out of business.

   Shuttle, wood, made into candle-
     holder $8-12
   Spool, wood, for paper towels (ill.) . . . 6- 9

Threaded Glass

Supposedly made at Sandwich, the glass
threading around the object was put on by
hand, later by machine. Attributed to
Nicholus Lutz, probably more than one person made it to keep up with demand in the
mid-1800s. All colors were used, including
cranberry. Another repro item.

   Atomizer, red/blue . . . . $ 82- 92
   Basket 118-142
   Biscuit jar, cranberry/clear 161-171
   Bowl, 5" high, applied white feet . 187-199

Threaded Glass

Decanter, blue on clear, 11½"
   high 109-118
Jam jar, silver-plated lid and bail . 132-152
Pitcher, 12" high, cranberry,
   floral decor, clear handle (ill.) . . 188-198
Tumbler, cranberry 121-131
Vase, cranberry, green shading . . 162-172

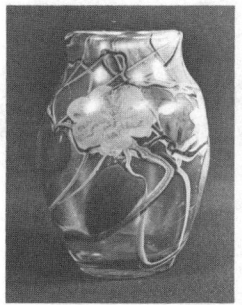

Tiffany

Tiffany

Louis Comfort Tiffany was an artist, an interior decorator, and a genius at making art
glass in many forms. Today, all his creations
are world-famous and highly sought after.
His Favrile trademark was registered in
1894. In 1896 a permanent numbering
system was instituted, as follows: A to N
prefix, 1896-1900; O to Z prefix, 1901-1905; A
to N prefix, 1906-1912; O to Z prefix, 1913 to
1920. Numbers only, before 1896. Early
pieces were not signed, having only fragile
paper labels. All numbers were acid-signed
as were the signatures, "Louis C. Tiffany,"
"L.C. Tiffany," and the initials "L.C.T."
Most lamp bases were stamped "Tiffany Fur-
naces." Look out for forgeries.

 (continued)

Ashtrays
Gold Dore, nest of 4, all
signed, all . . . . $ 550-   620
Zodiac, symbol in center,
signed   238-   268

Blotter Ends
Sea Horse, 12″ high,
stamped Tiffany
Studios, pr.   170-   188
Spanish pattern, 12″ high,
stamped Tiffany
Studios, pr.   235-   265
Zodiac, 12″ high, stamped
Tiffany & Co., pr.   275-   288

Bonbons
Blue iridescent, signed
L.C.T. Favrile   382-   392
Gold iridescent, signed as
above   347-   367

Bookends
American Indian pattern,
signed Tiffany Studios,
pr.   432-   462
Buddha, 6″ high, signed as
above, pr.   352-   366
Owl's head, signed as
above, pr.   392-   420

Bowls
Blue iridescent, floral vine,
signed L.C.T., 7″ high .   1,950- 2,300
Blue iridescent, ribbed,
signed L.C. Tiffany, 10″
dia. 2,275- 2,465
Blue iridescent, scalloped
rim, signed L.C. Tif-
fany, 5½″ high   510-   542
Gold iridescent, crystal
stem, green/white base,
7″ dia.   322-   342
Gold iridescent, fluted
edge, signed, 5″ dia. . . .   288-   320
Gold iridescent, scalloped
edge, signed L.C. Tif-
fany, 8¼″ dia.   565-   670

Boxes
Blue iridescent, ribbed
panels, signed L.C.T. . . .   750-   820
Gold iridescent, hexagon,
Gold Dore, signed   520-   560

Candlesticks
Blue iridescent, twisted
stem, 14¼″ high, signed   3,700- 3,900
Gold iridescent, Favrile/
bronze, 8″ high, signed
L.C. Tiffany, pr. 3,900- 4,300
Gold iridescent, Favrile/
bronze, 15″ high, signed   10,200-10,400

Chalices
Gold iridescent, pink high-
lights, signed L.C.T., pr.
(ill.) 1,500- 1,700
Paperweight base, signed
L.C.T.   875-   975

Champagnes
Gold iridescent, grape
design, 6¼″ high,
signed L.C.T.   295-   325
Gold iridescent, hollow
stem, 7½″ high, signed   468-   497
Lavender pastel, 8″ high,
signed   488-   522

Compotes
Gold/blue iridescent, 5″
high, signed L.C. Tif-
fany   795-   845
Gold iridescent, pedestal
base, 8″ high, signed
L.C.T.   652-   710
Gold iridescent, wafer
stem, 7½″ high, signed
L.C. Tiffany   590-   640
Green iridescent, 8″ high,
signed   665-   722

Dishes
Gold iridescent, Favrile,
scalloped edge, 4″ dia. .   352-   378
Nut, blue iridescent,
signed, 4¼″ dia.   495-   542
Nut, gold iridescent,
scalloped border, 3-
footed, 4″ dia., signed
L.C. Tiffany   562-   633

Goblets
Flower form, pink, 5¾″
high, signed   462-   492
Gold iridescent, hollow
stem, intaglio, 6¼″
high, signed   388-   420
Gold iridescent, swirl
stem, 7″ high, signed
L.C.T.   467-   522
Gold luster, iridescent on
amber, 7″ high, signed .   542-   582

Lamps
Floor, Dragonfly, 22″ dia.,
signed Louis C. Tiffany
on shade, Tiffany
Studios on base 79,000- 87,000
Lily, 5-light, shades and
base signed 6,200- 6,800
Lily, 12-light, floor, 4′ 8¼″
high, all pcs. signed . . . 38,700- 44,500
Table, Arrowroot, 20″ dia.
shade, both shade and
base signed . . . .   37,000+
Table, Daffodils, shade
20″ dia., all pcs.
signed . . . .   67,000+
Table, Peony Wisteria
shade, all pcs. signed . . 178,000-192,000

Pitchers
Blue iridescent, 3″ high,
signed L.C.T. 3,200- 3,500
Gold iridescent, etched
grapes, 7″ high, signed
L.C. Tiffany 1,800- 2,200

Green iridescent, tea,
applied leaves, 7½"
high 1,900- 2,200
Plates
Gold opalescent, Feather
design, 11" dia., signed . 492- 526
Pastel blue, yellows,
signed L.C.T. Favrile . . 488- 522
Purple iridescent, 6" dia.,
signed 452- 482
Salts
Amber, ruffled edge, 4
feet, 3½" dia., signed
L.C.T. 420- 480
Blue iridescent, ruffled
edge, 2¾" dia., signed . 272- 296
Gold iridescent, twisted
pulls, 2" dia., signed
L.C.T. 320- 344
Rainbow iridescent, ruf-
fuled edge, 2½" dia.,
signed L.C.T. 262- 288
Shades
Gold Drape, brown
ground, 8½" dia.,
signed 542- 566
Gold iridescent, tan
ground, 6½" dia.,
signed 520- 542
Purple opalescent, green
feathers, 7" dia., signed 542- 566
Sherbets
Blue iridescent, pinched
sides, 2¼" dia. 442- 449
Gold iridescent, 3" dia.,
signed L.C.T. 390- 462
Gold iridescent, 2½" dia.,
set of 6, all signed, all . . 1,900- 2,400
Toothpicks
Gold iridescent, blue
feathers, 3½" high,
signed 762- 790
Gold iridescent, green
feathers, 2¼" high,
signed 820- 860
Tumblers
Amber, paperweight base,
signed L.C.T. and
numbered 785- 940
Blue iridescent, Twist pattern, 5¼" high, signed . 962- 1,100
Clear, green feathers, 6"
high, signed L.C.T. and
numbered 372- 399
Vases
Amber iridescent, signed . 2,900- 3,300
Blue iridescent, scalloped
top, fluted stem, 9"
high, signed L.C. Tif-
fany and numbered 3,400- 3,700
Bud, blue iridescent,
Feather design, 8½"
high, signed 1,400- 1,600

Flower form, ribbed, gold
interior, 7½" high,
signed 3,600- 3,900
Multi-colored, paper-
weight base, 5½" high,
signed L.C. Tiffany
and numbered 375 T
(ill.) 6,975- 7,400

Tiffin Glass

One of the prettiest wares made by the Tif-
fin Glass Company, Tiffin, Ohio, was their
Black Satin glass. It was also made by the
U.S. Glass Company, Pittsburgh, late 1800s.
All prices listed are for Black Satin.

Basket, 10" high . . . . $ 74- 83
Bottle, perfume, brass plunger . . 51- 61
Bowl, 4" high, 7" dia. at top 55- 65
Compote, crystal stem, 7" high . . 59- 68
Tumbler 28- 37
Urn, 5½" high 64- 74
Vase, 7" high, flower decor in
gold trim 59- 69
Vase, 6½" high, gold decoration
around top 68- 78
Wine set, 6 wines and decanter,
all 120-130

Tiles

Ⓐ

TRENT TILE
TRENTON, N.J.
U.S.A.

*Low Art
Tile Co.
Chelsea
Mass. est. 1888*

Tiles

Decorative tiles have been used for floors,
benches, fireplaces, for centuries; table tiles
for the same length of time. Made in every
country in the world.

Blue/gold, flower decor, Austria . $ 26- 35
Delft, sailing scene, in frame 34- 43
Fireplace type, floral decor,
6"×6" 37- 42

(continued)

Mercer tile, Moravian Pottery
  & Tile Works, Doylestown, Pa.,
  octagonal, brown glaze 35- 42
Mercer tile, octagonal, blue
  glaze, cutout grape design 34- 39
Mercer tile, octagonal, "Rain,"
  terra-cotta, 6½" high 64- 72
Rookwood, blue/green, dated
  XVII 80- 90
Roseville, flowers, multicolored ..   52- 62
Spanish dancers 22- 32

Tin Containers

Tin Containers

Bennett, Sloan & Co., clove can,
  pull off lid, 3½"×2¼" ...... $ 14- 18
Bleecker & Simmons, tea can,
  hinged lid, 2"×4" 12- 21
Chase & Sanborn, Orange Pekoe
  tea can, screw lid, 4½"×3¾" ...   11- 21
Chicago Fire Appliance Co.,
  Eclipse fire extinguisher, snap
  in lid, 22"×6½" 21- 29
Conant, Patrick & Co., Milk Maid
  brand coffee, in cream pail with
  pull-off top, 7¼"×13" 46- 54
Co-Operative Mfg. Co., Bull Dog
  brand fire extinguisher, snap
  in lid, 22"×6½" 23- 33
Eureka Powders Works (gun),
  circular tin, screw cap,
  4¾"×10" 34- 42
Hazard Powder Co. (gun), circular
  tin, screw cap, 7½"×19½" ...   51- 61
Huntley & Palmers biscuit tin,
  log chest, hinged lid, 4¼"×7" .   56- 66
Huntley & Palmer biscuit tin,
  stack of Worcester plates, circular, hinged lid, 2"×26½" ... 118-132
Kings Great Western Powder Co.
  (gun), screw cap, 7¾"×6" 34- 44
Larus & Bros. Co. Hand Bag Cut
  Plug, hinged lid, 6"×4½" 38- 48
Mayo's Tobacco Co. Brownie,
  Roly-Poly tin, pull-off lid,
  7"×19" 288-298
Mayo's Tobacco Co., Negro
  mammy, Roly-Poly tin, pull-off
  lid, 7"×19" 287-296

United States Tobacco Co., North
  Pole Cut Plug, pull-off lid,
  5"×6" 64- 74
Savings bank, hinged lid, key,
  5"×8" (ill.) 21- 32

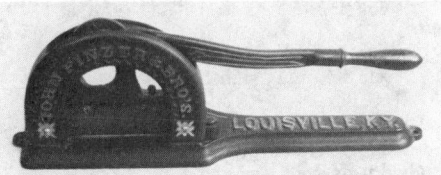

Tobacco Cutters

Tobacco Cutters

Before the advent of cigarettes, plug tobacco and snuff were the thing along with foul-smelling cigars. Plug tobacco came in bars and had to be cut. The cutter was used for that purpose. See **Clubs and Publications,** this Price Guide.

Black Beauty .... $ 68- 78
Brown Mule, iron 66- 76
Climax Plug 52- 62
Imp Thumbing Nose, iron   90-108
John Finzer & Bro's, Louisville,
  Ky., iron, gilded letters (ill.) ...   71- 81
Ordinary types, iron 62- 72
R.J.R.T. Co. (R. J. Reynolds
  Tobacco Co.), iron 71- 81

Tobacco Jars, Containers

Tobacco Jars, Containers

Usually made of porcelain, wood, or metal with a lid, they were used as humidors for cigars or pipe tobacco. In vogue in the mid-1800s. See **Clubs and Publications,** this Price Guide.

Black boy, straw hat	$134-142
Bulldog, Bristol glass	91-107
Dutch scene, glazed pottery, pipe finial on lid (ill.)	98-109
Elephant toe, ivory handle on lid, 10″ high (ill.)	91-101
Human skull, white, black bones	162-177
Indian chief, Majolica	172-182
Kitten holding friends, porcelain	141-151
Lion's head, 7″ high	77- 87
Mayo's Roly Poly, litho-on-tin, fat man w/pipe	252-262
Monkey's head, Majolica	133-139
Owl, Majolica, 7½″ high	81- 91
Pig with broom	134-139
Pirate, Staffordshire	187-206
Rookwood, brown tan, 1909	182-192
Royal Bayreuth, tapestry ware, pasture scene	164-174
Sea captain, Majolica, pipe in mouth	188-198

Toby Jugs

Supposedly taken from Sterne's *Tristam Shandy*, Uncle Toby was a popular shape for ale mugs in the early 1800s. The better ones came from England, in every color. Hundreds of fakes are on the market, especially from Japan.

Cat, 9″ high	$173-183
Creamer, Delft type, blue/white	228-242
Creamer, Rockingham-type glaze, man with tricornered hat, 6″ high	177-188
Jug, Napoleon, 10″ high	320-350
Jug, Santa Claus, 8″ high	172-182
Jug, Staffordshire, 1850s, old gentleman holding jug	442-452
Jug, Staffordshire, 1850s, squat, embossed figure	510-530
Jug, Toby Philpot, Pratt ware, 11″ high	832-844
Jug, George Washington head, American made (N.J.), probably Trenton	600-621
Jug, Ralph Wood, seated man with tricorn hat	462-482
Jug, identical to above, except marked Japan	72- 82

Toleware (Tin)

This is a misnomer as "tole" originally meant items made of sheet iron and then decorated. Popular use has caused tole to be known as decorated tin items, especially those coming from the Pennsylvania Dutch country in the mid-1800s. Scarce today because so much was thrown away when it became dented. Being reproduced.

Candle box with loop for hanging	$248-268
Coffeepot, black, orange, red, green decor, 12″ high	272-292
Coffeepot, blue/yellow, 6″ high	265-275
Creamer, 6″ high, initialed M.B.	281-291
Deed box, original stenciling, black, green, red decor	400-442
Document box, handled black, gold floral stenciling, red/yellow striping, 3″×3¼″	162-172
Document box, handled, stenciled	281-291
Food warmer, stenciled flowers	197-225
Jug, typical colors, 5″ high	540-562
Lantern, processional type, cross on staff, original stenciling	262-272
Muffineer, fruit/flowers, 4¼″ high	177-192
Pitcher, red/yellow, hinged lid, 7″ high	192-208
Syrup pitcher, green/black, red flowers, 5½″ high	212-228
Tea canister, red/green, 6″ high	220-240
Tray, black, gold stenciled flowers, leaves and borders, red/green/yellow	132-152
Tray, red, pink, white flowers, original paint	332-361

Tools

Tools

Handmade tools are being collected; even early factory-made tools are avidly sought. For a comprehensive look at old tools, see *Pictorial Guide to Early American Tools and Implements* by Robert W. Miller—another Wallace-Homestead publication. A lot of old tools have been altered through necessity, but too many are showing up at auctions and shows that have been deliberately altered to enhance their value. Also, see **Clubs and Publications**, this Price Guide.

387

(continued)

Cast iron, 5-lbs., 6½" high	28- 38
Hexagonal, Sargeant steel, 3½" high	22- 32
Witchet (adjustable rounding), Mockridge & Francis/Newark	115-138
Wooden, steel tip, 3½" high	27- 32

Rules

Ivory, 4-fold, bound in German silver, Stephens & Co., No. 99¼	162-172
Ivory, 4-fold, brass hinges	152-162
Meter, brass, folding type, Wien (Vienna)	44- 53

Saw Sets

Chas. Croissant & Bros., 1872 patent	14- 19
Foley, Pat. Oct. 5, 1916	13- 18
Leach's Patent	8- 12
Taintor's Positive No. 7, Patented 1891-1907	11- 16

Saws

Back, Fletcher/London, early 19th century	51- 61
Bow, beech frame, I & H Sorby, 8¼" blade	60- 70
Coping, typical gunsmith's, 12" overall	118-127
Keyhole	11- 15

Screwdrivers

Drummond's Patent, 1870	19- 27
Goodell Pratt, ratchet type	11- 14
A. H. Reid, Philadelphia, archimedian	25- 33
Yankee No. 10, ratchet type	11- 18

Shaves

Double, cast iron	31- 40
Ram's horn, beech, 11½" overall	46- 54
Spoke, bent inshave, beech	88- 98
Spoke, Sorby, ebony	52- 62

Squares

Try, fruitwood stock, 21½"	21- 31
Try, mahogany stock, brass bound, 16"	28- 37
Try, W. Tower & Co., brass bound stock, 15"	32- 42

Travelers

Hand-forged, 6" dia.	60- 70
Hand-forged, wooden handle, 10" dia.	34- 44
Manufactured, Green River style	28- 37

Toothpick Holders

In the 1800s it was considered polite to pick one's teeth after eating. The holders were made of every type of material, usually glass or a pot metal, silver-plated, with the toothpicks being made from wood slivers or shaved quills from birds' feathers. Wealthy

Toothpick Holders

gentlemen carried gold toothpicks, usually attached to their watch chains. See **Clubs and Publications**, this Price Guide.

Baby's bootie, clear glass	$ 32- 41
Boot, star on heel, blue glass	37- 40
Butterfly, glass	37- 42
Canoe, green glass	35- 41
Carnival glass, marigold, kittens	62- 68
Chick-in-egg	70- 78
Chicken on wishbone, quadruple plate No. 346	30- 40
Chicks eating grain, wicker basket pattern, clear glass	50- 61
Colorado pattern	23- 30
Diamond Fan	24- 29
Dog with hat, light blue glass	46- 52
Glass, Diamond Fan, 2" high	19- 27
Glass, flint	20- 28
Horse and cart, clear glass (ill.)	32- 37
Lizard holding container on back, clear glass	55- 62
Monkey on log, blue	45- 52
Ribbed, opal glass	44- 53
Saddle on barrel, frosted base, glass	54- 63
Satin glass	24- 32
Seashell, amber glass	44- 52
Souvenir type, red/clear, 1910, glass	26- 36
Uncle Sam's hat, painted milk glass	64- 73

Tortoiseshell Glass

A German chemist developed this glassware in imitation of tortoiseshell. The pro-

389

(continued)

Tortoiseshell Glass

cess involved blowing several bulbs of different shades of brown glass. These were broken into fragments, etc., then rolled among fragments of brown glass. It's a scarce glass and was made by the Sandwich Glass Company and a few firms in Germany.

Basket, gold enamel rim $160-170
Bowl, 8" dia. 40- 50
Box, jewelry, three-tiered 95-110
Finger bowl, ruffled, metallic
  flecks throughout, 6" dia.,
  Sandwich (ill.) 80- 90
Rose bowl, enameled flowers 60- 70
Vase, silver rim, 9" high 48- 58

Touraine Pattern China

Touraine Pattern China

The Alcock family made this semivitreous paste porcelain in England in the mid-1800s, using dark blue decorations and a faint gold band around the border.

Butter dish, covered . . . . $ 37- 46
Cheese dish, covered 42- 50
Creamer 36- 44
Cup/saucer 41- 51
Pitcher/bowl set, signed (ill.) both 260-270
Pitcher, milk 47- 54
Plates, 6½", 8¼", 10", 11½" dia. 39- 52
Platter, 12" long 47- 57
Teapot, 6 cups/saucers, all 172-182

Toys

Carved from wood, stone, cast from iron, machine-pressed, soldered, the very old, and the not-so-old—all highly collectible today.

Airplane, by Marx, tin
  mechanical windup,
  1940s . . . .$ 65- 75
Amos 'n' Andy Fresh Air Taxi-
  cab, tin mechanical windup,
  1930s 675- 775
Amos 'n' Andy radio script,
  "Amos' Wedding," 1935 . . . 162- 172
Amos walking toy, tin
  mechanical windup,
  1930s 170- 180
Andy walking toy, tin mechani-
  cal windup, 1930s 220- 240
Animated cow, 1920s, moving
  the tail made it "moo" 65- 75
Are-E-Go-Round, tin mechani-
  cal windup, Reeves, Milford,
  Conn., early 1900s, patent
  applied for 262- 272
Baby carriage, go-cart sleeper,
  sateen parasol, wire wheels,
  1900s 172- 182
Baby carriage, tin, cloth top
  2½' long, 1920s 88- 98
Baby Grand piano, Schoenhut,
  tin, 1900s 320- 360
Balky mule, tin mechanical
  windup, 1920s, by Lehmann, 95- 107
Bear-on-a-ball, composition,
  mechanical windup, 1940s . . 84- 94
Bellringers, cast iron and
  brass, 7" long, 1892 . . . . 144- 152
Blocks, lithograph on card-
  board, alphabet, mid 1800s,
  set 88- 98
Boat, tin, steam-operated,
  1900 975-1,100
Brake, four seat, iron, Pratt &
  Litchford, Conn., 28" long,
  1906, iron . . . . 13,500+
Buckboard, cast iron, Wilkens,
  1895, 14" long 320- 340
Bus, cast iron, Arcade Mfg.
  Co., 1920s 282- 292
Buster Brown in Cart, 7½"
  long, 1900s 295- 320
Busy Bee seesaw, tin mechani-
  cal, sand operated, litho,
  1920s 128- 132
Cab, No. 662, iron, Hubley, late
  1800s, 9¾" long 188- 198
Calliope, cast iron, Hubley,
  1920s, 16" long 340- 362
Cannon, wooden, 1900s 88- 98
Cannon, "Big Bang" type, 3"
  barrel, 1930s, carbide type . . 75- 90
Car, VW, cast iron, 1950s 55- 70

Carousel, tin mechanical
windup, bisque-headed dolls,
1880s .... 2,800+
Casey Jones, rider type, metal,
late 1930s 262- 282
Cash register, tin, "Benjamin
Franklin," by Kamkap,
1930s 99- 109
Cat with ball, tin mechanical
windup, U.S. Zone, Ger-
many, 1940s 46- 56
Chalkware hearth cat, early
1900s 99- 107
Charlie Chaplin squeeze toy,
Germany, 1920s 330- 350
Charlie McCarthy radio by
Majestic, c. 1930s, price if
radio works (ill.) 142- 152
Chicken in a basket, tin
mechanical windup, 5½"
high, 1920s 137- 152
Chimes, wooden Trinity, litho-
graph on wood, 8 buttons,
late 1800s 152- 162
Clown and monkey, celluloid/
tin mechanical windup,
1930s 88- 98
Columbia tin pull toy steamboat, late 1800s 540- 620
Crapshooter, by Cragston, tin
windup, 1930s 92- 107
Dog-and-cat fight, bell toy, cast
iron, 1890s, 9" long 260- 280
Double-decker, friction toy,
1930, 13" long 262- 272
Drum, lithograph decorated,
w/sticks, early 1900s 99- 107
Figure on horse, wooden, clockwork mechanism, 1900s 172- 192
Galloping horse and buggy, tin
mechanical clockwork, 1882,
18" long 395- 440
Girl-with-doll-on-sled bell toy,
cast iron, Daisy, 1893, 9"
long.................. 188- 196
Greyhound bus, cast iron,
1930s, 9" long........... 99- 107
Gyroscope, pot metal, com-
plete with instructions,
1930s 82- 92
Hanson, No. 661, iron, Hubley,
late 1800s, 9¼" long 262- 271
Harmonica, Original Emmet
Richter, tin/wood, 1920s ... 66- 72
Horse in hoop, Merriam Mfg.
Co., Durham, Conn., 1870s . 552- 570
Horse, wooden, pull toy, 1900s 432- 462
Hose reel, cast iron, Hubley,
20" long, 1900s 775- 840
Howdy Doody tumbling toy,
tin windup, c. 1950s (ill.) 82- 92
Ice skates, wood/iron, hand-
forged, 1880s 120- 140
Irish mail velocipede, 1910.... 975+

Charlie McCarthy Radio
Photo courtesy Hake's Americana & Collectibles

Howdy Doody
Photo courtesy Hake's Americana & Collectibles

Jazzbo Jim
Photo courtesy Hake's Americana & Collectibles

391

(continued)

Joe Penner
Photo courtesy Hake's Americana & Collectibles

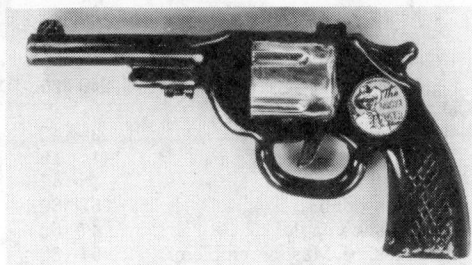

Lone Ranger Popgun
Photo courtesy Hake's Americana & Collectibles

Mickey Mouse Band
Photo courtesy Hake's Americana & Collectibles

Steam engine, horizontal, heated electrically, by Weeden, early 1900s	520-	542
Steamroller, tin, Buddy L, rider type, 1930s, 12½" high	232-	252
Stereoptican (stereoscope), Buckeye Stereoptican Co., Cleveland, 1900s	170-	190
Streetcar, tin, friction, doors open and close, c. 1920s	278-	294
Stove, Hubley, No. 893S, 4¾" high, cast iron, 1900s	162-	172
Sulky, cast iron, Hubley type pull toy, 8½" long, early 1900s	288-	320
Superman Fighting Airplane, tin mechanical windup, litho, Marx, 1940	310-	342
Tally Ho, iron, 1893, 18" long ..	522-	546
Taxi, cast iron, by Arcade, painted, 5" long, 1928	262-	282
Teddy bear, miniature by Steiff, 1920s, 2½" high	142-	152
Temple toy, India, brass mid-19th century, Bankura bronze	228-	261
Tin Lizzie, 1920s, friction type .	242-	261

Toonerville Trolley, tin mechanical windup, made by Nifty, 1922, 6¾" high	770-	799
Toy soldier, friction type, 1920s	122-	142
Traffic B squad car, tin mechanical windup, Marx, 1930s ...	288-	328
Train, cardboard puzzle, Milton-Bradley, early 1900s	82-	92
Train, lithograph on wood, 3-pc., 1850s	340-	362
Train, miniature, tin, lithographed, 6½" long, 4-pc., late 1800s	420-	452
Train, tin, lithographed, mid-1800s, 7" long	375-	422
Truck, metal Buddy "L", 1920s	288-	310
Truck, tin, Metalcraft Corp., St. Louis, 1930	262-	282
Tricycle, Tom Thumb, metal, wooden hubs, spokes, 1910 ..	392-	420
Tut, Tut, tin mechanical windup by Lehmann, 1904	472-	488
Walking-on-hands clown, by Chien, 1920s	102-	114
Waterloo game, Parker Bros., 1895	126-	135
Wells Fargo stage-coach, Tootsietoy, 1920s	98-	107
Wheelbarrow, tin, 29" long, 1920s	84-	93
Wheelbarrow, wooden, 1920s, 18" long	52-	67

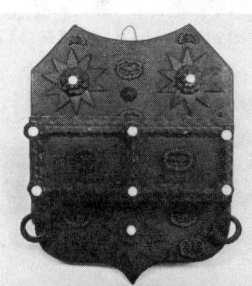

Tramp Art

Tramp Art

Supposedly, the tramps (hoboes), during the depression years, carved boxes, birdcages, chests, etc., to pass the time. The art was known before the 1930s and is still being practiced.

Birdcage, green trim	$235-247
Box, porcelain knobs, hinged lid .	84- 94
Magazine rack, wall type, 24" high	112-118
Rack, wall type, inlaid wood designs, 11" high (ill.)	78- 87

(continued)

Trevais Glass

Trevais Glass

In 1907 the Boston and Sandwich Glass Factory was reopened by the Alton Manufacturing Company. One of the items they made was Trevais ware, a glass to compete with Tiffany. It was quite good but the life of the company was short. This glass is occasionally found on Cape Cod and is expensive. It's mentioned only because it was associated with one of the world's great glass manufacturers.

Vase, gourd shape, green with
silver pearlized effect,
orange liner, silver floral
and leaf overlay, 9"
high (ill.) $1,600-1,750
Most pieces are in the $1,550 to $1,850 range.

Shield	188-199
Turtle	92-107
George Washington, 18th century	240-265
Cast Iron	
Crisscross	35- 42
Enterprise	14- 19
Heart (ill.)	38- 47
Hearts, double	52- 60
Horseshoe, eagle	47- 52
Horseshoe, Masonic emblem	51- 62
Jenny Lind	60- 70
Lacy Urn, wavy railing	47- 57
Lantz, No. 1, 2, 3, 4, 5, ea.	42- 52
Lyre	44- 52
Odd Fellows	42- 52
Order of Cincinnati	44- 52
Six Petal	35- 42
Star and Sunburst	52- 61
Target	42- 52
Turtle	47- 57
Urn with Fern	38- 47
George Washington	150-160
Tile	
Donkeys	27- 37
Leaves and Flowers	38- 47
Square with Loops	27- 47
Tulips	28- 40
Wire	
Coils with X	19- 24
12-spoke Wheel	19- 26
24-spoke Wheel	27- 37

Trivets

Trivets

Old wrought-iron types of the 1830s were equipped with tall legs for use over a fire or with a ring to hold a pot. A 3-legged trivet was called a spider; 6-legged, a cat. Those with short legs were used to hold hot dishes. What you find in shops today are cast iron and were used to hold a sadiron (flat iron). Beware of reproductions flooding the market.

Brass

English Fern	$ 98-107
Odd Fellows	112-127
Petal	94-107

Trunks

Trunks

American trunks date back to before the American Revolution. Immigrants brought thousands with them from Europe. Size and condition are important. W.W. Winship & Sons, Boston, have been making trunks for years.

Brass-studded, bound in clipped
calf hide, rounded top $172-190

Union Porcelain

Tucker China

William Ellis Tucker
China Manufacturer
Philadelphia
1828

Tucker China

Made only from 1825 to 1838 in Philadelphia, this rare china is believed to be the first porcelain made commercially in America. It is similar to Sevres. William Tucker made the first. In 1828, Thomas Hulme joined the firm. Judge Joseph Hemphill and William's brother, Thomas, took over the firm in 1832 when William died. In 1837 the Judge withdrew from the firm, and Thomas Tucker continued for one more year. All pieces were hand-decorated and rare.

Bowl, delicate florals, 3" high
  (ill.)..................... $ 260- 280
Cup/saucer, tea, no handle,
  floral pattern............   460- 485
Dish, oval, covered 1,200-1,400
Dish, round, covered   892-1,200
Pitcher, floral pattern 792- 888
Plate, 6¾" dia., landscapes of
  Philadelphia, set of 6...... 1,900-2,200
Plate, 7¼", 8¼" dia., set of 6 .   672- 722
Platter, floral pattern ....   1,900+
Urn, 3½" high, floral pattern,
  gold decoration on base,
  pr. 2,520-2,700
Urn, 10¼" high, floral pat-
  tern, gold painted base,
  handled, pr.............   2,975+

Union Porcelain

Thomas C. Smith purchased the Union Porcelain Works, Greenport, New York, just after the Civil War. It is one of the few American potteries to manufacture hard porcelain and is still in business. Several marks were used; one is shown here.

Pitcher, Parian, eagle/hunter,
  11" high (ill.) $458-482

Val St. Lambert

Val St. Lambert   Val St Lambert

Founded in the late 1700s, this Belgian firm made a cameo glass which featured cased glass bodies lavishly cut with the lapidary wheel and acid-engraved. They also made other types of glass.

Biscuit jar, blue/green floral,
  silver cover, signed $572-596
Bottle, perfume, frosted crystal
  cut to yellow, silver stopper,
  6½" high   352-372
Bowl, crystal/cranberry, 11½"
  dia.   270-282
Box, blue/rose poppies, 4" sq.,
  signed   318-327
Cologne bottle, blue/red flowers,
  frosted ground, signed   325-338

(continued)

Dish, blue, clear ground, 5″ dia., signed	320-342
Jewelry box, pink flowers, frosted ground, hinged lid, signed	381-399
Plate, game bird, 8″ dia., signed	182-192
Tray, dresser, etched crystal, clear/green, 6″ long	186-196
Vase, blue/purple, frosted ground, signed (ill.)	782-950
Vase, red-to-clear, signed	572-662

Valentines

Valentines

In early Christian times and based on a pagan feast called Lupercalia, churches adopted February 14, the day of the martyrdom of Bishop Valentine in 270 A.D., as Valentine's Day. The first written valentines in America date back to the late 1600s, but they really didn't get started until the mid-1700s. Lithographed valentines date from the 1840s. The lace-paper type is credited to Esther Howland, 1840s. Fun to collect today.

| Assortment, 1920s-1930s | $3- 5 |
| Lacy type, mid-1800s (ill.) | 7-12 |

What you're willing to pay is about what they're worth.

Vallerystahl Glass

This French/German glass has been made for years at Vallerystahl, Lorraine, France. After the Franco-Prussian War the area became part of Germany. Returned to France in 1918, the factory was destroyed by Allied bombers in World War II. What you find in shops today is from the mid-1800s to about 1915.

Bottle, perfume, blue, swirl ribbed, gold star decor	$129-152
Box, covered, blue milk glass, 3½″×4″	72- 82
Candlestick, carved frosted glass	131-142
Compote, fluted top, milk glass	89-101
Covered dish, swan, milk glass	99-117
Dish, covered, cow motif	88-107
Goblet, footed, blue, signed	70- 80
Jam jar, Grape and Leaf	71- 81
Plate, Thistle pattern, 6″ dia., signed	84- 93
Salt dip, Ram's Head, white	77- 88
Tumbler, cobalt, 4″ high	64- 75

Van Briggle Pottery

Van Briggle Pottery

Artus Van Briggle worked at Rookwood Pottery in the late 1800s, then moved to Colorado Springs for his health. The company is still in business. Van Briggle's work at Rookwood was far superior to anything he ever made in Colorado. He died in 1904.

Bookends, maroon/green, pr.	$ 98-122
Bowl, blue, 1924, paper label	52- 62
Bowl, Persian Rose, dated 1918 in bottom, 3″ dia.	63- 73
Candleholder, red/brown	60- 70
Candlesticks, Persian Rose, 3¾″ high, Pat. #733, signed	60- 70
Creamer, blue, Grecian Key	66- 76
Figurine, Indian maiden, turquoise	150-160

Lamp, Art Deco style, figural
  lady, Oriental, 10½" high,
  monogram mark 70- 80
Pitcher, maroon, 5" high, 1932 (ill.) 77- 82
Planter, oval shape, green/blue,
  incised signature 60- 70
Plaque, Indian maiden, blue,
  signed 77- 87
Tulip bowl, turquoise, 8½" long,
  3" high, signed 62- 72
Tulip flower frog, 20 holes, signed 40- 60
Vase, floral decor, Colorado
  Springs mark 63- 73
Vase, plum color, handled, incised
  signature, 1934 . . . . 67- 75
Vase, red/green, Greek Key, 6"
  high 60- 70
Vase, turquoise, daffodils, 9½"
  high, signed 88- 98
Vase, turquoise, 2½" high, scal-
  loped rim, signed 52- 62

Vasa Murrhina Glass

Vasa Murrhina Glass

Made by the Vasa Murrhina Art Glass
Company, Sandwich, Massachusetts, in
1884, this was a glass in which the body was
transparent, showing imbedded pieces of colored glass and mica flakes. Another repro
item.

Art glass basket, pink and white
  swirls, silver mica, clear handle $176-185
Bowl, multicolored, mica flecks . . 147-155
Bride's basket, tan/gold flecks,
  white casing 232-260
Creamer, rainbow, cased, 5" high   85- 95
Decanter, cranberry, gold flecks,
  ribbed handle 182-192
Fairy lamp, green/blue mottling . 242-260
Lamp, amber, mica flakes, 9"
  high 188-206
Tumbler, blue/white, silver mica
  flecks 118-132
Vase, pink/blue, silver flecks, 8"
  high 137-152
Vase, blue/pink, silver flecks,
  ruffled, 8" high 128-142
Vase, clear, red and silver flecks,
  3¾" high 74- 84

Vase, Persian rose, 9"
  high (ill.) 65- 75

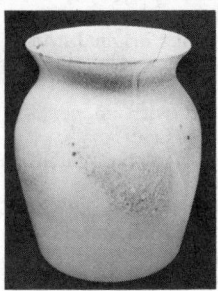

Vasart Glass

Vasart Glass   *Vasart*

Made in Scotland by the Streathearn Glass
Company, this is a fairly new art glass.
"Vasart" is usually engraved on the base.

Basket, blue/yellow, loop handle,
  6" high, signed $122-130
Bowl, yellow on base, speckled at
  top, 4" dia., signed 98-109
Mug, handled, green/blue, signed   79- 88
Tumbler, blue/white, striped,
  signed 84- 93
Vase, Cluthra type, apricot to
  clam broth, 9" high, signed (ill.) 366-384

Vaseline Glass

Vaseline Glass

A greenish-yellow glass that looks like
petroleum jelly. A product of the 1870s, it's
still being made.

Basket, 5" high . . . .$ 46- 56
Berry set, Wildflower, clear, 7-pc.   97-108
Bowl, embossed flowers, footed . . 72- 82
Butter dish, covered, Diamond
  Quilted 77- 86
Cake stand, opaline swirl 74- 90

(continued)

Candleholder, twisted stem, 11"
  high 45- 62
Compote, dolphin stem, opales-
  cent rim   95-120
Cruet, Argonaut, original stopper 182-220
Dish, candy, covered 42- 52
Mug, kitten pattern 47- 57
Perfume bottle with stopper (ill.) .   64- 74
Pitcher, Maple Leaf 110-122
Salt/pepper, Diamond Quilted, pr.   52- 62
Spooner, Alaska   98-109
Teaberry gum stand 88- 99
Toothpick holder, flower decor,
  ribbed, footed 49- 56
Tumbler, Wreath and Shell
  pattern, opalescent   88-107
Vase, swirl, 6" high   77-109
Wine, clear stem and foot 49- 57

Venetian Glass

Venetian Glass

A lot of people confuse it with Carnival because of its iridescence. It isn't and was first made 700 years before Carnival on an island near Venice, Italy. The factory was government-owned and continued until the early 1900s. It was usually colored, fragile, and very thin.

Basket, swirled blue/pink threads,
  handled . . . . $ 54- 63
Bowl, ruffled edge, blue/gold
  threads, 4" dia. 62- 72
Candlesticks, yellow with cobalt
  edging, applied pink and white
  violets, green leaves, 10½"
  high, pr. (ill.) 118-127
Candy dish, typical Venetian,
  6" dia.   77- 84
Compote, Dolphin, early 1800s . . 220-240
Cup/saucer, pink, lacy 77- 87
Epergne, pink/blue opalescent,
  23" high 172-192
Goblet, blue/gold threads, 8"
  high, clear stem 64- 73

Paperweight, twisted red/blue
  threads   95-108
Vase, blue swirl design, 7½" high,
  fluted top   97-108

Verlys Glass

Verlys Glass

This glass was made in France in the 1930s. A lot was made in America by Heisey. It's both blown and molded. The American glass is signed with a diamond-point-scratched name. The French has a molded signature. It brings brisk prices.

Ashtray, doves, French signature $ 50- 58
Bowl, blue acorns, signed, French 162-177
Bowl, Daisy pattern, 6-sided,
  American   92-120
Box hinged, flower decor,
  American   90-107
Plate, fish swimming, clear and
  frosted, 5" dia. (ill.) 72- 82
Tray, child with animal in relief,
  American 101-109
Vase, flowers in relief, 7" high,
  American 121-131
Vase, frosted lovebirds, 5" high,
  French 130-140
Vase, lovebirds, flowers 132-142

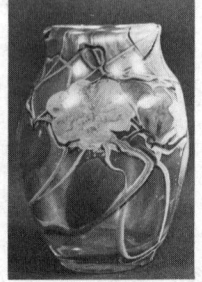

Villeroy and Boch

Villeroy and Boch

This firm of potters began in Luxembourg around 1875. Later known as Boch and Buschmann, besides making the world-famous Mettlach steins, the firm made plaques, cider sets, breadboards, and garden tiles.

Bowl, punch, floral decor $132-152
Butter dish, covered, design in
   heavy relief 108-121
Compote, creamware, 9″ high . . . 92-107
Cup/saucer, Dresden pattern 52- 62
Mug, advertising Detroit beer
   company, 5″ high 47- 57
Pitcher, gravy, tray attached,
   flower decor 62- 72
Plaque, ocean liner at sea, 11″ dia. 107-112
Plate, windmill, cows in field,
   9½″ dia. 64- 74
Plate, Dresden pattern, 10″ dia. . 75- 90
Stein, American eagle, pewter
   top, 9″ high 552-620
Teapot with 6 cups/saucers,
   flower decor 148-152
Vase, garden scene, 8″ high 77- 87
Vase, ancient German castle,
   11½″ high 82- 92

Volkstadt Porcelain

Volkstadt Porcelain

Georg Heinrich Macheleid established a porcelain factory at Sitzendorf, moving it later (in 1762) to Volkstadt. Crossed hay-forks was the original mark. Beyer and Bock manufactured it after 1890. Figurines, por-traits, and vases were made.

Figurine, dancing maiden, yellow/
   blue, 7¼″ high $350-372
Figurine, elkhound, blue/green,
   6½″ high 348-366
Figurine, gray/blue, spiral bands,
   11″ high 221-242
Group, cockatoos, polychrome,
   signed, 9½″ high (ill.) 252-272

Walking Sticks (Canes)

They were considered stylish in Europe during the late 17th century. Usually they were made of rattan; later some had con-cealed guns, swords, liquor flasks. In the 1800s wealthy gentlemen had canes with 14k gold heads, some inlaid with diamonds.

Gold-headed, insert tube for ¼
   pint whiskey $160- 190
Silver-plated head, Malacca
   type 62- 72
Sterling-silver head, Malacca
   type 188- 198
Sword concealed in handle,
   Malacca type, English, 18th
   century 272- 292
Two-shot pistol concealed in
   handle, Malacca type 1,100-1,400
Walking stick, carved burl
   head, thorn wood 44- 52

Warwick China

Warwick China

Made in Wheeling, West Virginia, from 1887 until 1951. Much of their wares were decal-decorated.

Ale set, pitcher, 10½″ high,
   6 mugs, 5″ high, "B.P.O.E.,
   Akron" on all pieces, brown
   ground, all $525-545
Bookends, Indian head, 7″ high,
   pr. 24- 32
Creamer, dairy maid, 5½″
   high 23- 30
Dish, floral decor, 7″ dia. 16- 22
Ewer, floral decor, 8¼″ high 47- 54
Humidor, monk's head, brown,
   6½″ high 155-163
Mug, Indian head, brown,
   5″ high 65- 73
Mug, monk holding beer stein,
   brown 60- 68

(continued)

Mugs, various fraternal orders,
  4½" high, ea. 38- 45
Pitcher, cows, blue 44- 52
Pitcher, floral decor, 6¼" high
  (ill.) 43- 52
Pitcher, monk, brown, 8½"
  high 48- 56
Plate, Indian, 8¼" dia. 68- 75
Platter, floral decor, blue/gold
  border, 16" long 35- 44
Spittoon, English village scene,
  flared top 165-180
Vase, "B.P.O.E., Cincinnati,"
  8¼" high 63- 74
Vase, gypsy lady, 10" high 65- 73
Vase, pine needles/cones, 7¼"
  high 63- 72
Vase, poppies, brown/green,
  Helmet mark, 8" high 75- 84
Vase, portrait of dog, 9" high . . .   74- 83
Vase, portrait of woman, twig
  handles, 11" high 133-142

Pink lustre bowl and pitcher,
  Sailor's Farewell, 1840s (ill.) . . . 628-682
Weller pottery bowl, pitcher,
  toothbrush holder, soap dish,
  all 510-527

Washboards

They are mentioned here because those from the early 1900s made of wood, brass, or glass are being collected for use in the kitchen and den as bulletin boards.

  Average price, in good condition . . . $15-27

Watch Chains and Fobs

Wash Sets

Wash Sets

A water pitcher and large bowl, usually with toothbrush holder, soap holder, and a smaller pitcher for hot water, were called a wash set. They were used before the days of indoor plumbing. Some were run-of-the-mill, some were ironstone, others were made by Haviland. Highly collectible. Many new sets are on the market.

Haviland, complete 7-pc. set,
  yellow/pink flowers, signed . . . $452-575
Ironstone, Mason's Patent, bowl
  and pitcher, smaller pitcher . . . 242-272
Meakin, floral decor, bowl and
  pitcher 275-298

Watch Chains and Fobs

Some are very ornate; all had the same purpose. See **Clubs and Publications**, this Price Guide.

Chains

Curb, 3-strand, 14k, hand-
  engraved slide $675- 775
14k gold, double strand, locket
  inset w/diamonds, pen/pen-
  cil holder, c. 1875 950-1,100
14k gold, single strand, 12"
  long 380- 420
Onyx charm, gold-filled, 8"
  long 48- 58
Rope, 2-strand, gold-filled, 11"
  long 52- 72
10k gold, single strand, 10"
  long 67- 77
Woven hair vest guard, gold-
  filled mountings, 8½"
  long 38- 48

Fobs

A.M.P. Co., Chicago (milk pro-
  ducts), silver, c. 1905 . . . . . .   42- 52
Banigan rubbers (footwear),
  bronze, c. 1910 . . . .   27- 32

Best on Earth (Wells' shoes),
  silver, c. 1909   41-   52
Chicago Tailoring Co., bronze,
  c. 1900s   14-   18
Commercial Travelers, Utica,
  N.Y., multi-color enamel,
  c. 1920   11-   17
Deutsches Haus, a German-
  American club in Rochester,
  N.Y., bronze, c. 1916   8-   11
FOE—Liberty, Truth, Justice,
  Equality—bronze, c. 1918 . . .   7-   11
Iceman's Convention, silver,
  c. 1920   40-   50
Joy silver streak (drilling co.),
  silver, c. 1950s   32-   52
LeRoi pneumatic air tools (drill-
  ing co.), bronze, c. 1950s   14-   18
LeTourneau, certified operator
  (driver's name, etc.), bronze,
  c. 1930s   34-   42
Lincoln (Lincoln story contest,
  awarded by Pittsburgh
  Press), bronze, c. 1922   9-   12
Patriotic 1917 victory ("V" 17),
  bronze, c. 1917   7-   10
U.S. Navy, sailor, bronze, c.
  1918   8-   11

Watches

Watches

The Europeans were far ahead of us when it
came to making watches. We got around to
making them in the 1830s. Until then every
one we used was imported from Europe.
Keyless watches came into being around
1700; with a second hand, around 1780;
radium dials, around 1898; the wristwatch,
around World War I. Any Elgin, Hamilton,
or Waltham numbered under 1,000 is collectible today. Abbreviations used are as
follows: DS—double sunk dial; GF—gold
filled; HC—hunter case; LS—lever set;
OF—open face; RR—railroad; S#—serial
number; SW—stem wind; WGF—white gold
filled; YGF—yellow gold filled. See **Clubs
and Publications**, this Price Guide.

Ball (Webb C. Ball Co., Cleveland, Ohio)
  Official Standard, 21 jewels, LS,
    YGF OF case, c. late 1890s . . . $ 84- 94
  Official Standard, 17 jewels, YGF
    case, OF, c. 1890s 82- 94
  Official Standard, 19 jewels, 10k
    YGF case, OF, c. 1910 . . . . . .   84- 94
**Columbus (Columbus Watch Co., Columbus,
Ohio)**
  Champion, OF, transparent back,
    YGF, c. 1895 . . . .   52- 62
  Coin silver, keywind, OF, en-
    graved case, c. 1890s 138-152
  17 jewels, swingout OF case,
    Roman dial, nickel silver case . 141-151
Elgin
  Coin silver, HC, keywind, 15
    jewels 138-162
  Father Time, YGF, OF, 21 jewels   132-150
  Keystone, silveroid OF case 72- 82
  Model 349, 21 jewels, LS, coin
    silver OF case 152-170
  Veritas, 21 jewels, LS, YGF OF
    case 171-181
  Veritas, 21 jewels, OF silveroid
    case 152-162
  Wheeler, 15 jewels, keywind, coin
    silver HC 152-160
  Wheeler, 17 jewels, silveroid OF
    case 70- 80
Hamilton (Hamilton Watch Co., Lancaster, Pa.)
  Model 924, YGP OF case, 17
    jewels, nickel case   88-107
  Model 935, 17 jewels, DS, HC . . .   92-109
  Model 937, 17 jewels, OF, trans-
    parent back case 142-152
  Model 940, coin silver HC, 21
    jewels 180-192
  Model 940, 21 jewels, LS, YGF
    OF 120-130
  Model 940, 21 jewels, RR, OF
    case   92-118
Illinois (Illinois Watch Co., Springfield, Ill.)
  Bunn Special, 24 jewels, LS,
    silveroid OF case 158-172
  Bunn Special, 24 ruby jewels, LS,
    YGF OF case 310-335
  Coin silver, keywind, HC, 15
    jewels 147-152
  Columbia, keywind, 15 jewels,
    silveroid OF case 80- 90
  Hoyt model, keywind, OF silver
    case 142-152
  Santa Fe Special, 21 jewels, LS,
    YGF OF case 162-172
Ingersoll (Robert H. Ingersoll, Trenton, N.J., and

(continued)

Waterbury, Conn.)

American Pride, back wind, c. 1891	66-	76
Ingersoll Trenton, yellow OF	29-	38
Ingersoll Trenton, 19 jewels, OF, YGF, Windsor patented case	77-	87
Midget, OF	45-	55
Reliance, OF, 7 jewels, white base metal	42-	52
Yankee, back keywind, paper dial	52-	61

New York Standard (New York Standard Watch Co., Jersey City, N.J.)

Columbia, 7 jewels, OF case	32-	47
15 jewels, YGF OF case (ill.)	67-	77
Keystone, 15 jewels, white nickel OF case	27-	37
New Era, 7 jewels, RR, silveroid OF case	61-	71
Perfection, 15 jewels, 14k YGF OF case	34-	44

Seth Thomas (Seth Thomas Watch Co., Thomaston, Conn.)

Alaska, swing out-cup OF case	82-	92
Bay State Imperial, coin silver OF case, enamel dial	88-	99
Centennial, 7 jewels, YGF OF case, engine turned case	67-	77
Coin silver HC, Series 2 model, cut-out movement	162-177	
Wadsworth, 15 jewels, OF case, enamel dial	128-142	

Swiss

Agassiz, 21 jewels, 18k gold OF case, high grade	210-221	
Agassiz, 21 jewels, HC, multi-color gold, original velvet box	540-562	
Bulova, 17 jewels, YGF OF, 8 adjustments	182-192	
Hebdomas, YGF OF case, visible balance, 8-day	107-117	
Hebdomas, OF case, exposed escapement, multi-color dial, 8-day	121-132	
Longines, 17 jewels, 14k YGF OF, 10-sided case	162-172	
Longines, 17 jewels, YGF OF case, blue Arabic numerals	121-131	
Tiffany, Movado round OF 14k YGF, 8-day	127-142	
Tiffany, 17 jewels, 18k YGF OF, double gold back covers	292-320	

Waterford Glass

This fine glass was first made in Ireland in 1729. The chandeliers are world-famous. A flint-type glass, it was dark in color before the 1830s. Then the formula was improved and the color became whiter and more brilliant. They shut down in 1852 and didn't reopen for

Waterford Glass

100 years. Now back in production, the glass they're making is marvelous. Don't confuse the old with the new.

Celery, Diamond Point Fan	$ 65- 74
Cracker jar, etched, silver lid	152-172
Cruet, cut stopper, 11½" high, old mark, pr.	282-296
Goblet, large (ill.)	177-192
Knife rest, signed Waterford	182-192
Lustres, 13" high, cut prisms, pr.	710-735
Mustard jar, contemporary, 3½" high	52- 62
Pitcher, ornate silver lid, 11" high	228-352
Salt, new	32- 42
Souvenir-type wines, Queen Elizabeth II Coronation, ea.	64- 73
Toothpick	35- 45
Tumbler, cut	107-120
Urn, cut, square base, 10" high	410-462
Vase, Diamond Cut, square base	420-438

Wave Crest Ware

The C.F. Monroe Company, Meriden, Connecticut, bought its blanks abroad and also from the Pairpoint Manufacturing Company, c. late 1890s. Reminiscent of Crown Milano, all pieces were formed from opaque white glass, blown into shape in full-size molds. Five backmarks were used to identify Wave Crest: Black Mark—Wave Crest Trade Mark; Red Banner Mark—"Wave Crest" on pennant, The C.F.M. Co.; Kelva—Kelva Trade Mark; Nakara—Nakara C.F.M. Co.; paper labels—Wave Crest Ware, Pat. Applied For.

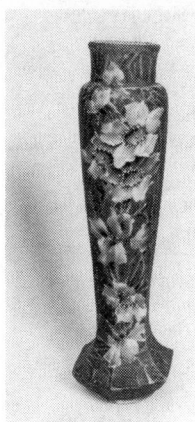

Wave Crest Ware

Tray, jewel, handled, Bishop's
Hat blank, 5½" high 582- 620
Tray, trinket, Nakara,
Bishop's Hat blank, 4½"
high 582- 628
Vase, Kelva, floral, signed,
13" high (ill.) 800- 875
Vase, Kelva, florals, brass
ormolu feet, 7¼" high 575- 620
Vase, Red Banner mark,
maiden riding butterfly,
ormolu handles and feet,
13½" high 3,100-3,400
Vase, Red Banner mark, white
florals, mauve cartouches
around entire piece, brass
handles and feet, 14" high . 2,600-2,700

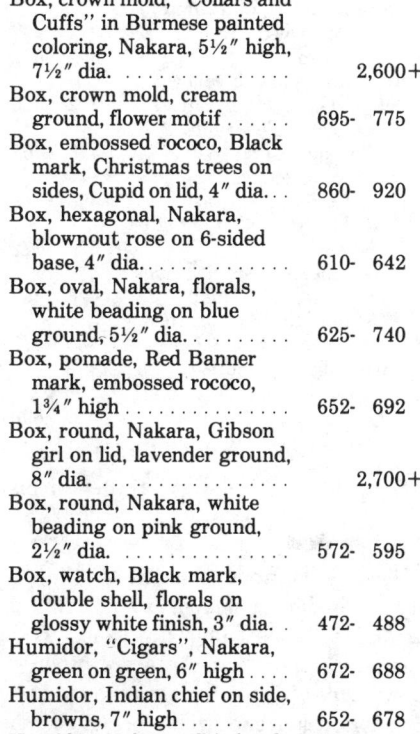

Box, blownout, enameled
flowers, brass collar . . . . . .$ 671- 692
Box, crown mold, "Collars and
Cuffs" in Burmese painted
coloring, Nakara, 5½" high,
7½" dia. . . . . 2,600+
Box, crown mold, cream
ground, flower motif 695- 775
Box, embossed rococo, Black
mark, Christmas trees on
sides, Cupid on lid, 4" dia. . . 860- 920
Box, hexagonal, Nakara,
blownout rose on 6-sided
base, 4" dia. 610- 642
Box, oval, Nakara, florals,
white beading on blue
ground, 5½" dia. 625- 740
Box, pomade, Red Banner
mark, embossed rococo,
1¾" high 652- 692
Box, round, Nakara, Gibson
girl on lid, lavender ground,
8" dia. . . . . 2,700+
Box, round, Nakara, white
beading on pink ground,
2½" dia. 572- 595
Box, watch, Black mark,
double shell, florals on
glossy white finish, 3" dia. . 472- 488
Humidor, "Cigars", Nakara,
green on green, 6" high 672- 688
Humidor, Indian chief on side,
browns, 7" high 652- 678
Humidor, Nakara, elk's head
w/B.P.O.E., 7½" high 842- 872
Jar, biscuit, C.F.M. Co., lilacs
on shiny finish, silver-plated
trim, 8" high 500- 562
Jar, biscuit, Egg Crate (Puffy),
clovers on 4 sides, plated
trim, 8" high 585- 662

Weather Vanes

Weather Vanes

They were usually in the shape of birds,
animals, racing sulkies, ships. Scarce today,
the old ones are being stolen in New England
from atop old barns and homes.

Angel Gabriel, remounted
on iron bracket . . . . $23,000+
Automobile, early brass, on
orb 2,600- 2,900
Bear, copper, gilded w/gold
leaf 1,500- 1,700
Cigar, on orb, copper w/gold
leaf 1,400- 1,600
Cow, copper, made by J.W.
Fiske, c. 1893 . . . . 1,875- 2,200
Deer running, hollow
copper, N.E.S.W. on orb,
directional arrow . . . . 1,700+
Dexter with jockey, copper
w/gold leaf 1,800- 2,000

(continued)

Eagle, spread wings, hollow
copper, complete (ill.) ... 2,600- 2,975
Fish, on orb, brass, 3' long . 1,400- 1,700
Fish, 30" long, made by
J.W. Fiske, c. 1898 ..... 1,600- 1,900
Hackney stallion, copper
w/gold leaf, 48" long,
c. 1893 .... 2,700- 2,900
Hog, tin, on orb 952- 1,110
Horse over hurdle, 30" long,
J.W. Fiske............ 2,300- 2,500
Indian, with bow and arrow,
Mashamoquet......... 37,000+
Owl, on broom, 3' long,
copper w/gold leaf...... 1,700- 1,900
Peacock, copper, on ball,
complete 11,650-12,500
Pigeon on ball, w/arrow,
copper, w/gold leaf,
complete 1,600- 1,800
Rooster and arrow, com-
plete, J.W. Fiske....... 1,100- 1,450
Rooster on milk glass light-
ning ball, complete 1,700- 1,900
Sulky driver, complete with
horse 2,650- 2,775
Tiffany scroll, 6' long,
complete 1,475- 1,650
Wagon and scroll banneret,
4' 6" long, copper w/gold
leaf 1,100- 1,375
Wagon wheel and arrow, 7'
long, copper w/gold leaf . 1,100- 1,375

Webb Glass

Webb Glass

Thomas Webb and Sons operated their factory at Stourbridge, England, and made
some of the finest glass the world has ever
known. Poor imitations are being made.

Bowl, cameo, cranberry/white
carving, signed Thomas
Webb................$1,700-2,220
Fairy lamp, Burmese glass,
scalloped top, signed Webb   540- 572
Fairy lamp, Sociable, Burmese
glass, 11" high, 3 decorated
Fairy size shades, 3 Bur-
mese shade holders, 3 small
flower holders, 1 larger
flower holder, 1 connecting
piece, all in a brass frame,
signed Thomas Webb 1,900-2,200
Match holder, rose to yellow,
3" high 352- 372
Pitcher, blue/white, cameo
carved leaves, 9½" high ... 925- 982
Pitcher, rose to yellow, cameo
carved, flowers, 11¼" high,
signed 925- 952
Perfume bottle, acid finish,
rose to yellow, signed 690- 722
Perfume bottle, brown/white,
cameo carved leaves, signed 742- 781
Perfume bottle, pink/white,
cameo carved, sterling
silver cap............. 652- 671
Rose bowl, pink to yellow,
fluted lip, 3" high, signed .. 392- 420
Rose bowl, yellow/white, 2¾"
high, signed............ 430- 462
Tumbler, rose to yellow, cameo
carved flowers, signed 395- 440
Vase, blue ground, 12" high,
signed 620- 672
Vase, pink opalescent, enameled flowers, 13" high 420- 452
Vase, pink to yellow, ruffled
top, 10½" high 460- 472
Vase, yellow to white, cameo
carved flowers, 11¼" high,
signed 1,550-1,800

WEDGWOOD
ENGLAND

Wedgwood   WEDGWOOD

Josiah Wedgwood founded the first pottery at Burslem, England, around 1759. Jasperware is the best known product. Basalt,
Creamware and Terra-Cotta are other well-
known types. Jasperware was made in over
25 colors, blue and white being the most
popular over the years. Wedgwood's history
is equally as confusing as that of Haviland.
See **Clubs and Publications**, this Price Guide.

Ashtray, Jasperware, blue/
white ....$ 115- 132
Biscuit barrel, hunting scene,
c. 1860, 9½" high 284- 320

Biscuit barrel, village scene,
    silver metal top, 10″ high .. 268- 292
Biscuit jar, Jasperware,
    brown/white, 10″ high,
    silver metal lid 272- 288
Biscuit jar, Jasperware, pink/
    white, hunting scene, 8¾″
    high 294- 320
Biscuit jar, pottery, blue/
    yellow/green, flowers, 9½″
    high 198- 220
Bowl, basalt, 4″ dia. 242- 262
Bowl, Fairyland luster, pixies
    and elves, 2½″ high 720- 782
Bowl, Jasperware, green/
    white, Grecian scenes, 3″
    dia. 240- 262
Bowl, Jasperware, lavender/
    white, floral decor, 2½″ dia. 242- 277
Box, basalt, hinged lid, 4¾″
    square 188- 210
Box, Jasperware, blue/white,
    hinged lid, late 130- 142
Box, red, flower decor, 5″
    square 127- 146
Bust, Lincoln, basalt, 9″ high . 227- 242
Bust, Shakespeare, basalt,
    13¼″ high 960-1,150
Candlesticks, Jasperware,
    brown/white, floral decor,
    8½″ high, pr............ 288- 320

Wedgwood

Candlesticks, Jasperware,
    Classic design, blue, 6″
    high, pr. (ill.) 262- 272
Candlesticks, Jasperware,
    Grecian maidens, 8¼″ high,
    pr. 320- 362
Compote, creamware, green/
    white, dancing ladies, 6¼″
    high 274- 285
Compote, Jasperware, blue/
    white, court scene, 7″ high . 275- 320

Creamer, basalt, flower decor,
    4″ high 199- 221
Creamer, Blue Willow design,
    4″ high 126- 137
Creamer, caneware, blue
    ground, leaves, 3¼″ high .. 262- 292
Cup/saucer, demitasse, basalt,
    after 1900 .... 42- 52
Cups/saucers, basalt, set of
    12 2,175-3,310
Cups/saucers, caneware,
    Oriental scene, set of 6, all . 875- 985
Decanter, Jasperware, red/
    white, Grecian dancers,
    stopper, 12″ high 385- 420
Dish, cheese, Jasperware,
    Grecian design, 6″ dia. 172- 192
Dish, relish, Jasperware, blue/
    white, 5½″ dia. 198- 220
Hair receiver, basalt 242- 262
Hair receiver, Jasperware,
    blue/white 199- 221
Humidor, seashell finial,
    coral/shell decor, 6½″ high . 242- 262
Jardiniere, dark blue, floral
    decor, 7″ high 472- 492
Jardiniere, Grecian ladies,
    green/white, 7½″ high 352- 382
Jug, Jasperware, brown/white,
    tavern scene, 6½″ high 320- 350
Jug, Jasperware, green/white,
    dancing ladies, 6″ high 229- 282
Medallion, basalt, Roman
    statesman, 3¼″ dia. 199- 221
Pitcher, blue/white, 6¼″ high . 232- 262
Pitcher, crimson, 5″ high 221- 252
Pitcher, green/white, 7″ high . 262- 282
Plate, Ivanhoe, Friar Tuck,
    10″ dia. 110- 127
Plate, pink/white, 9″ dia. 128- 142
Plates, blue/white, 10″ dia.,
    set of 6, all 372- 410
Sugar bowl, blue/white, 4¼″
    high 126- 137
Tea set, Jasperware, blue/
    white, 4-pc., all 597- 652
Tea set, Jasperware, yellow/
    white, 3-pc. 442- 482
Teapot, basalt, classical
    figures, 5″ high 242- 273
Teapot, Majolica, seashell
    finial, 6″ high 225- 262
Tiles, calendar, 1900-1909, ea. 92- 110
Tray, blue/white, medallion
    center, 6″ wide 162- 184
Tray, Jasperware, handled,
    Grecian maidens, 11″ dia... 175- 197
Urn, basalt, 9″ high 224- 262
Urn, Jasperware, green/white,
    5¼″ high 325- 362
Vase, basalt, cherubs, 7½″
    high 252- 287

405 (continued)

Vase, Fairyland luster, hum-
mingbirds, 7¼" high . . . . .   1,250+
Vase, Jasperware, blue/white,
dancing nudes, 7" high 282- 320
Vase, Queensware, blue, fruit
decor, 7½" high 98- 107

Weller Pottery

Seth Thomas, 1870s)   442-461
Decanter, handled, flower decor,
10" high   110-121
Mug, Etna, blue/red decor   99-117
Pitcher, ivory ground, multi-
colored panels, kingfisher
decor, 8" high 62- 71
Spittoon, floral decor on brown
glaze   92-109
Tankard, Dickens Ware, handled,
6½" high   252-271
Umbrella stand, Louwelsa,
brown/flowers, 19" high   346-362
Vase, blue/pink flowers, signed
McLaughlin, 11½" high   135-147
Vase, dogwood flowers, pink/
blue, incised Weller 89- 98
Vase, lavender flowers, white
background, 10" high   112-127
Vase, 6" high, signed Sicard . . . .   625+
Vase, 7" high, signed Weller,
LaSa   212-228
Vase, 7¾" high, signed
Weller (ill.) 28- 35

Aurelian

Weller Pottery   WELLER

In 1872 Sam Weller made Bluebird pottery
on his Fultonham, Ohio, farm; in 1882 he
moved to Zanesville. In 1890 he produced
glazed ware, cuspidors, umbrella stands, and
jardinieres. In 1895 he organized the Lonhuda Faience Company with William A.
Long. Pieces made were marked with an "L"
and "F" and an impressed shield. Weller got
rid of Long in 1896, changing the name of the
pottery to Louwelsa, a combination of letters
from his and his daughter's names. Many
kinds of pottery were made by Weller including Sicard, Thurada, Eosian, Floretta,
Aurelian, Dickens Ware, and LaSa. Weller
competed with Roseville and Rookwood. His
quality matched Roseville's, but other than
Sicard and LaSa, he never matched the Rookwood quality, The factory closed in 1949.

Basket, hanging, fruit decor,
9" dia. . . . .$ 97-109
Bowl, flowers, blue/pink, artist-
signed 88- 97
Candlestick, Louwelsa mark,
brown/green, 9" high   132-142
Clock case, flowers, green leaves,
Louwelsa, 7" high (clockworks,

Whieldon

Whieldon   WHIELDON

Thomas Whieldon started his first factory
at Fenton Low in 1719. Josiah Wedgwood
was in business with him from 1754 until
1759. Whieldon made Agate Ware, a deep
cream-colored earthenware of the Astbury
type, decorated with a mottled lead glaze
stained brown, blue and yellow, green,
grayish-black. Whieldon stayed in business
until 1795. His pieces are highly collectible.

Creamer, Flower pattern, lid
attached by metal chain, 1750s $695-752
Mug, Flower pattern, 1760s (ill.) .   420-462
Plate, Tortoiseshell ware, 18th
century   361-390
Plate, mottled browns, 1750s   272-288
Pitcher, Flower pattern, 1760s
(ill.)   499-562

Whisk Brooms

Whisk Brooms

Here we're talking about the porcelain-type body, usually a "doll" type. The doll was used either as a top for a pincushion or a whisk broom. The whisk is usually straw or grass.

Bisque baby, molded/painted hair, 6¼" high	$ 40-	50
Bisque, molded/painted hair, 8" tall overall	50-	60
China, Austria, #8034, molded features, 7" high	58-	67
China, Germany, molded/painted hair, features, 7" high	44-	54
China, Germany, molded/painted, lady with hat (ill.)	41-	52
China, Japan, molded/painted hair, features, 8" high	66-	76

Whiskey Sample Glasses

Whiskey Sample Glasses

In the late 1800s and early 1900s, salesmen and drummers carried these little shot glasses to impress the customer that their product was best.

Big 6 Gin shot glass, 1 oz.	$ 19-	27
Calvert, 2¼" high (ill.)	12-	19
Dilley's No. 5 Pure Rye shot glass, 2 oz.	18-	24

Habenero Piza Tabasco, ½ oz.	11-	18
Hanover Rye, Cincinnati, Ohio, shot glass, 2 oz.	16-	20
Hayner Distilling Co., Dayton, Ohio, and St. Louis, 3 oz.	19-	21
Vino Chinato bitters/wine shot glass, 1 oz.	12-	21

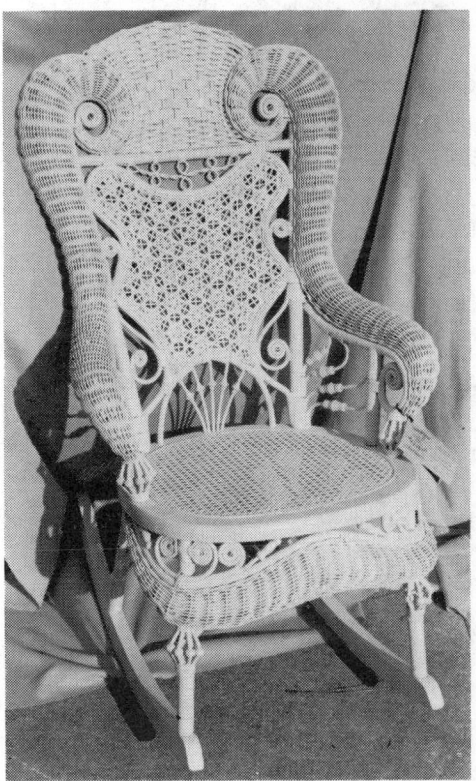

Wicker Items

Wicker Items

Wicker is a name used to describe many types of materials such as willow, cane, rattan, reed, and rush, even twisted paper. At one time it was quite common. Now, too many collectors have driven prices up, and many pieces are being reproduced, worldwide. Most pieces were handwoven or loomwoven, from the materials mentioned or from man-made fibers. Prices are for pieces in good-to-fine condition.

Baby Furnishings

Baby carriage, willow, handwoven, complete	$875-966
Bassinet, reed, handwoven	142-156

(continued)

Bird Cages

Reed, metal stand, handwoven . .	170-180
Willow, hanging type, hand-woven	160-180

Chairs

Child's high, reed, handwoven . . .	92-118
Child's, rocking, willow, man-made fibers	77- 92
Fireside, cane, handwoven	250-280
Fireside, willow, loom-woven	288-320
Rocking, ornate, willow, hand-woven (ill.)	352-371
Rocking, willow, handwoven	262-282
Straight, cushioned seat and back, willow, handwoven	320-342
Straight, magazine racks at arms, reed, handwoven	362-390

Chaise Lounges

Grass, handwoven	420-495
Reed, loom-woven	425-525

Davenports

Cushioned back and seat, reed, handwoven	520-650
Cushioned back and seat, willow, handwoven	466-488

Desks

Reed, handwoven	295-320
Rush, loom-woven	288-325
Man-made fibers, handwoven . . .	275-320

Fern Stands

Box-type, w/hanging bird cage, reed, handwoven	362-382
Box-type, willow, loom-woven . . .	225-262
Floor-type, reed, handwoven	199-246

Lamps

Floor, reed, handwoven	282-342
Hanging, willow, handwoven	220-227
Phonograph cabinet, floor model, willow, handwoven	440-472
Table, reed, handwoven	182-192

Settees

Grass, handwoven	395-495
Reed, loom-woven	395-495

Sewing Stands

Man-made fibers, handwoven . . .	140-160
Reed, handwoven	152-172

Swings

Porch, reed, handwoven	342-362
Porch, willow, handwoven	352-372

Tables

Bridge, reed, handwoven	282-292
Dining, willow, handwoven	388-422
End, reed, handwoven	92-108
Library, reed, handwoven	262-288
Parlor, reed, loom-woven	162-188

Tea Carts

Reed, removable tray, solid rubber tires, handwoven	352-377
Willow, removable tray, solid rubber tires, handwoven	392-425

Umbrella Stand

Reed, handwoven	99-122

Willow Ware

Willow Ware

This was first made in England in 1772, in America about 1880. It was made in every quality, from Spode and Minton to the 5¢ and 10¢ store variety. Chinese legend says two escaping lovers were turned into doves. Found in light and dark blue, also in pink and green. Red is rare. Lots of scenes other than the dove bit were used. Maker, year, and quality dictate prices here.

Bowl, Ridgway, 8″ dia. . . . . $	24- 32
Bowl, soup, marked Allerton, England, 6″ dia.	17- 25
Bowl, vegetable, 9¾″ dia.	32- 39
Butter pat, marked Allerton	7- 11
Butter pat, Ridgway	7- 11
Butter pat, Wedgwood	9- 14
Creamer, Buffalo Pottery, 4¼″ high	14- 22
Creamer, Johnson Bros., 4½″ high	12- 19
Creamer, Made in Japan, 4″ high	10- 16
Cup/saucer, Japan	16- 24
Cup/saucer, marked Allerton	28- 38
Cup/saucer, Ridgway	26- 34
Cup/saucer, Wedgwood	35- 45
Egg cup, Japan	7- 12
Egg cup, marked Allerton	10- 16
Pitcher, Buffalo Pottery, 10½″ high	34- 44
Pitcher, bulbous, Japan, 7″ high	25- 33
Pitcher, miniature, 3″ high	17- 24
Pitcher, Ridgway, 8½″ high	34- 42
Plate, Japan, 6″ dia.	14- 22

Plate, marked Allerton, 7¼" dia.	24-	32
Plate, marked Ridgway, 7¼" dia.	24-	32
Plate, marked Wedgwood, 7" dia.	24-	33
Plate, Royal Worcester, 7¼" dia.	24-	32
Plate, unmarked, 7" dia.	16-	24
Plates, 8", 8½", 10" dia., made in Ohio, ea. (ill.)	29-	39
Platter, Buffalo Pottery	36-	44
Platter, England	26-	34
Platter, Japan	23-	32
Platter, marked Ridgway	34-	40
Relish, Japan	9-	14
Relish, marked Ridgway	15-	23
Sauce, England	10-	14
Sauce, Japan	8-	11
Sugar/creamer, England	55-	63
Sugar/creamer, Japan	35-	44
Tea set, child's, Japan, 22 pcs.	35-	45
Tea set, England, 25 pcs.	57-	64
Tea set, Occupied Japan, 10 pcs.	39-	48
Wash bowl/pitcher, Allerton	235-255	
Wash bowl/pitcher, Wedgwood	265-325	

Witch Balls

From the early 1820s until the late 1890s these glass globes, usually placed in a stand or hung in the window, were supposed to prevent disease or ward off evil spirits. Wiping daily removed whatever evil was lurking in the neighborhood. Highly collectible today. Don't confuse them with the heavier glass balls used to float fishing nets.

Witch ball	$ 59-	72

Wood Carvings

Carrying on probably the oldest form of art, whittlers have been around since the days of the Romans. European woodcarvers, especially the German and French, decorated many of the finest palaces in the world. What we find today usually was carved in the mid-1800s. See **Clubs and Publications**, this Price Guide.

Angel heads (probably from a church), c. early 1800s, pr.	$ 328-	362
Buddha, lacquered, late 18th century	175-	192
Drunk under lamp post, 10" high; removable head is a bottle opener, lamp a cork-screw	44-	52

Wood Carvings

Duck, outspread wings, hand-painted, c. 1880s	230-	260
Eagle, outstretched wings over flag shield, c. mid-1800s	710-	742
Hunter with dog, European, c. early 19th century	305-	328
Japanese God, rosewood, 6" high (ill.)	110-	130
Mother with child, Italian, 7" high	71-	81
Sailing ship, in oval walnut frame, New England, c. 1850s	272-	292
Sinister eagle (looking to left), stern shield for ship		1,700+
Swiss couple, 5" high, early 20th century, pr.	62-	72
Wine maker, French, 8" high	64-	72

Wood, Enoch and Sons

ENOCH WOOD & Co.

Wood, Enoch and Sons

About 1784 Enoch Wood established his factory at Burslem, England. Later his sons

409   (continued)

joined him and they exported a large quantity of ceramics to the U.S. From 1819 until the 1840s the firm produced more marked American historical views than any other Staffordshire firm.

Jug, Sunderland Lustre, impressed mark (ill.) $522-562
Plate, dark blue, Pass in the Catskill Mountains, 7½" dia. . . 328-361
Plate, dark blue, The Capitol, Washington, 8¼" dia. 228-247
Plate, soup, dark blue, City of Albany, 10" dia. 232-252
Platter, dark blue, Highlands, Hudson River 542-592
Platter, dark blue, Military Academy, West Point, 9¼"×12" 652-672
Platter, dark blue, Niagara from the American side, 15" long . . . 492-522

Woodenware

Woodenware

Today, these wooden items used in the home in the last half of the 19th century are collectible. Dough bowls are scarce.

Bootjack, cherry, dated 1830 . . . . $108-121
Bowl, maple burl, 4" dia. 77- 87
Breadboard, maple, 11" dia. 74- 83
Breadboard, pine 68- 78
Broom, 1-pc., oak splint 77- 87
Bucket, oak, for well 52- 62
Butter paddle 32- 42
Calf yoke, with bow 188-197
Candle box, pine, sliding top, 16" long 86- 96
Candy mold (ill.) 30- 40
Candy scoop, poplar, 5" long 40- 50
Canteen, round 137-146
Cheese ladder, cherry 77- 87
Churn, barrel, with crank 92-107
Churn, bucket type 110-118
Churn, complete with dasher and lid 210-224
Cider funnel, poplar, 5½" long . . . 40- 50

Cookie board, Carved Daisy pattern, walnut, 6"×8" 62- 72
Cranberry picker, maple, child's size 132-142
Cream skimmer, pine, handled . . . 71- 81
Cup, burl walnut, handled 84- 94
Cutting board, walnut 37- 47
Darning knob, maple, 8" long . . . 49- 57
Dough bowl, maple, hand-carved . 138-147

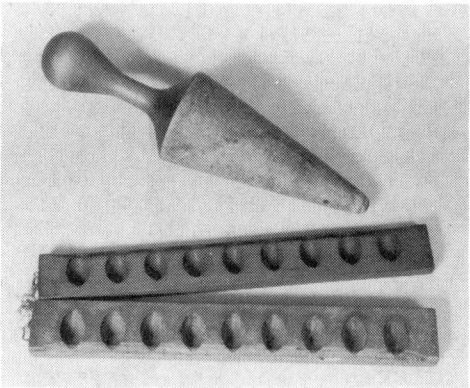

Woodenware

Egg carrier, 1 doz., wooden dividers 61- 71
Flour scoop 64- 74
Knife tray, 2-compartment w/handle, cherry 74- 84
Ladle, 14" long 62- 72
Lemon squeezer 50- 60
Letter box, cherry, hinged lid . . . 128-137
Oak keg, staved and hooped with hickory bands 120-142
Ox yoke, large, with bows 220-238
Pickle bucket, original lid 91- 99
Pie crimper, walnut wheel 88- 97
Piggin, staved and hooped 89-107
Plane, maple, signed L. Cook, 7" long 62- 72
Potato masher, pine, 9" long 32- 47
Rice molds, Japanese, hand-carved, 19th century, 16" and 18" long, ea. (ill.) 40- 45
Rolling pin, pine, solid, 15" long . 42- 52
Sap bucket, hickory bands 72- 82
Scriber, maple, 5½" long 52- 62
Shoulder yoke, pine 132-142
Spoke shaver, maple, brass insert and handle 62- 72
Spoon rack, pine, 8 carved slots, 16" high 272-282
Spoon rack, walnut, 6 carved slots, hanging type 240-262
Stirrup, pine (great for holding paper napkins) 37- 47
Sugar bucket 65- 75

Worcester Porcelain

This was Tonquin, originally (in 1751) called Worcester Tonquin Manufacture. Dr. John Wall (and partners) founded the firm at Worcester, England. The Dr. Wall or First Period ended in 1783, when Thomas Flight purchased all assets. In 1793, Martin Barr came in as a partner. Flight and Barr changed in 1807 to Flight, Barr and Barr. The name changed again in 1813. In 1840 Chamberlin and Company consolidated with the parent company. The firm was sold in 1852 to Kerr and Binn which is still in existence. What you find of the early Worcester is from the 1870-1900 period. Royal Worcester entered the picture in 1862. Reproductions of the Dr. Wall period are in shops today, having been reproduced over 60 years ago.

Basket, dark blue. c. 1910,
  8½" x 10½" $235-360
Bowl, blue enamel, gilt rim, Dr.
  Wall period, 6¼" dia. 285-310
Bowl, blue/gold, 7" dia. 93-102

Bowl, blue/white transfer,
  dancing ladies, 18th century .. 190-230
Cachepot, roses/fruit/birds, gold
  trim, c. 1910, 2½" x 2½" 218-233
Candle snuffer, monk, purple
  mark 80- 90
Creamer, floral decor, marked
  Flight, Barr and Barr,
  5" high 175-190
Cup/saucer, floral decor, Dr.
  Wall period 215-230
Cup/saucer, multicolored floral,
  gold trim, c. 1900 .... 75- 85
Cup/saucer, pansy decor on light
  blue, gold rim 205-215
Dish, Blind Earl, Dr. Wall period,
  6" dia. 475-525
Dish, cream ground, rust flowers,
  7½" dia. 160-180
Dish, shell-shaped, blue/green,
  gold rim, 7½" dia. 90-110
Jar, biscuit, peach/cream, silver
  bail and lid, c. 1905 115-130
Jug, milk, Scottish coat-of-arms,
  c. 1850 95-125
Plate, Blind Earl, Dr. Wall period,
  7½" dia. 475-550
Plate, green, floral decor, Dr.
  Wall period, 7¾" dia. 185-220
Plates, cream ground, castle
  scenes, 7" dia., pr. (ill.) 195-230
Platter, blue/gold, birds/flowers,
  c. 1900, 10½" long 165-190
Saucer, peacocks, c. 1900 .... 69- 78
Teapot, monk, rust color, 5½"
  high 275-300
Teapot, Queen Charlotte, Dr.
  Wall period, 5¾" high 335-370
Vase, Bengal tiger, 8½" high 275-330
Vase, blue/gold, floral decor,
  gold handles, 11" high 275-310

Worcester Porcelain

411

(continued)

Vase, pilgrim, bulbous shape,
18th century 235-245

Umbrella, paper, New York
World's Fair, 1939 . . . . 21- 31

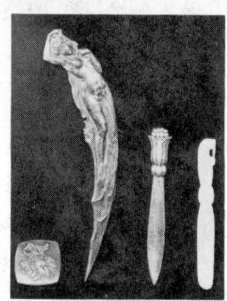

Writing Accessories

World Expositions and Fairs

World Expositions and Fairs

The first exhibition opened at the Crystal Palace in London in 1851. The first World's Fair opened at the Crystal Palace in New York City in 1853. The first exposition opened in Philadelphia in 1876. Mementos of these great events are highly collectible today, the older the better. What you find in shops is from the late 1800s in the form of spoons, glass mugs, toothpick holders, in metal or glass. These items stayed in vogue until the Sesquicentennial Exposition in Philadelphia, 1926. See **Clubs and Publications,** this Price Guide.

Arlington Mills woven advertis-
ing display, Columbus,
12"×18" $118-127
Bottle, milk glass, New York
World's Fair, 1939 . . . .   30- 40
Creamer, Chicago Exposition,
1893 . . . .   37- 47
Discovery of America medal 36- 46
Elongated (rolled-out) dime 37- 47
Elongated (rolled-out) penny 14- 21
Handkerchief, panorama of
fairgrounds 19- 27
Holy Bible, souvenir of
Exposition 42- 56
Match holder, New York World's
Fair, 1939 . . . .   19- 27
Photo album, red velvet cover,
color pages of buildings 77- 87
Pin, Simoniz (ill.) 2- 3
Plate, St. Louis Exposition, 1904   27- 36
Rain Bonnet (ill) 2- 4
Spoon, Chicago Exposition, 1893   34- 42

Writing Accessories

The pieces illustrated are sterling silver. Many writing sets were made of plated materials, metal-over-glass. As a complete set or individually, these accessories are collectible, especially if you find a piece stamped Tiffany Studios, New York.

Letter opener, Art Nouveau lady,
brass, 10" long (ill.) $72- 85
Letter opener, Eskimo, 6¾" long
(ill.) 118-127
Letter opener, sterling silver, 6¼"
long (ill.) 68- 79
Stamp box, Japan, bronze/brass,
1¾" high (ill.) 77- 86

Yellow Ware

Yellow Ware

This heavy earthenware varies in color from a rich orange to lighter shades of tan. Most of what you find are kitchen pieces, although occasionally you will find other items. English pieces have a harder body.

Bowl, blue band at top, 12½"
dia. . . . . $ 66- 72
Bowl, plain, 7½" dia. (ill.) 19- 26
Bowl, relief exterior, 9" dia. 52- 62
Crock, covered, large, brown
bands 81- 90
Crock, small, white bands 47- 56
Custard cup, small, blue band . . . 9- 15
Mold, Grape pattern, large 44- 52
Mold, Sunflower pattern, medium 38- 47
Pie plate, 8" dia. 37- 46
Pie plate, 9½" dia. 52- 62
Pitcher, blue band, 7" high 112-130
Pitcher, 5" high 88- 97
Rolling pin, wooden handles,
8" long 54- 63

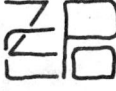

Zane Pottery

Zane Ware was originally the Peters and Reed Pottery in Zanesville, Ohio, 1921. Garden wares and such art lines as Powder Blue and Sheen were made. In 1941 the firm was sold to Lawton Gonder, of Gonder pottery fame. Prices and items are comparable to Roseville and Weller.

Zanesville
Art Pottery   LA MORO

The Zanesville Art Pottery Company began making jardinieres, tableware, umbrella stands, and vases in 1900. The company's major line was La Moro, a hand-painted, slip-decorated ware. Sam Weller bought the firm in 1920.

Bowl, La Moro, signed, 7" high . . $ 47- 56
Bowl, light blue matt glaze, 7¼"
high 46- 56

Zanesville Art Pottery

Coffeepot, dark green matt glaze,
5½" high 38- 52
Jardiniere w/stand, mottled
brown/green, 29" high 108-121
Plate, green matt glaze, signed,
6½" dia. 45- 62
Vase, blue flowers, La Moro,
artist-signed, 6½" high 220-242
Vase, blue orchids, La Moro,
signed by artist, 8¼" high 210-221
Vase, pansies, brown glaze, 6"
high 72- 82

Zsolnay Porcelain

In the 1850s the factory was established at Funfkirchen, Hungary, by Vilmos Zsolnay. It made soft-paste porcelains, usually enameled in many colors, and highly glazed.

Bowl, harbor, blue, gold, signed . . $260-280
Dish, castle, gold, green, iridized,
4½" dia. 121-140
Pitcher, floral decor, multi-
colored, signed, 7" high 192-220
Tea set (teapot, creamer, sugar,
6 cups/saucers), signed 262-270
Vase, blue, green, gold, reticu-
lated at top, signed, 6½" high . 310-342
Vase, enameled, signed, 10" high . 288-299

Section of Pattern Glass
Alphabetical by Pattern Name

The discovery of a mechanical means for producing press-molded glass articles was probably the most significant contribution made by American craftsmen to the glass industry's development in the 19th century. That it would prove to be of great national importance is now an accepted fact from an historical point of view.

The unfortunate fire of December 17, 1836, which destroyed much of the Patent Office and its records, left the patent records for the first half of the 19th century somewhat incomplete; therefore the controversy of who was first, in Pattern Glass, and with what, still rages.

Generally, Joseph Magouun's patent for a manually operated glass press (December 6, 1845); Frederick McKee and Charles Ballinger's patent for a steam-operated glass press (March 29, 1864); William King's patent for a revolving block-type press and Henry Leasure's patent for an air-cooled glass press (March 5, 1872) are usually accepted as milestones in the industry. Certainly, there were others, such as Hiram Dillaway's patent for a glass mold (August 21, 1841) in which ten glass stoppers for decanters or cruets could be pressed in one operation. Equally important was Daniel Ripley's patent (October 20, 1868) for a mold that pressed two or more articles of glass in one operation.

There are three methods of pressing glass: (1) Block Molding, the simplest; (2) Split Molding, where the mold is made up of two or more parts; and (3) Font Molding whereby each article is made absolutely identical in form and dimension.

For those who could not afford expensive, hand-cut pieces, pressed glass, which gave way to Pattern Glass with a clear, rather than a stippled background, conferred a great benefit of beauty and utility. This inexpensive glass for everybody revolutionized the glass industry in America.

Guide to Pattern Glass
with Duplicate Names

Acme—see Butterfly with Spray
Acorn— see Willow Oak
Alexis—see Priscilla
Amberette—see Klondike
Andes—see Beaded Tulip
Arched Fans—see Caprice
Artic—see Polar Bear
Ashland—see Snowdrop
Atlanta—see Clear Lion's Head
Austrian—see Fine Cut Medallion

Baby Thumbprint—see Dakota
Ball—see Notched Bar
Banded Prism Bar—see Doyle's 400
Beaded Bull's Eye and Drape—see Alabama
Beaded Mirror—see Beaded Medallion
Bean—see Egg in Sand
Bearded Man—see Queen Anne
Bearded Prophet—see Bearded Head
Beatty Rib—see Ribbed Opal
Berkley—see Blocked Arches
Big Block—see Henrietta
Blazing Pinwheels—see Shoshone
Blazing Star—see Pinwheels
Block and Pleat—see Persian
Block with Stars—see Hanover
Blockade—see Diamond Block with Fans
Bluebird—see Bird and Strawberry
Boswell—see Seashell
Bosworth—see Star Band
Brilliant—see Stars and Stripes
Broughton—see Pattee Cross
Bryce—see Ribbon Candy
Bullet—see Atlas
Buttressed Loop—see Buttressed Arch

Cable with Ring and Star—see Cable with Ring
California—see Beaded Grape
Cameo—see Classic Medallion, also see Ceres
Candlewick—see Banded Raindrop
Cannonball—see Atlas
Centennial—see Liberty Bell
Centennial Shield—see American Shield
Chain Lightning—see Lightning
Challinor's No. 313—see Challinor's Tree of Life
Challinor's Thumbprint—see
  Barrelled Thumbprint

Clear Lily—see Daisy and Button
  with Narcissus
Clear Panels with Cord Band—see Rope Bands
Colossus—see Lacy Spiral
Columbia—see Heart with Thumbprint
Columbian—see Coin
Column Block—see Panel and Star
Coral—see Fishscale
Crescent and Fan—see Starred Scroll
Cross Roads—see Ashman
Crow-Foot—see Yale
Crown Jewels—see Chandelier
Crystal Anniversary—see Crystal Wedding
Crystal Ball—see Atlas
Cut Log—see Cat's-eye and Block,
  also see Ethol

Daisy—see Thousand Eye
Daisy in Oval Panesl—see Bull's Eye and Fan
Daisy in Panel—see Two Panel
Daisy in Square—see Two Panel
Deer and Doe—see Deer and Pine Tree
Derby—see Pleat and Panel
Dewey—see Spanish-American
Diamond (Lippman)—see Flat Diamond
Diamond and Concave—see Diamond
  Thumbprint
Diamond Bar—see Lattice
Diamond Horseshoe—see Aurora
Dinner Bell—see Cottage
Dogwood—see Art Novo
Doll's Eye—see Memphis
Double Arch—see Interlocking Crescents
Double Loop—see Ribbon Candy
Double Pear—see Gypsy
Draped Top—see Victoria
Duquesne—see Wheat and Barley
Dynast—see Radiant

Egyptian—see Parthenon
Elite—see Pillow and Sunburst
English Hobnail Cross—see Klondike
Enigma—see Wyoming
Excelsior—see Ruby Thumbprint,
  also see Giant Bull's-Eye

Fancy Diamonds—see Three-in-One
Figure Eight—see Ribbon Candy

Fine Cut Bar—see Panama
Finecut and Blazing Star—see Pinwheels
Finecut and Feather—see Cottage
Finger Print—see Almond Thumbprint
Fisheye—see Torpedo
Flamingo—see Frosted Stork
Flat Panel—see Pleating
Flora—see Opposing Pyramids
Floral Diamonds—see Shoshone
Florida—see Herringbone, also see Emerald
   Green Herringbone
Flower Flange—see Dewey
Flowered Scroll—see Duncan 2000
Fluted Diamond Point—see Panelled Sawtooth
Flying Robin—see Hummingbird
Forest Ware—see Ivy-in-Snow
45 Colonis—see Colonis
Frosted Fleur-de-Lis—see Stippled Fleur de Lis
Frosted Flower—see Twinkle Star
Frosted Magnolia—see Water Lily
Frosted Waffle—see Hidalgo

Galloway—see Virginia
Gem—see Nailhead
Georgia—see Peacock Feather;
 also Pattee Cross
Gloria—see Pattee Cross
Goddess of Liberty—see Ceres, also see Act
Golden Agate—see Holly Amber
Good Luck—see Horseshoe
Guardian Angel—see Cupid and Venus

Hand—see Pennsylvania
Hartley—see Panelled Diamond Cut and Fan
Hearts and Spades—see Medallion
Hinoto—see Diamond Point with Panels
Honeycomb—see New York
Hops and Barley—see Wheat and Barley
Hops Band—see Maple

Iceberg—see Polar Bear
Ida—see Sheraton
Indian Tree—see Barley
Indiana—see Cord Drapery
Indiana Swirl—see Feather
Inverted Prism—see Masonic
Inverted Thumbprint with Daisy Band—see
   Honeycomb with Flower Rim
Irish Column—see Broken Column

Japanese—see Grace
Jersey Swirl—see Swirl
Jewel Band—see Scalloped Tape
Job's Tears—see Art

Kamomi—see Balder
Kansas—see Jewel with Dewdrop

King's Crown—see Ruby Thumbprint

Lace—see Drapery
Lacy Medallion—see Princess Feather
Large Thumbprint—see Ashburton
Late Sawtooth—see Cobb
Lawrence—see Bull's Eye
Leaf—see Maple Leaf
Lily—see Sunflower
Lion's Leg—see Alaska
Locust—see Grasshopper with Insect
London—see Picket
Long Spear—see Grasshopper with Insect
Loop—see Pillar
Loop and Jewel—see New England Pineapple,
   also see Jewel and Festoon
Loop with Pillar—see Michigan
Loop with Stippled Panels—see Texas
Looped Cord—see Beaded Chain

Magic—see Rosette
Maltese—see Jacob's Ladder
Maple—see Panelled Grape
"The Martyrs' Mug"—see Assassination Mug
Maryland Pear—see Gypsy
Mikado—see Daisy and Thumbprint Cross Bar
Mitred Diamond Points—see Mitred Bars

N.P.L.—see Pressed Leaf
Nautilus—see Argonaut Shell
Neptune—see Queen Anne
New Century—see Delaware
New Grand—see Grand
New Jersey—see Loops and Drops
North Pole—see Polar Bear
Notched Rib—see Broken Column
No. 11—see Thousand Eye

Oak Leaf—see Willow Oak
Oaken Bucket—see Pail
Oats and Barley—see Wheat and Barley
O'Hara—see Loop
Old Acorn—see Chestnut Oak
Old Man of the Mountain—see Bearded Head
Oregon—see Beaded Loop
Orion—see Cathedral
Owl in Fan—see Parrot

Panel with Diamond Point—see Late Diamond
   Point Band
Panelled Agave—see Cactus
Panelled Daisy and Button—see Queen
Panelled Diamond and Fine Cut—see Carmen
Panelled Flower, Stippled—see Maine
Peerless—see Lady Hamilton
Pennsylvania—see Pavonia

Pert—see Ribbed Forget-Me-Not
Pillar and Bull's Eye—see Thistle
Pioneer—see Westward Ho
Pittsburgh Daisy—see Floral Oval
Plain Sunburst—see Diamond Sunburst
Pointed Panel—see Queen
Pointed Thumbprint—see Almond Thumbprint
Portland Petal—see Loop
Potted Plant—see Flower Pot
Prayer Rug—see Horseshoe
Pretty Band—see Flower and Quill
Pride—see Beveled Star
Prism and Diamond Band—see Diamond Band
Prism Arc—see X-Log
Pygmy—see Torpedo

Question Mark—see Oval Loop
Quixote—see Harvard

Ray—see Lutz
Regal—see Panelled Forget-Me-Not
Rib—see U.S. Rib
Ribbed Leaf—see Bellflower
Ribbed Pineapple—see Prism and Flattened
  Sawtooth
Ripple Band—see Ripple
Roanoke—see Sawtooth
Rochelle—see Princess Feather
Romeo—see Block and Fan
Royal—see Sprig
Royal Crystal—see Harvard

Sampson—see Teardrop and Tassel
Sandwich Loop—see Hairpin
Santa Claus—see Queen Anne
Sawtooth Band—see Amazon
Scalloped Daisy Red Top—see Button Arches
Scalloped Diamond Point—see Late Diamond
  Point Band
Scalloped Loop—see Yoked Loop
Sedan—see Panelled Star and Button
Shell and Scroll—see Garland and Roses
Shield in Red, White and Blue—see Bullet
  Emblem
Shields—see Tape Measure
Single and Double Vine—see Bellflower
The Sisters—see Three Faces
Smocking Bands—see Double Beetle Band
Spades—see Medallion
Spanish Coin—see Coin
Sprig—see Ribbed Palm, also see Barley
Square—see Shell and Tassel
Square and Dot—see Spirea Band
Squared Dot—see Spirea Band
Star Galaxy—see Effulgent Star
Star and Punty—see Early Moon and Star
Star and Honeycomb—see Laverne

Stemless Daisy—see Cosmos
Stippled Scroll—see Scroll
Stippled Star—see Willow Oak
Stawberry—see Fairfax Strawberry
Stiped Dewdrop—see Panelled Dewdrop
Style—see Arrowhead in Oval
Sultan—see Curtain
Sun and Star—see Priscilla
Sunburst Medallion—see Daisy Medallion
Sunburst Rosette—see Frosted Medallion
Swirl—see Jersey Swirl

Tall Baby Thumbprint—see Challinor
  Thumbprint
Teardrops and Diamond Block—see Art
Teepee—see Wigwam
Texas—see Loop with Stippled Panels
Theatrical—see Actress
Thistle—see Willow Oak
Three Stories—see Persian
Thumbprint—see Argus
Thumbprint Band—see Dakota
Tidal—see Florida Palm
Tippecanoe—see Westward Ho
Tooth and Claw—see Esther
Trilby—see Valentine
Triple Bar—see Scalloped Prism
Tulip—see Tulip with Sawtooth
Tulip Petals—see Church Windows
Twin Pear—see Gypsy

U.S.—see Coin

Valencia Waffle—see Block and Star
Victor—see Shell and Jewel, also see Shoshone
Viking—see Bearded Head
Virginia—see Banded Portland

Washboard—see Adonis
Water Lily—see Frosted Magnolia,
  also Rose Point Band
Winged Scroll—see Ivorina Verde,
  also see Louis XV
Winona—see Barred Hobnail
Wisconsin—see Beaded Dewdrop
Wreath—see Willow Oak

Zephyr—see Pressed Diamond
Zipper—see Cobb

Acorn

Maker and date unknown, probably c. 1870s. Don't confuse it with Hobbs' opaque colors, c. 1890, or Beaumont's crystal colors, c. late 1890s.

Butter dish, covered, acorn finial . . .	$ 36-44
Celery	32-42
Compote	
Covered, acorn finial.	57-68
Open	46-52
Creamer	47-59
Egg cup	28-37
Goblet	37-42
Pitcher	52-62
Sugar bowl	
Covered, acorn finial.	45-62
Open	35-46

Probably other pieces. Goblet being reproduced.

Aberdeen

Aberdeen

Maker unknown, c. early 1870s. Clear, nonflint.

Butter dish, covered.	$ 37-45
Compote, open	27-36
Creamer	36-42
Egg cup.	22-32
Goblet	22-32
Pitcher, water.	47-54
Sauce, flat	18-27
Sugar bowl (ill.)	26-34

Acanthus Scroll

Maker and date unknown. Clear, possibly color, possibly engraved.

Butter dish, covered.	$ 36-50
Cake stand	26-35
Creamer	35-43
Goblet	21-29
Pitcher	36-43
Spoonholder	22-32
Sugar bowl, covered.	24-35

If color, if engraved, 50 percent higher than clear prices listed.

Actress

Actress

(Theatrical; Goddess of Liberty): La-Belle Glass Company, Bridgeport, Ohio, about 1872; probably Crystal Glass Company, same town, 1879. Clear; clear and frosted prices given, 20 percent less for clear.

419

(continued)

Bowl, footed, 6″	$ 57-68
Butler dish, covered	86-96
Cake stand, 7″ high	134-144
Candlesticks, pr.	221-232
Celery "Pinafore"	160-170
Cheese dish, covered, scene from "The Lone Fisherman"	205-218
Compote	
Covered, clear, 8″ high standard	160-170
Covered, low standard	162-172
Creamer	70-80
Goblet, clear, footed	97-108
Honey dish, covered	77-84
Marmalade jar, w/cover	122-132
Pickle dish, "Love's Request"	49-62
Pitcher	
Milk (ill.)	225-246
Water	230-250
Platter	
Scene from "Pinafore"	143-166
"Miss Nielson"	132-148
Relish dish	48-59
Salt/Pepper, pr.	74-84
Sauce	
Flat	39-49
Footed	39-55
Spoonholder, clear or frosted	79-93
Sugar bowl	91-108
Tray, bread, "Give Us This Day"	96-118

Pickle jar is being reproduced; possibly other pieces.

Adonis

McKee & Bros., Pittsburgh, 1897. Crystal, canary, blue, green, other.

Celery	
Oval	$ 24-36
Tall	27-38
Compote, stemmed	
Covered	35-44
Open	31-38
Dish, round	
1½″	12-18
4″	16-19
8″	22-31
Jelly, footed, 4½″ high	32-42
Molasses can, pewter top	34-38
Pitcher	
1 quart (ill.)	37-44
1 gallon	47-56
Plate, 10″	14-19

Tumbler	15-24

Color 50 percent higher than clear prices listed.

Adonis   Alabama

Alabama

(Beaded Bull's Eye and Drape): U.S. Glass Company, Pittsburgh, 1898. First of the extensive "States" series made by this company. Clear; probably in colors with gilt trim.

Butter dish, covered	$ 43-52
Cake stand	45-53
Celery	35-42
Compote	
Covered	39-47
Open, 5″	37-44
Creamer	41-50
Goblet	24-32
Honey dish, covered (rare)	55-64
Nappie, handled	24-32
Pitcher	
Milk (ill.)	56-64
Syrup	40-47
Water	56-64
Relish dish, oblong, 3 sizes, ea.	17-24
Spoonholder	28-36
Sugar bowl, covered	45-52
Tumbler	24-35

Alaska

(Lion's Leg): Northwood Glass Company, 1897. Opalescent, pearl blue, pearl yellow, pearl flint, green.

Berry set	
Bowl, berry, op. blue	$ 79-86
Bowl, berry, vaseline	74-83
Butter dish, covered, op. blue	321-342

Alaska

Creamer, green (ill.)	82-92
Creamer, sugar, square, pr., pearl blue	218-227
Jewel tray	47-56
Pitcher, water, decorated, vaseline . . .	362-381
Rose bowl, op. blue, vaseline, or emerald on stand, round pedestal foot	87-99
Spoonholder, emerald green	84-92

Probably other pieces.

Alligator Scales

Alligator Scales

Maker unknown, c. 1870s. Clear flint.

Goblet (ill.)	$ 35-43

Other pieces?

Almond

U.S. Glass Co., c. 1890s.

Decanter	$ 29-35
Goblet	26-34
Salt, footed	19-27
Wine (ill.)	18-22

Probably other pieces.

Almond

Almond Thumbprint

Almond Thumbprint

(Pointed Thumbprint; Finger Print): Bryce Bros., Pittsburgh, 1890. Clear, colors.

Butter dish, covered, cable edge	$86-108
Celery vase	72-80
Creamer (ill.)	70-80
Compote, covered High standard 4¾", 7", 10"	66-73
Low standard	62-72
Egg cup	36-44
Goblet, several styles	20-27
Pitcher, water	88-94
Sugar bowl, covered	64-72
Tumbler	45-55

Probably other pieces. Color, 150 percent higher than clear prices listed.

421

Amazon

Amazon

(Sawtooth Band): Bryce Bros., Pittsburgh, c. 1890. Crystal, plain and engraved. Reissued by U.S. Glass Company after 1891. Set consisted of 65 pieces.

Bowl, waste	$ 29-35
Butter dish, covered.	66-73
Cake stand, large	57-64
Compote, 6¾″ high	52-62
Creamer	37-46
Goblet	36-45
Pitcher, water, milk	53-62
Salt/Pepper, pr.	45-54
Sugar bowl (ill.)	58-66
Wine	36-44

American Shield

(Centennial Shield): Maker unknown, probably made for 1876 Centennial. Clear, nonflint.

Butter dish, covered	$160-170
Creamer	118-122
Spoonholder	121-130
Sugar bowl, covered	152-160

Only known pieces.

Angora

Maker unknown, c. late 1880s. Clear, nonflint.

Butter dish, covered.	$ 32-40
Creamer	23-32
Goblet	26-35
Spoonholder	22-29
Sugar bowl, covered	28-34

Probably other pieces.

Anheuser Busch

"A" ale glass possibly LaBelle Glass Company, Bridgeport, Ohio, c. 1880. Clear, nonflint.

Ale glass	$ 29-39

Anthemion

Anthemion

Model Flint Glass Company, Findlay, Ohio, 1890. Crystal glass only; possibly emerald green, others.

Bowl, berry, 7″	$ 23-32
Butter dish, covered (scarce)	58-67
Cake plate, high standard, 9¼″ high	37-46
Celery	19-26
Creamer	27-36
Marmalade jar	32-40
Pitcher	
Milk (ill.)	38-45
Water	39-47
Plate, 10″	17-26
Relish dish	10-15
Sauce, flat, square.	10-13
Spoonholder	23-30
Sugar bowl, covered.	41-50
Tumbler	32-40

Anvil

Toothpick (or match holder, anvilshaped), Windsor Glass Company, Pittsburgh, c. 1887.

Amber	$ 60-72
Blue.	47-56
Canary	38-48
Clear	35-42

Apollo

Apollo

Adams & Company, Pittsburgh, 1875; also, McKee Bros., same city, 1894. Clear and frosted. Prices are for clear; frosted, 15 percent more. Red stain, 20 percent more.

Bowl, 9½" d., also w/red stain	$ 34-42
Butler dish, covered	49-54
Cake stand	42-51
Celery, frosted (ill.)	24-32
Cheese dish (scarce)	49-54
Compote	
Covered, high standard	55-63
Open, low standard	37-46
Creamer.	39-44
Egg cup	23-30
Goblet	37-44
Pickle.	21-28
Pitcher, water	48-52
Pitcher, syrup	34-37
Sauce	
Flat	8-10
Footed.	12-16
Spoonholder	28-36
Sugar bowl, covered	44-50
Tray, water	38-42
Tumbler	29-36
Wine	27-32

Apple Blossom

Northwood Glass Company, Indiana, Pennsylvania, c. 1896, decorated milk glass.

Butter dish, covered	$ 70-78
Cake stand	62-72
Compote	60-68
Creamer.	38-42
Goblet	41-50
Pitcher, syrup	105-109
Sugar bowl, covered	88-94
Sugar shaker	82-92
Tumbler	52-61

Probably other pieces.

Aquarium

Aquarium

U.S. Glass Company, c. 1890s. The water pitcher is occasionally seen. Probably tumbler to match.

Tumbler	$ 33-41
Water pitcher (ill.)	152-166

Probably other pieces.

Arabesque

Arabesque

Bakewell, Pears & Company, Pittsburgh, before 1864. Clear, non-flint.

Butter dish	$ 48-53
Celery	38-44
Compote	
Covered, 6" and 8", high standard	59-63
Covered, 6" and 8", low standard	44-52

(continued)

Creamer, applied handle	49-54
Goblet	35-39
Pitcher, applied handle (ill.).	56-62
Sauce, flat	12-16
Spoonholder	28-33
Sugar bowl, open	40-44

**Arch and Fern
with Snake Medallion**

Arch and Fern
with Snake Medallion

Sandwich glass, mid-1800s. This is NOT
Pressed glass. It is blown 3-mold; just that,
blown into a mold, not plunger-pressed. It
is shown as a comparison only.

Arch and Forget-Me-Not Bands

Arch and Forget-Me-Not
Bands

Maker unknown, 1880s.

Berry bowl	$ 28-34
Butter dish, covered.	42-46
Creamer	34-42
Pitcher, water (ill.)	47-56
Saucedish.	14-20
Spoonholder	28-32
Sugar bowl, covered	44-52
Tumbler	24-32

Probably other pieces.

Arched Grape

Arched Grape

Sandwich glass, 1870s. Clear glass.

Butter dish, covered	$ 54-62
Celery vase	42-51
Compote	
Covered, high standard	54-63
Covered, low standard	51-60
Cordial	27-37
Creamer (ill.)	43-52
Goblet	35-42
Pitcher, water	64-72
Saucedish, 4"	14-22
Spoonholder	27-36
Sugar bowls	
Covered.	48-52
Open	40-47

Probably other pieces.

Arched Leaf

Arched Leaf

Maker unknown, c. 1870s. Clear, flint, nonflint.

Goblet	$ 24-32
Plate, 7″, 10″	24-34
Salt, footed	25-35
Sugar bowl (base ill.)	52-62

Flint, 50 percent higher than nonflint prices listed.

Arched Ovals

U.S. Glass Company, c. 1900. Clear, flashed with red; cranberry-flashed (rose), emerald green.

Goblet	$ 32-42
Toothpick holder	31-42
Tumbler	35-42
Wine	28-34

"Rose" and emerald green, 25 percent higher than clear, flashed with red prices listed. Probably other pieces.

Argonaut Shell (Nautilus)

Northwood Glass Company, about 1900. Custard, colors, clear, opalescent. Custard decorated in dark green and gold.

Berry set	Custard	Color
Large bowl	$340-352	$144-152
Small bowl	218-222	58-64
Butter dish, covered. .	265-280	250-262
Compote	172-188	270-288
Pitcher, water.	332-342	170-188
Salt/Pepper, pr.. . . .	98-110	362-371
Sugar bowl, covered . .	229-242	240-262
Tumbler	261-271	135-145

Probably other pieces. Custard bowl being reproduced. Also, blue opalescent toothpick.

Argus

Argus

(Thumbprint): Bakewell, Pears & Company, 1870. Crystal, colors (rare).

Ale glass, 7½″	$120-130
Butter dish	94-103
Celery vase, 2 types	72-81
Champagne	58-62
Cordial	62-72
Creamer, applied handle.	69-78
Decanter, quart	78-87
Goblet	51-62
Mug, applied handle (scarce)	81-91
Sauce	19-28
Spoonholder	38-42
Sugar bowl, covered	77-82
Tumbler, footed jelly, water	52-62
Tumbler, whiskey, handled	51-60
Wine	34-42

Arrowhead in Oval

425

(continued)

Arrowhead in Oval

Higbee Glass Company, c. 1890. Clear, nonflint. Not all pieces marked with "bee."

Cup, punch	13-20
Goblet (ill.)	24-32
Wine	19-28

Undoubtedly other pieces.

Art

Art

(Job's Tears, Teardrops and Diamond Block): Adams & Company, Pittsburgh, 1870s. Clear.

Basket, fruit	$ 78-87
Bowl, berry, 8″	46-52
Butter dish, covered	56-62
Cake stand, 10″	59-69
Compote	
Covered, footed, 7″	64-72
Open, footed, 7½″	46-56
Cracker jar	49-59
Creamer	38-47
Cruet	48-57
Dish, banana	42-44
Goblet	39-46
Mug	27-32
Pitcher, water (ill).	54-62
Relish	25-32
Sauce, footed, flat	14-18
Spoonholder	32-42
Sugar bowl, covered	45-52
Tumbler	28-37
Wine	27-32

Art Novo

Art Novo

(Dogwood): Co-Operative Flint Glass Company, Beaver Falls, Pennsylvania, 1905. Clear.

Butter dish	$ 28-34
Creamer	24-32
Lamp (ill.)	32-40
Spoonholder	23-32
Sugar bowl	28-34

Probably other pieces.

Artichoke

Artichoke

Probably Dalzell, Gilmore and Leighton, Findlay, Ohio, 1890s. crystal, opaque white, also with the figure work in satin finish, colors.

Bowl, 8″	$ 32-40
Butter dish	58-64
Cake stand	46-53
Compotes	
Covered, high standard	56-62
Open, high standard	50-57
Creamer	35-42

Assassination Mug

Assassination Mug

(Also called "The Martyrs' Mug"): Garfield on one side, Lincoln on other. Obviously made after 1881, the year Garfield was assassinated. By whom this mug was made is not known. Clear glass.

Mug, 2¼" high (ill.) . . . . $ 66-77

Atlas

Atlas

(Cannon Ball, Bullet): Adams & Company, Pittsburgh, 1889. Clear, vari-colors, ruby flashed.

Bowls, open	$ 17-24
Butter dish, covered	39-47
Cake stand, 10" high, clear	32-42
Creamer, covered, applied handle . . .	35-43
Goblet	31-40
Pitcher, water	44-52

Tumbler, water or whiskey	24-33
Wine	35-42

Probably other pieces.

Ball and Bar

Ball and Bar

Westmoreland Glass Company, Grapeville, Pennsylvania, 1896. Clear.

Butter dish	$ 44-52
Creamer	37-42
Pitcher (ill.)	64-72
Spoonholder	35-46
Sugar bowl	45-53

Probably other pieces.

Balloon

(continued)

Balloon

Made in lower Ohio Valley in early 1850s. Clear.

Creamer	$192-220
Goblet	75-87
Pitcher (ill.)	294-299
Sugar bowl	199-220

Probably a few other pieces but considered extremely rare today.

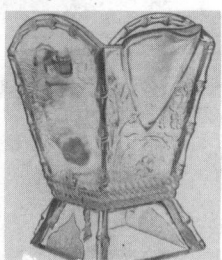

Bamboo

Bamboo

LaBelle Glass Company, Bridgeport, Ohio, 1883. Plain and engraved crystal glass.

Butter dish	$ 46-56
Celery	28-31
Compotes, 7″, 8″, 9″, covered	45-60
Creamer	35-42
Dish, 7″, 8″, 9″, oblong	24-33
Pitcher, water	43-52
Salt/Pepper, pr.	34-42
Sauce, 4″	14-19
Spoonholder (ill.)	22-29
Sugar bowl, covered	39-47
Tumbler	26-37

Banded Buckle

Sandwich glass, mid-1850s; other factories, Pittsburgh, 1870s. Clear glass.

Bowls, open	$ 22-34
Butter dish	47-52
Compote	
Open, low standard	49-57
Covered, low standard	39-52
Cordial	35-42
Creamer	42-50
Egg cup	27-31
Goblet	32-42
Pitcher, water	49-58

Banded Buckle

Salt, footed	14-20
Spoonholder	22-31
Sugar bowl (ill.)	38-50
Tumbler	24-32

Probably other pieces.

Banded Fleur-de-Lis

Banded Fleur-de-Lis

Imperial Glass Company, Bellaire, Ohio, 1890s. Clear.

Butter dish	$ 39-47
Creamer (ill.)	27-36
Pitcher	44-52
Spoonholder	27-31
Sugar bowl	29-40

Probably many other pieces.

Banded Icicle

Bakewell, Pears & Company, 1870s. Clear.

Butter dish	$ 44-52
Compote	
Covered, 6″, 8″, high standard	59-69
Open, 8″, low standard	35-41

Banded Icicle

Creamer (ill.)	39-42
Goblet	29-38
Pitcher	72-81
Sauce	22-32
Spoonholder	29-34
Sugar bowl	42-51

Probably other pieces.

Banded Portland (Virginia)

Banded Portland (Virginia)*

U.S. Glass Company, 1901. Crystal and rose flashed.

Bottle, water	$ 42-50
Butter dish, covered	49-56
Celery	39-46
Compote	
Covered	81-90
Covered, jelly	80-88
Cruet	47-56
Dish, sardine	18-27
Jar, jam	19-26
Pitcher, syrup (ill.)	32-41
Relish boat	27-36

Salt/Pepper, pr.	55-62
Sugar	
Bowl, covered	38-45
Shaker	39-44
Toothpick holder	47-52
Tumbler	34-42
Wine	44-52

Probably other pieces. 50 percent higher for colors than for clear prices listed. *Only called Virginia where rose flashed.

Banded Raindrops

Banded Raindrops

(Candlewick): Clear, rare in amber, opalescent blue and milk glass. These pieces 100 percent more than clear pieces listed.

Butter dish	$ 45-52
Celery	28-35
Compote, 7″, covered	34-43
Creamer	32-41
Cup and saucer	28-35
Goblet	34-40
Pitcher, water (ill.)	52-60
Plates, 7½″ and 8¾″	27-37
Relish	19-28
Sauce	22-31
Spoonholder	27-35
Sugar bowl	44-52
Wine	35-42

Banner Butter Dish

Probably Bryce, Walker and Company, made for Centennial, 1876. Clear, blue and amber. A rare pattern!

Butter dish (ill.)	
Clear	$136-144
Blue	182-192
Amber	277-292

431

(continued)

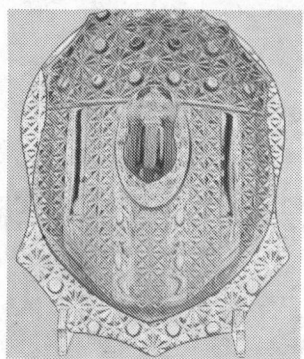

Banner Butter Dish

Barberry

Barley

Barley

(Sprig; Indian Tree): Campbell-Jones Company, late 1870s. Clear, any piece in color, rare; 100 percent more than clear.

Butter dish, covered	$ 35-44
Cake stand, 9″, 9¼″, 9½″, 9⅝″	27-34
Celery.	21-30
Compote, covered and open	27-49
Cordial	18-27
Creamer.	32-40
Dish, oval	16-23
Goblet	25-33
Jam jar, with lid (scarce).	54-62
Pickle.	18-27
Pitcher, water, (ill.)	46-57
Plate, 6″ (scarce)	25-32
Platter, oval, 6″ (scarce)	25-31
Sauces, footed, 4″, 5″	16-24
Spoonholder	15-25
Sugar bowl, covered and open	35-42
Wine	23-33

Barberry

Boston & Sandwich Glass Company, Sandwich, Massachusetts, 1860s. Later reproduced by several companies in Pittsburgh area, 1880s. Clear and colors; amber and blue, 50 percent and 70 percent more.

Bowl, covered, 8″	$ 45-52
Butter dish	68-78
Cake plate	47-56
Celery	46-55
Compote, covered, high and low standard	52-62
Cordial	42-52
Creamer (ill.)	56-66
Egg cup, oval berries	44-52
Goblet, oval berries	44-54
Pickle.	19-27
Pitcher, water.	94-107
Plate, 6″ deep	45-54
Salt, footed, 6″	40-50
Sauce, flat and footed	21-30
Spoonholder	32-42
Sugar bowl, covered	74-80
Syrup jug, pewter top	77-85
Wine	28-35

Barred Forget-Me-Not

Barred Forget-Me-Not

Canton Glass Company, Canton, Ohio, 1883. Clear, canary, vaseline amber, blue, apple green.

Butter dish	$ 42-50
Cake plates	
Closed handles, 9″	44-52
Extra large, on stand	47-56
Compote	
Covered, on high foot	47-56
Covered, low foot, 8″.	40-50
Open, small, on high foot	38-47
Cordial	19-27
Creamer	32-40
Goblet	35-42

Pickle dish, square handles 17-26
Pitcher (ill.). 42-52
Spoonholder 27-37
Sugar bowl, square handles,
   covered 34-43
Wine 23-30

Probably other pieces. Canary, 30 percent; blue, 60 percent; apple green, 100 percent higher than clear prices listed.

Barred Hobnail

Barred Hobnail

(Winona): Brilliant Glass Works, Brilliant, Ohio, 1888. Clear, opalescent, varicolored.

Bowls . . . . $ 18-28
Butter dish, covered 36-45
Creamer. 32-42
Goblet 31-38
Pitcher, water, ½ gallon (ill.) 47-52
Salt shaker 21-25
Sauce, flat. 21-26
Spoonholder 21-24
Sugar bowl, covered 35-42

Probably other pieces.

Barred Oval

Barred Oval

George Duncan & Sons, Pittsburgh, c. 1890, clear, frosted or color flashed. Reissued after 1891 by U.S. Glass Company.

Bottle, water . . . . $ 38-44
Butter dish, covered 35-46
Celery. 32-46
Compote, open 32-39
Creamer. 32-41
Goblet 32-44
Pitcher, water 57-66
Plate, small 31-40
Sugar bowl, covered (ill.) 49-59

Frosted or color flashed, 50 percent higher than clear prices listed.

Barred Star

(Spartan): Gillinder & Company, Pittsburgh, c. early 1880s. Clear, nonflint.

Butter dish, covered. . . . . $ 37-42
Cake stand 35-42
Celery 32-46
Compote, covered 36-41
Creamer 42-47
Pitcher 45-52
Salt/Pepper, pr. 21-27
Spoonholder 28-34
Sugar bowl, covered 40-52

Probably other pieces.

Barrel Excelsior

Sandwich, early; later, McKee Bros., Pittsburgh, 1850s and 1860s. Clear.

Ale glass . . . . $ 46-54
Butter dish, covered, early. 89-107
Celery
   Plain top 54-61
   Scalloped top 84-90
Decanters, pint, quart, 3 pints,
   early 87-96
Goblets, flaring and
   straight sides 42-52
Lamp, early. 150-160
Mug 54-63

(continued)

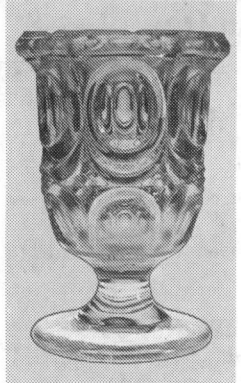

Barrel Excelsior

Spoonholder (ill.)	52-61
Sugar bowl, covered, early.	166-170
Tumbler, water, whiskey	46-52
Wine bottle, with tumble-up,	
early	152-162

Probably other pieces.

Barrelled Thumbprint
(Challinor's Thumbprint

Barrelled Thumbprint
(Challinor's Thumbprint)

Challinor, Taylor, Ltd., Tarentum, Pennsylvania, 1880s.

Butter dish	$ 52-60
Celery	42-52
Creamer	49-51
Goblet	49-60
Pitcher (ill.).	67-72
Spoonholder	43-46
Sugar bowl	48-58
Wine	37-52

Probably other pieces.

Basket Weave

Basket Weave

Mid-1880s. Clear, amber, blue, canary, milk white, apple green.

Bowl	
Berry	$ 19-27
Covered, flat.	21-29
Large, finger.	24-33
Butter dish	35-42
Cake plate.	29-37
Compote, covered	36-44
Cordial	25-32
Creamer.	34-42
Cup and saucer	34-42
Egg cup, double	17-27
Goblet	28-32
Lamp	29-37
Mug.	22-31
Pickle	21-30
Pitcher	42-52
Syrup, metal top, clear.	32-41
Water (ill.)	44-52
Plate, sheaf or wheat handles	27-36
Salt	9-12
Salt/Pepper, pr.	28-34
Sauce, round, flat	18-26
Spoonholder	22-31
Sugar bowl	34-43
Tray, round, 12″ dia..	32-41

Probably other pieces. Goblet and water pitcher being reproduced. Color pieces 25 to 75 percent higher than clear pieces listed.

Basket Weave
with Frosted Leaf

A design of the 1880s, it was made by many companies in many patterns. Clear, canary, yellow, blue, green.

Basket Weave with Frosted Leaf

Bowl, berry	$ 24-30
Cake plate.	42-45
Compote, covered	41-47
Cordial	22-28
Egg cup, double	25-28
Cups/saucers	19-22
Goblet	24-32
Pitcher, water (ill.)	56-66
Saucedish, round, flat	15-19
Syrup, metal top	32-40
Tray, water	32-42

Prices are for clear. Canary, yellow, green, 40 percent more; blue, 100 percent more. Probably other pieces.

Bead and Scroll

Bead and Scroll

Maker and date unknown.

Berry bowl, 8″.	$ 24-32
Butter dish, covered.	32-41

Compote, jelly	25-32
Creamer (ill.)	35-40
Goblet	22-29
Pitcher, water	39-44
Saucedish, flat	16-21
Spoonholder	29-37
Sugar bowl, covered	36-42
Tumbler	28-34

Probably other pieces.

Bead Column

Bead Column

Maker and date unknown.

Butter dish, covered.	$ 32-39
Creamer	27-34
Pitcher (ill.).	39-45
Spoonholder	27-32
Sugar bowl	29-35

Possibly other pieces were made.

Beaded Acorn Medallion

The Boston Silver-Glass Company, East Cambridge, Massachusetts, c. 1869. Clear, nonflint.

Butter dish, covered.	$ 62-72
Creamer	62-70
Goblet	45-54
Pitcher	66-77
Spoonholder	34-42
Sugar bowl, covered	66-69
Wine	32-41

Probably other pieces.

Beaded Arch Panels

Maker and date unknown.

Goblet	$ 32-42
Mug, handled (ill.)	34-41

Probably other pieces.

(continued)

Beaded Arch Panels

Beaded Band

Beaded Band

Maker unknown, c. 1884. Clear, color (rare).

Butter dish, covered. . . . . $ 38-46
Compote, open   46-52
Creamer   27-34
Jug, syrup.   22-31
Pitcher, water.   55-63
Spoonholder   27-36
Sugar bowl, open,
  (base ill.)   30-37
Wine   27-34

If color, 100 percent higher than clear prices listed.

Beaded Chain

(Looped Cord): Maker unknown, c. 1870s. Clear, nonflint.

Butter dish, covered . . . . $ 52-60

Celery.   41-44
Creamer.   44-50
Goblet   34-42
Pitcher, water   55-62
Plate, 6″.   38-42
Sauce, flat.   22-28
Spoonholder   35-41
Sugar bowl, covered   44-52

Probably other pieces.

Beaded Dart Band

Beaded Dart Band

Geo. Duncan & Sons, c. 1894. Pittsburgh. Clear, colors.

Butter dish . . . . $ 36-45
Celery holder   15-19
Compote   32-40
Creamer.   31-40
Goblet   19-28
Pickle caster with fork (ill.) 66-70
Spoonholder   18-21
Sugar bowl, covered   32-41

Probably other pieces.

Beaded Dewdrop

(Wisconsin): U.S. Glass Company, Gas City, Indiana, 1898.

Bottles, oil, vinegar . . . . $ 22-28
Bowl
  Covered, oblong, 6″, 8″   28-34
  Covered, round, 7″, 8″   32-40
Butter dish, large, small,
  covered   66-77
Celery tray   27-36
Celery vase   34-42
Compote
  Covered, 6″, 7″, 8″   57-66
  Open, 8½″, 9½″, 10½″   49-59

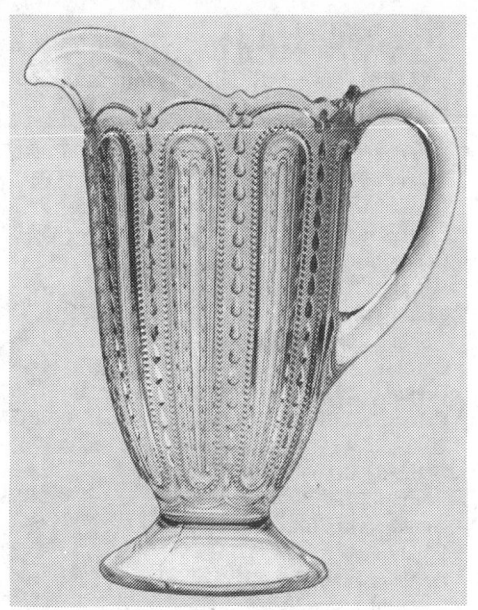

Beaded Dewdrop

Condiment, set, 4-piece in holder . . .	107-112
Creamer, individual and large	34-42
Cruet	34-42
Dish	
Candy	22-31
Oval, handled, covered, 6″	49-53
Oval, handled, open, 6″	22-29
Sweetmeat	26-29
Goblet	43-47
Mug, large	35-39
Pitcher	
3 pints	43-48
1 quart (ill.)	52-58
Salt/Pepper, short, tall, pr.	37-48
Sauce, flat and handled	19-27
Spoonholder	34-38
Sugar bowl, large and small,	
covered	33-50
Syrup jug, with cover	42-47
Toothpick holder	34-39
Tumbler	41-52
Wine	42-51

Beaded Ellipse

Cambridge Glass Company, Cambridge, Ohio, late 1890s. After 1906, all products permanently marked "Near-Cut" on inside base. Clear.

Butter dish	$ 40-50
Creamer	27-32

Beaded Ellipse

Compotes	42-50
Goblet	28-32
Pitcher	
Milk	42-47
Water (ill.)	44-52
Spoonholder	22-31
Sugar bowl	37-47
Wine	19-29

Probably other pieces.

Beaded Fan

Beaded Fan

Maker unknown, 1875-1880. Clear.

Butter dish	$ 29-36
Celery vase	24-30
Compote	34-40
Creamer	30-41
Pitcher (ill.)	32-42
Spoonholder	25-30
Sugar bowl	
Covered	40-49
Open	20-26

Probably other pieces.

Beaded Fine-Cut   **Beaded Flange**

Beaded Fine-Cut

Maker and date unknown. Clear; possibly in colors.

Butter dish	$ 29-36
Creamer	29-35
Goblet	31-40
Pitcher (ill.)	44-51
Spoonholder	28-31
Sugar bowl	29-36

Probably other pieces.

Beaded Flange

Fostoria Glass Company, 1891. Crystal and colors.

Butter dish	$ 29-35
Creamer	39-40
Goblet	31-34
Pickle dish	27-29
Spoonholder	24-27
Sugar bowl	38-44

Probably other pieces. Colors, 50 percent higher than clear prices listed.

Beaded Grape

(California): U.S. Glass Company, Pittsburgh, 1880s. Clear and emerald green.

Bowl, rectangular	$ 36-47
Butter dish, covered	69-78
Cake plate on stand	54-62
Celery tray, oblong	34-38
Compote	
High foot, 7″, 8″, 9″	47-52
Shallow, on standard	37-39
Small, 4″ high (rare)	42-50
Cordial	47-52
Creamer	48-56
Cruet	68-77
Dish	
Oblong, deep	23-28
Square, 5¼″, 6¼″, 7¼″, 8″	24-35
Goblet, green (ill.)	36-44
Pickle	25-32
Pitcher, water	
Round, several sizes	67-80
Square, several sizes	72-88
Plate, square, 8½″	24-33
Platter, oblong (rare)	47-54
Salt/Pepper, metal tops, pr.	57-66
Sauce, 3½″, 4″, 4½″	19-27
Spoonholder	34-42
Sugar bowl, covered	58-66
Toothpick holder	55-62
Tumbler, water	32-39
Vase, 6″	24-31

Probably other pieces. Green pieces, 50 percent higher than clear prices listed. Almost every piece being reproduced.

Beaded Grape Medallion

Boston Silver-Glass Company, East Cambridge, Massachusetts, late 1860s. Clear.

Butter dish, acorn finial	$ 55-62
Celery vase	38-47
Compote, covered, high, low,	
oval	66-82
Creamer, applied handle (ill.)	49-52
Egg cup	22-31
Goblet, various sizes	27-36
Pitcher, water	107-118
Salt, footed, oval and round, flat	24-32
Spoonholder	34-42
Sugar bowl, acorn finial,	
covered	56-63

Probably other pieces.

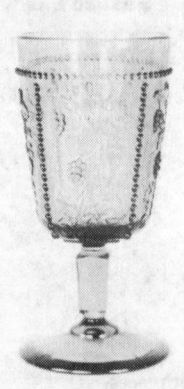

Beaded Grape

Beaded Grape Medallion

Cordial	23-34
Creamer	29-37
Dish, oval, 7½", 9½", 10½"	20-30
Goblet	38-44
Mug, handled	32-41
Pickle dish, boat shape	21-29
Pitcher	
Milk (ill.)	42-51
Syrup	42-52
Water, ½ gallon	54-62
Saucedishes, 2 types	23-29
Shakers	
Salt/Pepper, pr.	38-45
Sugar	31-42
Spoonholder, footed and flat	49-56
Sugar bowl	
Covered	38-45
Open	22-29
Tray, bread	43-49
Tumbler	32-46
Vase, toothpick holder	28-37
Wine	31-40

Beaded Loop

Beaded Loop

(Oregon): U.S. Glass Company, 1906-08. Clear, ruby-flashed.

Bowl, berry, covered, 6", 7", 8"	$ 18-28
Butter dish, 2 types	48-54
Cake stand, 6", 9½"	42-46
Celery	32-41
Compote	
Large, covered	42-47
Open, jelly	38-48

Beaded Medallion

Beaded Medallion

(Beaded Mirror): Sandwich glass, late 1860s, or early 1870s. Clear only.

Butter dish, covered	$ 65-75
Compote, covered	55-62
Creamer	61-70
Egg cup	37-44
Goblet	47-54
Pitcher (ill.)	92-107
Relish dish	37-42
Salt dish, footed	35-43
Sauce, flat and footed	21-27
Spoonholder	32-41
Sugar bowl, covered	44-49

Probably other pieces.

Beaded Oval and Scroll

Beaded Oval and Scroll

(Dot): Bryce Bros., Pittsburgh, late 1870s. Clear.

Bowl, 6½″.	$ 32-42
Butter dish, covered	49-56
Cake stand	42-52
Compote	
High standard, covered	47-54
High standard, open	44-52
Cordial	23-29
Creamer.	39-42
Dish, oval	24-34
Goblet	42-47
Pickle dish	35-42
Pitcher, water (ill.)	66-69
Salt/Pepper, pr.	32-42
Sauce	19-23
Spoonholder	52-57
Sugar bowl	
Covered	67-70
Open	48-52

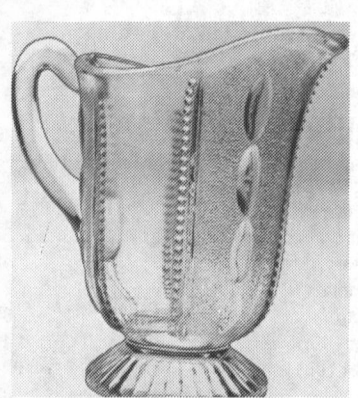

Beaded Panels

Beaded Panels

Crystal Glass Company, Pittsburgh, 1877. Crystal.

Butter dish	$ 35-42
Compote	42-50
Creamer	34-42
Egg cup	27-29
Goblet	24-29
Honey dish	17-21
Pitcher, water (ill.)	35-40
Salt/Pepper, pr.	24-31
Sauce	22-29
Spoonholder	23-30
Sugar bowl	39-45
Tumbler	32-41
Wine	22-29

Probably other pieces.

Beaded Panels

Beaded Panels

Maker unknown, late 1880s. Clear, non-flint.

Goblet	22-28
Spoonholder	22-29

Undoubtedly other pieces.

Beaded Swirl and Disc

Beaded Swirl and Disc

Maker and date unknown.

Butter dish, covered	40-47
Cake stand	32-39
Celery	32-40

Compote, covered   38-44
Creamer, covered   32-38
Cruet   21-27
Pitcher
  Milk (ill.)   46-54
  Syrup   32-41
  Water   54-62
Salt/Pepper, pr.   28-32
Sugar bowl, covered   40-50

Probably other pieces, possibly in colors.

Beaded Tulip

Beaded Tulip

(Andes): McKee Bros., Pittsburgh, c. 1894. Clear, nonflint; possibly, blue.

Bowl, oblong . . . . $ 19-27
Butter dish, covered.   42-51
Cake stand, 9″ high   53-61
Creamer   34-39
Goblet (ill.)   27-34
Pickle, oval   21-28
Pitcher, water, ...   55-63
Spoonholder   34-39
Sugar bowl, covered   48-54
Tray, water   57-62
Wine   24-29

Tray, water, blue, 100 percent higher than tray, water, clear, listed.

Bearded Head

(Viking; Bearded Prophet; Old Man of the Mountain): Hobbs, Brockunier & Company, Wheeling, West Virginia, 1876. Clear. The bearded head is that of a Roman Warrior, NOT a Viking.

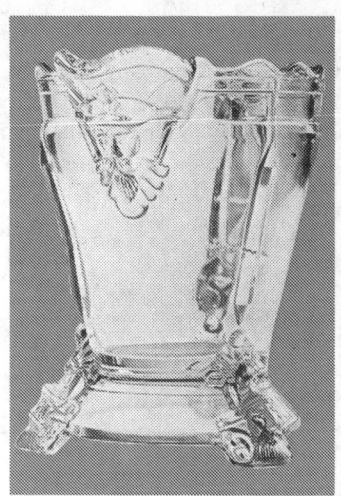

Bearded Head

Bowl, covered, large . . . . $ 60-67
Butter dish, covered.   62-67
Celery   36-40
Compote, covered, 7″, 8″.   67-72
Creamer, 3 heads   44-51
Pickle dish   29-35
Pitcher, water (ill.)   57-64
Platter   49-56
Relish, footed   39-47
Salt   34-42
Sauce   32-41
Spoonholder   34-42
Sugar bowl, covered   56-62

Goblets and tumblers were not made. This pattern apparently was reproduced before World War II. In what pieces it is not known. Careful!

The Bedford

441

(continued)

The Bedford

Fostoria Glass Company, Moundsville, West Virginia, 1901-1905. Clear. Over 60 pieces were made in this popular pattern. Nonflint.

Butter dish	$ 39-42
Celery vase	22-29
Creamer	37-42
Goblet	35-45
Pitcher (ill.).	49-57
Spoonholder	28-37
Sugar bowl	39-46
Tumbler	32-41

Many other pieces.

Bellflower

Bellflower

(Ribbed Leaf): Sandwich Glass Company, 1840s; McKee Bros., Pittsburgh, 1868; others. Clear, cobalt blue, amber, opaque. Amber considered rarest, blue next. One could write an entire book on Bellflower. Its many qualities and types must be taken into consideration when giving a price on a particular piece. A silvery-looking "lace glass" would probably be Sandwich; the dull-looking glass, some of it with worn designs, would be the lesser glass, probably made after the Civil War. Prices given here are for what one generally finds in shops. If you can authenticate a piece as being genuine Sandwich, it's worth at least 75 percent more than the prices given here. Know your dealer, please!

Bowl
Berry, flat, scalloped	$120-130
Deep, oval.	120-128
Flat, scallop and point edge.	136-142

Round, 6″, 8″ edge	126-134
Butter dish, covered	
Beaded edge.	97-118
Rayed edge	96-109
Scalloped edge	122-142
Cake stand (rare) if found	1,800+
Caster sets, 5 bottles (rare)	270-290
Celery vase (rare)	170-190
Compotes, any and all, 6 types.	42-69
Creamer, Double or Single	
Vine.	128-142
Decanter, 3 types (rare)	162-172
Egg cup (rare in colors)	42-52
Goblets, 6 types	34-42
Honey dish, 3″, 3¼″, 2½″	30-38
Lamps, 3 types	143-162
Mug, handled, small (rare)	238-250
Pitcher	
Milk, Double Vine (rare).	575+
Syrup, 10-sided (rare)	678+
Water, 2 sizes	92-107
Plate, 6″ (rare)	120-130
Salt	
Covered, footed (rare)	170-180
Open, footed	58-68
Sauce	24-32
Spoonholder	
Double Vine.	77-87
Single Vine	62-72
Sugar bowl	
Double Vine, covered	120-130
Octagonal (rare).	345+
Single Vine, covered	108-120
Tumbler, footed, fine rib	228-260
Whiskey—small tumbler	
(rare)	166-172
Wine, Single Vine	90-107

Belted Worchester

442

Belted Worchester

Maker unknown, c. 1850s. Clear, flint.

Champagne	$ 41-50
Cordial	32-40
Goblet (ill.)	32-42
Sugar bowl, covered	54-62
Whiskey, handled	31-40
Wine	28-32

Another member of the Worchester family.
Probably other pieces.

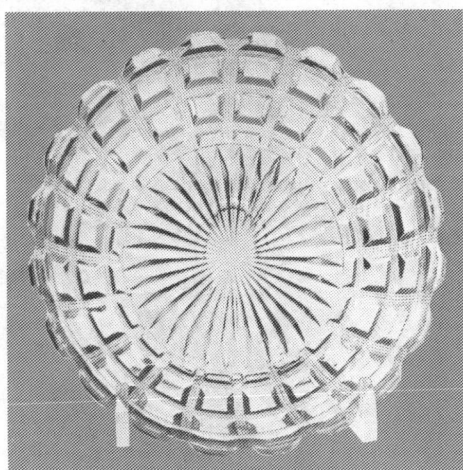

Berlin

Berlin

Adams & Company, Pittsburgh, 1874.
Clear.

Butter dish	$ 34-42
Compote	
Covered	52-60
Open	41-50
Creamer. . . :	32-42
Dish, oval	21-30
Egg cup	25-34
Honey dish	22-31
Pickle dish	22-29
Pitcher	
Milk.	66-72
Water	66-72
Plate (ill.), 7″	27-32
Salt/Pepper, pr.	29-34
Sauce	22-31
Spoonholder	26-35
Sugar bowl	39-47
Tumbler	36-47
Wine	32-46

Berry Cluster

Berry Cluster

Maker unknown, 1880s. Clear.

Butter dish	$ 48-57
Celery vase	26-32
Creamer.	42-46
Goblet	27-32
Pitcher, water (ill.)	59-62
Spoonholder	27-34
Sugar bowl	
Covered	42-52
Open	22-31

Probably other pieces.

Bethlehem Star

Bethlehem Star

Maker unknown, 1880s. Clear, nonflint.

Butter dish	$ 32-40
Celery.	19-28
Creamer.	22-27
Goblet	22-27
Pitcher (ill.)	39-42
Sauce	11-19

Beveled Diagonal Block

Beveled Diagonal Block

Challinor, Taylor & Company, 1880s. Also by Bryce Bros., 1888. Clear, nonflint.

Butter dish	$ 42-47
Cake stand	45-55
Celery vase (ill.)	34-42
Compote	44-52
Cordial	22-29
Creamer.	44-49
Goblet	29-36
Marmalade jar	30-40
Pitcher, water	35-42
Plate	22-29
Salt/Pepper, pr.	32-41
Spoonholder	27-37
Sugar bowl	42-50
Tumbler	27-29
Wine	22-31

Probably other pieces.

Beveled Star

(Pride): Model Flint Glass Company, Findlay, Ohio, 1890, called this pattern Pride. Clear, emerald green, cobalt, amber.

Butter dish, covered.	$ 45-52
Celery	29-33
Compote, covered, high standard . . .	54-61
Creamer	37-47
Goblet	32-42
Pitcher, water (ill.)	53-61

Beveled Star

Salt/Pepper, pr..	32-42
Spoonholder	35-42
Sugar bowl	39-43

Probably other pieces. Emerald green, cobalt, 50 percent higher, amber, 100 percent higher than clear prices listed.

Bicycle Girl

Bicycle Girl

Dalzell, Gilmore and Leighton, Findlay, Ohio, 1880s; later by National Glass Company, Greentown, Indiana.

Pitcher, water, clear (ill.)	$ 395+
Possibly tumbler to match.	170+

Bigler

Boston & Sandwich Glass Company, Sandwich, Massachusetts, c. 1850s. Clear, flint.

Bowls	$ 64-74
Celery	78-84
Champagne.	90-103
Cordial	84-88
Decanter, bar type	80-90

Bigler

Goblet	66-72
Mug, handled.	68-77
Tumblers.	56-64
Wine	55-62

Possibly creamer and sugar bowl (rare).

Birch Leaf

Birch Leaf

Maker unknown, c. 1870s. Clear, milk glass, flint.

Butter dish, covered, on pedestal (ill.)	$ 64-72
Creamer	35-42
Egg cup	24-29
Goblet	24-29
Salt, master, footed	22-27
Spoonholder	25-32
Sugar bowl, covered	55-63

Milk glass, 100 percent higher than clear prices listed. Probably other pieces.

Bird and Strawberry

Bird and Strawberry

(Bluebird): 1890s, berries, birds, leaves. Colored, clear; nonflint.

Bowl, footed, berry, round.	$ 25-33
Butter dish, covered.	89-96
Cake stand, 9″ diameter	62-72
Compote, open, 2 sizes	82-96
Creamer, w/color	53-63
Goblet	45-49
Pitcher (ill.).	218-242
Relish, heart-shaped	29-39
Sauce, clear	27-32
Spoonholder	49-52
Sugar bowl, covered	68-78
Tumbler	44-53
Wine	36-44

Probably other pieces.

Bird Napkin Ring

Bird Napkin Ring

With salt (in bird's back) and pepper. Sandwich glass; considered scarce. There is

445

(continued)

a pair of these at the Houston Museum, Chattanooga, Tennessee.

Bird napkin ring w/Salt/Pepper,
pr. (ill.) . . . . $ 390+

Bird on Nest Mug

Bird on Nest Mug

Challinor & Taylor, Ltd., Tarentum, Pennsylvania, 1880s.

Mug . . . . $ 67-74

Birds and Harp Mug

Birds and Harp Mug

A novelty drinking mug for children in the late 1800s.

Mug. . . . . $ 48-54

Birds at Fountain

Birds at Fountain

Early 1880s. Clear, opaque.

Bowl . . . . $ 31-42
Butter dish 48-54

Cake stand 49-55
Compote, covered, 8″ 67-73
Creamer. 39-42
Goblet 49-54
Mug, (ill.) 32-42
Spoonholder 22-31
Sugar bowl, covered 34-42
Probably other pieces.

Blackberry

Blackberry

William Leighton, Jr., Wheeling, West Virginia, 1870. Clear, milk, white.

Butter dish, covered . . . . $ 64-72
Celery vase (rare) 66-75
Champagne. 42-51
Compote
  Covered, high foot 79-88
  Covered, low foot 62-70
Creamer 57-67
Dish, oval, 8¼″ × 5½″ 18-27
Egg cup, double and single 37-49
Goblet (rare) 35-43
Honey dish 18-27
Pitcher, water (rare) (ill.) 162-172
Salt, footed, 2 styles 25-36
Sauce, flat 17-22
Spoonholder 55-64
Sugar bowl, open 60-67
Syrup 22-31
Tumbler 29-37

Milk glass, 80-90 percent higher than clear prices listed. Being reproduced in butter dish, celery vase, creamer, egg cup (single), goblet, water pitcher, sugar bowl. Possibly others. Careful!

Blaze

New England Glass Company, East Cambridge, Massachusetts, c. 1869. Clear, flint.

Butter dish, covered. . . . . $ 75-82
Celery. 75-83

Compote, covered, low standard
7", 8" 77-85
Creamer. 86-92
Goblet 57-62
Plate, 6", 7" 36-44
Sauce, 4", 5" 19-26
Spoonholder 47-52
Sugar bowl, covered 75-83
Tumbler 49-52
Wine 62-72
Possibly other pieces.

Bleeding Heart

Bleeding Heart

Sandwich Glass Company, 1860-1875, other companies later. Clear, opaque.

Bowl, waste. . . . . $ 34-43
Butter dish 58-74
Cake plate on stand, 9½" high 64-73
Compote
  Covered, high foot 69-77
  Covered, low foot 62-72
  Oval, covered 60-70
Cordial 19-27
Creamer, applied handle 59-66
Dish, oval, large 21-28
Egg cups
  Barrel shape 38-42
  Straight side 31-40
Goblet
  Plain and knob stem 28-44
  Thin, design low on bowl (ill.) 26-34
Mug, handled. 34-44
Pickle dish, oval 26-32
Pitcher, water, (ill.) 132-142
Plates (rare) 70-80
Platter, oval 66-77
Salt, oval and round, footed. 19-27
Sauces, 3 types 27-36
Spoonholder 32-42
Sugar bowl 69-74
Tumbler
  Footed 35-44
Water 25-32
Wine 69-74

Block and Circle

Block and Circle

Maker and date unknown. Clear, non-flint.

Goblet . . . . $ 24-31
Lamp, miniature 31-40
Pitcher, water (ill.) 47-52
Tumblers to match 24-32
Possibly other pieces.

Block and Fan

Block and Fan

(Romeo): Richards & Hartley Glass Company, Tarentum, Pennsylvania, 1880s. Clear; clear with red flashing.

Bowl, berry, 8" dia., flat . . . . $ 42-51
Butter dish, covered. 39-44
Cake stand, 10" dia. 39-47
Celery tray 19-22
Compote 37-44
Cordial 22-28
Creamer 34-39
Cruet (ill.) 31-40
Goblet 56-66
Lamp 58-67
Jam jar 32-42
Pitcher, water, pedestal base 34-42
Plate, large 27-36
Salt/Pepper, pr. 44-50
Sauce, flat and footed 27-32
Spoonholder 29-38

(continued)

Sugar, covered and open.   42-50
Tumbler   35-42
Wine   45-52

Red flashing, 120 percent higher than clear prices given.

Block and Honeycomb

Block and Honeycomb

McKee & Bros., Pittsburgh, 1874. Clear,
nonflint.

Butter bowl . . . . $ 45-51
Goblet   35-40
Pitcher (ill.).   74-81
Sugar bowl   55-62

Probably other pieces.

Block and Palm

Beaver Falls Co-Operative Glass Company, Beaver Falls, Pennsylvania, c. 1890.
Clear, milk glass, nonflint.

Butter dish, covered. . . . . $ 27-32
Cake stand   29-36
Celery   19-26
Creamer   19-25
Goblet   18-24
Pitcher, water.   39-44
Salt/Pepper, pr..   38-44
Sauce, flat   19-27
Spoonholder   16-27
Sugar bowl, covered   22-27

Milk glass, 25 percent higher than clear prices
listed. Probably other pieces.

Block and Rib

Block and Rib

Maker and date unknown. Chalk white
glass, also clear.

Butter dish, covered. . . . . $ 37-41
Celery holder   24-30
Creamer   25-29
Goblet   26-31
Pitcher, water (ill.)   43-51
Spoonholder   38-47
Sugar bowl, covered   35-42

Probably other pieces.

Block and Star

Block and Star

(Valencia Waffle): 1885-1895. Clear, canary, blue, amber.

Butter dish, covered . . . . $ 32-42
Celery.   31-42
Compote
  Covered   38-44
  Open   32-41

Creamer. 29-37
Goblet (ill.) 27-31
Sauce
   Flat 22-29
   Footed. 22-29
Spoonholder 28-37
Sugar 34-42
   Covered 32-42
   Open 21-31
Relish 24-34
Wine 29-37

Probably other pieces. Color, 60 percent more than clear prices listed.

Block and Sunburst

Block and Sunburst

George Duncan and Sons, Pittsburgh, 1880. Clear, ruby flashed, nonflint.

Butter dish . . . . $ 46-53
Compote 48-54
Cream tankard 45-54
Goblet 32-42
Mug. 32-42
Pitcher, water (ill.) 77-81
Sauce 22-31
Spoonholder 29-38
Sugar bowl 42-51
Tumbler 35-42
Wine 29-38

Probably other pieces.

Block and Thumbprint

Possibly Union Glass Company, Somerville, Massachusetts, c. 1860s. Clear, flint and nonflint.

Butter dish, covered. . . . . $ 42-51
Celery (ill.) 32-42
Compote, covered 38-47
Creamer. 38-44

Block and Thumbprint

Spoonholder 32-42
Sugar bowl, covered 37-44
Tumbler, footed 37-42

Flint, 40 percent higher than nonflint prices listed. Probably other pieces.

Blockade

Blockade

Challinor, Taylor, Ltd., Tarentum, Pennsylvania, 1885. Clear only.

Butter dish, covered (stemmed) . . . . $ 32-42
Celery (stemmed) 32-39
Compotes, covered,, 6″, 7″, 8″, 9″
   flared or straight. 27-42
Creamer (stemmed) 24-32
Goblet (ill.) 29-37
Pitcher, qt., ½ gal. 49-56
Sugar bowl, covered (stemmed) 44-52
Tumbler 29-37

Many other pieces. Lower half of stem is hollow.

Blocked Arches

Blocked Arches

(Berkley); U.S. Glass Company, c. 1893. Clear, nonflint, possibly stained ruby.

Bowl, finger	$ 25-32
Creamer.	39-47
Cup/saucer	27-33
Goblet.	29-36
Jug, syrup	48-54
Shaker, salt	24-33
Spoonholder.	21-31
Sugar bowl (base ill.)	45-52
Tumbler	28-36
Wine	31-40

If stained ruby, 50 percent higher than clear prices listed. Other pieces.

Bosc Pear

Bosc Pear

Maker unknown, 1920s. Clear, flashed purple pears, gold flashed leaves, nonflint.

Butter dish, covered	$ 44-52
Celery.	32-41
Creamer (ill.)	48-54
Pitcher, water	53-62
Spoonholder.	34-42
Sugar bowl	36-45
Tumbler	22-27

Probably other pieces.

Bow-Tie

The Thompson Glass Company, Uniontown, Pennsylvania, c. 1886. Clear, nonflint.

Bowl, fruit, 10″ deep.	$ 68-76
Butter dish, covered	69-77
Creamer.	65-74
Goblet.	49-54
Pitcher, water	77-85
Spoonholder.	36-44
Sugar bowl, covered	73-82

Firm only in business for three years. Possibly other pieces.

Boxed Star

Boxed Star

Maker unknown, 1890s. Clear, nonflint.

Butter dish	$ 34-42
Creamer (ill.)	23-30
Pitcher, water	37-42
Spoonholder.	27-29
Sugar bowl	34-42
Tumbler	32-41

Probably other pieces.

Bradford Grape

Bradford Grape

Maker unknown, c. 1850s or 1860s. Clear, flint.

Butter dish, covered	$106-116
Champagne	77-85
Cordial	75-84
Creamer.	108-112
Goblet (ill.)	84-93
Pitcher, water	198-210
Spoonholder	58-67
Sugar bowl, covered	112-122
Tumbler (rare)	119-124
Wine	88-99

Possibly other pieces.

Branched Tree

Branched Tree

Probably National Glass Company, Greentown, Indiana, 1890s. Nonflint.

Butter dish	$ 56-62
Celery	32-40
Compote, covered, high,	
low standard	52-61
Creamer	35-41

Goblet	36-46
Pitcher, water (ill.)	79-86
Spoonholder	35-44
Sugar bowl	45-55

Probably others.

Brickwork

Brickwork

Probably National Glass Company, Greentown, Indiana, around 1900. Clear and caramel slag, nonflint.

Butter dish	$ 43-52
Celery	32-40
Creamer (ill.)	31-40
Goblet	36-51
Pitcher, water	49-57
Salt/Pepper, pr.	28-34
Spoonholder	32-42
Sugar bowl, covered	39-44

Caramel slag, 70 percent higher than clear prices listed.

Brilliant   **Brilliant**

Possibly McKee Bros., Pittsburgh, c. 1870s. Clear, flint.

Goblet (ill.)	$ 64-77

There should be other pieces.

451

Bringing Home the Cows

Bringing Home the Cows

Dalzell, Gilmore and Leighton Company, 1870s. Clear.

Butter dish, covered	$198-220
Creamer	142-160
Pitcher, milk (ill.).	320-342
Spoonholder	107-118
Sugar bowl, covered	173-192

Probably other pieces.

Britannic   Britannic

McKee Bros., Pittsburgh, 1893. Clear crystal with ruby stain. Popular after Columbian Exposition of 1893. Also found in amber and green.

Butter dish, covered	$ 47-54
Cake stand, small, large.	46-55
Compote	
Covered.	59-68
Open	54-63
Creamer	40-50
Cruet.	37-47
Cups, custard.	24-32
Goblet	28-34
Pitcher (ill.)	47-56
Salt/Pepper, pr.	34-44
Spoonholder	35-44
Sugar bowl, covered	55-65
Tumbler	42-52

Wine	32-41

Red flashing, 65 percent higher; amber flashing, 45 percent higher than clear prices listed.

Broken Column

Broken Column

(Irish Column, Notched Rib): U.S. Glass Company, 1892, before that by Columbia Glass Company, Findlay, Ohio, 1891. Clear, clear with ruby-stained depressions.

Banana dish	$ 70-80
Basket, handled	88-92
Bowl	
8½″ diameter.	42-51
Covered, various sizes.	40-50
Butter dish, covered	50-60
Cake stand, large	52-58
Celery	40-50
Celery tray	40-50
Compote	
Covered, high standard	60-70
Open, high standard	40-50
Creamer	39-58
Cruet.	39-47
Custard cup	20-27
Finger bowl.	20-27
Goblet, lady's.	40-50
Pickle caster, complete	80-88
Pitcher, water (ill.)	50-58
Plate, 7″ (rare)	50-58
Salt/Pepper, pr.	32-40
Sauce, flat	16-20
Spoonholder	30-40
Sugar	
Bowl, open	30-38
Shaker (rare)	40-48
Syrup jug.	52-60
Tumbler, plain	30-38
Water bottle	42-51
Wine	50-60

Goblet is being reproduced. Ruby-stained depression pieces, 150 percent higher than clear prices listed.

Brooklyn

Brooklyn

Maker unknown, c. late 1860s, early 1870s. Clear, flint. Possibly a Bakewell, Pears product.

Compote	
Covered.	$ 70-80
Open	40-46
Creamer	58-62
Decanter	60-70
Goblet (ill.)	52-61
Pitcher, water.	72-81
Sugar bowl, covered.	72-80

Probably other pieces.

Buck and Doe

Maker and date unknown.

Goblet . . . . $ 155+

Buckingham

Buckingham

U.S. Glass Company, 1906. Clear, cranberry and green, nonflint.

Bowl, 8¼" dia. (ill.)	$ 52-60
Butter dish, covered	50-59
Celery	27-31
Compote	
Covered.	48-52
Open	34-42
Creamer	45-60
Goblet	31-39
Pitcher, water.	64-72
Spoonholder	32-39
Sugar bowl, covered.	54-62
Tumbler	24-29

Probably other pieces. Color, 25 percent higher than clear prices listed.

Buckle   **Buckle**

Sandwich Glass, early 1870s; also Gillinder & Sons, Philadelphia, same period. Clear, sapphire blue (rare); flint and nonflint.

Bowl, wire basket container.	$ 63-70
Butter dish, covered, flat	57-62
Champagne.	22-29
Compote, open, low standard	38-46
Cordial.	19-27
Creamer, applied handles, pedestal foot	38-46
Egg cup	33-42
Goblets, 2 types.	29-38
Pickle dish, large, oval	13-19
Pitcher, water, applied handle	80-88
Salt dip	
Footed	19-27
Oval, flat (rare)	24-32
Saucedish, 4".	17-26
Spoonholder, scalloped rim	32-41
Sugar bowl, covered, flint	49-58
Tumbler	27-36

Color, 80 percent more than clear prices listed. Flint, 50 percent higher than nonflint prices listed.

Buckle with Diamond Band

Maker unknown, c. 1880s. Clear, non-flint.

Butter dish, covered	$ 47-56
Creamer.	39-40
Goblet	42-52
Pitcher, water	44-52
Spoonholder	32-40
Sugar bowl, covered	48-55

Probably other pieces.

Buckle with Star

Buckle with Star

(Orient): Bryce, Walker & Company, Pittsburgh, c. 1875. Clear, nonflint.

Bowls, oval, round.	$ 22-27
Butter dish, covered	34-44
Celery.	30-36
Compote, covered	56-64
Creamer (ill.)	39-48
Goblet	33-42
Pitcher	52-66
Relish, oval	15-23
Sauce, flat.	11-18
Spoonholder	23-32
Sugar bowl, covered	28-32
Wine	27-32

Probably other pieces.

Bulldog with Hat Toothpick

A scarce novelty from Sandwich. Supposedly clear only, but the Houston Museum, Chattanooga, Tennessee, has one in amber and one in blue. Being reproduced in all colors.

Bulldog with Hat Toothpick

Amber	$ 185+
Blue.	170+
Clear	88-97

Also made by Belmont Glass Company, Bellaire, Ohio, c. 1885.

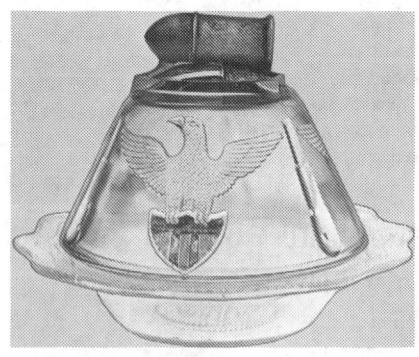

Bullet Emblem

Bullet Emblem

(Shield in red, white and blue): Clear, Spanish-American War souvenir, made in 1898.

Butter, covered (ill.)	$290-335
Creamer	184-196
Spoonholder	146-159
Sugar bowl, covered	265-320

Possibly other pieces.

Bull's Eye

Bull's Eye

(Lawrence): New England Glass Company; also Sandwich. Clear, milk-white, other colors (rare).

Bitters bottle	$ 40-48
Butter dish, covered	184-194
Caster bottle	38-47
Celery vase (ill.)	74-83
Champagne	89-107
Cologne bottle	79-86
Compote	
Open, large, high, standard	52-61
Open, low standard	47-53
Cordials, 2 styles	21-28
Creamer	131-138
Cruet	37-47
Decanter	
Bar lip, pint and quart	131-140
Usual type, pint and	
quart	129-140
Egg cup, covered (rare)	169-177
Goblet, knob and plain stem	78-85
Jar, covered, small	77-85
Lamp	89-96
Pickle dish, oval	38-45
Salt	
Footed	31-40
Footed, oblong, covered	
(rare)	112-116
Spoonholder	39-47
Sugar bowl, covered	122-131
Tumbler, water	79-88
Water bottle with tumble-up	118-127

Colored pieces, 50 percent higher than clear prices listed.

Bull's Eye and Daisy

Maker unknown, c. 1890s. Clear, clear with bull's eyes in red, purple, green, gilt rims; nonflint.

Bull's Eye and Daisy

Butter dish, covered	$ 50-60
Creamer	48-55
Goblet	30-37
Pitcher, water	58-64
Salt	21-29
Spoonholder	31-38
Sugar bowl, handled (ill.)	30-38
Tumbler	21-29
Wine	20-27

Colors, 60-80 percent higher than clear prices listed.

Bull's Eye and Fan

Bull's Eye and Fan

(Daisies in Oval Panels): Mid-1890s. Clear; sometimes combined with color.

Bowl	$ 17-23
Butter dish, covered	31-40
Creamer	49-58
Goblet	24-29
Pitcher, water (ill.)	48-56
Sauce, flat	22-29
Spoonholder	22-30
Sugar	
Covered	35-44
Open	24-30

Probably other pieces. Pieces with colored dots in eyes, 20 percent higher than clear prices listed.

Bull's Eye and Prism

Bull's Eye and Prism

Maker unknown, c. late 1840s, early 1850s. Clear, flint.

Goblet (ill.) . . . . $ 140+
Other pieces unknown.

Bull's Eye and Spear Head

Bull's Eye and Spear Head

Dalzell, Gilmore & Leighton, Findlay, Ohio, c. late 1870s. Clear, nonflint.

Bottle, caster	$ 34-42
Butter dish, covered	63-70
Compote	
Covered	32-41
Open	66-75
Creamer.	44-52
Decanter (ill.)	54-63
Goblet	48-58
Lamp, night	42-50
Spoonholder	39-46
Sugar bowl, covered	71-80
Wine (ill.)	38-44

Probably other pieces.

Bull's Eye with Fleur-de-Lis

Bull's Eye with Fleur-de-Lis

Boston & Sandwich Glass Company, mid-1800s; probably Union Glass Company, Somerville, Massachusetts, 1860s. Clear and amber, flint only.

Ale glass (rare)	$167-183
Butter dish, covered	181-191
Celery . . . . :	93-102
Compote	
Open, high standard	126-134
Open, low standard	112-119
Creamer (rare)	262-271
Decanter	
Pint	82-90
Quart	92-101
Goblet	107-114
Lamp	
Glass only	62-71
Glass bowl, brass stem	
marble base	290-315
Pitcher, water (rare) (ill.)	288-320
Salt, footed	62-71
Sugar bowl, covered	144-152

Amber, 60 percent higher than clear prices listed.

Butterfly

Butterfly

U.S. Glass Company. Clear or clear with frosted handles, nonflint.

Butter dish, covered.	$ 56-64
Celery	32-41
Creamer	40-50
Mustard, covered, handled	25-32
Pickle dish	22-31
Pitcher, water (ill.)	66-74
Relish dish, oval.	28-37
Salt/Pepper, pr..	37-46
Sugar bowl, covered	63-72

Probably other pieces.

Butterfly and Grape

Butterfly and Grape

Fenton Art Glass Company, Williamstown, West Virginia, early 1920s, Golden Iridescent only. Nonflint.

Bowl, berry	$ 54-59
Butter dish, covered.	66-73
Creamer	51-60
Pitcher, water, jug, not footed	62-72
Spoonholder	35-43
Sugar bowl, covered, footed	66-73
Tumbler	27-36

Butterfly with Spray

Butterfly with Spray

(Acme): Bryce, Higbee and Company, Pittsburgh, early 1800s. Clear, nonflint.

Butter dish, covered	$ 53-60
Celery	21-28
Compote, covered, high, low standard	39-42
Creamer	30-37
Goblet	29-37
Mug (ill.)	34-39
Pitcher, water	55-61
Spoonholder	31-38
Sugar bowl, covered	47-54
Tumbler	22-30

Probably many other pieces.

Button Arches

Button Band

Button Arches

(Scalloped Daisy, Red Top): Duncan & Miller Glass Company, Washington, Pennsylvania, 1897. Clear, clear with red top.

Bowl, 8″.	$ 31-42
Cake stand	44-52
Compote, jelly	24-33
Creamer	29-37
Cruet	34-42
Goblet	46-56
Mug	28-37
Pitcher, water (ill.)	42-51
Salt/Pepper, pr..	29-37
Spoonholder	25-31

(continued)

Sugar bowl, covered 42-52
Toothpick holder 44-53
Tumbler 25-32
Wine 22-30

Probably other pieces. Red top pieces, 35 percent more than clear prices listed. Reproduced in butter dish, wine, goblet and creamer.

Button Band

Early 1880s. Clear, nonflint.

Bowl . . . . $ 22-28
Butter dish, covered 45-52
Cake stand, 10″ 49-54
Compote,, open, small 52-61
Creamer. 33-42
Goblet 34-42
Pitcher, water (ill.) 49-56
Sugar bowl, covered 34-42
Tumbler 24-27
Wine (rare) 42-51

Probably other pieces.

Buttressed Arch

Buttressed Arch

(Buttressed Loop): Possibly Adams Glass Company, Pittsburgh, mid-1880s. Clear, nonflint.

Butter dish, covered . . . . $ 42-48
Celery vase 32-42
Creamer (ill.) 34-39
Goblet 26-35
Pitcher, water 56-63
Sauce 21-28
Spoonholder 27-36
Sugar bowl, covered 38-47

Probably other pieces.

Cabbage Leaf

Cabbage Leaf

Maker unknown, 1870s and 1880s. Clear amber, heavily stippled and frosted, opalescent.

Butter dish, covered $98-107
Celery 68-78
Compote, covered,
  high standard 115-122
Creamer (ill.). 73-82
Pickle dish, large leaf shape 42-52
Pitcher, water 92-107
Plate, rabbit head in center 60-68
Spoonholder 42-52
Sugar bowl, covered 90-99

Stippled and frosted pieces, 20 percent more; amber, 50 percent more than clear prices listed. Tumbler not known but probably made. BEWARE! Every piece—even goblets—has been reproduced in almost every color.

Cabbage Rose

Cabbage Rose

Central Glass Company, Wheeling, West Virginia, 1880s; possibly at Sandwich earlier. Clear, nonflint.

Butter dish, covered	$ 49-56
Cake plate on standard, 11″	67-74
Celery vase	49-54
Compotes, 6″, 7″, 8″, 9″	40-74
Cordial	18-23
Creamer, applied handle	63-70
Egg cup	25-34
Goblet	54-63
Pickle dish	46-54
Pitcher	
Quart (ill.).	110-118
Three pints (rare)	121-132
Salt, footed, master	29-35
Saucedish	12-16
Spoonholder	39-47
Sugar bowl, open	32-39
Sugar bowl, with lid	62-71
Tumbler, water	44-53
Wine (rare)	47-54

Goblet being reproduced.

Cable

Cable

Possibly Sandwich glass of the 1850s. Clear, flint; rare in opaque, blue opaque, green opaque, silver-stained panels.

Butter dish, covered	$ 69-76
Compote, open	49-56
Creamer (rare)	365-425
Egg cup, open	79-86
Goblet	66-74
Lamp, marble base	94-103
Pitcher, water (rare)	360-420
Spoonholder (ill.)	39-47
Sugar bowl, covered	92-102
Tumbler, footed (rare)	162-180

Colors, 120-140 percent higher than clear prices listed.

Cable with Ring

Cable with Ring

Sandwich Glass Company, 1860s. Clear only, flint.

Butter dish	$ 67-72
Compote, open, 8¼″	65-72
Creamer	66-74
Honey dish	28-37
Lamp	91-106
Pitcher (ill.)	119-132
Sauce, flat	18-28
Sugar bowl, covered	94-112

No goblet or tumbler known.

Cactus   Cactus

(Panelled Agave): Indiana Tumbler & Goblet (National) Company, 1903. Crystal, chocolate (caramel slag); Nonflint.

Berry bowl	$112-122
Butter dish	140-150
Butter dish, stemmed	240-260
Celery tray	66-76
Compote	
Large	191-220
Medium	152-162
Small	109-118
Cracker jar	140-150
Creamer	132-142
Cruet	118-127
Mug	77-84
Mustard jar	130-140
Pitcher, water (ill.)	205-215

(continued)

Relish dish	88-97
Salt/Pepper, pr.	77-87
Spoonholder	76-86
Sugar bowl	97-106
Syrup, Dewey or metal lid	98-109
Toothpick.	67-75
Tumbler, water and lemonade	71-80

Prices listed are for chocolate. Being reproduced—careful!

Canadian

Canadian

Burlington Glass Works, Canada, 1870s. Clear.

Butter dish, covered	$ 56-64
Celery.	42-52
Compote	
Covered, 6″, 7″, 8″	54-63
Open, high and low	
standard.	47-52
Cordial	18-24
Creamer (ill.)	59-66
Goblet	69-74
Jam jar, covered	39-46
Pitcher, water	
Large	79-85
Small	62-70
Plate, 6″, 8″, 10″	34-54
Sauce, flat and footed, 4″	13-18
Spoonholder	45-52
Sugar bowl, covered	57-66
Wine	40-47

Cane

Sandwich Glass Company, 1875-1885. Also Gillinder Glass Company and McKee

Cane

Glass Company, same period. Clear, amber, apple green, blue, yellow.

Bowl, berry, 3-panel, footed	$ 22-27
Bowl, finger.	18-25
Butter dish, covered.	46-54
Creamer	25-35
Goblet	25-35
Jam jar	22-31
Pickle dish, oval.	14-18
Pitcher, water (ill.)	47-52
Salt/Pepper, pr.	32-40
Sauce	
Covered.	12-16
Flat	9-12
Spoonholder	22-28
Sugar bowl, covered	54-63
Toddy plate.	14-20
Tray, water	35-42
Tumbler, water	22-31

Green, common. Amber and blue, 15-20 percent higher than clear prices listed.

Cane Column

Mid-1800s. Clear, canary, amber, blue, nonflint.

Butter dish, covered.	$ 42-52
Creamer	40-50
Goblet	35-42
Pitcher (ill.).	45-55
Sauce, flat	24-32
Spoonholder	29-37
Sugar bowl	
Covered	45-52
Open	32-42
Wine	34-43

Cane Column

Probably other pieces. Colored pieces, 80 to 100 percent higher than clear prices listed.

Cane Insert

Cane Insert

Tarentum Glass Company, Tarentum, Pennsylvania, 1898-1906. Clear, clear with gold gilt, emerald green with gold gilt, pink with gold gilt, custard, pea green custard; nonflint.

Butter dish, covered.	$ 48-54
Cake stand	47-53
Compote	40-48
Creamer (ill.)	38-42
Goblet	40-47
Pitcher, water.	61-70
Sugar bowl, covered	40-47

Made in a full line of ware. Gold gilt, custard, 75 percent higher than clear prices listed.

Cane Medallion

Cane Medallion

Westmoreland Glass Company, Grapeville, Pennsylvania, 1896. Clear, opaque, nonflint.

Bowl, berry, oblong, oval.	$ 22-28
Butter dish	31-40
Creamer (ill.)	34-40
Pickle	18-22
Pitcher, water	49-54
Spoonholder	29-34
Sugar bowl, covered	42-52
Toothpick.	27-34
Tumbler	24-29

Probably other pieces.

Cape Cod

Probably Sandwich, c. 1870s. Clear, nonflint.

Bowl, handled.	$ 23-28
Butter dish, covered	57-62
Celery.	33-40
Compote	
Covered, 6″, 7″, 8″	60-79
Open, 6″, 7″, 8″.	34-44
Creamer.	32-41
Goblet	34-42
Jar, jam,.	44-52
Pitcher, water	54-63
Spoonholder	32-40
Sugar bowl, covered	56-64
Wine	34-42

Probably other pieces.

461

(continued)

Capitol Building

Capitol Building

Souvenir glass of the 1920s. Different buildings on different pieces.

Dessert plate . . . . $ 28-33
Goblet (ill.) 41-50
Sherbet 40-50
Tumbler 42-52
Wine 34-44

Caprice

Cambridge Glass Company, Cambridge, Ohio, 1936. It is known to have been produced in clear crystal, pink, blue, and satin.

Candleholder, crystal, 2⅝″ high. . . . $ 9-12
Dish, candy, crystal 21-28
Pitcher, blue, 80 oz. 78-86
Sherbet, footed, crystal, 7 oz. 6-11
Sherbet, tall, blue. 15-20
Sugar, blue 15-19
Sugar, crystal. 6-11
Tumbler, footed, crystal, 12 oz. 8-12

Caramel Strigil

Probably Indiana Tumbler and Goblet

Caramel Strigil

Company, before 1903, when the factory burned. McKee Bros. made an identical pattern in 1897, calling it Nelly, only in clear glass. In 1900, both firms joined National Glass Company, so either firm could have made this pattern.

Tankard, cream (ill.) . . . . $ 180+
Probably other pieces made.

Cardinal Bird

Cardinal Bird

Probably Ohio Flint Glass Company, Lancaster, late 1870s. This company was the ancestor of the Anchor-Hocking Glass Company. Clear. Of course it's a cardinal!

Butter dish, covered. . . . . $ 45-53
Creamer 54-62

Goblet	34-42
Pitcher, water	110-118
Sauce	
Flat, round	17-24
Footed, 4", 5½"	22-27
Spoonholder (ill.)	38-44
Sugar bowl, covered	82-91

Possibly other pieces were made. Goblet being reproduced.

Carmen

(Panelled Diamond and Fine-Cut): Fostoria Glass Company, Moundsville, West Virginia, c. 1896. Clear, clear flashed with yellow, nonflint.

Bowls, berry, 7", 8"	$ 22-27
Butter dish, covered	39-46
Cake stand	37-45
Celery	24-32
Compote	
High standard, 7", 8"	37-46
Low standard	25-37
Creamer	39-43
Cruet, oil	24-32
Goblet	27-36
Pitcher, water, tankard	42-52
Spoonholder	28-37
Sugar bowl, open	34-43
Wine	27-36

Yellow flashing, 20 percent higher than clear prices listed.

Cat on a Hamper

Cat on a Hamper

Indiana Tumbler & Goblet (National) Company, Greentown, Indiana, before 1903. Chocolate, amber, blue, green, clear. Two types made, short and tall. Prices listed, same for both.

Amber	$ 170+
Blue	198-220
Chocolate	220+
Clear	120-135
Green	170-190

Extremely rare when top of hamper is in red, as shown in photo. It is believed no museum except the Houston has this type hamper. Rare!

Catawba Grape

Catawba Grape

Fairly new glass. Clear, also colors. Lots of it around.

| Goblet | $ 24-33 |
| Wine (ill.) | 22-29 |

Cathedral

463

(continued)

Cathedral

(Orion): Bryce Bros., Pittsburgh, late 1880s. Crystal, amber, vaseline, blue amethyst.

Bowl, berry, 5″, 6″, 7″, 8″	$ 21-32
Butter dish, covered	59-66
Cake plate on stand	43-52
Compote	
Covered, large, high standard	56-64
Open, low standard	29-38
Creamer, tall	44-52
Dish, round, footed	19-26
Egg cup	29-34
Goblet	39-46
Pitcher, water, 3 quart	59-66
Saucedish	
Flat, 4″	12-15
Footed, 4″, 4½″	17-22
Spoonholder	29-38
Sugar bowl, covered	35-43
Tumbler, water	29-34
Wine glass	33-42

Vaseline and amber, 30 percent; blue, 40 percent; amethyst, 100 percent higher than clear.

Cat's Eye and Block

(Cut Log): Westmoreland Specialty Company, c. 1896. Clear, sometimes in camphor glass, nonflint.

Butter dish, covered	$ 66-73
Cake stand	66-71
Celery	60-68
Creamer, 3″, 5″	24-32
Goblet	33-41
Pitcher, water	52-62
Sugar bowl, covered	59-69
Tumbler	32-42
Wine	41-50

Camphor, 50 percent higher than clear prices listed.

Celtic Cross

Duncan, Miller Glass Company, Pittsburgh, c. 1888. Clear, etched, nonflint.

Butter dish, covered	$ 53-63
Compote, covered	42-52

Creamer	37-41
Goblet	28-36
Spoonholder	32-40
Sugar bowl, covered	42-46

Etched, same price. Probably other pieces.

Centennial Beer Mug

Centennial Beer Mug

This was made by M. Daniel Connolly, or designed by him.

Beer mug	$ 59-66

Centennial Beer Mug

Centennial Beer Mug

Hobbs, Brockunier & Company, designed for Philadelphia Centennial, 1876.

Butter dish	$ 72-81
Centennial mug (ill.)	47-56

Ceres

Ceres

(Cameo, Goddess of Liberty): Possibly Indiana Tumbler & Goblet Company, 1898-1900. Crystal, opaque white, opaque turquoise, clear, amber, purple-black opaque.

Butter dish . . . . $ 48-54
Candy jar, covered   29-34
Compote, open, low standard   45-54
Creamer   29-37
Mug, handled   40-50
Pitcher, water.   49-54
Spoonholder (ill.)   26-31
Sugar bowl, covered   47-52

Probably other pieces. Colored pieces, 50 percent higher than clear prices listed.

Chain

Chain

Fort Pitt Glass Works, Pittsburgh, c. early 1880s. Clear, nonflint.

Butter dish, covered . . . . $ 50-60
Compote, covered.   43-53
Cordial   32-42
Creamer   24-29
Goblet   27-34
Spoonholder   22-29
Sugar bowl (base ill.)   48-57
Wine   31-40

Probably other pieces.

Chain

Chain

Possibly Sandwich, early. The creamer shown here is almost identical with one made by R. B. Curling & Sons, Fort Pitt. This glassworks was located in Pittsburgh. Prices are for curling.

Butter dish . . . . $ 44-52
Creamer, cheaper version   22-28
Goblet, cheaper version   24-28
Pitcher, water (ill.)   39-43
Platter   29-37
Spoonholder   18-27
Sugar bowl, covered   39-47
Wine   17-26

Chain and Shield

Late 1870s. Clear, nonflint.

Butter, covered . . . . $ 39-47
Creamer.   29-37
Goblet   30-37
Pitcher (ill.)   38-44
Platter, oval   35-39

(continued)

Chain and Shield

Sauce, flat.	16-22
Spoonholder	22-28
Sugar, covered.	35-42

Undoubtedly other pieces.

Chain with Star

Chain with Star

Possibly A. J. Beatty & Company, Steubenville, Ohio, 1880s. Later, U.S. Glass Company, c. 1890s. Clear.

Bowl, footed, small and large	$ 18-23
Butter dish, covered	39-44
Cake stand, 10½″	34-40
Compote, covered, high and low standard	49-54
Creamer (ill.).	28-37
Dish, oval	11-17
Goblet.	22-31
Pickle dish.	12-17
Pitcher, water	45-52
Plate, 7″, 9″, 10″, 12″	16-27

Plate, bread, handled	29-34
Salt/Pepper, pr.	22-30
Sauce, flat and footed	14-26
Spoonholder.	24-32
Sugar bowl, open.	30-36
Wine	22-27

Challinor Thumbprint

(Tall Baby Thumbprint): Challinor, Taylor & Company, Ltd., Tarentum, Pennsylvania, c. 1880s. Clear, nonflint.

Bottle, water	$ 34-40
Bowl	31-39
Butter dish, covered.	40-47
Creamer.	36-42
Goblet	34-42
Spoonholder	34-42
Sugar bowl, covered	37-47
Tumbler	35-42

Other pieces.

Challinor's Tree of Life

Challinor's Tree of Life

(Challinor's No. 313): Challinor, Taylor, Ltd., Tarentum, Pennsylvania, 1885-1893. Opal, olive green, roseblush pink, turquoise blue, yellow. Pieces were plain or hand decorated in colors. Nonflint.

Butter dish, covered	$ 52-60
Can, molasses	27-32
Creamer.	29-34
Dish, diamond-shaped	18-24
Jar, cracker (ill.)	59-68
Salt/Pepper, pr.	34-42
Spoonholder	32-40
Sugar bowl, covered	51-60

Hand-decorated pieces, 75 percent higher than plain prices listed.

466

Chandelier

Chandelier

(Crown Jewels): O'Hara Glass Company, Ltd., 1880s. Nonflint.

Bowl, finger.	$ 18-27
Celery	39-47
Compote	
Covered.	57-62
Open	42-50
Creamer, clear or etched.	39-46
Pitcher, water (ill.)	56-66
Salt, footed	20-25
Sauce, flat	14-19
Spoonholder	35-42
Sugar	
Covered.	45-52
Open	30-37

Probably other pieces.

Checkerboard

Westmoreland Glass Company, Grapeville, Pennsylvania, c. 1900. Clear, nonflint.

Bowls	
Large	$ 27-33
Small	18-22
Butter dish, covered.	38-44
Celery	27-37
Cheese dish	27-36
Creamer	28-35
Cruet	26-32
Goblet	22-29
Pitcher, milk	31-40
Salt/Pepper, pr.	23-32
Spoonholder	19-28
Sugar bowl, covered	30-38
Tumbler, iced tea	17-24
Wine	16-24

Kemple Glass Company, East Palestine, Ohio, reproducing some pieces in milk glass.

Cherry

Cherry

Bakewell, Pears & Company, Pittsburgh, c. 1870. Clear, opal, flint.

Butter dish, covered	$ 68-74
Compote	
Covered, high standard	66-74
Open, high and low	
standard.	48-54
Creamer.	45-55
Goblet (ill.)	37-47
Sauce	20-29
Spoonholder	29-34
Sugar bowl, covered	60-62
Wine	22-27

Opal, 50 percent higher than clear prices listed. Being reproduced in most pieces. Know the original or leave it alone!

Cherry and Fig

Possibly Sandwich, 1880s. Clear. Usual pieces; prices could be compared with those of Circled Scroll.

Cherry Lattice

Northwood Glass Company, 1890s, 1900s. Clear, nonflint.

Berry set	
Large bowl.	$ 51-60
Small bowl	18-22
Butter dish, covered	48-56
Compote	47-56
Creamer (ill.)	52-60
Spoonholder	49-58
Sugar bowl, covered	64-69

Possibly other patterns.

467 (continued)

Cherry and Fig

Cherry Lattice

Chestnut Oak

Chestnut Oak

(Old Acorn): Possibly Sandwich, early 1870s. Clear.

Butter, covered	$ 42-50
Celery.	25-32
Compote	
Covered	47-56
Open	32-43
Egg cup	19-25
Goblet	24-31
Pitcher, water.	42-51
Sauce, flat.	19-27
Spoonholder	28-37
Sugar	
Covered	57-67
Open	31-40

Chrysanthemum Sprig

Chrysanthemum Sprig

Northwood Glass Company, 1890s. Custard, nonflint.

Banana boat.	$195-215
Berry set	
Large bowl.	166-175
Small bowl	69-78
Butter dish, covered (ill.).	190-220
Creamer.	90-110
Pitcher, water	188-200
Salt/Pepper, pr.	128-134
Spoonholder.	82-92
Sugar bowl, covered	118-122
Tumbler, water (rare in blue)	67-74

Probably others. Rare in blue, 100 percent higher than custard prices listed.

Church Windows

(Tulip Petals): U.S. Glass Company, c. 1903. Clear, nonflint. They called it No. 15,082. Previous maker or date are not known.

Butter dish, covered.	$ 56-64
Cake stand	32-40
Celery	27-36
Compote, jelly, covered	46-50
Creamer	32-42
Dish, sardine	24-30
Goblet	27-33
Pitcher, ½ gal.	47-56
Spoonholder	26-36
Sugar bowl	
Covered	64-72
Open	47-57

Many other pieces.

Circled Scroll

Circled Scroll

Produced 1880s, 1890s. Clear, canary, green, blue, with opalescent edge and trim; nonflint.

Bowl, berry	
Covered	$ 44-52
Open	34-39
Creamer (ill.)	52-61
Pitcher, water	71-80
Sauce, clear	22-31
Sugar	
Covered	56-62
Open	30-38
Tumbler	38-47

Probably other pieces. Colored pieces, 65 percent higher than clear prices listed.

Circular Saw

Circular Saw

Maker and date unknown. Clear, some have gilt trim, nonflint.

Bowl	
Berry	$ 25-32
Punch	52-62
Butter dish, covered.	35-42
Cracker jar	22-30
Creamer (ill.)	37-46
Saucedish	20-24
Spoonholder	27-36
Sugar bowl, covered	37-42
Tumber	22-29

Probably other pieces.

Classic

Classic

Gillinder & Sons, 1880s, open and closed feet. Clear, frosted.

Bowl, footed, 6¼″ dia.	$132-141
Butter dish, covered, log feet	220-235
Celery vase, 6 log feet	134-143
Compote	
Covered, open feet	162-172
Open, 6″ standard.	128-137
Creamer	110-120
Goblet	195-220

469

(continued)

Pitcher
    Collared base   286-294
    Open, log feet (ill.)   280-290
Plate
    President Cleveland.   172-182
    Blaine, Hendricks, Logan   172-182
    Warrior.   162-170
Sauce, open, log feet   39-46
Spoonholder, open, log feet   108-120
Sugar bowl, covered, very
    large   161-170

Footed type brings 25 percent more than collared base type.

Classic Medallion

Classic Medallion

(Cameo): Another good clear, nonflint glass of the 1880s.

Butter dish, covered. . . . . $ 37-42
Celery vase   29-34
Compote
    Covered   49-53
    Open   38-44
Creamer.   33-42
Pitcher, water (ill.)   54-63
Spoonholder   29-37
Sugar bowl
    Covered   38-47
    Open   27-35

Probably other pieces.

Clear Diagonal Band

Late 1880s. Clear, nonflint.

Butter dish . . . . $ 46-52
Celery vase   29-34
Compote
    Covered, high standard   47-56
    Covered, low standard   37-46

Clear Diagonal Band

Cordial   19-27
Creamer.   32-39
Goblet   28-36
Marmalade jar, covered   32-42
Pitcher, water (ill.)   38-46
Platter, "Excelsior"   55-62
Salt/Pepper, pr.   33-42
Sauces, flat and footed   11-18
Spoonholder   26-35
Sugar bowl
    Covered   46-56
    Open   24-32

Probably other pieces.

Clear Lion's Head

Clear Lion's Head

(Atlanta): Fostoria Glass Company, Moundsville, West Virginia, 1895. Plain, etched and engraved, nonflint.

Bowl, berry (ill.). . . . . $ 49-54
Butter dish, covered   59-67
Cake stand, large, square   108-119
Compote
    Covered, 5", square stem 144-152
    Open, 5", square stem 139-150
Creamer.   57-64
Goblet   54-62
Jam jar   69-74
Pickle dish   49-54
Salt, master   53-62

Sauce, flat.	33-42
Spoonholder	45-54
Sugar bowl, covered	55-62
Sugar bowl, open	40-47
Toothpick holder	39-46

Clear Stork

Clear Stork

Possibly Mosaic Glass Company, Fostoria, Ohio, 1890-91. Nonflint.

Butter dish	$ 52-60
Compote	70-80
Creamer	50-60
Goblet	45-54
Pitcher, water (ill.)	82-92
Spoonholder	29-34
Sugar bowl, covered	58-66
Tumbler	25-35

Probably other pieces. Frosted Stork prices, 60 percent higher than clear prices listed.

Clio

Clio

Challinor, Taylor, Ltd., Tarentum, Pennsylvania, 1885-1891. Clear, amber, blue, nonflint.

Butter dish, covered.	$ 46-54
Celery	25-29
Compote, covered (ill.)	34-42
Goblet	24-32
Pitcher, qt., ½ gal.	45-54
Spoonholder	22-29
Sugar bowl, covered	46-54

Probably other pieces.

Coach Bowl

Coach Bowl

McKee & Bros., 1886. Crystal, amber, canary, blue (draft tongue in photo broken off). Also being reproduced in milk glass, amber, purple, blue, other colors.

Coach Bowl (ill.)	$ 225+

In colors, 50 percent higher.

Coarse Cut and Block

Coarse Cut and Block

Model Flint Glass Company, Findlay, Ohio, 1880s. Clear, nonflint.

Butter dish	$ 32-41

(continued)

| Celery . . . . | 22-29 |

Compote	
Covered, high standard	37-44
Open, low standard	27-36
Creamer	34-38
Goblet	20-27
Pitcher, water (ill.)	35-42
Spoonholder	24-27
Sugar bowl, covered	40-47

Probably other pieces.

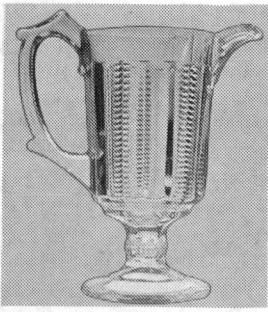

Cobb

Cobb

(Late Sawtooth; Zipper): Richards & Hartley, Tarentum, Pennsylvania, 1888. Clear, nonflint.

Butter dish, covered	$ 47-55
Compote, covered	49-56
Creamer	
High.	37-46
Low	34-42
Goblet	22-30
Pitcher (ill.)	47-56
Salt/Pepper, pr.	24-34
Spoonholder	35-42
Sugar bowl	36-46
Tumbler	19-24

Probably other pieces.

Coin

Coin

(Columbian; Spanish, Coin): Made by one of the factories mentioned in Coin, U.S., where they used Spanish coins and possibly some English coins, same date, 1892. Spanish coins are bronzed. Never as collectible as U.S. coins.

Bowl	
Berry, 10″.	$112-121
Finger	70-78
Butter dish, covered (ill.)	144-156
Cake stand	60-64
Compote	
Covered, 6″, 7″, 8″	95-120
Open, 7″, 8″, 10″.	69-79
Creamer	82-92
Goblet	70-80
Pitcher, water	78-88
Salt/Pepper, pr.	66-74
Sugar bowl, covered	75-84
Toothpick holder	38-48
Tumbler	44-52

Being reproduced. Know your seller.

Coin

Coin

(U.S.): Central Glass Company and Hobbs, Brockunier, Wheeling, West Virginia, for a few months in 1892. Space doesn't allow us to tell all about this glass. Because real coins were used, the Treasury Department made the company stop after only a few months' production. Very scarce today: 5¢ piece, 10¢, 25¢, 50¢ and the silver dollar. Clear, frosted, sometimes silvered or gilded. Prices given for indicative pieces. Being skillfully reproduced. Careful! Demand a receipt.

Bowl, berry
25¢. $255-270
$1.00 295-320
Bread platter, frosted coins. 540-552
Butter dish
$1.00 500-525
50¢ 470-480
Cake stand
$1.00, frosted 400-425
50¢ 425-432
Celery, 50¢ 300-340
Celery, 25¢ 230-242
Compote, covered
50¢, 8″ dia. 500-525
25¢ (ill.) 460-470
$1.00, frosted, finial. 620-632
Creamer, 25¢ 325-345
Goblet
$1.00 320-340
10¢ 310-332
Mug, $1.00 220-240
Pitcher
Milk, 50¢ 400-452
Water, $1.00 525-562
Sugar bowl
Covered, 50¢, finial 520-540
Covered, 25¢ finial 485-520
Toothpick holder, $1.00 158-170
Tumbler
$1.00 on base (rare) 258-275
10¢ 230-240
Wine, one-half dime (rare) 322-342

The toothpick holder was reproduced in Indiana several years ago, before the government stopped it. A few reached the market. Now, bread tray (50¢) and tumbler ($1.00 on base) are being reproduced.

Colonial

Colonial

Sandwich Glass, 1850-1860. Clear, opal or other colors, rare.

Ale glass, tall, footed. . . . . $ 67-75
Celery glass 68-76
Champagne 68-78
Egg cup 22-32
Goblet, knob stem. 45-55
Pitcher (ill.) 78-87
Spill holder 45-55
Sugar bowl 95-115

Possibly other pieces. Colors, 150 percent higher than clear prices listed.

Colonis

Colonis

(45 Colonis): U.S. Glass Company, 1913. Clear, nonflint.

Butter dish . . . . $ 38-42
Cake stand, 8″ 32-39
Celery vase 27-35
Compote
Covered, high standard 37-47
Open, low standard 34-42
Cordial 24-32
Creamer. 31-40
Dish, oval 21-29
Egg cup 21-27
Goblet 25-32
Pitcher
Milk (ill.) 45-54
Water 46-56
Sauce 19-27
Spoonholder 42-52
Sugar bowl, covered 29-39
Tray 32-41
Tumbler 27-32

Colorado

Colorado

U.S. Glass Company, 1897, another of their "States" series. Crystal glass, both plain and engraved, and crystal with ruby stain; green and deep blue with gold decorations, and amethyst—rare in this color.

Banana bowl	$ 29-34
Bowl, berry, 6″	15-19
Butter dish, covered	56-64
Cheese dish, low, footed	21-30
Creamer, individual and large	25-37
Dish	
Crimped edge, 4″, 8″	25-34
Flared edge, 4″, 8″	26-35
Pitcher, water (ill.)	32-39
Salt/Pepper, pr.	22-27
Spoonholder	25-32
Sugar bowl	
Individual	25-32
Large, covered	48-54
Toothpick holder	25-35
Tumbler	19-27

Ruby, 20 percent; blue, 55 percent; green, 75 percent; amethyst, 200 percent higher than clear prices listed.

Columbia

U.S. Glass Company, 1907. Clear, non-flint. Probably others earlier.

Bowl, 7″, 8″, 9″, 10″	$ 31-38
Butter dish, covered	34-42
Celery tray	24-31
Creamer (ill.)	25-32
Custard cup	24-32
Dish	17-21
Olive	24-32
Sundae	32-42

Columbia

Pitcher, water	35-42
Relish bowl	24-32
Salt/Pepper, pr.	24-34
Spoonholder	25-32
Sugar bowl, covered	35-44
Tumbler	24-33

At least 125 different pieces were made in this pattern.

Comet

Comet

Sandwich Glass, c. late 1840s. Clear, flint. Don't confuse this rare glass with McKee Bros.' glass of the same name, c. 1887.

Butter dish, covered	$244-258
Goblet (ill.)	92-103
Pitcher, water	420-450
Tumbler, whiskey, water	150-162

Possibly other pieces.

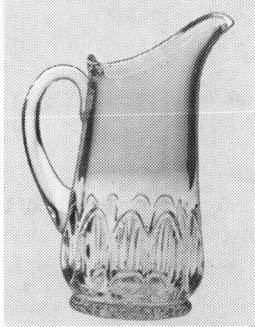

Concaved Almond

Concaved Almond

Maker unknown, used for souvenir purposes in 1890s, a style created at the Chicago Exposition in 1893. Emerald green, ruby stain.

Goblet . . . . $ 32-41
Pitcher, water (ill.) 52-62
Toothpick. 29-39

Probably other pieces. Colors, 60 percent higher than clear prices listed.

Connecticut

U.S. Glass Company, c. 1898. Clear, non-flint.

Bowls, 4″, 6″, 8″ . . . . $ 15-26
Butter dish, covered. 28-38
Cake stand, 10″ 42-52
Celery tray 19-24
Creamer 29-34
Pitcher, tankard, 3 types 37-46
Salt/Pepper, pr.. 22-32
Tumbler 15-27
Wine 19-27

Many other pieces.

Continental

A. H. Heisey Company, Newark, Ohio, 1903. Not all pieces marked with "Diamond H."

Butter dish
  Covered . . . . $ 45-55
  Covered, footed 52-60
Creamer
  Flat 42-51
  Footed. 45-32

Continental

Pitcher, water (ill.) 82-92
Spoonholder
  Flat 36-46
  Footed. 44-54
Sugar bowl
  Covered 52-62
  Covered, footed 68-74

Prices are for signed pieces.

Continental Bread Tray

Continental Bread Tray

Another in the series of historical plates sold at the Philadelphia Exposition in 1876. Clear only. Atterbury and Company, Pittsburgh.

Plate, 13″ by 9″ (ill.) . . . . $ 155+

Coolidge Drape

Coolidge Drape

Maker unknown, 1880. Clear and cobalt (blue) in several sizes. Lamp is famous because this was pattern of lamp in room in which Coolidge took presidential oath after Harding's sudden death.

Any size in clear $122-131
Any size in cobalt 182-194

Cord and Tassel

Cord and Tassel

Central Glass Company, 1872. Clear.

Bowl, oval.	$ 27-32
Butter dish, covered.	45-52
Cake stand, high standard.	34-42
Celery.	38-45
Compote, high standard.	56-62
Cordial.	18-22
Creamer, applied handle.	38-47
Egg cup.	28-37
Goblet.	31-40
Lamp, applied handle.	65-73
Mug.	39-44
Pitcher, water (ill.).	59-68
Sauce.	15-21
Spoonholder.	38-46
Sugar bowl, covered.	45-52
Wine.	45-52

Probably other pieces.

Cord Drapery

Cord Drapery

(Indiana): Indiana Tumbler & Goblet (National) Company, Greentown, Indiana, 1899. Clear, amber, blue, green, chocolate, opal.

Berry bowl.	$ 24-29
Butter dish, clear.	68-77
Cake plate.	49-58
Compote	
Stemmed, covered, jelly.	43-53
Stemmed, fluted.	47-56

Stemmed, large.	74-79
Creamer.	47-56
Goblet.	49-58
Pitcher, water (ill.).	52-60
Salt/Pepper, pr..	32-41
Spoonholder.	34-40
Tumbler (rare).	29-36

Chocolate, 200 percent higher; other colors, 30 percent higher than clear prices listed.

Cordova

Cordova

O'Hara Glass Company, Pittsburgh, 1890. Clear, nonflint.

Bowl	
Covered.	$ 29-36
Finger.	19-28
Open.	15-22
Butter dish, covered.	39-47
Cake stand.	42-52
Celery.	30-37
Compote, covered and open,	
high standard.	41-50
Creamer, regular.	29-37
Cruet.	44-53
Inkwell (rare).	89-95
Pitcher	
Syrup (ill.).	40-44
Water.	44-54
Spoonholder.	24-32
Sugar bowl, covered.	34-42
Tumbler.	25-31

Probably made in other pieces.

Coreopsis

Possibly Dalzell, Gilmore & Leighton Company, Findlay, Ohio, c. 1888, white opaque.

Butter dish, covered.	$ 98-108
Creamer.	78-83
Spoonholder.	58-67
Sugar bowl, covered.	92-103

Probably other pieces.

Cornucopia

Cornucopia

Maker unknown, 1885-1890. Clear, fine fruit group on reverse side.

Butter dish, covered.	$ 37-42
Celery	24-33
Compote, covered	46-56
Creamer	27-36
Goblet	21-28
Pitcher, water (ill.)	52-62
Spoonholder	19-28
Sugar bowl, covered	35-44

Probably other pieces.

Cosmos   Cosmos

(Stemless Daisy): Probably Dithridge & Son, New Brighton, Pennsylvania, 1900. Opaque.

Butter dish, open and covered (ill.)	$227-232
Caster set; salt/pepper, mustard	251-262
Creamer	140-150
Lamps	
Large, round with shade	190-198
Miniature, base only	98-118
Miniature with shade	120-130
Lemonade pitcher with 6 mugs	340-360
Pitcher, water, 8¾″ high	182-192

Salt/Pepper, pr.	118-127
Spoonholder	116-122
Sugar bowl, covered	177-190
Tumbler	100-110

Probably other pieces.

Cottage

Cottage

(Dinner Bell; Fine Cut Band): Adams & Company, Pittsburgh, 1874. Clear, dark green (rare), amber.

Butter dish, covered	$ 39-44
Cake stand, 9″ high	36-45
Celery vase	24-29
Compote, covered and open, high standard	42-52
Creamer.	22-29
Cruet, w/stopper	42-50
Fruit bowl, high standard	25-32
Goblet	27-35
Pitcher, pint, quart, half gallon, amber	38-54
Plate, 6″, 7″, 8″, 9″	14-24
Salt/Pepper, pr.	39-47
Spoonholder	23-32
Sugar bowl, covered	34-40
Tray, water	29-34
Tumbler	20-27
Wine	26-31

Probably other pieces made. Colors, 70 percent higher than clear prices listed. Dark green considered rare.

Cow

Maker unknown, c. 1870s. Clear, nonflint.

Butter dish, covered, 6″ long	$ 97-110

Cradled Prisms

Probably Challinor, Taylor, Ltd., c. late 1880s. Clear, nonflint.

Butter dish, covered	$ 42-51
Creamer, footed	32-41
Spoonholder	22-30
Sugar bowl, covered	34-42

Probably other pieces.

Croesus

Croesus

Riverside Glass Works, Wellsville, West Virginia, 1897. Crystal. Emerald, royal purple (amethyst), gold trim, made by McKee in 1899.

Bowl, berry	$ 79-88
Butter dish, covered	109-119
Celery	69-79
Creamer, regular	69-77
Cruet	82-92
Pickle dish	37-48
Pitcher, water (ill.)	98-107
Salt/Pepper, pr.	52-64
Spoonholder	49-54
Sugar bowl, covered	92-103
Toothpick holder	44-53
Tumbler	33-102

Emerald green, 100 percent; amethyst, 250 percent higher than clear prices listed. Entire table set being reproduced in Japan.

Crossed Block

Possibly Hartley & Richards, late 1800s. Clear, nonflint.

Butter dish, covered.	$ 46-56
Creamer (ill.)	36-47

Crossed Block

Spoonholder	27-32
Sugar bowl, covered	58-67

Probably other pieces.

Crossed Fern

Atterbury & Company, Pittsburgh, c. 1876. Clear, opal, turquoise, nonflint.

Bowl, collared	$ 22-29
Butter dish, covered.	34-39
Compote, covered	36-43
Creamer	22-29
Pitcher	36-47
Spoonholder	23-30
Sugar bowl, covered	25-34
Tumbler	21-30

Opal, turquoise, 40 percent higher than clear prices listed.

Crossed Ferns with Ball and Claw

Atterbury & Company, c. 1876. Clear, opal, turquoise, nonflint. Same prices as Crossed Fern—see.

Crossed Shield

478

Crossed Shield

Fostoria Glass Company's No. 1303, late 1890s. Clear, nonflint.

Butter dish, covered.	$ 39-46
Creamer	46-51
Compotes, several sizes	32-46
Cordial	22-29
Decanter	52-60
Egg cup	24-32
Goblet	24-33
Pitcher, water, (ill.)	57-63
Spoonholder	24-32
Sugar bowl, covered	34-46
Tumbler	24-33

Probably other pieces.

Crystal

McKee Bros. Pittsburgh, c. 1859. Clear, flint.

Ale glass	$ 39-47
Bowl, covered	42-50
Butter, covered	69-74
Celery	39-46
Compote, covered, high standard . . .	
Creamer	59-68
Decanter, qt.	66-73
Egg cup	29-34
Goblet	32-40
Pitcher, water.	92-107
Spoonholder	29-34
Sugar bowl, covered	54-64
Tumbler	
bar	32-40
footed	38-46

Crystal Wedding

Crystal Wedding

(Crystal Anniversary): Adams Glass Company, early 1880s. Clear, amber, canary, blue, nonflint.

Banana stand	$107-118
Butter dish, covered	52-61

Cake stand, high standard	61-70
Celery	40-47
Compote	
Open, low standard	74-83
Covered, high standard (ill.)	77-89
Covered, low standard	72-81
Creamer, clear	59-68
Goblet	33-42
Pitcher, water, square	154-164
Salt/Pepper, pr.	52-61
Spoonholder	44-50
Sugar bowl, covered	63-70
Tumbler	49-58

Probably other pieces. Goblet and compote being reproduced. Colors, 100 percent more than clear prices listed.

Cube with Fan

U.S. Glass Company, c. 1900. Clear, nonflint.

Bowl, finger	$107-118
Celery	24-34
Dish, jelly	20-24
Goblet	19-25
Plates, 5″, 7½″	18-29
Sugar bowl, covered	34-42
Tumbler	19-28

Many other pieces.

Cupid and Venus

Cupid and Venus

(Guardian Angel): Richard & Hartley Glass Company, Pittsburgh (Birmingham), 1875-1884. Clear, yellow, amber, nonflint.

(continued)

Butter dish, covered	$ 81-90
Cake plate, 11″	36-44
Celery	45-52
Champagne (rare)	108-116
Compote	
Covered, high and low	
standard	57-74
Open, high standard	56-62
Creamer, footed	37-42
Jam jar, covered (ill.)	94-102
Mug, 2″, 2½″, 3½″	26-36
Pickle caster	18-22
Pitcher, large and small	60-72
Plate, bread, 10½″, round	38-46
Plate, bread, handles	39-45
Sauce	
Flat, round	7-11
Footed, 3½″, 4″, 5″	10-13
Spoonholder	45-52
Sugar bowl, covered	64-72
Wine (scarce)	88-99

Probably other pieces. Color, 40 percent higher than clear prices listed.

Currant

Sandwich glass, 1870s. Later, Campbell, Jones & Company, Pittsburgh, 1870s. Crystal.

Butter dish	$ 59-67
Cake plate on stand, 2 types	64-72
Celery vase	47-52
Compote	
Covered 8″ high foot	60-69
Covered, 8″, 9″, low foot	49-58
Cordial	35-43
Creamer, applied handle	55-64
Dish, oval, 6″ × 9″, 5″ × 7″	27-32
Egg cup	25-34
Goblets, 5½″, 6″	34-44
Pitcher, water (ill.)	83-93
Spoonholder	32-38
Sugar bowl, covered	49-58

Tumbler, footed	32-41
Wine	34-42

Probably other pieces.

Currier and Ives

Currier and Ives

Bellaire Goblet Company, Findlay, Ohio, 1880s. Clear, rare in colors—amber, blue, nonflint.

Butter dish, covered	$ 59-63
Cordial	28-37
Creamer	34-42
Cup and saucer	36-47
Goblet, knob stem	29-38
Lamp, No. 2, complete w/ burner	
and chimney	37-46
Pitcher, large and small	42-59
Salt/Pepper, pr.	50-60
Spoonholder	25-34
Sugar bowl, covered	47-53
Tray, "Balky Mule on RR	
Tracks"	64-72
Wine	24-32

Probably other pieces. Color, 300 percent higher than clear prices listed.

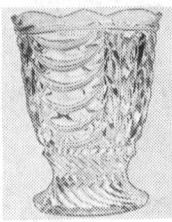

Curtain

Curtain

(Sultan): Bryce Bros., Pittsburgh, 1875-1885. Clear, nonflint.

Bowl, covered, 6″, 7″, 8″	$ 24-33
Bowl, open, 6″, 7″, 8″	20-30

Butter dish 57-64
Cake plate on stand 34-42
Celery boat 36-42
Compote
  Covered, high standard,
  6″, 7″, 8″ 51-60
  Open, high standard
  7″, 8″, 10″ 45-60
Creamer 47-56
Goblet 37-46
Mug, large 27-34
Pitcher, quart, half gallon 61-66
Salt/Pepper, pr.. 34-39
Spoonholder (ill.) 37-42
Sugar bowl 47-52
Tumbler 32-38

Probably other pieces.

Curtain Tieback

Maker unknown, c. mid-1880s. Clear, nonflint. Two types of feet.

Bowl, berry, 7″ square . . . . $ 18-24
Butter dish, covered 33-38
Celery. 17-21
Creamer. 22-31
Goblet 26-36
Pitcher, water 40-50
Spoonholder 23-32
Sugar bowl, open 21-31
Tumbler 19-27
Wine 19-31

Other pieces.

Dahlia

Dahlia

Canton Glass Company, Canton, Ohio, 1880s. Clear, amber, vaseline, blue, green. Amber and yellow are scarce.

Butter dish, covered. . . . . $ 35-42
Cake plate on stand, 10″. 35-43
Champagne 87-94
Compote, large, covered, high
  standard 57-62
Cordial 34-41
Creamer 27-36
Egg cup, double (rare). 52-60
Goblet, etched (scarce) 52-61
Mug, handled, 2 sizes 34-39
Pitcher, water, milk (ill.) 39-47
Platter, grape handles, oval 32-41
Spoonholder 24-32
Sugar bowl, covered 44-53
Wine 39-46

Colors, 30-50 percent higher than clear prices listed. Amber, yellow, 100 percent higher.

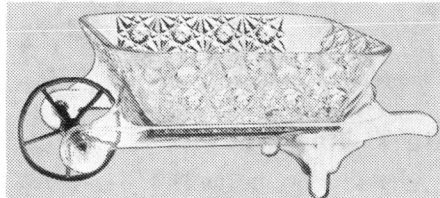

Daisy and Button

Daisy and Button

Gillinder and Sons, Philadelphia, 1876, in time for the Centennial; also, Hobbs, Brockunier and Company, Wheeling, West Virginia. Souvenir items were extremely popular at the Fair. This D and B wheelbarrow with metal wheel is rare today. It can be seen at the Houston Museum.

No single glass pattern has been or is being reproduced more than Daisy and Button in all its variations. Collect it if you like it but not because you think you're getting a bargain. Know your dealer!

Daisy and Button

Daisy and Button

One of the rarest pieces ever made is this "Helmet" covered butter dish. Don't look for it in shops. You can see this one at the Houston Museum in Chattanooga.

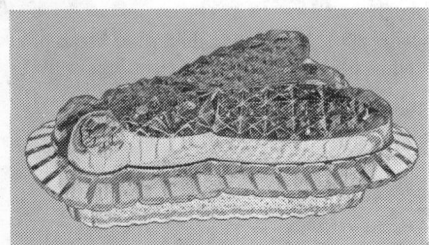
Daisy and Button

Daisy and Button

Another rarity in the D & B pattern is the "Bee" covered dish. I honestly believe that every original D & B pattern is being reproduced today. Be extremely careful when you buy. Make sure your dealer is an authority before you buy! This "Bee" is at the Houston Museum.

Daisy and Button

Daisy and Button

This is a rare blue creamer with clear handle. Probably Hobbs, Brockunier and Company. We're including four different D & B pieces to show you how many, many different pieces were made. Enjoy looking, but save your money!

**Daisy and Button,
Oval Medallion**

Daisy and Button, Oval Medallion

One of the most popular patterns ever produced in this country.

Usual D & B prices. But do be careful!

Daisy and Button, Oxford

Daisy and Button, Oxford

Sandwich, early. Clear and colored.

Amber, canary shoe . . . . $ 56-62
Blue shoe 68-74
Clear shoe. 57-61

What one sees today in shops are reproductions. Watch it!

Daisy and Button, Panelled

Here again another of the D & B patterns. Too many reproductions to take a chance on this or any other D & B pattern.

Daisy and Button, Panelled

This pattern is rare in two colors—amber and clear—but don't worry about finding it outside a museum such as the Houston Museum in Chattanooga, Tennessee. Save your money.

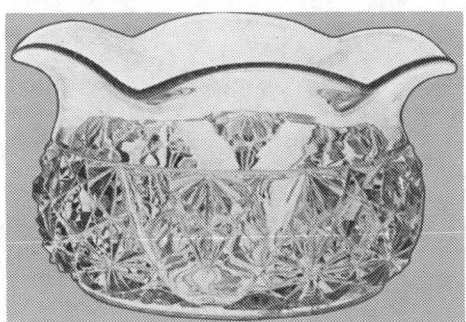

Daisy and Button "V"

Daisy and Button "V"

A. J. Beatty & Company, 1886-1887. Clear.

Just as many patterns reproduced in this "V" as in D & B. Not worth discussing. You're buying new unless you're an expert.

Daisy and Button with Narcissus

(Clear Lily): Another D & B, maker unknown, late 1880s. Clear, sometimes flashed with gold, nonflint.

Butter dish	$ 39-47
Celery, flat, footed, ea.	24-31
Compote, open	39-48
Creamer.	32-41
Decanter, w/stopper.	56-62
Goblet	27-35

Daisy and Button with Narcissus

Pickle dish	16-24
Pitcher, water (ill.)	67-74
Salt/Pepper, pr.	45-52
Sauce, 4″	16-20
Spoonholder	24-30
Sugar bowl, covered	34-42
Tumbler	19-27
Wine	19-27

Probably other pieces. Wine being reproduced, also bowls and vases.

Daisy and Button with Prisms

Daisy and Button with Prisms

It sounds like a broken record, but save your breath on these D & B patterns with variations such as shown. Just about every genuine piece has been reproduced and they're good. Buy it for what it is—new—and enjoy it as such. Don't put your money into it unless you know it yourself. Few dealers can tell you whether it's old.

Daisy and Thumbprint Cross-Bar

Daisy and Thumbprint Cross-Bar

(Mikado): Richards and Hartley Flint Glass Company, 1888. Clear, yellow, amber, light and dark blue; nonflint.

Bowl, flat, 6″, 8″	$ 22-29
Butter dish, flat, footed	37-43
Catsup bottle	29-34
Compote	
Covered, 7″, 8″	46-54
Open, 7″, 8″	30-40
Creamer, regular (ill.)	27-32
Cruet	26-34
Goblet	29-35
Lamps, 4 sizes	29-44
Pitcher, quart, half gallon	41-51
Salt/Pepper, pr.	22-31
Spoonholder	24-33
Sugar bowl, covered	32-40
Tumbler	22-30
Wine	19-27

Probably other pieces. Amber, yellow, 40 percent higher; blue, 100 percent higher than clear prices listed.

Daisy in Diamond

O'Hara Glass Company, Pittsburgh, 1886. Crystal, amber, rose, blue, nonflint.

Butter dish, covered	$ 32-42
Celery	23-32
Creamer	27-37
Egg cup	18-22
Goblet	19-28
Pitcher, water (ill.)	35-42
Spoonholder	24-33
Sugar bowl, covered	29-38
Tumbler	22-31

Probably other pieces. Colors, 110-130 percent higher than clear prices listed.

Daisy in Diamond

Daisy Medallion

Daisy Medallion

(Sunburst Medallion): Maker unknown, 1880s. Clear, nonflint.

Butter dish, covered	$ 28-37
Cake stand	26-34
Compote	27-34
Creamer	24-34
Pitcher	30-37
Spoonholder	19-27
Sugar bowl (ill.)	29-38

Probably other pieces.

Daisy Whorl

Maker unknown, 1870s. Clear, also in colors.

Butter dish, covered	$ 31-38
Compote	
Covered	32-41
Open	26-34

Daisy Whorl

Goblet	24-30
Pitcher, water (ill.)	44-52
Spoonholder	17-27
Sugar bowl	
Covered	34-43
Open	24-32

Probably other pieces. Colors, 50-75 percent higher than clear prices listed.

Dakota   Dakota

(Baby Thumbprint; Thumbprint Band): Doyle & Company, Pittsburgh, 1890s. Clear, red-flashed, nonflint.

Bowl, berry, 8″	$ 32-41
Butter dish, covered, etched	64-73
Cake stand, 10″	77-84
Celery, flat base	27-33
Compote, covered, 5″, 6″, 7″, 8″	44-62
Creamer, pedestal base (ill.)	59-67
Goblet, etched.	36-44
Pitcher, water, ...	82-93
Salt/Pepper, pr.	72-82
Spoonholder	57-64
Sugar bowl, covered, etched	68-74
Tray, water, 13″ (rare)	66-75
Tumbler	42-50
Wine	46-52

Probably other pieces. Red-flashed, 60 percent higher than clear.

Dancing Goat

Possibly LaBelle Glass Company, Bridgeport, Ohio, c. 1878. Clear, nonflint.

Ale glass.	$ 75+

Dart

Maker unknown, c. 1880. Clear, nonflint.

Butter dish, covered.	$ 32-40
Creamer	23-31
Goblet	22-30
Sauce	12-17
Spoonholder	18-24
Sugar bowl, covered	31-39

Other pieces.

Deer and Oak Tree

Deer and Oak Tree

Dalzell, Gilmore & Leighton, Findlay, Ohio; also, Indiana Tumbler & Goblet (National) Company, Greentown, Indiana. National took over both factories in 1889.

Pitcher, water (ill.)	$185-250

Chocolate color, 150 percent higher than clear price listed.

Deer and Pine Tree

(Deer and Doe): Sandwich glass, 1860s. Clear, blue, amber, green, yellow, nonflint. Later, Belmont Glass Co. and McKee Glass Co., c. early 1880s. Prices are for Belmont and McKee.

Bowl, waste	$ 44-52
Butter dish, covered.	66-74

(continued)

Deer and Pine Tree

Cake plate on standard	78-84
Celery	49-54
Compote, covered, oblong, large	44-56
Creamer	42-52
Goblet	34-39
Jam jar, covered.	49-54
Pickle dish, oblong, deep	24-32
Pitcher, large and small	82-107
Plate, bread.	42-50
Platter, 13¼" × 8"	57-64
Sauce, flat and footed	18-24
Spoonholder	45-52
Sugar bowl, covered	56-64
Tray, large, 11" × 15", handled	79-86

Probably other pieces. Colors, 60 percent higher than clear prices listed. Colored pieces have been reproduced.

Delaware

Delaware

(New Century): U.S. Glass Company, 1899. Crystal glass with rose stain and gilt trim; also, green glass with gilt trim, amethyst (rare), nonflint.

Bowl, round, fluted, boat-shaped, banana	$ 47-56
Butter dish	87-96
Celery.	35-44
Creamer.	24-32
Cruet	109-118
Pitcher, water (ill.)	72-82

Spoonholder	25-34
Sugar bowl, covered	74-82
Toothpick holder	24-32
Tumbler	24-33

Probably other pieces. Colors, 100 to 150 percent higher than clear prices listed. Amethyst, rare, 400 percent higher.

Dewdrop and Flowers

Dewdrop and Flowers

Probably originated at Sandwich; late 1870s, early 1880s. Clear.

Butter dish, covered.	$ 35-42
Compote	
Covered	45-52
Open	31-40
Creamer	32-42
Goblet	29-37
Pitcher, milk (ill.)	45-54
Spoonholder	14-22
Sugar bowl	
Covered	32-39
Open	28-34
Wine	19-27

Dewdrop and Raindrop

Dewdrop and Raindrop

Kokoma Glass Manufacturing Company, Kokomo, Indiana, 1900-1905. Clear, clear/gilded, clear/ruby, nonflint.

Bowl, berry . . . . $ 44-55
Butter dish 59-67
Cordial, set of 6, each 29-34
Creamer 41-45
Cup, sherbet 10-12
Goblet 41-47
Pitcher, water (ill.) 70-80
Sauce 13-17
Salt/Pepper, pr.. 50-58
Spoonholder 31-40
Sugar bowl 41-44
Tumbler 17-26
Wine 30-37

Cordial, goblet, sherbet cup, and wine being reproduced.

Dewdrop in Points

Dewdrop in Points

Greensburg Glass Company, Greensburg, Pennsylvania, probably 1875-1885. Clear, nonflint.

Butter dish, covered. . . . . $ 56-65
Cake stand, large 44-52
Compote
  Covered. 51-61
  Open 47-50
Creamer, covered 38-44
Goblet 38-47
Pickle dish, oval. 19-25
Pitcher (ill.). 66-72
Plate, bread. 27-32
Sauce, footed 19-27
Spoonholder 32-41
Sugar bowl, covered 49-54

Probably other pieces.

Dewdrop with Star

Dewdrop with Star

Campbell, Jones & Company, Pittsburgh, 1877. Clear, nonflint.

Butter dish, covered, star base. . . . . $ 71-81
Cake plate on standard 64-72
Celery, star in base 32-41
Compote
  Covered, high and low
    standard. 79-84
  Covered, footed, 6", 7",
    star base. 66-74
Creamer, star base. 44-52
Pickle dish 14-20
Pitcher, water (ill.) 92-107
Plates, 4½" through 11" 19-36
Sauce, flat and footed 9-14
Spoonholder 37-46
Sugar bowl, covered, star base 48-58
Tumbler 29-37

Probably other pieces. The 7¼" plate and salt and probably footed sauces are being reproduced.

Dewey   Dewey

(Flower Flange): Indiana Tumbler & Goblet Company, 1898. Crystal, canary, green, amber, blue, chocolate.

Bowl, berry . . . . $ 20-29
Butter dish, covered (ill.) 35-42

(continued)

Creamer.	29-36
Cruet	32-42
Mug.	36-45
Pitcher, water, 9½" high.	48-57
Salt/Pepper, pr.	34-41
Serpentine tray	22-28
Spoonholder	25-32
Sugar bowl, covered	35-42
Tumbler	29-37

Other pieces were made. Chocolate, 300 percent higher; other colors, 70 percent higher than clear prices listed.

Diagonal Band

Diagonal Band

A pattern of the 1800s; clear. Apple green scarce.

Prices almost identical to Diagonal Band with Fan, except apple green 100 percent higher than clear prices listed.

Diagonal Band with Fan

Diagonal Band with Fan

U.S. Glass Co., c. 1891. Nonflint.

Butter dish, covered.	$ 39-47
Celery vase	24-29
Compote, high and low foot	37-49
Cordial	19-27
Creamer	26-32
Goblets, 3 sizes, ea.	22-34
Pitcher, milk, 8" (ill.)	56-62
Plate, 6", 7", 8"	14-18
Salt/Pepper, pr.	49-57
Sauce, footed, 4", 4½"	15-19
Spoonholder	24-32
Sugar bowl, covered	39-46
Wine	27-36

Probably other pieces.

Diamond and Sunburst

Diamond and Sunburst

Maker unknown, late 1860s. Clear, nonflint.

Butter dish, covered.	$ 39-47
Cake stand	34-43
Celery vase	24-32
Compote	
Covered	44-52
Open	32-38
Creamer, applied handle	34-41
Decanter	28-34
Egg cup	18-22
Goblet	28-36
Pitcher, water (ill.)	27-39
Spoonholder	19-26
Sugar bowl, covered	38-42
Tumbler	22-31

Probably other pieces.

Diamond Band

(Prism and Diamond Band): Central Glass Company, Wheeling, West Virginia, c. 1870. Clear, nonflint.

Butter dish, covered.	$ 38-46
Celery	24-35
Compote, small, footed	37-46
Creamer	36-42
Dish, shallow	12-18
Goblet	24-32
Pitcher, water.	37-44
Spoonholder	19-27
Sugar bowl, covered	41-50
Wine	21-27

Other pieces.

Diamond Block with Fans

(Blockade): Challinor, Taylor, Ltd., c. 1880s. Clear, nonflint. It was their No. 309. The pattern may have been continued by U.S. Glass Company after 1891.

Bowl, waste	$ 24-32
Butter dish, covered	45-52
Celery.	24-33
Creamer.	29-38
Goblet	33-42
Pitcher, water	49-57
Spoonholder	24-37
Sugar bowl, covered	51-61

Many other pieces.

Diamond Mirror

Diamond Mirror

Maker unknown, late 1880s. Clear, nonflint.

Butter dish, covered.	$ 34-42
Celery.	19-25
Creamer.	21-28
Spoonholder (ill.)	21-27
Sugar bowl	
Covered	33-42
Open	22-31

Probably other pieces.

Diamond Point

Diamond Point

Sandwich glass, 1830. Bryce, Richards & Co., Pittsburgh, c. 1854; others, c. 1880s. Clear, rare in colors, flint. Prices are for Sandwich.

Ale glass	$ 25-34
Butter dish, covered	105-115
Celery	72-81
Compote	
Covered, 6″, 7″, 8″, high and low standard	72-81
Open, 6″, 7″, 8″, high and low standard	59-67
Creamer, footed, scalloped	92-103
Egg cup (rare in color)	27-36
Goblet, large and small	42-62
Pitcher, half pint, pint, quart	70-162
Plates, 3″ through 8″	32-55
Spoonholder	49-55
Sugar bowl, covered	88-99
Tumbler, water, whiskey	64-82

Probably other pieces. Color, 400 percent higher; opaque, 200 percent higher than clear prices listed.

Diamond Point Discs

(continued)

Diamond Point Discs

Probably made at Findlay, Ohio, late 1880s. Clear, nonflint.

Butter dish, covered.	$ 29-37
Cake stand	35-44
Celery	18-27
Compote	
Covered, 7", 8", high	
standard	37-47
Covered, 7", 9", colored base	44-52
Creamer	27-36
Goblet	20-27
Pitcher	47-56
Salt/Pepper, pr.	17-27
Spoonholder	22-31
Sugar bowl, covered	34-52

Probably other pieces.

Diamond Point with Panels

Diamond Point with Panels

(Hinoto): Boston and Sandwich Glass Company, 1850s. Clear, flint.

Celery	$125-142
Champagne	77-86
Goblet	94-103
Pitcher (ill.)	152-161
Salt, footed	52-61
Spoonholder	57-67
Sugar bowl	92-104

Diamond Quilted

Maker unknown, c. 1880s. Clear, many colors, nonflint.

Diamond Quilted

Butter dish, covered.	$ 46-52
Creamer	34-38
Goblet	34-42
Pitcher, water	42-52
Sauce, footed (ill.)	14-19
Spoonholder	34-44
Sugar bowl, covered	38-47
Tray, water	35-44
Tumbler	39-44

Canary, 100 percent; light blue, 150 percent; light, dark amethyst, 200 percent higher than clear prices listed. Probably many other pieces. Goblet being reproduced. Also tumbler.

Diamond Rosettes

Diamond Rosettes

Several Pittsburgh factories, 1870s until early 1900s. Clear, sometimes found in colors—yellow, blue, light green; nonflint.

Bowl	$ 19-27
Butter dish, covered.	36-47
Celery holder	25-34
Compote	39-47
Compote, covered	48-53
Creamer	26-36
Goblet	22-29
Pitcher, water	45-52
Spoonholder	19-29
Sugar bowl	
Covered	32-43
Open (ill.)	19-27

Tumbler 19-26

Probably many other pieces. Color, 50 percent higher than clear prices listed.

Diamond Sunburst

(Plain Sunburst): Bryce, Walker & Company, Pittsburgh, c. 1860s. Clear, nonflint.

Butter dish, covered.	$ 42-52
Cake stand	36-47
Celery.	32-41
Compote, covered, high standard . . .	54-63
Creamer.	37-44
Goblet	37-44
Lamp	36-44
Pitcher, milk	37-47
Spoonholder	26-34
Sugar bowl, covered	44-54
Tumbler	27-37
Wine	26-36

Probably other pieces.

Diamond Thumbprint

Diamond Thumbprint

(Diamond and Concave): Sandwich glass; McKee & Bros., 1850s. Clear, green-tinted, amethyst (due to improper mixing of metal), and yellow (rare), flint.

Bowl, waste.	$ 92-107
Butter dish, covered	160-170
Cake stand, 2 sizes	99-118
Celery	134-142
Champagne (rare)	240+
Decanter, original stopper, qt.	112-118
Goblet (rare)	370+
Pitcher, water, rare (ill.)	350+
Spoonholder	72-82
Sugar bowl, 2 styles, covered	134-144
Wine jug, places for holding	
glasses, set	575+

This glass is extremely rare. Goblet being reproduced.

Diapered Flower

Diapered Flower

Probably Westmoreland Glass Company, 1890s. Opaque blue. It was a container for mustard or other condiments. Nonflint.

Creamer (ill.)	$ 42-51
Mustard jar	50-60
Sugar bowl	45-53

Probably other pieces.

Dickinson

Dickinson

Sandwich glass, 1860s. Clear, flint.

Butter dish, covered	$ 55-62
Compote	
Covered	84-92
Open (ill.)	62-70
Creamer.	120-140
Goblet	101-112
Sauce, flat.	29-38
Spoonholder	68-78
Sugar	
Covered	58-64
Open	42-52
Pitcher, water	88-98
Wine	34-44

Possibly other pieces.

Divided Block with Sunburst

Divided Block
with Sunburst

(Variant): U.S. Glass Company, after 1891. Crystal, plain, and with ruby stain, nonflint.

Butter dish, covered.	$ 40-48
Celery vase	18-24
Compote, covered, high or low	
standard.	29-36
Creamer.	27-32
Goblet	19-27
Pitcher, water (ill.)	42-51
Salt/Pepper, pr.	22-31
Spoonholder	24-35
Sugar bowl, covered	39-47
Tumbler	22-31

Probably other pieces.

Divided Hearts

Boston & Sandwich Glass Company, c. early 1860s. Clear, flint.

Butter dish, covered	$152-170
Compote	
Covered.	132-150
Open	127-142
Creamer	121-140
Egg cup	79-89
Goblet	92-103
Lamp, marble base	130-144
Sugar bowl, covered	142-152

Possibly other pieces.

Dog

Possibly Sandwich, c. 1870s. Clear, nonflint.

Compote, covered, low	$ 87-96
Compote, covered, high	100-109

"Dog and Child" Mug

Dog and Child Mug

Indiana Tumbler & Goblet Company (National), Greentown, Indiana, 1902. Chocolate, Nile green, nonflint.

Chocolate.	$230-242
Nile green.	248-271

Rare!

Dog Hunting

Dog Hunting

One of a series of animal designs put out by National Glass Company, Greentown, Indiana, before the plant was destroyed by fire in 1903. Nonflint.

Pitcher, water (ill.)	$222-231
Probably tumber to match	89-93

Dolphin

Dolphin

Sandwich, 1850s; McKee Bros., 1868; Bakewell, Pears & Company, 1868. Clear. Don't confuse it with Greentown's Dolphin covered dish.

Butter dish, covered. $168-172
Compote, high standard. 99-107
Creamer 120-130
Goblet 118-122
Pitcher, water (ill.) 172-182
Spoonholder 91-101
Sugar bowl, covered 118-132
Possibly other pieces.

"Dolphin"

Dolphin

Covered dish, Indiana Tumbler & Gob-

let Company, 1899. Clear, chocolate, blue, nonflint.

Blue $267-288
Chocolate. 194-207
Clear 134-142

Double Beetle Band

Double Beetle Band

(Smocking Bands): Columbia Glass Company, Findlay, Ohio, 1880s. Clear, yellow, amber, blue, nonflint.

Butter dish, covered . . . . $ 37-43
Creamer. 29-41
Goblet 24-34
Pitcher (ill.) 52-61
Sauce, footed, flat 24-32
Spoonholder 22-32
Sugar bowl
   Covered 37-44
   Open 27-37
Probably other pieces. Yellow, 50 percent higher; amber and blue, 100 percent higher than clear prices listed.

Double Dahlia and Lens

Possibly an early Northwood or Fenton pattern of the late 1880s or early 1890s. The background is stippled on each panel, the flowers are stained purple, foliage green, on crystal background. Scrolls at top and over lip are in bright gold, at least in table set and probably other pieces. Nonflint.

(continued)

Double Dahlia and Lens

Butter dish, covered	$ 58-64
Creamer (ill.)	49-57
Spoonholder	38-47
Sugar bowl, covered	57-67

Double Donut

Double Donut

Findlay, Ohio, 1880s. Clear, nonflint.

Butter dish	$ 35-45
Cake stand	32-52
Celery.	24-33
Compote, open, low standard	37-47
Creamer.	26-32
Goblet	25-30
Pitcher (ill.)	42-52
Salt/Pepper, pr.	22-31
Spoonholder	26-32
Sugar bowl	32-40

Probably other pieces.

Double Greek Key

This is Canadian glass, made by the Burlington Glass Works, Hamilton, Ontar-

Double Greek Key

io, 1880s. Clear, stippled, opaque white, blue.

Butter dish, covered	$118-132
Compote, covered	77-85
Creamer.	46-52
Pitcher (ill.)	89-99
Spoonholder	40-50
Sugar bowl, covered	66-74
Tassi (small compote), 6″	57-64
Tumbler	47-54

Probably other pieces. Don't overlook Canadian glass. Most of it is well made and most collectible. Color, 50 percent more than clear prices listed.

Double Ribbon

Double Ribbon

Made by many factories in the 1870s. Frosted and clear, flint.

Butter dish	$ 54-63
Compote	
Covered, high foot	49-58
Open, high foot	43-52
Creamer	32-42

Egg cup	27-36
Goblet	41-51
Pickle dish	19-27
Pitcher (ill.).	49-58
Platter, bread, frosted.	38-47
Sauce, footed, 4½″	12-17
Spoonholder	34-42
Sugar bowl, covered	36-47

Probably other pieces.

Double Spear

Double Spear

Maker unknown, 1880s. Clear, nonflint.

Butter dish, covered.	$ 35-42
Celery	27-35
Compote, covered, high standard . . .	46-54
Creamer	34-42
Dish, oval, deep	18-24
Goblet	25-34
Pickle dish	19-27
Pitcher, water (ill.)	52-62
Sauce	18-22
Spoonholder	27-37
Sugar bowl, covered	34-44

Probably other pieces.

Draped Fan

Doyle and Company, Pittsburgh, c. 1880s. Clear, nonflint. Pattern reissued by U.S. Glass Company in 1890s.

Butter dish, covered.	$ 38-44
Cake stand	39-42
Celery	22-32
Compote	
Covered	34-43
Open	22-31
Creamer	29-39
Goblet	24-32

Pitcher, water.	45-54
Spoonholder	27-37
Sugar bowl, covered	42-52

Many other pieces.

Drapery

Drapery

(Lace): Sandwich, early and later; Doyle & Company, Pittsburgh, 1870. Clear, nonflint.

Butter dish, covered	$ 49-57
Compote, covered	37-42
Creamer, applied handle.	35-43
Dish, oval	18-27
Goblet	27-36
Pitcher (ill.)	49-54
Plate, 6″.	14-18
Saucedish, flat, 4″	18-22
Spoonholder	35-42
Sugar bowl, covered	29-38

Probably other pieces.

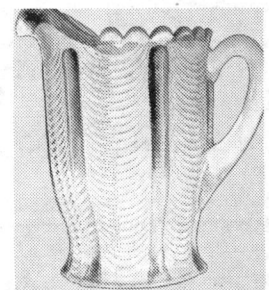

Drapery   Drapery

Northwood & Company, late 1890s.

	Marigold	Vivid	Pastel
Pitcher (ill.) . . .	$110-118	$155-162	$198-200
Rose bowl . . .	52-59	62-69	81-88
Vale, 4″, 5″, 10″ high,			
flared top . . .	34-40	46-52	55-61

Drinking Scene on Mug

Drinking Scene on Mug

Indiana Tumbler & Goblet (National) Company, late 1890s. Nonflint.

Amber $118-131
Blue milk   47-56
Chocolate   77-85
Clear   34-39
Nile green   46-56
White milk   48-58

With lip, regular size, 100 percent higher; large steins, 350 to 400 percent higher.

Drum   Drum

Bryce, Higbee & Company, Pittsburgh, 1880s. Clear and milk glass. Finials are tiny cannon.

Butter dish, covered, cannon
   finial (ill.) . . . . $ 68-77
Creamer (ill.)   66-75
Mustard jar, covered, cannon
   finial   69-78
Spoonholder (ill.)   67-77
Sugar bowl, covered, cannon
   finial (ill.)   75-84

Possibly a few other pieces. Milk glass, 80 percent higher than clear prices listed.

Duncan 2000

(Flowered Scroll): George Duncan's Sons & Company, Washington, Pennsylvania, c. 1893. Clear, sometimes flowered scroll is colored amber, nonflint.

Butter dish, covered . . . . $ 42-48
Creamer   39-46
Pitcher, milk   45-55
Spoonholder   21-31
Sugar bowl, covered   36-47
Tumbler   37-46

Amber flowered scroll, 50 percent higher than clear prices listed. Possibly other pieces.

E Pluribus Unum

E Pluribus Unum

Gillinder & Sons, Philadelphia, Pennsylvania, mid-1800s. Clear, nonflint.

Mug, handled . . . . $ 88-101
Pickle dish   47-57
Platter (ill.)   94-107

Ear of Corn

Ear of Corn

Challinor, Taylor & Company, Tarentum, Pennsylvania, c. 1885. Clear, colored, opal, nonflint.

Butter dish, covered . . . . $ 65-75
Creamer, souvenir-type, green
   "corn" in burnished gold 84-93

Creamer, standard size, clear
   colored, opal.   71-80
Vase, clear-to-opal, 7″ high (ill.)   88-98
Probably other table pieces.

Early Moon and Star

Early Moon and Star

(Star and Punty): Sandwich, 1840s. Clear, canary, probably other colors.

Creamer	$177-185
Lamp, small handle	180-200
Lamp, whale oil	205-220
Lilac water bottle	175-190
Pomade jar	125-135
Spoonholder	85-95
Sugar bowl, open (ill.)	184-193
Tumbler, footed.	90-110
Vase, spill type	160-170

Possibly other pieces. This is an extremely rare pattern.

Early Panelled Grape Band

Early Panelled Grape Band

Maker unknown, 1870s. Clear, nonflint.

Butter dish, covered.	$ 42-52
Celery	28-38
Creamer	38-48
Egg cup.	28-37
Goblet	38-47
Pitcher, water.	52-62
Spoonholder	37-46
Sugar bowl (ill.)	46-52

Probably other pieces.

Effulgent Star

Effulgent Star

(Star Galaxy): Central Glass Company, Wheeling, West Virginia, 1880. Crystal and colored glass.

Butter dish, covered.	$ 58-69
Cake stand	65-73
Celery.	32-41
Creamer.	42-52
Goblet	57-67
Pitcher, water (ill.)	75-85
Spoonholder	32-41
Sugar bowl, covered	54-62
Tumbler	27-36

Probably other pieces.

Egg in Sand

(continued)

Egg in Sand

(Bean): Maker unknown, 1880s. Clear and amber, nonflint.

Butter dish	$ 45-52
Cake stand	47-53
Compote, covered	49-56
Cordial	18-27
Creamer	39-47
Goblet	32-41
Pitcher, water (ill.)	47-56
Salt/Pepper, pr.	49-56
Sauce	17-26
Spoonholder	37-46
Sugar bowl	44-52
Tray, bread	33-42
Tumbler	22-29
Wine	27-35

Probably other pieces. Amber is 60 percent higher than clear prices listed.

Elk Medallion

Elk Medallion

Maker and date unknown. The elk is shown in three different panels; the piece is acid etched.

Goblet (ill.)	$ 45-52

Ellipse

Ellipse

Richards & Hartley Flint Glass Company, Pittsburgh; later, Tarentum, Pennsylvania, 1875-1893. Clear only. Standard pieces made. Only goblet made after 1888.

Butter dish, covered	$ 38-44
Celery	27-33
Creamer	24-32
Goblet (ill.)	21-28
Pitcher, water	57-64
Salt/Pepper, pr.	16-19
Spoonholder	21-29
Sugar bowl, covered	35-42
Tumbler	22-29

Emerald Green Herringbone

Emerald Green Herringbone

(Florida): U.S. Glass Company, 1880s. Clear, emerald green, nonflint.

Bowl, berry, large, deep	$ 32-40
Butter dish	38-42
Celery	27-32
Compote, open, high foot	37-50
Creamer (ill.)	28-37
Goblet	29-42
Pitcher, water	52-61
Plates, square, 7¼", 9¼"	17-27
Salt/Pepper, pr.	34-42
Spoonholder	34-45
Tumbler, water	24-32
Wine	22-30

Probably other pieces. Emerald green, 200 percent higher than clear prices listed. Goblet is being reproduced, especially in green. Probably in clear, amber, and blue. Watch it!

Ellipse

English

Etched Grape

English

Westmoreland Glass Company, 1896. Clear, opal ware, nonflint.

Butter dish . . . . $ 42-50
Celery   32-41
Compote   35-43
Creamer   29-39
Goblet   24-32
Pitcher, water (ill.)   50-59
Salt/Pepper, pr..   28-39
Spoonholder   34-42
Sugar bowl, covered.   34-42
Tumbler   29-35

Probably other pieces. Opal ware is 65 percent higher than clear prices listed.

Esther

(Tooth and Claw): Riverside Glass Company, Wellsburgh, West Virginia, c. 1896. Clear, emerald green, nonflint.

Compote
  Covered . . . . $ 55-64
  Open   42-50
Creamer   94-103
Cruet   52-61
Goblet   39-47
Relish.   18-22
Spoonholder   39-47
Sugar bowl
  Covered   59-64
  Open   37-42
Toothpick holder   54-62

Emerald green, 100 percent higher than clear prices listed. Other pieces.

Etched Grape

U.S. Glass Company, 1900-1905. Clear, emerald green, with and without acid-etch, with vineyard design; nonflint.

Butter dish . . . . $ 36-42
Celery vase   24-35
Creamer.   27-37
Goblet   34-42
Pitcher, water (ill.)   54-63
Tumbler   22-29

Probably other pieces. Emerald green is 50 percent higher than clear prices listed.

Ethol   Ethol

(Cat's Eye and Block; Cut Log): Greensburg Glass Company, Greensburg, Pennsylvania, c. 1885. Clear, nonflint.

Bowls, round, oblong . . . . $ 24-32
Butter dish, covered   47-54
Creamer.   34-42
Goblet (ill.)   32-42
Pitcher, milk   48-57

(continued)

Sugar bowl, covered   42-50
Tumbler   22-28
Wine   26-35

Probably other pieces. Don't confuse this pattern with that made by Westmoreland Specialty Company.

Etruscan

Bakewell, Pears & Company, Pittsburgh, c. 1874. Clear, flint.

Butter dish, covered . . . . $ 77-86
Cake stand   92-103
Compote
  Covered, high standard   115-128
  Covered, low standard   88-98
Creamer   64-74
Egg cup   54-63
Goblet   52-62
Sauce   49-58
Spoonholder   72-81
Sugar bowl, covered   74-83
Tumbler   34-43

Eugenie

McKee & Bros., Pittsburgh, c. 1850s. Clear, flint.

Butter dish, covered . . . . $ 82-91
Celery   79-87
Compote, covered, on standard   109-115
Creamer (rare)   210-228
Egg cup   52-62
goblet   58-68
Spoonholder   77-87
Sugar bowl, covered, dolphin
  finial (rare)   87-96
Tumbler   47-57
Wine   52-62

Probably other pieces.

Excelsior

Sandwich, 1850s; McKee Bros., 1868. C. Ihmsen and Company, 1851; others. Clear.

Ale glass . . . . $ 62-70
Bitters bottle   29-38
Butter dish, covered   110-118
Candlesticks, pr   260-280
Compote
  Covered, low foot   133-142
  Open, high foot   92-103
Creamer, 2 styles   77-84
Decanter, small, pint, quart   47-52

Excelsior

Egg cup, double and single   39-47
Goblet, barrel, Maltese Cross . . . . .
Pitcher
  Milk (rare), Sandwich . . . .   225+
  Syrup   62-70
  Water, rare,
  Sandwich (ill.) . . . .   300+
Spoonholder   82-91
Sugar bowl, 2 styles   98-108
Tumbler, footed, jelly, water   36-55
Whale oil lamp w/Maltese
  Cross, Sandwich   162-180
Wine   47-56

Excelsior Variant

Excelsior Variant

(Excelsior with Double Ringed Stem): Probably McKee & Bros., 1868. Clear, nonflint.

Butter dish	$ 52-62
Celery	
Plain top	40-48
Scalloped top	54-63
Cordial	25-35
Creamer (scarce)	118-127
Goblet	37-47
Spoonholder (ill.)	38-48
Sugar bowl, covered	56-66

Probably other pieces.

Eye-Winker

(Crystal Ball): Maker unknown, c. 1889; possibly made by one of several factories in Findlay, Ohio. This pattern is not "Diamond Point Discs." Clear, nonflint.

Butter dish, covered	$ 82-92
Cake stand	77-83
Compote, open, scalloped edge	86-94
Creamer	45-53
Dish, banana	106-110
Lamp, kerosene	92-107
Pitcher, syrup	62-70
Plate, scalloped edge, 8½″	36-45
Sauce, flat	42-52
Spoonholder	28-37
Sugar bowl	
Covered	59-68
Open	40-47

Butter dish, creamer, lamp, pitcher, sauce, covered sugar bowl, toothpick holder, and tumbler being reproduced.

Faceted Flower

Faceted Flower

Maker unknown, probably Midwest, late 1800s. Clear, nonflint.

Butter dish, covered	$ 43-52
Celery	24-34
Creamer	25-34
Goblet	26-35
Pitcher, water (ill.)	48-54

Spoonholder	24-31
Sugar bowl, covered	69-75
Tray, water	36-42

Probably other pieces.

Fairfax Strawberry

Fairfax Strawberry

(Strawberry): Clear and milk glass, late 1860s, some made at Sandwich. Also made at Bryce, Walker and Company, 1870. Nonflint.

Butter dish	$122-140
Compote, covered, 8″, high, low	152-162
Creamer	121-131
Egg cup	60-70
Goblet	79-88
Honey dish	52-62
Pitcher	
Syrup	90-100
Water	152-162
Sauce	44-53
Spoonholder	72-82
Sugar bowl (ill.)	92-107

Probably other pieces. Prices listed are for milk glass. Clear, 50 percent less. Egg cup, goblet, probably other pieces, being reproduced both in clear and milk glass. Careful!

Falling Leaves

Maker and date unknown. Otherwise ordinary glass, this pattern is unusual because the leaves are embossed on the **inside** of the body. So far, no mold-maker has figured out how it was done. Can anyone tell us? Apparently the usual pieces were made. Nonflint.

Berry bowl (ill.)	$ 37-46
Butter dish, covered	51-60
Creamer	34-42

(continued)

Spoonholder   31-38
Sugar bowl, covered   42-51
Probably other pieces.

Falling Leaves

Fan

Fan

Northwood Glass Company, late 1880s. Blue with opalescent trim; made in Custard glass and Carnival glass. Nonflint.

	Carnival	Colors
Berry set	Custard	Marigold
Large bowl	$118-127	
Small bowl	44-52	37-42
Butter dish, covered .	77-88	
Creamer (ill.)	66-74	
Spoonholder	61-70	
Sugar bowl, covered .	77-87	

Probably other occasional pieces made in Marigold, Vivid, Pastel.

Fan and Star

Challinor, Taylor, Ltd., c. 1880s. Clear, opaque white, decorated with enamelled flowers in different colors, nonflint.

Bowl	$ 16-22
Butter dish, covered	27-35
Celery	22-31

Compote, covered   27-36
Goblet   19-24
Pitcher, water   34-43
Sauce   11-18
Spoonholder   19-27
Sugar bowl, covered   32-42

Opaque white, 100 percent higher than clear prices listed.

Fancy Diamonds

Fancy Diamonds

Maker unknown, late 1880s, early 1890s. Clear, nonflint.

Bowl	$ 19-27
Butter dish, covered	33-38
Creamer	29-38
Goblet	26-34
Pitcher (ill.)	48-56
Spoonholder	22-31
Sugar bowl, covered	34-42
Wine	18-22

Probably other pieces.

Fan with Diamond

Fan with Diamond

Maker unknown, late 1870s. Clear, non-flint.

Butter dish	$ 39-46
Compote	
Covered, high foot	49-56
Covered, low foot	32-37
Cordial	19-27
Creamer, applied handle.	21-29
Dish, oval, 9″ × 6¾″.	19-27
Egg cup	20-30
Goblet (ill.)	24-29
Pickle dish	16-21
Pitcher, water	39-47
Sauce, flat, 4″	18-22
Spoonholder	24-32

Probably other pieces.

Feather

Feather

(Finecut and Feather; Indiana Swirl): McKee Glass Co., 1890s. Clear and green, rare in amber, red, chocolate.

Bowl, 7½″, 8½″	$ 22-29
Butter dish, covered	54-63
Cake stand, 8½″, 11″ (rare)	47-54
Celery vase	22-29
Compote, high standard	54-62
Cordial	68-75
Creamer	32-42
Cruet, original stopper	50-60
Goblet	54-63
Pitcher, water (ill.)	62-70
Plate, 10″.	32-39
Spoonholder	28-35
Sugar bowl, covered	51-60
Toothpick holder	54-62
Tumbler	35-47
Wine	32-46

Probably other pieces. Green, 250 percent; amber, red, chocolate, 400 percent higher than clear prices listed.

Feather Duster

Feather Duster

U.S. Glass Company, 1880s. Clear and emerald green, nonflint.

Bowl, berry	$ 21-27
Butter dish	32-38
Compote, covered, 6″ high	47-56
Creamer	29-37
Egg cup	23-32
Goblet	40-50
Pitcher, water (ill.)	43-52
Spoonholder	27-32
Sugar bowl, covered	39-46
Tumbler	19-27

Probably other pieces. Emerald green, 80 percent higher than clear prices listed.

Feather with Quatrefoil Center

Feather with Quatrefoil Center

Sandwich Glass Company, probably c. 1850s or 1860s. Clear, flint.

Center plate, 9¼″ (ill.)	$164-173

Fern Garland

McKee Glass Company, Jeannette, Pennsylvania, c. 1894. Clear, nonflint. Pieces marked "Pres-Cut."

(continued)

Butter dish, covered.	$ 37-42
Celery	22-31
Compote	
High standard.	35-44
Low standard	22-29
Creamer	27-36
Goblet	28-34
Pitcher	48-58
Spoonholder	22-31
Sugar bowl, covered	29-36
Tray, celery	22-28
Vase, violets	19-27

Probably other pieces.

Fern Sprig

Bellaire Goblet Company, Bellaire, Ohio, and Findlay, Ohio, c. 1800s. Clear; nonflint. Pattern reissued after 1891 by U.S. Glass Company.

Butter dish, covered.	$ 44-53
Creamer.	42-51
Goblet	34-42
Spoonholder	24-34
Sugar bowl, covered	42-51

Should be many more pieces.

Festoon

Festoon

Portland Glass Company, Portland, Maine, 1860s. Nonflint.

Bowl, berry, 9″, 10″, finger	$ 18-27
Butter dish, covered	54-63
Cake plate on stand, 9″, 10″, dia.	44-52
Celery.	29-39
Compote, high foot	28-35
Creamer.	24-32
Pickle jar	50-60
Pitcher, water (ill.)	62-68
Plate, 7″, 8″, 9″	42-50
Spoonholder	30-40

Sugar bowl, covered	62-69
Tumbler	32-42
Wine	25-33

Probably other pieces.

File

File

Columbia Glass Company, Findlay, Ohio, 1890-1907. Clear, nonflint.

Butter dish	$ 34-42
Celery.	19-27
Creamer.	34-42
Goblet	25-34
Lamp, tall.	58-64
Pitcher, (ill.)	54-64
Spoonholder	32-42
Sugar bowl	42-52
Tumbler	24-32

Probably other pieces.

Fine Cut   Fine Cut

Bryce Bros., Pittsburgh, 1870s. U.S. Glass Co., c. 1891. Crystal, blue, amber, yellow. Nonflint.

Bowl, finger, small	$ 23-32
Butter dish, covered	46-54
Compote, covered . . . . ᾽	46-56

Creamer	32-37
Dish, oblong, deep	23-33
Goblet	28-37
Pitcher, water (ill.)	46-54
Plates, 6¼", 7¼", 10¼"	27-37
Saucedish	14-18
Spoonholder	34-38
Sugar bowl, covered	36-38
Toothpick holder.	20-28
Tray, bread, water	42-51

Probably other pieces. Amber, yellow, 35 percent; blue, 70 percent higher than clear prices listed.

Fine Cut and Panel

Creamer	32-41
Goblet	28-36
Pitcher (ill.)	39-47
Salt/Pepper, pr..	27-36
Sauce, flat, square.	12-16
Spoonholder	28-34
Sugar bowl, open	25-32
Tumbler	23-32
Wine	19-26

Probably other pieces. Amber, yellow, 35 percent; blue, 100 percent higher than clear prices listed.

Fine Cut and Block

Fine Cut and Block

King Glass Company, Pittsburgh, 1880s. Clear, amber, sapphire blue, clear with color blocks.

Butter dish, covered.	$ 47-56
Cake stand	
Large	44-52
Small	32-52
Compote, jelly	34-40
Creamer	66-71
Goblet, buttermilk	28-35
Lamp, handled, flat	32-39
Pitcher, water (ill.)	46-56
Spoonholder	34-39
Sugar bowl	48-54
Tumbler	28-36

Probably other pieces. Colors, 60 percent higher; colored blocks, 125 percent higher than clear prices listed.

Fine Cut and Panel

Probably Bryce Bros., Pittsburgh, 1880s; reissued by U.S. Glass Company in early 1890s. Clear and color, nonflint.

Butter dish, covered, square.	$ 45-52
Celery	
Compote, open, high standard.	39-47

Fine Cut and Rib

Fine Cut and Rib

Maker unknown, late 1880s. Clear.

Butter dish, covered.	$ 39-47
Celery vase	24-32
Creamer	34-42
Goblet	22-31
Pitcher, water (ill.)	40-49
Spoonholder	27-32
Sugar bowl, covered	35-47
Tumbler	22-31

Fine Cut Medallion

Fine Cut Medallion

(Austrian):l Indiana Tumbler and Goblet Company, Greentown, Indiana, 1897-1898. Clear, canary, chocolate, green, nonflint.

Banana dish.	$ 55-62
Bowl, berry	32-41
Butter dish	48-56
Compote	
Jelly.	34-42
Open, large	36-41
Creamer.	27-32
Goblet	35-42
Pitcher, water (ill.)	57-62
Punch cup.	14-21
Rectangular bowl	52-61
Rose bowl	
Large	48-56
Small	45-52
Spoonholder	35-42
Tumbler	39-47

The miniatures in chocolate are rare and expensive. Chocolate, 350 to 450 percent higher than clear; other colors are 300 percent higher than clear.

Fishscale

Fishscale

(Coral): Bryce Bros., Pittsburgh, 1880s. Clear, nonflint.

Bowl, 6″, 7″, 8″, open.	$ 19-28

Butter dish	55-62
Cake plate on stand, 9″, 10″, 11″	29-36
Celery vase	34-42
Compote	
Covered, high standard, 6″, 7″, 8″	62-73
Open, high standard, 4″, 7″, 8″, 9″, 10″	33-42
Creamer.	36-44
Goblet	33-42
Pickle dish	25-29
Pitcher, qt. and ½ gal..	48-52
Plate, round, 7″, 8″	26-32
Sauce, flared, footed, 4″	10-16
Spoonholder	29-37
Sugar bowl, covered	46-52
Tumbler	27-34

Probably other pieces.

Flared Top Belted Worchester

Maker unknown, c. 1850s. Clear, flint.

Cordial	$ 34-42
Goblet	27-34
Sugar bowl, covered	42-50
Tumbler	24-27
Whiskey, handled	27-36
Wine	26-32

Possible other pieces.

Flared Top Hairpin

Same prices as Hairpin—see.

Flat Diamond

Flat Diamond

(Diamond): Richards & Hartley Glass Company, Tarentum, Pennsylvania, 1885-1893. Clear only, nonflint.

Butter dish, covered.	$ 58-66
Creamer	45-52
Goblet (ill.)	21-30
Spoonholder	34-42
Sugar bowl, covered	45-52
Tumbler	22-30

Should be other pieces.

Flattened Diamond and Sunburst

Flattened Diamond and Sunburst

Maker unknown, 1800s. Clear, colors, nonflint.

Butter dish, miniature	$ 22-29
Celery	17-26
Creamer, miniature	24-32
Goblet	19-27
Pitcher (ill.).	44-52
Saucedish, 4", 5"	19-27
Spoonholder	24-32
Sugar bowl, covered	35-42

Probably other pieces. Color is 60 percent higher than clear prices listed.

Flattened Sawtooth

George Duncan & Sons, Pittsburgh, c. 1880. Clear, flint.

Bowl
Finger.	$ 43-47
Flat, 10".	73-80
Celery	66-73
Compote, covered.	65-71
Creamer	49-52
Goblet	55-62
Pitcher	96-107

Spoonholder	65-75
Sugar bowl, covered	63-73
Wine	37-46

Probably other pieces.

Fleur-de-Lis and Tassel

U.S. Glass Company, c. 1892. Clear, opal, green with gilt decoration, nonflint.

Bottle, water.	$ 44-52
Butter dish, covered	49-56
Cake stand	54-63
Celery.	27-34
Compote, covered	35-42
Creamer.	34-39
Pitcher, milk	61-72
Pot, mustard	19-27
Spoonholder.	24-32
Sugar bowl, covered	35-42
Tumbler.	26-35
Wine	19-24

Colors, 40 percent higher than clear prices listed.

Flickering Flame

Flickering Flame

Westmoreland Glass Company, 1896. Clear, some stained with ruby color, nonflint.

Creamer (ill.)	$ 37-46
Sugar, covered.	42-51

Possibly others in this pattern.

Floral Oval

(Pittsburgh Daisy): Bryce, Higbee Co., c. 1880s, non-flint.

Celery.	$ 16-24
Plate, 7¼" square	35-44
Pitcher (ill.)	62-71

(continued)

Floral Oval

Spoonholder 24-32
Wine 18-26

Probably usual pieces.

Florida Palm

(Tidal): Greensburg Glass Company, Greensburg, Pennsylvania, c. early 1900s. Clear, nonflint.

Bowls, berry, 7″, 8″, 9″ . . . . $ 19-29
Cake stand 33-42
Celery 24-32
Creamer 32-40
Goblet 27-33
Spoonholder 22-31
Sugar bowl, covered 34-42

Probably other pieces.

Flower and Quill

(Pretty Band): Possibly McKee Bros., 1880s. Clear, nonflint.

Butter dish, covered . . . . $ 44-52
Celery, footed 32-41
Creamer 34-41
Nappy, flange handle, 4″ 19-26
Pickle caster 49-56
Pitcher, water (ill.). 37-46
Plate, large, square 27-36
Spoonholder 35-42
Sugar bowl, covered 37-44

Probably other pieces.

Flower and Quill

Flower Band

Maker unknown, c. 1870s. Clear, nonflint; possibly frosted.

Butter dish, covered . . . . $ 76-84
Celery 43-50
Compote, covered 152-160
Creamer 75-82
Goblet 75-82
Pitcher, milk 86-94
Spoonholder 54-63
Sugar bowl
Open 56-62
Covered 84-93

If it was made in frosted, 40 percent higher than clear prices listed.

Flower Pot

Flower Pot

(Potted Plant): Possibly Adams Glass Company, 1800s. Clear, nonflint.

Butter dish, covered. . . . . $ 62-70

Cake stand, 10½" dia..	57-63
Compote, covered	55-62
Creamer	44-52
Goblet	36-43
Pitcher, milk (ill.)	44-52
Sauce, open, on standard	16-22
Spoonholder	36-42
Sugar bowl, covered	55-61
Tray, bread	49-55
Tumbler	23-29

Flower with Cane

Flower with Cane

Maker unknown, 1895-1905, flower stained pea green with gilt center. Upper part is gilded. Ruby probably also used; flower also in other than green. Nonflint.

Creamer	$ 42-48
Pitcher (ill.)	53-62
Sugar bowl, covered	33-37

Probably other pieces. Colors don't affect prices listed.

Flute

Flute

Many factories made this clear glass, 1850s and 1860s. It went by many names: Bessimer Flute, Sexton Flute, Reed Stem Flute, Sandwich Flute, Duchess Flute. Prices listed are basic prices and not specific to any one pattern. All nonflint.

Ale glass	$ 34-43
Bitters bottle (6 and 8 flute)	42-51
Bowl, scalloped	33-38
Candlesticks, pr. (6 flute,	
no sockets)	44-52
Creamer	29-35
Decanter, quart size	49-54
Goblet	27-34
Lamp, whale oil	69-75
Mug	35-42
Tumbler, half pint, jelly, one	
gill, half gill (toy), each	11-22
Wine	14-20

Many other pieces.

Flute and Cane

Flute and Cane

Maker unknown, late 1870s. Clear, nonflint.

Butter dish	$ 38-46
Celery vase	24-30
Creamer	26-32
Goblet	19-28
Pitcher	
Milk	43-52
Tankard (ill.)	44-52
Spoonholder	22-29
Sugar bowl, covered	26-35
Tumbler	19-28

Probably other pieces.

Fluted Scrolls

Fluted Scrolls

Harry Northwood Glass Co., Indiana, Pennsylvania, c. 1897. Flint, sapphire blue, canary, white opalescent.

Bowl, berry	$ 31-44
Butter dish, covered	64-70
Creamer	55-64
Jewel (or puff) tray	21-29
Pitcher, water (ill.)	62-72
Saucedish	11-15
Spoonholder	22-28
Sugar, covered	54-63

Sapphire blue, 125 percent; vaseline, 200 percent; white, 125 percent higher than flint prices listed.

Flying Birds

Maker unknown, c. 1870. Clear, nonflint.

Goblet . . . . $ 68-73
There should be other pieces.

Flying Swan

Flying Swan

By Westmoreland Specialty Company, Grapeville, Pennsylvania, 1890s. Clear, slag, nonflint.

Butter dish	$ 46-52
Celery	27-31
Creamer	32-38
Pitcher (ill.), slag	129-141
Spoonholder	28-34
Sugar bowl, covered	48-57
Toothpick holder	35-42
Vase	34-40

Probably other pieces. Colors, 75 percent higher than clear prices listed.

Forget-Me-Not-in-Scroll

Forget-Me-Not-in-Scroll

Maker unknown, c. 1870s. Clear, nonflint.

Butter dish, covered	$ 36-41
Creamer	34-39
Goblet (ill.)	29-34
Pitcher	45-54
Spoonholder	24-31
Sugar bowl, covered	37-45

Probably other pieces.

Fostoria's Number 952

Fostoria Glass Company, Fostoria, Ohio, late 1800s. Clear, nonflint.

Pitcher, water	$ 45-52
Tumbler to match	27-37

Probably other pieces, including four-piece table set.

Fostoria's Number 952

Four Petal

Four Petal

Bryce, McKee & Company or McKee & Bros., c. 1850s. Clear, blue, flint.

Compote, open, 6" high	$ 64-69
Creamer	87-96
Sugar bowl, open (ill.)	70-80
covered	84-92

Only known pieces. Should be others. Blue, 50 percent higher than clear prices listed.

The Fox and the Crow

The Fox and the Crow

Indiana Tumbler & Goblet (National) Company, late 1890s. Nonflint.

Pitcher, water, clear (ill.) $155-166
Probably tumbler to match.

Framed Blocks

Framed Blocks

A member of the Block-and-Thumbprint family, c. 1870s. Clear, flint, nonflint.

Goblet	$ 55-64
Wine (ill.)	45-54

Flint, 40 percent higher than clear prices listed. Should be other pieces.

Framed Circles

Framed Circles

Maker unknown, c. 1840s. Clear, flint.

Goblet	$ 48-54
Wine (ill.)	49-53

Probably other pieces.

Framed Ovals

Framed Ovals

Possibly Sandwich, c. 1840s. Clear, gilt, trimmed, flint. Could also be New England Glass Company, same era.

Brandy (or pony ale),
  footed (ill.) . . . . $ 97-106

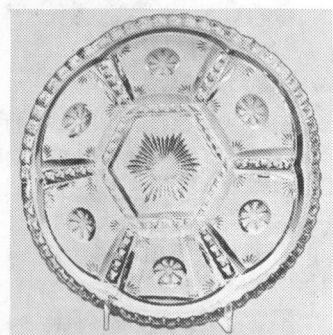

Frost Crystal

Frost Crystal

Tarentum Glass Company, Tarentum, Pennsylvania, 1906. Clear, nonflint

Butter dish	$ 43-52
Celery boat	26-32
Creamer.	25-34
Custard cup	19-27
Plate (ill.)	32-42
Spoonholder	36-45
Sugar bowl, open	44-52

Probably other pieces.

Frosted Block

Indiana Glass Company, Dunkirk, Indiana, 1913. Clear, amber, yellow, blue, green, pink; also, vaseline with opalescent border. This is a "new" glass. It compares to Oatmeal glass. It comes in many pieces. If you like it, buy it.

Frosted Block

Berry bowl	$ 18-26
Butter dish, covered.	33-40
Celery	21-29
Compote, jelly	27-34
Creamer	23-32
Pitcher, water (ill.)	35-42
Salt/Pepper, pr.	23-29
Spoonholder	19-27
Sugar bowl, covered	32-41

Other pieces.

Frosted Circle

Frosted Circle

Bryce Bros., 1870s, U.S. Glass Company, after 1891. Clear, nonflint.

Bowl, covered and open, 7", 8"	$ 39-47
Butter dish, covered.	66-73
Cake stand, 8", 9", 10",	
(10½" with pedestal)	59-66
Celery	35-42
Compote, covered, open, 7", 8".	77-84
Creamer	55-61
Goblet	44-54
Pickle jar	38-47

Pitcher, water (ill.)	79-87
Plates, 4", 5", 7", 9"	23-30
Salt/Pepper, pr..	59-62
Spoonholder	35-42
Sugar bowl	57-67
Tumblers, 2 types.	28-34
Wine	44-53

Probably other pieces. Goblet being reproduced.

Butter dish, covered	$ 44-52
Cake stand (ill.)	52-60
Creamer.	47-56
Goblet	65-72
Sauce, flat, deep, large.	24-32
Sugar bowl, covered	40-50
Syrup jug	57-67

Probably other pieces.

Frosted Fruits

Frosted Fruits

Maker unknown, 1880-1890s. Clear and frosted, nonflint.

Butter dish	$ 64-72
Celery	32-41
Creamer	44-52
Goblet	40-50
Pitcher, water (ill.)	82-90
Sauce.	22-28
Sugar bowl	55-62
Tumbler	42-52

Probably other pieces. Frosted is 40 percent higher than clear prices listed.

Frosted Medallion

Frosted Medallion

(Sunburst Rosette): Maker unknown, late 1880s. Clear, nonflint.

Bowl, oval.	$ 18-27
Butter bowl, covered	36-42
Creamer.	30-38
Compote	
Covered	42-51
Open	23-32
Goblet	27-35
Pitcher, syrup (ill.)	33-42
Spoonholder	24-32
Sugar bowl, covered	32-39
Tumbler	19-27

Probably other pieces.

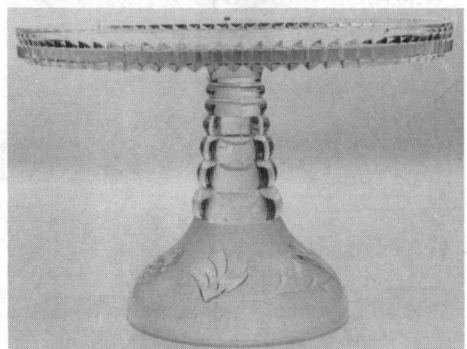

Frosted Magnolia

Frosted Magnolia

(Water Lily): Dalzell, Gilmore & Leighton, West Virginia factory, or Findlay, Ohio, late 1800s. Frosted and clear, nonflint.

Frosted Ribbon

Frosted Ribbon

Bakewell, Pears and Company; also George Duncan and Sons, 1878s. Nonflint.

(continued)

Ale glass.	$ 30-35
Bitters bottle	39-46
Bowl, waste	46-54
Butter dish	47-54
Celery.	44-53
Compote	
Covered, high standard	44-52
Covered, low standard	39-46
Open, Dolphin standard	85-93
Creamer.	41-50
Egg cup	30-38
Goblet	32-39
Pitcher, water, quart, and	
½ gallon.	38-45
Spoonholder	29-36
Sugar bowl	43-52
Tumbler	32-37
Wine	27-33

Probably other pieces. Goblet being reproduced.

Frosted Stork

Frosted Stork

(Flamingo): Crystal Glass Company, Bridgeport, Ohio, 1879. Nonflint.

Bowl, waste	$ 46-54
Butter dish	82-91
Creamer	52-59
Goblet	61-70
Jam jar, covered.	69-74
Pitcher, water (ill.)	120-130
Plate, 9″	49-57
Sauce	22-27
Spoonholder	34-42
Sugar bowl, covered, with finial	45-54
Tray, large, oval.	52-61

Probably other pieces. This is a rare pattern. Being reproduced in most pieces

Fuchsia

Sandwich, early; possibly Hobbs, Brockunier & Company, 1865. Clear, nonflint.

Fuchsia

Butter dish, covered.	$ 53-62
Cake stand	39-49
Celery vase	31-40
Compote, open	48-54
Creamer	37-46
Goblet	37-43
Pitcher (ill.).	57-64
Plate, 8″, 10″	46-52
Spoonholder	39-46
Tumbler	26-35

Possibly other pieces.

Gaelic

Gaelic

Maker and date unknown, possibly 1890-1905 period. Undoubtedly one of the glass companies absorbed by the giant U.S. Glass Company. This water pitcher has a gold band at top and green leaves. Nonflint.

Bowl, oval, 9″.	$ 25-31
Pitcher, water (ill.)	66-75
Punch cup	18-25

Relish dish, 7¼"   15-23
Probably tumbler to match   32-41

Garden of Eden

Garden of Eden

(Lotus): Probably McKee & Bros., 1865. Clear, nonflint.

Butter dish, covered. . . . . $ 82-91
Cake stand   53-62
Creamer   44-53
Goblet, plain, and serpent head   66-73
Mug, handled   54-63
Pickle dish, oval.   23-30
Pitcher (ill.).   52-60
Platter   39-47
Platter, bread   44-52
Sugar bowl, covered   56-63
Tray, bread   39-45

Probably other pieces.

Garfield Drape

Garfield Drape

Adams & Company, Pittsburgh, 1880s. Clear. One of the Garfield Memorial plates was produced by Campbell, Jones & Company, in 1881. Clear, nonflint.

Bowl . . . . $ 28-36
Butter dish, covered.   61-67
Cake plate on stand   67-74
Celery   41-52

Compote, covered, high and
  low standard   99-108
Creamer   45-53
Goblet   34-39
Honey dish   22-28
Pickle dish, oval.   22-26
Pitcher, water, milk   62-71
Plate
  "We Mourn Our Nation's Loss" (ill.).   95-106
  "Memorial," 11"   68-76
Sauce, footed and round.   8-11
Spoonholder   34-42
Sugar bowl, covered   53-62

Probably other pieces.

Garland of Roses

Garland of Roses

Maker unknown, 1880. Clear, vaseline, nonflint.

Butter dish . . . . $ 25-34
Celery.   19-27
Creamer (ill.)   24-32
Egg cup   22-29
Salt, open footed   18-22
Spoonholder   23-32
Sugar bowl, covered   34-42

Probably other pieces. Vaseline, 50 percent higher than clear prices listed.

Garter Band

Maker unknown, c. late 1880s. Clear, nonflint.

Butter dish, covered. . . . . $ 35-43
Celery.   36-44
Goblet   22-28
Sugar bowl, covered   32-39
Wine   22-31

Probably other pieces.

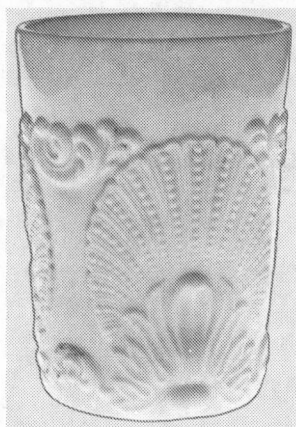
Geneva

Geneva

(Shell and Scroll): Northwood Glass Company, 1900. Clear, custard, with ruby or green decorations; nonflint.

Bowls, 3 scroll feet.	$ 54-62
Butter dish, covered	55-64
Creamer, covered	53-62
Pitcher, syrup	67-74
Salt/Pepper, pr.	63-72
Spoonholder	42-50
Sugar bowl, open, covered	67-75
Tumbler (ill.)	58-67

Probably other pieces. Custard, 150 percent higher than clear prices listed.

Giant Bull's Eye

Giant Bull's Eye

(Excelsior): Belmont Glass Company, Bellaire, Ohio, 1880s. Clear, nonflint.

Butter dish, covered	$ 45-52
Celery.	30-39
Creamer.	36-45
Goblet	32-41
Pitcher, water (ill.)	72-82
Spoonholder	32-39
Sugar bowl, covered	37-44

Probably other pieces. Possibly in color.

Giant Sawtooth

Giant Sawtooth

Maker unknown, 1830. Clear, flint.

Goblet	$ 80-88
Lamp, whale oil (ill.)	215-230
Spill holder	55-63
Tumbler	64-72

Probably other pieces.

Gibson Girl

Kokomo Glass Co., c. early 1900s. Clear, nonflint. Considered rare.

Butter dish	$ 79-89
Creamer	63-72
Pitcher, water (ill.)	252-272
Plate, 10″.	84-92
Spoonholder	57-65
Sugar bowl, covered	85-93
Tumbler	74-83

Possibly other pieces.

Gibson Girl

Gladstone "For the Million"

Girl with Flower

Maker unknown, 1870s. Clear, green, blue, nonflint.

Plate, 6″, blue (ill.) . . . . $ 49-53
Sauce, clear   44-52

Probably other pieces. Colors, 50 percent higher than clear.

Gladstone "For the Million"

This pattern honors William Ewart Gladstone, four times Prime Minister of England (1809-1898).

Bowl, 8½″ dia. . . . . $ 82-94
Creamer (ill.)   255-263
Mug, amethyst   84-93
Plate, aqua   69-78

Of English make, fairly rare, but found on occasion. This is an unusual piece as the words are reversed—backwards. Possibly the only one in the world. Houston Museum.

Girl with Flower

Goat's Head

Hobbs, Brockunier & Company, Wheeling, West Virginia, c. 1878. Clear, nonflint.

Butter dish, covered . . . . $ 57-64
Celery   57-63
Compote, 6″   78-85
Creamer   58-65
Sugar bowl
  Open   45-54
  Covered   55-62

Probably other pieces.

(continued)

Gooseberry

Gothic

Gooseberry

Sandwich glass, 1870s. Others also made it. Clear, opaque, white, nonflint.

Butter dish, covered	$ 47-55
Cake stand, 9½" dia.	48-56
Compote	
Covered, high foot, large	56-64
Covered, high foot, 6"	43-52
Creamer	24-30
Goblet	29-37
Honey dish	19-25
Lemonade glass.	36-44
Pickle dish	16-22
Pitcher, water (ill.)	72-80
Saucedish	19-29
Spoonholder	27-34
Sugar bowl	47-56
Tumbler, applied handle	33-42

Probably other pieces. Opaque white, 65 percent higher than clear prices listed. Being reproduced in opaque white.

Gothic

McKee & Bros., 1850s. Clear, flint.

Butter dish.	$ 69-77
Cake stand	65-74
Caster bottle, each	23-29
Champagne (rare)	88-98
Compote	
Covered, on standard	57-66
Open, footed	37-44
Cordial.	32-40

Creamer (ill.)	25-34
Egg cup	18-27
Goblets, 2 styles	28-39
Pitcher	69-78
Plate (rare)	37-45
Sauce	12-16
Spoonholder	28-37
Sugar bowl, covered	49-54
Tumbler	34-43
Wine (rare)	52-61

Probably other pieces.

Gothic Arch and Panels

Gothic Arch and Panels

Maker and date unknown. Clear, flint.

Butter dish, covered.	$ 64-72
Jar, horseradish	45-52
Paperweight	46-52
Sauce, footed	34-39
Spoonholder	46-54
Sugar bowl (base ill.)	66-75

Should be other pieces.

Grace

Grace

(Japanese): Richards & Hartley Flint Glass Company, Pittsburgh, 1870s. Pattern was discontinued prior to the company's removal to Tarentum in 1884. Scene is different on each individual table piece, though top and bottom horizontal borders are the same.

Butter dish, covered.	$ 54-63
Compote	37-44
Creamer	37-46
Goblet	37-44
Spoonholder	38-47
Sugar bowl, covered	58-64

Possibly other pieces.

Grand

Grape and Festoon

Grand

(New Grand): Bryce, Higbee & Company, 1885. Clear, nonflint.

Butter dish, covered, flat	$ 39-46
Cake stand, 8″, 10″	32-44
Celery vase (ill.)	25-29
Compote	44-52
Creamer.	28-37
Goblet	24-32
Pitcher, water	39-46
Sauce	9-13
Spoonholder	21-28
Sugar bowl, covered	31-41
Tumbler	45-52
Wine	19-27

Probably other pieces.

Grape and Festoon

Sandwich, early; they probably produced the clear leaf. Doyle & Company, Pittsburgh, 1870s, stippled leaf; probably other factories. Nonflint.

Butter dish	$ 77-85
Celery.	57-64
Compote, covered, high and low standard.	64-72
Cordial	36-44
Creamer, 2 styles	54-62
Egg cup, 2 styles.	24-33
Goblet, 2 styles	47-56
Pickle dish, oval.	24-32
Pitcher, water (ill.)	66-74
Plate, 6″.	34-43
Saucedish, flat, 4″	22-35
Spoonholder	37-46
Sugar bowl, acorn knob	64-73
Wine	25-35

Probably other pieces.

Grape and Festoon with Shield

Possibly produced by Doyle & Company, 1860s. Clear, blue, other colors, nonflint.

Butter dish	$ 37-42
Celery.	19-26
Compote, covered, high and low standard.	55-64
Creamer.	34-42

519

(continued)

Grape and Festoon with Shield

Egg cup	24-29
Goblet	27-34
Mug, blue	20-21
Pitcher, water (ill.)	56-64
Saucedish, flat, 4″, 6″	19-25
Spoonholder	29-38
Sugar bowl	42-51

Probably other pieces.

Grape Band

Grape Band

Bryce, Walker & Company, Pittsburgh, c. 1869. Clear, nonflint.

Butter dish, covered.	$ 56-64
Compote	46-55
Creamer	29-36
Goblet (ill.)	27-36
Pitcher, water.	59-66

Spoonholder	28-37
Sugar bowl, covered	39-47
Wine	29-38

Made in flint at an earlier date, late 1850s. 50 percent higher than nonflint prices listed.

Grape Bunch

Grape Bunch

Sandwich, c. 1870s. Clear, nonflint.

Butter dish, covered.	$ 45-52
Compote	38-46
Creamer	35-43
Egg cup (ill.)	34-42
Goblet	34-42
Pitcher, water.	42-52
Spoonholder	34-43
Sugar bowl, covered	35-42

Probably other pieces.

Grape Jug

This is one of the late fruit patterns, made in the late 1890s and early 1900s and should not be considered as Early American glass. Nevertheless, it's collectible today. Clear.

Grape jug (ill.)	$ 37-45

Brings higher price because collectors buy it as a pitcher.

Grape Jug

Grape with Thumbprint

Grape with Thumbprint

Maker unknown, 1890s. Clear, nonflint.

Berry dish, covered	$ 42-51
Butter dish	44-47
Celery vase	29-34
Creamer.	34-42
Goblet	44-52
Pitcher, water (ill.)	48-54
Spoonholder	29-36
Sugar bowl, covered	39-44
Syrup jug, several sizes	35-43
Toothpick holder	22-29
Tumbler	24-34

Probably other pieces.

Grape with Overlapping Foliage

Grape with Overlapping Foliage

Probably Sandwich, early. Later, other factories in Pittsburgh area, 1880s. Clear and milk-white.

Butter dish	$ 42-48
Celery vase	34-42
Creamer	39-46
Goblet	36-42
Pitcher	44-53
Spoonholder	35-43
Sugar bowl	39-47

Probably other pieces. Milk-white, 50 percent higher than clear prices listed.

Grape with Vine

Grape with Vine

Maker unknown, 1890s. Original pieces, red paint and gilt. Nonflint.

Butter dish	$ 36-44
Celery.	24-31
Creamer.	29-38
Goblet	35-43

(continued)

Honey dish	23-30
Pitcher, water (ill.)	36-42
Spoonholder	25-33
Sugar bowl	34-42

Probably other pieces.

Grasshopper with Insect

Grasshopper with Insect

(Locust: Long Spear): Possibly Belmont Glass Works, Bellaire, Ohio, early 1880s. Clear and amber.

Butter dish	$ 66-74
Celery vase (ill.)	43-49
Compote, covered	74-82
Creamer	44-52
Goblet	77-84
Pickle dish, oval	27-34
Pitcher, water · · · · · · · · · ·	77-86
Sauce	19-28
Spoonholder	35-42
Sugar bowl, covered	55-65

Probably other pieces. Goblet being reproduced. Amber, 90 percent higher than clear prices listed.

Grasshopper, with or without Insect

When grasshopper is present, he's climbing up side, directly above floral motif. With insect, 100 percent higher in price. Clear. Nonflint.

Bowl, covered	$ 34-42
Butter, covered	42-50
Compote, covered	57-64
Pitcher (ill.)	52-60
Plate, large	24-29
Sauce, flat	12-17
Spoonholder	24-30
Sugar, covered	38-43

Probably other pieces. Goblet being reproduced.

Grasshopper, with or without Insect

Greensburg's 130

Greensburg's 130

Greensburg Glass Company, Greensburg, Pennsylvania, late 1880s. Plain and engraved crystal. Nonflint.

Butter dish	$ 39-45
Celery dish	24-32
Creamer	33-37
Goblet	31-40
Honey dish	26-29
Pitcher, water, milk (ill.)	44-53
Sauce	20-28
Spoonholder	24-32
Sugar bowl, covered	41-50

Other pieces. Engraved crystal, 25 percent higher than plain prices listed.

Gridley Pitcher

A. J. Beatty & Sons, Dunkirk, Indiana, 1898. Clear.

Gridley pitcher	$ 165+

Highly collectible today.

Gridley Pitcher

(Wm.) Haley's Glass Basket

Hairpin

(Sandwich Loop): Sandwich, c. 1850s. Clear, milk glass, flint.

Celery	$ 60-68
Champagne	55-64
Compote, covered, low standard	84-93
Egg cup	23-30
Goblet	39-46
Pitcher	134-144
Spoonholder	40-50
Sugar bowl	
Open	39-46
Covered	64-73
Tumbler	42-50

Milk glass, 100 percent higher than clear prices listed.

Hairpin with Rayed Base

Same prices as Hairpin—see.

Wm. Haley's Glass Basket

Two dates appear in the bottom: July 21, 1874, and April 5, 1881. Where it was made is not known.

Basket . . . . $ 84-92

Hamilton

Hamilton

Sandwich, early 1860s. Clear, flint.

Butter dish, covered	$ 82-92
Caster set, in standard	
Celery	39-45
Compote, covered	82-90
Creamer, applied or pressed	
handle	80-88
Decanter, w/stopper	70-80
Egg cup	22-30
Goblet	39-47
Pitcher	
Syrup, metal top	70-77
Water	133-142
Saucedish, 4", 5"	
Spoonholder, 2 styles	38-49
Sugar bowl, covered (ill.)	82-91

(continued)

Tumbler, whiskey 101-109
Wine 82-92
Probably other pieces.

Hamilton with Leaf

Hamilton with Leaf

Sandwich, 1870s. Clear and frosted. Other factories, 1890s on. Sandwich prices shown.

Butter dish	$ 82-92
Celery vase	39-45
Compote, open, high and	
low standard	67-74
Cordial	
Creamer	80-88
Egg cup	22-30
Goblet	39-47
Lamp, 2 sizes	72-90
Pitcher (ill.)	133-142
Salt, footed	26-34
Spoonholder	38-43
Sugar bowl, covered	82-91
Tumbler, water	70-79
Wine	82-92

Possibly other pieces.

Hand

(Pennsylvania): O'Hara Glass Company, Ltd., 1880. Clear.

Bowl, 7″, 8″, 9″, 10″	$ 18-36
Butter dish, covered	92-103
Cake plate on stand, 10″	42-52
Celery vase	51-60
Compote	
Covered, high foot	97-108
Open	53-62

Hand

Creamer	45-52
Goblet	72-82
Honey dish	18-25
Jam jar	56-62
Pickle dish	21-27
Pitcher, water (ill.)	57-64
Platter, 8″ × 10½″	35-43
Saucedish, flat, 4″	15-24
Spoonholder	30-37
Sugar bowl, covered	54-63

Probably other pieces.

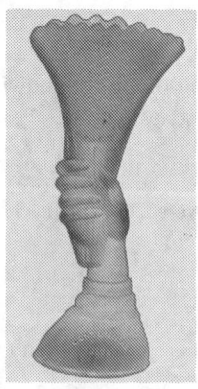

Hand vase

Hand vase

Gillinder and Sons, Philadelphia, for Centennial, 1876. Clear and frosted.

Hand vase (ill.)	$118-129

Highly collectible by "Hand" collectors.

Hanging Basket

Possibly Mosaic Glass Company, Fostoria, Ohio, 1890s. Clear, colors, nonflint.

Butter dish	$ 66-74

Hanging Basket

Compote	56-65
Creamer	45-52
Goblet	32-40
Pitcher (ill.)	125-135
Spoonholder	47-56
Sugar bowl, covered	68-73
Tumber	42-52

Colors, 50 percent higher than clear prices listed.

Hanover

(Block with Stars): Richards & Hartley Glass Company, Tarentum, Pennsylvania, c. 1888. Clear, nonflint.

Butter dish, covered	$ 45-54
Cake stand	37-47
Celery	40-47
Compote	
Open	34-42
Covered	44-52
Creamer	29-38
Goblet	29-36
Pitcher, water	46-54
Spoonholder	22-29
Sugar bowl, covered	42-52
Tumbler	24-32
Wine	18-25

Probably other pieces.

Harp

Bryce Bros., Pittsburgh, 1840s or 1850s. Clear, green, other colors.

Butter dish, two sizes	$140-145
Compote, covered, low standard	194-208
Dish, covered, low foot	
Goblet (rare)	
Flared sides	410+

Harp

Straight sides	280+
Lamps, whale oil	
Handled, double wick	
with snuffers	182-192
Larger, on glass standard	150-160
Saucedish	58-68
Spill holder (ill.)	72-82
Spoonholder	77-86

Possibly other pieces.

Hartford

Hartford

Fostoria Glass Company, 1900s. Clear, yellow, amber, possibly green, nonflint.

Bowl, 4½″, 5½″, 6″, 7″, 8″, 9″	$ 34-46
Butter dish, covered	47-56
Celery vase	38-46
Creamer (ill.)	37-46
Salt/Pepper, pr.	35-43
Sauce, 4½″	28-36
Spoonholder	32-42
Sugar bowl, covered, footed, plain base	47-56
Syrup jug	34-43
Tumbler	29-39

Possibly other pieces.

Harvard Harvard

(Quixote): Tarentum Glass Company, Tarentum, Pennsylvania, 1898-1912. Clear, custard, emerald green, pea green, ruby-stained, nonflint.

Bowl, finger	$ 19-26
Butter dish, covered	42-50
Compote	33-42
Cup, punch	18-27
Goblet	29-36
Pitcher, water	63-72
Plate, 10½″	24-34
Sugar bowl, covered	42-51
Wine (ill.)	22-27

Many other pieces. Colors, 100 percent higher than clear prices listed.

Heart   **Heart and Thumbprint**

Heart

Sandwich, very early. Clear. One of many Sandwich pieces at the Houston Museum, Chattanooga. It's shown here because it's pressed glass and still around.

Heart and Thumbprint

(Columbia): Sandwich, early; Tarentum Glass Company, 1889-1912. Crystal, sometimes gold rims. Natural and green custard.

Bowl, berry, 9″	$ 35-43
Butter dish, covered	56-64
Celery vase	45-52
Creamer, individual, regular	38-46
Cruet with stopper	66-74
Goblet	54-62
Pitcher	56-64
Salt, master (ill.)	33-42
Sauce	11-14
Spoonholder	36-45
Sugar bowl	
Covered	45-54
Individual	30-37
Tumbler	35-43
Vases, 10″, pr.	83-92
Wine	45-54

Probably other pieces. Prices are for Tarentum.

Heart and Waffle

Heart and Waffle

Probably Sandwich, mid-1850. Clear.

Lamp	$221-240

Heart Band

Heart Band

McKee Glass Company, 1897. Crystal glass with ruby stain, nonflint.

Butter dish, covered	$ 51-60
Celery.	32-40
Compote	45-54
Creamer.	34-42
Goblet	37-47
Pitcher, water (ill.)	66-75
Spoonholder	38-46
Sugar bowl, covered	47-55
Tumbler	33-42

Probably other pieces.

Heart Stem

Heart Stem

Maker unknown, late 1880s or 1890s. Clear.

Butter dish	$ 55-62
Celery	38-45
Compote, covered, 7″ high	57-65
Creamer (ill.)	32-41
Goblet	38-45
Pitcher	54-62
Spoonholder	37-46
Sugar bowl	52-60
Tumbler	32-41

Probably other pieces.

Heavy Drape

Fostoria Glass Company, 1904. Clear, nonflint.

Bowl, berry, flat and footed	$ 25-32
Butter dish, covered.	39-47
Celery	32-41
Compote, covered and open	42-51
Creamer	27-36
Egg cup	24-33

Heavy Drape

Goblet	36-45
Pitcher, milk, water (ill.)	67-74
Salt/Pepper, pr..	36-45
Spoonholder	34-42
Sugar bowl, covered	39-47
Tumbler	37-46
Wine	28-35

Probably other pieces as there were some 50 pieces comprising the set.

Heavy Gothic

Heavy Gothic

U.S. Glass Company, 1892. Clear, clear stained with ruby, nonflint.

Butter dish.	$ 90-110
Compote.	62-72
Creamer	75-85
Egg cup	29-37
Goblet	42-52
Pitcher (ill.)	98-115
Spoonholder	42-52
Sugar bowl, two types	49-60
Tumbler	47-56
Wine.	38-47

Probably other pieces. Ruby stained has no effect on prices listed.

Heavy Jewel

Heavy Jewel

Fostoria Glass Company, 1900s. Clear, nonflint.

Butter dish . . . . $ 34-42
Celery 30-40
Compote, covered and open 42-52
Creamer 35-44
Goblet 30-38
Pitcher (ill.). 38-46
Spoonholder 32-42
Sugar bowl
   Covered 39-47
   Open 26-34
Tumbler 28-36

Henrietta

Henrietta

(Big Block): Adams and Company, 1874. Also Columbia Glass Company, 1889. Clear, blocks flashed in red, nonflint.

Bowl, berry . . . . $ 19-27
Butter dish 28-36

Celery. 23-30
Compote 34-40
Creamer. 34-43
Goblet 30-37
Pitcher, water (ill.) 44-52
Spoonholder 33-42
Sugar bowl, covered 35-42
Tumbler 27-37

Probably other pieces. Red flashing, 60 percent higher than clear prices listed.

Heron

Heron

Another of the animal (and bird) series put out by Indiana Tumbler & Goblet (National) Company, late 1890s. Clear and chocolate.

Pitcher, water
   Chocolate $274-283
   Clear (ill.) 155-172
Probably tumblers to match.

Herringbone

Herringbone

Indiana Tumbler & Goblet (National) Company, late 1890s. Nonflint.

	Amber	Green	Clear
Butter dish,			
covered . . .		$105-115	$58-67
Cake stand . .		74-83	57-67
Cordial	$94-106	78-88	46-56
Creamer. . . .		98-110	38-48
Pitcher . . .		109-119	66-76
Salt/Pepper			
pr..		64-73	45-54
Spoonholder .		54-63	49-59
Sugar bowl . .		65-75	48-55
Wine	88-98	66-75	44-53
			Chocolate
Mug (ill.), chocolate			84-93

Probably other pieces.

Herringbone

Herringbone

(Florida): U.S. Glass Company, 1890s. Clear and colors, nonflint.

Berry set, 5 pc., all	$ 45-54
Bowl, 7½", 9" dia..	15-24
Butter dish	45-54
Compote	46-53
Creamer	28-37
Goblet (ill.)	34-42
Pickle dish	24-32
Pitcher, water.	34-42
Salt/Pepper, pr..	31-40
Sauce	16-21
Spoonholder	28-37
Sugar bowl, covered	34-43

Probably other pieces. Color, 50 percent more than clear prices listed.

Hexagonal Bull's Eye

Hexagonal Bull's Eye

Maker unknown, early 1890s. Clear, nonflint.

Butter dish, covered.	$ 56-62
Celery vase	39-47
Creamer	36-47
Pitcher (ill.).	67-72
Sauce	25-32
Spoonholder	37-46
Sugar	
Covered	52-60
Open	35-43
Tumbler	38-47
Wine	34-42

Probably other pieces.

Hidalgo

Hidalgo

(Frosted Waffle): Adams & Company, Pittsburgh, 1880. Crystal, plain and engraved; also frosted.

Bowl, large, small	$ 32-38
Butter dish	54-63
Celery	37-46
Compote, covered, open, high	
or low standard	38-47
Cup and saucer	19-27
Goblet	24-32
Pitcher, milk (ill.)	42-51

(continued)

Salt/Pepper, pr............... 20-25
Sauce, flat and footed......... 12-17
Spoonholder............... 29-38
Sugar bowl, covered.......... 44-52
Tumbler............... 35-44

Probably other pieces. Frosted, 15 percent higher than clear prices listed.

Hobbs Diamond and Sunburst

Hobbs Diamond and Sunburst

Hobbs, Brockunier & Company, 1880s. Clear, nonflint.

Butter dish, covered.......... $ 38-45
Cake stand.............. 34-40
Compote
Covered............... 42-48
Open................. 32-41
Creamer, applied handle....... 38-47
Egg cup............... 24-32
Goblet................ 29-37
Pitcher (ill.).............. 56-64
Sauce, flat............... 19-28
Spoonholder............. 29-37
Sugar bowl, covered.......... 47-55
Tumbler............... 32-42

Probably other pieces.

Hobnail

Hobnail

So many companies made a Hobnail pattern, including New Brighton Glass Company, A. J. Beatty Company, McKee & Bros., Gillinder Bros., and others. It came in clear and colors and is heavily reproduced today in about every color.

Some of the **many** pieces made were berry bowls, perfume bottles, creamers, celerys, cordials, bone dishes, mugs, pitchers, salts (ill.), glass shades, spoonholders, sugar bowls, toothpick holders, trays, tumblers, vases, wines.

Hobnail Band

Hobnail Band

One of the Hobnail group, around 1890. Clear, nonflint.

Butter dish.............. $ 46-54
Creamer................ 29-36
Goblet................ 24-34
Pitcher, water (ill.).......... 36-45
Spoonholder............. 25-34
Sugar bowl.............. 34-43
Tumbler, water........... 13-20

Many other pieces.

Hobnail in Big Diamonds

Challinor, Taylor & Company, 1888. Clear.

Butter dish, covered.......... $ 46-54
Creamer................ 34-39
Pitcher (ill.).............. 55-64

Hobnail in Big Diamonds

Spoonholder	35-44
Sugar	
Covered	44-52
Open	33-42

Probably other pieces. Hobnail in Diamond same, except hobs are confined inside bars and do not cover the pieces.

Holly

Holly

Sandwich glass, late 1860s, early 1870s. Clear, nonflint. Others made this pattern in custard.

Butter dish	$132-141
Cake stand, 11″	92-101
Compote, covered, high or	
low standard	118-142
Creamer, applied handle	61-70
Egg cup	42-51
Goblet (rare) (ill.)	88-96
Pitcher, water	112-121
Sauce	24-32
Spoonholder	37-46
Sugar bowl	79-88

Tumbler, footed	98-107
Wine	52-61

Probably other pieces.

Holly Amber

Holly Amber

(Golden Agate): Indiana Tumbler & Goblet (National) Company, January to June, 1903, only. Holly amber and clear.

Butter dish (ill.)	$1,600+
Candy dish, covered	690+
Compote	
Covered, large	975+
Covered, small	950+
Cruet	1,600+
Parfait	675+
Pitcher, water	2,600+
Salt/Pepper, pr.	1,100+
Spoonholder	750+
Sugar bowl	700+
Tumbler	675+

Other pieces made. Clear, 20 to 50 percent of the amber prices listed. Butter dish, covered compote, jelly compote, creamer, cruet, 7½″ plate, toothpick, and tumbler being reproduced. A **highly overrated** glass.

Holly Band

531

(continued)

Holly Band

Maker unknown, 1870s. Clear, nonflint.

Butter dish	$ 44-53
Celery (ill.)	29-38
Compote	35-44
Creamer	31-41
Pitcher, applied handle	68-77
Spoonholder	29-37
Sugar bowl	39-44
Tumbler	27-36

Probably other pieces.

Home

Home

Pioneer Glass Company, Pittsburgh, late 1880s; later reproduced by McKee Bros. in 1894. Clear, upper and lower bands sometimes decorated in ruby color; nonflint.

Butter dish, covered	$ 48-56
Celery.	33-42
Creamer.	31-40
Goblet	27-32
Pitcher, water (ill.)	50-60
Spoonholder	34-43
Sugar bowl covered	40-50
Tumbler	23-30

Probably other pieces. Ruby color has little or no effect on clear prices listed.

Honeycomb with Flower Rim

Honeycomb with Flower Rim

(Inverted Thumbprint with Daisy Band): Greentown, Indiana, around 1903. Clear, blue, green, custard; nonflint.

Butter, covered	$ 40-47
Celery.	24-36
Compote	
Covered	48-54
Open	34-42
Creamer.	33-42
Pitcher (ill.)	51-60
Sauce, footed	17-26
Sugar bowl	
Covered	46-54
Open	37-46
Tumbler	28-34

Other pieces. Blue and custard, 90 percent; amber, 65 percent; others, 20 percent higher than clear prices listed.

Horn of Plenty

Horn of Plenty

Sandwich glass, early 1830s; Bryce, McKee, Pittsburgh, 1868, nonflint. Prices are for Sandwich. Opalescent white, canary, clear, flint.

Butter dish	
Conventional knob,	
6″ dia.	$133-142
Washington's head (rare)	450+
Celery.	172-182
Compote	
Covered, oblong, on	
standard.	172-180
Open, low standard	115-124
Oval, on standard	325+
Creamer, large.	187-195
Decanter, pint, quart, ½ gallon	110-135

Egg cup	47-56
Goblet	79-86
Lamp, all glass	172-182
Mug, applied handle, 3″ (rare)	162-172
Pitcher, water (ill.)	340-362
Spoonholder	47-56
Sugar bowl, 2 types	122-138
Tumbler, whiskey	58-64
Wine (rare)	135-142

Probably other pieces. Canary, amber, blue, 85 percent higher than clear prices listed. Amber goblet and water tumbler being reproduced. Also, glass lamp.

Horsehead's Medallion

Horsehead's Medallion

Portland Glass Company, Portland, 1870s. Clear; rare in milk-white, nonflint.

Celery	$ 89-97
Compote	
Covered	136-145
Open	118-127
Creamer	99-108
Spoonholder	59-69
Sugar bowl	
Covered	84-94
Open (ill.)	84-93

Probably other pieces. Milk-white, 100 percent higher than clear prices listed.

Horseshoe Stem

Maker unknown, 1880s. Clear, nonflint.

Cake stand	$ 66-75
Compote	
Covered	77-86

Horseshoe Stem

Open	72-80
Creamer	52-62
Goblet	58-68
Pitcher (ill.)	127-140
Sauce	38-47
Sugar	
Covered	67-75
Open	46-55
Tumbler	47-55

Probably other pieces.

Hour Glass

Maker unknown, c. 1880s. Clear, yellow, amber, blue; nonflint.

Butter dish, covered	$ 45-54
Creamer	39-48
Dish, sauce, large	34-43
Goblet	37-46
Pitcher, water	42-52
Spoonholder	37-45
Sugar bowl, covered	32-42

Yellow, 65 percent; amber, blue, 100 percent higher than clear prices listed.

Huber

Huber

Several firms made this pattern—Sandwich, New England Glass Company, Bakewell, Pears & Company, probably others, 1860s and earlier. Clear, flint. Sandwich prices listed.

(continued)

Bitters bottle	$ 47-56
Bowl, covered, 6″, 7″.	39-47
Butter dish	64-72
Celery (ill.)	48-62
Compote, covered, high and low standard, 7″, 10″. . .	79-88
Creamer, scalloped rim	57-66
Decanter	
Bar lip, pint, quart.	48-58
With stopper, pint, quart	62-72
Egg cup, handled	45-55
Goblet, hotel, large, small	32-46
Jug, quart, 3 pints	35-45
Mug, beer, pony beer	35-48
Pitcher, water, 2 styles.	66-75
Plate, 6″, 7″	22-31
Salt, celery dip, footed.	12-20
Spoonholder	28-37
Sugar bowl, covered	56-66
Tumbler, gill, ½ pt., large and small, taper bar	23-32
Wine	24-33

Hummingbird

Hummingbird

(Flying Robin): Maker unknown, late 1880s. Clear, canary, amber, blue; nonflint.

Butter dish, covered.	$ 49-56
Celery.	48-57
Creamer, footed	36-44
Goblet	34-42
Pickle dish	13-20
Pitcher, milk, water, 8″ high (ill.)	48-57
Sauce, flat.	13-19
Spoonholder	34-42
Sugar bowl, covered	45-53
Tray, water	58-67
Tumbler	32-42

Canary, 25 percent; amber and blue, 50 percent higher than clear prices listed.

Hundred Leaved Rose

Hundred Leaved Rose

Possibly Model Flint Glass Company, Findlay, Ohio, 1890s. Clear, frosted, stippled; nonflint.

Bowl	$ 25-35
Butter dish, covered.	46-54
Creamer.	46-54
Pitcher (ill.)	50-60
Sauce, flat.	22-29
Spoonholder	35-42
Sugar bowl	
Covered	58-67
Open	35-54

Probably others. Frosted and stippled, 40 percent higher than clear prices listed.

Imperial

Imperial Glass Company, Bellaire, Ohio, c. 1901. Clear, nonflint.

Butter dish, covered.	$ 48-56
Cake stand	41-51
Celery tray	25-35
Compote	36-45
Creamer	47-56
Goblet	37-47
Pitcher, milk, water	52-62
Salt/Pepper, pr..	33-42
Spoonholder	37-42
Sugar bowl, covered	46-54
Tumbler	46-54
Wine	37-46

Probably other pieces.

In Remembrance Platter

A memorial platter issued after Garfield's assassination in 1881. Garfield shares a place with Lincoln and Washing-

In Remembrance Platter

ton. Clear only, nonflint.

Platter (ill.) $165-174

Intaglio
Intaglio

Northwood Glass Company, 1890. Clear, custard, opalescent, blue, deep green, non-flint.

Berry set	Colors	Custard/ Opalescent
Large bowl	$ 77-86	$141-147
Small bowl	41-50	68-78
Butter, covered . . .	77-86	190-220
Compote, jelly . . .	63-72	160-170
Cruet	81-88	152-162
Sugar, covered	83-93	132-141
Creamer	69-78	92-108
Pitcher (ill.).	82-92	250-262
Spoonholder	73-84	87-89
Pitcher, water.	107-117	182-192
Salt/Pepper, pr.. . . .		184-192
Tumbler, water	48-57	101-108

Interlocked Hearts

Interlocked Hearts

Possibly Northwood Glass Company, Indiana, Pennsylvania, late 1890s, early 1900s. Nonflint.

Creamer	$ 38-46
Goblet	33-42
Pitcher, water (ill.)	48-58
Tumbler	22-32
Wine	30-40

Probably other pieces.

Interlocking Crescents

(Double Arch): The King Glass Company, Pittsburgh, c. late 1880s. Clear, non-flint.

Butter dish, covered	$ 42-52
Creamer.	40-50
Goblet	38-47
Spoonholder	26-34
Sugar bowl, covered	42-51

Only known pieces.

Iron Kettle

Adams & Company, 1874; Challinor Taylor & Company, 1885. Clear, colors, nonflint.

Butter dish, covered	$ 49-58
Creamer (ill.)	34-42

(continued)

Iron Kettle

Spoonholder	37-47
Sugar bowl, covered	56-64

Probably other pieces. Colors, 60 percent higher than clear prices listed.

Ivorina Verde

Ivorina Verde

A. H. Heisey Company, Newark, Ohio, 1899. Opaque white with green trim (custard), nonflint.

Bowls	$ 99-115
Butter dish, covered	120-130
Celery	77-87
Creamer	95-106
Cruet	77-86
Pitcher, water	140-150
Spoonholder	61-70
Sugar bowl, covered (ill.)	110-122

Probably other pieces.

Ivy-in-Snow

(Forest Ware): Cooperative Flint Glass Company, Beaver Falls, Pennsylvania, late 1880s. Clear, foliage stained red, gold leaf.

Butter dish, flat	$ 68-78
Cake stand, square	50-60
Celery	60-70

Ivy-in-Snow

Compote, covered, small, medium, large, high standard	74-82
Creamer	45-55
Cup and saucer	28-34
Goblet	34-43
Jam jar	31-40
Pitcher, water (ill.)	67-77
Sauce, flat, round, 4", 6"	24-34
Spoonholder	27-36
Sugar bowl	58-66
Tumbler	47-57
Wine	34-42

Probably other pieces. Butter dish, cake stand, celery, creamer, goblet, pitcher, sugar bowl being reproduced.

Jacob's Coat

Jacob's Coat

Maker unknown, 1800s. Clear, amber, nonflint.

Bowl, berry	$ 24-32
Butter dish, covered	39-47
Celery	28-37
Creamer	26-34
Goblet	34-42
Pickle dish	19-24
Pitcher (ill.)	51-60
Saucedish	10-15
Spoonholder	23-29
Sugar bowl, covered	36-45

Probably other pieces. Amber, 50 percent higher than clear prices listed.

Jacob's Ladder

Jacob's Ladder

(Maltese): Bryce Bros., Pittsburgh, 1870s. Clear, amber, yellow; colors scarce; nonflint. Cheap version reissued in 1890.

Bowl, 6″ dia.	$ 22-29
Butter dish, covered, Maltese	
Cross finial	68-77
Cake plate on stand	38-47
Celery	35-44
Compote, covered, open, large	
standard	45-54
Creamer, footed	48-58
Cruet, Maltese Cross stopper	65-74
Dish, oval	19-27
Dolphin compote (rare)	270-290
Goblet, knob stem	66-74
Mug	35-42
Pitcher, water (ill.)	89-92
Sauce	
Flat, round, footed, 3½″,	
4″, 5″	10-17
Footed, 4½″	15-23
Spoonholder	39-45
Sugar bowl, covered, Maltese	
Cross finial	62-70
Tumbler, handled	62-69
Wine	39-47

Probably other pieces. Colors, 150 percent higher than clear prices listed.

Jardiniere

Maker unknown, c. 1887. Clear, nonflint.

Butter dish, covered	$ 38-45
Creamer	34-41
Spoonholder	34-42
Sugar bowl, covered	35-45

Possibly other pieces.

Jefferson's Number 251

Jefferson's Number 251

Jefferson Glass Company, Steubenville, Ohio, 1904. Plain, colored and opalescent, nonflint.

Berry bowls, 8″, 6″, 4½″	$ 25-36
Butter dish, covered	38-47
Condiment set	44-53
Creamer	34-44
Cruet, handled (ill.)	40-50
Jug, ½ gal.	37-46
Salt/Pepper, pr.	26-35
Spoonholder	30-40
Sugar bowl, covered	37-46
Toothpick, blue, opalescent	
(rare)	

Probably other pieces. Colors and opalescent, 60 percent higher than clear prices listed.

Jefferson's Number 271

Jefferson's Number 271

Jefferson Glass Company, Follansbee, West Virginia, 1907. Crystal, blue, green,

(continued)

also gold trimmed, with gold rims. Non-flint.

Butter dish, blue	$ 52-64
Creamer.	34-42
Jug, ½ gal.	44-53
Nappy, 4″ and 8″	25-34
Pitcher, water, green	58-68
Spoonholder	27-37
Sugar bowl, covered	58-68
Tumbler (ill.)	35-45

Probably others.

Jersey

Jersey

McKee Bros., 1894. Clear, nonflint.

Butter dish, covered	$ 39-47
Compote	
High standard	46-53
Low standard	42-50
Celery.	34-41
Creamer.	39-48
Goblet	34-42
Pitcher, ½ gal., small	56-66
Spoonholder	37-47
Sugar bowl, covered	49-61
Tumbler	34-42

Probably other pieces.

Jersey Swirl

Jersey Swirl

(Swirl): Windsor Glass Company, Pittsburgh, 1887. Clear and color: canary, amber, blue; nonflint.

Butter dish, covered	$ 45-54
Compote	
Covered.	38-46
Open	30-35
Creamer	36-44
Goblet	
Buttermilk (ill.).	44-53
Regular size.	27-36
Pitcher, water	39-47
Plate, bread	16-22
Salt dip.	11-15
Sauce.	12-16
Sugar bowl	
Covered.	32-41
Open	19-26
Tumbler	18-25
Wine	43-52

Canary, 40 percent; blue or amber, 60 percent higher than crystal prices listed. Being reproduced in goblets, covered compotes, nappies, plates (2 sizes), salt dips and sauces.

Jewel and Dewdrop

Jewel and Dewdrop

(Kansas): Cooperative Flint Glass Company, 1870s; reproduced by U.S. Glass Company, in 1907 as Kansas pattern. Clear and opalescent, nonflint.

Bowl, berry, 6″, 7″, 8½″	$ 20-30
Butter dish, covered.	58-64
Cake stand, 8″, 9″, 10″	53-70
Celery	35-44
Compote	
Covered, high standard,	
deep bowl	68-77

Open, high standard	60-64	
Creamer	25-32	
Goblet (rare)	49-57	
Pitcher, water (ill.)	46-54	
Salt/Pepper, pr.	57-66	
Spoonholder (rare)	39-46	
Sugar bowl, covered	45-54	
Syrup	42-52	
Toothpick holder	50-60	
Tumbler	29-38	
Wine	45-53	

Probably other pieces. Goblet and mug being reproduced.

Jewel and Festoon

Jewel and Festoon

(Loop and Jewel): Maker unknown, Ohio, late 1880s. Clear, nonflint.

Bowls, several sizes	$ 34-43	
Butter dish, covered	45-54	
Creamer	42-52	
Goblet	38-47	
Pitcher (ill.)	68-77	
Relish dish	24-30	
Salt/Pepper, pr.	25-30	
Sherbet cup	22-28	
Spoonholder	35-42	
Sugar bowl, covered	44-53	

Probably other pieces. Tumbler being reproduced.

Jeweled Heart

Northwood Glass Company, 1900s. Clear, colored, Carnival; nonflint.

	Clear	Color
Butter	$72-81	$138-150
Cruet, clear, colored (ill.).		55-64
Lamp	70-77	95-104

Pitcher	52-59	134-150
Pitcher, Carnival		195-221
Syrup	50-57	69-78
Tumbler		
Carnival		68-77

Probably other pieces. Toothpick, goblet, creamer and sugar being reproduced.

Jeweled Heart

Jeweled Moon and Star

Jeweled Moon and Star

Maker unknown, Ohio, 1880s. Clear and frosted moons, blue or red; amber and blue; red and amber; nonflint.

Bowl, relish, oval	$ 28-37	
Butter dish, covered	45-54	
Compote		
Covered	52-60	
Open	50-58	
Goblet	48-58	
Pitcher, water (ill.)	64-72	
Sugar bowl, covered	55-65	
Tray, water	44-53	
Tumbler	42-50	
Wine	39-49	

Probably other pieces.

539

Jubilee

Jubilee

McKee Glass Company, 1894. Clear, nonflint.

Celery vase	$ 37-45
Compote	
Covered	34-42
Open	33-40
Creamer	32-42
Goblet	40-48
Pickle dish	23-33
Pitcher, water (ill.)	42-52
Salt/Pepper, pr.	24-33
Spoonholder	29-38
Sugar bowl, covered	43-50
Tumbler	34-42

Probably other pieces.

Jumbo

Photo: Mr. and Mrs. A.M. Zinkeler, Chattanooga, Tenn.

Jumbo

Canton Glass Company, Canton, Ohio, 1883. Also made by Aetna Glass Co., Bellaire, Ohio, same period. Clear, nonflint.

Butter dish	
Round, Barnum's Lead	$ 335-365
Oblong, Jumbo	240-260
Caster set, 3 bottles	570-630
Compote, covered	330-360
Creamer	225-240
Cup and saucer	160-170
Dish, covered, frosted	177-184
Goblet (rare)	375-420
Spoon rack (rare) (ill.)	850-925
Spoonholder	162-180
Sugar bowl, covered	320-360

Possibly other pieces. The spoon rack is one of the rarest pieces of pattern glass in America today. Prices are for Canton pieces.

King's Curtain

King's Curtain

Maker unknown, 1880s. Clear, nonflint.

Butter dish, covered	$ 52-60
Cake stand	58-67
Creamer	34-39
Goblet	37-47
Pitcher, water (ill.)	40-49
Plate	28-37
Salt shaker	29-38
Saucedish, flat	22-29
Spoonholder	29-38
Sugar bowl	
Covered	42-52
Open	38-47

Probably other pieces.

King's 500

(Parrot): King, Son & Company, Pittsburgh, 1891. Clear, transparent blue, possibly other colors; nonflint.

Bowl, berry, blue	$ 73-83
Butter, covered, cobalt, gold eyes	99-110
Cruet, blue (ill.)	84-92

King's 500

Photo: Mr. and Mrs. A.M. Zinkeler, Chattanooga, Tenn.

Probably the usual patterns, the usual prices for a glass of this date. The cruet shown is a beautiful blue.

Klondike

Klondike

(Amberette; English Hobnail Cross): A. J. Beatty Company, Findlay, Ohio, 1870s. Other companies, 1880s. Clear or frosted with color: amber, lilac/gold; nonflint.

Bowl, 6″ sq.	$148-162
Butter dish, covered	325-350
Compote, covered, 8″	232-240
Creamer (ill.)	177-182
Pitcher, square, tankard	650-680
Salt/Pepper, pr.	260-270
Sauce, footed, flat, other	82-92
Spoonholder	188-202
Sugar bowl	
Covered	320-330
Open	232-240
Syrup	520-545
Toothpick holder, 2 types	270-280

Tray, square, 5½″, 7″, 8½″	225-245
Tumbler	142-152
Vase, bud, 8½″ high	385-420

Many other pieces. Colors, 50 percent higher than clear prices shown.

Knights of Labor

Knights of Labor

Bakewell, Pears & Company, Pittsburgh, 1879. Clear, canary, amber, blue; nonflint.

Mug	$ 65-77
Plate, bread (ill.)	108-116

Colors, 65 percent higher than clear prices listed.

Krom

Krom

Maker unknown, c. 1830s. Clear, flint.

Goblet (ill.)	$ 77-86
Whiskey, several sizes	37-46

Lacy Dewdrop

Co-Operative Flint Glass Company, Beaver Falls, Pennsylvania, c. 1890. Clear, milk glass, nonflint. Possibly other colors.

(continued)

Bowl, berry	$ 34-43
Butter dish, covered.	46-54
Creamer	37-46
Goblet	48-58
Mug	35-44
Pitcher, water.	56-64
Spoonholder	34-42
Sugar bowl	
Open	34-44
Covered	60-64
Tumbler	25-33

Milk glass, 30 percent higher than clear prices listed. Probably other pieces.

Lacy Medallion

Lacy Medallion

U.S. Glass Company, 1890s. Souvenir-type, gilded in opaque white, sometimes with flowers painted on sides. Nonflint.

Cup.	$ 40-47
Mug (ill.)	50-58
Toothpick.	35-44
Tumbler	34
Wine	42-51

Other pieces.

Lacy Spiral

Lacy Spiral

(Colossus): Maker unknown, late 1880s. Clear, nonflint.

Butter dish, covered.	$ 47-57
Compote	
Covered	49-55
Jelly, open.	36-40
Open	36-42
Creamer	45-52
Pitcher, water (ill.)	55-62
Spoonholder	37-44
Sugar bowl, covered	57-65
Relish dish	32-41

Probably other pieces.

Lady Hamilton
Photo: Mrs. Paul Brown, Chattanooga, Tenn.

Lady Hamilton

(Peerless): Richards & Hartley Flint Glass Company, Pittsburgh, 1875. Clear.

Celery vase	$ 48-55
Compotes (22 different types)	24-120
Creamer, low and high stem	47-54
Goblet	44-53
Mustard jar	47-56
Spoonholder	35-44
Sugar bowl	64-72
Tumbler	48-58

"Lafayet"

Boat-shaped saltcellar: This is a rare piece because it's one of the few, if not the **only,** piece of glass signed at the Boston & Sandwich Glass Company, Sandwich, Massachusetts.

"Lafayet"

No price given because there are few, if any, available. Shown only because Sandwich made some of the finest glass the world has ever known.

Large Stippled Chain

Large Stippled Chain

Probably Gillinder & Sons, 1870s. Clear, nonflint.

Creamer.	$ 52-61
Goblet	50-60
Pitcher (ill.)	66-74
Sugar bowl	
Covered	55-65
Open	47-56

Probably other pieces.

Late Crystal

Richard & Hartley Company, 1888; also, McKee Bros., 1894, and U.S. Glass Company, 1898. Clear, nonflint.

Late Crystal

Celery	$ 24-33
Compote	
Covered, low and high foot	47-52
Open, low foot only	29-35
Creamer	35-44
Egg cup.	19-27
Goblet	35-43
Pitcher, water (ill.)	42-54
Salt/Pepper, pr..	22-32
Sauce, flat and footed	18-22
Spoonholder	27-36
Sugar bowl	45-54
Tumbler	32-42

Probably other pieces.

Late Diamond Point Band

Late Diamond Point Band

(Scalloped Diamond Point, Panel with Diamond Point): Central Glass Company, Wheeling, West Virginia, 1870s. Nonflint.

(continued)

Bowl, round, oval	$ 24-32
Butter dish, covered	29-36
Cake stand, small, large	32-42
Cheese dish, covered	44-53
Creamer	37-47
Goblet	33-42
Pitcher (ill.)	51-60
Sugar bowl, covered, open	32-40

Probably other pieces.

Late Panelled Grape

Late Panelled Grape

Another of the Grape patterns, late 1890s. Clear, nonflint.

Bowl, berry	$ 23-30
Butter dish, covered	35-42
Creamer (ill.)	34-41
Dish, covered	24-29
Goblet	23-32
Pitcher, milk, water	46-52
Wine	24-32

Goblet being reproduced.

Late Panelled Grape, Variant

Late Panelled Grape, Variant

Maker unknown, 1890s. Clear, probably premium glass at grocery stores. Nonflint.

Bowl, berry	$ 17-23
Butter dish, covered	26-31
Creamer (ill.)	27-32
Goblet	22-27
Pitcher	
Milk	31-41
Syrup	31-40
Water	30-40
Wine	22-29

Probably other pieces.

Late Swan, Opaque

Late Swan, Opaque

Westmoreland Specialty Company, Grapeville, Pennsylvania, 1891-1892. Opaque white and opaque turquoise, nonflint.

Sugar bowl, covered	
Opaque white	$ 94-105
Opaque turquoise (ill.)	92-103

Probably other pieces.

Late Thistle

Pittsburgh, late 1890s. Clear, nonflint.

Butter dish, covered	$ 47-53
Cake stand, small	40-47
Compote	
Covered	49-54
Open	38-46
Honey dish, covered	35-43
Pitcher, milk (ill.)	61-67
Sugar bowl	47-57
Tumbler	39-48

Probably other pieces.

Late Thistle

Lattice

Lattice

(Diamond Bar): King, Son & Company, Pittsburgh, 1880. Clear, nonflint.

Butter dish, covered	$ 45-52
Cake stand	47-54
Celery	24-32
Compote, covered, high standard . . .	47-54
Cordial	23-30
Creamer	37-46
Egg cup	20-27
Goblet	28-36
Pitcher, water (ill.)	54-62
Plate, 6½″, 7¼″, 10″, 12″	14-32
Platter, clear, "Waste not, want not"	67-72

Salt/Pepper, pr.	108-112
Sauce, flat, footed	27-32
Spoonholder	98-107
Sugar bowl, covered	99-107
Wine	28-32

Probably others.

Leaf and Flower   **Leaf Bracket**

Leaf and Flower

Hobbs, Brockunier & Co., Wheeling, West Virginia. A Wheeling, West Virginia, product made in the 1890s. Clear, clear and frosted with amber or green flowers. Red has been reported.

Bowl, finger or waste	$ 24-32
Butter dish, covered	43-52
Caster set	49-58
Creamer	35-42
Creamer, amber stained flowers	60-70
Pitcher, water (ill.)	51-60
Sauce, flat	27-37
Tray, celery	30-40

Probably other pieces. Clear and frosted, 30 percent higher; amber, green, 70 percent higher; red, 100 percent higher than clear prices listed.

Leaf Bracket

Indiana Tumbler & Goblet (National) Company, Greentown, Indiana, 1900. Crystal, opal, chocolate, Nile green; nonflint.

Berry bowl	$ 55-63
Butter dish	81-90
Celery tray	59-68
Creamer	61-70
Cruet (ill.)	118-126
Salt/Pepper, pr.	62-72

(continued)

Spoonholder 62-70
Tumbler 50-60

Probably other pieces. Chocolate, 80 percent higher; opal and Nile green, 30 percent higher than clear prices listed.

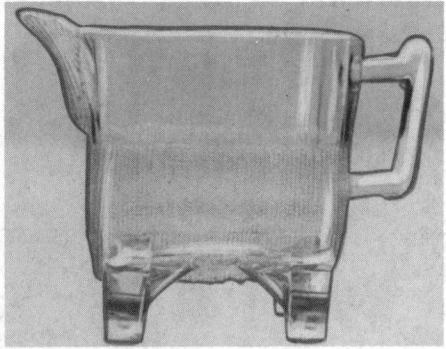

Legged Trough

Legged Trough

Maker and date unknown. How many pieces (creamer, sugar, tumbler, etc.) were made is unknown to this writer. It must have taken some doing to remove it from the mold! If you know—**write!**

Lens and Star

O'Hara Glass Company, Pittsburgh, c. 1886. Clear, nonflint.

Bowl, waste . . . . $ 16-25
Butter dish, covered. 42-51
Celery 23-31
Creamer 32-41
Pitcher, water. 45-54
Spoonholder 28-36
Sugar bowl, covered 35-44
Tray, handled. 49-59
Tumbler 19-27

Probably other pieces.

Leverne

(Star in Honeycomb): Maker unknown, c. early 1870s. Clear, nonflint.

Butter dish, covered. . . . . $ 47-56
Celery 34-42
Compote
Open 36-44
Covered 50-57
Goblet 27-35

Pitcher 48-54
Relish, oval 24-28
Sauce, flat, footed 21-29
Spoonholder 28-36
Sugar bowl, covered 50-55

Probably other pieces.

Liberty Bell

Liberty Bell

(Centennial): Gillinder & Company, Philadelphia. Made for 1876 Centennial. Rare in milk glass. Nonflint.

Butter dish, covered $140-150
Celery 80-90
Child's table set (4 pc.) 170-178
Compote, open, 6″, 8″ 109-118
Creamer
Plain handle 102-112
Reeded handle 170-180
Goblet 68-75
Pitcher, water 575-660
Plate, 6″, 8″, 10″ 75-102
Platter, 9¼″ × 13″, Independence
signers' names on border (ill.) 255-270
Salt
Celery dip, master salt 38-44
Shaker top, bell-shaped 78-84
Salt/Pepper, pr. 138-148
Spoonholder, pedestal base 111-122
Sugar bowl, covered 121-132
Sugar bowl, open 47-57

Probably other pieces. Milk glass, 150 percent higher than clear prices listed.

Liberty Bell Novelty Bank

This bell was made for the St. Louis Exposition in 1903.

Liberty Bell Novelty Bank

Liberty Bell bank (ill.). . . . . $ 49-58
Others were made and it gets confusing. If you like them, buy them.

Lightning   Lightning

(Chain Lightning): Tiffin Glass Company, Gas City, Indiana, 1890s. It was called Chain Lighting in the factory by the men. Clear, nonflint.

Bowls, several styles.	$ 22-30
Butter, covered	41-50
Celery vase	28-34
Compote	
Covered	45-53
Open	34-42
Creamer (ill.)	38-42
Goblet	34-42
Pitcher, water	47-56
Spoonholder	37-45

Probably others.

Lily-of-the-Valley

Lily-of-the-Valley

Sandwich, 1870s. Clear, etched, nonflint.

Butter dish, footed, on	
three feet	$ 59-68
Celery	38-44
Compote, covered, high standard . . .	84-93
Cordial	46-54
Creamer, on three feet.	92-102
Cruet, tall stopper.	74-83
Dish, oval	35-42
Goblet	44-52
Pitcher, milk, scarce (ill.)	97-106
Sauce, flat	22-27
Spoonholder, on three feet	29-39
Sugar bowl, on three feet	68-76
Wine (scarce)	58-65

Probably other pieces.

Lincoln Drape

Lincoln Drape

Sandwich, late 1860s. Clear, milk-white, sapphire blue (both rare); flint.

Butter dish	$110-125
Celery	98-106
Compote	
Open, low standard	77-86
Covered.	92-102

(continued)

Creamer	132-140
Decanter	100-108
Egg cup	46-54
Goblet (ill.)	88-97
Pitcher, water	362-371
Plate, 6″	58-67
Spoonholder	71-80
Sugar bowl, open	65-74
Tumbler	48-56

Probably other pieces. Colors, 45 to 75 percent higher than clear prices listed.

Lined Band Round Thumbprint

Lined Band Round Thumbprint

Maker unknown, c. 1860. Clear, flint.

Champagne	$ 50-56
Compote, open	48-55
Goblet (ill.)	32-41
Tumbler, footed	27-36
Wine	37-46

Probably other pieces.

Lion

Lion

(Atlanta): Gillinder & Sons, Philadelphia, 1870s. Clear and frosted, milk glass.

Bread plate, frosted	$ 70-78
Butter dish, Lion's head finial	110-117
Celery, etched	79-87
Compote	
Covered, large, high standard	155-164
Covered, low 5⅝ standard	115-122
Creamer, frosted lion on base	68-77
Goblet	69-78
Paperweight, milk glass, lions reclining	142-152
Pitcher	
Milk	370-410
Syrup, metal top	238-244
Water	210-224
Sauce, footed, small medium, large	23-28
Spoonholder	57-64
Sugar bowl, rampant lion finial (ill.)	69-77
Tumbler	98-107
Wine, frosted	159-168

Probably other pieces. Butter dish, celery, cordial, egg cup, goblet, water pitcher, sauce, etc., being reproduced. Don't buy it for genuine.

Lion and Baboon

Lion and Baboon

Maker unknown, a humorous design of the 1880s. Clear.

Butter dish, covered	$ 70-78
Creamer	80-87
Compote, covered	100-110
Miniature, 4-piece table set	128-137
Pitcher (ill.)	100-107
Spoonholder	42-52
Sugar bowl, covered	67-77

Probably other pieces.

Lion's Head

Lion's Head

Miniature set, possibly Gillinder & Sons, c. 1870s. Clear, nonflint.

5-piece table set (ill.) $330-365

Little Owl

Little Owl

Bryce, Higbee & Company, Pittsburgh, mid-1880s. This is part of a Menagerie Toy Set, which includes "Bear" covered sugar, "Fish" spoonholder, "Turtle" butter dish. Crystal, old gold, blue and white opaque, amber, other colors. You see too few of these to price them. Don't buy one of these as Sandwich, especially the owl.

Little River

Possibly Sandwich, 1870s. Clear, possibly colors.

Pickle caster . . . . $ 87-97
Pickle jar (ill.). 55-65

The scene shown in photo (windmill) is unknown to collectors. Probably other pieces.

Little River

Log Cabin

Log Cabin

Central Glass Company, Wheeling, West Virginia, 1875. Clear, nonflint.

Butter dish . . . . $ 88-97
Compote, covered, on
   stand (ill.) 250-260
Creamer 127-142
Mustard 79-88
Pitcher, water. 287-294
Sauce. 42-51
Spoonholder 104-115
Sugar bowl (rare), covered. 193-204

Probably other pieces.

Loganberry and Grape

Loganberry and Grape

Dalzell, Gilmore & Leighton, mid-1880s. Clear, nonflint.

Butter dish, covered.	$ 44-50
Celery	30-40
Creamer	43-52
Goblet	34-42
Pitcher, water (ill.)	50-60
Tumbler	35-45

Probably other pieces.

Long Maple Leaf

Long Maple Leaf

Possibly Westmoreland Specialty Company, late 1800s. Clear, nonflint.

Butter dish, covered.	$ 42-50
Celery	24-31
Creamer	35-42
Goblet	22-31
Mug with cap	28-35

Pitcher, water (ill.)	57-62
Salt/Pepper, pr..	30-38
Spoonholder	22-31
Sugar bowl, covered	40-44

Probably other pieces.

Loop

Loop

(O'Hara): O'Hara Glass Company, Pittsburgh, late 1850s or 1860s. Also made by Gillinder & Sons, 1860s, and by Portland Glass Company, Portland, Maine, 1870s. They called it Portland Petal.

Butter dish, covered	$ 56-64
Cake stand	78-87
Celery.	29-36
Compote	
Covered, high standard	65-72
Open	38-46
Creamer, 6″ high	66-72
Egg cup	31-40
Goblet, 3 styles	28-38
Pitcher, water, applied	
handle.	78-86
Spoonholder	28-37
Sugar bowl	
Covered	64-72
Open	38-43
Wine	34-39

Probably other pieces.

Loop and Dart

Loop and Dart

Sandwich, early; Richards & Hartley, Portland Glass Company, Portland, Maine, 1860s. Clear.

Butter dish, covered, round	
ornaments	$ 42-50
Celery vase, diamond band	35-44
Compote, 8″, low foot	39-50
Cordial	42-51
Creamer, diamond ornaments	42-52
Egg cup, round ornaments	28-37
Goblet, buttermilk	44-52
Pitcher, water (ill.)	69-74
Plate, 6″ (rare)	70-80
Salt, footed	33-40
Spoonholder, round ornaments	32-40
Sugar bowl, covered	48-54
Tumbler, footed, water	29-37
Wine	34-43

Probably other pieces.

Loop and Dart with Round Ornaments

Loop and Dart with Round Ornaments

Portland Glass Company, Portland, Maine, c. 1869. Clear, nonflint and flint.

Butter dish, covered	$ 49-55
Butter patty	17-23
Compote, covered	70-77
Creamer	84-92
Egg cup	25-34
Goblet (ill.)	29-34
Pitcher, water	69-79
Spoonholder	32-41

Sugar bowl	
Covered	60-70
Open	38-45

Flint, 25 percent higher than nonflint prices listed. Sauce being reproduced.

Loop and Moose Eye

Loop and Moose Eye

Maker unknown, c. 1870s. Clear, flint.

Creamer	$ 35-42
Decanter	44-52
Goblet (ill.)	37-47
Spoonholder	32-42
Sugar bowl, covered	45-55

Probably other pieces.

Loop with Dewdrops

Loop with Dewdrops

Earlier maker unknown; reproduced by U.S. Glass Company, 1892. Nonflint.

Bowl, 5″, 6″, 7″, 8″	$ 15-25
Butter dish, covered	42-51
Cake plate on stand, 9″, 10″	52-61
Celery vase	37-46
Compote	
Covered, 5″, 6″, 7″, 8″,	
high foot	47-66

(continued)

Open, 5″, 6″, 7″, 8″,	
high foot	30-43
Creamer	40-48
Dish, oval, 7″, 8″, 9″	24-32
Goblet, knobbed stem	38-42
Mug, with cap.	30-38
Pitcher, ½ gal. (ill.)	47-55
Salt/Pepper, pr..	32-41
Spoonholder	32-41
Sugar bowl, covered	42-51
Tumbler	27-36
Wine	31-41

Probably other pieces.

Loop with Stippled Panels

Loop with Stippled Panels

(Texas): U.S. Glass Company, 1900 and 1907. Crystal, crystal with gilded top, ruby in the body, nonflint.

Bowl, berry, 7½ ⅝, 8½ ⅝, 9½ ⅝,	
flat, footed	$ 26-32
Butter dish	37-41
Cake stand, footed, 10⅝, high	
and low standard	48-56
Celery	29-37
Creamer (ill.)	32-42
Cruet, faceted stopper.	41-50
Goblet	36-45
Pitcher, 3 pts..	40-46
Salt/Pepper, pr., large, small	33-42
Spoonholder	23-32
Sugar bowl, small	40-45
Toothpick holder	22-29
Tumbler	24-33
Wine	27-36

Probably other pieces. Colors same price.

Loops and Drops

Loops and Drops

(New Jersey): Maker unknown, c. 1890s. Clear, ruby-flashed, nonflint.

Butter dish, covered (ill.)	$ 62-72
Creamer.	49-53
Goblet	39-47
Spoonholder	34-41
Sugar bowl, covered	58-63

Ruby-flashed, 50 percent higher than clear prices listed. Probably other pieces.

Louis XV

Louis XV

(Winged Scroll): Northwood Glass Company, Indiana, Pennsylvania, 1898. Custard, "ivory and gold," green, other colors. Nonflint.

	Color	Custard
Berry set		
Large bowl.	$115-122	$172-186
Small bowl	64-69	98-110
Butter dish, covered . .	98-107	210-230

Compote		128-134
Creamer.	91-100	116-121
Cruet	101-118	169-177
Pitcher, water	118-127	172-190
Salt/Pepper, pr. . . .	77-86	153-162
Spoonholder	94-103	120-130
Sugar bowl, covered (ill.).	91-101	130-138
Tumbler, water . . .	70-80	84-93

Louisiana Purchase Exposition

Louisiana Purchase Exposition

The World's Fair held in St. Louis, Missouri, 1904, to commemorate the centennial of the Louisiana Purchase 100 years before. Plates and iced tea (or beverage) glasses were popular souvenirs. Crystal, crystal with frosted center, milk-glass.

Beverage glass.	$ 47-52
Plate	42-54
Tumbler (ill.)	39-45

Probably other pieces.

Lutz

Lutz

McKee Bros., Jeannette, Pennsylvania, 1894. Clear, nonflint.

Goblet	$ 41-50
Mustard jar	35-42
Pickle jar	32-39
Pitcher, water (ill.)	58-66

Probably other pieces.

Madison

Madison

Maker and date unknown. Clear, flint.

Compote, covered	$ 90-98
Creamer	118-122
Goblet	54-62
Spoonholder	55-64
Sugar bowl (base ill.)	108-120

Should be other pieces.

Magnet and Grape, Frosted Leaf

Magnet and Grape, Frosted Leaf

Sandwich glass, early. Clear glass with frosted leaf.

Butter dish	$131-140
Celery	200-207
Champagne.	128-140
Compote, open (scarce)	148-162

Magnet and Grape

Magnet and Grape

Sandwich glass, 1870s. Clear glass with stippled leaf, nonflint.

Butter dish, acorn knob	$ 54-62
Compote, open	37-45
Cordial	40-47
Creamer (ill.)	50-58
Goblet, knob stem.	34-41
Pitcher	90-101
Salt, footed	22-29
Saucedish, 4″	10-16
Spoonholder	37-46
Sugar bowl	34-42
Tumbler	29-37

Maine

Maine

(Panelled Flower, Stippled): U.S. Glass Company, Pittsburgh, early 1890s. Clear, emerald green.

Bowl, 6″, 7″, 8″	$ 25-38
Creamer	32-38
Dish, relish	21-26

Mug, handled	31-40
Pitcher (ill.).	52-61
Sauce, flat	20-27
Spoonholder	32-39
Sugar bowl, covered	34-44
Toothpick holder	24-31
Tumbler	27-36

Probably other pieces. Green, 100 percent higher than clear prices listed.

Maize

Maize

Libbey & Son Company, Toledo, Ohio, 1889. Crystal, ivory, pale celadon green.

Bowl	
Berry, 9″	$ 52-62
Finger, 5″	40-47
Celery vase	38-47
Creamer	70-80
Decanter, pt., qt.	77-82
Pitcher	
Syrup (ill.)	92-106
Water.	101-118
Spoonholder	62-72
Sugar bowl	70-80
Toothpick holder	66-72
Tumbler	48-52

Probably other pieces. Ivory and pale celadon green, 30 percent higher than Crystal prices listed. Being reproduced in many sizes and shapes. Careful here!

Manhattan

U.S. Glass Company, 1902. Clear, gilt in the sunken circles, red-flashed, amber; nonflint.

Bowl, berry, 7″, 8″, 8½″, 9½″,	
10″, 11″, 12½″.	$ 27-32
Bowl, punch, large, cups	120-140
Butter dish	37-44
Cake stand	45-55
Celery vase, tall.	22-29

Manhattan

Compote, 9½″, 10½″	40-47
Creamer, individual, large.	17-23
Pitcher, syrup (ill.)	50-58
Plate, 5″, 9½″, 11″, 12″	15-22
Sauce, 5″, footed, 4½″, flat	10-15
Spoonholder	19-24
Sugar bowl	
Covered.	37-44
Open, individual	21-29
Tumbler, iced tea, water	24-32
Water bottle	37-42

Probably other pieces. Red-flashed, 25 percent higher than clear. Amber, 50 percent higher. Being reproduced in bowls, creamer and sugar, goblets, iced teas, plates, sherbets and wines.

Manhattan

Manhattan

Tarentum Glass Company, Tarentum, Pennsylvania, 1895. Clear only, nonflint.

Butter dish, covered (ill.)	$ 35-42
Cake stand	35-42
Celery.	21-30
Creamer.	18-22
Pitcher, water.	37-43
Spoonholder	26-34
Sugar bowl, covered	37-42
Wine	23-32

All standard pieces made.

Maple

(Hops Band): King, Son & Company, Pittsburgh, c. 1870s. Clear.

Butter dish, covered.	$ 37-44
Cake stand, large	48-52
Celery	41-52
Compote, covered	44-52
Creamer	34-43
Egg cup.	34-42
Goblet	30-37
Pitcher	46-53
Salt, footed	32-41
Spoonholder	27-36
Sugar bowl	
Open	24-32
Covered	38-44

Probably other pieces.

Maple Leaf

Maple Leaf

Northwood Glass Company, 1890s. Custard, Carnival, nonflint.

Berry set	
Large bowl, stemmed,	
Custard.	$127-136
Small bowl, stemmed,	
Custard.	60-70
Butter dish, covered, Custard	108-117
(Carnival marigold)	70-80
(Carnival vivid)	106-111
Creamer, Custard.	81-90
(Carnival marigold)	44-53
(Carnival vivid)	73-83
Ice cream set, Carnival	
Large bowl, stemmed,	
marigold	54-63
(Carnival vivid)	117-123
Small bowl, stemmed,	
marigold	51-61

(continued)

(Carnival vivid)	72-81
Pitcher, Custard	180-190
(Carnival marigold)	78-87
(Carnival vivid) (ill.)	150-160
Spoonholder, Custard	107-116
(Carnival marigold)	60-70
(Carnival vivid)	71-80
Sugar bowl, covered, Custard	110-118
(Carnival marigold)	41-50
(Carnival vivid)	70-77
Tumbler, Custard	89-97
(Carnival marigold)	40-50
(Carnival vivid)	42-52

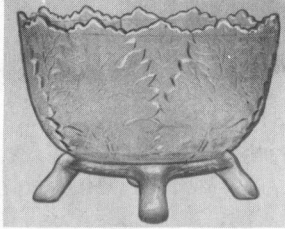

Maple Leaf

Maple Leaf

(Leaf): Gillinder & Sons, Greensburg, Pennsylvania, late 1880s. They called it Leaf. Clear, canary, amber, vaseline, blue, sapphire, other colors; nonflint.

Butter dish	$ 72-80
Celery vase	40-42
Compote	
Covered, high standard	88-98
Round, open, footed	42-52
Goblet	48-54
Pitcher, large	64-72
Plate, 10″, 10½″, Grant Peace	45-52
Sauce, 5″, 6″, footed	17-24
Spoonholder	28-35
Sugar bowl (ill.)	42-51
Tumbler	30-38

Probably other pieces. Colors, 40 to 60 percent higher than clear prices listed. Being heavily reproduced in various sizes and colors.

Marquisette

Co-Operative Flint Glass Company, Beaver Falls, Pennsylvania, c. early 1880s. Clear, flint.

Butter dish, covered	$ 66-73
Celery	47-54

Compote	
Open	42-51
Covered	70-77
Creamer	49-57
Goblet	28-36
Spoonholder	29-37
Sugar bowl	
Open	37-42
Covered	57-64
Wine	29-36

Probably other pieces.

Marsh Fern

Riverside Glass Works, Wellsburg, West Virginia, c. 1889. Clear, nonflint. This was their No. 327.

Bowl	$ 28-35
Compote, high standard	38-47
Creamer, tankard	42-51
Goblet	37-46
Spoonholder	28-34
Sugar bowl, covered	47-54

Other pieces.

Marsh Pink

Marsh Pink

Maker unknown, Ohio, 1880s. Clear, rare pieces in amber; nonflint.

Bowl, open and covered	$ 20-27
Butter dish, covered	45-54
Cake stand, small	27-32
Compote, covered	52-62
Jam jar	42-51
Pitcher (ill.)	49-57
Spoonholder	22-29
Sugar bowl, covered	35-43

Probably other pieces. Amber, 150 percent higher than clear prices listed.

Maryland

Maryland

U.S. Glass Company, one of their States series. Clear, with gold, nonflint.

Bowl	$ 33-42
Butter dish, covered.	42-50
Compote, open	41-50
Custard.	27-32
Creamer	35-44
Cruet.	27-35
Honey dish	22-29
Goblet	37-44
Pitcher, water, with gold (ill.)	45-53
Plate, bread.	28-34
Sauce.	22-29
Spoonholder	40-44
Sugar bowl, covered.	37-46
Tumbler	39-47
Wine	37-46

Mascotte

Ripley & Company, Pittsburgh, c. 1884, clear, plain or engraved. Reissued by U.S. Glass Company after 1891. Nonflint.

Butter dish	
Plain	$ 57-63
Horseshoe-shaped, marked "Maud S." (rare)	88-107
Celery, etched.	41-50
Compote	
Open	44-52
Covered.	81-92
Dish	22-31
Goblet, etched	36-44
Sugar bowl, covered.	47-56
Tumbler	27-36
Wine	27-35

Other pieces. Ripley prices listed.

Masonic

(Inverted Prism): McKee Glass Company, Jeannette, Pennsylvania, c. 1894. Clear, nonflint.

Bowl, berry	$ 34-43
Butter dish, covered.	47-54
Cake stand, high standard.	50-57
Creamer	30-38
Pitcher, water.	58-66
Spoonholder	24-29
Sugar bowl, covered.	44-54
Tumbler	28-33

Probably other pieces.

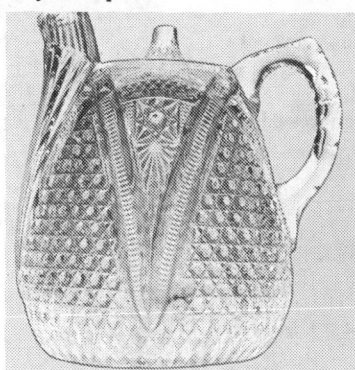

Massachusetts

Massachusetts

U.S. Glass Company, 1898. Clear, nonflint.

Butter dish, covered.	$ 58-64
Cruet, miniature with stopper	70-78
Dish, candy	27-36
Creamer	28-42
Pitcher, water.	73-82
Plate, 8″	39-43
Shot glass.	24-32
Table lamp	64-73
"Teapot" (intended as rum jug) (ill.).	109-121
Water carafe	54-63

Probably other pieces.

William McKinley Campaign Items

Most were made by McKee & Bros. in 1896. Nonflint.

Bread plate, "His Will Be Done" (ill.)	$ 88-97

(continued)

William McKinley Campaign Items

Goblet, bust.	54-63
Gold tray	98-107
Mug (cup), covered	50-58
Plate, "Protection and Plenty"	70-79
Tumbler, clear	52-62
Tumbler, frosted	54-63

Other pieces.

Medallion

Medallion

(Spades, Hearts and Spades): Maker unknown, 1880s. Clear, yellow, amber, blue, apple green; nonflint.

Butter dish	$ 38-47
Cake stand	40-47
Celery vase	27-34
Compote, covered, high	
standard.	46-54
Creamer.	28-34
Goblet	29-37
Mug.	27-34
Pitcher, water (ill.)	60-70
Sauce, flat, footed	16-23
Spoonholder	27-34
Sugar bowl, covered	29-38

Tumbler	22-29
Wine	27-36

Probably other pieces. Yellow, amber, blue, 40 percent; apple green, 75 percent higher than clear prices listed.

Melrose

Greensburg Glass Company, Greensburg, Pennsylvania, c. 1890s. Clear, plain or etched; nonflint.

Butter dish, covered	$ 43-52
Cake stand	41-50
Celery.	40-50
Compote, covered, high	
standard, 6″, 8″	24-28
Creamer, tankard	27-36
Goblet	25-34
Mug.	24-35
Pitcher	
Quart	40-46
½ gal.	42-47
Spoonholder	27-35
Sugar bowl, covered	33-39
Tumbler	18-25
Wine	22-27

Etched, 20 percent higher than clear prices listed. Other pieces.

Memphis

Memphis

(Doll's Eye): Northwood Glass Company, 1908-1910. Clear, colors, Carnival.

Berry set (clear, colors only)

Large bowl	$ 40-46

Small bowl	25-34
Butter dish, covered (clear	
colors only)	47-56
Fruit bowl and base.	62-71
Pitcher	
Syrup.	61-70
Water.	159-167
Punch set	
Bowl and base	61-70
Cup.	22-32
Spoonholder (clear, colors	
only)	47-56
Sugar bowl, covered (clear,	
colors only)	48-55

Colors, 50-75 percent; Carnival, 60 percent higher than clear prices listed. Probably other pieces.

Mephistopheles

Mephistopheles

Germany; also made in this country, late 1800s. Clear, frosted.

Ale glass, "Germany"	$ 42-51
Goblet	48-53
Mug (ill.)	54-63
Pitcher, applied handle	62-68

Probably other pieces made.

Michigan

(Loop with Pillar): U.S. Glass Company, c. 1893. Clear; gilted, some pieces with painted decorations; nonflint.

Bowl, berry, 7½″, 8½″, 10″	$ 32-44
Butter dish, covered	

Michigan

Large	42-50
Small	46-55
Creamer	
Individual.	28-37
Large	27-35
Cruet	34-42
Goblet (ill.)	42-51
Pitcher, tankard	45-54
Salt/Pepper, pr..	47-56
Spoonholder	44-53
Sugar bowl, covered.	54-63
Tumbler	39-42
Wine	34-42

Minerva

Minerva

Sandwich glass, 1870s. Clear, nonflint.

Butter dish, covered.	$ 69-77
Cake plate, on standard, 13″.	115-125
Compote, high and low	
standard	92-101
Creamer	43-52

(continued)

Goblet	88-97
Marmalade jar, w/lid	79-88
Pitcher, water.	160-170
Plate, small, closed handles, 9″	54-63
Platter, "Give Us This Day".	66-74
Sauce, flat round, footed round	33-41
Spoonholder	34-39
Sugar bowl, (ill.)	82-91

Probably other pieces.

Minnesota

U.S. Glass Company, c. 1898. Clear, green with gold decoration, nonflint.

Bowl	
Berry, round, 6″, 7″, 8″	$ 38-46
Flared edge, 4½″, 7½″, 8½″, 9½″	35-44
Butter dish, covered	49-54
Celery tray, 10″, 13″	19-27
Compote	
Round, 6″, 7″, 8″	60-70
Square, 6″, 7″, 8″	58-68
Creamer.	41-51
Goblet	44-53
Pitcher, water	48-56
Sugar bowl, covered	49-56
Tumbler	37-46

Green with gold decoration, 25 percent higher than clear prices listed.

Mirror

Mirror

McKee Bros., Pittsburgh, c. 1870s. Clear, flint.

Ale	$ 28-36
Champagne	37-44

Compote, 6″	55-64
Cordial	37-46
Goblet	35-43
Jar, pickle	32-47
Spoonholder	15-20
Tumbler (ill.)	36-45
Wine	39-46

Probably other pieces.

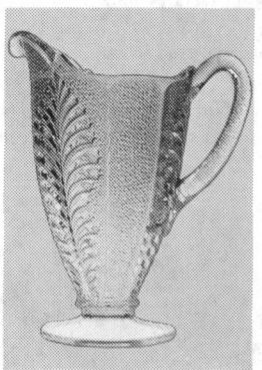

Missouri

Missouri

U.S. Glass Company, after 1891. Clear, blue, emerald green, canary, amethyst.

Butter dish, covered	$ 39-46
Celery	27-32
Compote, high and low standard	39-42
Creamer.	32-39
Goblet	39-47
Pitcher, pint, ½ gallon (ill.)	44-52
Spoonholder	27-35
Sugar bowl, covered	39-47
Tumbler	28-37

Probably other pieces. Blue, green, 50 percent higher; canary, amethyst, 100 percent higher than clear prices listed.

Mitred Bars

(Mitred Diamond Points): Bryce Bros., Pittsburgh, c. 1885. Clear, nonflint.

Bowl, oval.	$ 25-34
Butter dish, covered.	38-44
Cake stand	31-40
Celery	37-46
Creamer, covered	42-52
Goblet	38-47
Spoonholder	28-31
Sugar bowl, covered.	38-47
Wine	26-30

Other pieces.

Monkey

Monkey

George A. Duncan and Sons, Pittsburgh, 1880s. Clear and opalescent, nonflint.

Bowl, waste.	$115-127
Butter dish, covered	171-180
Celery	61-70
Creamer	118-126
Jar, pickle	59-68
Mug, 2 styles	80-90
Pitcher (ill.)	258-266
Spoonholder	120-130
Sugar	
Covered.	177-187
Open	96-105
Toothpick holder	77-86
Tumbler	82-90

Probably other pieces. Opalescent, 90 percent higher than clear prices listed. Spoonholder and toothpick holder being reproduced.

Monroe

Maker unknown, made well before the Civil War. Clear and brilliant. Extremely

Monroe

rare in lamp. Shown here because too many patterns remain unidentified as to maker, etc. If you know, write to the Houston Museum, Chattanooga, Tennessee.

Lamp (rare) (ill.)	$ 875+

Moon and Star

Moon and Star

Pioneer Glass Company, 1892; Wilson Glass Company, 1890, same name. Imperial, Cooperative Flint Glass Company, 1890s. Mold sold to Phoenix Glass Company, 1937. Many reproductions on market today. Clear, some pieces with color added, also milk glass.

(continued)

Bowl, berry, 6", 12½" . . . . $ 23-29
Butter dish, covered 62-70
Cake stand, 6" dia.. 62-72
Celery. 50-60
Compote, covered, 7", 8", 10",
  high standard 49-80
Creamer. 64-72
Goblet, clear, frosted 44-52
Pitcher, water (ill.) 122-130
Sugar bowl, covered, jeweled. 62-71
Tumbler, footed, flint 58-68
Wine 34-42

EVERY item being reproduced. Careful!

Morning Glory

Morning Glory

Sandwich, c. 1860s. Clear, flint.

Compote, open $195-218
Creamer (rare) . . . . 365+
Egg cup. . . . . 170+
Goblet (ill.) 274-285
Wine 158-167

Goblet and wine being reproduced in clear and in color.

Nail

Bryce Bros., Pittsburgh, 1885. Crystal glass with ruby stain, etched.

Bowl, footed . . . . $ 22-27
Butter, covered 31-40
Creamer 34-42
Goblet 35-46
Pitcher, water (ill.) 68-72
Salt/Pepper, pr.. 18-27
Sauce, footed 24-32

Nail

Spoonholder 22-27
Sugar bowl
  Covered 34-38
  Open 18-26
Tumbler 24-32

Probably other pieces. With ruby stain, 100 percent higher than clear prices listed.

Nailhead

Nailhead

(Gem): Sandwich, early; later, Bryce, Higbee & Co., Pittsburgh. Clear orange in the grooves, clear aquamarine; nonflint.

Butter dish . . . . $ 45-52
Cake stand, 4" high 46-53
Celery 28-34
Compote, covered, open,
  scalloped 46-59
Cordial 34-38
Creamer 29-34
Goblet 32-36
Pitcher, water (ill.) 55-64

Plate, round, 9″, square, 7″	25-34
Salt/Pepper, pr.	36-42
Saucedish	12-17
Spoonholder	25-27
Sugar bowl, covered, scalloped	35-43
Tumbler	26-34
Wine	23-32

Probably other pieces. Colors, 50 percent higher than clear prices listed.

New England Pineapple

New England Pineapple

(Loop and Jewel): Boston & Sandwich Glass Company, c. 1860s. Clear, flint. Colored pieces considered rare.

Butter dish, covered	$143-155
Champagne.	112-122
Compote, open	84-93
Creamer	170-184
Decanter, with or without	
stopper	120-142
Goblet (ill.).	54-63
Sauce.	24-29
Spoonholder	50-60
Sugar bowl, covered	112-122
Tumbler, water	84-92

Other pieces. Goblet and wine being reproduced.

New York (Honeycomb)

Many firms made this pattern, among them Bakewell, Pears & Company, 1860s on. Early in clear; later in yellow, blue, amber, green, opalescent.

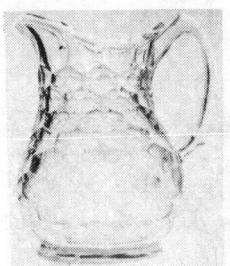

New York (Honeycomb)

Bowl, 6″, 7″, 8″, 9″, 10″	$ 29-39
Butter dish	47-56
Caster bottle	22-27
Celery, Laredo, flint	58-66
Creamer	47-56
Decanter, pint, quart	51-60
Goblet	40-50
Jug, ½ pt., pt., qt., 3 pts.	40-47
Pitcher, water (ill.)	62-69
Salt/Pepper, pr..	41-50
Spoonholder	34-41
Sugar bowl	50-58
Tumbler, ½ pt., ⅓ pt., footed.	42-51
Wine	44-52

Many other pieces. Colors, 40 to 60 percent higher than clear prices listed.

Niagara

Fostoria Glass Company, Fostoria, Ohio, c. 1900. Clear, nonflint.

Bowl, berry	$ 24-32
Butter dish, covered	38-47
Creamer.	34-44
Pitcher	
Tankard.	32-41
Water	41-50
Spoonholder	19-27
Sugar bowl, covered	35-44
Tumbler	22-29

Other pieces.

Notched Bar

(Ball): McKee & Bros., Jeannette, Pennsylvania, c. 1894. Clear, nonflint.

Bottle, caster	$ 45-52
Butter dish, covered	70-80
Creamer.	60-70
Cruet	51-62
Jar, jam	78-84
Spoonholder	31-42

(continued)

Sugar bowl, covered   64-72
Wine   42-52
Probably other pieces.

Nova Scotia Grape and Vine

Nova Scotia Grape and Vine

Nova Scotia, Canada, late 1880s. Non-flint.

Pitcher, water (ill.) . . . . $ 47-54
Tumbler to match   25-33
Probably other pieces.

Nursery Tales

A product of Pennsylvania, 1880s. Each piece shows different characters from old nursery tales. Clear and opal glass, non-flint.

Child's 4-piece set (butter
  dish, creamer, spoonholder,
  sugar bowl), miniature
  Clear $166-174
Punch set with 6 cups,
  miniature, Clear 225-232
Sauce.   58-67

Opal, 100 percent more than clear prices listed.

Octagonal Beehive Deep Dish

Sandwich, early. Clear glass only. It is 9¼-inch in diameter and was used to hold a compote.

Beehive dish (ill.). $182-191
Compote to match
  (extremely rare). . . . .   685+

Odd Fellow

Probably Adams & Company, Pittsburgh, early 1880s. This firm specialized in

Octagonal Beehive Deep Dish

Odd Fellow

selling their wares in Central and South America. If traveling there, look for Adams, if you know their patterns. Much has been found south of the border. Clear, nonflint.

Butter dish, covered . . . . $ 50-58
Cake stand, 8″, 9″, 10″   42-52
Celery   29-37
Creamer   39-44
Goblet, knob and round
  stem (ill.)   35-42
Pitcher, large, small.   50-58
Spoonholder   35-42
Sugar bowl   40-44

Many other pieces, some being reproduced, such as horseshoe-handled platter.

O'Hara Diamond

U.S. Glass Company, c. 1891, 1892. Clear, plain, flashed with ruby stain, nonflint.

Bowl, 8″.	$ 24-32
Celery	30-38
Creamer	35-42
Cup/saucer, custard	21-32
Goblet	34-39
Pitcher, tankard	45-54
Spoonholder	34-42
Sugar bowl, covered	34-42
Tray, piecrust edge	30-37

Ruby stain, 40 percent higher than clear prices listed.

One-Hundred-and-One

One-Hundred-and-One

Probably Bellaire Goblet Company, Findlay, Ohio, late 1870s. Clear, nonflint.

Butter dish	$ 64-72
Celery.	59-67
Compote, covered, high foot, 8″	70-77
Creamer.	42-50
Goblet	51-60
Lamp, handled, flat	98-109
Pickle, oval, tapered	33-42
Plate	
7″, 8″, 9″, 10″, 11″	27-58
Bread, round, 11″, "Give us this day"	70-75
Salt/Pepper, pr.	42-52
Sauce, flat, 4″	15-21
Spoonholder	50-54
Sugar bowl	52-59
Relish dish, oval, deep.	21-27

Probably other pieces.

Opposing Pyramids

(Flora): Greensburg Glass Company, 1889. Clear, nonflint.

Butter dish, covered	$ 40-50
Creamer	34-39
Goblet (ill.).	33-42
Pitcher, water	47-56

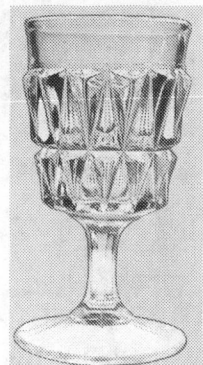

Opposing Pyramids

Sugar bowl, covered	43-51
Tumbler	40-50
Wine	32-37

Probably other pieces.

Optic

U.S. Glass Company, c. 1892. Clear, often ruby stained or engraved or both; nonflint.

Bowl, berry	$ 25-32
Butter dish, covered	37-44
Celery.	25-32
Creamer.	31-38
Goblet	24-29
Pitcher, water	42-51
Spoonholder	31-39
Sugar bowl, covered	37-42
Toothpick holder	24-35

Ruby stained and/or engraved, 20 percent higher than clear prices listed.

Oregon

Richards & Hartley Flint Glass Company, Tarentum, Pennsylvania, c. 1888. Clear, clear, flashed with ruby blocks; nonflint.

Butter dish, covered	$ 42-51
Celery.	35-42
Compote, covered	48-57
Creamer.	24-29
Goblet	37-42
Pitcher, water	50-57
Sauce, footed	27-35
Spoonholder	25-37
Sugar bowl, covered	35-46

Ruby blocks, 50 percent higher than clear prices listed.

Oriental   <small>Oriental</small>

Probably LaBelle Glass Works, Bridgeport, Ohio, 1875-1880. Clear, nonflint.

Butter dish, covered.	$ 39-44
Celery	37-41
Compote, covered	40-47
Creamer	39-46
Goblet	29-35
Pitcher	40-47
Spoonholder	27-32
Sugar bowl	
Covered (ill.)	48-52
Open	30-35
Tumbler	19-28

Probably other pieces.

Orion Inverted Thumbprint

Orion Inverted Thumbprint

Canton Glass Company, Canton, Ohio, 1894. Clear, amber, blue, green, milk-white, yellow, black; nonflint.

Butter dish, covered	$ 40-45
Celery	29-35
Compote	
Covered.	39-46
Open	32-41
Creamer	31-40
Pitcher, water (ill.)	42-46
Sauce, footed	25-27

Spoonholder	30-32
Sugar bowl	
Covered.	39-42
Open	25-34

Probably other pieces. Milk-white, 25 percent; yellow, 45 percent; amber, green, 65 percent; blue, 100 percent higher than prices listed for clear.

Oval Loop

(Question Mark): Richards & Hartley Flint Glass Company, Pittsburgh, c. 1880. Clear, nonflint.

Bowls, round, oval	$ 31-36
Butter dish, covered	47-54
Celery	24-30
Compote, covered.	44-50
Creamer	27-31
Goblet	26-32
Pitcher	47-51
Shaker, sugar	33-42
Spoonholder	35-42
Sugar bowl, covered.	40-42
Tumbler	36-39
Wine	32-37

Other pieces.

Oval Miter

McKee & Bros., Pittsburgh, c. 1865. Clear, flint.

Butter dish, covered	$ 77-82
Compote	
Open, 6″, 8″	52-59
Covered, high standard	68-72
Goblet	51-59
Sauce, flat	18-23
Spoonholder	41-50
Sugar bowl	
Open	73-78
Covered.	51-60

Probably other pieces.

Oval Panels

Maker unknown, c. late 1880s. Nonflint.

Goblet		
Amber.	$ 32-37
Blue.	42-48
Clear	32-39
Yellow.	31-40

Other pieces?

Owl and Possum

Owl and Possum

Maker unknown, 1880s. Clear, nonflint.

Goblet (ill.) . . . . $ 77-84
Pitcher, water 110-118
Sauce, footed 42-51
Probably other pieces.

Paling

Paling

Maker unknown, c. 1880s. Clear, non-flint.

Butter dish, covered . . . . $ 39-44
Creamer (ill.) 29-34
Goblet 27-32
Spoonholder 22-30
Sugar bowl, covered 39-44
Other pieces.

Palm Beach

U.S. Glass Company, c. 1895. Yellow, blue/opalescence, nonflint.

Butter dish, covered $265-274
Creamer 55-62
Pitcher, water 222-240
Sauce 33-42
Spoonholder 68-74
Sugar bowl, covered 77-84
Tumbler 52-61
Butter dish, 75 percent higher.

Palm Leaf Fan

Palm Leaf Fan

Maker unknown, early 1890s. Clear.

Bowl, large . . . . $ 31-42
Butter dish, covered 42-48
Cake stand, large 38-45
Celery vase 35-44
Compote
  Covered 41-48
  Open 26-37
Creamer 30-37
Pitcher, water (ill.) 43-49
Sugar, covered 42-51
Wine 24-29
Probably other pieces.

Palmette

Maker unknown, c. 1870s. Clear, nonflint.

Butter dish, covered . . . . $ 59-65
Cake stand 44-48
Celery 35-42

(continued)

Palmette

Compote
  Covered, low standard.   65-74
  Open, 8″ high   34-39
Creamer (with applied handle,
  rare)   49-54
Goblet   37-44
Pitcher (with applied handle,
  rare)   72-81
Salt, master (ill.)   22-28
Spoonholder   28-34
Sugar bowl, covered   39-45
Tumbler, water, footed   59-66
Wine   29-34

Probably other pieces.

Panama   Panama

(Fine Cut Bar): U.S. Glass Company, c. 1890s. Clear, nonflint.

Butter dish, covered. . . . . $ 34-39
Compote, covered   34-38
Cordial   22-27
Creamer.   29-38
Decanter   33-41
Goblet   34-39

Salt/Pepper, pr.   24-28
Spoonholder   29-37
Sugar bowl, covered   40-42
Tumbler   24-28
Wine (ill.)   31-39

Many other pieces.

Panel and Cane

Panel and Cane

Maker unknown, 1890s. Clear, nonflint.

Butter dish, covered. . . . . $ 42-51
Celery vase   28-32
Goblet   33-42
Pitcher (ill.)   40-44
Spoonholder   24-32
Sugar bowl, covered   32-41

Probably other pieces.

Panel and Star

(Column Block): O'Hara Glass Company, Ltd., Pittsburgh, c. 1880. Clear, nonflint.

Butter dish, covered. . . . . $ 48-55
Celery.   31-37
Creamer.   32-36
Goblet   35-41
Jar, pickle.   28-32
Pitcher, ...   44-52
Sauce, footed   23-28
Shaker, salt   29-37
Spoonholder   25-32
Sugar bowl, covered   34-43

Other pieces.

Panelled Acorn Band

Sandwich, early; other factories later. Clear, opaque. Sandwich prices listed.

Panelled Acorn Band

Butter dish, covered . . . .$ 92-105
Compote
  Covered 88-96
  Open 66-74
Celery vase 85-93
Creamer, applied handle. 64-72
Egg cup 35-42
Goblet 40-45
Pitcher (ill.) 88-97
Sauce, flat, footed 26-34
Spoonholder 35-42
Sugar bowl, covered 71-77

Probably other pieces. Goblet being reproduced.

Panelled Cable

Panelled Cable

Sandwich made a Cable pattern in the 1860s to commemorate the laying of the Atlantic Cable. There's a certain similarity between the Sandwich product and Panelled Cable, except this was made much later, probably in the 1890s. Sandwich closed its doors in 1888. Another of those "who-where-when" patterns.

Panelled Cane

Panelled Cane

(Cane Column): Possibly A. H. Heisey, Newark, Ohio, c. 1897. Clear, canary, amber, blue; nonflint.

Butter dish, covered. . . . . $ 34-39
Creamer 40-45
Goblet (ill.) 32-39
Sauce, flat 11-16
Spoonholder 23-31
Sugar bowl, open 28-34
Wine 20-27

Canary, 75 percent; amber, 85 percent; blue, 100 percent higher than clear prices listed.

Panelled Cherry

Northwood Glass Company, 1880s. "N" sometimes found in bottom. Clear, cherries red, leaves gold; nonflint.

Butter dish, covered. . . . . $ 83-92
Compote, covered, low
  standard 82-88
Creamer 49-54
Goblet 40-48
Pitcher
  Syrup 72-79
  Water (ill.) 80-88
Sauce, flat, footed 24-29
Spoonholder 39-47
Sugar bowl, covered 72-82
Tumbler 28-33

(continued)

Panelled Cherry

Panelled Daisy

Panelled Daisy

(Brazil): Bryce Bros., Pittsburgh, c. 1888. Clear, nonflint; amber, rare.

Bowl, waste	$ 17-25
Butter dish, covered, footed	48-54
Cake stand, 8″, 9″, 10″, 11″, high standard	37-55
Creamer (rare)	35-41
Goblet	27-35
Pitcher	
Water	65-74
Syrup	60-62
Plate, 7″ square (ill.)	30-34
Salt/Pepper, pr.	47-54
Spoonholder	28-35
Sugar bowl, covered	44-52

Amber, 300 percent higher than clear prices listed. Goblet being reproduced.

Panelled Dewdrop

(Striped Dewdrop): Campbell, Jones & Company, Pittsburgh, c. 1878. Clear, nonflint. Two types: plain base; rows of dewdrops on base.

Panelled Dewdrop

Butter dish, covered	$ 62-69
Celery	38-45
Cordial	32-41
Creamer, applied handle	37-44
Goblet, dewdrops on base	39-45
Pitcher, water	42-48
Sauce, footed	9-12
Spoonholder (ill.)	39-47
Sugar bowl, covered	39-47

Other pieces. Rows of dewdrops on base, 20 percent higher than plain base prices listed.

Panelled Diamond Cut and Fan

Panelled Diamond Cut and Fan

(Hartley): Richards & Hartley, late 1800s. Clear, amber, blue, canary; nonflint.

Bowl	$ 27-36
Butter dish, covered	42-51
Cake stand	49-56
Celery	27-36
Compote	
Covered	52-61
Open	33-41
Creamer	40-45
Goblet (ill.)	35-42
Pitcher, water	48-57
Sauce, flat	22-27
Spoonholder	28-32
Sugar bowl	
Covered	39-44
Open	25-35
Wine	24-32

Probably other pieces. Colors, 100 percent higher than clear prices listed.

Panelled Forget-Me-Not

Panelled Forget-Me-Not

(Regal) Bryce Bros., Pittsburgh, 1870s. Clear, amber, yellow, blue, green. Amethyst, rare.

Bowl, covered	$ 28-35
Butter dish, covered	44-52
Cake plate on standard	27-32
Celery	49-54
Compote, covered, high	
standard, 8″ high	57-63
Cordial	36-42
Creamer	28-34
Goblet	39-48
Jam jar	38-46
Pickle dish, oval	22-27
Pitcher, two sizes	36-49
Sauce, flat, rounded footed	18-25
Spoonholder	23-30
Sugar bowl, covered	34-39

Probably other pieces. Colors, 40-50 percent higher than clear prices listed. Amethyst, 175 percent higher.

Panelled Grape (Number 507)

Panelled Grape (Number 507)

Kokoma Glass Manufacturing Company, Kokoma, Indiana, 1904. Clear, colors, rare in milk glass. Westmoreland reproduced it in crystal and milk glass. Non-flint.

Bowl, round, covered	$ 49-58
Butter dish	61-67
Compote, covered	51-60
Creamer	48-57
Pitcher, applied handle (ill.)	60-68
Sauce, footed and flat	20-27
Spoonholder	20-27
Sugar bowl	
Covered	20-27
Open	28-32

Probably other pieces. Milk glass, 60 percent higher than clear prices listed. All items made being reproduced.

Panelled Heather

(continued)

Panelled Heather

Maker unknown, early 1890s. Clear, nonflint.

Butter dish	$ 38-44
Cake stand	40-48
Compote, covered	49-58
Creamer	30-37
Goblet	34-39
Pitcher	
Milk	48-56
Water (ill.)	40-44
Spoonholder	32-37
Sugar bowl, covered	26-34

Probably other pieces.

Panelled Hobnail

Panelled Hobnail

Bryce Bros., 1875-1885. Clear, amber, blue, opaque-white, vaseline, canary; nonflint.

Butter dish, covered	$ 34-38
Compote	
Covered	32-37
Open	28-32
Creamer	31-40
Goblet	27-36
Pitcher (ill.)	40-48
Sugar bowl	
Covered	37-45
Open	24-32
Wine	22-29

Probably other pieces. Amber, canary, opaque-white, 60 percent higher; blue, green, 80 percent higher than clear prices listed.

Panelled Honeycomb

Bryce, Walker & Company, 1880. Clear, nonflint.

Butter dish	$ 39-46

Panelled Honeycomb

Celery	25-31
Compote	39-44
Creamer	37-42
Goblet	32-41
Pitcher (ill.)	49-54
Spoonholder	24-32
Sugar bowl, covered	38-46

Probably other pieces.

Panelled Ivy

Panelled Ivy

Possibly Bryce Bros., late 1880s; later U.S. Glass Company. Clear, possibly colors; nonflint.

Butter dish, covered	$ 38-44
Cake stand	33-42
Celery	25-38
Compote	
Covered	48-57
Open	32-37
Goblet	35-42
Pitcher (ill.)	39-44

Probably other pieces. If in color, at least 60 percent higher than clear prices listed.

Panelled Oak

Panelled Oak

Maker unknown, 1890s, early 1900s. Clear, nonflint.

Butter dish, covered.	$ 40-46
Celery vase	27-32
Creamer.	32-35
Goblet	37-45
Pitcher (ill.).	48-54
Spoonholder	35-42
Sugar bowl, covered	40-47
Tumbler	26-31

Probably other pieces.

Panelled Ovals

Maker unknown, c. 1860s. Clear, flint.

Butter dish, covered.	$ 72-77
Compote	
Open	32-39
Covered	57-66
Creamer	60-68
Egg cup.	37-42
Goblet	48-57
Spoonholder	51-57
Sugar bowl	
Open	25-34
Covered	42-48

Other pieces.

Panelled Pleat

Robinson Glass Company, Zanesville, Ohio, c. 1894. Clear, nonflint.

Butter dish, covered	$ 36-42
Creamer	29-38
Goblet	26-32

Spoonholder	24-31
Sugar bowl, covered.	30-34

Possibly other pieces.

Panelled Primula

Panelled Primula

Maker unknown, 1900s. Clear, nonflint.

Butter dish, covered	$ 37-44
Cake stand	38-46
Celery vase	34-39
Compote	
Covered, high standard	49-54
Open, high and low standard	42-51
Creamer	25-34
Goblet	21-28
Pitcher, water (ill.)	43-52
Salt/Pepper, pr..	28-34
Spoonholder	21-28
Sugar bowl, covered.	32-37
Tumbler	24-29

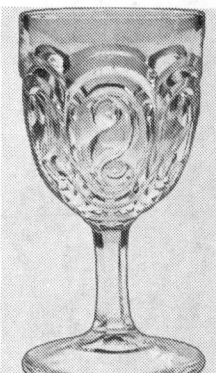

Panelled "S"

Panelled "S"

Maker unknown, 1880s. Clear, nonflint.

Butter dish, covered.	$ 45-52
Celery	31-38

(continued)

Compote	34-39
Creamer	38-45
Goblet(ill.)	32-42
Plate, 5″, 6″, 7½″	24-32
Pitcher, water.	58-62
Spoonholder	40-44
Sugar bowl, covered	47-56

Probably other pieces.

Panelled Sawtooth

Panelled Sawtooth

(Fluted Diamond Point): Duncan & Miller Glass Company, Washington, Pennsylvania, 1880s. Clear, nonflint.

Butter dish, covered	$ 48-56
Cake stand	38-43
Celery.	27-36
Goblet	32-41
Pitcher (ill.)	54-63
Spoonholder	21-29
Sugar	
Covered	41-50
Open	30-37
Wine	24-32

Probably other pieces.

Panelled Star and Button

Panelled Star and Button

(Sedan): Maker unknown, late 1880s. Clear, nonflint.

Butter dish, covered	$ 30-36
Creamer.	27-35
Goblet	29-37
Pitcher (ill.)	38-47
Spoonholder	34-41
Sugar bowl	
Covered	38-47
Open	30-40
Wine	29-34

Probably other pieces.

Panelled Stippled Scroll

Panelled Stippled Scroll

Maker unknown, early 1900s. Clear, amber, blue; nonflint.

Celery vase	$ 22-31
Compote	34-39
Creamer.	26-32
Goblet (ill.)	28-38
Pitcher, water	42-50
Spoonholder	21-29
Sugar bowl, covered	35-44
Tumbler	26-29

Probably other pieces. Color, 40 percent more than clear prices listed.

Panelled Strawberry

Maker unknown, late 1890s. Clear, foliage and berries burnished gold; also, maroon to pink; nonflint.

Butter dish	$ 48-54
Celery.	26-30
Creamer.	32-37
Goblet	31-38

Panelled Strawberry

Pitcher (ill.)	55-62
Sauce, 5″, 6″, 6½″	27-37
Spoonholder	30-38
Sugar bowl, covered	39-47
Tumbler	22-29

Colors don't affect price.

Panelled Sunflower   **Panelled Thistle**

Panelled Sunflower

Maker unknown, 1880s. Clear, blue, nonflint.

Butter dish	$ 37-42
Celery	26-33
Creamer	31-36
Goblet (ill.)	35-42
Spoonholder	27-38
Sugar bowl	29-39

Probably other pieces. Blue, 65 percent higher than clear prices listed.

Panelled Thistle

J. B. Higbee Glass Company, Bridgeville, Pennsylvania, 1910, possibly earlier. Clear, nonflint.

Bowl, berry, 6½″, 7″, 8½″, 9″, footed	$ 32-44
Butter dish	45-52
Cake plate on stand, large, small	25-34
Celery, 11″	28-34
Compote, open, small, medium, large	26-33
Creamer, knob feet, Bee	34-39
Cruet	58-66
Dish, honey, oblong, oval, round with Bee	48-54
Goblet, 2 styles	39-50
Pickle dish, 7½″, 8¼″	22-28
Pitcher, 2 sizes	59-69
Plate, 7¼″, 8¼″, 9½″, 10¼″	29-39
Salt/Pepper, pr.	55-64
Spoonholder	28-36
Sugar bowl, 2 handles	52-61
Tumbler, water	28-32
Wine, 2 styles	27-34

Probably other pieces. With Bee mark, 25 percent higher. Practically every piece being reproduced.

Panelled Wheat

Panelled Wheat

Hobbs, Brockunier & Company, Wheeling, West Virginia, 1871. Crystal and milk glass.

(continued)

	Clear	Milk Glass
Butter dish, covered . . .	$37-42	$47-52
Compote		
Covered, footed	47-52	110-120
Open		50-58
Creamer	28-37	49-57
Goblet	30-37	98-107
Pitcher, water (ill.)		118-124
Sauce, flat	12-18	23-32
Spoonholder	22-30	31-38
Sugar bowl		
Covered.	38-47	47-54
Open		

Possibly other pieces.

Pansy and Moss Rose

Pansy and Moss Rose

Maker and date unknown. Clear, nonflint.

Prices comparable to Panelled Strawberry.

Parrot

Parrot

(Owl in Fan): Possibly Richards & Hartley, Tarentum, Pennsylvania, 1880s. Clear, nonflint.

Bowl	$ 42-48
Celery.	33-42
Goblet (ill.)	47-53
Wine (rare)	58-62

Doubtful if other pieces were made.

Parthenon

(Egyptian): Sandwich glass, c. 1870s. Clear, flint.

Butter dish, covered.	$ 58-58
Celery.	47-52
Compote	
Open, high, low standard.	44-52
Covered, high, low standard.	50-52
Creamer.	49-57
Goblet	47-52
Pitcher, water	62-68
Platter	
Figure of a woman	58-67
Salt Lake Temple	69-78
Spoonholder	39-48
Sugar bowl, covered	50-60

Possibly other pieces.

Pattee Cross

(Broughton; Gloria): U.S. Glass Company, c. 1900. In 1912, Sears, Roebuck listed it in their catalog under the name Gloria. Clear, green, nonflint.

Butter dish, covered.	$ 38-42
Celery.	24-29
Creamer.	30-39
Goblet	19-26
Pitcher	34-44
Sugar bowl, covered	34-39

Green, 40 percent higher than clear prices listed. Prices of 1900 pieces listed. Probably other pieces.

Pavonia

(Pineapple Stem): Ripley & Company, Pittsburgh, 1885. Clear, red-flashed, etched; nonflint.

Butter dish, covered, etched . . . . . $ 74-82

Pavonia

Cake stand, etched
   Large   44-52
   Small   40-42
Celery, etched.   37-42
Compote
   Covered, high standard   48-54
   Open, high standard.   34-39
Creamer, pedestal base, etched   54-62
Goblet, pineapple stemmed,
   etched.   35-44
Pitcher, water, pineapple
   stemmed   68-74
Spoonholder, etched   24-33
Sugar bowl, covered.   66-73
Tumbler, etched (ill.)   33-39
Wine, etched   35-39

Probably other pieces. Red-flashed, 35 percent higher than clear.

George Peabody

George Peabody

A hero in the War of 1812, a great philanthropist, honored both in England and America (1795-1869).

Mug, English registry mark . . . . $ 92-101
Bowl, English registry mark   107-114
Creamer, English registry
   mark (ill.)   88-98

Considered rare today.

Peacock Eye

Peacock Eye

An early Sandwich pattern. Clear, flint. Don't confuse it with Peacock Feather (Georgia).

Bowl, 8″ dia. (ill.) . . . . $ 182-194

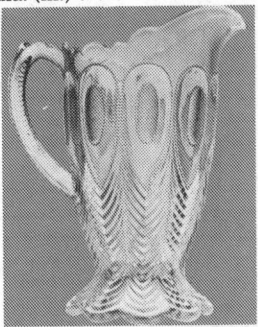

Peacock Feather

Peacock Feather

(Georgia): Originally an old Sandwich pattern. In 1907, U.S. Glass Company made same pattern and called it Georgia as part of their States series. Clear, blue, amethyst, other colors.

577

(continued)

Bowl, berry . . . . $ 27-35
Butter dish, covered. 48-54
Cake stand, 9″, 10″, 11″ 36-52
Celery boat   29-37
Compote
  Shallow, high standard   26-35
  Covered, deep, high
  standard   44-53
Creamer   33-42
Dish, oval   20-25
Lamp, handles, oil, blue 46-54
Pitcher, water (ill.) 68-74
Salt/Pepper, pr.. 45-53
Spoonholder 24-29
Sugar bowl, covered 66-72
Tumbler   33-40

Probably other pieces. Colors, 50 percent higher.

Peerless

Richards & Hartley Flint Glass Company, Pittsburgh, c. 1875. Clear, nonflint.

Bottle, caster . . . . $ 37-42
Champagne   40-48
Creamer, round, angular.   41-50
Egg cup 31-40
Goblet   31-41
Jar, pickle. 40-45
Pitcher, water, ½ gal. 54-62
Spoonholder 30-34
Sugar bowl, covered 55-63
Tumbler 32-41

Many other pieces. Twenty-two compotes alone!

Pendelton

Pendelton

Maker unknown, late 1860s, early 1870s. Clear, nonflint.

Butter dish . . . . $ 40-47
Celery vase 32-37
Creamer   26-31

Goblet   29-38
Pitcher, syrup, metal cap (ill.) 47-52
Spoonholder 27-36
Sugar bowl, covered.   37-46
Tumbler   25-33

Probably other pieces.

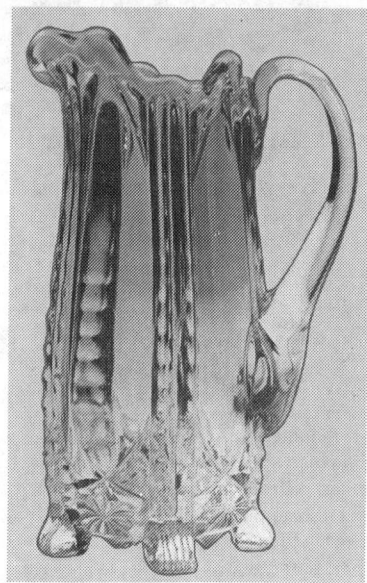

Pentagon

Pentagon

George Duncan & Sons, Pittsburgh, 1880. Clear, nonflint.

Creamer, individual . . . . $ 39-44
Creamer, tankard type 42-48
Pitcher, water, tankard
  type (ill.) 57-67

Other pieces probably exist in this pattern.

Persian

Persian

(Three Stories; Block and Pleat): Bryce, Higbee & Company, Pittsburgh, c. 1885. Clear, nonflint.

Bowls, oval, 8″, 9″, 10″	$ 23-31
Butter dish, covered.	46-52
Celery	30-37
Creamer (ill.)	32-41
Goblet	37-46
Mug	31-41
Nappies, fruit, 6″, 7″, 8″	19-27
Pitcher, ½ gal.	50-60
Sugar bowl, covered	47-54

Many other pieces.

Pert

Pert

(Ribbed Forget-Me-Not): Bryce Bros., 1880. Clear, nonflint.

Butter dish, covered.	$ 39-44
Creamer (ill.)	34-38
Spoonholder	28-33
Sugar bowl, covered	37-42

Probably these pieces made for a whist table.

Petal and Loop

Sandwich, early; later produced by O'Hara Glass Company, Pittsburgh; they called it the O'Hara pattern (see Loop). The piece shown here is Sandwich; smaller petals and loop designs on base of standard.

Petal and Loop

Compote (ill.).	$127-140
Dish, honey.	42-52

Philadelphia

New England Glass Company, c. 1860s. Clear, flint.

Bowl, covered	$ 43-52
Celery	38-48
Egg cup	38-46
Goblet	50-60
Spoonholder	23-42
Sugar bowl	
Open	29-38
Covered	40-49
Wine	39-46

Possibly other pieces.

Picket

Picket

(London): King Glass Company, Pittsburgh, late 1880s. Clear, stippled, nonflint.

Butter dish, covered	$ 54-63
Celery vase	45-52
Compote	
Covered, 6″, 8″, high foot	58-64

 (continued)

Open, high, low foot	38-47
Creamer.	35-42
Goblet	39-44
Marmalade jar	42-50
Match holder	32-37
Pickle jar, with cover	42-48
Pitcher, water (ill.)	54-64
Salt, flat, oblong.	17-26
Sauce, footed	12-16
Spoonholder	37-45
Sugar bowl, covered	48-56
Tray for water set	55-62

Pigs in Corn

Pigs in Corn

Maker unknown, 1875-1885. Clear, goblet only.

Goblet (ill.) $140-147

Pilgrim Bottle

Pilgrim Bottle

Variant; maker and date unknown. May come in colors or trimmed with ruby or gilt. Nonflint.

Bottle (ill.) . . . . $ 64-78

Pillar

Pillar

(Loop): Bakewell, Pears & Company, Pittsburgh, c. 1850s. Clear, flint.

Ale (ill.).	$ 52-61
Bottle, bar, 7″	44-52
Cordial	70-78
Creamer.	77-84
Decanter, no stopper	59-64
Sauce, flat.	24-29
Sugar bowl, covered	74-84

Should be other pieces.

Pillow and Sunburst

Pillow and Sunburst

(Elite): Westmoreland Specialty Company, 1891; again in 1896, and again in 1917. Clear, nonflint.

Butter dish, covered	$ 40-47
Celery.	28-34

Compote
Covered 45-54
Open 29-37
Creamer (ill.) 40-50
Goblet 32-39
Pitcher, water 47-54
Spoonholder 28-32
Sugar bowl 38-47
Probably other pieces.

Pillow Bands

Pillow Bands

Maker unknown. Clear and colors, nonflint.

Berry bowl . . . . $ 28-34
Butter dish 38-44
Celery 30-37
Compote
Covered 40-47
Open 38-41
Creamer 24-29
Cruet, cobalt blue 47-54
Goblet 39-49
Pitcher (ill.) 39-47
Spoonholder 32-42
Sugar bowl, covered 39-44
Probably others. Colors, 50 percent more than clear prices listed.

Pillow Encircled

Maker unknown, early 1890s. Clear and ruby flashed, nonflint.

Butter dish, covered . . . . $ 40-42
Compote
Covered 47-53
Open 38-47
Creamer 29-39
Dish, oval 17-25
Pitcher (ill.) 48-54
Sauce 19-23

Pillow Encircled

Spoonholder 27-34
Sugar bowl
Covered 32-42
Open 22-29
Tumbler 19-27
Probably other pieces. Ruby flashing, 60 percent higher than clear prices listed.

Pineapple

Pineapple

Hobbs, Brockunier & Company, Wheeling, West Virginia, 1886. Clear, opalescent, colors, nonflint.

Butter dish, covered . . . . $ 48-54
Celery 28-37
Pitcher (ill.) 58-64
Spoonholder 38-48
Sugar bowl
Covered 40-50
Open 28-36
Other pieces. Opalescent and colors, 50 percent higher than clear prices listed.

Pineapple and Fan

Adams & Company, Pittsburgh; later by

(continued)

Pineapple and Fan

U.S. Glass Company, 1891. Clear, emerald green, milk white, gold trimmed. Nonflint.

Bowl, berry, 8″, 9″	$ 17-27
Butter dish, covered	44-52
Cake stand	24-30
Celery, medium, tall	27-34
Creamer, individual, large	26-32
Mug	26-33
Pitcher	
½ gal., ¾ gal., tankard	38-46
1 qt., 1 pt., water	32-36
Sauce, 4″, 4½″	11-16
Spoonholder, laydown type	24-32
Sugar bowl	
Individual, covered	42-49
Large, covered	45-54
Tumbler, water	18-26

Probably other pieces. Emerald green, 50 percent, milk white, 100 percent higher than clear prices listed.

Pioneer's No. 15

Pioneer's No. 15

Pioneer Glass Company, Pittsburgh, c. 1890s. Clear with ruby stain, nonflint.

Butter dish, covered	$ 29-38
Compote, covered	32-46
Creamer	29-38
Goblet	30-36
Pitcher, milk	40-47
Salt/Pepper, pr.	24-33

Spoonholder	25-33
Sugar bowl, covered	29-38
Tumbler (ill.)	25-33
Wine	19-28

Probably other pieces.

Pioneer's Victoria

Pioneer's Victoria

Pioneer Glass Company, 1885. Crystal glass with ruby stain. Some pieces are engraved.

Butter dish, covered	$ 39-43
Celery	28-33
Compote, high, low standards	34-37
Creamer	32-40
Egg cup	29-37
Goblet	24-29
Pitcher, water (ill.)	34-43
Sauce	22-29
Spoonholder	30-34
Sugar bowl	38-47

Probably other pieces. Ruby stain has no effect on price.

Plaid

582

Plaid

Maker unknown, rare pattern of the 1880s. Clear, nonflint.

Celery . . . . $ 34-40
Creamer   29-33
Goblet   32-39
Pitcher, water (ill.)   49-56
Sugar bowl, open   37-47

Possibly other pieces.

Plain Tulip

Plain Tulip

Possibly Sandwich, 1850s. Clear, nonflint.

Celery . . . . $ 24-29
Compote
  Covered, large, high
    standard   60-66
  Open, large   47-57
Creamer   44-52
Goblet   35-43
Pitcher
  Syrup (ill.)   40-43
  Water.   52-58
Spoonholder   30-38
Sugar bowl   30-39
Tumbler   28-32
Wine   26-32

Probably other pieces.

Pleat and Panel

(Derby): Bryce Bros., Pittsburgh, 1870s; they called it Derby. It is better known as Pleat and Panel today. Clear, amethyst, yellow, blue, nonflint.

Butter dish, covered. . . . . $ 49-54
Cake plate, square, on standard
  9″, 9¼″   54-63

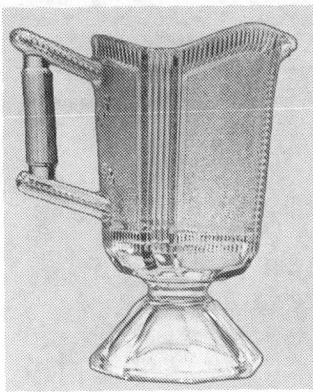

Pleat and Panel

Compote, covered and open   38-58
Creamer   34-39
Dish, oblong and square.   25-29
Goblet, 2 types   25-37
Lamp, 9¼″ high.   37-46
Pickle dish   19-27
Pitcher, water (ill.)   55-66
Plate, square 3½″, 6″, 7½″, 8½″. . . .   24-35
Platter, closed, open handles   39-47
Salt/Pepper, pr.   53-60
Spoonholder   29-37
Sugar bowl, covered.   48-55

Probably other pieces. Colors, 75 percent higher than clear prices listed. 7″ plate, 7½″ plate and goblet being reproduced.

Pleating

(Flat Panel): Bryce Bros., Pittsburgh; Gillinder & Sons, Philadelphia, c. 1880s. Reissued by U.S. Glass Company, c. 1891. Clear, flashed in red; nonflint.

Butter dish, covered. . . . . $ 39-44
Cake stand   38-42
Celery   22-28
Compote
  Open   30-37
  Covered   40-48
Creamer   32-47
Pitcher, water.   39-46
Spoonholder   29-37
Sugar bowl, covered   41-50

Flashed in red, 60 percent higher than clear; Bryce Bros. prices listed.

Plume

Adams Glass Company, 1874. Clear, redflashed, nonflint.

(continued)

Plume

Bowl, berry, finger	$ 23-33
Butter dish, covered	54-62
Cake stand	43-50
Celery	38-44
Compote	
Covered	44-52
Open, scalloped top	35-43
Creamer	33-42
Goblet	44-52
Pickle dish	23-30
Pitcher, water (ill.)	58-66
Sauce	12-17
Spoonholder	29-33
Sugar bowl, covered	43-48
Tray, water	65-73
Tumbler	19-27

Probably other pieces. Red-flashed, 25 percent higher than clear prices listed. Goblet being reproduced.

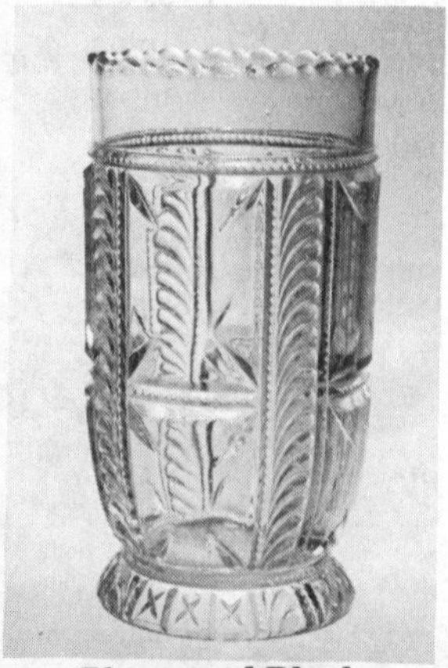

Plume and Block

Plume and Block

Richards & Hartley Glass Company, Tarentum, Pennsylvania, 1885-1891. Clear, clear with ruby stain; nonflint.

Butter dish, covered	$ 38-45
Celery (ill.)	28-36
Compotes, 4″, 6″, 8″	34-43
Creamer	28-37
Pitcher, ½ gal., gal.	59-68
Spoonholder	27-36
Sugar bowl, covered	38-44

Possibly other pieces.

Plutec

Plutec

McKee Glass Company, Jeannette, Pennsylvania, c. early 1900s. Clear, nonflint. Most pieces marked "Prescut."

Bowl, nut	$ 31-39
Butter dish, covered	34-43
Cake stand	40-47
Compote, covered	31-40
Creamer	30-38
Dish, pickle	19-24
Goblet (ill.)	34-42
Pitcher, water	47-55
Spoonholder	32-41
Sugar bowl, covered	34-37

Many other pieces.

Pointed Cube

Maker unknown, c. 1880s. Clear and frosted, nonflint.

Decanter	$ 40-47
Tray, wine	34-41
Wine (ill.)	32-40

Frosted, 20 percent higher than clear prices listed. Probably other pieces.

Pointed Cube

Pointed Jewel

Polar Bear

Pointed Jewel

Columbia Glass Company, Findlay, Ohio, 1880s; later U.S. Glass Company, 1892. Clear, nonflint.

Butter dish, covered . . . . $ 49-56
Creamer. 43-52
Custard cup 17-23
Goblet 25-32
Pitcher (ill.) 58-64
Spoonholder 22-28
Sugar bowl, covered 49-54
Tumbler 29-37
Wine 22-29

Probably other pieces.

Polar Bear

(Iceberg; Arctic; North Pole): Crystal Glass Company, Bridgeport, Ohio, 1880s. Clear; partly frosted, nonflint.

Bowl, waste . . . . $ 89-94
Butter dish, clear 112-121
Creamer, clear. 80-88

Goblet
   Clear 89-97
   Frosted 108-114
Pickle dish 34-43
Pitcher, water, frosted (ill.) 284-293
Platter, oval, handled 109-118
Sauce 15-23
Spoonholder 35-43
Sugar bowl, covered 48-54
Tray, water, round, oval 152-170

Probably other pieces.

Popcorn   Popcorn

Sandwich, 1860s. Crystal only. Some pieces have "popcorn ears."

Butter dish, covered . . . . $ 68-77
Cordial 44-52
Creamer 54-62
Goblet, with and without ear 29-58
Pitcher, water (ill.) 106-114
Sauce 14-18
Spoonholder 35-42
Sugar bowl, covered 52-61
Wine, with ear 66-69

Probably other pieces. "Popcorn ear" pieces, 25 percent higher than clear prices listed.

Portland

Portland, Maine,1880s. Cranberry, ruby, green, yellow, nonflint.

Bride's basket in frame . . . . $ 92-105
Butter dish, covered 50-58
Celery 32-41
Compote, covered, jelly 40-47
Creamer 32-40
Cruet (ill.) 41-48
Goblet 35-43
Jam jar 27-37
Pitcher, water. 49-58
Punch bowl. 52-60
Spoonholder 26-35
Sugar bowl, covered. 45-54

(continued)

Sugar shaker 47-54
Wine 28-34
Many other pieces made.

Portland   Powder and Shot

Powder and Shot

Originally Sandwich; other makers unknown. Clear, nonflint and flint.

Butter dish . . . . $ 88-95
Caster bottle 41-50
Celery 54-62
Compote, covered, high
  standard 88-95
Creamer 74-82
Egg cup, flint 67-74
Goblet, both styles 38-60
Pitcher, water (ill.) 82-90
Sauce 27-36
Spoonholder 39-46
Sugar bowl, covered 68-74
Tumbler 46-54

Pressed Diamond

Pressed Diamond

(Zephyr) Central Glass Company, Wheeling, West Virginia. Clear, yellow, amber, blue (scarce); nonflint.

Butter dish, covered. . . . . $ 50-58
Celery 39-46
Creamer 32-36
Compote
  Covered 51-50
  Open 34-43
Goblet 35-44
Pitcher (ill.) 49-54
Spoonholder 28-37
Sugar bowl, covered 58-66
Tumbler 30-37

Probably other pieces. Yellow, 70 percent higher; amber, blue, 125 percent higher than clear prices listed.

Pressed Leaf

Pressed Leaf

(N.P.L.): Sandwich, early; Central Glass Company, Wheeling, West Virginia, 1881; McKee Bros., Pittsburgh, 1868, called it N.P.L. Clear, nonflint.

Bowl, open, high and low foot
  7″, 8″ . . . . $ 29-37
Butter dish, covered 44-52
Cake plate on stand 65-78
Compote, covered, high, low
  standard, 6″, 7″, 8″ 54-66
Cordial 44-51
Creamer, applied handle (ill.) 45-53
Dish, oval, 5″, 6″, 8″, 9″ 25-38
Egg cup 22-27
Goblet 27-35
Lamp, applied handle 51-60
Pitcher, water 88-96
Sauce 14-19
Spoonholder 23-28
Sugar bowl, covered 38-44
Wine 38-42

Probably other pieces.

Primrose Primrose

Canton Glass Company, Canton, Ohio, 1880s. Crystal, amber, canary, blue, apple green, opaque-white, turquoise, purple slag, opaque-black. Apple green and yellow, rarest colors. Nonflint.

Bowl, berry, round, deep.	$ 24-29
Butter dish	45-53
Cake plate on standard	48-56
Compote, covered, 6″, 7½″, 8″, 9″ . . .	30-56
Creamer.	33-40
Goblet, plain, knob stem.	24-33
Pickle dish	14-18
Pitcher, milk (ill.)	38-47
Plate, 4½″, 6″, 7″, 8¾″, cake.	17-32
Sauce, footed, 4″, 5½″	16-25
Spoonholder	24-32
Sugar bowl, covered	34-42

Probably other pieces. Yellow and amber, 20 percent higher; blue, green, 30 percent higher than clear prices listed.

Princess Feather

(Lacy Medallion; Rochelle): Sandwich called it Princess Feather; Bakewell, Pears, Blackwell & Company called it Rochelle. It was also called Lacy Medallion by U.S. Glass Company, late 1880s. Clear, opaque white, nonflint.

Butter dish, covered.	$ 69-77
Celery	45-53
Compote	
Covered, 6″, 7″, high	
standard	56-63

Princess Feather

Open, 8″, low standard.	28-34
Creamer (ill.)	54-62
Egg cup.	36-40
Goblet	38-46
Honey dish	17-21
Pitcher, ½ gal.	79-86
Plate, 6″, 7″, 8″, 9″, cake	34-53
Spoonholder	29-35
Sugar bowl, open	34-42

Opaque white, 50 percent higher than clear.

Printed Hobnail

Printed Hobnail

Maker unknown, 1880s. Clear, amber, canary, blue, green, amethyst; nonflint.

Butter dish	$ 44-48
Celery vase	37-43

587 (continued)

Creamer	30-36
Goblet	30-37
Mug, handled	22-27
Pitcher, water (ill.)	48-54
Saucedish, 4″	14-21
Spoonholder	30-35
Sugar bowl	41-50
Tray for water set	38-46
Tumbler	24-29
Wine	24-29

Probably other pieces. Amber, canary, 60 percent higher; blue, green, amethyst, at least 125 percent higher than clear prices listed.

Priscilla   Priscilla

(Alexis; Sun and Star): Dalzell, Gilmore & Leighton Company, Findlay, Ohio, 1890s. Clear, with red dots, nonflint.

Bowl, square, 8″, flat, 10½″, rose	$ 52-58
Butter dish, covered	74-78
Cake stand, 10″ dia.	54-63
Celery	58-66
Compote	
Covered, 7″	57-62
5″ high	45-50
Open, 7½″	30-36
Creamer	28-36
Goblet	29-37
Mug	18-22
Pitcher, water	81-91
Spoonholder	23-32
Sugar bowl, covered	38-47
Toothpick holder	54-62
Tumbler (ill.)	25-34
Wine	29-37

Probably other pieces. With red dots, 40 percent higher than clear prices listed. Being reproduced in volume.

Prism   Prism and Flattened

Prism   Sawtooth

Maker unknown, c. 1860s. Flint and nonflint. Don't confuse it with Prism and Flute—their trade name was also Prism, a nonflint product.

Champagne	$ 42-52
Compote, open	48-57
Creamer	68-78
Decanter	59-67
Goblet (ill.)	49-53
Pitcher	84-92
Wine	49-57

Nonflint, 50 percent lower than flint prices listed. Probably other pieces.

Prism and Flattened Sawtooth

(Ribbed Pineapple): Maker unknown, 1850s. Clear.

Goblet (ill.)	$ 60-68
Lamp	74-81
Spoonholder (or spill)	50-58
Sugar bowl, open	69-77

Probably other pieces.

Prism with Diamond Points

Possible Sandwich Glass, early; or Midwest, c. 1860s. Clear, flint.

Butter dish, covered	$ 79-86
Compote, covered, knob stem	103-112
Cordial	34-43
Creamer	68-76
Egg cup, double	48-55
Goblet	
Plain stem	48-57

Knob stem.	60-68
Pitcher, 6½" high	106-116
Spoonholder	47-55
Sugar bowl, covered	54-62
Tumbler	38-45
Wine	55-64

Covered.	40-47
Tub, ice	38-46

Many other pieces. If clear with colored top, 30 percent higher than clear prices listed.

Quatrefoil

Psyche and Cupid

Psyche and Cupid

Possible Hartley Glass Company, Tarentum, Pennsylvania, 1880s. Clear, nonflint.

Butter dish, covered	64-72
Celery	47-53
Compote, high, low standard	56-77
Creamer	58-66
Goblet	42-51
Jam jar	35-42
Pickle dish	27-32
Pitcher, water (ill.)	71-81
Sauce	15-19
Spoonholder	57-62
Sugar bowl	47-56
Wine	29-36

Probably other pieces.

Quartered Block

George Duncan's Sons & Company, Washington, Pennsylvania, c. 1894. Clear, nonflint; possibly clear with colored top.

Butter dish, covered	$ 39-44
Cake plate, flat, high	29-37
Celery	30-38
Compote	
Low standard	31-40
High standard	44-52
Creamer, pt.	32-38
Dish, horseradish	25-35
Goblet	31-40
Spoonholder	25-34
Sugar bowl	
Open	29-38

Quatrefoil

Maker unknown, 1880s. Clear, apple green, nonflint.

Bowl	$ 24-29
Butter dish, covered	41-50
Compote, covered.	40-47
Creamer	36-44
Goblet (rare)	100-108
Pitcher (ill.)	49-54
Salt/Pepper, pr.	24-33
Spoonholder	22-31
Sugar bowl	
Covered.	31-40
Open	21-29
Tumbler (some say it was never	
made)	180+

Colors, 75 percent higher than clear prices listed.

Queen

(Sunk, Pointed Panel; Panelled Daisy and Button): McKee Glass Company, Jeannette, Pennsylvania, 1894; other factories same period. Clear, yellow, amber, apple green, blue.

Butter dish, covered.	$ 40-50
Compote	
Covered	41-50
Open	35-44
Creamer	34-42
Goblet	30-40
Pitcher, water (ill.)	45-54
Sauce, oval	20-27
Spoonholder	26-35

(continued)

Sugar bowl
Covered.	40-48
Open	28-36
Tumbler	34-42

Probably other pieces. Yellow, 50 percent; amber, apple green, 60 percent; blue, 80 percent higher than clear prices listed.

Quilt and Flute

Queen Anne   Queen

Queen Anne

(Bearded Man; Santa Claus; Neptune): LaBelle Glass Company, Bridgeport, Ohio, 1878. Clear, colors, nonflint.

Butter dish, covered	$ 54-62
Celery.	28-36
Compote, covered, 7″, 8″	52-63
Creamer.	34-42
Pitcher, water, (ill.)	55-63
Sauce, footed, 4½″	33-40
Spoonholder	29-36
Sugar bowl, open	32-37

Probably other pieces. Colors, 25 percent higher than clear prices listed.

Quilt and Flute

Maker and date unknown. Probably made for use as a container for mustard. Clear, nonflint.

Creamer (ill.)	$ 28-37
Mustard jar	24-33
Sugar bowl	35-44

Possibly other pieces.

Quixote

Quixote

Tarentum Glass Company, Tarentum, Pennsylvania, 1899. Nonflint.

Butter dish	$ 43-47
Celery	25-35
Goblet	30-37
Pitcher	47-55
Spoonholder (ill.)	22-30
Sugar bowl	33-37

Probably other pieces

Racing Deer

Probably Indiana Tumbler & Goblet Company, late 1890s. Clear, chocolate.

Pitcher, water—chocolate	$245-260
Pitcher, water—clear (ill.).	118-130

Radiant

(Dynast): Maker unknown, c. late 1880s. Clear, etched, nonflint.

Butter dish, covered.	$ 40-48
Cake plate	41-50
Celery	24-32

Racing Deer

Compote
Open 27-36
Covered 38-44
Creamer 37-46
Goblet 40-50
Pitcher, syrup. 40-47
Salt/Pepper, pr. 37-46
Spoonholder 24-33
Sugar bowl, covered 40-47
Tumbler 25-34
Wine 24-32

Clear, etched, same price. Probably other pieces.

Rainbow

McKee & Bros., Pittsburgh, c. 1894,
Rose pink, gold decorated. McKee was the
first of the manufacturers to use a permanent trademark, "PRES-CUT" 1894, in
the glass. Nonflint.

Butter dish, covered. . . . . $ 49-56
Carafe 47-54
Creamer 40-47
Goblet 42-47
Jar, cigar, gold or silver lid. 38-47
Pitcher, water. 28-35
Tumbler 28-35
Wine 38-42

Many other pieces.

Raindrop

Maker unknown, c. 1880s. Clear, canary,
amber, blue, light green (rare); nonflint.

Bowl (ill.) . . . . $ 12-16

Raindrop

Butter dish, covered, round 32-40
Compote, open, high, low
standard 28-34
Creamer 24-32
Egg cup, double 27-35
Pitcher, syrup. 22-27
Sauce, flat, footed 10-14
Tray, large 38-47

Canary, 70 percent higher; amber, blue, 100 percent higher; light green, 150 percent higher than
clear prices listed.

Raspberry

Raspberry

Maker unknown, late 1870s. Clear, nonflint.

Butter dish, covered . . . . $ 35-42
Celery 21-28
Compote
Covered 39-46

591

(continued)

Open	27-30
Creamer.	29-34
Goblet	26-32
Pitcher, water (ill.)	47-54
Spoonholder	29-34
Sugar bowl, covered	37-46
Tumbler	26-34

Probably other pieces.

Ray

Ray

McKee Bros., 1894. Plain or engraved or ruby-stained or frosted on the plain parts. Nonflint.

Bowls, round, 6″, 7″	$ 30-37
Celery vase, tall	28-32
Dish, oblong, deep, 7″, 9″	27-36
Pitcher (ill.)	47-54
Plate, 6″	27-36
Saucedish, round, 4″, 5″, footed	24-32
Sugar bowl	
Covered	39-42
Open	35-45

Probably other pieces. Ruby-stained, 60 percent higher than clear prices listed.

Red Block

Doyle & Company, reproduced by U.S. Glass Company, 1892 and later. Clear, blocks painted red; nonflint.

Butter dish, covered	$ 68-74
Celery vase	54-62
Creamer, individual	73-80
Dish	
Cheese	75-82
Oblong, 8″, 9″, 10″	34-41
Goblet	38-45
Pitcher, water (ill.)	110-120
Salt/Pepper, pr.	84-93
Spoonholder, double handled	42-52

Red Block

Sugar bowl, covered	64-72
Tumbler	45-52
Wine bottle	60-65
Wine glass	40-47

Probably other pieces. Red, 25 percent higher than clear prices listed. Many reproductions. Goblet and mug being reproduced. Also, wine.

The Regent

The Regent

H. Northwood and Co., Wheeling, West Virginia, 1880s. Clear, blue-green, amethyst (extremely rare), decorated with gold; also in crystal. Clear prices given.

Bowl	$ 42-48
Butter dish	70-78
Compote	89-97
Creamer	70-73
Cruet set	80-88
Pticher, water (ill.)	118-127
Salt/Pepper, pr.	50-58
Sherbet	47-53
Spoonholder	59-65
Sugar bowl	77-84

Probably other pieces. Colors, 40 percent to 250 percent higher than clear prices given.

Reticulated Cord

Reticulated Cord

Maker unknown, 1880s. Clear, color scarce; nonflint.

Butter dish, covered.	$ 40-47
Cake stand, large	46-52
Celery vase	28-35
Creamer	44-52
Pitcher, water (ill.)	49-57
Relish.	18-27
Spoonholder	29-36
Sugar bowl	
Covered.	44-53
Open	39-45
Tumbler	25-34
Wine	18-26

Probably other pieces. Color, 125 percent higher than clear prices listed.

Rexford

Rexford

Tarentum Glass Company, Tarentum,

Pennsylvania, 1912-1918. Clear glass only, nonflint. Pieces were made with flared, straight, or belled edges.

Butter dish, covered.	$ 31-40
Cake stand, 9¾″	35-42
Celery	22-31
Creamer	25-34
Goblet	24-32
Pitcher	37-44
Spoonholder (ill.)	26-29
Sugar bowl, covered	30-42
Wine	24-32

Many other pieces.

Ribbed Forget-Me-Not

Ribbed Forget-Me-Not

(Pert): Bryce, McKee & Company, 1880. Clear, nonflint.

Butter dish, covered	$ 31-38
Creamer.	30-39
Cup, handled	22-29
Mustard jar with cover	32-42
Pitcher (ill.)	47-54
Spoonholder	30-38
Sugar bowl, covered	40-47

Probably other pieces.

Ribbed Grape

Maker unknown, possibly Sandwich, 1850s. Clear, flint. If colors, rare.

Butter dish, covered	$105-111
Celery vase	61-67
Compote	
Covered, 6″, high	
standard	147-156
Open, low foot	77-87
Cordial.	70-72
Creamer	142-148

(continued)

Ribbed Palm

Ribbon Candy

Ribbed Grape

Goblet	50-58
Pitcher (ill.)	170-180
Spoonholder	71-80
Sugar bowl, covered	99-106

Probably other pieces. If colors, 250 percent higher than clear prices listed.

Ribbed Opal

Ribbed Opal

(Beatty Rib): A. J. Beatty Glass Company, Steubenville, Ohio, 1888. Crystal, amber, blue, canary, three opalescent colors.

Creamer, individual (ill.)	47-54
Mug.	37-46
Pitcher, water	58-64
Relish.	34-38
Sugar	
Bowl	42-51
Shaker	40-47
Tumbler, 2 types	40-47
Wine	34-38

Probably other pieces. Blue opalescent, 90 percent higher; yellow opalescent, 150 percent higher than clear prices listed.

Ribbed Palm

(Sprig): McKee & Bros., Pittsburgh, 1868. Clear, flint.

Butter dish	$ 88-97
Celery	87-94
Compote, 7″, 8″, 10″, high,	
low standard	77-152
Creamer, applied handle	182-192
Dish, 6″, 7″, 8″, 9″, deep	49-58
Goblet	38-47
Lamp, three types.	98-107
Pitcher, 9″ high, applied	
handle (rare) (ill.)	152-170
Sauce, 4″	24-29
Spoonholder	50-60
Sugar bowl, covered	66-69
Tumbler, whiskey.	87-94
Wine	57-64

Probably other pieces. Color, 100 percent higher than clear prices listed.

Ribbon

Bakewell, Pears & Company, Pittsburgh, c. 1870. Clear, frosted, nonflint.

Butter dish, covered.	$ 68-75
Compote	
Dolphin stem, scalloped	355-370
Round, rectangular bowl.	162-170
Creamer	50-60
Dish, cheese, covered	109-114
Goblet	38-47
Spoonholder	34-42
Sugar bowl, covered	69-77
Tray, water	108-116
Wine (rare)	89-97

Other pieces. Goblet being reproduced.

Ribbon Candy

(Figure Eight; Double Loop; Bryce): Bryce Bros., 1880s; U.S. Glass Company, 1898. Clear, nonflint.

Bowls, various.	$ 34-42
Butter dish, covered.	48-55
Celery	29-38
Cruet	50-54
Cup/saucer	32-42
Creamer	34-39
Honey dish	40-47
Pitcher, water (ill.)	69-74
Sugar bowl	
Covered	41-50
Open	36-45
Tumbler	29-34

Probably other pieces.

Richmond

Richmond

Nickel Plate Glass Company, Fostoria, Ohio, 1889, early 1890s. Clear, nonflint.

Butter dish	$ 35-42
Celery.	28-35
Creamer.	29-37
Compote	
Covered	40-47
Open	40-48
Creamer.	46-54
Goblet	31-41
Pitcher, water (ill.)	58-68
Salt/Pepper, pr.	29-37
Spoonholder	28-37
Sugar bowl	47-56
Tumbler	37-46
Wine	35-43

Probably other pieces.

Richmond

Richards & Hartley Glass Company,

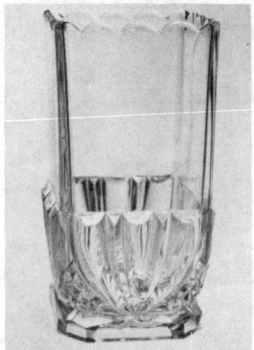

Richmond

Tarentum, Pennsylvania, 1885-1891. Clear glass only, nonflint.

Butter dish, covered	$ 36-42
Celery (ill.)	29-35
Compotes, 4″, 6″, 7″, 8″	24-33
Creamer.	22-31
Goblet	24-32
Pitcher, qt., ½ gallon	47-56
Sugar shaker	28-37
Sugar bowl, covered	40-48
Tumbler	22-32
Wine	33-43

Probably other pieces.

Ringed Framed Ovals

Ringed Framed Ovals

An "Oval" pattern originating at Sandwich Glass Company in the 1840s. Clear, vaseline, apple green, flint.

Goblet	$ 87-96
Tumbler (ill.)	90-103

Vaseline, 25 percent; apple green, 50 percent higher than clear prices listed.

Ripple

(Ripple Band): Sandwich, last 1870s.

595

(continued)

Clear, nonflint. Inferior as far as Sandwich glass is concerned.

Bowl, oval	$ 26-35
Butter dish, covered	33-39
Compote	
Open	31-40
Covered	37-47
Creamer	30-40
Goblet	31-40
Lamp	29-38
Salt, footed, oval	19-26
Spoonholder	23-32
Sugar bowl, covered	48-57
Wine	30-37

Probably other pieces.

Roanoke

Gillinder & Sons, Greensburg, Pennsylvania, 1885; later by U.S. Glass Company, 1898. Clear, amber, emerald green; nonflint.

Butter dish, covered	$ 38-45
Celery	22-27
Creamer	28-34
Goblet	24-32
Spoonholder	34-38
Sugar bowl, covered	69-76
Tumbler	28-34
Water pitcher	69-76

Probably many other pieces. Colors, 100-150 percent higher than for clear prices listed.

Robin Hood

Fostoria Glass Company, 1898. Clear, nonflint.

Butter dish	$ 35-42
Celery	30-36
Creamer (ill.)	28-31
Compote	
Covered	40-45
Open	34-43
Goblet	30-37
Pitcher, water	38-43
Spoonholder	28-37
Sugar bowl	37-41
Tumbler	28-34

Probably other pieces.

Rock Crystal

McKee Glass Company, Jeannette, Pennsylvania, c. 1894. Clear, colors, nonflint.

Butter dish, covered	$ 38-44
Cake stand	37-43
Celery	28-38
Creamer	30-37
Cup, custard	21-28
Glass, sundae	20-27
Goblet	25-32
Pitcher	35-41
Spoonholder	22-29
Sugar bowl, covered	32-40

Colors, 50 percent higher than clear prices listed. Many other pieces.

Robin Hood

Roman Rosette

Roman Rosette

Bryce, Walker & Company, 1875. Reproduced by U.S. Glass Company, in 1892, again in 1898. Clear; few pieces in color; clear pieces sometimes decorated with ruby on vertical ribbing; nonflint.

Bowl, 5″, 6″, 7″, 8″ . . . . $ 25-42
Butter dish, covered 44-51
Cake plate on stand, 9″, 10″
  (rare) 87-96
Caster set 70-79
Celery 35-43
Compote, covered, high, low
  standard, 5″, 6″, 7″, 8″ 49-66
Creamer, one pint 29-36
Goblet 39-46
Mug, large, medium 16-24
Pickle dish 27-32
Pitcher, syrup (ill.) 57-63
Salt/Pepper, pr. 49-54
Sauce, flat, footed 15-22
Spoonholder 65-73
Sugar bowl, covered 49-56
Tumbler 42-51
Wine 34-42

Probably other pieces. Red color, 25 percent higher than clear prices listed. Goblet being reproduced.

Rope Bands

Rope Bands

(Clear Panels with Cord Band): Possibly McKee & Son, Pittsburgh, late 1870s.

Clear; color, scarce.

Cake stand, large . . . . $ 44-53
Celery 30-38
Compote, covered 40-44
Creamer (ill.) 29-36
Goblet 25-32
Platter 34-42
Sugar
  Covered 40-50
  Open 35-42
Tumbler 24-29

Probably other pieces. Color, 100 percent higher than clear prices listed.

Rose-in-Snow

Rose in Snow

Bryce Bros., Pittsburgh, in the square shape. 1870s. Clear, amber, blue, yellow; nonflint.

Butter dish, round . . . . $ 44-53
Compote, covered, high low
  standard 49-56
Creamer, square 30-39
Dish, oval, large, small 18-27
Goblet 28-35
Mug 37-46
Pitcher, water (ill.) 102-112
Plate, 5″, 6″, 7¼″, 9″, (5″ rare) 19-37
Sauce, flat, round, square 18-26
Spoonholder, round, square 34-42
Sugar bowl, round, square 47-56
Tumbler, water 42-50

Probably other pieces. Colors, 20 percent higher than clear prices listed. Pieces made in the round shapes by the Ohio Flint Glass Co. Goblet, mug and 9″ plate being reproduced.

Rose Leaves

Rose Leaves

Maker unknown, c. 1880s. Clear, non-flint.

Goblet (ill.) . . . . $ 35-42
Other pieces?

Rose Point Band

Rose Point Band

(Water Lily): Maker unknown, early 1900s. Clear, nonflint.

Butter dish	$ 30-33
Celery	22-28
Creamer (ill.)	34-42
Goblet	28-37
Spoonholder	22-28
Sugar bowl, covered	36-40

Probably other pieces.

Rose Sprig

Campbell, Jones & Company, Pittsburgh, 1886. Clear, amber, yellow, blue; nonflint.

Butter dish . . . . $ 40-47

Rose Sprig

Cake plate on stand	28-36
Celery vase	32-40
Creamer	35-42
Dish, three styles	30-36
Goblet	38-45
Mug, handled	32-40
Pitcher, water, two sizes (ill.)	53-61
Plate, 6½″, 10½″, square	29-36
Platter	42-50
Salt, sleigh	24-32
Spoonholder	24-31
Sugar bowl, covered	46-52
Tray, water	51-60
Tumbler	27-35

Probably other pieces. Colors, 40-50 percent higher than clear prices listed. Salt, sleigh being reproduced.

Rosette **Rosette**

(Magic): Bryce Bros., Pittsburgh, called it Magic. Later produced by U.S. Glass Company, Tiffin, Ohio, who also called it Magic. Clear, nonflint.

Butter dish, covered.	$ 35-43
Cake plates on stand, 9″, 10″, 11″ . . .	21-32
Celery	33-37
Compote	
Covered, high standard, 6″, 7″, 8″	49-53
Open, footed, 6″, 7″, 8″, 9″, 10″.	44-52

Creamer	22-27
Goblet	29-36
Pitcher, water, half gallon (ill.)	39-47
Plate, 7″, 9″, handled	14-18
Relish (fish shape)	15-19
Spoonholder	25-33
Sugar bowl, covered	28-34
Tumbler	29-36
Wine	31-37

Probably other pieces.

Rosette with Pinwheels

Rosette with Pinwheels

Possibly U.S. Glass Company, after 1895. Clear, nonflint.

Butter dish, covered	$ 39-46
Celery	26-34
Creamer	30-40
Pitcher, water (ill.)	50-58
Spoonholder	27-39
Sugar bowl, covered	32-40

Probably other pieces.

Royal

Royal

Belmont Glass Company, Bellaire, Ohio, 1881. Clear, nonflint.

Butter dish	$ 40-47

Celery	30-37
Compote, covered 8″ high	37-44
Creamer	34-39
Goblet	28-36
Pitcher, water	41-48
Spoonholder	31-38
Sugar bowl (ill.)	40-48
Tumbler	32-41

Probably other pieces.

Royal Crystal

Royal Crystal

Tarentum Glass Company. Also known as Atlanta. Tarentum, Pennsylvania, 1894. Clear, ruby flashed; nonflint.

Butter dish, covered	$ 50-58
Celery	27-36
Compote, open, 7¾″	47-52
Creamer	28-36
Pitcher (ill.)	57-67
Sauce, flat	24-29
Spoonholder	35-44
Sugar bowl	
Covered	40-48
Open	38-47

Probably other pieces. Red or amber flashing, 50 percent higher than clear prices listed.

Royal Ivy

(continued)

Royal Ivy

Northwood Glass Company, Martins Ferry, Ohio, 1889-1890. Clear, deep pink/clear; deep pink/clear, acid finished; pink/clear, amber mottled; nonflint.

Bowl, open, 7″	$ 50-55
Butter dish, covered, clear to frosted	177-186
Creamer	57-64
Pitcher	
Syrup	68-77
Water	118-127
Shakers	
Salt/Pepper, pr.	108-117
Sugar bowl, covered.	116-122
Toothpick holder	65-72
Tumbler	54-63

Probably other pieces. All color patterns at least 50 percent higher than clear prices listed.

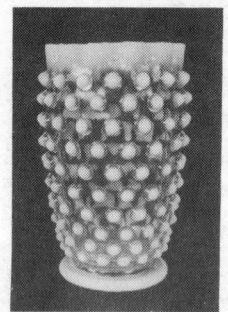

Ruffled Edge Hobnail

Royal Oak

Royal Oak

Northwood Glass Company, Martins Ferry, Ohio, 1889-1890. Flint, deep pink/clear; deep pink/clear, acid finished; pink/clear, amber mottled. Nonflint.

Prices same as Royal Ivy, nonflint and colors.

Ruffled Edge Hobnail

Maker and date unknown. Nonflint.

Bowl, finger	$ 34-42
Butter dish, covered.	40-47
Celery, opalescent (ill.)	23-32
Creamer	37-41
Sugar bowl, squat	44-52
Tumbler	30-37

Probably other pieces.

Ruffled Eye

Ruffled Eye

Indiana Tumbler & Goblet (National) Company, 1890s. This pattern is similar to Indiana's Dewey. Known to have been made in water pitcher. Nonflint.

Amber	$168-176
Blue	171-177
Green.	148-154

Probably other pieces but not known to this writer.

S Repeat

Northwood Glass Company, then National Glass Company, Pittsburgh, 1903. Clear, colors: amethyst and gold; translucent sapphire; light green without gilt; nonflint.

S Repeat

Butter dish	$ 48-56
Celery	30-38
Compote, high, low standard	50-59
Creamer	39-47
Goblet	36-42
Pitcher, water.	57-65
Salt/Pepper, pr.	36-44
Spoonholder	30-34
Sugar bowl, covered	51-60
Tumbler (ill.)	55-64

Probably other pieces. Colors, 50 percent higher than clear prices listed.

Saint Bernard

Fostoria Glass Company, Moundsville, West Virginia, c. 1894. Clear, nonflint.

Bowl, berry	$ 25-32
compote, covered	40-48
Creamer	30-36
Goblet	25-32
Jar, jam, covered	40-48
Spoonholder	30-39
Sugar bowl, covered	30-38

Many other pieces.

Sandwich Block

Sandwich, early. Flint.

Piece shown in photo is blue perfume with stopper. Rare. No price available, but probably $650+.

Sandwich Covered Sugar

Sandwich glass, early. Not pressed glass in the truest sense as it's blown-molded but nevertheless absolutely beautiful and still to be found. Flint.

Covered sugar (ill.) . . . . $ 850+

Sandwich Block

Sandwich Covered Sugar

Sandwich Glass Sugar Bowl

Sandwich, later period. Blue, amethyst, flint.

Sugar bowl with lid	$380-410
Probably creamer to match	290-320

(continued)

Sandwich Glass Sugar Bowl

Sandwich Star

Open, supported by 3	
dolphins, flint	850+
Amethyst, tall (rare),	
flint	1,350+
Cordial, flint	425+
Creamer, flint	335-365
Decanter, qt.	158-166
Goblet (rare), flint.	390-420
Pitcher, flint (ill.)	1,400+
Relish dish	78-84
Spill holder	85-95
Spoonholder	67-75

Probably other pieces.

Sandwich Spill

Sandwich Spill

Sandwich glass, early 1850s. Another example of magnificent glass. Flint.

Sandwich Star

Sandwich, early. Clear and amethyst (rare).

Compote
Covered, high standard . . . . $ 350+

Sawtooth

Sawtooth

(Roanoke): New England Glass Company, and Sandwich, 1860s. Later called Roanoke and made by Ripley & Company, Pittsburgh, 1885. Also made by U.S. Glass Company (Gillinder-merge) Nonflint.

Bowl, berry	$ 56-64
Butter dish	100-109
Cake stand, 9″, 10″	90-97
Celery vase	70-80
Compote	
Covered, 6″, 7″, 8″, 9″,	
10″, 11″, knob stem	118-126
Open, 6″, 7″, 8″, 10″	67-75

Creamer.	101-111
Decanter, qt.	140-150
Egg cup	58-67
Goblet	57-65
Pitcher, water, ½ gal. (ill.).	118-127
Sauce, 4", 5".	19-25
Spill holder, octagonal.	42-51
Spoonholder	47-56
Sugar bowl	90-108
Tumbler, footed, water	52-61

Probably other pieces. Goblet, iced tea, sherbet and wine being reproduced in pink.

Sawtoothed Honeycomb

Sawtoothed Honeycomb

Steiner Glass Company, Buckhannon, West Virginia, 1906; again in 1908 by Union Stopper Company, Morgantown, West Virginia. Crystal; crystal with central honeycombs in ruby with rims in gold; nonflint.

Celery	$ 24-29
Creamer (ill.)	60-70
Goblet	20-29
Pitcher, milk, bulbous.	45-53
Spoonholder	30-37
Sugar bowl, covered.	40-47

Probably other pieces.

Saxon

Adams & Company, Pittsburgh, Pennsylvania, c. 1880. Clear, plain and engraved, opal. Reissued after 1891 by the U.S. Glass Company. Nonflint.

Bowl, oval.	$ 32-41

Butter dish, covered.	59-66
Creamer	37-46
Compote	
Open	21-28
Covered	40-47
Goblet	32-42
Plate, 6"	33-42
Spoonholder	28-35
Sugar bowl, covered.	42-49
Tumbler	27-34
Other pieces.	

Scalloped Diamond Point

Possibly Central Glass Company, Wheeling, West Virginia, c. 1870s. Clear, nonflint.

Bowls, round, oval.	$ 23-32
Butter dish, covered.	37-41
Cake stand, large, 10"	39-47
Creamer	38-47
Dish, cheese.	36-46
Sauce, flat, footed.	18-27
Spoonholder	27-36
Sugar bowl, covered.	41-48
Wine	36-44

Probably other pieces.

Scalloped Prism

(Triple Bar): Doyle & Company, Pittsburgh, c. early 1880s. Clear, nonflint. Originally called No. 84 by Doyle. Reissued by U.S. Glass Company in 1891.

Butter dish, covered.	$ 45-54
Goblet	28-37
Spoonholder	26-36
Sugar bowl, covered.	41-51
Tumbler	26-34
Other pieces.	

Scalloped Tape

603

(continued)

Scalloped Tape

(Jewel Band): Maker unknown, 1880s. Clear, amber, canary, blue, apple green.

Butter dish, covered	$ 39-46
Cake stand	32-40
Celery	
Creamer	22-29
Egg cup	19-27
Goblet	28-36
Pitcher, water (ill.)	45-54
Sauce	19-26
Sugar	
Covered	27-36
Open	19-27
Wine	19-27

Probably other pieces. All colored pieces, at least 40 percent higher than clear prices listed.

Scarab

Scarab

Maker; date unknown. Clear, flint.

Goblet (ill.)	$118-130

Other pieces? The goblet is beautiful!

Scroll

(Stippled Scroll): Maker unknown, 1880s. Clear, nonflint.

Butter dish, covered	$ 43-49
Celery	30-38
Compote, covered, high, low	
standard	34-42
Creamer	22-28
Egg cup	14-23
Goblet	18-26
Pitcher, tankard type (ill.)	43-52
Spoonholder	21-29
Sugar bowl, covered	37-42

Scroll and Daisy

Scroll and Daisy

Northwood Glass Company. Opaline and Carnival; usual Carnival colors; nonflint.

Compote, candy or jelly	52-60
Creamer (probably a mustard jar, with lid, originally) (ill.)	41-50

Colors, 50 percent higher than crystal, marigold prices listed.

Scroll with Acanthus

Scroll with Acanthus

Central Glass Company, Wheeling, West Virginia. Clear, sapphire blue, purple slag. This pattern also was made by Northwood, only in the Mosaic or slag type. The prices shown are Northwood, 1902. Nonflint.

Creamer (ill.)	$ 67-74
Compote, jelly, tall, stemmed	60-70
Sugar bowl, open	60-69

Scroll with Flowers

Scrolled Sunflower

Scroll with Flowers

Central Glass Company, late 1870s. Clear, later made by Northwood in apple green, amber and blue. Possibly other colors made. Prices listed are for Northwood. Nonflint.

Butter dish	$ 45-53
Cake plate, handled	24-32
Celery	32-41
Creamer	29-37
Egg cup, 2 handles	28-37
Goblet	28-35
Mustard, covered	34-42
Pitcher (ill.).	77-86
Salt/Pepper, pr..	41-50
Sugar bowl, covered	38-42

Supposedly a rare pattern. Colors, 50 percent higher than crystal/marigold prices listed. Probably other pieces.

Scroll with Star

Challinor, Taylor & Company, Tarentum, Pennsylvania, c. 1885. Clear, nonflint.

Butter dish	$ 40-48
Cup.	25-29
Creamer	30-40
Goblet	25-32
Sauce	19-25
Spoonholder	29-32
Sugar bowl, covered	32-40

Probably other pieces.

Scrolled Sunflower

Another of those patterns lost on the back roads of time. Possibly Northwood who made several Scroll patterns. Shown for identification only. If you know, tell me.

?   ?

Because that's just what it is! An absolutely beautiful pattern. Maker and date unknown and no prices available. Anyone know its name?

Seashell

(Boswell): Maker unknown, c. late 1870s. Clear, nonflint.

Butter dish, covered . . . . $ 40-47
Cake stand   35-42
Celery   24-29
Creamer   27-36
Goblet   35-42
Pitcher   38-47
Salt/Pepper, pr.   30-38
Spoonholder   31-41
Sugar bowl, covered   40-48

Probably other pieces.

Shell and Jewel

Butter dish, covered . . . . $ 55-65
Cake stand   50-60
Compote, open, high foot 42-52
Creamer   34-42
Pitcher, water (ill.) 44-53
Spoonholder   32-40
Sugar bowl   42-51
Tumbler   25-34

No goblet made. Probably other pieces. Colors, 100 percent higher than clear prices listed.

Seesaw

Seesaw

Probably Gillinder & Sons, c. 1870s.

Plate, 10″ dia. (ill.) $97-106

Serenade Plate

Indiana Tumbler & Goblet (National) Company, 1890s. Chocolate, white-milk glass.

Serenade plate, large . . . . $ 175+
Serenade plate, small . . . . 165+

Prices given are for chocolate; milk-white, 50-60 percent lower.

Shell and Jewel

(Victor): Westmoreland Glass Company, 1893, originally called it Victor. Better known today as Shell and Jewel. Clear, blue, green, nonflint.

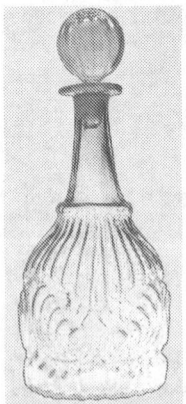

Shell and Ribbing

Shell and Tassel

Shell and Ribbing

This is blown, 3-mold glass, probably very early Sandwich. Not Pressed glass but we thought you'd like to see one of the rarest types of glass in the world.

Shell and Tassel

(Square): George A. Duncan & Sons; Shell and Tassel, Round: 10 years later, 1890, Duncan & Heisey. On the Round, the finial on the covered pieces was a dog in a reclining position. Round prices given. Square, 100 percent more.

Berry set, 7 pcs.	$102-108
Butter dish, round, covered, dog finial	55-64
Cake stand, large	48-54
Celery vase, round	19-24
Compote	
Covered	30-37
Open, 4½″, high standard	27-34
Creamer, round, square	44-52
Goblet, 2 types	32-46
Pitcher, round, (ill.)	43-52
Platter, bread	30-36
Salt shaker	18-27
Spoonholder, round	19-27
Sugar bowl, round	70-78
Vases, pr.	155-165

Probably other pieces. Colors, rare. 100 percent higher than prices listed for clear. Goblet being reproduced.

Sheraton

Sheraton

(Ida): Bryce, Higbee & Company, Pittsburgh, 1880s, called it Ida. Clear, amber, blue, green; and possibly yellow; nonflint.

Bowl, berry	$ 14-21
Butter dish	28-36
Compote, covered	36-44
Creamer	24-33
Goblet	39-45
Pitcher, water	29-39
Sauce, flat	12-16
Sugar bowl, covered	32-41
Tumbler	29-37
Wine	28-37

Amber, blue, 40-50 percent higher than color prices listed. Probably other pieces.

Shimmering Star

Shimmering Star

Maker unknown, 1880s. Probably made at an earlier date also. Clear, nonflint.

Butter dish, covered	$ 40-50
Cake stand	37-46
Pitcher (ill.)	42-51
Sauce, flat	22-27
Spoonholder	29-36
Sugar bowl	
Covered	57-66
Open	41-50
Tumbler	30-40

Probably other pieces.

Shoshone

Shoshone

(Victor; Blazing Pinwheels): U.S. Glass Company c. 1895. Crystal, ruby-stained, emerald green; nonflint.

Banana stand (ill.)	$ 40-47
Butter dish, covered	43-52
Compote, covered and open, 7″, 8½″	44-52
Creamer, 3½″, 5″ high	38-47
Goblet	34-42
Mug	30-37
Pitcher, milk, several sizes	68-74
Spoonholder	26-34

(continued)

Sugar bowl   38-46

Colors, 100 percent higher than clear prices listed.

Shrine

Maker unknown, c. 1880s. Clear, nonflint.

Bowl	$ 32-37
Butter dish, covered.	44-52
Compote, jelly	37-42
Creamer	33-42
Goblet	34-43
Sauce	16-24
Spoonholder	25-33
Sugar bowl	
Open	37-42
Covered	45-52
Tumbler, regular	35-46

Probably other pieces.

Shuttle

Shuttle

Indiana Tumbler & Goblet (National) Company, 1900. Chocolate, clear, caramel, nonflint.

	Chocolate	Clear
Cordial		$ 20-25
Creamer		38-47
Goblet		29-47
Mug (ill.)	$ 84-92	44-52
Pitcher, syrup	77-86	48-56
Punch cup	61-66	24-28
Salt/Pepper, pr. . . .		40-44
Saucedish		26-31
Spoonholder	60-70	38-47
Tumbler	47-54	28-37
Wine	37-46	29-39

Caramel, 200 percent more than clear prices listed.

Singing Birds

Singing Birds

Northwood Glass Company, Wheeling, West Virginia, 1900s. Clear, custard, Carnival, other; nonflint.

Berry set	
Large bowl, marigold	$ 60-68
Large bowl, vivid	77-84
Small bowl, marigold	24-32
Small bowl, vivid	37-46
Butter dish, covered, clear	38-44
Butter dish, covered, marigold	70-77
Butter dish, covered, vivid	124-129
Creamer, clear (ill.)	52-62
Creamer, marigold	56-64
Creamer, vivid	70-75
Mug, custard, marigold, vivid	37-42
Mug, color, non-iridescent	40-46
Pitcher, marigold	80-88
Pitcher, vivid	132-142
Sherbet (custard) (rare)	50-56
Sugar bowl, covered, clear	48-57
Sugar bowl, covered, marigold	62-72
Sugar bowl, covered, vivid	77-86
Spoonholder, clear	38-42
Spoonholder, marigold	50-60
Spoonholder, vivid	67-74
Tumbler, marigold	35-44
Tumbler, vivid	35-44

Custard, Carnival, 100 percent higher than clear prices listed.

Single Rose

Probably Westmoreland Specialty Company, c. 1890-1900. Clear, opaque white; sometimes colored, in rose and green, gilded; nonflint.

Butter dish, covered	$ 52-61
Creamer	40-47
Pitcher, water	42-51
Spoonholder	26-34
Sugar bowl, covered	47-52

Tumbler 25-34

Opaque white, 25 percent; rose, 30 percent; green, gilded, 40 percent higher than clear prices listed. Possibly other pieces.

Siskyou

Siskyou

A member of the Block family, c. 1880s. Clear, nonflint.

Same values as Block and Fan—see.

Slashed Swirl

Slashed Swirl

Riverside Glass Company, Wellsburg, West Virginia, 1891. Clear, nonflint.

Butter dish, covered.	$ 39-47
Celery	28-37
Compote	40-47
Creamer	30-38
Goblet	29-37
Pitcher, water (ill.)	40-49
Salt/Pepper, pr..	28-38
Sugar bowl	36-45

Tumbler 26-36

Wine 24-29

Probably other pieces.

Slewed Horseshoe

Slewed Horseshoe

Possibly Imperial Glass Company, Bellaire, Ohio, after 1906. Clear, nonflint.

Butter dish	$ 36-44
Cake stand	33-42
Celery	27-37
Creamer	32-41
Compote	35-44
Goblet	34-42
Pitcher, syrup (ill.)	41-51
Spoonholder	24-27
Sugar bowl, covered.	28-37
Tumbler	24-34

Probably other pieces.

Smocking

(continued)

Smocking

Sandwich Glass, 1840s. Clear, flint.

Butter dish, covered.	$ 90-99
Compote, footed, open, 6" high	72-81
Creamer, applied handle (rare)	101-109
Goblet	70-78
Lamp, 9" high	136-144
Spill, holder.	56-64
Sugar bowl, covered (ill.)	90-107

Probably other pieces.

Smooth Diamond

Smooth Diamond

Possibly McKee Bros., late 1880s. Clear, nonflint.

Butter dish	$ 40-47
Compote	33-42
Creamer	35-44
Goblet	34-42
Pitcher, water (ill.)	50-60
Sugar bowl, covered.	40-48
Tumbler	36-45

Probably other pieces.

Snail

George Duncan & Sons, Pittsburgh, c. 1880s, clear. After 1891, by U.S. Glass Company, who added ruby color to the plain bands, sometimes engraving through the color. Nonflint.

Bowls, berry.	$ 47-56
Butter dish, covered.	88-96

Cake stand	77-85
Celery.	47-54
Compote, covered	47-54
Creamer, regular	38-46
Goblet	50-60
Pitcher, water.	88-97
Spoonholder	38-44
Sugar bowl	
Individual, covered	54-62
Large, covered	42-50
Tumbler	37-45

Ruby colored bands, 100 percent higher than clear prices listed. Many other pieces.

Snakeskin with Dot

Snakeskin with Dot

Maker unknown, late 1870s. Clear, occasionally found in deep blue and amber.

Celery vase	$ 29-36
Creamer	37-47
Goblet	31-40
Pitcher, water (ill.)	46-55
Plates, 4½" to 7"	24-32
Sugar bowl, covered.	41-50

Probably other pieces. Deep blue and amber, 50 percent higher than clear prices listed.

Snow Band

(Puffed Bands): Maker unknown, c. early 1880s. Clear, blue, possibly other colors; nonflint.

Butter dish	$ 37-43

Compote
Open	26-34
Covered	40-47
Creamer	35-44
Goblet	26-35
Pitcher, water	40-50
Relish	24-33
Sauce, flat	18-25
Spoonholder	24-35
Sugar bowl, covered	38-42
Wine	25-29

Blue, 40 percent higher than clear prices listed. Probably other pieces.

Snowdrop

(Ashland): Portland Glass Company, Portland, Maine, c. 1880s. Clear, nonflint.

Dish, ice cream, leaf-shaped	$ 35-44
Goblet	30-40
Tray, ice cream	38-46

Should be other pieces.

Snowflake

Snowflake

Probably U.S. Glass Company, early 1900s. Clear, nonflint.

Butter dish	$ 40-46
Cake stand	42-51
Celery	26-36
Compote, covered, high, low	
standard	32-41
Creamer	30-38
Goblet	30-39
Pitcher	
Milk (ill.)	40-47
Water	50-57
Spoonholder	26-34
Sugar bowl, covered	39-48
Tumbler	26-35

Probably other pieces.

Southern Ivy

Southern Ivy

Maker unknown, mid-1800s. Clear, nonflint.

Bowl, berry	$ 19-27
Butter dish, covered	27-36
Creamer	27-35
Cruet, small	26-36
Egg cup	18-26
Pitcher, water (ill.)	34-39
Saucedish, 4″	19-26
Spoonholder	19-27
Sugar bowl, covered	27-36
Tumbler, water	24-33

Probably other pieces made. No goblet made.

Spanish-American

Spanish-American

(Dewey):Beatty-Bradly Glass Co., Dunkirk, Indiana, late 1890s.

| Pitcher, water, Admiral Dewey, cannon balls around base (ill.) | $ 66-75 |
| Tumbler, matches pitcher | 38-46 |

(continued)

Pitcher, water, "You may fire
when ready, Gridley"   67-77
Tumbler, matches pitcher (rare)   85-95

Spearpoint Band

Spearpoint Band

Maker and date unknown. Clear with ruby stain, nonflint.

Butter dish . . . . $ 34-42
Creamer.   29-32
Pitcher, water (ill.)   39-44
Sugar bowl, covered   30-40

Probably other pieces.

Spiral and Maltese Cross

Maker unknown, c. early 1880s. Clear, nonflint.

Butter dish, covered . . . . $ 40-47
Creamer.   29-38
Spoonholder   21-29
Sugar bowl, covered   40-43

Should be other pieces. We're always glad to hear from collectors and dealers alike. Constructive criticism is welcome; it helps us produce a better price guide for you.

Spiralled Ivy

Another of the Ivy patterns, mid-1880s. Clear, nonflint.

Butter dish, covered   42-50
Creamer.   27-36
Pitcher, water (ill.)   48-57

Spiralled Ivy

Sauce   9-12
Spoonholder   24-29
Sugar bowl, covered   34-42
Tumbler   21-29

Probably other pieces.

Spirea Band

Spirea Band

(Square and Dot; Squared Dot): Bryce, Higbee & Company, c. 1885. Nonflint.

Butter dish, covered . . . . $ 35-44
Cake stand   33-42
Celery   28-36
Compote
Covered   32-41
Open   24-30
Creamer   24-32
Goblet   19-27
Pitcher, water (ill.)   39-46
Platter   23-33
Salt/Pepper, pr..   22-26
Spoonholder   24-29
Sugar bowl, open   19-27
Tumbler   17-22

Wine   18-26

Probably other pieces. Amber, canary, blue, 65
percent higher; green, 100 percent higher than
clear prices listed.

Sprig

Sprig

(Royal): Bryce, Higbee & Company,
Pittsburgh, early 1880s. Clear, with and
without sprig decoration; nonflint.

Bowl, berry	$ 29-34
Butter dish	43-52
Cake stand	31-40
Celery	48-52
Compote	
Covered, high, standard,	
12″	52-61
Open, low standard	35-42
Creamer	24-32
Goblet	31-40
Pitcher, water (ill.)	54-63
Platter, oval.	36-44
Sauce, flat, footed	11-15
Spoonholder	27-36
Sugar bowl, covered	37-44
Tumbler	17-24
Wine	47-52

Probably other pieces.

Squared Star

Maker unknown, 1890s. Clear, nonflint.

Butter dish	$ 31-39
Creamer	24-30
Spoonholder (ill.)	30-35
Sugar bowl	45-50

Probably other pieces.

Squared Star

Squirrel

Squirrel

Indiana Tumbler & Goblet (National)
Company, Greentown, Indiana, 1880s.
Clear. Finials are squirrels. Nonflint.

Butter dish, covered, squirrel	
knob	$130-140
Creamer.	106-114
Goblet (extremely rare)	585+
Pitcher, water	130-140
Sauce, footed, flat	48-60
Sugar bowl	
Covered (ill.)	99-107
Open	66-74

Possibly other pieces. Chocolate (water pitcher
is known) would be 200 percent higher than
clear prices listed.

Star and Dart

Celery.	32-41
Creamer.	50-60
Goblet	31-40
Pitcher, water	70-77
Salt/Pepper, pr.	36-45
Spoonholder	40-45
Sugar bowl, covered	51-60
Tumbler	30-39
Wine	30-38

Probably other pieces.

Star and Dart

Maker unknown, c. 1850s. Clear, flint.

Butter dish, covered (ill.)	$ 50-58
Creamer.	45-53
Spoonholder	27-35
Sugar bowl, covered..	50-58

Should be other pieces. A note to you nice people who have been kind enough to buy this Price Guide. If you have information concerning **any** pattern, please let us hear from you. If you don't agree with the prices quoted, please, let us hear from you. If you think the piece illustrated is a spoonholder rather than a celery (etc.), please let us hear from you. Constructive criticism is **always** welcome.

Star and Punty

Star and Punty

Sandwich, early. One of the finest patterns ever made at Sandwich. Clear.

Cologne bottle	$227-240
Creamer	230-240
Pitcher (ill.).	585+
Sugar bowl	282-292
Whale-oil lamp	750+

Relatively few pieces made. Possibly a few more, but doubtful.

Star and Pillar

Star and Pillar

Possibly Nickel Plate Glass Company, 1891. Clear, nonflint.

Butter dish, covered, also footed	$ 49-56

Star Band

(Bosworth): A "new" glass as far as age goes, 1900s. Clear, nonflint.

Butter dish	$ 30-39
Celery	24-33
Compote	32-40
Creamer	38-45
Goblet	30-37
Pitcher (ill.).	30-38
Spoonholder	29-31

Star Band

Sugar bowl   30-37

Probably other pieces. As it gets older, it will probably become more collectible.

Star-in-Bull's Eye

Star-in-Bull's-Eye

U.S. Glass Company, 1907, probably before. Clear, gold trim, nonflint.

Bowl, berry	$ 25-34
Butter dish	30-39
Cake stand	31-40
Celery vase	26-32
Compote	
Covered	44-56
Open, 6″ high	41-50
Creamer · · · · · · · · · · · · ·	26-35
Goblet	31-40
Pitcher, water	45-54
Spoonholder	30-38
Sugar bowl, covered	40-47
Tumbler, gold band (ill.)	27-36

Probably other pieces.

Star in Honeycomb

Bryce Bros., Pittsburgh, late 1880s. Clear, nonflint.

Star in Honeycomb

Butter dish, covered	$ 44-53
Compote	
Covered	40-47
Open	35-44
Cake stand	42-51
Creamer	40-47
Goblet	25-37
Pitcher (ill.)	40-49
Sauce, flat	23-32
Spoonholder	24-33
Sugar bowl, covered	50-60
Tumbler	31-40

Probably other pieces.

Star Pattern

(continued)

Star Pattern

Not specific name; given only for filing purposes. No one can find it in any book. 8-pointed stars. Not made by U.S. Glass Company. Anyone know?

Star Rosetted

Star Rosetted

McKee & Bros., Pittsburgh, 1875. Clear, nonflint.

Butter dish	$ 37-46
Compote, open, high, low standard.	38-52
Creamer.	34-43
Goblet	29-38
Pitcher, water	49-58
Plate, 10″, "A Good Mother" (ill.)	56-64
Spoonholder	28-37
Sugar bowl, covered	49-54

Probably other pieces.

Starlyte

Lancaster Glass Company, Lancaster, Ohio, 1910. Clear.

Butter dish	$ 33-42
Celery vase	26-35
Compote	40-44
Creamer.	40-47
Goblet	26-35
Pitcher, water (ill.)	34-42
Spoonholder	26-35
Sugar bowl, covered	40-48

Probably other pieces.

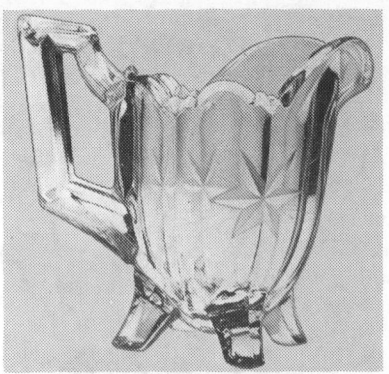

Starlyte

Starred Scroll

Starred Scroll

(Crescent and Fan): Maker unknown, c. early 1900s. Clear, nonflint.

Butter dish, covered.	$ 30-37
Celery.	29-35
Jug, syrup (ill.)	28-34
Spoonholder	23-29
Sugar bowl, covered	30-37
Wine	24-32

Stars and Bars

Stars and Bars

(With Stippled Leaf): This is a clear

glass of the late 1870s, or early 1880s. Most
books show it without stippled leaf.

Butter dish	$ 32-41
Celery dish	22-28
Creamer (ill.)	35-42
Dish, oval, 7″, 8″, 9″, 10″, 11″	25-34
Dollhouse set of creamer, butter dish, sugar, set	59-69
Goblet	26-35
Jam jar	25-34
Night lamp, small	31-40
Pitcher, milk	47-52
Spoonholder	26-34
Sugar bowl, covered	35-42

Undoubtedly many more pieces.

Stars and Stripes

Stars and Stripes

(Brilliant): Called Brilliant in an 1899
Ward Catalog. Nonflint.

Butter dish	$ 38-45
Celery	26-32
Compote	31-40
Creamer	27-35
Goblet	37-42
Pitcher (ill.)	37-42
Spoonholder	28-31
Sugar bowl	28-37
Tumbler	26-35

Probably other pieces. If there are milk glass
pieces, 50 percent higher than clear prices listed.

The States

U.S. Glass Company, 1905. Clear, some
pieces gold trimmed, nonflint.

Butter dish, covered	$ 48-56
Celery	18-25

The States

Compote, 7″, open	33-42
Creamer, individual	18-26
Dish, handled, round	20-27
Pitcher, water, gold trimmed (ill.)	54-62
Plate, large, 10″	37-45
Sugar bowl, covered	41-50
Toothpick holder, handled	38-46
Tumbler	28-32

Probably other pieces. Gold trim doesn't affect
price of clear prices listed.

Stippled Band

(Panelled Stippled Bowl): Maker unknown, c. 1870s. Clear, nonflint.

Butter dish, covered	$ 50-58
Celery	35-43
Creamer	40-48
Goblet	30-38
Pitcher	50-59
Spoonholder	27-36
Sugar bowl, covered	40-47
Tumbler	27-36

Other pieces.

Stippled Chain

Gillinder & Sons, 1870s. Nonflint.

Butter dish, covered	$ 48-54
Creamer, applied handle	24-31
Goblet	20-26
Pickle dish	15-22
Pitcher, water (ill.)	45-53
Salt, footed	17-22
Sauce	8-12
Spoonholder	29-35
Sugar bowl, covered	34-42
Tumbler	16-23

Probably other pieces.

(continued)

Stippled Chain

Stippled Cherry

Stippled Cherry

Probably Lancaster Glass Company, 1880s. Clear, nonflint.

Bowl, berry, 6″, 8″	$ 22-28
Butter dish	43-48
Celery	35-39
Creamer	25-33
Pitcher, water (ill.)	48-54
Plate, 6″, 9¼″	16-25
Saucedish, 4″	13-19
Spoonholder	26-32
Sugar bowl, covered.	31-38
Tumbler, water	20-28

Probably other pieces.

Stippled Daisy

Maker unknown, 1880s. Nonflint.

Compote, open	$ 26-31
Creamer	25-31
Relish, oval	18-24
Sauce, flat	8-13
Spoonholder (ill.)	21-28
Sugar bowl	
Covered	34-39
Open	16-24

Stippled Daisy

Tumbler	26-31
Wine	23-28

Probably other pieces.

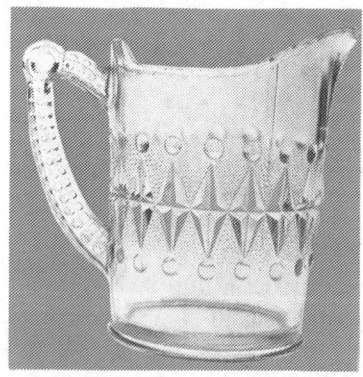

Stippled Dart and Balls

Stippled Dart and Balls

Another product of the 1890s. Clear, nonflint.

Butter dish, covered.	$ 30-35
Creamer	24-30
Goblet	22-27
Pitcher, (ill.)	38-44
Sugar bowl, covered	30-37
Tumbler	22-29
Wine	18-24

Probably other pieces.

Stippled Double Loop

Made in Pennsylvania in the late 1880s. Scarce and in demand. Nonflint.

Stippled Double Loop

Butter dish, covered	$ 38-45
Creamer.	29-33
Goblet	29-36
Pitcher (ill.)	49-52
Spoonholder	28-34
Sugar bowl, covered	39-44
Tumbler	29-34

Stippled Fleur-de-Lis

Stippled Fleur-de-Lis

(Frosted Fleur-de-Lis): Maker unknown, c. late 1880s. Clear, amber, blue, green, milk glass; nonflint.

Butter dish, covered	$ 44-51
Cake stand	29-39
Creamer (ill.)	34-39
Goblet	34-39
Spoonholder	31-38
Sugar bowl, covered	41-50

Amber, blue, milk glass, 40 percent higher; green, 60 percent higher than clear prices listed.

Stippled Forget-Me-Not

Stippled Forget-Me-Not

Bryce Bros., 1880s, also Model Flint Glass Company, after 1891. Clear, color, extremely rare (amber, opal); nonflint.

Butter dish	$ 53-58
Cake plate on stand, large,	
small	49-55
Celery	38-44
Compote, covered, 6″, 7″, 8″	48-56
Creamer	34-37
Goblet	28-32
Mug	22-28
Pitcher, water (ill.)	54-59
Plate, baby center, 7″, star	
center, 7″, kitten center, 9″	43-52
Sauce, flat, footed.	24-32
Spoonholder	28-34
Sugar bowl	38-47
Tumbler, bar, ½ pt., gill	
footed.	24-30
Wine	38-44

Amber, opal, 200 percent higher than clear pieces listed.

Stippled Fuchsia

Probably Sandwich, c. 1870s. Clear and stippled, nonflint.

Butter dish, covered	$ 40-43
Compote	
Open	41-47
'Covered	51-59
Creamer.	48-54
Goblet	39-47
Pitcher	58-64
Spoonholder	28-34
Sugar bowl, covered	47-53

Probably other pieces.

Stippled Grape and Festoon

Stippled Grape and Festoon

Doyle & Company, Pittsburgh, 1870. Clear and stippled (this pattern with stippled background is the scarcest of the grape and festoon family.) Nonflint.

Butter dish	$ 86-94
Celery	58-63
Compote, covered, low	
standard	74-82
Cordial	38-47
Creamer	60-70
Egg cup	30-37
Goblet	47-53
Pitcher, water, applied	
handle (ill.)	110-118
Spoonholder	40-47
Sugar	
Open	45-53
Covered	58-64
Wine	38-46

Probably other pieces.

Stippled Leaf and Flower

Stippled Leaf and Flower

Maker unknown, 1870s. Clear, nonflint.

Butter dish, covered	$ 42-51
Creamer	34-39

Dish, sauce	20-24
Decanter, stopper	33-42
Goblet	35-44
Pitcher, water (ill.)	88-94
Spoonholder	24-33
Sugar	
Covered	50-56
Open	34-42
Tumbler	39-44

Probably other pieces.

Stippled Medallion

Stippled Medallion

Union Glass Company, Somerville, Massachusetts, late 1860s. Clear, nonflint.

Butter dish, covered	$ 46-52
Celery	32-41
Creamer	35-44
Goblet (ill.)	37-45
Pitcher, water	45-54
Spoonholder	28-36
Sugar	
Covered	40-47
Open	30-38

Probably other pieces.

Stippled Peppers

Sandwich glass, 1870s. Clear, nonflint.

Creamer	$ 34-38
Egg cup	22-25
Goblet	29-36
Pitcher, water	48-55
Salt, footed (rare)	17-24
Sauce	7-10
Spoonholder	27-34
Sugar bowl, covered	37-42

Probably other pieces.

Stippled Peppers

Stippled Sandbur

Stippled Sandbur

(Stippled Star Variant): Maker unknown, early 1890s. Clear, nonflint.

Bowl	$ 35-42
Butter, covered	38-46
Celery, vase	29-37
Compote, covered	37-44
Creamer.	32-41
Goblet	25-29
Sauce, flat.	28-35
Spoonholder	27-35
Sugar bowl, covered	35-44
Wine	29-36

Probably other pieces.

Stippled Star

Gillinder & Sons, Greensburg, Pennsylvania, 1870s. Probably Sandwich, much earlier. Nonflint.

Butter dish	$ 43-48
Celery.	35-42
Compote, large, high standard, covered	68-75

Stippled Star

Creamer (ill.)	47-52
Dish, oval, 8″	18-24
Egg cup	28-34
Goblet	33-42
Pickle dish	14-20
Pitcher, water (ill.)	79-85
Sauce, flat, 4″, 6″	14-19
Spoonholder, 5½″ high	27-34
Sugar bowl, covered	48-55
Tumbler	22-28

Probably other pieces. Creamer, goblet, salt dip, sugar bowl and wine being reproduced in clear (original) and new colors.

Stippled Star Flower

Stippled Star Flower

(With the band, called Star Flower Band): Maker unknown, late 1880s. Clear, nonflint.

Butter dish	$ 38-45
Celery	24-31
Creamer	21-27
Goblet (ill.)	26-34
Salt, footed	18-24
Spoonholder	22-29
Sugar bowl, covered	31-38
Tumbler	21-29
Wine	18-26

Other pieces.

Stove

Stove

Maker and date unknown, clear, colors. A novelty of the late 1800s. Nonflint.

Clear (ill.) $132-150
Color, 125 percent higher than clear price listed.

Strawberry

Strawberry

Sandwich Glass, 1850-1860. Clear, opaque white (milk glass); nonflint.

Butter dish, covered. . . . . $ 57-63
Compote, covered, 8″ high,
   low standard 66-78
Creamer 54-62
Egg cup. 28-34
Goblet 28-32
Honey dish 26-34
Pickle dish 24-26
Pitcher
   Syrup 57-64
   Water (ill.) 68-74
Salt, footed 35-44
Saucedish, flat 25-33
Spoonholder 34-39
Sugar bowl 42-48

Probably other pieces. Prices listed are for milk glass. Clear, 85-100 percent less. Egg cup and goblet being reproduced.

Strawberry Jar

Strawberry Jar

Don't confuse this with the Sandwich Glass Strawberry. This was a container for grocery products—mustard, etc. Possibly made by Specialty Glass Company and Indiana Tumbler & Goblet Company. Nonflint.

Strawberry jar (ill.) . . . . $ 39-49

Strigil

Strigil

Possibly McKee Bros., Pittsburgh, late 1880s. Clear, nonflint.

Butter dish . . . . $ 35-44
Celery. 34-39
Compote 40-48
Creamer. 38-45
Egg cup 22-31

Goblet	27-35
Pitcher	47-54
Sauce	22-29
Spoonholder	26-32
Sugar bowl	39-48
Tumbler	27-34

Probably other pieces.

Strutting Peacock

Strutting Peacock

Possibly Westmoreland Glass Company, late 1880s. Clear, other colors, nonflint.

Bottle, decanter type	$ 42-48
Butter dish, covered	49-54
Creamer, covered (ill.)	34-39
Goblet	40-48
Mug 4" high	19-27
Pitcher, ½ gal.	64-72
Plates, 6", 7", 8", 9"	40-48
Spoonholder	28-37
Sugar bowl, covered	41-50
Tumbler, 4" high	26-32

Probably other pieces. Blue, purple, green, 50 percent higher; opalescent white or white Carnival, 125 percent higher; reds, 125 percent higher than clear/marigold prices given.

Stylized Flower

Stylized Flower

Challinor, Taylor & Company, Tarentum, Pennsylvania, 1885. "Mosaic glass" in brown and other colors. Also, crystal and opal. Only six pieces known in this pattern.

Butter dish	$ 45-49
Creamer	23-29
Pitcher	
Quart (ill.)	52-59
½ gal.	47-54
Spoonholder	29-33
Sugar bowl, covered	48-56

Opal, 50 percent higher than clear prices listed.

The Summit

Thompson Glass Company, Uniontown, Pennsylvania, c. 1895. Clear, flint.

Butter dish, covered	$ 60-64
Celery	35-41
Creamer	40-47
Pitcher, large, tankard	65-75
Spoonholder	25-34
Sugar bowl, covered	47-57

Possibly other pieces.

Sunbeam

Sunbeam

McKee & Bros., Jeannette, Pennsylvania, c. 1898. Clear; later, emerald with gold decorations; nonflint.

Bowl, berry	$ 18-26
Celery	19-25
Compote, jelly (ill.)	19-27
Creamer, individual	18-26
Sauce	15-24
Sugar bowl, covered	26-34

(continued)

Tumbler 22-29
Emerald with gold decorations, 50 percent higher than clear prices listed.

Sunburst

Sunburst

McKee & Bros., 1898. Clear, nonflint.

Butter dish	$ 48-54
Cake plate on standard,	
two types	39-45
Celery	30-37
Compote, covered, low	
standard	46-52
Cordial	28-36
Creamer	37-45
Egg cup	27-33
Goblet	28-35
Pitcher, large, small	46-53
Plate, 6″, 7″, 11″	27-35
Spoonholder	31-40
Sugar bowl	40-48
Wine	24-32

Probably other pieces.

Sunflower

Sunflower

(Lily): Atterbury & Company, Pitts-

burgh, 1881. Crystal, amber, blue, opal, mosaic glass.

Butter dish, covered.	$ 50-57
Creamer	34-42
Goblet	24-33
Nappy	32-41
Pitcher (ill.).	60-70
Spoonholder	28-37
Sugar bowl	
Covered	53-62
Open	35-44

Probably other pieces. Amber, 50 percent higher; mosaic, 100 percent higher than clear prices listed.

Sunflower Container

Sunflower Container

Westmoreland Specialty Company or Specialty Glass Company. This is a creamer, originally made as a commercial jelly container.

Sunflower container (ill.) . . . . . . $ 28-36

Sunk Daisy

Co-Operative Flint Glass Company, Beaver Falls, Pennsylvania, 1898. Clear and green, nonflint.

Butter dish, covered	$ 37-45
Compote	39-46
Creamer	27-31
Goblet	20-38
Pitcher (ill.)	43-51

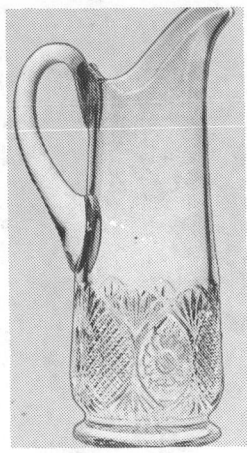

Sunk Daisy

Sugar bowl, covered 26-35
Wine 19-27
Probably other pieces. Green, 50 percent higher than clear prices listed.

Sunk Diamond and Lattice

Sunk Diamond and Lattice

Maker unknown, 1885-1890. Clear, nonflint.

Butter dish . . . . $ 34-43
Celery vase 32-39
Compote
  Covered 37-44
  Open 20-26
Creamer. 23-32
Pitcher, water (ill.) 39-44
Salt/Pepper, pr. 24-29
Spoonholder 19-27
Sugar bowl, covered 35-42
Tumbler 22-29

Probably other pieces.

Sunk Honeycomb

This by McKee; later, Greensburg. Clear

Sunk Honeycomb

as well as with a ruby top, nonflint.

Celery . . . . $ 32-41
Creamer, clear 32-41
Cruet with stopper 80-88
Decanter, 12½" high, original,
  stopper; ruby top 62-71
Pitcher, water, ruby top (ill.) 79-83
Spooner, ruby top 39-41

Sunken Buttons

Sunken Buttons

Maker unknown, Ohio, late 1880s. Clear canary, amber, blue; nonflint.

Butter dish, covered. . . . . $ 31-40
Compote
  Covered 35-42
  Open 31-40
Creamer 34-42
Goblet 29-38
Pitcher, syrup (ill.) 40-47
Platter 32-42
Salt/Pepper, pr. 24-32

(continued)

Sugar bowl
Covered   37-40
Open   30-36
Wine   20-28

Probably other pieces. Canary, 50 percent higher; amber, blue, 125 percent higher than clear prices listed.

Swag with Brackets

Swag with Brackets

Jefferson Glass Company, Steubenville, Ohio, late 1800s. Crystal, sapphire with whitened rims, amethyst, opalescent white; nonflint.

Butter dish, covered . . . . $ 58-67
Celery   32-41
Creamer   34-43
Pitcher, water (ill.)   59-67
Spoonholder   41-51
Sugar bowl, covered.   43-53
Tumbler   28-37

Probably other pieces. Colors, 90 percent higher than clear prices listed.

Swan

Maker unknown, 1880s. Clear, light amber, yellow, deep blue. Possibly Westmoreland. Nonflint.

Butter dish, covered, 5″ dia. . . . . . . $ 40-48
Creamer   19-27
Dish, oval, covered   32-37
Goblet, (rare)   62-71
Marmalade jar, covered, swan
finial   57-64
Pitcher, water (ill.)   74-83
Sauce, footed, round, flat, 4″   11-14
Spoonholder   34-43

Swan

Sugar bowl, covered   52-61

Probably other pieces. Amber, yellow, 45 percent higher; blue, 65 percent higher than clear prices listed.

Swan with Tree

Swan with Tree

U.S. Glass Company, Gas City, Indiana, late 1880s. Clear, nonflint.

Goblet . . . . $ 52-58
Pitcher, water (ill.)   61-68

At least these two pieces; possibly more.

Swirl

(Jersey Swirl): Windsor Glass Company, Pittsburgh, c. 1887. Clear, amber, blue, yellow; nonflint.

Butter dish, covered . . . . $ 49-55

Cake stand	49-56
Celery.	37-46
Compote, covered	52-61
Creamer.	41-51
Goblet	
Buttermilk, large	45-54
Regular	42-52
Pitcher, water.	50-58
Spoonholder	32-38
Sugar bowl, covered	47-56

Yellow, 30 percent; amber, blue, 50 percent higher than clear prices listed. Many repros in the colored glass; also in clear buttermilk goblet.

Swirl and Diamond

Sugar bowl	
Covered	47-55
Open	27-36

Probably other pieces.

Swirl and Cable

Swirl and Cable

Sandwich, mid-1850s. Clear.

Creamer.	$ 40-47
Pitcher, milk (ill.)	60-68

Probably other pieces.

Swirl and Diamond

(America): Riverside Glass Works, Wellsburg, West Virginia, called it America. Also made by Riverside's successor, American Glass Company, Anderson, Indiana, in 1899. Crystal.

Bowl	$ 23-30
Butter dish, covered.	47-54
Creamer.	29-37
Pitcher, water (ill.)	54-63
Sauce, flat.	22-29
Spoonholder	27-34

Sydney

Sydney

Fostoria Glass Company, 1905, possibly earlier. Clear, nonflint.

Butter dish, covered.	$ 39-48
Celery	22-29
Compote	
Covered	45-53
Open	31-41
Creamer	27-36
Goblet	34-43
Molasses jug	24-32
Pickle dish, 6", 8", 9"	19-27
Pitcher (ill.).	55-62
Salt shaker	17-25
Spoonholder	19-28
Sugar bowl, covered	35-42

Probably other pieces.

Syrup Jug with Applied Handle

Syrup Jug with Applied Handle

Maker and date unknown. Bird on lid, Britannia lid. Nonflint.

Syrup jug (ill.) . . . . $ 54-63
Anyone have information on it?

Tackle Block

Tackle Block

Maker unknown, c. 1840s. Clear, flint.

Goblet (ill.) . . . . $ 60-67
Possibly other pieces.

Tall Argus

Maker unknown, 1850s. Clear, flint.

Goblet . . . . $ 80-87
Pitcher, water (ill.) 163-169
Possibly other pieces.

Tall Argus

Tape Measure

Tape Measure

(Shields): Portland Glass Company, early 1870s. Clear, nonflint.

Butter dish . . . . $ 44-52
Goblet   31-38
Pitcher, water (ill.)   55-64
Sauce, flat   22-28
Probably other pieces.

Teardrop and Tassel

Teardrop and Tassel

(Sampson): Original name was Sampson, made by Indiana Tumbler & Goblet Compay, 1890s. Better known today as Teardrop and Tassel. Clear, blue; nonflint.

	Blue	Green	Clear
Butter dish . .	$58-66	$78-85	$40-46
Creamer . . .	34-42	55-62	19-27
Goblet, rare. .	77-84	97-106	62-68
Pitcher (ill.) .	92-102	112-118	72-81
Relish tray . .	82-91	62-72	45-52
Spoonholder .	47-54	67-74	33-39
Sugar bowl . .	67-73	89-107	50-57
Tumbler . . .	47-52	68-74	32-39
Wine (rare) . .	84-93	97-106	67-74

Probably other pieces.

Teardrop and Thumbprint

Teardrop and Thumbprint

Ripley & Company, Pittsburgh; later, U.S. Glass Company, early 1900s. Plain or engraved, clear, blue; pattern on blue enameled on white. Nonflint.

Bowl	$ 22-28
Butter dish, covered	38-47
Cake stand	45-52
Celery	22-29
Creamer, covered	28-34
Compote, open	34-38
Goblet	25-32
Pitcher, water (ill.)	50-59

Sugar		
Covered		41-50
Open		24-32
Wine		27-36

Probably other pieces. Blue, 100 percent higher than clear prices listed.

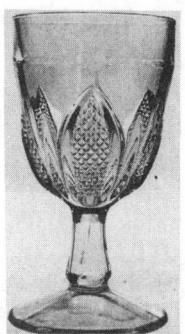

Teasel

Teasel

Bryce Bros., Pittsburgh, 1870s. Clear.

Butter dish, covered	$ 35-42
Cake stand	25-29
Celery	17-26
Compote	28-36
Creamer	25-35
Cruet	22-31
Goblet (ill.)	30-34
Sauce, square footed	18-26
Spoonholder	18-24
Sugar bowl, covered	35-42

Probably many other pieces.

Tennessee

(continued)

Tennessee

U.S. Glass Company, 1900. One of their States series. Clear, nonflint.

Butter dish	$ 47-53
Cake stand, 9½"	37-42
Celery	20-26
Creamer	25-27
Goblet (rare)	33-38
Jam jar	37-46
Pitcher, water (ill.)	47-54
Relish, oval	27-35
Spoonholder	22-27
Sugar bowl, covered	38-47
Tumbler	24-29

Probably others.

Tennessee Mug

Tennessee Mug

So-called camphor glass, American flag, 16 stars on one side, Cherokee rose on other. Nonflint.

Mug (ill.)	$ 36-44

Texas

(Loop with Stippled Panels): U.S. Glass Company, c. 1900, as No. 15,067. In their 1907 catalog, given name of Texas. Clear, clear with gilded top; also with ruby in the body. Nonflint.

Butter dish, covered	$ 47-55
Cake stand, 10"	48-53
Compote, open	29-38
Creamers, 2 types	11-27
Goblet	33-42
Pitcher, water	54-62
Spoonholder	23-32
Sugar bowl, covered, regular	38-44
Tumbler	27-34

Color, gilded top, 50 percent higher than clear prices listed. Other pieces.

Thistle

Thistle

(Pillar and Bull's Eye): Bakewell, Pears and Company, 1872. Nonflint.

Bowl, berry, covered	$ 32-41
Butter dish, covered	62-70
Cake plate on standard	55-63
Compote	
Covered, high standard	57-64
Open, low standard, 8"	33-42
Cordial	50-58
Creamer	63-72
Egg cup	34-42
Goblet	41-50
Pickle dish, tapered at one end	24-29
Pitcher (ill.)	63-69
Plate, 10¾" dia.	31-38
Sauce, flat, deep, 4"	20-26
Spoonholder	29-37
Sugar bowl, covered	60-67
Tumbler, footed, water	40-47
Wine	42-50

Probably other pieces.

Thousand Eye

(Daisy; No. 11): Richards & Hartley, 1888, called it Daisy; New Brighton Glass Company, New Brighton, Pennsylvania, 1889, also made it. It's also No. 11 in an old Adams Glass Company catalog. Clear and just about every color; nonflint.

Bowl, banana . . . . $ 40-47
Bowl, berry, waste 40-46
Butter dish, knob, plain stem 53-60
Cake stand, knob, plain stem 54-61
Compote, covered. 47-54
Creamer, knob, plain stem 43-52
Goblet, knob stem 34-39
Pitcher, large knob,
    plain stem (ill.) 78-86
Spoonholder, knob, plain stem 29-37
Sugar bowl, knob, plain stem 43-52
Tumbler, water. 24-29

Many other pieces. Amber, yellow, blue, 20 percent higher; apple green, 60 percent higher than clear prices listed. Cruet, plain stem, goblet, hat (match holder), mug, 8″ sq. plate, tumbler and wine being reproduced.

Thousand Eye

Threading

(Threaded): Maker unknown, c. late 1870s. Clear, nonflint.

Butter dish, covered. . . . . $ 33-39
Compote
    Open 29-36
    Covered 38-46
Creamer. 37-46

Spoonholder 37-45
Sugar bowl
    Open 23-29
    Covered 40-46
Probably other pieces.

Three Birds

Three Birds

Dalzell, Gilmore & Leighton Company, Findlay, Ohio, 1880s. Clear, nonflint.

Pitcher, water (ill.) . . . . $ 66-75
Probably tumbler and other pieces to match.

Three Face

Three Face

(The Sisters): George A. Duncan's Sons, Pittsburgh, 1878. Clear and crystal-with-frosted-faces.Some pieces etched and engraved. Nonflint.

Butter dish. $157-166

(continued)

Cake Stand
8″, 9½″	114-122
Frosted base	135-145
Celery, pedestal base	106-109
Celery, scalloped top	77-87

Compote
Covered, large	138-146
Covered, 6″, small.	118-123
Open, high standard	82-91
Creamer, 2 styles	108-118
Goblet	88-97
Pitcher, milk, etched	272-281
Pitcher, water, ½ gal., rare (ill.). . . .	310-322
Salt/Pepper, pr.	77-86
Spoonholder	79-86
Wine	87-94

Probably other patterns. Butter dish, cake stand, champagne, 6½″ covered compote, claret, creamer, goblet, lamp, sauce, salt/peppers, spoonholder, sugar bowl, being reproduced. Advice is cheap. This advice won't cost you a thing: DON'T BUY IT! Some dealers sell the new for the same price as the old! All pieces being skillfully reproduced.

Three-in-One

Three-in-One

(Fancy Diamonds): Imperial Glass Company, Bellaire, Ohio, c. late 1880s. Clear, nonflint. Toothpick in Carnival (?).

Bowl	$ 17-27
Butter dish, covered	40-47
Creamer	28-37
Goblet (ill.)	15-24
Spoonholder	19-27

Sugar bowl
Covered.	40-46
Open	27-36
Wine	12-19

Probably other pieces.

Three Leaf Clover

Three Leaf Clover

Maker and date unknown. Any information on this lovely piece of flint glass would be deeply appreciated.

Three Panel

Three Panel

Hartley & Company, Tarentum, Pennsylvania, 1888. Clear, canary, amber, blue; nonflint.

Bowl, 8½"	$ 18-26
Butter dish, covered	38-47
Celery	19-27
Compote, open, 7", 8½", 9", 10",	
low standard	28-42
Creamer	27-32
Cruet	20-24
Goblet	27-32
Mug	19-26
Pitcher, water (ill.)	41-50
Sauce	13-20
Spoonholder	23-29
Sugar bowl	37-44
Tumbler	20-27

Probably other pieces. Colors, 40-90 percent higher than clear prices listed.

Tic-Tac-Toe

Tick-Tac-Toe

Maker unknown, c. late 1880s. Clear, nonflint.

Goblet (ill.)	34-42
Salt, master, footed	17-24

Should be other pieces.

Tiebacks

Tiebacks

Boston & Sandwich Glass Company, c. 1850s, opalescent. They were used to hold the window curtains in place.

2" dia., pr.	$ 54-63
3" dia., pr. (ill.)	58-67
4¼" dia., pr.	80-85

Tiny Lion

Tiny Lion

Maker unknown, Ohio, early 1880s. Clear; clear and frosted; nonflint.

Butter dish, covered.	$ 35-43
Celery, 2 handles (ill.)	42-51
Compote	45-51
Creamer	30-38
Pitcher, water.	42-51
Spoonholder	27-36
Sugar bowl	
Covered	38-42
Open	36-41

Probably other pieces.

Tom Thumb—Humpty Dumpty Mug

Tom Thumb— Humpty Dumpty Mug

(Humpty Dumpty shown): maker unknown, a novelty of the 1880s. Clear only.

Mug (ill.)	$ 58-67

Torpedo

Torpedo

(Pygmy, Fisheye): Thompson Glass Company, Uniontown, Pennsylvania, 1889. Clear, nonflint.

Bowl
Berry, 8″, covered	$ 42-50
Rose, 4″ (scarce).	49-56
Open, 8″, 8¼″, 9″, 9½″, flared rim	35-44
Waste, scalloped top.	27-34
Butter dish, covered.	78-85
Cake stand, 9″, 10″	53-62
Compote	
Covered, jelly, 4″	52-60
Open, jelly, flared rim	38-43
Covered, 6″, 8″, 9″	42-50
Creamer, flat, footed, large and medium.	42-51
Decanter	67-74
Goblet	54-62
Pitcher, syrup (ill.)	67-74
Salt, individual	13-17
Salt/Pepper, pr., 2¼″ high, 3″ high	53-62
Sauce, 4½″ footed honey, 3½″ flat honey	11-14
Spoonholder	38-47
Sugar bowl, open	52-61
Tumbler	32-40
Wine	31-39

Undoubtedly other pieces.

Tree of Life

Portland Glass Company, Portland, Maine, c. 1867. Clear, amber, blue, purple, canary, green, and etched.

Bowl, flat, 8″, 10″, finger	$ 33-39
Butter dish, hand/ball on cover	58-66

Tree of Life

Celery vase, silver plated frame	
Compote	
Open, 10″, "Davis".	128-138
Covered	89-94
Creamer, in plated holder	77-86
Goblet, plain	34-43
Pitcher, water.	78-84
Spoonholder	37-46
Sugar bowl, covered (ill.)	48-55
Tumbler, footed	47-54
Wine	51-60

Probably other pieces. Colors, 50-100 percent higher than clear prices listed. Some pieces came in a plated holder. No change in value. Some pieces signed "P.G. Co. Patent." Others, "Davis" (woven in design).

Tree of Life with Hand

Tree of Life with Hand

George A. Duncan's Sons, 1884. Clear, blue; probably other colors. Nonflint.

Bowl, finger.	$ 34-43
Butter dish, covered	78-85
Celery	43-50
Compote, covered.	67-73
Creamer	62-70
Dish, berry	25-34

Plate, berry.	26-35
Saucedish.	18-26
Sugar bowl	
Covered.	67-74
Open	35-43

Probably other pieces. No goblet seems to have been made in hand stem.

Tree of Life with Sprig

Tree of Life with Sprig

Portland Glass Company, Portland, Maine, 1870s. Clear, possibly colors; non-flint.

Butter dish	$ 48-54
Celery	39-47
Creamer	38-42
Spoonholder	40-48
Sugar bowl, covered	45-53
Syrup jug, top missing (ill.)	37-45

Probably other pieces. Creamer has little wheels at base; other pieces don't. Don't let this confuse you.

Triangular Prism

Triangular Prism

Maker unknown, c. 1850s. Clear, flint and nonflint.

Bowl, shallow.	$ 22-28
Butter dish, covered	45-53
Celery	40-47
Compote	
Low pedestal	24-29
Tall pedestal	33-42
Cup, handled	19-27
Goblet, ladies' or gents'.	49-53
Salt, master, footed.	27-36
Spoonholder	37-42
Sugar bowl, covered	54-62
Tumbler	22-29
Wine (ill.)	38-46

Flint, 25 percent higher than clear prices listed. Probably other pieces.

Triple Triangle

Triple Triangle

Doyle & Company, Pittsburgh, c. 1885. Clear and ruby-stained, nonflint.

Butter dish, covered.	$ 44-51
Cup, punch	19-25
Creamer	29-39
Goblet (ill.)	55-62
Mug	37-45
Sugar bowl, covered	44-52
Wine	39-47

Ruby-stained, 25 percent higher than clear prices listed. Other pieces.

Troubadour Scene

Indiana Tumbler & Goblet (National) Company, late 1890s. See colors with price.

(continued)

Troubadour Scene

Amber (ill.)	$150-160
Blue milk	66-73
Chocolate	87-96
Clear	44-50
Nile green	67-73
White milk	50-58

With lip, regular size, 100 percent higher. Large steins, 350-400 percent higher.

Tulip with Sawtooth

Tulip with Sawtooth

(Tulip): Bryce, Richards and Company, Pittsburgh, c. 1854. Flint.

Butter dish, covered	$128-136
Celery vase	63-72
Compote	
Covered, large high standard	96-105
Covered, small, high standard	77-84
Open, large	55-63
Covered, low standard	50-54
Creamer	108-116
Decanter, quart	155-163
Goblet, knob stem, 7″ high	64-72
Jug	
Pint	82-90
Quart	123-127
Pitcher (ill.)	170-177

Spoonholder	37-44
Sugar bowl, open	48-54
Tumbler, footed, water	53-62
Wine	57-62

Probably other pieces. Wine being reproduced.

Twin Teardrops

Twin Teardrops

Maker unknown, c. 1890s. Clear, non-flint; possibly in emerald green.

Celery	$ 28-35
Compote, open (ill.)	34-40
Cruet	29-38
Dish, banana, flat	32-41
Plate, 7⅝″ square	24-32

If emerald green, 100 percent higher than clear prices listed. Should be other pieces.

Twinkle Star

Twinkle Star

(Frost Flower): U.S. Glass Company, 1901. Clear, clear and frosted. Six-pointed stars on **inside** of glass. Nonflint.

Butter dish, covered	$ 44-51

Celery.	32-41
Creamer.	38-45
Goblet	32-41
Pitcher, water (ill.)	56-62
Spoonholder	37-46
Sugar bowl, covered	32-40
Tumbler	34-39

Probably other pieces.

Two Band

Two Band

Maker unknown, c. late 1880s. Clear, nonflint.

Butter dish, covered	$ 39-44
Creamer (ill.)	31-40
Goblet	28-36
Spoonholder	32-39
Sugar bowl, covered.	40-47
Also made in child's set:	
Butter dish, covered.	77-83
Creamer	60-67
Spoonholder	64-72
Sugar bowl, covered	79-83

Probably other pieces in adult size.

Two Panel

(Daisy in Panel; Daisy in Square): Richards & Hartley Flint Glass Company, Tarentum, Pennsylvania, c. 1880s. Clear, apple green, amber, blue, canary; nonflint.

Bowls, 3 sizes	$ 25-35
Butter dish, covered.	42-51
Celery	32-41
Compote	
Covered, open, high	
standard	38-46
Open, low standard	31-40

Two Panel

Creamer	37-42
Goblet (ill.)	28-37
Lamp	60-70
Mug, large	28-37
Pitcher	51-60
Spoonholder	32-40
Sugar bowl, covered	37-44

Apple green, 80 percent; canary, 60 percent; amber, blue, 50 percent higher than clear prices listed. Many other pieces. Goblet being reproduced, especially in color.

Umbilicated Sawtooth

Umbilicated Sawtooth

Another of the Sandwich patterns.

Bowl, 8″	$ 35-46
Butter dish, covered, on	
pedestal (ill.)	54-62
Egg cup	34-41
Plate, 6″	29-37
Salt, master, footed	22-31
Sauce.	15-22
Tumbler	29-38
Wine	34-43

Probably other pieces.

Unique

Unique

Co-Operative Flint Glass Company, 1898. Clear, nonflint.

Butter dish	$ 42-47
Celery vase	35-42
Creamer	35-41
Goblet	24-33
Pitcher	
Syrup metal cap (ill.)	34-42
Water	46-53
Spoonholder	20-37
Sugar bowl, covered	37-46
Tumbler	28-35

Probably other pieces.

U.S. Rib

U.S. Rib

(Rib): U.S. Glass Company, 1900. Green glass with gold rims; possibly crystal and other colors.

Butter dish	$ 53-62
Celery	37-44
Creamer (ill.)	49-57
Pitcher, water	78-84
Spoonholder	43-52
Sugar bowl, covered	49-56
Tumbler	36-45

Probably other pieces. Crystal, 50 percent less than green prices listed.

Valentine

Valentine

(Trilby): U.S. Glass Company, Pittsburgh, late 1870s. Clear, nonflint.

Butter dish	$ 60-67
Celery	38-47
Cologne bottle	36-42
Creamer	34-42
Goblet	38-45
Match holder	28-37
Pitcher, water (ill.)	166-172
Tumbler	45-51

Victoria

Victoria

Bakewell, Pears & Company, early 1860s. Clear, canary, possibly other colors; flint.

Bowl, 8½" dia. (ill.)	$ 91-97
Butter dish, low foot, 8"	112-122
Cake stand	
9"	88-98
15"	128-132
Celery	36-47

Compote
Covered, 10" 137-142
Open 62-71
Creamer 92-106
Dish, sweetmeat 70-77
Sugar bowl (scarce) 172-190

Possibly other pieces. Colors, 140-170 percent higher than clear prices listed.

Victoria

(Draped Top): **Not** Bakewell, Pears but another pattern, made by Riverside Glass Works, Wellsburg, West Virginia, c. 1894. Clear, with red, nonflint.

Butter dish, covered . . . . $ 39-47
Cake stand 42-50
Celery 28-36
Compote 34-42
Creamer 40-47
Goblet 28-37
Pitcher, water 46-56
Salt/Pepper, pr. 37-44
Spoonholder 29-38
Sugar bowl, covered 42-51

With red, 100 percent higher than clear prices listed.

Virginia

Virginia

(Galloway): U.S. Glass Company, 1901, Glassport, Indiana. Clear, red-flashed; nonflint.

Butter dish, covered . . . . $ 48-54
Celery 38-47
Compote
Covered, footed, 6", 7", 8" 55-60
Open, footed, 6", 7", 8" 44-52
Creamer, individual, large 29-38
Goblet 37-44
Pitcher, water (ill.) 55-64

Sauce, flared, 4"; straight,
4", 4½" 19-27
Spoonholder 37-46
Sugar bowl
Covered, large 49-56
Open, small 32-42
Tumbler 37-46
Wine 39-46

Probably other pieces. There are several "Virginia" patterns; don't get them confused, price-wise. Red-flashed, 25 percent higher than clear prices listed.

Waffle

Waffle

Bryce, Walker & Company, Pittsburgh, 1860s. Flint.

Butter dish, covered $128-134
Celery, 9" high (ill.) 108-117
Champagne goblet 106-112
Claret 49-54
Compote
Open, large, high
standard 68-74
Open, small, high
standard 54-60
Open, small, low
standard 50-58
Creamer, pint and quart
(rare) 118-124
Decanter, pint and quart 127-134
Goblet, knob stem 62-72
Pitcher, water (rare) 9½" high 124-132
Spoonholder 60-68
Sugar bowl, covered 129-141
Tumbler, water, footed 78-86
Wine 64-73

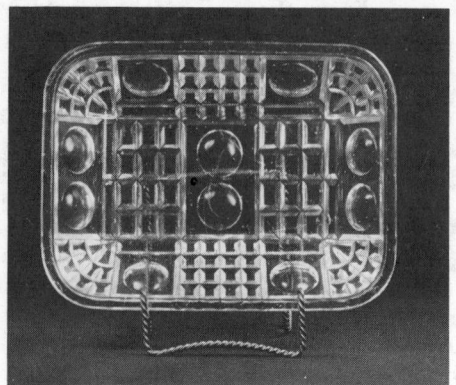

Waffle and Thumbprint

Waffle and Thumbprint

Possibly New England Glass Company or Sandwich, early; later, Ohio Valley, c. 1850s, 1860s. Clear, flint and nonflint.

Bowl, rectangular (ill.)	$ 63-73
Butter dish, covered.	152-161
Cordial	82-91
Creamer	125-140
Decanter	
Pint	82-90
Quart	122-131
Goblet	60-67
Sugar bowl, covered	121-130

Nonflint, 50 percent lower than flint prices listed. Possibly other pieces.

Waffle with Fan Top

Waffle with Fan Top

Maker unknown, c. 1880s. Clear, nonflint.

Goblet (ill.)	$ 35-41

Another member of the Waffle family. There should be other pieces.

Washboard

McKee & Bros., Pittsburgh, c. 1897. Clear, canary, blue, nonflint.

Bowls, round, oval.	$ 24-32
Butter dish, covered	32-41
Cake stand, large	47-53
Creamer.	35-44
Goblet	38-43
Pitcher	50-58
Sauce, flat.	18-27
Spoonholder	27-36
Sugar bowl, covered	35-43

Colors, 35 percent higher than clear prices listed. Probably other pieces.

Washington

Washington

New England Glass Company, Cambridge, Massachusetts, c. early 1860s. Clear, flint.

Butter dish, covered, on	
pedestal	$178-185
Celery	98-107
Compote, covered, tall, 10″	177-184
Cordial	153-162
Creamer	205-210
Egg cup	79-87
Goblet	78-85
Pitcher	
Syrup.	132-144
Water.	270-295
Sugar bowl (base ill.)	108-117
Tumbler	88-95
Wine	68-78

Possibly other pieces.

Washington Centennial

Gillinder & Sons, Philadelphia, c. 1876. Clear, nonflint.

Bowl, oval	$ 34-38
Butter dish, covered	84-93
Celery	60-70
Champagne	67-73
Creamer	78-85
Goblet	43-52
Pitcher, water	99-108
Platters	
Washington's head	118-126
"The Nation's Birthplace"	112-120
Carpenter's Hall	108-114
Relish, flat, oval, marked	
"Centennial 1776-1876"	42-50
Sugar bowl, covered	75-83
Wine	57-63

Probably other pieces.

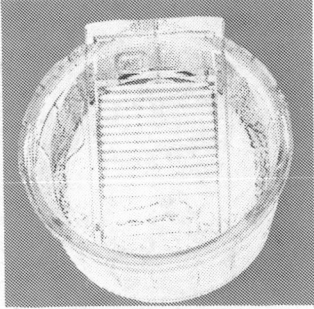

Washtub Soap Dish

Washtub Soap Dish

Maker and date unknown. A novelty item of the 1860s. Clear glass; also canary, amber, blue. Nonflint.

Washtub, clear	$ 58-64
Washtub, canary or amber	68-73
Washtub, blue (rare) (ill.)	88-94

Water Lily

(Frosted Magnolia): Dalzell, Gilmore & Leighton Company, Findlay, Ohio, c. 1890. Clear, nonflint.

Butter dish, covered	$ 44-53
Cake stand, large	32-40
Creamer	18-27
Goblet	14-19
Pitcher, syrup	18-26
Sauce, flat	11-15
Sugar bowl, covered	29-38

Probably other pieces.

Waterfall

Waterfall

O'Hara Glass Company, Pittsburgh, 1880s. Clear, light blue, canary; nonflint.

Butter dish	$ 41-50
Celery	24-32
Compote	47-52
Creamer	31-40
Goblet	31-40
Pitcher, water (ill.)	60-66
Spoonholder	32-42
Sugar bowl, covered	40-48

Probably other pieces. Colors, 50 percent higher than clear prices listed.

Waterlily and Cattails

Waterlily and Cattails

Northwood Glass Company, later Fenton, 1889. Clear, colored w/opalescence (blue, green Carnival glass); Lavender (rare). Northwood prices given. Nonflint.

Butter dish, covered	$ 50-58
Celery vase	27-36

 (continued)

Creamer	41-50
Goblet	40-47
Pitcher, water (ill.)	50-58
Plate, 9", 10"	34-41
Spoonholder	35-44
Sugar bowl, covered	57-62
Tumbler	37-46

Probably other pieces. Sapphire and purple, 100 percent higher than clear prices listed.

Way's Colonial

Way's Colonial

Maker unknown, c. 1840s. Clear, flint. Possibly Central Glass Company, c. 1870s.

Sugar bowl, covered	$ 64-70
Tumbler (ill.)	40-47
Whiskey, handled	41-50

Wedding Bells

Wedding Bells

Fostoria Glass Company, Moundsville, West Virginia, 1900. Clear, amethyst gold, possibly green, pink flashed; flint.

Butter dish, covered	$ 55-63
Celery	29-37
Creamer	40-44
Compote, covered, high, low foot	47-53
Cruet, with stopper	42-50
Egg cup	32-41
Goblet	44-53
Pitcher, half gallon tankard (ill.)	72-80
Spoonholder	37-46
Sugar bowl	45-53
Tumbler	34-44

Probably other pieces. Colors, 60 percent higher than clear prices listed.

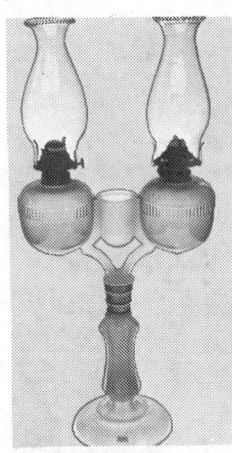

Wedding Lamp

Wedding Lamp

On July 14, 1870, Daniel C. Ripley patented a mold for producing twin-fountain oil lamps, both by pressing and blowing. Extremely rare today, the one shown here is on display at the Houston Museum, Chattanooga, Tennessee.

Lamp (rare) (ill.)	$ 900+

Wedding Ring

Wedding Ring

Maker unknown, 1870s. Clear, flint.

Champagne	$ 32-39
Creamer.	42-51
Decanter	44-52
Goblet	33-42
Pitcher, syrup (ill.)	43-51
Wine	27-34

Probably other pieces.

Westward Ho!

Westward Ho!

(Pioneer; Tippecanoe): Gillinder & Sons, Philadelphia, about 1879. Originally called Pioneer, also Tippecanoe. This last name was never popular. Clear, frosted; nonflint.

Butter dish, covered	
standard	$ 167-174
Celery	109-118
Compote	
Covered, 6″, high	
standard	262-271
Covered, 6″, low standard	181-191
Oval, 9″.	88-97
Creamer (ill.)	89-97
Goblet, frosted	87-96
Jar, jam, covered (scarce)	181-191
Pitcher, milk	218-224
Pitcher, water	208-212
Sauce, 4″, footed	42-51
Spoonholder	90-98
Sugar bowl, covered	152-160
Wine	138-144

Probably other pieces. Butter dish, 6″ compote, 9″ compote, cordial, goblet, clear and frosted, water pitcher, sauce, wine being reproduced in amethyst, blue green, clear and frosted. Goblets originally clear or frosted. Careful!

Wheat and Barley

Wheat and Barley

(Duquesne; Hops and Barley; Oats and Barley): Original trade name was Duquesne. Made by Bryce Bros., Pittsburgh, late 1870s, early 1880s. Clear, amber, blue, yellow. Reproduced by U.S. Glass Company, 1889. Nonflint.

Butter dish, covered.	$ 24-33
Cake stand, 8″, 9″, 10″	19-36
Compote	
Covered, 7″, 8″, high	
standard	34-45
Open, high standard	34-42
Creamer, plain and footed.	27-36
Goblet	20-27
Pitcher	
Water (ill.)	47-54
Milk, syrup	28-36
Plate, 7″, 9″	19-25
Salt/Pepper, pr.	33-40
Sauce, footed, 4″, flat	12-17
Spoonholder	24-32
Sugar bowl, covered	34-42
Tumbler, footed, water	18-26

Probaby other pieces. Canary, amber, 50 percent higher; blue, 65 percent higher than clear prices listed.

Wheat Sheaf

Maker unknown, late 1870s. Clear.

Butter dish.	$ 39-44
Celery vase.	29-35
Compote, low standard	36-44
Creamer	34-41
Goblet	29-38
Pitcher, water (ill.)	45-55
Spoonholder	27-36

(continued)

Wheat Sheaf

Sugar bowl   39-48
Tumbler   29-36
Probably other pieces.

Wheel in Band

Wheel in Band

Maker unknown, 1870s. Clear, nonflint.

Butter dish, covered . . . . $ 39-43
Celery   25-32
Creamer   34-42
Goblet   28-38
Jam jar, covered   38-46
Pitcher, water (ill.)   52-60
Spoonholder   27-35
Sugar bowl, covered   40-45
Wine   29-37

Probably other pieces.

Whirled Sunburst in Circle

Maker and date unknown, 1890-1895. Clear.

Whirled Sunburst in Circle

Butter dish, covered . . . . $ 51-60
Creamer.   39-44
Pitcher, water (ill.)   61-68
Spoonholder   29-36
Sugar bowl, covered   41-50

Probably other pieces.

Wigwam

(Teepee): Iowa Glass Company, Iowa City, Iowa, c. late 1880s. Clear, nonflint.

Butter dish, covered . . . . $ 52-58
Creamer.   42-51
Goblet   39-46
Spoonholder   42-51
Sugar bowl, covered   57-66

Probably other pieces.

Wild Bouquet

Wild Bouquet

Northwood Glass Company, 1900-1905. White, green, blue opalescense.

	White	Green	Blue
Bowl, berry . . .	$ 50-55	$ 82-92	
Butter dish . . .	92-98	194-197	
Compote	99-107	182-189	$180-190

Cruet	175-182	197-204	196-199
Pitcher, water			
(ill.)	182-188	250-270	250-260
Tumbler . . .	40-48	40-48	43-52

Probably other pieces.

Wild Rose and Lady Lamp

Wild Rose and Lady Lamp

Riverside Glass Company, Wellsburg, West Virginia. The Millersburg Glass Company, Millersburg, Ohio, made nine of these lamps to honor the wives of the company officials. When Millersburg went out of business in 1914, Riverside Glass Company somehow obtained the Wild Rose and Lady Lamp mold. Millersburg had the familiar wild rose and honeycomb on the outside of the lamp; Riverside has these on the underside. Also, Riverside had "Riverside Clinch on Collar" in raised letters on the outside at the base. All these lamps, both Millersburg and Riverside, are highly collectible today.

Lamp, Millersburg (rare) (ill.)	$ 875+
Lamp, Riverside	225-235

Wild Rose with Bow-Knot

Maker unknown, late 1880s. Clear, colors, frosted.

Bowl	$ 36-42
Butter dish	47-54
Creamer	33-42

Wild Rose with Bow-Knot

Pitcher (ill.)	64-72
Sauce	21-28
Spoonholder	32-42
Sugar bowl, covered	59-64
Tumbler	40-47

Probably other pieces. Water pitcher had cover, meaning it was originally made as condiment holder—mustard, jelly, etc. Colors, 50 percent higher than clear prices listed.

Wild Rose with Scrolling

Wild Rose with Scrolling

Possibly Dithridge & Company, Pittsburgh, 1870s. Clear; possibly opaque white, other colors. It's almost as if this miniature table set were made for the wee people. Tiny and dainty.

Butter dish, covered (ill.)	$ 77-84
Creamer	65-73
Spoonholder	38-47
Sugar bowl, covered	66-75

Probably other pieces.

Wildflower

Wildflower

Adams & Company, Pittsburgh, 1874; other factories later; reproduced by U.S. Glass Company, 1898. Clear, canary, amber, blue, green, amethyst, vaseline; nonflint.

Butter dish, collared base, covered	$ 43-47
Cake stand, large, small	52-61
Celery	30-37
Compote	
6″, 8″, covered, high standard	37-47
8″, low standard	35-42
Open, high standard	32-38
Creamer	22-28
Goblet	32-42
Pitcher, water (ill.)	47-54
Salt/Pepper, pr.	43-48
Sauce, flat, round, square	9-12
Spoonholder	19-28
Sugar bowl, covered	34-39
Tumbler, water	23-29
Wine	32-38

Probably other pieces. Amber, yellow, blue, 40 percent higher; green, 100 percent higher than clear prices listed. Goblet, 10″ plate, round, flat sauce, tumbler, wine being reproduced.

Willow Oak

(Oak Leaf; Stippled Star; Acorn; Thistle; Wreath): Bryce Bros., Pittsburgh, made it in the 1880s and called it Wreath. It is also

Willow Oak

known by the other names listed here. Clear, amber, blue; nonflint.

Bowl, waste, berry	$ 22-27
Butter dish, covered	49-56
Cake stand, 8½″	47-56
Celery	33-42
Compote, covered, 7½″, 9″ high standard	44-53
Creamer	34-39
Goblet	37-44
Mug	37-43
Pitcher, large, (ill.)	48-56
Plates, 7″, 9″, closed handles	27-29
Salt/Pepper, pr.	43-50
Sauce, flat, footed, round	9-17
Spoonholder	32-39
Sugar bowl, covered	38-47
Tumbler	22-28

Probably other pieces. Amber, 40 percent higher; blue, 60 percent higher than clear prices listed.

Wiltec

646

Wiltec

McKee & Bros., Pittsburgh, c. 1890s. Clear, flint.

Butter dish, covered. . . . . $ 52-61
Creamer.   39-46
Spoonholder   34-43
Sugar bowl, covered (ill.) 43-53

Obviously other pieces.

Windflower

Windflower

Maker unknown, late 1870s. Clear, nonflint.

Butter dish, flat, covered . . . . $ 54-62
Celery   34-39
Compote, covered, high,
  standard 66-73
Cordial   40-47
Creamer (ill.)   19-27
Egg cup   24-32
Goblet   49-54
Pitcher, water   42-52
Salt, footed, Master   27-32
Sauce, 4″   10-14
Spoonholder   22-29
Sugar bowl, covered   34-43
Tumbler, water   28-37
Wine   33-42

Probably other pieces.

Wooden Pail

(Oaken Bucket): Bryce Bros., 1880s. Clear, amber, blue, canary. Probably a container for candy, mustard, baking powder,

Wooden Pail

coffee. Bryce Bros. called it their Bucket Set. Made in miniature and full size. Amethyst, rare; nonflint.

Butter dish, covered. . . . . $ 64-71
Creamer   52-57
Pitcher (ill.). 54-63
Spoonholder   32-41
Sugar bowl
  Covered.   47-56
  Open   34-42

Undoubtedly other pieces. Miniature same price as large. Yellow, amber, 60 percent higher; blue, 85 percent higher; amethyst, 275 percent higher than clear prices listed.

Woodflower

Sandwich, 1870s. Clear and stippled.

Creamer . . . . $ 68-74
Goblet 66-73
Sugar bowl, covered. 84-92

Probably other pieces.

Wreath and Shell

(continued)

Wreath and Shell

Albany, Indiana, Glass Company. late 1880s. Opaque colors.

Butter dish, covered. . . . . $ 87-94
Rose bowl (ill.) 67-74
Tumbler 77-86

Probably many other pieces.

Wyoming

Wyoming

(Enigma): U.S. Glass Company, Gas City, Indiana, 1907. Crystal, colored glass, including mosaic glass; nonflint.

Butter dish, covered. . . . . $ 47-54
Cake stand, 9″. 74-83
Creamer. 35-44
Goblet 34-41
Pitcher, milk, water (ill.). 39-47
Spoonholder 31-38
Sugar bowl
　Covered 37-45
　Open 32-40
Tumbler 29-37
Wine 47-54

Probably other pieces.

X-Log

X-Log

(Prism Arc): Maker unknown, c. mid-1880s. Clear, nonflint.

Bowl, vegetable, oval (ill.). . . . . . . $ 24-32
Butter dish, covered 38-47
Cake stand 48-55
Creamer 39-47
Goblet 32-41
Mug 29-38
Spoonholder 34-42
Sugar bowl, covered 39-46
Wine 32-41

Probably other pieces.

Yale

Yale

(Crow-Foot): McKee Glass Company, Jeannette, Pennsylvania, 1894. Clear, nonflint.

Butter dish, covered . . . . $ 29-36
Cake stand 50-57
Celery 28-32
Compote, covered. 34-39
Cordial 16-20
Creamer, regular 24-29
Goblet 28-34
Pitcher
　Syrup. 32-38
　Water 37-46
Plate 24-32
Salt/Pepper, pr. 42-51
Saucedish, 4″, 6″ 19-27
Spoonholder (ill.) 29-36
Sugar bowl, covered 38-44
Tumbler 23-32

Probably other pieces.

Yoked Loop

Yoked Loop

(Scalloped Loop): Maker unknown, c. 1860s. Clear, flint.

Goblet . . . . $ 39-46
Sugar bowl
   Covered. 57-64
   Open (ill.). 40-48
Should be other pieces.

York Colonial

York Colonial

Possibly Sandwich, c. 1850s, clear, flint; also opalescent, amethyst, blue. Later, Central Glass Company, c. 1870s, clear, nonflint.

Ale, footed . . . . $ 56-64
Celery 108-119
Compote, covered. 109-120
Creamer 117-124
Goblet 80-87
Sugar bowl (base ill.) 65-75
Tumbler 45-54

Colors (rare), 200 percent higher than clear prices listed. Central Glass pieces, 50 percent lower than Sandwich prices listed.

York Herringbone

York Herringbone

Maker unknown, late 1880s. Clear; clear with ruby stain; nonflint. Souvenir pieces sold at 1893 World's Fair.

Celery . . . . $ 37-44
Creamer, green, individual
   (ill.). 57-62
Spoonholder 45-53
Probably other pieces.

Yuma Loop

(continued)

Yuma Loop

O'Hara Glass Company, late 1850s or early 1860s. Clear, flint. Contemporary of Loop (O'Hara). Same values.

Zigzag Band

Zigzag Band

Possibly Gillinder & Sons, 1870s. Clear.

Butter dish, covered	$ 47-52
Celery vase	38-45
Creamer	37-44
Goblet	38-43
Pitcher, water (ill.)	66-71
Spoonholder	29-37
Sugar bowl, covered	48-56
Tumbler	41-50

Probably other pieces.

Zipper

Richards & Hartley Glass Company, Tarentum, Pennsylvania, c. 1880s. Clear, nonflint.

Butter dish, covered	$ 40-47
Celery	19-27

Compote	
Open	24-32
Covered	45-53
Jar, jam, covered	29-37
Pitcher, water	45-54
Sugar bowl	
Open	18-24
Covered	33-39

Probably other pieces.

Zipper Slash

Zipper Slash

George A. Duncan's Sons, Washington, Pennsylvania, 1893. Stained ruby-red above pattern; sometimes in yellow; nonflint.

Butter dish, covered	$ 62-71
Creamer (ill.)	50-55
Spoonholder	38-47
Sugar bowl	62-29
Wine	40-48

Probably other pieces. Yellow, 50 percent higher; with souvenir marking, 50 percent less than clear prices listed.

Glass Companies

An asterisk indicates firms which exhibited their wares at the Centennial Exhibition in Philadelphia, Pennsylvania, in 1876.

* Adams & Company, Pittsburgh, 1861; joined U.S. Glass Company in 1891 as Factory A.

Aetna Glass & Manufacturing Company, Bellaire, Ohio, 1880.

American Glass Company, Anderson, Indiana, 1889.

Anchor-Hocking Glass Company (see Ohio Flint Glass Company).

* Atterbury & Company, Pittsburgh, about 1858.

Bakewell & Company (also called Bakewell & Page), 1809.

Bakewell & Ensell, Pittsburgh, 1807.

Bakewell, Page & Bakewell, 1824.

* Bakewell, Pears & Company, 1836.

Bay State Glass Company, Cambridge, Massachusetts, about 1849.

Beatty, Alexander J. & Sons, Steubenville, Ohio, about 1850. Moved to Tiffin, Ohio, in 1890.

Beatty-Brady Glass Company, Steubenville, then to Dunkirk, Indiana, in 1898. Both taken over by the U.S. Glass Company; Factory S at Steubenville and Factory T at Tiffin.

Beaumont Glass Company, Martins Ferry, Ohio, 1895. Sold to Hocking Glass in 1905.

Beaver Falls Co-Operative Glass Company, Beaver Falls, Pennsylvania, 1879.

Beaver Falls Glass Company, Beaver Falls, Pennsylvania, 1887.

Bellaire Goblet Company, Bellaire & Findlay, Ohio, 1878; merged with U.S. Glass Company in 1891. Both plants were moved to Tiffin, Ohio, under the name Factory M.

Belmont Glass Company, Bellaire, Ohio, 1866.

* Boston & Sandwich Glass Company, Sandwich, Massachusetts, 1825.

Boston Silver-Glass Company, East Cambridge, Massachusetts, 1857.

Brilliant Glass Works, Brilliant, Ohio (originally called Novelty Glass Company), 1880.

Bryce, McKee & Company, Pittsburgh, 1850.

Bryce, Richards & Company, Pittsburgh, 1854.

Bryce, Walker & Company, Pittsburgh, 1865.

Bryce Bros., Pittsburgh, 1882. Taken over by U.S. Glass Company around 1889 and named Factory B.

Bryce Bros. again entered the business Hammondsville, Pennsylvania, 1896.

Bryce, Higbee & Company (also known as Homestead Glass Works), Pittsburgh, 1879.

J. B. Higbee Glass Company, Bridgeville, Pennsylvania, 1900.

* Excelsior Glass Works, Wheeling, West Virginia; moved to Martins Ferry, Ohio, in 1879 under the name Buckeye Glass Company.

Campbell, Jones & Company, Pittsburgh, 1865.

Canton Glass Company, Canton, Ohio, 1883; factory moved to Marion, Indiana, in 1894. In 1899 it joined with National Glass Company. In 1903 the factory site changed to Cambridge, Ohio. Another Canton Glass Company was founded in Marion, Indiana, in 1904.

Jones, Cavitt & Company, Ltd., Pittsburgh, 1886.

*Central Glass Company, Wheeling, West Virginia, 1863. (Famous for their Coin pattern.) Joined U.S. Glass Company in 1891 as Factory O.

Challinor, Taylor, Ltd., Tarentum, Pennsylvania, 1884-1894.

Columbia Glass Company, Findlay, Ohio, 1886; incorporated into U.S. Glass Company in 1891 as Factory J.

Consolidated Lamp & Glass Company, Pittsburgh and Coraopolis, Pennsylvania, 1894.

Co-Operative Flint Glass Company, Beaver Falls, Pennsylvania, 1889.

*Crystal Glass Company, Pittsburgh, 1868; later moved to Bridgeport, Ohio, in 1882.

Craig & Ritchie, Wheeling, West Virginia, 1824 or 1826—said to be the first plant in the U.S. for pressing glass. Before Sandwich on Cape Cod.

R. B. Curling & Sons (originally called Curling, Price & Company), Pittsburgh, 1827.

Dalzell, Gilmore & Leighton Company, Findlay, Ohio, 1888.

Diders, McGee, Brilliant, Ohio, date unknown.

Dithridge & Company, Pittsburgh, 1860s; also a factory at Martins Ferry, Ohio.

Doyle & Company, Pittsburgh, 1866; purchased by Phoenix Glass Company, Phillipsburgh, New Jersey, in the early 1880s. In 1891, firm was purchased by U.S. Glass Company, known as Factory P.

Dugan Class Company, Indiana, Pennsylvania, in 1892 (originally known as Indiana Glass Company).

*George Duncan & Sons, Pittsburgh, 1874; George A. Duncan & Sons, Washington, Pennsylvania, 1894; Duncan & Heisey Company, 1886-1889, Pittsburgh; Duncan & Miller Glass Company, Washington, Pennsylvania, 1870s—U.S. Glass Company's Factory D.

East Liverpool Glass Company, East Liverpool, Ohio, 1882.

Elson Glass Company, Martins Ferry, Ohio, 1882.

Enterprise Glass Works, Ravenna, Ohio, 1878.

Fenton Art Glass Company, Martins Ferry, Ohio, 1906; factory moved to present location in Williamstown, West Virginia, in 1906. The firm is still in business.

Findlay Flint Glass Company, Findlay, Ohio, 1888.

Fort Pitt Glass Works—better known as Dithridge & Company.

Fostoria Glass Company, Fostoria, Ohio, 1887; the factory was moved to Moundsville, West Virginia, in 1891, and is still in operation today.

Franklin Flint Glass Company, Philadelphia, 1861.

Gillinder & Bennett, Philadelphia, 1863.

*Gillinder & Sons, Philadelphia, 1867; later sold to U.S. Glass Company and named Factory G.

Graham Glass Works, Brilliant, Ohio, 1895.

Greensburg Glass Company, Greensburg, Pennsylvania, 1889 (previously operated as Brilliant Glass Works, Brilliant, Ohio).

A. H. Heisey Glass Company, Newark, Ohio, 1895.

Hemingray Glass Company, Cincinnati, Ohio, and Covington, Kentucky, founded in Cincinnati around 1848.

Hipkins Novelty Mold Shop, Martins Ferry, Ohio, 1884.

*Hobbs, Brockunier & Company, Wheeling, West Virginia, 1863; factory known as J. H Hobbs Glass Company. Taken over by U.S. Glass Company in 1891, calling their new acquisition Factory H.

Homestead Glass Works, Pittsburgh, 1879.

Huntington Glass Company, Huntington, West Virginia, 1891. Originally called Central City until incorporated as Huntington in 1909.

C. Ihmsen & Company, Pittsburgh, 1850s.

Imperial Glass Company, Bellaire, Ohio, 1901. Still in business today.

Indiana Glass Company, Dunkirk, Indiana, 1897. Joined National Glass Company merger in 1899.

Indiana Tumbler & Goblet Company, Greentown, Indiana, 1894. In 1899, firm merged with nineteen other factories to become National Glass Company.

Jefferson Glass Company, Steubenville, Ohio, 1901; moved to Follansbee, West Virginia, in 1907.

Jenkins Glass Company, Greentown, Indiana, 1894.

Jersey Glass Company, Jersey City, New Jersey, 1825.

Jones, Cavitt & Company, Pittsburgh, 1884.

*Keystone Tumbler Works, Rochester, Pennsylvania, 1897.

King Glass Company, Pittsburgh, 1880. This firm was absorbed into the U.S. Glass Company in 1891, thereafter known as Factory K.

King, Son & Company, Pittsburgh, 1869.

Kokomo Glass Company, Kokomo, Indiana, 1899. It was destroyed by fire but rebuilt in 1906 as the D. C. Jenkins Glass Company.

*LaBelle Glass Company, Bridgeport, Ohio, 1872.

Lancaster Glass Company, Lancaster, Ohio, 1915.

McKee & Brothers Glass Works, Pittsburgh, 1853-1888. Moved to Jeannette, Pennsylvania; known as McKee-Jeannette Glass Works, 1889-1908. Called McKee Glass Company from 1908-1951, when purchased by Thatcher Glass Manufacturing Company. Now owned by Jeannette Glass Company.

Model Flint Glass Company, Findlay, Ohio, 1888.

Mosaic Glass Company, Fostoria, Ohio, 1887.

Muhleman Glass Works, LaBelle, Ohio, 1888.

National Glass Company, Bellaire, Ohio, 1877. Not bthe aNational Glass Company.

National Glass Company, Cambridge, Ohio, 1901 (also called Cambridge Glass Company).

New Brighton Glass Company, New Brighton, Pennsylvania, 1884. Originally known as American Ferroline Company.

*New England Glass Company, Cambridge, Massachusetts, early 1800s. Later New England Glass Works.

Nickel Plate Glass Company, Fostoria, Ohio, 1888. Joined the U.S. Glass Company in 1891, becoming their Factory N.

Northwood: Union Glass Works, Martins Ferry, Ohio, 1887; Elwood City, Pennsylvania, 1890; Indiana, Pennyslvania, 1895; Wheeling, West Virginia, 1901 (this factory is probably where he made most of his Carnival Glass.)

Novelty Glass Company, LaGrange, Ohio, 1880; later became U.S. Glass Company's Factory T.

* O'Hara Glass Company, 1848. Joined U.S. Glass Company in 1891 as Factory L.

Ohio Flint Glass Company, Lancaster, Ohio, 1899. Soon merged with the National Glass Company—out of these combines emerged today's giant Anchor-Hocking Glass Company.

Oriental Glass Company, Pittsburgh, early 1890s.

Phoenix Glass Company, Monaca, Pennsylvania, 1880.

Pioneer Glass Company, Pittsburgh, 1891.

Portland Glass Company, Portland, Maine, 1864.

* Richards & Hartley Glass Company, Tarentum, Pennsylvania, 1884-1893.

* Ripley & Company, Pittsburgh, 1866; joined U.S. Glass Company in 1891 as Factory F.

Riverside Glass Company, Wellsburgh, West Virginia, 1879.

Robinson Glass Company, Zanesville, Ohio, 1893.

* Rochester Tumbler Company, Rochester, Pennsylvania, 1872.

Steiner Glass Company, Buckhannon, West Virginia, 1870s.

Tarentum Glass Company, Tarentum, Pennsylvania, 1894-1918.

Thompson Glass Company, Uniontown, Pennsylvania, 1889.

* Union Glass Company, Somerville, Massachusetts, 1851.

United States Glass Company, 1891 (see Factories A-T).

Specialty Glass Company, East Liverpool, Ohio, 1889.

West Virginia Glass Company, Martins Ferry, Ohio, 1861.

Westmoreland Glass Company, during World War I.

Westmoreland Specialty Company, early 1890s.

Windsor Glass Company, Pittsburgh, 1887.

Whitla Glass Company, Beaver Falls, Pennsylvania, 1887. In 1890 the company reorganized as Valley Glass Company.

NOTE: There were probably many other glass companies, but as some stayed in business less than a year. Since many never published a catalog or advertised their products in newspapers, etc., the above list gives a fairly comprehensive list of the "better known" producers of pressed glass in the United States from 1824 until the early 1900s.

Silver Definitions

Coin
Made from melted American currency, usually before 1860, usually with 800 or 900 parts of silver. Coin silver spoons are fragile, often found in a repaired condition.

EPNS
Electroplate on nickel silver is nickel metal dipped in a silver solution as electricity is run through the piece.

EPWN
Electroplate on white metal—same process as above.

Plated
The base of plated silver is usually Britannia Ware, 10 parts tin, 1 part antimony. After shaping, the article was plated by an electrolytic method which placed a thin coating of silver over the base metal. Less silver was used than in Sheffield silver.

Sheffield Plate
This is a plated product produced by placing thin sheets of silver on either side of a heavy copper sheet. The basic standard was 8 pounds copper to 2 pounds silver. Dishonest silversmiths used much less silver. There was a heavy penalty if and when they were caught. Pieces you see today that show more copper than silver are examples of this cheaper method.

Silver Plate
Silver plate in England is the equal to our sterling in this country. Solid English silver was marked with the familiar hallmarks: Lion passant, leopard's head, king's (or queen's) head, plus maker's touchmark.

Sterling Silver
By law, it must contain 92.5 parts of pure silver, both here and in England. "Sterling" —Irish, after 1720 (rare), or American, after the 1860s.

Quadruple Plate
Four times dipped.

Triple Plate
Three times dipped.

African Silver
English plate after 1850, by Hills, Monke and Company.

Brazil Silver
Globe Nevada Silver Works, Birmingham, England; on a nickel silverware that was not silver plate.

German Silver
Silver-colored metal from nickel, copper and zinc.

Oregon Silver
Just another trade name used on silver-plated English wares after the 1800s.

Siberian Silver
Silver on copper, English; Hayman and Company, late 1800s.

Please note: In 1980 the price of 925/1000 (sterling) silver shot to nearly $60 an ounce. That price has since dropped, but the manufacturers of sterling (flatware, holloware) have raised their prices 300 to 500 percent. This does not indicate the intrinsic (antique) value of the silver piece.

Index

China (cont'd)

Dresden, 182-83
Fischer, 195
flow blue, 196-97
gaudy Dutch, 213-14
gaudy Welsh, 214
Geisha girl, 214-15
Haviland, 138, 221
Imari, 228
moss rose pattern, 272
Newhall, 282
Noritake, 139, 284-85
old ivory, 287-88
old Paris, 288
Pickard, 139, 314-15
pink lustre, 316
railroad, 329-30
rose medallion, 337
Rosenthal, 140, 337-38
Royal Rudolstadt, 344
Sarreguemines, 352-53
Sevres, 357-58
Touraine pattern, 390
Tucker, 395
Warwick, 399-400
China cabinets, 202
Chocolate glass, 117
Chocolate pots, 117, 220, 283, 347
Christmas collectibles/ornaments, 117-18
Christmas plates, 118-19
Chronometers, 65-66
Cigar cutters, pocket, 119
Cigar molds, 119
Cigar store figures, 119-20
Cinnabar, 120
Civil War collectibles, 120-21, 318
Clambroth glass, 121
Clevenger glass, 121
Clewell Metal Art, 121
Clews, Ralph and James, 121
Clifton Art Pottery, 122
Clocks, 122-31
Cloisonne enamel, 131-32
Clothing, 132-33
Clubs, antique and collectible, 27-43
Coal hods, 133
Coalport, 133
Coca-Cola collectibles, 133-34
Cocktails. See under type or
    manufacturer
Coffee grinders, 134
Coin, 362, 655
Coin spot glass, 134-35
Coin-operated machines, 135-36
Collar boxes, 136
Collectors' plates, 136-41
Combs, 141
Comic books, 141-42
Commemorative/historical/souvenir glass,
    142-43
Commemorative/souvenir plates, 143
Commemorative/souvenir spoons, 143
Compasses, 143-44
Compote. See under type or
    manufacturer
Confederate provisional stamps/envelopes,
    144
Cookbooks, 144, 288
Cookie jars, 283, 361
Cookie molds, 144-45
Coors pottery, 145
Copeland-Spode china, 145-46
Copper, 146
Copper lustre, 146-47
Coralene, 147
Cordey china, 147-48
Cordials. See under type or
    manufacturer
Coronation collectibles, 148
Cosmos glass. See Pattern glass
Country store collectibles, 148
Cowan pottery, 149

Cracker jars, 149, 151, 168, 283, 347, 353
Crackle (craquelle) glass, 149-50
Crackleware, Chinese, 150
Cradles, 202
Cranberry glass, 150
Craquelle glass, 149-50
Crazing, 150-51
Creamer. See under type or
    manufacturer
Crest china, 151
Crown Derby, 151
Crown Milano, 151-52
Cruets, 51, 152, 156, 222, 278
Cup/saucer. See under type or
    manufacturer
Cup plates, 152-53
Cupboards, 202
Cups, mustache, 277, 347
Currier and Ives, 153-54
Curtain tiebacks, 154
Cuspidors, 53, 72, 107, 154-55
Custard glass, 155, 188
Cut glass, 155-57
Cut glass trademarks, 157-58
Cut velvet glass, 158
Czechoslovakia, 158-59

Daguerreotype cases, 159
Daguerreotypes, 159
D'argental, 159-60
Daum Nancy, 160
Davenport china, 160-61
De Latte, 161
De Vez, 161
Decanters, 52, 61, 77, 107, 156-57, 161-62,
    222, 374
Decoys, 162-63
Dedham Pottery, 163
Degenhart glass, 163-64
Deldare. See Buffalo pottery
Delft, 138, 164
Depression glass, 164-69
Desk sets, 86, 169-70
Desks, 202-203, 208, 211, 408
DeVilbiss, 170
Dishes. See under type or manufacturer
Disneyana collectibles, 170. See also
    Character collectibles
Doll furniture and accessories, 170-71
Dolls, 171-80
    Kewpies, 240
Donald Duck, 74, 113, 117, 170
Door knockers, 180-81
Doorstops, 181
Dorflinger glass, 181
Dough troughs, 203
Doulton pottery, 182. See also Royal
    Doulton pottery
Dresden china, 182-83
Dressers, 203
Dry sinks, 203
Durand art glass, 183

EPNS, 362, 655
EPWM, 362, 655
ES Germany, 185
Easter eggs, 183, 186-87
Edged weapons, 183-84. See also Japanese
    war items
Enamel
    Battersea, 67
    cloisonne, 131-32
End-of-day glass. See Spatter glass
Engravings, etchings, 184-85
Epergnes, 108, 185
Eskimo art, 186
European art glass, 186
Ewers, 182, 283, 299

Faberge, 186-87
Faience, 187. See also Rorstrand faience
Fairy lamps, 187, 404

Famille rose, 187-88
Fans, 188
    ceiling, 111
Feather work, 188
Fenton Art Glass, 138, 188-89
Fiesta ware, 189-90
Figurines. See also under type or
    manufacturer
    bisque, 75, 367
    Hummel, 226-27
    Royal Doulton, 341-43
    Staffordshire, 371-72
    Steuben glass, 374
Finger bowls, 190
Fire fighting collectibles, 190-91
Firearms, 191-94
Fireglow, 194
Fireplace accessories, 194-95
Fischer China, 195
Fish sets, 195
Flashed and overlay glass, 216
Flasks, 72, 195-96, 309, 321-22, 364
Florentine art "cameo," 196
Flow blue, 196-97
Fluting irons, 197
Folk art, American, 197
Footstools, 203-204
Fostoria glass, 197-98
Foval glass, 200
Frakturs, 198
Francesware, 198
Frankoma Pottery, 138, 198
Fraternal order collectibles, 199, 360
"French ivory." See Celluloid
Fruit jars, 199
Fry glass, 199-200
Fulper pottery, 200
Furniture
    American, 200-207
    English, 207-10
    French, 210-11
    garden, 213
    wicker, 407-408

Galle cameo glass, 211-12
Game plates, 212
Games, 135, 212-13
Garden furniture, 213
Gaudy Dutch, 213-14
Gaudy ironstone, 214
Gaudy Welsh, 214
Geisha girl china, 214-15
German silver, 655
Gibson girl plates, 215
Gillinder glass, 215
Girandoles, 215-16
Girl Scouts, 216
Glass
    agata, 50
    akro agate, 50
    alexandrite, 50
    amberina, 51-52
    aventurine, 60
    Baccarat, 60-61
    bells, 71
    black amethyst, 75-76
    Bohemian, 77
    bottles, 80-85
    Bristol, 88-89
    Burmese, 93-94
    Cambridge, 97-99
    cameo. See Cameo glass
    camphor, 100
    carnival (taffeta), 104-109
    cased, 216
    chocolate, 117
    clambroth, 121
    Clevenger, 121
    coin spot, 134-35
    commemorative, 142-43
    coralene, 147